ASIAN ECONOMIC INTEGRATION REPORT 2023

TRADE, INVESTMENT, AND CLIMATE CHANGE IN ASIA AND THE PACIFIC

FEBRUARY 2023

ASIAN DEVELOPMENT BANK

ADB

© 2023 Asian Development Bank
6 ADB Avenue, Mandaluyong City, 1550 Metro Manila, Philippines
Tel +63 2 8632 4444; Fax +63 2 8636 2444
www.adb.org

Some rights reserved. Published in 2023.

ISBN 978-92-9270-031-7 (print); 978-92-9270-032-4 (electronic); 978-92-9270-033-1 (ebook)
Publication Stock No. TCS230031-2
DOI: http://dx.doi.org/10.22617/TCS230031-2

The views expressed in this publication are those of the authors and do not necessarily reflect the views and policies of the Asian Development Bank (ADB) or its Board of Governors or the governments they represent.

ADB does not guarantee the accuracy of the data included in this publication and accepts no responsibility for any consequence of their use. The mention of specific companies or products of manufacturers does not imply that they are endorsed or recommended by ADB in preference to others of a similar nature that are not mentioned.

By making any designation of or reference to a particular territory or geographic area, or by using the term "country" in this publication, ADB does not intend to make any judgments as to the legal or other status of any territory or area.

Please contact pubsmarketing@adb.org if you have questions or comments with respect to content, or if you wish to obtain copyright permission for your intended use that does not fall within these terms, or for permission to use the ADB logo.

Corrigenda to ADB publications may be found at http://www.adb.org/publications/corrigenda.

Notes:
In this publication, "$" refers to United States dollars, "€" refers to euros, "B" refers to baht, "NZ$" refers to New Zealand dollars, "SLRs" refers to Sri Lanka rupees, "SUM" refers to sum, and "Tk" refers to taka.

ADB recognizes "Brunei" as Brunei Darussalam; "China" as the People's Republic of China; "Hong Kong" as Hong Kong, China; "Korea" and "South Korea" as the Republic of Korea; "Kyrgyzstan" as the Kyrgyz Republic; "Russia" as the Russian Federation; and "Vietnam" as Viet Nam.

Cover design by Erickson Mercado.

All masthead photos are from ADB.

CONTENTS

Tables, Figures, and Boxes v

Foreword x

Acknowledgments xii

Abbreviations xiv

Highlights xvi

1. REGIONAL COOPERATION FOR TRANSFORMATIVE ECONOMIC RECOVERY 1

References 15

2. TRADE AND GLOBAL VALUE CHAINS 18

Recent Trends in Asia's Trade 18

Asia's Intraregional Trade.. 21

Progress of Global and Regional Value Chains 25

Special Topic: Food and Energy Crisis and Asia's Trade 30

Asia's Free Trade Agreement Policy.. 38

Digital Economy Agreements and Policy Interventions 40

Trade-Related Measures and Temporary Restrictions... 46

References...53

3. CROSS-BORDER INVESTMENT 57

Recent Trends in Foreign Direct Investment 57

Policy Focus: Investment Tax Incentives in Asia and the Pacific....................................... 69

Policy Recommendations 83

References... 84

Annex 3a: Foreign Direct Investment Regulatory Restrictiveness in the Telecommunications Sector...................... 88

4. FINANCIAL COOPERATION...89

Special Topic: The Issue of Dollar Dependence in Financing and Trade Invoicing 103

References...109

5. MOVEMENT OF PEOPLE...111

Migration...111

Remittances.. 121

Tourism...132

References...147

6. UPDATES ON SUBREGIONAL COOPERATION INITIATIVES **156**
    Integration Index Estimates for Subregional Initiatives 156
    Central Asia Regional Economic Cooperation Program...158
    Greater Mekong Subregion Program...165
    Brunei Darussalam–Indonesia–Malaysia–Philippines East ASEAN Growth Area and Indonesia–Malaysia–
        Thailand Growth Triangle 169
    Bay of Bengal Initiative for Multi-Sectoral Technical and Economic Cooperation 172
    South Asia Subregional Economic Cooperation 176
    South Asian Association for Regional Cooperation...180
    The Pacific: Regionalism to Support Resilience 183
    Promoting Climate Change Agenda as a Cross-Cutting Theme..186
    References...189
    Annex 6a: Subregional Integration Indexes 191

7. THEME CHAPTER: TRADE, INVESTMENT, AND CLIMATE CHANGE IN ASIA AND THE PACIFIC **193**
    Introduction...193
    The Trade/Investment and Climate Change Nexus...195
    Emissions from Production, Demand, and Trade..196
    Impact of Industrial Structure and Technique 202
    Foreign Direct Investment Impact on Environmental Outcomes 207
    Challenges in Greening Trade and Investment 215
    How Can Trade and Investment Policies Be Integrated with Climate Action?................................... 221
    Promoting Trade in Environmental Goods and Services 222
    Nurturing Green Businesses..224
    Bilateral, Regional, and International Cooperation..228
    Carbon Pricing Mechanisms...235
    Background Papers 244
    References 245
    Annex 7a: Potential Impact of Trade Facilitation on Greenhouse Gas Emissions 256
    Annex 7b: Analyzing the Environmental Content of International Investment Agreements 259
    Annex 7c: Measures of Asia's Exposure and Vulnerability to the European Union' Carbon Border
        Adjustment Mechanism 260

8. STATISTICAL APPENDIX..**263**
    Regional Groupings...263
    Table Descriptions 263
    Methodological Note and Update—AEIR Cross-Border Investment Firm-Level Data 266

TABLES, FIGURES, AND BOXES

TABLES

1.1	Comparison of Digital Trade Provisions in Regional Agreements	13
2.1	New Regional Trade Agreements in Asia and the Pacific, December 2021–December 2022	39
2.2	Recently Upgraded/Expanded Trade Agreements—Asia and the Pacific	40
2.3	Selected Digital Trade Agreements in Asia and the Pacific	42
3.1	Top 10 Destinations of Foreign Direct Investment—World and Asia and the Pacific	58
3.2	Top Recipients of Increased Foreign Direct Investment in Asia and the Pacific, Firm-Level	61
3.3	Average Project and Deal Size by Sector—Asia and the Pacific	62
3.4	Top 10 Sources of Foreign Direct Investment—World and Asia and the Pacific	67
3.5	Explicit Restrictions in Investment Laws—Selected Asia and Pacific Economies	71
3.6	Economies Providing Investment Tax Incentives with Sector Conditions	76
3.7	Investment Tax Incentives by Domestic Laws and Granting Authorities	79
3.8	Examples of Green Incentives Used in Selected Asia and Pacific Economies	79
5.1	Top Extraregional Host Economies of Asia and Pacific Migrants	112
5.2	Top 10 Migrant Sending Economies in Asia and the Pacific and COVID-19 Indexes	113
5.3	Status of Policies to Facilitate the Global Compact on Migration in Major Migrant Host Economies	119
5.4	Remittance Inflows by Recipient Region	123
5.5	Remittance Inflows by Recipient Subregions	124
5.6	International Tourism: Export Revenues and Contribution to Gross Domestic Product—Asia and the Pacific	136
6.1	Selected Economic Indicators, 2021—Central Asia Regional Economic Cooperation Program	158
6.2	Selected Economic Indicators, 2021—Greater Mekong Subregion	165
6.3	Selected Economic Indicators, 2021—Bay of Bengal Initiative for Multi-Sectoral Technical and Economic Cooperation	173
6.4	Selected Economic Indicators, 2021—South Asia Subregional Economic Cooperation	177
6.5	Selected Economic Indicators, 2021—South Asian Association for Regional Cooperation	180
7.1	Examples of Low-Emissions or Green Certification Schemes	226
A1	Asia-Pacific Regional Cooperation Integration Index	269
A2	Regional Integration Indicators—Asia and the Pacific	271
A3	Trade Shares—Asia and the Pacific, 2021	272
A4	Free Trade Agreement Status—Asia and the Pacific, as of November 2022	273
A5	Cross-Border Portfolio Equity Holdings—Asia and the Pacific, 2021	274
A6	Cross-Border Portfolio Debt Holdings—Asia and the Pacific, 2021	275
A7	Foreign Direct Investment Inflow Share—Asia and the Pacific, 2021	276
A8	Remittance Inflows Share—Asia and the Pacific, 2019	277
A9	Outbound Migration Share—Asia and the Pacific, 2020	278
A10a	Inbound Tourism Share—Asia and the Pacific, 2020	279
A10b	Outbound Tourism Share—Asia and the Pacific, 2020	280

FIGURES

1.1	Merchandise Trade Value Growth—Asia and the Pacific	2
1.2	Trade-Related Measures Imposed on Asia and the Pacific	2
1.3	Services Trade Value Growth—Asia and the Pacific	3
1.4	Inward Foreign Direct Investment—Asia and the Pacific	3
1.5	Average Statutory Corporate Income Tax Rate and New Investment Incentives by Region	4
1.6	Nonresident Portfolio Inflows—Asia and the Pacific	4
1.7	Perceived Solvency Risk—Asia and the Pacific	5
1.8	Remittances Growth—Selected Asian Economies	6
1.9	International Tourist Arrivals—Selected Asian Economies	6
1.10	Overall and Dimensional Integration Indexes—Asia and the Pacific	7
1.11	Indexes of Regional Integration	8
1.12	Carbon Intensive and Non-Carbon Intensive Foreign Direct Investment by Host Region	9
1.13	Digital Services Trade Restrictiveness—World and Asia and the Pacific	11
2.1	Merchandise and Services Trade Volume and Real Output Growth— Asia and the Pacific versus World	18
2.2	Monthly Trade, by Value and Volume—Asia and the Pacific	20
2.3	Shipping Costs and Freight Rates—Weekly Indicators	20
2.4	Manufacturing Purchasing Managers' Index	21
2.5	Confidence and Production Indexes versus Asia and Pacific Trade	22
2.6	Confidence and Production Indexes versus Asia and Pacific Trade by Commodity	23
2.7	Intraregional Trade Share—Merchandise versus Services Trade	24
2.8	Merchandise and Services Trade of Asia and the Pacific, By Partner	24
2.9	Intraregional Trade Shares by Asian Subregion	25
2.10	Global and Regional Value Chain Participation Rates and Shares of Their Components	27
2.11	Global and Regional Value Chain Participation Rate—Asia and the Pacific	27
2.12	Regional Value Chain–Global Value Chain Intensity By Region	28
2.13	Regional Value Chain–Global Value Chain Intensity by Major Sector—Asia and the Pacific	28
2.14	Regional Value Chain–Global Value Chain Intensity—Asian Subregions	29
2.15	Decline in Global and Regional Value Chain Participation in Asia and the Pacific	30
2.16	Changes in Asia's Simple and Complex Global and Regional Value Chain Participation Rates	30
2.17	Growth of Trade Values and Volumes in Selected Food and Energy Commodities—Asia and the Pacific	31
2.18	Average Prices of Food and Energy Commodities in Selected Major Commodity Markets	32
2.19	Number of Effective Food Trade Restrictions, 2022	33
2.20	Food and Energy Net Trade—Selected Asian Economies	34
2.21	Foreign Exchange Rates of Asian Economies	35
2.22	Changes in Estimated 2022 Import Prices of Food and Energy Commodities in Local Currency—Asia and the Pacific	37
2.23	Newly Effective Free Trade Agreements—Asia and the Pacific	39
2.24	Digital Policy Interventions—Selected Asian Economies	46
2.25	Trade-Related Measures—Asia and the Pacific	47
2.26	Share of Total Trade Covered by Restrictive and Liberalizing Interventions by Region—World	48
2.27	Share of Total Trade Covered by Restrictive and Liberalizing Interventions by Asian Subregion	49
2.28	Share of Total Trade Subject to Trade Interventions from 2019 to 2022, by Selected Commodity Group—Asia and the Pacific	50
3.1	Total Inward Foreign Direct Investment—Balance of Payments	58

3.2	Quarterly Global Inward Foreign Direct Investment—Firm-Level	59
3.3	Foreign Direct Investment by Mode of Entry—Asia and the Pacific, Firm-Level	60
3.4	Quarterly Inward Foreign Direct Investment—Asia and the Pacific, Firm-Level	61
3.5	Total Inward Foreign Direct Investment to Asia and the Pacific by Sector—Firm-Level	62
3.6	Inward Greenfield Foreign Direct Investment Job Creation—Asia and the Pacific	63
3.7	Intraregional Foreign Direct Investment—Asia and the Pacific, Firm-Level, by Mode of Entry	64
3.8	Greenfield Investment in Asia and the Pacific, by Selected Business Activity—2003–2007 versus 2017–2021	65
3.9	Foreign Direct Investment Concentration Index—Firm-Level Investment	66
3.10	Global Outward Foreign Direct Investment by Source—Balance of Payments	67
3.11	Quarterly Outward Foreign Direct Investment—Asia and the Pacific, Firm-Level	68
3.12	Average Statutory Corporate Income Tax Rate by Region and Subregion, 1980–2021	72
3.13	Corporate Income Tax Revenue, 2010 and 2019	72
3.14	Revenue Forgone in Corporate Income Tax and Investment in Selected Asia and Pacific Economies, 2019	73
3.15	Average Revenue Forgone by Tax Type—Selected Economies	74
3.16	Investment Incentives By Type, 2011–2021	75
3.17	Broadband and Mobile Subscriptions and Service Cost in 2020	81
3.18	Regulatory Framework for Infrastructure Sharing in the Telecommunications Sector	82
4.1	Selected Commodity Prices	89
4.2	Federal Open Market Committee Participants' Assessments of Appropriate Monetary Policy	90
4.3	Benchmark Monetary Policy Rate	90
4.4	Policy Rate Differential with the United States Policy Rate—Selected Asian Economies	91
4.5	2-Year Bond Yields and Foreign Exchange Rate—Selected Asian Economies and the United States	91
4.6	10-Year Bond Yields and Foreign Exchange Rate—Selected Asian Economies and the United States	92
4.7	Credit Default Swaps—Selected Asian Economies	92
4.8	High Yield Indexes	92
4.9	Nonresident Portfolio Flows—Selected Asian Economies	93
4.10	Foreign Exchange Rate—Selected Asian Currencies	93
4.11	Volatility Index	94
4.12	Financial Stress Index	94
4.13	Sovereign Stripped Spreads	95
4.14	Stock Price Index—Selected Asian Economies	95
4.15	Total Bond Return Index—Selected Asian Economies	96
4.16	Volume of Corporate Bond Issuance and Policy Rate—Selected Asian Economies	96
4.17	Variance Decomposition for Equity Returns—Asia and the Pacific	97
4.18	Variance Decomposition of Bond Returns—Asia and the Pacific	97
4.19	Debt Service Ratio of the Nonfinancial Private Sector	97
4.20	Sectoral Debt Ratio—Selected Asian Economies	98
4.21	Corporate Financing—Emerging Asia	99
4.22	Bank Profitability Indicators—Selected Asian Economies	100
4.23	Bank Nonperforming Loan Ratio—Selected Asian Economies	101
4.24	Cross-Border Assets—Asia and the Pacific	101
4.25	Change in Outward Portfolio Investment—Asia and the Pacific	102
4.26	Cross-Border Loans and Deposit Flows—Asia and the Pacific	102
4.27	Cross-Border Liabilities—Asia and the Pacific	103
4.28	Change in Inward Portfolio Investment—Asia and the Pacific	104

4.29	Currency Composition of Asia and the Pacific's International Total Investment, 2021	104
4.30	Currency Composition of Asia and the Pacific's International Debt Investment, 2021	105
4.31	Currency Composition of Latin America and the Caribbean's International Total Investment, 2021	106
4.32	Currency Composition of Latin America and the Caribbean's International Debt Investment, 2021	106
4.33	Currency Shares of Asia and the Pacific's International Investment Assets and Liabilities	107
4.34	Share of Trade with the United States and Trade Invoice in United States Dollar	108
5.1	Status of International Points of Entry—Global	111
5.2	Migration to and from Asia and the Pacific, by Region, 1990–2020	113
5.3	Outflow of Migrants from Selected Asian Economies	114
5.4	Distribution of Employed Migrants in Major Host Economies by Level of Skills	116
5.5	Visas Issued to Asian Migrants in Select Migrant Host Economies	117
5.6	Status of Policies to Facilitate Orderly, Safe, Regular, and Responsible Migration and Mobility of People, 2021	118
5.7	Remittance Inflows to Asia and the Pacific, and the World	121
5.8	Financial Flows in Selected Regions	122
5.9	Top 10 Remittance Recipient Economies in Asia and the Pacific	126
5.10	Average Total Cost of Remitting $200	131
5.11	International Tourist Arrivals	133
5.12	Monthly Tourist Arrivals by Asian Subregions	134
5.13	International Tourism Receipts	135
5.14	International Travel Restrictions	138
5.15	COVID-19 Vaccination Profile by Region	139
5.16	Fully Vaccinated Persons and COVID-19 Cases	139
5.17	Outbound Tourism from the Russian Federation and Ukraine, 2019	140
5.18	Crude Oil and Jet Fuel Price Indexes	140
5.19	Barriers to Recovery of Global Tourism	141
5.20	Source Markets for Inbound Tourism in Asia and the Pacific, 2019	142
6.1	Overall Integration Indexes, by Subregional Initiative	157
6.2	Dimensional Estimates by Subregional Initiative, 2020	157
6.3	Investments by Funding Source—Central Asia Regional Economic Cooperation Program	159
6.4	Investments by Sector—Central Asia Regional Economic Cooperation Program	159
6.5	Total Portfolio By Sector—South Asia Subregional Economic Cooperation, 2001–2022	177
6.6	ADB Regional Investment in the Pacific—Loans and Grants, 2010–2022	185
6.7	ADB Regional Investment in the Pacific—Loans and Grants by Sector, 2010–2022	185
7.1	Number of Disasters, 2000–2021	193
7.2	Production- and Demand-Based Carbon Emissions—Asia versus Non-Asia	197
7.3	Gross Domestic Product by Economic Activity	198
7.4	Share of Industrial Inputs in Total Imports—Asia and the Pacific, European Union, United States	198
7.5	Embodied Carbon Emissions in Exports	199
7.6	Embodied Carbon Emissions in Imports	200
7.7	Asian Subregions' Carbon Emissions Embodied in Exports by Destination, 2019	200
7.8	Asian Subregions' Carbon Emissions Embodied in Imports by Source, 2019	200
7.9	Average Annual Net Carbon Emissions Balance by Major Trade Partners, 2014–2019—Asian Economies	201
7.10	Net Carbon Emission Balance with the People's Republic of China, 2014–2019	202
7.11	Production Carbon Emission Factor by Region	202
7.12	Production Carbon Emission Factor by Asian Subregions	203
7.13	Carbon Emissions Intensity of Gross Exports and Imports, by Region	203

7.14   Carbon Emissions Intensity per Industry and Trade Shares per Region, 2018   204
7.15   Carbon Emissions Embodied in Exports By Sector, 2018   205
7.16   Carbon Intensive and Non-Carbon Intensive Foreign Direct Investment by Host Region   209
7.17   Carbon Intensive and Non-Carbon Intensive Foreign Direct Investment by Asian Subregions   210
7.18   Job Creation in Greenfield Foreign Direct Investment for Carbon Intensive and Non-Carbon Intensive Industries   210
7.19   Sources of Greenfield Foreign Direct Investment for Asia and the Pacific   211
7.20   Estimated Greenfield Foreign Direct Investment toward Environmental Goods and Services   212
7.21   Correlation of Stringency and Enforcement of Environmental Regulations   213
7.22   Total Environmental Goods Imports and Exports by Region   216
7.23   Share of Regional Environmental Services in Total Imports and Exports   217
7.24   Price of Solar Modules in the Top Producing Economies   217
7.25   Environment-Related Certifications by Region and in Asia and the Pacific   219
7.26   Preferential Trade Agreements and Environmental Provisions   220
7.27   International Investment Agreements with Environmental Reference, by Region and Treaty Element   221
7.28   Carbon Pricing Initiatives Implemented in Asia and the Pacific   222
7.29   International Investment Agreements with Environmental Reference, by Provision   231

BOXES

1.1   Regional Trade Agreements Help to Mitigate the Adverse Impact on Trade Flows During Crisis   10
2.1   Growing Global and Regional Export Shares of the People's Republic of China   19
2.2   Gravity Model Estimation of Bilateral Exports   26
2.3   Trade-Restricting Measures Arising from the Russian Invasion of Ukraine   52
3.1   Key Changes in Firm-Level Data Compilation   66
3.2   Investment Provisions in the Regional Comprehensive Economic Partnership   69
3.3   Adapting Investment Tax Incentives to New Tax Rules   78
3.4   Competition in the Telecommunications Sector in Asia and the Pacific   81
5.1   Economic Crisis and Remittance Inflows: The Cases of Sri Lanka and Pakistan   125
5.2   The Impact of the Russian Invasion of Ukraine on Money Transfers to Central Asia   128
5.3   The Sharpest Downturn in International Tourism Since 2000   136
5.4   Thailand's Tourism Transformation Approach: DASH Model   143
7.1   Carbon Dioxide Emissions Embodied in International Trade Data Set   197
7.2   Classification of Carbon Intensive and Non-Carbon Intensive Industries   208
7.3   Outbound Foreign Direct Investment of the People's Republic of China and the Belt and Road Initiative   214
7.4   Certification and Net-Zero Goals: The Case of Hydrogen   225
7.5   Innovative Approaches to Climate Financing and Catalyzing Private Sector Investments   227
7.6   Toward Consistent Methodologies for the Calculation of Embedded Emissions   228
7.7   Assessing the Investment Effects of Environmental and Climate Change Elements of International Investment Agreements   232
7.8   Singapore–Australia Green Economy Agreement   236
7.9   The Landscape of Carbon Pricing Instruments   237
7.10 The Process of Implementing the European Union's Carbon Border Adjustment Mechanism   238
7.11 Reaching Net Zero through an International Carbon Market: Evidence for Asia and the Pacific   241

FOREWORD

The COVID-19 pandemic, economic consequences of the Russian invasion of Ukraine, persistent geopolitical tensions on the trade and technology fronts, and growing investor jitters over high inflation and interest rates have created a challenging environment for governments to navigate a path toward inclusive and resilient recovery. Meanwhile, climate change is one of the biggest threats to achieving sustainable development. While climate goals are ambitious, difficulties in reaching global consensus on how to achieve them only add to concerns about how to rebuild economies on a sustainable footing.

Against this backdrop, the *Asian Economic Integration Report 2023* highlights the power of regional cooperation as a force for inclusive, resilient, and sustainable economic development. Despite continued disruption to economic activities, regional trade and cross-border investment demonstrate strong resilience. The reopening of borders is slowly allowing tourism to pick up speed, even as international arrivals remain well below pre-pandemic levels. However, more can be done to strengthen international trade and investment. Regional value chains remain tilted toward low value-added, low-tech sectors, while services trade continues to face regulatory hurdles. Broadening gains from digital trade requires better coordination to build coherent and comprehensive regulatory regimes across borders. These challenges underscore the need to intensify regional cooperation, including through implementing trade and investment agreements.

The report's theme chapter highlights the structural role of trade and investment in Asia and the Pacific in the fight against climate change in the context of Asia's fast-paced industrialization contributing significantly to global carbon emissions. At the same time, the region is more vulnerable to climate risks than any other part of the world. Carbon dioxide emissions from the region have tripled since 1995 and now account for half of global emissions. That scale of carbon output and Asia's position as a net exporter of emissions to the rest of the world puts the region on the frontline of climate change. The report stresses, however, that the right mix of policies and governance systems can make trade and investment an important part of the climate solution.

Regional and international cooperation in trade and investment are essential for tackling climate change and greening the global economy. The Asia-Pacific Economic Cooperation-led environmental goods list, intended to shepherd tariff reductions among members, is a good example of how regional commitments can advance global cooperation.

Policy makers can further support climate action by facilitating trade in environmental goods and services such as solar panels, wind turbines, and wastewater management that can improve resource efficiency and technology transfer. Efforts to support green business are also crucial for building a sustainable production and trading system, and reinforcing environmental and climate change chapters in free trade agreements and investment treaties is pivotal for decarbonizing trade and investment. Fostering innovative and flexible instruments to foster international carbon markets offers unique opportunities for reducing global carbon dioxide emissions and leakages across borders, especially when establishing and linking national emission trading systems based on concerted efforts by policy makers and stakeholders are emerging as a feasible solution.

I hope this report will encourage more discussions on how the region can make concerted efforts to tackle pressing climate issues, advance green trade and investment, and support economic recovery through stronger regional cooperation and voluntary compliance.

Albert Park
Chief Economist and Director General
Economic Research and Regional Cooperation Department
Asian Development Bank

ACKNOWLEDGMENTS

The Asian Economic Integration Report (AEIR) 2023 was prepared by the Regional Cooperation and Integration Division (ERCI) of the Asian Development Bank's (ADB) Economic Research and Regional Cooperation Department, under the overall supervision of ERCI Director Cyn-Young Park. Jong Woo Kang coordinated overall production assisted by Mara Tayag. ERCI consultants under Technical Assistance 6753: Asian Economic Integration: Building Knowledge for Policy Dialogue, 2021–2022 (Subproject 2) contributed data compilation, research, and analysis.

Contributing authors include Sanchita Basu-Das, Rolando Avendano, and Ryan Jacildo, with data support from Pilar Dayag and Lovely Ann Tolin (Regional Cooperation for Transformative Economic Recovery); Jong Woo Kang, Pramila Crivelli, Joshua Anthony Gapay, Kevin Daniel Quizon, Donna Faye Bajaro, and Gerald Gracius Yee Pascua (Trade and the Global Value Chains); Rolando Avendano, Clemence Fatima Cruz, Ryan Jacildo, John Lourenze Poquiz, and Lovely Ann Tolin, with data support from Kristine Anne Gloria (Cross-Border Investment); Jong Woo Kang and Ana Kristel Lapid, with data support from Carlos Cabaero (Financial Integration); and Kijin Kim, Sanchita Basu-Das, and Ma. Concepcion Latoja, with data support from Pilar Dayag and Zemma Ardaniel (Movement of People). The chapter "Updates on Subregional Cooperation Initiatives" was consolidated by Paulo Rodelio Halili, with data support from Pilar Dayag and based on contributions by regional departments in ADB: Central Asia Regional Economic Cooperation Secretariat including staff from the Regional Cooperation and Operations Coordination Division of the Central and West Asia Department and the Public Management, Financial Sector, and Regional Cooperation Division of the East Asia Department (Central Asia Regional Economic Cooperation subsection); Greater Mekong Subregion (GMS) Secretariat (GMS subsection); Regional Cooperation and Operations Coordination Division, Southeast Asia Department (Brunei Darussalam–Indonesia–Malaysia–Philippines East ASEAN Growth Area and Indonesia-Malaysia-Thailand Growth Triangle); Thiam Hee Ng, Dongxiang Li, Lani Garnace, and John Mercurio of the South Asia Department (Bay of Bengal Initiative for Multi-Sectoral Technical and Economic Cooperation); Thiam Hee Ng, Tadateru Hayashi, Pia Corrina Reyes, Esnerjames Fernandez, Jesusito Tranquilino, and Leticia de Leon of the South Asia Department (South Asia Subregional Economic Cooperation); Thiam Hee Ng, Dongxiang Li, Lani Garnace, and Subash Sharma of the South Asia Department (South Asian Association for Regional Cooperation); and Rosalind McKenzie and Cara Tinio of the Pacific Department (Pacific subsection).

Jong Woo Kang, Rolando Avendano, and Pramila Crivelli coordinated and contributed to the production of the theme chapter, "Trade, Investment, and Climate Change in Asia and the Pacific," with support from Mara Tayag. Background papers were provided by Emma Aisbett, Zemma Ardaniel, Sanchita Basu-Das, Wenting Cheng, Matthew Cole, Virender Kumar Duggal, Torsten Ehlers, Robert Elliot, Joshua Anthony Gapay, Bruce Jones, Jong Woo Kang, Kijin Kim, Jolly La Rosa, Christina Pak, John Lourenze Poquiz, Kevin Daniel Quizon, Wyatt Raynal, Prachi Srivastava, Shawn W. Tan, Mara Tayag, Lovely Ann Tolin, Lee White, Norihiko Yamano, and Liyun Zhang. Ricky Li, Joachim Monkelbaan, and Vesselina Ratcheva provided access to World Economic Forum's environmental regulations data and the Climate Trade Zero initiative. The theme chapter benefited from comments and suggestions provided by Lei Lei Song and the participants of the following workshops and events: "ADB Virtual Inception Workshop on Trade, Investment, and Climate Change in Asia" held on 2–4 March 2022; "ADB-ADBI Virtual Conference: Trade, Investment, and Climate Change in Asia" held on 20–21 July 2022; "AEIR 2023 Theme Chapter Internal Workshop: Impact of Trade and Investment on Climate

Change in Asia and the Pacific" held on 5 October 2022; and "Workshop: Asian Economic Integration Report 2023" held on 16 November 2022. The overall guidance and comments of ADB Chief Economist Albert Park on the theme chapter are gratefully acknowledged.

James Unwin and Eric van Zant edited the manuscript. Joseph Manglicmot typeset and produced the layout. Erickson Mercado created the cover design and assisted in typesetting. Tuesday Soriano proofread the report. Ana Kristel Lapid, Clemence Fatima Cruz, and Carol Ongchangco assisted in proofreading. Support for AEIR 2023 printing and publishing was provided by the Printing Services Unit of ADB's Corporate Services Department and by the Publishing and Dissemination Unit of the Department of Communications. Carol Ongchangco, Amiel Bryan Esperanza, Angel Love Roque, Marilyn Parra, Pia Asuncion Tenchavez, and Nanette Lozano provided administrative and secretarial support, and helped organize the AEIR workshops, launch events, and other AEIR-related webinars and briefings. Terje Langeland, with support from Lean Alfred Santos, of the Department of Communications coordinated the dissemination of AEIR 2023.

ABBREVIATIONS

ABEC	Almaty-Bishkek Economic Corridor
ADB	Asian Development Bank
AEIR	Asian Economic Integration Report
APEC	Asia-Pacific Economic Cooperation
ARCII	Asia Regional Cooperation and Integration Index
ASEAN	Association of Southeast Asian Nations
ASEAN+3	ASEAN plus the People's Republic of China, Japan, and the Republic of Korea
BCA	border carbon adjustment
BIMP-EAGA	Brunei Darussalam–Indonesia–Malaysia–Philippines East ASEAN Growth Area
BIMSTEC	Bengal Initiative for Multi-Sectoral Technical and Economic Cooperation
BIT	bilateral investment treaty
BOP	balance of payments
BRI	Belt and Road Initiative
CAREC	Central Asia Regional Economic Cooperation
CBAM	Carbon Border Adjustment Mechanism
CCESP	Climate Change and Environmental Sustainability Program
CDM	Clean Development Mechanism
CIT	corporate income tax
CO_2	carbon dioxide
COVID-19	coronavirus disease
CPIS	Coordinated Portfolio Investment Survey
CPTPP	Comprehensive and Progressive Trans-Pacific Partnership
CROP	Council of Regional Organisations of the Pacific
DTA	deep trade agreements
ECD	economic corridor development
ESCC	Energy Sector Coordinating Committee
ETM	Energy Transition Mechanism
ETS	emissions trading scheme
EU	European Union
FDI	foreign direct investment
FTA	free trade agreement
GCM	Global Compact for Safe, Orderly and Regular Migration
GDP	gross domestic product
GEA	green economy agreement
GHG	greenhouse gas
GloBE	Global Anti-Base Erosion
GMS	Greater Mekong Subregion
GVC	global value chain

HFTC	highly facilitated trade corridors
HS	Harmonized System
ICT	information and communication technology
IIA	international investment agreement
IMF	International Monetary Fund
IMT-GT	Indonesia–Malaysia–Thailand Growth Triangle
ISDS	investor–state dispute settlement
ISO	International Organization for Standardization
IT	information technology
JSI	joint statement of intent
km	kilometer
LAC	Latin America and the Caribbean
Lao PDR	Lao People's Democratic Republic
M&A	merger and acquisition
MC12	12th Ministerial Conference of the World Trade Organization
MNE	multinational enterprise
MOU	memorandum of understanding
MRA	mutual recognition agreement
MVNO	mobile virtual network operator
NAICS	North American Industry Classification System
NPL	nonperforming loan
NTB	nontariff barrier
OECD	Organisation for Economic Co-operation and Development
PRC	People's Republic of China
R&D	research and development
RCEP	Regional Comprehensive Economic Partnership
RED II	EU Renewable Energy Directive II
RIF	Regional Investment Framework
RTA	regional trade agreements
RVC	regional value chain
SAARC	South Asian Association for Regional Cooperation
SASEC	South Asia Subregional Economic Cooperation
SDG	Sustainable Development Goal
SEZ	special economic zone
SME	small and medium-sized enterprise
SO_2	sulfur dioxide
SRMTS	SAARC Regional Multimodal Transport Study
$TECO_2$	carbon dioxide emissions embodied in international trade
TVET	technical-vocational education and training
UK	United Kingdom
UNESCAP	United Nations Economic and Social Commission for Asia and the Pacific
UNFCCC	United Nations Framework Convention on Climate Change
US	United States
USP	University of the South Pacific
VCM	voluntary carbon market
WTO	World Trade Organization

HIGHLIGHTS

- **Regional integration in Asia and the Pacific is progressing steadily.** Regional integration, as measured by the Asia-Pacific Regional Cooperation and Integration Index, has progressed steadily over the past 15 years and remained stable in 2020 despite the pandemic. The Asia-Pacific Regional Cooperation and Integration Index subindexes such as trade and investment, infrastructure, and digital connectivity have been notably buoyant. Southeast Asia fares better than other subregions in the dimensions of trade and investment, money and finance, infrastructure and connectivity, institutional arrangements, and people and social dynamics. Looking ahead, it is critical to deepen regional cooperation to address pressing climate challenges and advance trade and supply chain resilience, the digital economy, and sustainable tourism recovery. With Asia's growing role in the fight against climate change, regional cooperation is vital for decarbonizing its production, and trade and investment.

Trade and Global Value Chains

- **Asia's trade growth remains strong, but headwinds are increasing.** After the strong rebound in 2021 pushed Asia's merchandise trade volume 11.3% higher than its pre-pandemic level, growth in trade has moderated in 2022. More recent high frequency data such as container freights and packing indexes as well as new export orders of global manufacturing purchasing managers point to a slowdown in the region's trade growth momentum. Tightening monetary policies to contain inflationary pressures in many advanced economies are affecting external demand and do not bode well for the region's exports. Overall, Asia's trade is more correlated with industrial production cycles inside and outside the region than with consumer confidence, reflecting the region's trade structure, which relies more heavily on intermediate goods exports (57% of Asia's total exports in 2021) and imports (70% of Asia's total imports in 2021) than on consumer goods.

- **Regional trade integration continues to deepen, although regional value chain linkages remain focused on less sophisticated sectors.** The region's intraregional trade share declined slightly to 58.2% in 2021 from 58.5% in 2020, which is higher than the average of 57.4% between 2015 and 2019. Whereas the European Union (EU) and North American intraregional trade shares have stagnated over the past 3 decades, Asia's has grown steadily, in part due to the weight of the People's Republic of China (PRC). While both Asia's global value chain and regional value chain (RVC) participation rates rose in 2021, its RVC relies more on simple networks—production involving border-crossing once—than complex ones. Likewise, its RVC displays stronger linkages in primary and low technology sectors than in high technology and business services, suggesting the possibility of cultivating closer value chain linkages in high value added, high technology sectors. Recent trade cooperation and liberalization momentum offered by the Regional Comprehensive Economic Partnership and other bilateral and regional trade agreements are expected to help deepen RVC linkages, laying the groundwork for regional production and trade to become more resilient to global shocks. The region's growing interest in establishing digital trade rules on the free flow of data across borders can also promote innovation, competitiveness, efficient value chains, and economic growth.

- **Regional cooperation is crucial to prevent harms from export bans and trade restrictions on food and energy prices.** Commodity price surges, prompted by the Russian invasion of Ukraine, have moderated lately. Export bans on food commodities such as wheat, corn, and palm oil have exacerbated food price inflation, and dozens of such restrictions are still in place. Weakening local currency values through 2022 also added to the pains of growing import bills for the major food and energy importers of the region. Food and energy price increases have varying impacts on Asian economies, depending on their status as a net importer or exporter, as well as the scale of their import bills and export revenues relative to economic size. Unlike crude oil and natural gas, major food importers are among the poorest economies in the region. To mitigate food security risks posed by supply shocks and logistical hurdles, policy makers should strengthen international cooperation to eliminate trade restrictions and streamline commodity supply chains, promote trade facilitation, and cultivate alternative transportation routes.

Cross-Border Investment

- **Global foreign direct investment (FDI) flows to Asia and the Pacific continue to recover to pre-pandemic levels.** Based on balance of payments data, inward FDI expanded by 64.3% in 2021 worldwide—nearly 7% higher than in 2019. FDI to Asia and the Pacific recovered in 2021, up 19.1% from 2020, accounting for 40% of global inward FDI in 2021, and down from 55% in 2020. The PRC remains the top destination for global FDI in Asia, followed by Hong Kong, China and Singapore. Firm-level data similarly highlight Asia's resilience in attracting FDI. Greenfield investment to the region grew a modest 0.8% in 2021 after declining 40.9% in 2020, while the value of mergers and acquisitions recovered by 10.1% after a 10.0% loss. Recent years have seen greenfield investments increase in other business activities besides manufacturing. From 2003 to 2021, the share of greenfield investment in Asia increased in activities such as electricity (from 4% to 13%), and information and communication technology and internet infrastructure (from 1% to 4%), while contracting in extraction activities (from 11% to 2%). Meanwhile, outward investment from Asia recovered by 15.2% in 2021, based on balance of payments data. Japan and the PRC remain the largest sources of FDI from Asia. Having been robust in 2021, FDI flows may subside in 2022, given the uncertain global environment. FDI to Asia is likely to remain resilient as the region attracts FDI from a more diversified pool of investors. Investment chapters in new megaregional agreements, such as the Regional Comprehensive Economic Partnership, may complement efforts to promote investment.

- **Tax incentives for foreign investment ought to be reexamined amid changes in international tax rules.** Corporate income tax (CIT) incentives are a significant component of investment packages, in the form of instruments such as tax rate reductions, tax holidays, investment tax allowances, and tax credits. In Asia, CIT incentives represented 50% of all tax-related investment measures from 2011 to 2021. While well-targeted, nonredundant tax incentives can foster new industries and support firms during downturns, they can also be costly and reduce the tax base. While CIT accounts for 21% of tax revenues in developing Asia, the estimated foregone revenue related to CIT measures in economies where information is available is about 2.2% of tax revenues—and can be as high as 5.8%. New global tax rules will limit tax competition and offset the use of tax incentives for foreign investment in the future. Economies in the region need to reassess their incentive structures accordingly and exercise caution when considering new ones. Greater premium can be placed on regulatory incentives that favor certain projects or sector characteristics. Cross-border cooperation will be critical for the region's effective adoption of global tax rules while balancing the use of tax incentives, and for designing appropriate incentives to encourage investment in key areas including green industries.

Financial Cooperation

- **Growing uncertainties in global economic growth prospects and worsening financial conditions could put pressure on capital inflows and local currencies.** Nonresident portfolio inflows of debts and equities rebounded strongly after plunging in March 2020 during the onset of the pandemic, and remained robust throughout 2021. Since the United States (US) Federal Reserve System's first interest rate hike in March 2022, however, net nonresident portfolio inflows turned negative although the scale of the net outflows are still relatively mild. Regional currencies have also seen a decline in their value relative to the US dollar. Stock market performances have been lackluster in 2022, reflecting tightening liquidity and financial conditions and a slowing economy. Debt-to-gross domestic product ratios across sovereign, corporate, and household sectors increased post-pandemic in many regional economies. Given the heightened financial uncertainties, policy makers need to remain vigilant in monitoring financial market conditions and guarding against a buildup of systemic risks and potential spillover effects. If financial uncertainty and evaporation of dollar liquidity trigger sharp exchange rate volatility, it could have negative impacts on balance sheets and debt management. Therefore, regional financial safety nets, such as the ASEAN+3's Chiang Mai Initiative Multilateralisation, need to be strengthened to provide a backstop in case of liquidity and balance of payment crunches. The ASEAN+3 Multi-Currency Bond Issuance Framework, a policy program under the Asian Bond Markets Initiative, could promote common bond issuance in the region based on a regionally standardized framework.

- **Asia's financial integration has progressed steadily.** Intraregional inward portfolio debt ratio increased to 29% in 2021, from 28% in 2017, while the inward equity ratio rose to 21% from 18%, and cross-border bank loan and deposit inflow ratio grew to 38% from 37%. Stronger regional financial integration could help recycle a greater portion of regional savings into regional investments. Growing financial interconnectedness, however, has also highlighted the risks of cross-border spillover and contagion effects, which might be triggered by regional shocks and financial distress. Economies in the region could strengthen an array of safety nets, such as their international foreign exchange reserves, bilateral swap arrangements, and regional financial arrangements such as the Chiang Mai Initiative Multilateralisation. Policy measures to help cushion impacts from global and regional shocks could include temporary capital flow management and foreign exchange measures, and macroprudential arrangements.

Movement of People

- **As more borders reopen and travel requirements ease, outbound migration from Asia and the Pacific continues to increase.** Asian migrants resumed emigration to major host economies where labor demand is improving, such as in the Middle East, North America, some European economies, and Oceania. In 2022, the aftermath of the Russian invasion of Ukraine aggravated the condition of Central Asian migrants, while the subregion experienced a sudden large jump in inflow of skilled Russian workers and businesses seeking safety. While work visa issuance in major developed host economies has yet to recover, labor shortages and demand for more high-skilled workers could open more opportunities for Asian migrants. Regional cooperation initiatives need to aim at improving international migration governance frameworks to uphold the tenets of the Global Compact for Migration, including migrant rights, cooperation and partnerships, and socioeconomic well-being. These could drive and sustain global recovery and revitalize the development impact of international migration.

- **Remittance inflows display resilience alongside rising relative economic contribution.** Inflows to the region recovered with a 3.4% growth in 2021, reaching $325.5 billion, after a 1.9% dip in 2020. Since 2019, remittance inflows also overtook tourism receipts as the second-largest type of financial inflow following net FDI inflows. Except for East Asia and Oceania, remittance inflows to Asian subregions improved in 2021, bolstered by recovery in major host economies in North America, the Middle East, and Europe. In 2022, the Russian invasion of Ukraine led to large money transfers from the Russian Federation to Central Asia, accompanied by Russian workers and companies. The average cost of sending $200 to Asia was 5% in the second quarter of 2022—still higher than the Sustainable Development Goal target of 3% by 2030. Advancing knowledge transfer on digital financial platforms, promoting greater transparency, and improving the remittance infrastructure could help lower remittance costs. An enabling legal and regulatory environment could also contribute to cross-border interoperability and further promote formal remittance channels.

- **Tourism recovery has picked up speed, but the level of international tourist arrivals remains much below the 2019 level.** International tourist arrivals in Asia and the Pacific rose 399% year-on-year for the first 8 months of 2022, but only to about 10.3% of the pre-pandemic 2019 numbers. Among the subregions, Southeast Asia reached 20% of the pre-pandemic level, while Central Asia and South Asia touched 50%. The variation is largely driven by differences in the pace of border reopening, public health protocols, and people's confidence in overseas travel. The PRC's zero-COVID policy held back the tourism recovery in East Asia. The Russian invasion of Ukraine also continued to pose a downside risk to Asian tourism—a potential loss of about one-third of the Russian Federation's outbound tourists, especially to the PRC, Thailand, and some Central Asian economies. Higher fuel prices translating to higher airfares and travel expenses, alongside weak global growth prospects, are dampening the recovery momentum. Experts foresee the global tourism sector rebounding to 2019 level by 2024. For post-pandemic recovery, economies in the region need to look at several policy options to build sustainability and resilience while addressing pre-pandemic challenges that include narrow source markets, mass tourism, lack of infrastructure, and high informality. While some policy options can be developed at the national level, greater regional cooperation is needed to deal with the prolonged challenges.

Theme Chapter: Trade, Investment, and Climate Change in Asia and the Pacific

- **Asia and the Pacific is one of the most vulnerable regions to climate change risks yet emits the largest volume of carbon dioxide.** Annual temperatures have risen faster in the last 30 years than in any other region, and are now 0.86°C above the 1981–2010 average. Asia is also increasingly facing more extreme precipitation incidences such as storms, floods, and landslides, having borne the brunt of almost 40% of disasters worldwide in the past 2 decades. Ironically, it is responsible for about a half of global annual carbon dioxide (CO_2) emissions.

- **CO_2 emissions embodied in Asia's production increased sharply, surpassing its demand.** Emissions embodied in production in the region have almost tripled since 1995, largely reflecting the unparalleled pace of economic growth and manufacturing to satisfy demand, both within the region and in export markets. Massive global demand for manufacturing goods, including carbon intensive ones, may not have been met without Asia's rapid expansion of production capacity, which also increased CO_2 emissions as a byproduct. Rapid growth has involved heavy resources consumption in the production of goods, with manufacturing's share now exceeding 20% of gross domestic product, which is higher than the 11% share in the US and 15% share in the EU. Asia's fast incorporation into the global value chain through industrialization, while helping promote economic growth and prosperity, has also contributed to this byproduct. Asia's CO_2 emissions embodied in production have grown much faster than the consumption side, with the region exporting CO_2 emissions to the rest of the world.

- **Many Asian economies are net exporters in their CO_2 emission balances with developed economies in Europe and North America.** In 2019, Asia's production-based CO_2 emissions were 17.2 giga tonnes. After exporting 4.5 giga tonnes and importing 3.5 giga tonnes, the region consumed 16.2 giga tonnes of CO_2 emissions. This left a 1.0 giga tonne positive CO_2 emissions balance for the region. Total CO_2 emissions from gross exports have risen almost threefold over 20 years although the trajectory has moderated recently. The region's CO_2 emissions from gross exports had overtaken Europe's in 2003, led by East Asia. On the other hand, Asia's total CO_2 emissions embodied in gross imports have risen more slowly than for exports over those years.

- **Better emissions-reducing technology, stricter environmental regulation, and growing environmental consciousness have moderated the emissions intensity in Asia's production and exports over the past 2 decades.** However, Asia still records the highest CO_2 emission intensities in both production and exports. This is partly due to the region's industrial structure, with high shares of traded products coming from carbon intensive industries. The share of carbon intensive exports in Asia was 62.3% in 2018, while it was 40.2% for the EU plus the United Kingdom, and 37.3% for North America. The share of industrial inputs in Asia's total imports, at about 60%, was also higher than for other regions, reflecting a significant import share of intermediate goods for production in Asia rather than final consumption goods. The region's relatively high dependence on manufacturing compared with primary and services sectors also contributes to high CO_2 emissions. The effect of this factor is likely to diminish as more Asian economies develop and transition to more services-driven and digital economies.

- **There is room to improve Asia's low carbon competitiveness in high carbon intensive industries.** With economic size and industrial structure held constant as factors, many Asian economies demonstrate higher CO_2 emission intensity (emissions per output or export value) than the US and EU economies in such sectors as utility and basic metals. However, significant heterogeneity is apparent across economies. For example, some Asian economies would show lower emission intensity than developed economies even in some carbon intensive sectors. This is because economies can use different energy sources and production technologies.

- **Asia has attracted the largest share of global FDI in carbon intensive industries, but its share in global non-carbon intensive FDI is increasing.** Trends in Asia's greenfield investment reflect its role as a global manufacturing hub. On average, Asia hosted 33.1% of global carbon intensive FDI flows from 2008 to 2016, above industrialized regions such as North America (29.7%) and Europe (22.5%). East Asia and Southeast Asia host nearly three-quarters of the region's carbon intensive FDI, mainly in manufacturing, retail trade, mining, gas and oil extraction, and utilities. At the same time, the region lags only Europe as a destination for FDI in non-carbon intensive industries, accounting for 20% of global greenfield investment in these sectors. By source, intraregional FDI flows—investments from other Asian peers—also reflect an important shift. They make up about 45% of the carbon intensive investments in the region, followed by investments from North America (28.5%) and Europe (24%). Yet, participation from Asian investors in non-carbon intensive industries is growing rapidly, having tripled from 9.8% to 31.5% from 2008 to 2016, suggesting an encouraging shift in regional investment toward cleaner industries.

- **FDI into environmental goods and services is also growing in Asia.** The region's estimated share of greenfield FDI in environmental goods and services grew from 3.4% in 2005 to 11.4% in 2021, with a major share concentrated on renewable energies. Indeed, an average 41.6% of foreign investment in environmental goods and services was destined for solar electric power projects and 20.5% for wind electric power. This could facilitate the transfer of green technology from foreign investment and firms, which is crucial for the adoption of emissions abatement technologies.

Trade and investment policies should be part of the climate action

- **Trade and investment in environmental goods and services can help mitigate climate change.** Clean and renewable energy goods—such as solar panels and wind turbines—and resource-efficiency goods are critical to reduce greenhouse gas emissions. They encourage low-carbon production techniques and reallocate resources toward activities with low-emission intensities. Asia's trade in environmental goods is remarkable in this regard as it accounts for more than 40% of the global volume, both as exporter of renewables and importer of environmental management appliances, among other products. On the other hand, the region's environmental services trade lags far behind other regions, accounting for less than 2% of the global total, suggesting there is great room to develop and cultivate its industrial potential.

- **With better and more affordable access to green technologies, Asian businesses have a massive opportunity to improve resource efficiency while reducing their environmental footprint.** However, challenges remain in leveraging this promise. A narrow scope and lack of consensus on the definition of environmental goods, along with tariff and nontariff measures on environmental products in some Asian economies, limit the benefits. Promoting trade in environmental goods will require preferential treatment for a broader range of goods, including rapidly changing technologies in areas such as energy and resource efficiency. Further, a regional initiative to define and liberalize environmental services is imperative.

- **Interoperability of certification schemes and mutual recognition could be pathways to lower regulatory burdens and facilitate green trade.** Interoperability should be an essential component of nationally developed certification schemes. An important step toward this is the alignment of embedded emissions—emissions over the supply chain or parts thereof—accounting methodologies. Recent experience suggests that interoperability can best be supported through a modular approach to boundary definition for embedded emissions accounting. This will ensure that embedded emissions are calculated for distinct modules along the supply chain. Likewise, mutual recognition agreements (MRAs) for conformity assessment can also facilitate access to markets. MRAs can simplify the verification process by a specific conformity assessment body. Adoption of MRAs will help reduce redundant efforts and technical duplication, while ensuring much-needed convergence to encourage green trade.

- **Trade agreements can be useful for fostering climate policies, yet further progress needs to be made.** Environmental provisions in preferential trade agreements across the world have increased dramatically from 2 provisions per agreement on average in 1990 to 87 provisions in 2018. They have been important in removing barriers to climate-friendly goods, services, and technologies. Trade agreements also outline other areas for climate mitigation such as the use of alternative energy and net-zero goals. In addition, trade facilitation measures, in particular those promoting digitalization, can help reduce carbon emissions by increasing transparency, simplifying customs procedures, improving border agency coordination, and shortening delays at borders. Raising the coverage and depth of environment and climate change provisions or incorporating a separate chapter on climate change mitigation efforts into regional trade agreements can help ensure their effectiveness in achieving climate goals.

- **International investment agreements (IIAs) could also be better utilized to promote climate action.** With climate-related litigation on the rise, there is further scope to align IIAs with net-zero commitments. As it stands, the existing IIA network falls far short of effectively supporting climate goals. Less than 10% of bilateral investment treaties in Asia contain environmental and climate-related references. Most of them aim to reserve policy space for environmental regulation, prevent lowering environmental standards to attract investment, and encourage environmental cooperation. Empirical assessments show that the inclusion of environmental and climate-related references in bilateral investment treaties has a moderate but positive impact on non-carbon intensive FDI inflows.

As investment frameworks become more ambitious in their climate policy, economies could pursue introducing a model agreement or "opt in" mechanism—a multilateral agreement where economies can flexibly join to modify old agreements—which includes substantive standards on environmental protection and access to investor–state dispute mechanisms in climate-related cases. Further, Asian agreements could expand coverage to areas beyond environmental regulation to support climate mitigation, including market access for climate investment, green investment incentives, and investment facilitation in green industries.

- **New modalities of international cooperation are emerging to implement climate action in trade and investment. Novel and practical international green economy collaborations are looming.** These can help Asian economies accelerate actions on the identification, certification, and freer trade of green products, and facilitate innovation and green technology transfers. Memorandums of understanding and joint statements of intent could build the entry level framework. While being low-cost in terms of required resources with low risk involved (as they are generally not legally binding), they could be a step toward more ambitious collaboration (including legally binding agreements). Further, green economy agreement (known as GEA) offers an innovative, promising avenue for cross-border collaboration to tackle climate change by combining green industrial policy objectives with the depth, commitment, and legal standing of a formal agreement. Through GEA, economies could pursue deep regulatory collaboration and facilitate trading in environmental goods and services across borders, among other achievements.

- **Carbon pricing is crucial for curbing emissions efficiently.** Momentum is growing for the use of market-based mechanisms, either through a carbon tax or carbon pricing system. However, Asian economies have yet to seize the momentum fully. New measures such as border carbon adjustments also loom large—particularly in the EU. While the details of its implementation are yet to be finalized, the Carbon Border Adjustment Mechanism will likely have a negative impact on the welfare of developing economies. Potential controversies remain, surrounding possible conflict with the principle of voluntary mitigation efforts, inadequacy in capturing the global social costs of carbon emissions, and questions on World Trade Organization compliance. Economies with a high exposure of trade in emission-intensive industries could be affected more than others. Asian economies need to be monitoring developments closely and to take steps to mitigate risks under the changing trade environment.

- **A global approach could offer the best solution for the reduction of emissions and carbon leakages across borders.** An international framework on cross-border carbon measures or a global carbon pricing mechanism can help resolve deficiencies in unilateral approaches. While a fully functional international emissions trading system as outlined in Article 6.4 of the Paris Agreement may not be feasible in the short term, bottom-up approaches can build the foundations for a global carbon market. As an intermediate process, direct and indirect linking of existing emissions trading schemes can be more effective than fragmented approaches in reducing mitigation costs, limiting carbon leakage, and fostering convergence in carbon prices. Regional carbon market alliances can also further facilitate trade of carbon assets, increase transparency, and harmonize standards. Regional economies will need support to take full advantage of these opportunities. Technical assistance and capacity building could provide knowledge on different carbon market models and help employ the most efficient technical options for implementation.

1 Regional Cooperation for Transformative Economic Recovery

While the COVID-19 risk dissipates, emerging challenges keep Asia's economic outlook modest.

Asia and Pacific economies are emerging from the lows of the protracted coronavirus disease (COVID-19) pandemic with reduced hospitalization and eased border restrictions.[1] However, the challenges are not altogether over. The growth slowdown in the United States (US) and Europe coupled with a dip in domestic activity in the People's Republic of China (PRC) are weighing on Asia's growth prospects. Policy rate hikes across the world to rein in surging inflation, exacerbated by the escalation of geopolitical tensions and the PRC's zero-COVID policy for a period that constrained the supply chains, provide another drag. In light of the buildup of headwinds, the *Asian Development Outlook 2022 Supplement* in December pared the growth forecast for developing Asia to 4.2% in 2022 and 4.6% in 2023 (ADB 2022a). The expected growth rate for the region is weaker than the 7.0% expansion rate recorded in 2021.

Cross-border economic activities are progressing unevenly across trade, investment, and tourism.

International flows were treading contrasting paths midway through 2022. The growth in value of the merchandise and services trade of Asian economies has remained robust although losing some traction amid persistent weakness in domestic conditions of key external markets and the tense geopolitical climate. Foreign portfolio investments have pulled back as near-term uncertainties rise, while foreign direct investment (FDI) inflows are seemingly holding up well, indicative of a robust longer-term investor outlook. In the meantime, tourist arrivals and remittances are recovering briskly in a number of economies.

Goods trade in the region continues to expand through the third quarter (Q3) of 2022, but the momentum is decelerating in line with the global trend. Asia's merchandise exports value growth has slowed to about 12% year-to-date from 29% in the same period the previous year (Figure 1.1). The region's merchandise imports largely follow a similar trend, rising by about 14% year-on-year from January to September 2022, down from 31% 12 months earlier. Notable drivers include the weakening global economy, as the US, the European Union (EU), and the PRC hobble; the ongoing Russian invasion of Ukraine; and some degree of base effects, owing to the strong growth the previous year.

There are some encouraging indications even though the economic outlook is still challenging. Besides slowly tapering food and fuel prices, the agreement reached on Ukraine's grain exports signals an openness to compromise, although the situation remains precarious overall.[2] The decline in shipping cost is another welcome development. The Global Container Freight index has notably fallen by about 75% since September 2021,

---

[1] Asia and the Pacific, or Asia, consists of the 49 regional member economies of the Asian Development Bank (ADB). The composition of economies for Central Asia, East Asia, the Pacific and Oceania, South Asia, and Southeast Asia are outlined in ADB. Asia Regional Integration Center. Economy Groupings. https://aric.adb.org/integrationindicators/groupings.

[2] The Government of the Russian Federation reportedly sought a review of the deal in September 2022 (Bland and Clyne 2022).

Figure 1.1: Merchandise Trade Value Growth—Asia and the Pacific (% change, year-on-year)

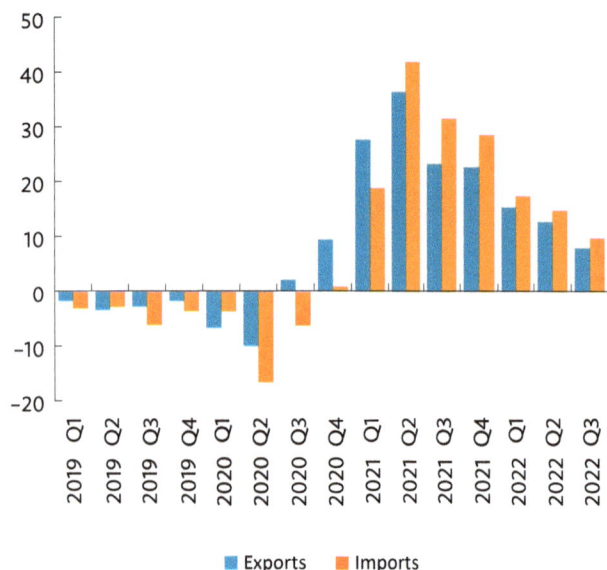

Q = quarter.

Note: Asia and the Pacific includes Hong Kong, China; India; Indonesia; Japan; Malaysia; Pakistan; the People's Republic of China; the Philippines; the Republic of Korea; Singapore; Taipei,China; Thailand; and Viet Nam.

Source: ADB calculations using data from CEIC Data Company.

Figure 1.2: Trade-Related Measures Imposed on Asia and the Pacific (number)

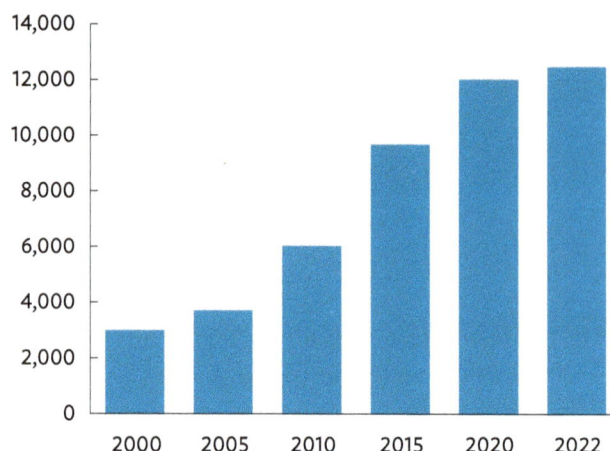

Note: Based on cumulative number of nontariff measures in force as of the end of each year.

Source: ADB calculations using data from World Trade Organization. Integrated Trade Intelligence Portal. https://i-tip.wto.org/goods/default.aspx (accessed July 2022).

although the prevailing rate is still high relative to the rate before the pandemic.[3] On the downside, the ongoing energy crisis in Europe could squeeze the region's economic activity, which could stifle Asia's trade in the coming months.

Structurally, as discussed in Chapter 2, Trade and Global Value Chains nontariff measures, such as sanitary and phytosanitary standards and technical trade barriers, remain a considerable trade hindrance. The number of active nontariff measures imposed on Asia exceeded 12,000 in 2020, which is more than threefold that in 2000 (Figure 1.2). Worryingly, the trend suggests a steady increase, with data as of July 2022 already exceeding the number for the entire 2020.

Growth in the region's services trade value was robust through the second quarter of 2022, although like merchandise trade, the rate is gradually declining. Total

services trade grew by about 20% through to the Q2 2022, compared with the same quarter of 2021 (Figure 1.3). Sectors leading that growth were transportation; telecommunications, computer, and information; and other business services. Gross transaction value rose close to that in the same period in 2019 before the pandemic hit.[4] Advanced estimates indicate that the global momentum is sustained (WTO 2022), which bodes well for the region's trade prospects.

Digital services trade gained importance in recent years with a rise in digitally enabled cross-border trade transactions. Evidently, its share in the total services trade in Asia is estimated to have risen from less than 35% in 2005 to over 55% in 2020 (ADB 2022b). However, digital regulations in Asian economies (e.g., telecom regulations, data protection, competition policy, cybersecurity act, and others) are found to be relatively

---

[3]   The weekly Freightos Baltic Index (Global Container Freight) dropped from over $11,100 in the second week of September 2021 to about $2,800 in the last week of November 2022. See Freightos Data. Freightos Baltic Index - Global Container Freight. https://fbx.freightos.com/ (accessed December 2022).

[4]   Annualized data refer to the four-quarter moving sum. The latest data are as of Q1 2022.

Figure 1.3: Services Trade Value Growth—Asia and the Pacific (% change, year-on-year)

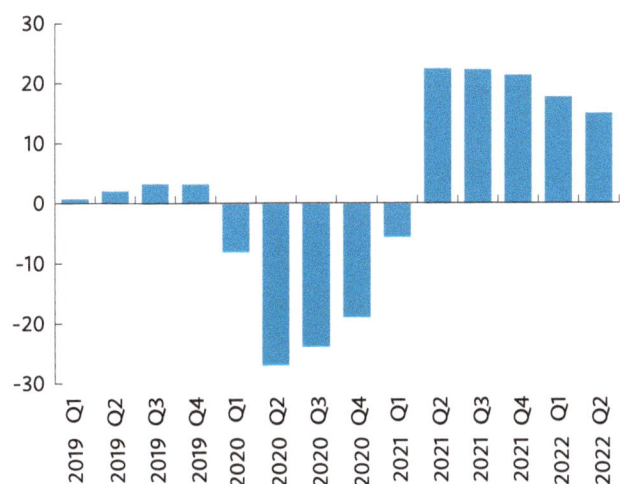

Q = quarter.

Notes: Trade in services is computed as trade in services credits plus debits. Asia and the Pacific includes Armenia; Australia; Cambodia; Georgia; Hong Kong, China; India; Indonesia; Japan; Kazakhstan; Malaysia; Nepal; New Zealand; Pakistan; the People's Republic of China; the Philippines; the Republic of Korea; Singapore; Taipei,China; and Thailand.

Source: ADB calculations using data from International Monetary Fund Balance of Payments and International Investment Position Statistics. https://data.imf.org/BOP (accessed November 2022).

Figure 1.4: Inward Foreign Direct Investment—Asia and the Pacific ($ billion)

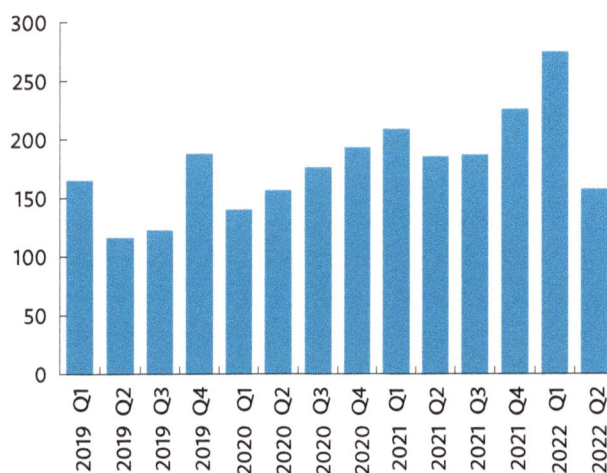

Q = quarter.

Notes: Asia and the Pacific includes Armenia; Australia; Bangladesh; Cambodia; Georgia; Hong Kong, China; India; Indonesia; Japan; Kazakhstan; the Kyrgyz Republic; the Lao People's Democratic Republic; Malaysia; Mongolia; New Zealand; Pakistan; the People's Republic of China; the Philippines; the Republic of Korea; Singapore; Sri Lanka; Taipei,China; Thailand; Uzbekistan; and Viet Nam. The data refer to net direct investment liabilities (i.e., foreign placements net of foreign withdrawals).

Source: ADB calculations using data from CEIC Data Company.

less integrated compared with traditional merchandise trade regulations (e.g., tariffs, quota, licensing standards, and procedures) (UNESCAP and OECD 2022).[5]

Net foreign direct investment (FDI) receipts of Asian economies show resilience in the first half of 2022, although data in the second quarter hint some growing apprehensions. Traditionally large FDI recipients appear to have had a mixed performance year-to-date (Figure 1.4). FDI inflows to Australia; Hong Kong, China; India; and Japan were bulkier than the previous year while inflows into the PRC and Singapore receded marginally. The year-to-date value of inflows into these economies are notably generally higher than they were in the same period in 2019. Inflows have also risen markedly in other developing economies in the region. Taipei,China in East Asia; and Armenia and Georgia in Central Asia have at least doubled their inflows year-to-date relative to the previous year.

While still robust, investors sentiment for the region in the medium and long terms is arguably weighed down by global economic uncertainties and the pressure for multinational companies to reshore (Knizek, Jenner, and Dharmani 2022). On the other hand, global and domestic infrastructure expansion plans that are a part of the recovery agenda will help sustain the momentum. For example, the Group of Seven economies have launched the 5-year, $600 billion Partnership for Global Infrastructure and Investment project (Savoy and McKeown 2022), which is said to mainly catalyze private finance and use official finance on a limited scale.

Enhancing the competitiveness of Asian economies' investment climate in the coming years may require a reexamination of domestic investment laws in the context of the international tax reform being pursued, the so-called inclusive framework. As discussed in Chapter 3: Cross-Border Investment, these may include

---

[5]   The definition of the Asia and Pacific region here is based on United Nations Economic and Social Commission for Asia and the Pacific (UNESCAP) and Organisation for Economic Co-operation and Development (OECD) (2022).

incentives in tax, research and development, and regulations. Corporate income tax (CIT) incentives are a significant component of that work. Tax Foundation data show that CIT rates across economy groups have steadily declined over the years (Figure 1.5a) and suggest that CIT rates in Asia in 2021 are lower than Africa, Latin America, and North America but higher than in the European Union and the Middle East. Asian economies have introduced several investment incentives in recent years, particularly CIT-based measures (Figure 1.5b). The aggregate number of measures in Asia is more than the tally in Europe and North America, and Latin America and the Caribbean, but less than in Africa.

Asia's net portfolio investments have receded in the first 9 months of 2022, reflecting near-term apprehensions about corporate earnings, debt yields, and narrowing interest rate differential between regional economies and advanced economies. Steep US Federal Reserve policy rate hikes were arguably pivotal in the direction of capital flows during the period. The Federal Reserve increased its policy rate by 425 basis points between mid-March and end-December 2022. Capital markets subsequently wobbled, while local currencies in the region depreciated considerably against the US dollar. Reversing the net

portfolio investment flows hinges on the effectiveness of inflation containment measures and the pace of stabilization in financial conditions (Figure 1.6).

Figure 1.6: Nonresident Portfolio Inflows—Asia and the Pacific ($ billion)

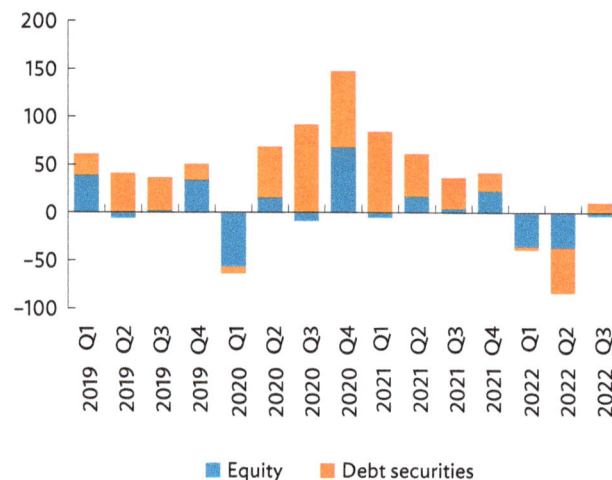

Q = quarter.

Note: Asia and the Pacific includes India; Indonesia; Malaysia; Mongolia; Pakistan; the People's Republic of China; the Philippines; the Republic of Korea; Sri Lanka (equity); Taipei,China (equity); Thailand; and Viet Nam (equity).

Source: ADB calculations using data from Institute of International Finance. Monthly Emerging Markets (EM) Portfolio Flows Database. https://www.iif.com/Research/Download-Data#PortFlows (accessed October 2022).

Figure 1.5: Average Statutory Corporate Income Tax Rate and New Investment Incentives by Region

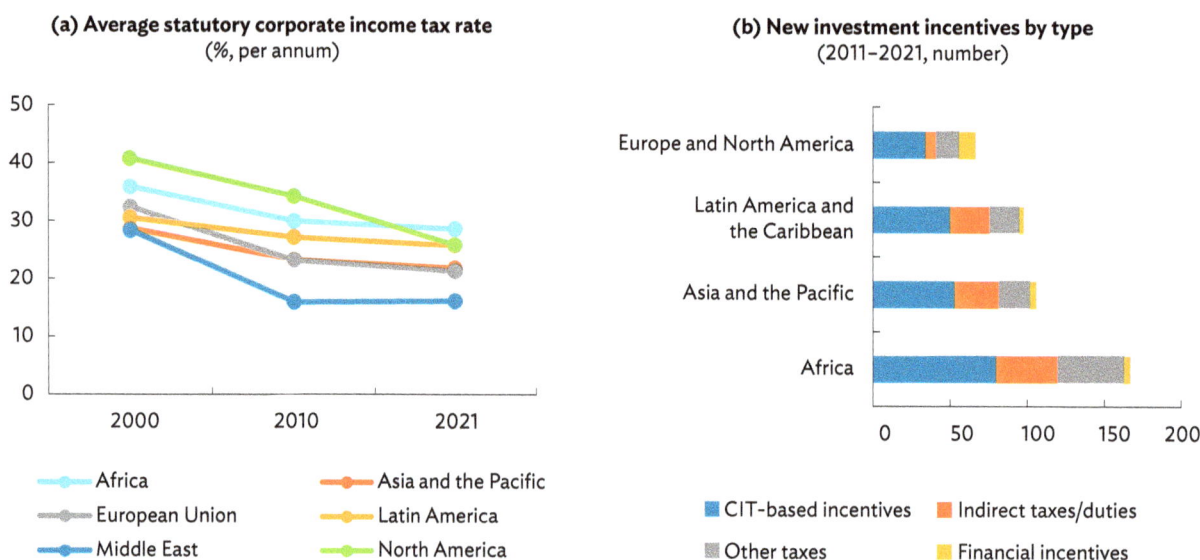

(a) Average statutory corporate income tax rate
(%, per annum)

(b) New investment incentives by type
(2011–2021, number)

CIT = corporate income tax.

Sources: ADB calculations using data from Tax Foundation. Corporate Taxes database. https://taxfoundation.org/publications/corporate-tax-rates-around-the-world/ (accessed August 2022); and United Nations Conference on Trade and Development (2022).

Reassuring investors arguably necessitates containment of solvency risks as debt has piled up in some economies in the region, as discussed in Chapter 4: Financial Cooperation. Asian economies' credit default swap spreads have been inching up generally since the start of 2022, although the wider dispersion indicates that the perceived risk is evolving in a dissimilar manner across the region (Figure 1.7a). The JP Morgan Emerging Markets Bond Index sovereign stripped spreads underline even more the divergence in risk perception for Asian economies with the inclusion in the sample of Mongolia, Pakistan, and Sri Lanka—economies facing more challenges than others in Asia (Figure 1.7b).

The buoyancy of remittances was pivotal in sustaining private consumption at the height of COVID-19 restrictions, while a recent revival of tourist arrivals brought some relief. Inflows of overseas-based individuals also partly supported the external positions of the economies. However, as with the previous year, data in recent months suggest a mixed picture. Robust inflow appears to continue in economies like Armenia, Georgia, Kazakhstan, and Samoa in 2022, with year-to-date rates

outpacing those in 2021 (Figure 1.8). Two factors that may underpin the strength on remittance inflows into Central Asia, as discussed in Chapter 5: Movement of People, are (i) the rise in energy prices that resulted in increased demand for migrants in several sectors in the Russian Federation, and (ii) the relocation of families and enterprises because of the Russian invasion of Ukraine.

In contrast, the decline in remittances persists, and even steepened in 2022 in Bhutan and Sri Lanka. The sharp fall of the value of the Sri Lankan rupee against the US dollar—about 80% between March and October 2022—resulting from the central bank's decision to float the currency, coupled with dire socioeconomic and political conditions domestically, possibly means that nationals offshore are holding up from sending money home. Bhutan's year-to-date remittance slump stems from the peculiar large drop in transfers coming from Australia.

Meanwhile, tourist arrivals are slowly picking up and providing much-needed support to ailing tourism and affiliated enterprises. The level is still far off from 2019 arrivals in many economies, but the trajectory is on the

Figure 1.7: Perceived Solvency Risk—Asia and the Pacific (basis points)

(a) Sovereign credit default swap spread range

(b) Sovereign stripped spread range

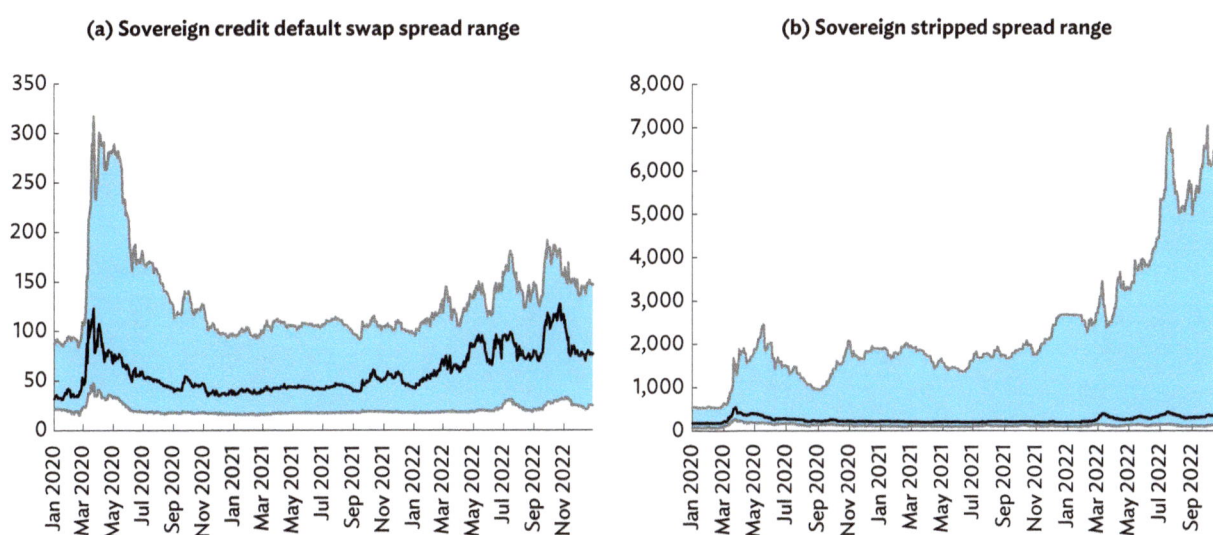

Notes: The black line refers to the median value. The gray lines refer to the upper and lower bounds. The blue shade refers to the range. For the credit default swap, Asia and the Pacific includes Indonesia, Japan, Malaysia, the People's Republic of China, the Philippines, the Republic of Korea, Thailand, and Viet Nam. The data refer to the mid-spreads based on 5-year senior sovereign US dollar bonds. For the sovereign stripped spreads, Asia includes Armenia, India, Indonesia, Kazakhstan, Malaysia, Mongolia, Pakistan, Papua New Guinea, the People's Republic of China, the Philippines, and Sri Lanka. The data refer to JP Morgan Emerging Markets Bond Index Sovereign Stripped Spreads.

Source: ADB calculations using data from Bloomberg.

Figure 1.8: Remittances Growth—Selected Asian Economies (%, year-on-year)

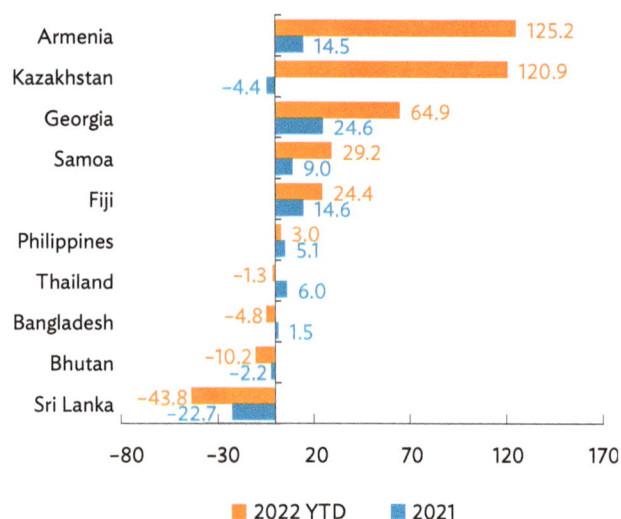

YTD = year to date.

Note: YTD data are as of October 2022 for Bangladesh; September 2022 for Armenia, Bangladesh, Georgia, Kazakhstan, Samoa, Sri Lanka, and Thailand; August 2022 for the Philippines and Fiji; and July 2022 for Bhutan.

Source: ADB calculations using data from domestic sources.

rise. The rate of recovery is however uneven across the region, with Georgia and Fiji enjoying larger increases than regional neighbors in annualized terms (Figure 1.9). It helps that many developing Asian economies rank well in tourism competitiveness compared with counterparts outside the region, but ample scope remains to build strategic partnerships and explore new source markets to maximize the potential of the sector, as noted in Chapter 5: Movement of People.[6]

Regional integration is progressing steadily, with Southeast Asia integrating faster than other Asian subregions.

Notwithstanding the COVID-19-induced disruption to economic activities across the world, the Asia-Pacific Regional Cooperation and Integration Index (ARCII) has remained relatively stable, declining only a marginal 0.3% from 2019 to 2020 (Figure 1.10).[7] Subindexes broadly support resilience in the overall index.

Figure 1.9: International Tourist Arrivals—Selected Asian Economies (January 2020 = 100, 12-month moving sum)

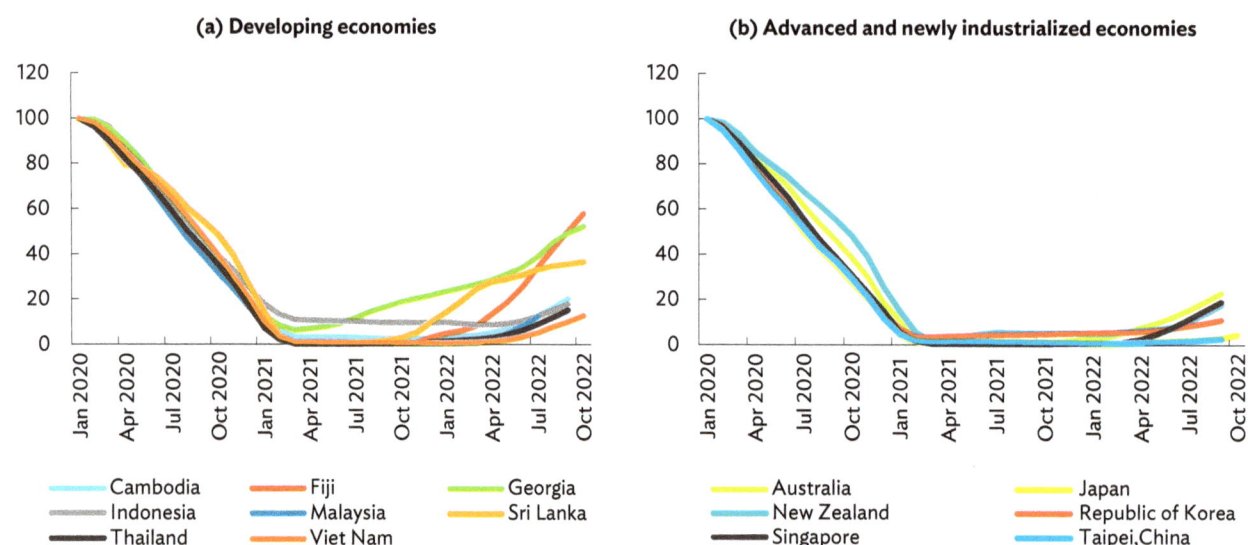

Source: ADB calculations using data from CEIC Data Company and domestic sources.

---

[6]   For tourism competitiveness, refer to Uppink and Soshkin (2022).

[7]   ARCII is a multidimensional measure of regional integration. The composite index captures the extent of integration with Asia in terms of trade and investment, money and finance, regional value chain, infrastructure and connectivity, people and social dimensions, institutional arrangements, technology and digital connectivity, and environmental cooperation. Subregional indexes measure integration of the subregion with Asia as a whole.

Figure 1.10: Overall and Dimensional Integration Indexes—Asia and the Pacific

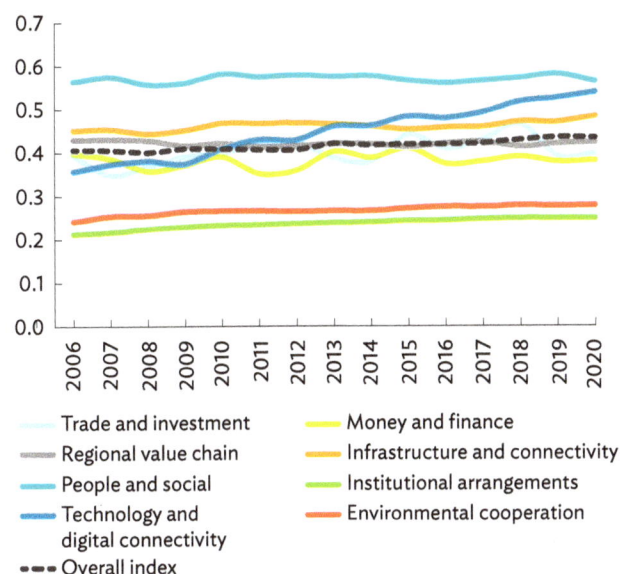

Notes: Based on ADB's Asia-Pacific Regional Cooperation and Integration Index (ARCII) estimates. Higher values denote greater regional integration.

Source: ADB. Asia Regional Integration Center. ARCII Database. https://aric.adb.org/database/arcii (accessed December 2022).

Relative to the other regional blocs, Asia trails the EU in its degree of regional integration while staying ahead of the Middle East, Africa, and Latin America (Figure 1.11a). Within the region, the highest degree of integration with Asia is in Southeast Asia, closely followed by East Asia. In comparison to other subregions, Southeast Asia fares better in the dimensions of trade and investment, money and finance, infrastructure and connectivity, institutional arrangements, and people and social dynamics (Figure 1.11b). East Asia has a slight edge in technology and digital connectivity integration while Central Asia also reports high scores in this dimension.

Economies covered by the subregional initiatives in Southeast Asia, specifically the Association of Southeast

Asian Nations (ASEAN) and the Greater Mekong Subregion (GMS), are relatively more integrated among them than economies in other subregional programs such as the Central Asia Regional Economic Cooperation Program (CAREC), and South Asia Subregional Economic Cooperation (SASEC) (Figure 1.11c). All subregional initiatives showed improvement in the extent of intrasubregional integration, except for SASEC, which experienced a decline.

Climate-related risks emanating from trade and investment call for deeper global cooperation.[8]

Asia is estimated to account for about 50% of the global emissions in 2019 as discussed in Chapter 7: Theme Chapter—Trade, Investment, and Climate Change in Asia and the Pacific.[9] Notably, Asia has become the net emissions exporter to non-Asian economies. Its carbon emissions in production have exceeded that of consumption as it is the major provider of products to meet growing global demand.

Asia hosts more FDI from carbon intensive industries than other regions. On average, Asia accounted for 33% of inward carbon intensive FDI flows from 2008 to 2016 on average, followed by North America (29.7%) and Europe (22.5%) (Figure 1.12). East Asia and Southeast Asia hosted about three-quarters of the carbon intensive FDI, mainly in manufacturing, retail trade, mining, gas and oil extraction, and utilities. Nevertheless, Asia's share of FDI in highly carbon intensive industries relative to non-carbon intensive industries remains within the global average. Indeed, for non-carbon intensive industries, Asia was the second destination for investments after Europe, making up for 20% of greenfield investment for the period.

---

[8]   This subsection is based on Chapter 7: Theme Chapter—Trade, Investment, and Climate Change in Asia and the Pacific.

[9]   ADB calculations using data from OECD. Carbon dioxide emissions embodied in international trade (TECO$_2$) data set.

Figure 1.11: Indexes of Regional Integration

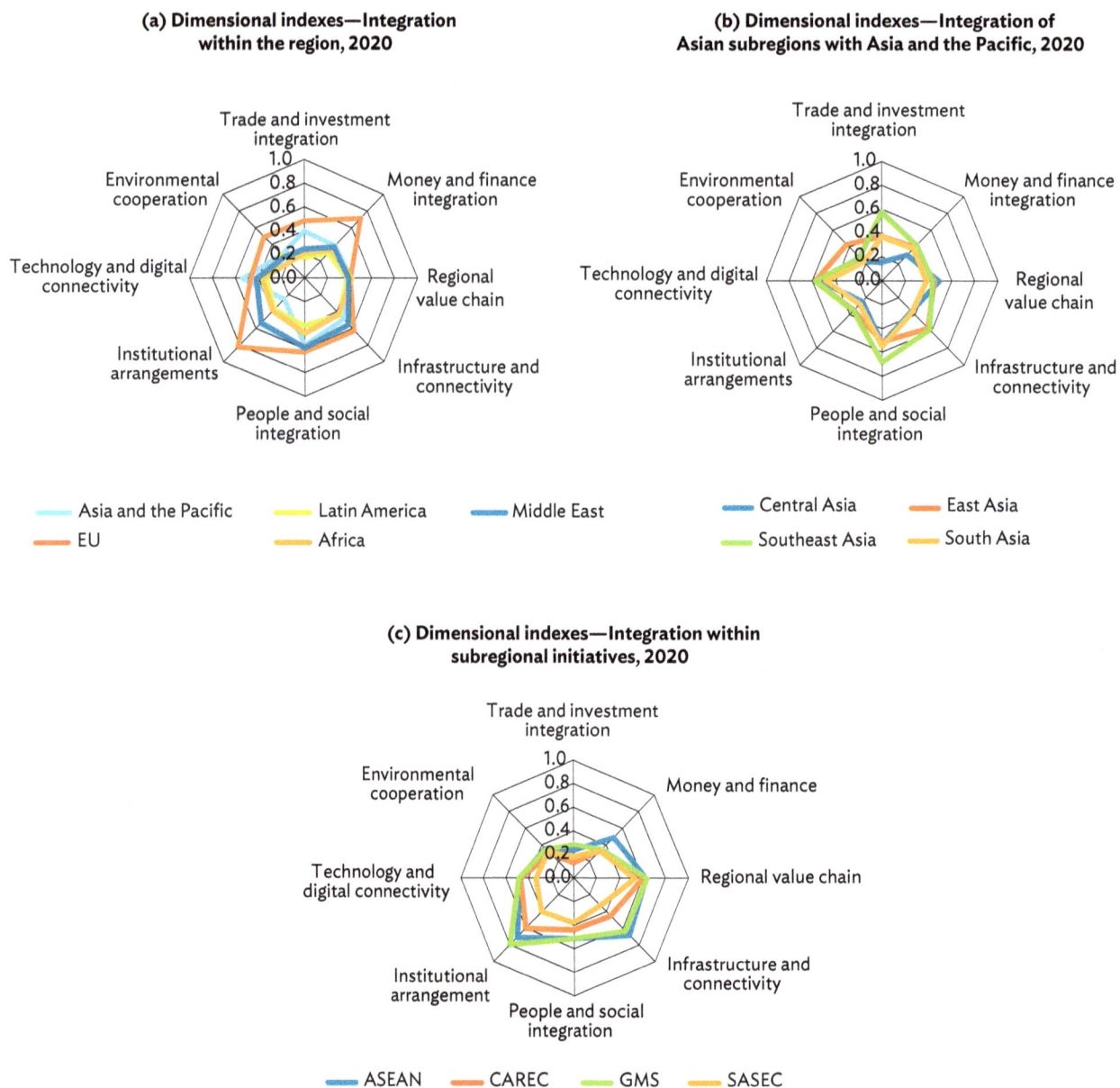

(a) Dimensional indexes—Integration within the region, 2020

Asia and the Pacific — Latin America — Middle East
EU — Africa

(b) Dimensional indexes—Integration of Asian subregions with Asia and the Pacific, 2020

Central Asia — East Asia
Southeast Asia — South Asia

(c) Dimensional indexes—Integration within subregional initiatives, 2020

ASEAN — CAREC — GMS — SASEC

ASEAN = Association of Southeast Asian Nations, CAREC = Central Asia Regional Economic Cooperation Program, EU = European Union (27 members), GMS = Greater Mekong Subregion, SASEC = South Asia Subregional Economic Cooperation.

Source: ADB. Asia Regional Integration Center. Asia-Pacific Regional Cooperation and Integration Database. https://aric.adb.org/database/arcii (accessed December 2022).

Moreover, the carbon dioxide (CO_2) content of trade involving Asia is high, which reflects the region's industrial structure with high dependence on the manufacturing sector relative to services. In 2018, carbon intensive exports comprise about 62% of the region's total exports, which is higher than EU+United Kingdom (UK) (40%) and North America (37%). Meanwhile, the proportion of carbon intensive imports in the region's total imports was 58%—also higher than the shares of EU+UK (41%) and North America (53%).

Figure 1.12: Carbon Intensive and Non-Carbon Intensive Foreign Direct Investment by Host Region (%)

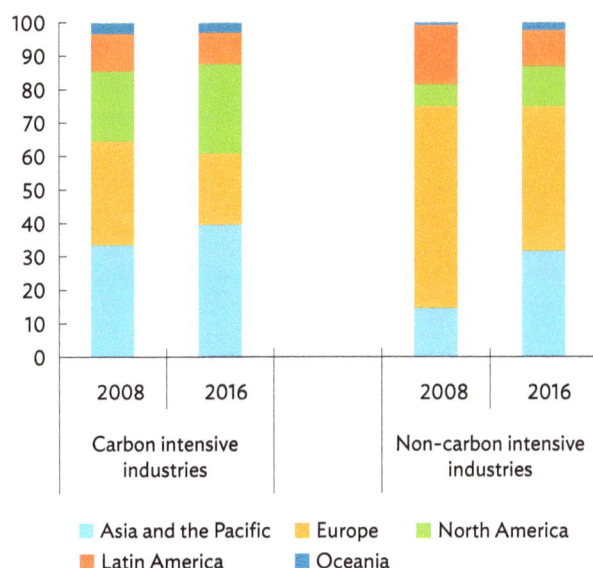

FDI = foreign direct investment.

Notes: The figure shows share of FDI by geographic location of destination economy in 2008 and 2016. The graph does not include data from Africa and the Middle East.

Sources: ADB calculations using data from Financial Times. fDI Markets; Groningen Growth and Development Centre. World Input-Output Database. https://www.rug.nl/ggdc/valuechain/wiod/?lang=en (accessed November 2022); and methodology based on Timmer et al. (2015).

In the coming years, a deepening of regional cooperation on trade in environmental goods, reinforcing environmental and climate change chapters in free trade agreements, along with trade facilitation, are going to be pivotal in the region's efforts to decarbonize production and trade. Coming up with an acceptable definition of environmental services or criteria in determining their environmental nature is a crucial first step. Encouraging environmental goods trade likewise necessitates going beyond Asia-Pacific Economic Cooperation's (APEC) list of 54 environmental goods that enjoy preferential treatment. Just as vital is the interoperability of certification systems that enable the use of mutual recognition agreements. A separate chapter on climate change mitigation policies in the regional trade agreements of developing Asia or increased utilization of green economy agreements will also be beneficial.

At the domestic level, it is crucial to nurture the production of green goods, encourage green business, and put together the appropriate financial incentives. To this end, investment policy frameworks can be made more in line with the climate change agenda. Having a trustworthy carbon pricing mechanism, which helps internalize the costs of pollution, is also key. This entails that policy makers have to keep up with carbon pricing instruments used in reducing emissions cost-effectively, depending on the economy context, and lay out the policies necessary to make them operable.

Regional cooperation remains crucial for a seamless supply chain, enhanced digital trade, and sustainable tourism recovery.

Regional cooperation is crucial in the region's efforts to chart a path for post-COVID-19 economic recovery while navigating geopolitical tensions. Climate change is fast emerging as a systemic challenge, and digital transformation is presenting both opportunities and threats. Addressing vulnerabilities in supply chains have become a key policy issue for Asian economies.

Regional trade agreements (RTAs), as one of the forms of regional cooperation, have potential to mitigate the adverse impact of supply chain disruptions. RTAs between participating economies promote strategic relations, enabling the flow of goods even during periods of crisis. Hayakawa and Imai (2021) acknowledge that even during the height of the export ban during COVID-19, exports of limited quantity of essential goods continued based on economies' bilateral relations and demographic ties. Similarly, Basu-Das and Sen (2022) agree that the onset of the pandemic hurt exports of essential goods. But the damage was not as great for economies engaged in RTAs, emphasizing the role of governments in committing to RTAs and implementing cooperation measures that lower trade barriers and create seamless logistics (Box 1.1).

The ongoing trend toward deeper trade agreements is argued to promote trade and boost global value chain integration (Rocha and Ruta 2022).[10] Implementation of trade facilitation measures, for instance, as committed to the World Trade Organization (WTO) Trade Facilitation

[10] Mattoo, Rocha, and Ruta (2020) define deep trade as "reciprocal agreements between countries that cover not just trade but additional policy areas, such as international flows of investment and labor, and the protection of intellectual property rights and the environment, among others."

Box 1.1: Regional Trade Agreements Help to Mitigate the Adverse Impact on Trade Flows During Crisis

Ensuring that trade channels for essential commodities remain unhampered in times of crisis is critical to lessen the impact of economic shocks. However, as circumstances at the onset of the coronavirus disease (COVID-19) pandemic showed, achieving such an objective requires more concerted and targeted cross-border multilateral policies.

Basu-Das and Sen (2022) noted that Asian economies' participation in the trade of COVID-19 essential medical goods tends to be influenced by their level of economic development. Low-income economies are largely dependent on imports, whereas selected middle- and high-income economies are part of two-way trade and engaged in the low end of the vaccine value chain (such as vaccine packaging materials and protective gears). The authors, who examined bilateral trade data for selected medical items that were clustered into seven categories, further point out the following:

(i)   The decline in global trade interdependence in selected categories of essential medical goods from 2019 to 2020 suggests that governments prioritized their own populations over others as infection rates grew.

(ii) The People's Republic of China and Japan were two economies whose overall trade interdependency in these goods dropped in 2020 from 2019.

(iii) Trade interdependencies are higher for Asian economies in personal protective equipment and the lower end of the vaccine value chain—a segment dominated by developed economies in Europe and North America.

In such conditions, the authors argue and empirically demonstrate that regional trade agreements (RTAs) are significant trade facilitation enablers that helped economies access essential medical goods when COVID-19 infection rates were rising and governments were focused on prioritizing their own populations. As shown in the box table, economies in RTAs appear more likely to engage in trade in essential medical goods, and this mitigates the impact of the pandemic on the vaccine and test kits supply chain in these economies. As bilateral trade costs are reduced, participation in RTAs or commitment to trade facilitation initiatives arguably provides a channel to access these essential medical goods like a form of insurance. Being part of an RTA also tends to strengthen participation in global vaccine value chains.

The authors opine that RTAs can be further utilized to identify different source economies for imports of essential goods and enhance investment in domestic production of these goods to diversify risks; lower or eliminate trade barriers; simplify border procedures; and enhance hard and soft infrastructure to improve access to essential medical goods between economies.

Effect of Regional Trade Agreements on Essential Medical Goods Trade Accounting for COVID-19 Cases

Variables	PPE	Test Kits	Vaccines	Ingredients	Vaccine Primary Packaging	Vaccine Storage and Distribution	Vaccine Administration
Export partner COVID-19	-0.116***	-0.015	-0.006	-0.047***	-0.047***	-0 046***	-0.009
	[0.017]	[0.017]	[0.034]	[0.015]	[0.011]	[0.015]	[0.010]
RTA	0.133***	0.043*	0.101**	0.090***	0.082***	0.060***	0.010
	[0.025]	[0.023]	[0.051]	[0.023]	[0.023]	[0.023]	[0.022]
Import partner COVID-19	0.050***	0.019	-0.020	0.008	-0.039***	-0.019	-0.042***
	[0.010]	[0.016]	[0.035]	[0.008]	[0.007]	[0.011]	[0.014]
RTA	-0.015	0.016	-0.030	-0.033	0.067***	0.070***	0.11***
	[0.022]	[0.024]	[0.051]	[0.03]	[0.02]	[0.022]	[0.025]
Log pseudo likelihood	-3.24E+11	-2.31E+11	-1.88E+10	-3.71E+10	-1.92E+10	-1.90E+10	-3.82E+10
Pseudo R^2	0.5095	0.6047	0.7245	0.4234	0.6134	0.4595	0.6370
Observations	115,473	57,327	14,064	86,400	28,800	86,400	28,800

COVID-19 = coronavirus disease, PPE = personal protective equipment, RTA = regional trade agreement.

Notes: Estimation results shown by the Poisson pseudo-maximum likelihood method. ***, **, and * denote 1%, 5%, and 10% levels of statistical significance, respectively. The standard errors reported in square brackets are those clustered by pairs of economies. In all specifications, we control for economy-pair fixed effects and trade flow-year fixed effects following Yotov et al. (2016) that proxies for multilateral resistance terms in the structural gravity equation first suggested by Anderson and van Wincoop (2003). COVID-19 indicates the number of confirmed cases.

Source: Basu-Das and Sen (2022).

Source: ADB staff based on Basu-Das and Sen (2022).

Agreement and the United Nations Economic and Social Commission for Asia and the Pacific (UNESCAP) digital trade, remains crucial. Addressing other challenges, such as export restrictions, narrow source market, and weaknesses in the human component, transport network, information technology systems, assumes priority given the macroeconomic impact of inflationary pressure due to supply chain disruptions (UNESCAP and ADB 2021).

In addition, not many developing economies have specific provisions to govern trade policy in crisis situations (Alisjahbana 2020). While RTAs generally include clauses to permit exceptions in time of emergencies, they do not feature provisions to effectively deal with trade disruptions in emergency situations for the most part. Shirotori et al. (2021) posit that it is relevant to have dedicated provisions in the trade agreements that distinctly define an "emergency situation" and list essential goods and services that ought not to be subjected to tight restrictions to avoid severe shortage. They also note the importance of establishing special government procurement arrangements and emergency mutual recognition of technical regulations.

As the fourth industrial revolution deepens, the importance of digitalization of trade becomes more pronounced. Digital services, digital payment, and digitally enabled trade have grown rapidly along with new technologies. Simultaneously, restrictions in digital space have increased in recent years, limiting the potential of digital trade for benefits of small and medium-scale enterprises and the marginalized population. Data from the OECD show that in general, digital trade restrictiveness globally has marginally risen since 2014 (Figure 1.13). In Asia, the policies are relatively more stable, although the region remains more restrictive than the rest of the world based on the median indexes. Addressing the challenges require coordination among economies to establish and modernize digital rules (e.g., privacy laws, cybersecurity act, data flow, etc.), and harmonize digital policies.

The Comprehensive and Progressive Trans-Pacific Partnership (CPTPP), Digital Economy Partnership Agreement, and the Singapore–Australia Digital

Figure 1.13: Digital Services Trade Restrictiveness— World and Asia and the Pacific (median)

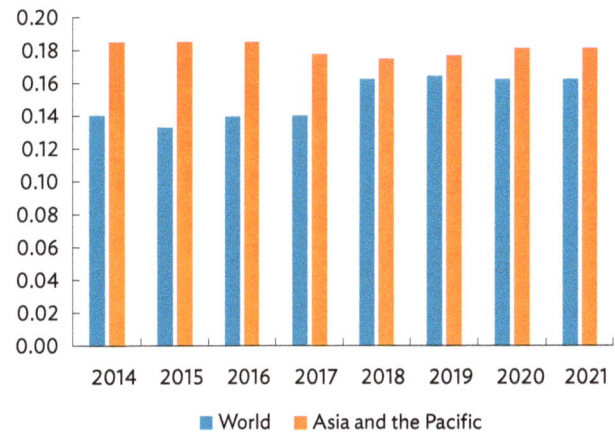

Notes: The index takes the value from 0 (completely open) to 1 (completely closed). There are 77 economies in the sample, 18 of which are in Asia. The Asian economies included in the database are Australia; Brunei Darussalam; Cambodia; Hong Kong, China; India; Indonesia; Japan; the Lao People's Democratic Republic; Malaysia; Nepal; New Zealand; Pakistan; the People's Republic of China; the Republic of Korea; Singapore; Thailand; Vanuatu; and Viet Nam.

Source: ADB calculations using data from Organisation for Economic Co-operation and Development. OECDStat: Digital Services Trade Restrictiveness Index. https://stats.oecd.org/?datasetcode=STRI_DIGITAL (accessed October 2022).

Economy Agreement are three agreements involving Asian economies that hold promise to address digital policy fragmentation. According to the World Economic Forum (WEF 2020), while the scope and coverage of the three agreements vary, they share common objectives: reducing trade barriers to the digital economy; building compatible standards and creating greater regulatory harmonization to facilitate interoperability and trust; and facilitating cooperation and capacity-building mechanisms, among others.

A comparison of the features of the trade agreements suggests that Singapore–Australia Digital Economy Agreement has more extensive provisions on digital issues than the other two (Table 1.1). The set of provisions include commitments to promote digital trade, pushing for paperless trading and electronic invoicing, online consumer protection, open government data, dispute settlement, and commonality in standards and protocols, among others. The CPTPP, on the other hand, has the least number of provisions, although it also covers a number of pertinent concerns.

The Digital Standards Initiative, under the auspices of the Asian Development Bank (ADB), the Singapore government, and the International Chamber of Commerce, is another highly relevant undertaking in that it aims to bridge gaps in digital standards and practices such as the use of digital ledgers and QR codes (ADB 2022c). The initiative mainly seeks to forge an agreement among exporters, shippers, ports, customs, warehousing/logistics, and importers concerning the standards and protocols to underpin digitalization. To this end, a proposed advisory board will bring stakeholders together "to promote and explain the measures that are needed, such as a model digitalization law designed by the United Nations."

As the tourism sector is on its path to recovery, building a sustainable one, leveraging on digitalization and addressing challenges of climate change concerns is important. Prior to the pandemic, digitally enabled tourism services have been growing rapidly in line with the deepening of digitalization. It is estimated that the global revenue of online travel platforms alone is already over $1 trillion in 2019 (Villafuerte, Narayanan, and Abell 2021), which is only lower than the e-commerce industry. The Asian region accounts for over 37% of the global revenue pie, which is roughly the same as the combined total of the US (20%) and the euro area (17%), largely driven by the PRC.

The appeal of digitalized services arguably hinges on the ease in scanning options and in conducting the transactions. According to the United Nations World Tourism Organization (UNWTO) the use of technologies has made tourism more efficient, inclusive, and economically and environmentally sustainable than previously. These tools are also deemed to have "facilitated innovation and rethinking of processes, with a view to tackling challenges such as seasonality and overcrowding and developing smarter destinations."[11]

Many regional organizations have strengthened their cooperation around digitalization of the tourism industry. They have either promised to encourage greater use of technology in tourism services delivery or have committed to developing the skills for tourism marketing and growth. For example, ASEAN governments, in 2020, adopted the ASEAN Declaration on Digital Tourism (ASEAN 2020) emphasizing the use of digital technology for tourism development to enhance competitiveness and growth.

Separately, the Pacific Tourism Organisation, with the support of the Government of New Zealand, has rolled out a 4-year digital transformation program (SPTO 2021a) in 2021. The program, which is in its second phase focuses on training and projects related to digital marketing, advocacy and communications, and sustainable development and research—all in accordance with the Pacific Tourism Organisation's Digital Strategy Framework (Solomon Times 2022, SPTO 2021b). Similarly, the Central Asia Regional Economic Cooperation Program (CAREC) Tourism Strategy 2030, reiterates the importance of cooperation to develop digital platforms and promote use of digital tools and data to identify opportunities to upscale cross-border tourism (ADB 2020).

Technology can also help pave the sustainable tourism pathways for the region.[12] Some of the technology-related opportunities ADB (2021) underscores for the sector are in waste, water, and energy management; travel and health requirement coordination; data collection for more informed decision-making; and emission containment through digitization of processes and transactions.[13]

---

[11]   UNWTO. Digital Transformation. https://www.unwto.org/digital-transformation.

[12]   As for the notion of sustainable tourism, UNWTO enumerates three broad parameters. First, environmental resources have to be used optimally in the sense that essential ecological processes are maintained, and natural heritage and biodiversity are conserved. Second, the sociocultural authenticity of the host communities has to be respected, and understanding and tolerance among cultures have to be promoted. Finally, economic benefits have to be fairly distributed among stakeholders, with activities geared toward poverty alleviation (see UNWTO. Sustainable Development. https://www.unwto.org/sustainable-development). European Commission (2016) succinctly lays out how sustainable tourism is related to concepts such as ecotourism, ethical tourism, and responsible tourism.

[13]   These are some of the risks and challenges identified by ADB (2021).

Table 1.1: Comparison of Digital Trade Provisions in Regional Agreements

Key		No.	Digital Trade Provisions	DEA	DEPA	CPTPP
✓	Provision is identical (or very close to identical)	1	Commitments to facilitate digital trade	✓	✓	✓
✓ (+)	Provision article is more comprehensive	2	No customs duties on electronic transmissions	✓ [5]	✓ [3.2]	✓ [14.3]
✓ (-)	Provision article is less comprehensive	3	Nondiscrimination of digital products	✓ [6]	✓ [3.3]	✓ [14.4]
✗	No similar provision articles	4	Domestic electronic transactions framework	✓ [8]	✓ [2.3]	✓ [14.5]
[ ]	Numbers in brackets refer to the agreement's article number	5	Electronic authentication and signatures	✓ (+) [9]	✗	✓ (-) [14.6]
		6	Paperless trading	✓ (+) [12]	✓ (+) [2.2]	✓ (+) [14.9]
		7	Electronic invoicing	✓ (+) [10]	✓ (-) [2.5]	✗
		8	Electronic payments	✓ [11]	✓ [2.7]	✗
		9	Express shipments	✓ [13]	✓ [2.6]	✓ [5.7]
		10	Online consumer protection	✓ [15]	✓ [6.3]	✓ [14.7]
		11	Cooperation on competition policy	✓ [16]	✓ [8.4]	✗
		12	Personal information protection	✓ (-) [17]	✓ (+) [4.2]	✓ (-) [14.8]
		13	Unsolicited commercial electronic messages	✓ (+) [17]	✓ (-) [4.2]	✓ (-) [14.8]
		14	Submarine telecommunications cable systems	✓ [22]	✗	✗
		15	Location of computing facilities for financial services	✓ [25]	✗	✗
		16	Data innovation	✓ (-) [26]	✓ (+) [9.4]	✗
		17	Open government data	✓ [27]	✓ [9.5]	✗
		18	Source code	✓ (+) [28]	✗	✓ (-) [14.17]
		19	Digital identities	✓ [29]	✓ [7.1]	✗
		20	Standards and conformity assessment for digital trade	✓ [30]	✗	✗
		21	Artificial intelligence	✓ [31]	✓ [8.2]	✗
		22	Fintech and regtech cooperation	✓ [32]	✓ [8.1]	✗
		23	Dispute settlement	✓ (+) [21]	✓ (+) [14]	✓ (-) [14.18]

CPTPP = Comprehensive and Progressive Trans-Pacific Partnership, DEA = Digital Economy Agreement (Singapore–Australia), DEPA = Digital Economy Partnership Agreement.
Source: World Economic Forum (2020).

The Southeast Asia Sustainable Tourism Hub was launched in March 2022 under the auspices of ADB in line with the post-COVID-19 regional cooperation agenda. The hub is geared toward accelerating a sustainable and inclusive recovery of the tourism industry through assistance to local tourism entrepreneurs, especially women and youth, including adoption of digital platforms to grow their businesses (ADB Knowledge Events 2022). Along the same lines, during the 11th APEC Tourism Ministerial Meeting in August 2022, the 21 member economies likewise agreed to a set of policy recommendations that emphasizes economic, social, cultural, and environmental actions (APEC 2022).

New emerging issues require collective actions.

In post-COVID-19 recovery, regional cooperation among Asian economies will be shaped by global, regional, and domestic forces. While developing economies cooperate at the global level through multilateral frameworks to resolve challenges around global public goods (such as climate change and future pandemics), they also simultaneously manage their own macroeconomic policies to serve domestic interest. Regional cooperation among like-minded economies will continue to assume importance to advance globalization.

In the coming years, cooperation will be sought in areas of hard and soft (regulations) infrastructure to address shared technological, environmental, and socioeconomic challenges. While the rise of nationalist sentiment and the expansion of geopolitics (driven by the shift in economic power, trade conflicts, technology rivalry, the Russian invasion of Ukraine, and others) will be considered as part of the new normal, unpacking the potential of digital transformation will be crucial for economic competitiveness and greater inclusiveness. Investment in the green economy will gain traction. And governments will cooperate to tackle the pressing issue of inequality, particularly in accessing social infrastructure.

References

Alisjahbana, A. S. 2020. Forging Resilient Regional Supply Chains and Connectivity. Op-Ed. 7 October. United Nations Economic and Social Commission for Asia and the Pacific (UNESCAP). https://www.unescap.org/op-ed/forging-resilient-regional-supply-chains-and-connectivity.

Anderson, J. E., and E. van Wincoop. 2003. Gravity with Gravitas: A Solution to the Border Puzzle. *American Economic Review*. 93 (1). pp. 170–192.

Asian Development Bank (ADB). 2020. *CAREC Tourism Strategy 2030*. Manila.

———. 2021. *Sustainable Tourism after COVID-19: Insights and Recommendations for Asia and the Pacific*. Manila.

———. 2022a. *Asian Development Outlook (ADO) 2022 Supplement: Global Gloom Dims Asian Prospects*. Manila.

———. 2022b. *Asian Economic Integration Report 2022: Advancing Digital Services Trade in Asia and the Pacific*. Manila.

———. 2022c. Global Supply Chains Need Upgrading for a Green, Inclusive, Resilient and Socially Responsible Future. Article. 22 June. Manila.

———. Asia Regional Integration Center. Asia-Pacific Regional Cooperation and Integration Index Database. https://aric.adb.org/database/arcii (accessed December 2022).

———. Asia Regional Integration Center. Economy Groupings. https://aric.adb.org/integrationindicators/groupings.

ADB Knowledge Events. 2022. ADB's Southeast Asia Sustainable Tourism Hub Launched at #SEADS2022. 16 March. https://events.development.asia/materials/20220316/adbs-southeast-asia-sustainable-tourism-hub-launched-seads2022.

Asia-Pacific Economic Cooperation (APEC). 2022. Policy Recommendations for Tourism of the Future: Regenerative Tourism. Prepared for the 11th APEC Tourism Ministerial Meeting. Bangkok. 19 August.

Association of Southeast Asian Nations (ASEAN). 2020. ASEAN Declaration on Digital Tourism. Prepared at the 37th ASEAN Summit. Ha Noi. 12–15 November.

Basu-Das, S., and R. Sen. 2022. Trade Interdependencies in COVID-19-Related Essential Medical Goods: Role of Trade Facilitation and Cooperation for the Asian Economies. *ADB Economics Working Papers*. No. 666. Manila: ADB.

Bland, W., and H. Clyne. 2022. Russia Seeks Review of Ukraine's Black Sea Grain Exports Deal. *S&P Global Commodity Insights*. 7 September. https://www.spglobal.com/commodityinsights/en/market-insights/latest-news/agriculture/090722-russia-seeks-review-of-ukraines-black-sea-grain-exports-deal.

European Commission. 2016. Why Going Sustainable? A Business Case for Sustainable Tourism. https://ec.europa.eu/programmes/erasmus-plus/project-result-content/94dc3fda-1b2a-427d-8532-4fdf9c16fe9a/Innoguide%20Advanced%20Sustainability.pdf.

Freightos Data. Freightos Baltic Index - Global Container Freight. https://fbx.freightos.com/ (accessed December 2022).

Global Future Council on International Trade and Investment. 2020. *Advancing Digital Trade in Asia*. Geneva: World Economic Forum.

Groningen Growth and Development Centre. World Input-Output Database. https://www.rug.nl/ggdc/valuechain/wiod/?lang=en (accessed November 2022).

Hayakawa, K. and K. Imai. 2021. Who Sends Me Face Masks? Evidence for the Impacts of COVID-19 on International Trade in Medical Goods. *The World Economy*. 45 (2). pp. 365-385.

Institute of International Finance. Monthly Emerging Markets (EM) Portfolio Flows Database. https://www.iif.com/Research/Download-Data#PortFlows (accessed October 2022).

International Monetary Fund (IMF). Balance of Payments and International Investment Position Statistics. https://data.imf.org/BOP (accessed November 2022).

Knizek, C., F. Jenner, and S. Dharmani. 2022. *Why Global Industrial Supply Chains Are Decoupling*. London: Ernst & Young Global Limited.

Mattoo, A., N. Rocha, and M. Ruta. 2020. *Handbook of Deep Trade Agreements*. Washington, DC: World Bank.

Organisation for Economic Co-operation and Development (OECD). OECD Digital Services Trade Restrictiveness Index database. https://stats.oecd.org/?datasetcode=STRI_DIGITAL (accessed October 2022).

Pacific Tourism Organisation (SPTO). 2021a. *Digital Transformation Project to Guide Pacific Tourism Recovery Efforts*. Suva.

———. 2021b. Digital Strategy Framework: Summary for Marketing Sub Committee. 31 March. https://southpacificislands.travel/wp-content/uploads/2021/07/Pacific-Tourism-Digital-Strategy-2021.pdf.

Rocha, N. and M. Ruta , eds. 2022. *Deep Trade Agreements: Anchoring Global Value Chains in Latin America and the Caribbean*. Washington, DC: World Bank.

Savoy, C. M. and S. McKeown. 2022. Future Considerations for the Partnership on Global Infrastructure and Investment. Commentary. Center for Strategic and International Studies. 29 June. https://www.csis.org/analysis/future-considerations-partnership-global-infrastructure-and-investment.

Shirotori, M., T. Ito, Y. Duval, R. Du, and G. Marceau. 2021. *Readying Regional Trade Agreements for Future Crises and Pandemics*. Geneva: United Nations Conference on Trade and Development.

Solomon Times. 2022. Miles Partnership to Design e-learning Modules for SPTO Members. 14 July. Honiara.

Tax Foundation. Corporate Taxes database. https://taxfoundation.org/publications/corporate-tax-rates-around-the-world/ (accessed August 2022).

Timmer, M. P., E. Dietzenbacher, B. Los, R. Stehrer, and G. J de Vries. 2015. An Illustrated User Guide to the World Input–Output Database: The Case of Global Automotive Production. *Review of International Economics*. 23 (3) pp. 575–605.

United Nations Conference on Trade and Development (UNCTAD). 2022. Corporate Income Taxes and Investment Incentives: A Global Review. *Investment Policy Monitor*. No. 8. Geneva.

United Nations Economic and Social Commission for Asia and the Pacific (UNESCAP) and ADB. 2021. *Asia-Pacific Trade Facilitation Report 2021: Supply Chains of Critical Goods amid the COVID-19 Pandemic—Disruptions, Recovery, and Resilience*. Bangkok and Manila.

UNESCAP and OECD. 2022. *Asia-Pacific Digital Trade Regulatory Review 2022: ESCAP-OECD Initiative on Digital Trade Regulatory Analysis*. Bangkok and Paris.

United Nations World Tourism Organization (UNWTO). Digital Transformation. https://www.unwto.org/digital-transformation.

———. Sustainable Development. https://www.unwto.org/sustainable-development.

Uppink, L. and M. Soshkin. 2022. Travel & Tourism Development Index 2021: Rebuilding for a Sustainable and Resilient Future. *Insight Report.* Geneva: World Economic Forum.

Villafuerte, J., B. Narayanan, and T. Abell. 2021. Digital Platforms, Technology, and Their Macroeconomic Impact. In C. Y. Park, J. Villafuerte, and J. T. Yap, eds. *Managing the Development of Digital Marketplaces in Asia.* Manila: ADB.

World Trade Organization (WTO). 2022. Trade Growth to Slow Sharply in 2023 as Global Economy Faces Strong Headwinds. Press release. 5 October. https://www.wto.org/english/news_e/pres22_e/pr909_e.htm.

———. Integrated Trade Intelligence Portal. https://i-tip.wto.org/goods/default.aspx (accessed July 2022).

Yotov, Y. V., R. Piermartini, J. Monteiro, and M. Larch. 2016. *An Advanced Guide to Trade Policy Analysis: The Structural Gravity Model.* Geneva: WTO.

2 Trade and Global Value Chains

Recent Trends in Asia's Trade

Asia and the Pacific recovered strongly in 2021 as its merchandise and services trade grew rapidly.[14]

As the coronavirus disease (COVID-19) lockdowns eased, the Asian economies grew 6.2% in 2021, contributing 37% of the world's economic growth. The region's merchandise trade volume grew by 13.2%, faster than world merchandise trade growth at 10.8%. Services trade volume in the region grew by 8.4%, which was also faster than global services trade growth, at 7.6% (Figure 2.1).

In 2021, Asia surpassed its pre-pandemic gross domestic product (GDP) and merchandise trade levels, but its services trade has yet to fully recover. In the same year, the region's economy was 5.4% higher than its 2019 level, while trade in merchandise goods was 11.3% higher than in 2019. The region's trade in services was still 11.1% below its level of 2019. Services trade may have been hit harder than merchandise trade, as COVID-19 lockdowns

Figure 2.1: Merchandise and Services Trade Volume and Real Output Growth— Asia and the Pacific versus World (%, year-on-year)

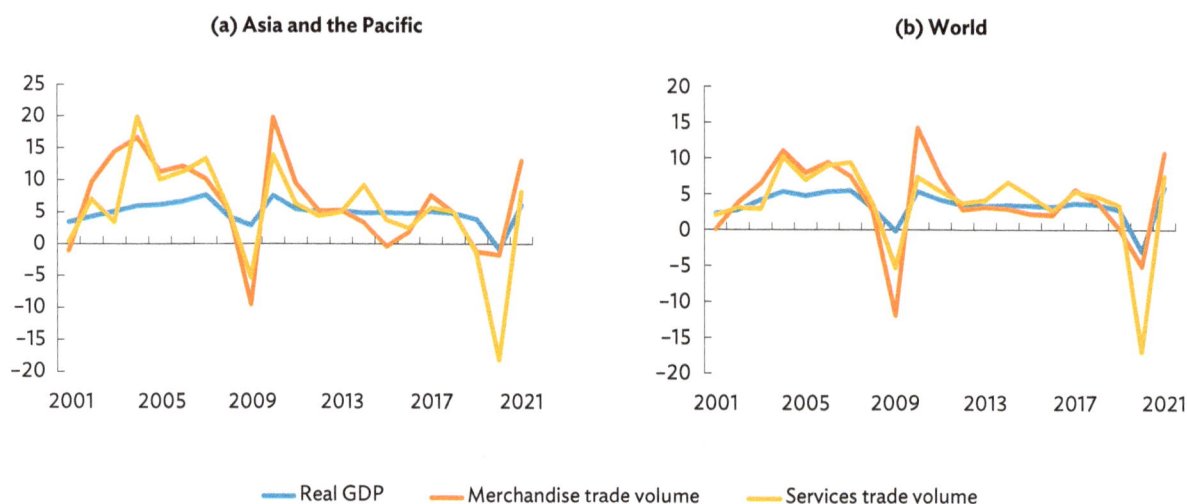

(a) Asia and the Pacific

(b) World

Real GDP — Merchandise trade volume — Services trade volume

GDP = gross domestic product.

Sources: ADB calculations using data from International Monetary Fund (IMF). World Economic Outlook October 2022 Database. https://www.imf.org/en/Publications/WEO/weo-database/2022/October; IMF. Direction of Trade Statistics. https://data.imf.org/dot; and WTO-OECD Balanced Trade in Services Dataset (BaTIS)—BPM6. https://www.wto.org/english/res_e/statis_e/trade_datasets_e.htm (all accessed December 2022).

---

[14] Asia and the Pacific, or Asia, consists of the 49 regional member economies of the Asian Development Bank (ADB). The composition of economies for Central Asia, East Asia, the Pacific and Oceania, South Asia, and Southeast Asia are outlined in ADB. Asia Regional Integration Center. Economy Groupings. https://aric.adb.org/integrationindicators/groupings.

curtailed people's movements and activities, hitting sectors such as tourism particularly hard.

Asia's economic recovery is driven particularly by the People's Republic of China (PRC), which accounted for 64.2% of total growth. The PRC also contributed 37.6% of the region's total trade growth in goods, and 44.6% of total trade growth in services (Box 2.1). The Association of Southeast Asian Nations (ASEAN), accounting for only 5.2% of Asia's economic growth, contributed 19.7% of Asia's growth in merchandise trade and 13.3% of its growth in services trade. Developed Asian economies—Australia, Japan, and New Zealand—accounted for 8% of the region's economic growth, 8.2% of trade in goods growth, and 5.3% of trade in services growth.

After the pandemic hit and Asia's merchandise trade shrank, it returned to positive growth in October 2020, peaking in June 2021 with double-digit growth rates. Nonetheless, Asia's trade growth slowed in the first months of 2022. The PRC seemed to lead the region with faster recovery and an earlier return to growth in July 2020, peaking in March 2021 in the double digits. However, the PRC's trade has been on the decline again since March 2022 amid renewed lockdowns to contain the COVID-19 Omicron variant and maintain its zero-COVID policy. Trade returned to growth in the PRC in July 2022 as it eased its lockdowns. Asia's trade values in particular seemed to be growing, with double-digit price increases since January 2021. The gap between trade value and volume growth is widening under persistent global inflationary pressures (Figure 2.2).

Box 2.1: Growing Global and Regional Export Shares of the People's Republic of China

Regional and global export value and volume shares of the People's Republic of China, in 2021, rose above their pre-pandemic levels. The economy's export value shares have been consistently higher than its trade volume shares.

In 2021, the electrical machinery and equipment commodity group contributed most to the economy's rising exports (26%) followed by mechanical appliances (14%) and vehicles (5%).

PRC's Growing Global and Regional Export Shares

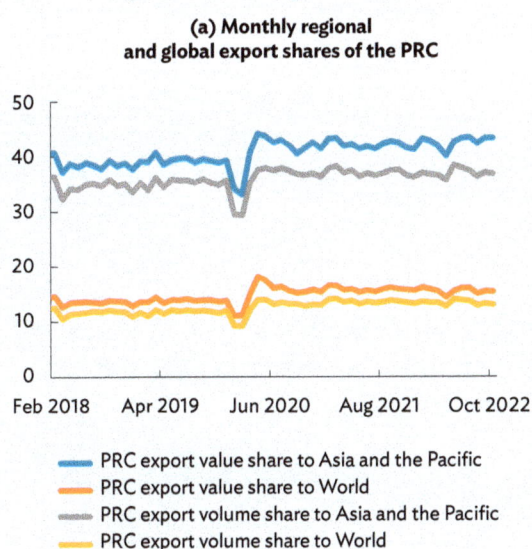

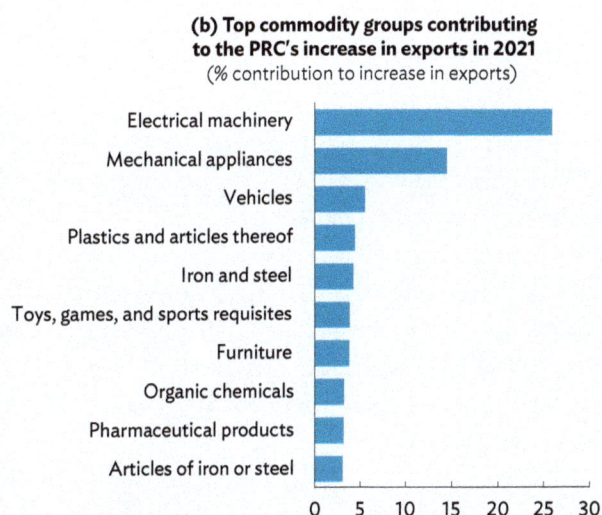

(a) Monthly regional and global export shares of the PRC

Legend:
— PRC export value share to Asia and the Pacific
— PRC export value share to World
— PRC export volume share to Asia and the Pacific
— PRC export volume share to World

(b) Top commodity groups contributing to the PRC's increase in exports in 2021
(% contribution to increase in exports)

PRC = People's Republic of China.

Note: Contribution to increase in exports is computed by dividing the change in export level of a specific commodity with the change in total export level.

Sources: ADB calculations using CPB Netherlands Bureau for Economic Policy Analysis. World Trade Monitor October 2022. https://www.cpb.nl/en/world-trade-monitor-october-2022; and United Nations. Commodity Trade Database. https://comtrade.un.org (both accessed January 2023).

Figure 2.2: Monthly Trade, by Value and Volume—Asia and the Pacific

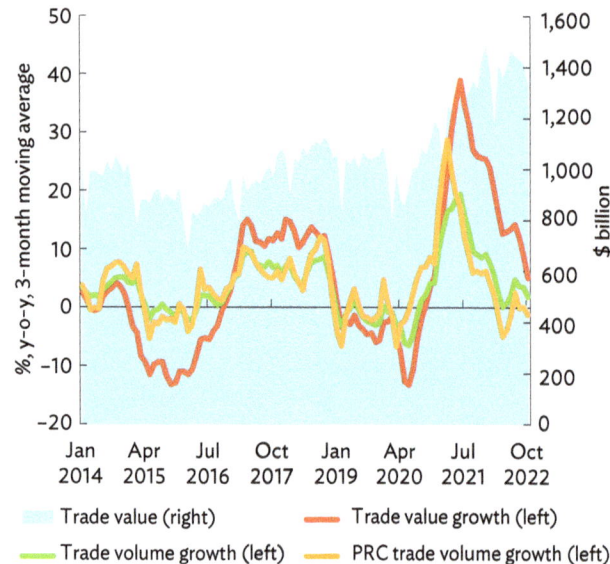

PRC = People's Republic of China, y-o-y = year-on-year.

Notes: Trade volume growth rates were computed using volume indexes. For each period and trade flow type (i.e., imports and exports), available data include indexes for the PRC and Japan, and aggregate indexes for selected Asia and Pacific economies: (1) advanced economies excluding Japan (Hong Kong, China; the Republic of Korea; Singapore; and Taipei,China); and (2) emerging economies excluding the PRC (India, Indonesia, Malaysia, Pakistan, the Philippines, Thailand, and Viet Nam). The aggregate index for Asia and the Pacific was computed using trade values as weights.

Sources: ADB calculations using data from CEIC Data Company; and CPB Netherlands Bureau for Economic Policy Analysis. World Trade Monitor. https://www.cpb.nl/en/world-trade-monitor-october-2022 (accessed January 2023).

Newly industrialized economies in Asia, and some ASEAN economies, sustained positive merchandise trade growth in 2021. Exports from Indonesia; the PRC; the Republic of Korea; Taipei,China; and Thailand managed to sustain growth in the first half of 2022, while growth rates in Hong Kong, China and Singapore declined. Imports of Hong Kong, China and the PRC declined in the first half of 2022, but increased in Indonesia; Malaysia; the Republic of Korea; Singapore; Taipei,China; and Thailand.

Rising shipping costs and freight rates could dampen global trade recovery, including Asia's. In 2021, container freight rates, as measured by Bloomberg and MSCI Containers and Packaging indexes, have been higher than in the past 3 years, before decreasing gradually by mid-June 2022. The cost of shipping goods, measured

by Baltic Dry Index, peaked in the middle of 2021 then tapered off (Figure 2.3).

S&P Global Manufacturing Purchasing Managers' Index New Export Orders subindex of Asia and the world point to the deteriorating trade environment over time since 2021. This finding is corroborated by the Purchasing Managers' Index Stocks of Finished Goods subindex of the world, which indicates the possible piling up of stocks due to weaker global demand (Figure 2.4).

Figure 2.3: Shipping Costs and Freight Rates—Weekly Indicators (z-scores)

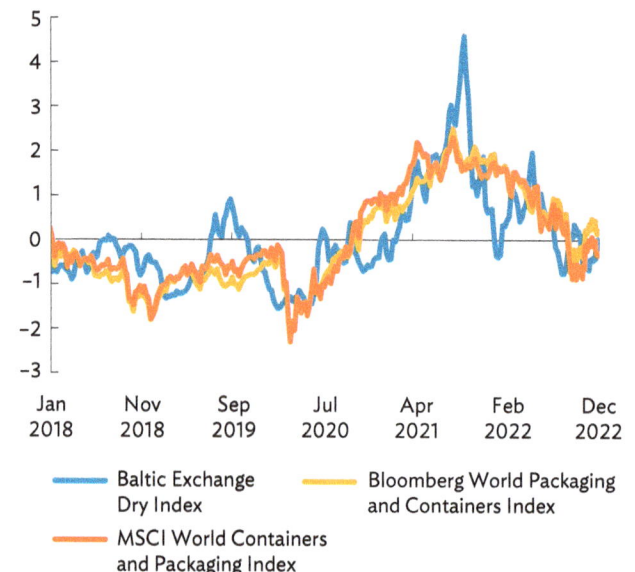

Notes: The indexes have been normalized using z-scores. Calculated mean and standard deviation of the indexes were for the period 5 January 2018 to 23 December 2022.

Sources: ADB calculations using data from Bloomberg; CEIC Data Company; Freightos. Freightos Baltic Index (FBX). https://fbx.freightos.com/ (accessed January 2023); and S&P Capital IQ Pro.

Asia's trade is mainly driven by industrial production on both the export and import fronts.

Asia's exports are less aligned with the consumer confidence and industrial production in the United States (US) and the euro area, reflecting its diversified export destinations (Figures 2.5a and 2.5c). Between the two, the US and euro area industrial production indexes are more correlated to Asia's exports than consumer confidence, hinting at Asia's importance as intermediate goods provider. For Asia's imports, between consumer confidence and industrial production, the latter is also more aligned with its imports, suggesting the region's greater significance as assembler (factory Asia) than as consumer (Figures 2.5b and 2.5d).[15]

For exports and imports at the commodity level, imports of consumer goods are well aligned with consumer confidence in Asia (Figure 2.6b), while exports are less so with consumer confidence in the US and the euro area (Figure 2.6a). For imports of intermediate and capital goods, Asia's industrial production is more aligned (Figures 2.6d and 2.6f), while the industrial production in the US and the euro area are modestly aligned with Asia's exports (Figures 2.6c and 2.6e).[16]

Figure 2.4: Manufacturing Purchasing Managers' Index

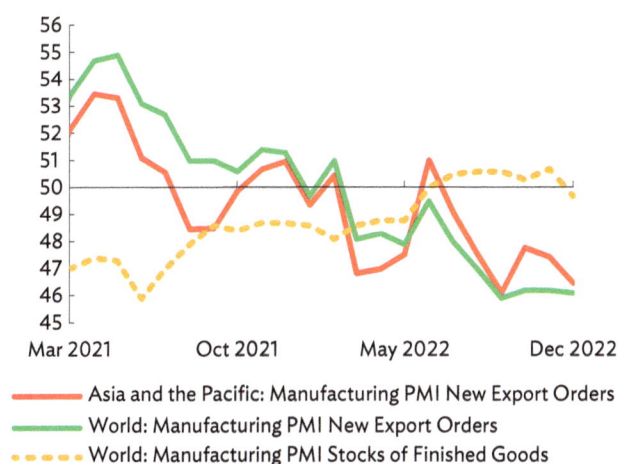

PMI = Purchasing Managers' Index.

Notes: The PMI new export orders index for Asia and the Pacific is the weighted average of economy-level indexes for Australia; Indonesia; India; Japan; Malaysia; the People's Republic of China; the Philippines; the Republic of Korea; Taipei,China; Thailand; and Viet Nam, using export values as weights. A PMI reading over 50 indicates growth or expansion of the manufacturing sector as compared with the previous month, while a reading under 50 suggests contraction.

Sources: ADB calculations using data from CEIC Data Company; and International Monetary Fund. Direction of Trade Statistics. https://data.imf.org/dot (all accessed January 2023).

Asia's Intraregional Trade

Asia's share of intraregional trade declined slightly in 2021 but was still higher than in the past 2 decades.

The intraregional merchandise trade linkages of Asia (including the PRC) weakened slightly to 58.2% in 2021 from 58.5% in 2020 as trade with outside the region grew faster than within the region.[17] The region's intraregional merchandise trade share remained higher than that of North America (39.9%) and lower than that of the European Union plus the United Kingdom (EU+UK) (63.6%). During the same year, the PRC maintained its role as a major trading partner of the region, as evidenced by the large gap between the intraregional trade shares of Asia with and without the PRC. This pattern is somewhat similar to the patterns of the intraregional trade in services shares from 2005 to 2019. Intraregional trade in services share of Asia (including the PRC) was also greater than that of North America and lower than that of the EU+UK (Figure 2.7). Moreover, the PRC was still a major trading partner, contributing to 22% of Asia's intraregional services trade. This is followed by Hong Kong, China (13%); Singapore (12%); Japan (11%); and the Republic of Korea (7%). The top sectors driving Asia's growth in intraregional trade in services in 2021 are wholesale trade, rental of machinery and equipment, and transport/travel services. Combined, these sectors contribute about 70% of Asia's intraregional trade in services growth.[18]

Excluding the PRC, Asia's intraregional merchandise trade share strengthened to 38.6% in 2021 from 38.2% in 2020. Asia (excluding the PRC) in 2019 enhanced trading services with itself, where intraregional trade in services share was at 34.8%, up from 34.3% in 2018 (Figure 2.7).

---

[15] The correlation coefficient of Asia's export volume with US consumer confidence is −0.1, while that with the euro area is 0.2, which are both lower than that with Asia. The correlation coefficient of the region's export volume with the US industrial production index is 0.4, while that with the euro area is 0.5, which are both lower than that with Asia. The correlation coefficient of Asia's import volume with consumer confidence is 0.4, while that with the region's industrial production index is 0.9.

[16] The correlation coefficient of Asia's consumption goods export volume with US consumer confidence is 0.03, while that with the euro area is 0.3, which are both lower than that with Asia. The correlation coefficient of Asia's consumption goods import volume with Asia's consumer confidence index is 0.8. The correlation coefficients of Asia's intermediate and capital goods export volumes with US industrial production index are both 0.3. The correlation coefficients of Asia's intermediate and capital goods export volumes with euro area industrial production index are both 0.5. These are all lower than that with Asia. The correlation coefficient of Asia's intermediate import volume with the region's industrial production is 0.7, while it is 0.9 with that of capital import volume.

[17] See intraregional and extraregional trade values annual growth rate by region in online Annex 1a: https://aric.adb.org/pdf/aeir2023_onlineannex1.pdf.

[18] ADB calculations using data from ADB. Multi-Regional Input–Output Tables.

Figure 2.5: Confidence and Production Indexes versus Asia and Pacific Trade

(a) Consumer confidence versus Asia and Pacific exports

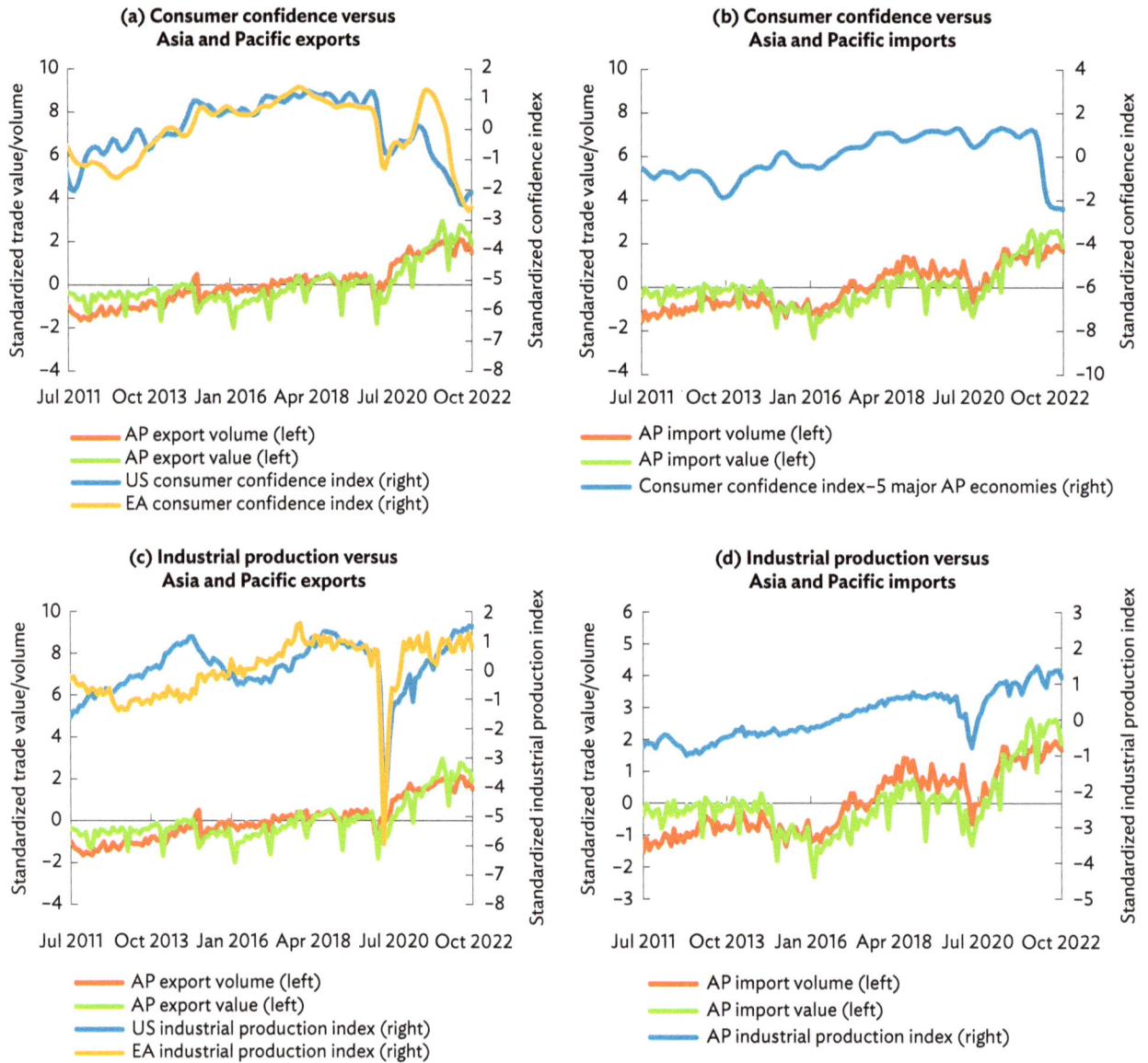

AP = Asia and the Pacific, EA = euro area, PRC = People's Republic of China, US = United States.

Notes: For export and import volume indexes, available data from CPB Netherlands Bureau for Economic Policy Analysis include indexes for Japan, the PRC, and aggregate indexes for selected Asia and Pacific economies: (1) advanced economies excluding Japan (Hong Kong, China; the Republic of Korea; Singapore; and Taipei,China); and (2) emerging economies excluding the PRC (India, Indonesia, Malaysia, Pakistan, the Philippines, Thailand, and Viet Nam). The aggregate export and import volume index for Asia and the Pacific was computed using trade values as weights and were subsequently standardized. The standardized industrial production index of Asia and the Pacific is the aggregated standardized industrial production indexes of India; Japan; the PRC; the Republic of Korea; Singapore; Taipei,China; and Thailand using gross domestic product as weights. The consumer confidence index of the 5 major Asian economies includes India, Indonesia, Japan, the PRC, and the Republic of Korea.

Sources: ADB calculations using data from CEIC Data Company; and CPB Netherlands Bureau for Economic Policy Analysis. World Trade Monitor. https://www.cpb.nl/en/world-trade-monitor-october-2022 (all accessed January 2023).

In 2021, Asia and the Pacific maintained its merchandise trade pattern observed in 2020. Asia and the Pacific (excluding the PRC) still traded merchandise mostly with itself. The PRC remains the region's most important trading partner. North America and the EU+UK followed respectively, with merchandise trade shares with these regions declining in 2021. The region's merchandise trade share with the rest of the world, on the other hand, increased in 2021. The merchandise trading pattern of the region shows how important intraregional trade is for Asia (Figure 2.8).

Figure 2.6: Confidence and Production Indexes versus Asia and Pacific Trade by Commodity

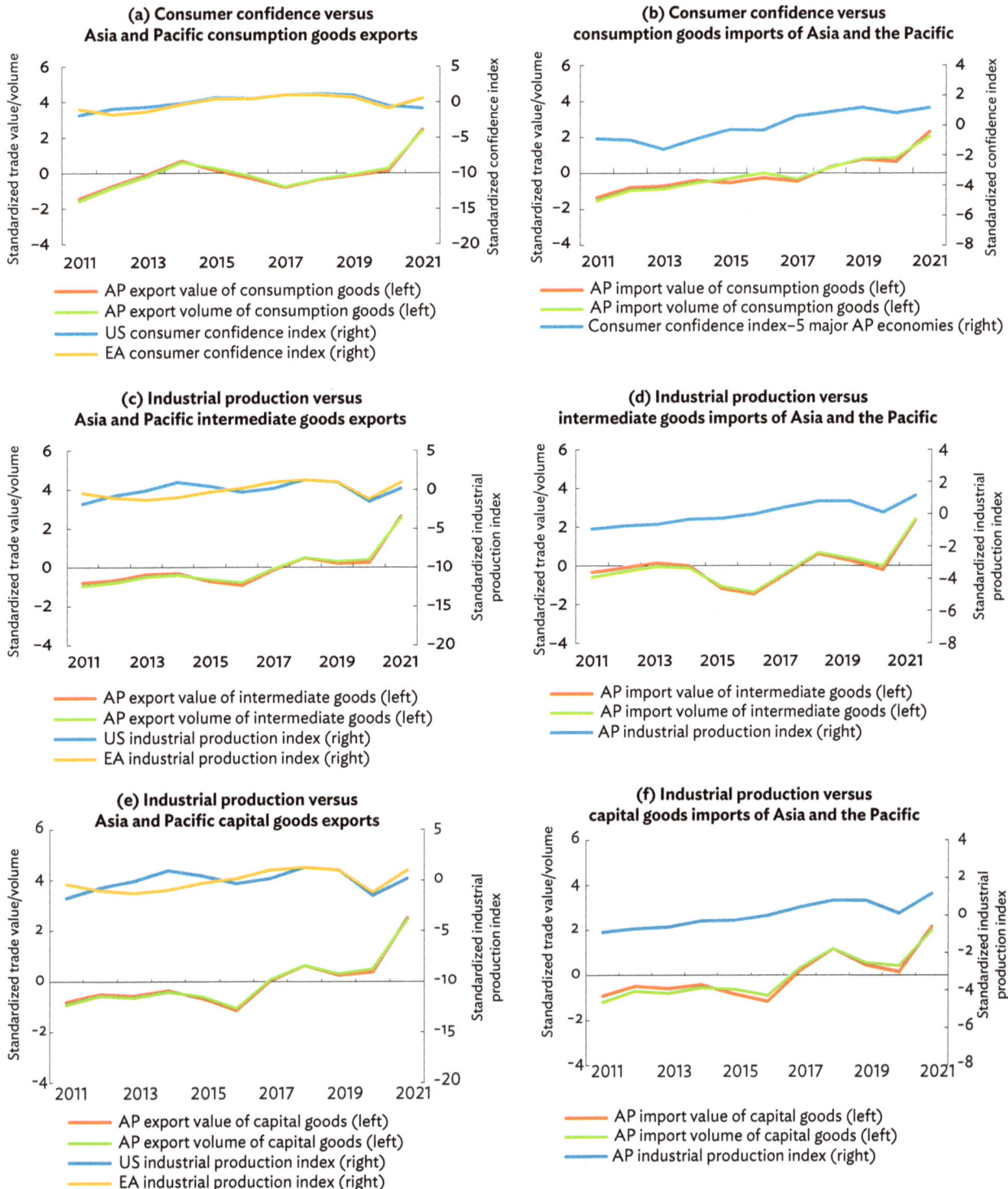

**(a) Consumer confidence versus
Asia and Pacific consumption goods exports**

- AP export value of consumption goods (left)
- AP export volume of consumption goods (left)
- US consumer confidence index (right)
- EA consumer confidence index (right)

**(b) Consumer confidence versus
consumption goods imports of Asia and the Pacific**

- AP import value of consumption goods (left)
- AP import volume of consumption goods (left)
- Consumer confidence index–5 major AP economies (right)

**(c) Industrial production versus
Asia and Pacific intermediate goods exports**

- AP export value of intermediate goods (left)
- AP export volume of intermediate goods (left)
- US industrial production index (right)
- EA industrial production index (right)

**(d) Industrial production versus
intermediate goods imports of Asia and the Pacific**

- AP import value of intermediate goods (left)
- AP import volume of intermediate goods (left)
- AP industrial production index (right)

**(e) Industrial production versus
Asia and Pacific capital goods exports**

- AP export value of capital goods (left)
- AP export volume of capital goods (left)
- US industrial production index (right)
- EA industrial production index (right)

**(f) Industrial production versus
capital goods imports of Asia and the Pacific**

- AP import value of capital goods (left)
- AP import volume of capital goods (left)
- AP industrial production index (right)

AP = Asia and the Pacific, EA = euro area, PRC = People's Republic of China, US = United States.

Notes: Export (import) volume was computed by deflating nominal export (import) values using export (import) price indexes. AP export and import volume includes Japan; Hong Kong, China; India; Indonesia; Malaysia; Pakistan; the Philippines; the PRC; the Republic of Korea; Singapore; Taipei,China; Thailand; and Viet Nam. Trade indicators were standardized after aggregation. AP standardized industrial production index is the aggregated standardized industrial production indexes of India; Japan; the PRC; the Republic of Korea; Singapore; Taipei,China; and Thailand using gross domestic product as weights. The consumer confidence index of the 5 major Asian economies includes India, Indonesia, Japan, the PRC, and the Republic of Korea.

Sources: ADB calculations using data from CEIC Data Company; and United Nations. Commodity Trade Database. https://comtrade.un.org (all accessed December 2022).

Similar to trade in merchandise goods, intraregional services trade remains vital for trade in services in Asia (excluding the PRC). In particular, the trade in services share of Asia (excluding the PRC) with the PRC grew to 10.6% in 2019 from 8.2% in 2005, while its share with the rest of the world grew to 14.3% in 2019 from 13.4% in 2005. For trade in services of Asia (excluding the PRC), the EU+UK and North America still account for a greater portion than for trade in goods (Figure 2.8).

Figure 2.7: Intraregional Trade Share—Merchandise versus Services Trade (%)

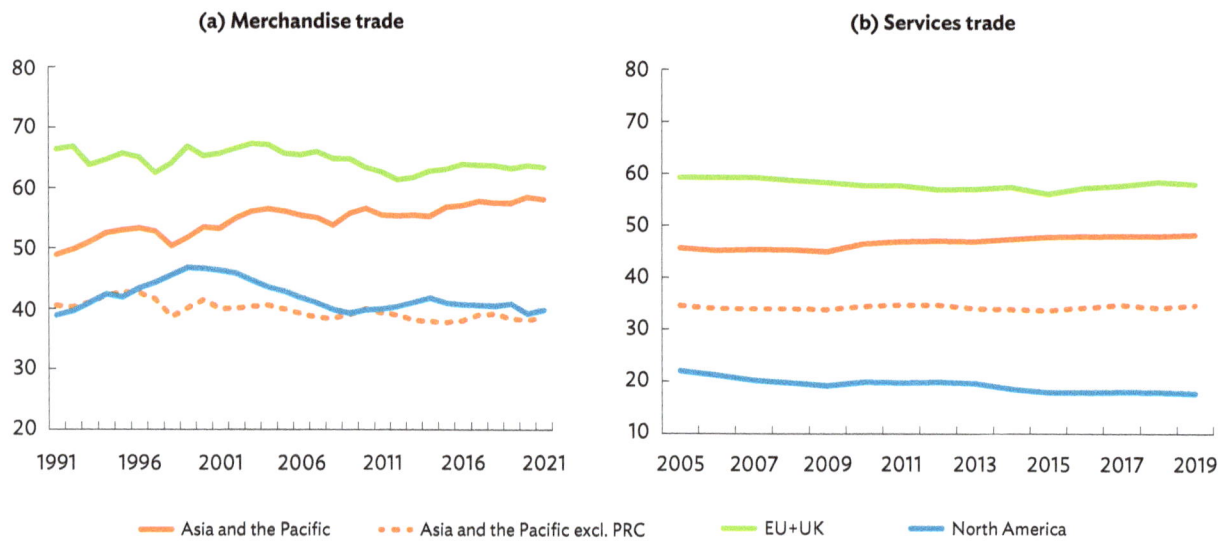

(a) Merchandise trade

(b) Services trade

Legend: Asia and the Pacific — Asia and the Pacific excl. PRC — EU+UK — North America

EU = European Union (27 members), PRC = People's Republic of China, UK = United Kingdom.

Notes: Values expressed as percentage of the region's total merchandise trade (sum of exports and imports). North America covers Canada, Mexico, and the United States.

Sources: ADB calculations using data from International Monetary Fund. Direction of Trade Statistics. https://data.imf.org/dot; and WTO-OECD Balanced Trade in Services Dataset (BaTIS)—BPM6. https://www.wto.org/english/res_e/statis_e/trade_datasets_e.htm (both accessed December 2022).

Figure 2.8: Merchandise and Services Trade of Asia and the Pacific, By Partner (% of total)

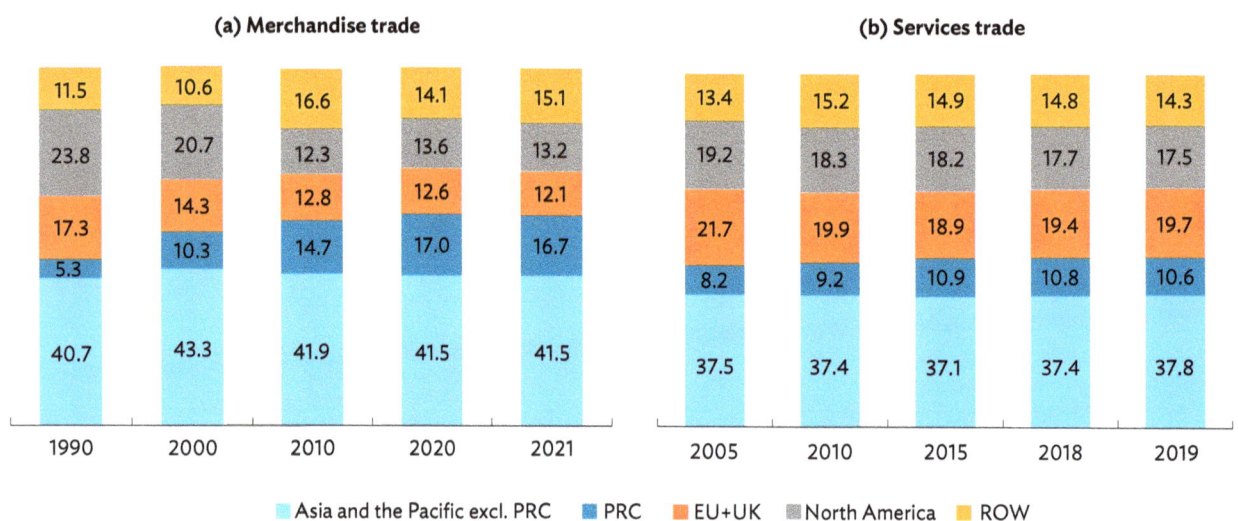

(a) Merchandise trade

	1990	2000	2010	2020	2021
ROW	11.5	10.6	16.6	14.1	15.1
North America	23.8	20.7	12.3	13.6	13.2
EU+UK	17.3	14.3	12.8	12.6	12.1
PRC	5.3	10.3	14.7	17.0	16.7
Asia and the Pacific excl. PRC	40.7	43.3	41.9	41.5	41.5

(b) Services trade

	2005	2010	2015	2018	2019
ROW	13.4	15.2	14.9	14.8	14.3
North America	19.2	18.3	18.2	17.7	17.5
EU+UK	21.7	19.9	18.9	19.4	19.7
PRC	8.2	9.2	10.9	10.8	10.6
Asia and the Pacific excl. PRC	37.5	37.4	37.1	37.4	37.8

Legend: Asia and the Pacific excl. PRC — PRC — EU+UK — North America — ROW

EU = European Union (27 members), PRC = People's Republic of China, ROW = rest of the world, UK = United Kingdom.

Notes: Values expressed as percentage of the region's total merchandise trade (sum of exports and imports). North America covers Canada, Mexico, and the United States.

Sources: ADB calculations using data from International Monetary Fund. Direction of Trade Statistics. https://data.imf.org/dot; and WTO-OECD Balanced Trade in Services Dataset (BaTIS)—BPM6. https://www.wto.org/english/res_e/statis_e/trade_datasets_e.htm (both accessed December 2022).

Intraregional trade linkages strengthened in the Pacific and Oceania in 2021.

In intraregional merchandise trade shares by Asian subregion, only the Pacific and Oceania region grew in 2021. By magnitude, the Pacific and Oceania still had the highest intraregional trade share in 2021, followed by Southeast Asia and East Asia. This 2021 intraregional trade share of the Pacific and Oceania was its highest since 2000. South Asia and Central Asia, however, continued to post intraregional trade shares below 50% (Figure 2.9).

Figure 2.9: Intraregional Trade Shares by Asian Subregion (%)

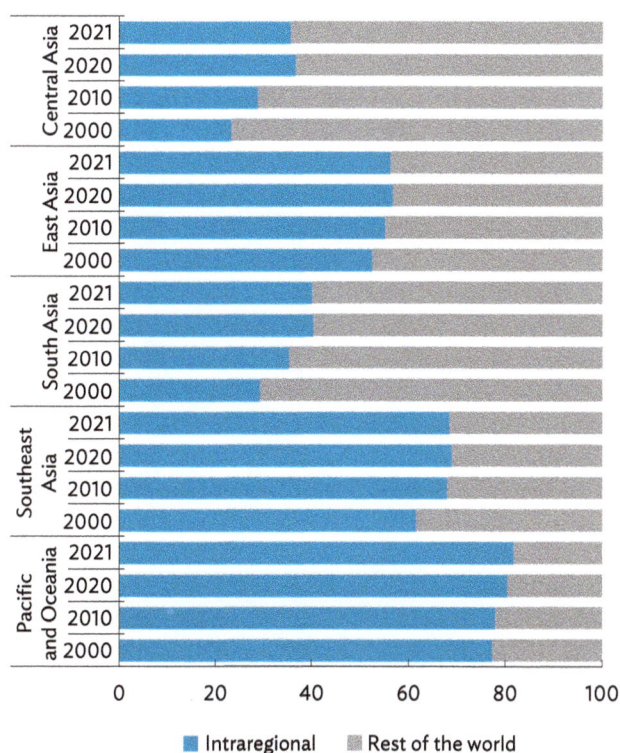

■ Intraregional   ■ Rest of the world

Source: ADB calculations using data from International Monetary Fund. Direction of Trade Statistics. https://data.imf.org/dot (accessed December 2022).

Intraregional trade shares by the Asian subregion can be decomposed into two components, the intrasubregional and the intersubregional. East Asia still had the strongest intrasubregional trade linkages, with a trade share of 35.1% in that component, while Southeast Asia followed with an intrasubregional trade share of 21%. Intrasubregional trade linkages in Central Asia, South Asia, and the Pacific and Oceania remained relatively weaker. In intersubregional trade, the Pacific and Oceania retained the highest share, at 80.8% in 2021. Southeast Asia, South Asia, Central Asia, and East Asia followed, in that order, all with intersubregional trade shares below 50%. The high and increasing intraregional trade share of the Pacific and Oceania is mainly attributable to the growing intersubregional trade share of Australia and New Zealand. Asia's trade integration can be further decomposed using dynamic gravity model estimation (Box 2.2).

Progress of Global and Regional Value Chains

Asia's global value chain and regional value chain linkages strengthened in 2021.

The world and Asia's global value chain (GVC) participation rates and Asia's gross regional value chain (RVC) participation rate increased in 2021. The world GVC participation increased to 73.4 in 2021 from 71.8 in 2020, as global exports involving cross-border production grew by 28.6%, while global exports of final goods made by single economies grew only at 18.4%. Asia's GVC participation increased to 67.7 in 2021 from 66.2 in 2020. Asia's gross RVC grew to 69.0 from 67.6 as GVC production within Asia surpassed the growth of non-GVC exports by Asia. Meanwhile, Asia's net RVC declined to 51.6 from 52.2 as GVC trade within Asia involving non-Asian third economies grew by 33.2%, while GVC trade within Asia involving only Asian third economies grew by 18.8% (Figures 2.10a and 2.10b).[19]

For the past 2 decades, complex GVCs have contributed the most in Asia-to-world GVC participation, while

---

[19]   Gross RVC is the share of exports that involves production in at least two economies using cross-border production networks to total gross exports with linkages all within the region. Net RVC is similar to gross RVC except that its denominator includes non-regional third economies.

Box 2.2: Gravity Model Estimation of Bilateral Exports

Gravity model estimation is employed to trace Asia's progress in regional trade integration. Economy pair specific effects such as distance, colonial relationship, common language, and contiguity among trading partners all present the expected signs with significance. After these effects along with exporter and importer time-varying fixed effects are controlled, the coefficient of dummy variable for both Asian exporter and importer suggests that intraregional

exports of goods are, on average, 58% less than Asia's export to the rest of the world for 2017–2021. Among the commodity groups, intermediate goods demonstrate the least negative intraregional trade bias. Overall, these results suggest that Asia's regional trade integration can be largely explained by its geographic vicinity and cultural and historical relationship, and that much remains to be done in cultivating closer economic interrelationship.

Gravity Model Estimation Results, 2017–2021

Dependent Variable: Bilateral Exports

Variables	All Goods	Capital Goods	Consumption Goods	Intermediate Goods
	(1)	(2)	(3)	(4)
Distance	−0.20***	−0.21***	−0.20***	−0.20***
	(.0051)	(0.0054)	(0.0053)	(0.0061)
Colonial relationship dummy	0.11**	−0.073	0.20***	0.17***
	(0.045)	(0.055)	(0.060)	(0.047)
Common language dummy	0.31***	0.43***	0.33***	0.29***
	(0.033)	(0.035)	(0.041)	(0.037)
Contiguity dummy	0.90***	0.82***	0.98***	0.94***
	(0.032)	(0.041)	(0.036)	(0.036)
Both in Asia dummy (base: Asia to ROW)	−0.86*** [−0.93***]	−1.30*** [−1.19***]	−1.20*** [−1.26]	−0.74*** [−0.81***]
	(0.072)	(0.083)	(0.085)	(0.075)
Constant	10.45***	9.54***	8.78***	9.787***
	(0.042)	(0.052)	(0.042)	(0.0483)
Observations	222,249	222,249	222,249	222,249
Pseudo R²	0.934	0.947	0.918	0.920

ROW = rest of the world.

Notes: *** = significant at 1%, ** = significant at 5%, * = significant at 10%. Estimates for 2014–2018 are in brackets. Robust standard errors in parentheses. Data cover 229 economies, of which 46 are from Asia and the Pacific. Poisson pseudo-maximum likelihood estimation was used to account for zero bilateral trade. Time-varying exporter and importer fixed effects are included but not presented for brevity. Each variable's increase or decrease in percentage is computed by natural number raised by the variable's coefficient minus one. Trade data are based on Broad Economic Categories.

Sources: ADB calculations using data from Centre d'Études Prospectives et d'Informations Internationales (the French Research Center in International Economics). GeoDist Database. http://www.cepii.fr/CEPII/en/cepii/cepii.asp; and United Nations. Commodity Trade Database. https://comtrade.un.org (both accessed December 2022).

Source: ADB staff.

simple RVCs contributed the most in the Asia-to-Asia gross RVC participation rate.[20] In 2021, the share of complex GVCs in Asia-to-world GVC participation rates has increased, while the shares of simple GVCs and non-

GVCs declined (Figure 2.11a). In the same year, the share of complex RVCs seems to be increasing the Asia-to-Asia gross RVC participation rate (Figure 2.11b).[21]

---

[20]   "Asia-to-world" refers to linkages in which the direct exporter is within Asia, while the direct importer is any Asian or non-Asian economy. "Asia-to-Asia" refers to linkages wherein both the direct exporter and importer are Asian economies.

[21]   Non-GVCs and non-RVCs contain final goods exports involving a single economy in their production. Simple GVCs and RVCs contain intermediate goods exports processed by the importing economy as final goods to be consumed domestically. Complex GVCs and RVCs contain final and intermediate goods exports that made at least two border crossings in their production.

Figure 2.10: Global and Regional Value Chain Participation Rates and Shares of Their Components

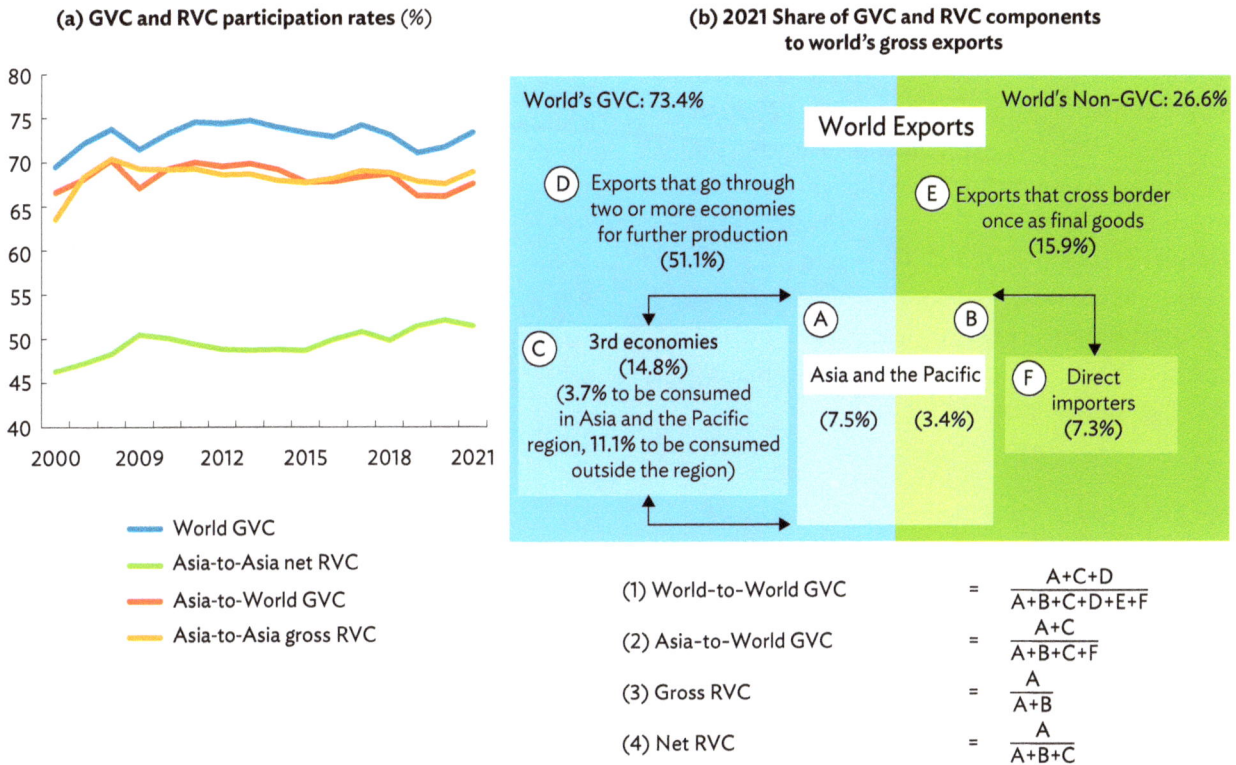

(a) GVC and RVC participation rates (%)

- World GVC
- Asia-to-Asia net RVC
- Asia-to-World GVC
- Asia-to-Asia gross RVC

(b) 2021 Share of GVC and RVC components to world's gross exports

World's GVC: 73.4%   World's Non-GVC: 26.6%

World Exports

D Exports that go through two or more economies for further production (51.1%)

E Exports that cross border once as final goods (15.9%)

A   B

C 3rd economies (14.8%) (3.7% to be consumed in Asia and the Pacific region, 11.1% to be consumed outside the region)

Asia and the Pacific (7.5%)   (3.4%)

F Direct importers (7.3%)

(1) World-to-World GVC $= \dfrac{A+C+D}{A+B+C+D+E+F}$

(2) Asia-to-World GVC $= \dfrac{A+C}{A+B+C+F}$

(3) Gross RVC $= \dfrac{A}{A+B}$

(4) Net RVC $= \dfrac{A}{A+B+C}$

GVC = global value chain, RVC = regional value chain.

Notes: The GVC participation rate is the share of gross exports that involves production in at least two economies using cross-border production networks. The RVC participation rate is the same as that of GVC, except that it only involves economies of the same region.

Sources: ADB calculations using ADB data. Multi-Regional Input–Output Tables; and methodology by Borin and Mancini (2019).

Figure 2.11: Global and Regional Value Chain Participation Rate—Asia and the Pacific (%)

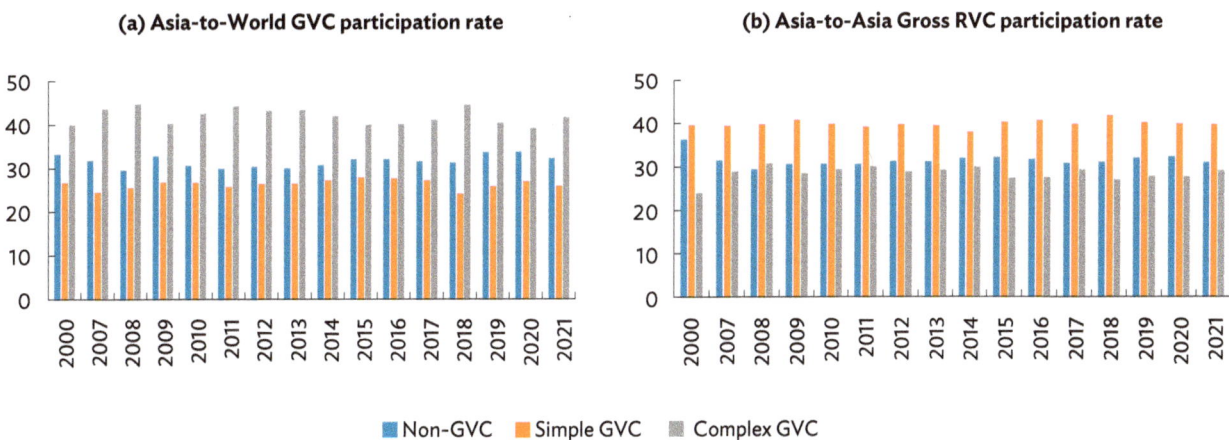

(a) Asia-to-World GVC participation rate

(b) Asia-to-Asia Gross RVC participation rate

■ Non-GVC   ■ Simple GVC   ▦ Complex GVC

GVC = global value chain, RVC = regional value chain.

Notes: Gross RVC participation is the share of Asia's intraregional value chain exports to its intraregional gross exports but excluding all non-Asian third economies in gross exports. Non-GVC refers to final goods exports. Simple GVCs are intermediate goods exports that cross borders only once or absorbed by the direct importer economy. Complex GVCs are intermediate exports that cross borders at least twice.

Sources: ADB calculations using data from ADB. Multi-Regional Input–Output Tables; and methodology by Borin and Mancini (2019).

Asia's RVC–GVC intensity surpassed the EU+UK in 2008 and North America in 2018 and continued to rise before slightly decreasing in 2021. North America's RVC–GVC intensity declined in 2018 then recovered slightly afterward, albeit to a lower level than 2000 to 2017. The EU+UK's RVC–GVC intensity has been slowly declining for the past decade. Even though it recovered sharply after its decline in 2018, its level in 2021 is still lower than its level in 2000 to 2016 (Figure 2.12). Lower RVC–GVC intensity for Asia does not necessarily mean regional value chain linkages are loosening as it could happen when RVC increases, yet more slowly than the GVC, which was the case in 2021.

Figure 2.12: Regional Value Chain–Global Value Chain Intensity By Region

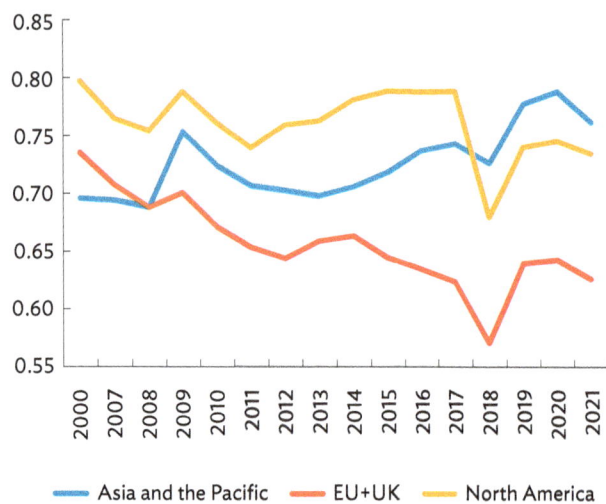

EU = European Union (27 members), GVC = global value chain, RVC = regional value chain, UK = United Kingdom.

Notes: RVC–GVC intensity is the ratio of RVC participation and GVC participation rates. North America here consists of the United States, Canada, and Mexico.

Sources: ADB calculations using data from ADB. Multi-Regional Input–Output Tables; and methodology by Borin and Mancini (2019).

Asia's RVC–GVC intensity peaked in 2020 in all four major sectors during the pandemic, as Asia's production networks outside the region declined more steeply than its intraregional production networks. In 2021, the region's GVC recovered and grew faster than the region's RVC, causing the RVC–GVC intensity values for the major sectors, especially high and medium technology, and the primary sector to decline. Nevertheless, their

intensity values remained much higher than pre-global financial crisis levels (Figure 2.13).

Figure 2.13: Regional Value Chain–Global Value Chain Intensity by Major Sector—Asia and the Pacific

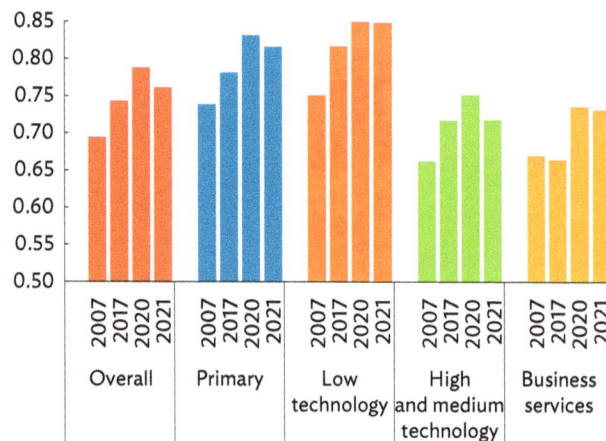

GVC = global value chain, RVC = regional value chain.

Notes: RVC–GVC intensity is the ratio of RVC and GVC participation rates. Sectoral classification is based on ADB (2015). Business services includes personal and public services.

Sources: ADB calculations using data from ADB. Multi-Regional Input–Output Tables; and methodology by Borin and Mancini (2019).

All Asian subregions have seen increasing RVC–GVC intensity. However, in subregional RVC–GVC intensity, only East Asia and South Asia were increasing (Figure 2.14).

In 2021, RVC–GVC intensity values declined in most Asian economies as their production linkages outside Asia recovered and grew faster. Out of 26 Asian economies, overall GVC participation rates increased in 21, and complex GVC participation rates increased in 24. However, overall RVC participation rates increased in only 9 out of 26 economies, while complex RVC participation rates increased in 17 out of 26. Overall RVC–GVC intensity rose in only 5 economies, while complex RVC–GVC intensity rose in only 4 economies.

Among all Asian exports in 2021 that involve at least one border crossing for production, they rose rapidly in almost all Asian economies, both within and outside of Asia. Value chain growth was higher within Asia than outside Asia in Bhutan, the Kyrgyz Republic, Singapore,

Figure 2.14: Regional Value Chain–Global Value Chain Intensity—Asian Subregions (3-year moving average)

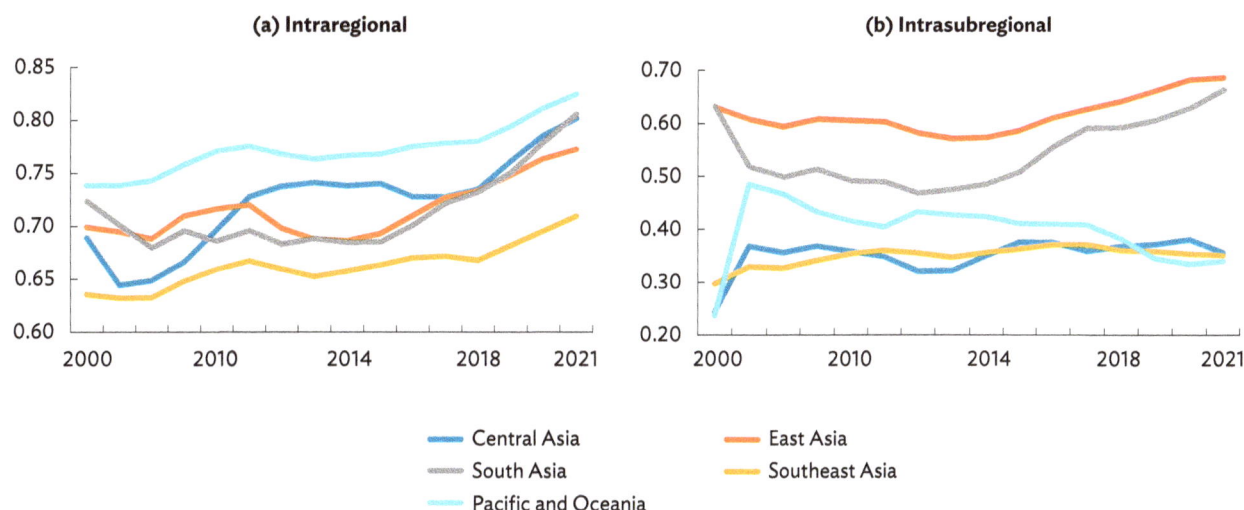

(a) Intraregional

(b) Intrasubregional

Central Asia
South Asia
Pacific and Oceania
East Asia
Southeast Asia

GVC = global value chain, RVC = regional value chain.

Note: RVC–GVC intensity is the ratio of RVC participation and GVC participation rates.

Sources: ADB calculations using data from ADB. Multi-Regional Input–Output Tables; and methodology by Borin and Mancini (2019).

and Sri Lanka, pushing up their RVC–GVC intensity. In most economies, however, growth rates outside Asia were higher than within Asia, reducing RVC-GVC intensity.[22] Fiji saw declining growth within Asia and increasing growth outside Asia. Meanwhile, Brunei Darussalam and Nepal saw declining growth within Asia and outside Asia. RVC-GVC intensity increased in Nepal as its production network outside Asia declined more rapidly than its network within Asia, while RVC–GVC intensity in Brunei Darussalam decreased as its production network within Asia declined more rapidly than outside Asia.[23]

In 2021, complex GVC network rose rapidly in almost all Asian economies, both within and outside Asia. In four economies—Kazakhstan, the Kyrgyz Republic, the Philippines, and Singapore—complex RVC–GVC intensities rose as their multi-border export production network within Asia increased more rapidly than outside Asia. Like overall GVCs, complex RVC–GVC intensities declined in most Asian economies, as their multi-border

export production network outside Asia increased more rapidly than within Asia.[24] Complex RVC-GVC intensities decreased in only Brunei Darussalam, Fiji, and Nepal, due to decreasing multi-border production within Asia.[25]

Asia's GVC and RVC Participation Excluding the Primary Sector

Asia's overall RVC participation seems to be dependent more upon primary-sector-related value chain linkages than its GVC linkages, although the degree has been declining since 2011. The decline in Asia's overall GVC participation rate hovers around 4 to 5 percentage points when the primary sector is taken out of the simple linkages, while net RVC declines by 6 to 8 percentage points, while the region's gross RVC declines the most, about 8 to 12 percentage points, under this scenario (Figure 2.15).

---

[22] These economies are Australia; Bangladesh; Cambodia; Hong Kong, China; India; Indonesia; Japan; Kazakhstan; the Lao People's Democratic Republic (Lao PDR); Malaysia; Maldives; Mongolia; Pakistan; the Philippines; the PRC; the Republic of Korea; Taipei,China; Thailand; and Viet Nam.

[23] See 2021 growth rates of RVC-GVC intensity components at economy level in online Annex 1b: https://aric.adb.org/pdf/aeir2023_onlineannex1.pdf.

[24] These economies are Australia; Bangladesh; Bhutan; Cambodia; Hong Kong, China; India; Indonesia; Japan; the Lao PDR; Malaysia; Maldives; Mongolia; Pakistan; the PRC; the Republic of Korea; Sri Lanka; Taipei,China; Thailand; and Viet Nam.

[25] See 2021 growth rates of RVC-GVC intensity components at economy level in online Annex 1b: https://aric.adb.org/pdf/aeir2023_onlineannex1.pdf.

Figure 2.15: Decline in Global and Regional Value Chain Participation in Asia and the Pacific (without the primary sector in simple linkages)

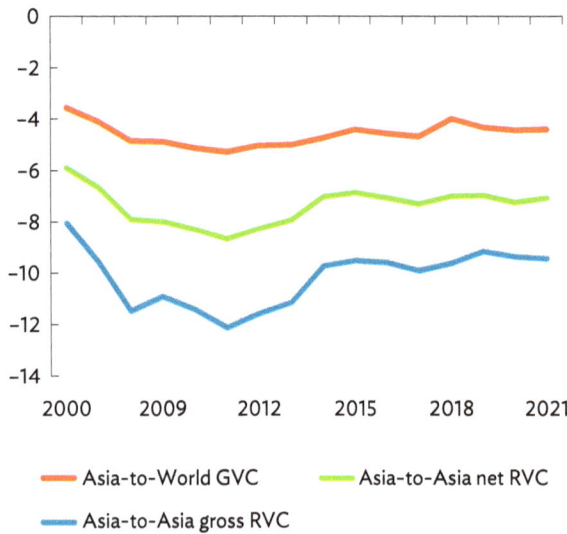

GVC = global value chain, RVC = regional value chain.

Note: The lines are the difference between the original participation rates and the participation rates without the primary sector in simple linkages in their numerators.

Sources: ADB calculations using data from ADB. Multi-Regional Input–Output Tables; and methodology by Borin and Mancini (2019).

Further decomposition into simple and complex GVC and RVC linkages suggests that this phenomenon is largely due to a high dependence of simple RVC linkages in the region, while complex RVCs are much less dependent on the primary sector (Figure 2.16). East Asia is the largest contributor to Asia's primary sector linkages with simple and complex GVCs, followed by Southeast Asia and the Pacific and Oceania. The Pacific and Oceania is the largest contributor to Asia's primary sector linkages in simple and complex RVCs, followed by Southeast Asia and East Asia.

Special Topic: Food and Energy Crisis and Asia's Trade

Recent Global Events Challenging the Food and Energy Industries

Economic recoveries from the pandemic globally have been hampered by spiraling inflation pressures, prompted in part by the Russian invasion of Ukraine

Figure 2.16: Changes in Asia's Simple and Complex Global and Regional Value Chain Participation Rates (without the primary sector in all linkages)

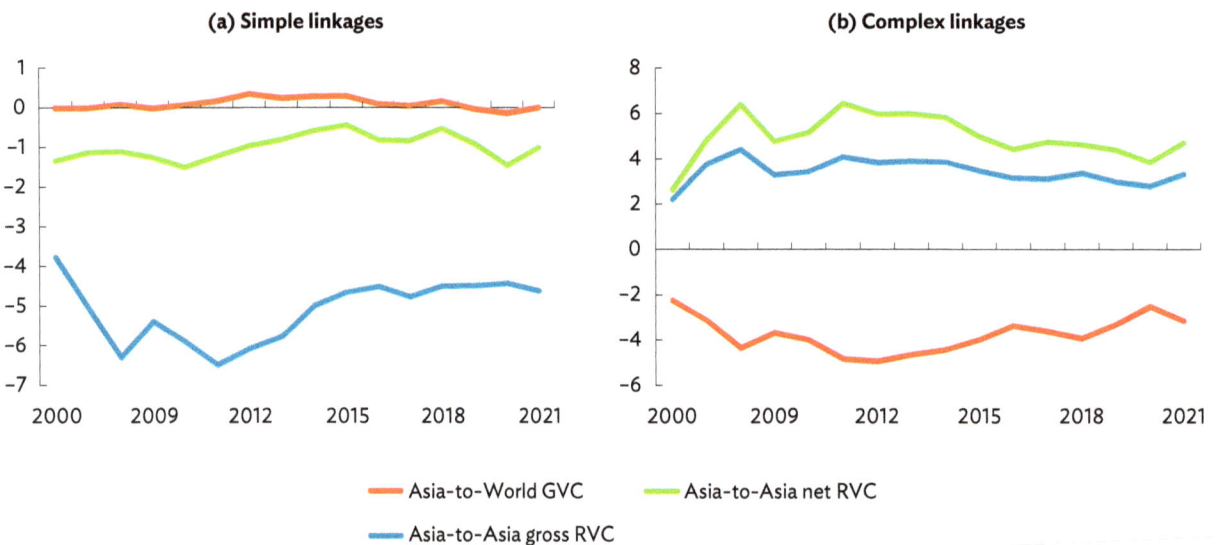

GVC = global value chain, RVC = regional value chain.

Note: The lines are the difference between the original participation rates and the participation rates without the primary sector in all linkages, both in their numerators and denominators.

Sources: ADB calculations using ADB data. Multi-Regional Input–Output Tables; and methodology by Borin and Mancini (2019).

in February 2022. Ukraine is one of the top exporters of wheat, corn, and sunflower oil, and the Russian Federation is one of the top exporters of wheat, crude oil, natural gas, and fertilizer. Supply chain disruptions in these food and energy essentials are expected to add to their price pressures. Notwithstanding nascent progress in removing Ukraine's Odesa port blockade and stabilizing many food and energy commodities, the outlook for global food and energy prices remains uncertain, volatile, and precarious. Major central banks, such as the US Federal Reserve, European Central Bank, and the Bank of England, have tightened monetary policy, compounding burdens in food and energy importing developing economies as these higher rates weaken the value of their domestic currency. Trade restrictions imposed during the period, such as export bans and export licensing, pose additional challenges to the recovery of economies. This includes recent bans imposed by major exporters such as Hungary, India, the Russian Federation, Serbia, and Ukraine for corn and/or wheat, and Indonesia for palm oil.[26]

Recent Trade and Price Trends of Food and Energy Commodities

Growth rates of food exports and imports have declined already since the second half of 2021, while those for energy commodities have increased. After the Russian invasion of Ukraine, the trade value growth of both food and energy commodities fell. The persistent gap between the growth rates of trade value and trade volume (the latter lower), presents the salient effect of prices on the trade of commodities (Figure 2.17).

For food commodities, export restrictions imposed by major food exporters in 2022 provide additional burdens to the prices of such staples (Figure 2.18). Food trade restrictions were more common for wheat and corn products, commodities that are mainly produced by non-Asian economies. Food trade restrictions imposed in 2022 peaked at around April 2022 and have been declining since (Figure 2.19).

Figure 2.17: Growth of Trade Values and Volumes in Selected Food and Energy Commodities—Asia and the Pacific
(%, year-on-year, 3-month moving average)

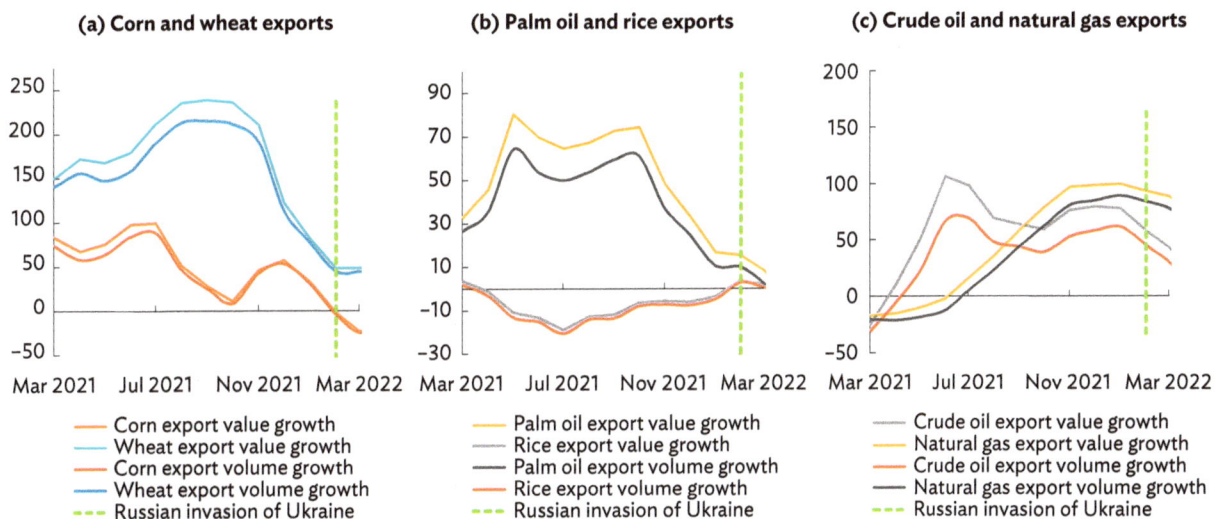

(a) Corn and wheat exports

— Corn export value growth
— Wheat export value growth
— Corn export volume growth
— Wheat export volume growth
--- Russian invasion of Ukraine

(b) Palm oil and rice exports

— Palm oil export value growth
— Rice export value growth
— Palm oil export volume growth
— Rice export volume growth
--- Russian invasion of Ukraine

(c) Crude oil and natural gas exports

— Crude oil export value growth
— Natural gas export value growth
— Crude oil export volume growth
— Natural gas export volume growth
--- Russian invasion of Ukraine

continued on next page

26   D. Laborde and A. Mamun. Food Export & Fertilizer Restrictions Tracker. https://public.tableau.com/app/profile/laborde6680/viz/ExportRestrictionsTracker/FoodExportRestrictionsTracker (accessed January 2023).

Figure 2.17 *continued*

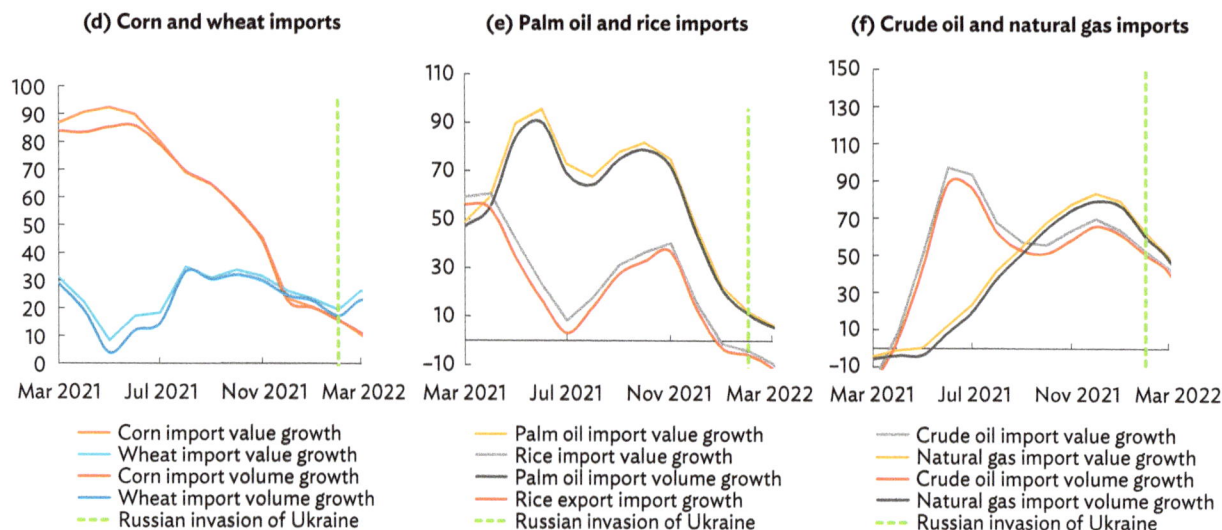

(d) Corn and wheat imports

- Corn import value growth
- Wheat import value growth
- Corn import volume growth
- Wheat import volume growth
- --- Russian invasion of Ukraine

(e) Palm oil and rice imports

- Palm oil import value growth
- Rice import value growth
- Palm oil import volume growth
- Rice export import growth
- --- Russian invasion of Ukraine

(f) Crude oil and natural gas imports

- Crude oil import value growth
- Natural gas import value growth
- Crude oil import volume growth
- Natural gas import volume growth
- --- Russian invasion of Ukraine

Notes: Export and import volumes are computed by deflating export and import values using commodity-level export and import price indexes. Asia and the Pacific includes Armenia; Australia; Azerbaijan; Bangladesh; Bhutan; Brunei Darussalam; Cambodia; the People's Republic of China; Hong Kong, China; Fiji; Georgia; India; Indonesia; Japan; Kazakhstan; Kiribati; the Kyrgyz Republic; the Lao People's Democratic Republic; Malaysia; Maldives; Mongolia; Nepal; New Zealand; Pakistan; Papua New Guinea; the Philippines; the Republic of Korea; Samoa; Singapore; Solomon Islands; Sri Lanka; Tajikistan; Thailand; Timor-Leste; Tonga; Turkmenistan; Tuvalu; Vanuatu; and Viet Nam.

Sources: ADB calculations using data from United Nations (UN). Commodity Trade Database (COMTRADE). https://comtrade.un.org/; and International Monetary Fund (IMF). Commodity Terms of Trade Database (CTOT). https://data.imf.org/ (all accessed November 2022).

Figure 2.18: Average Prices of Food and Energy Commodities in Selected Major Commodity Markets (15 July 2021 = 100)

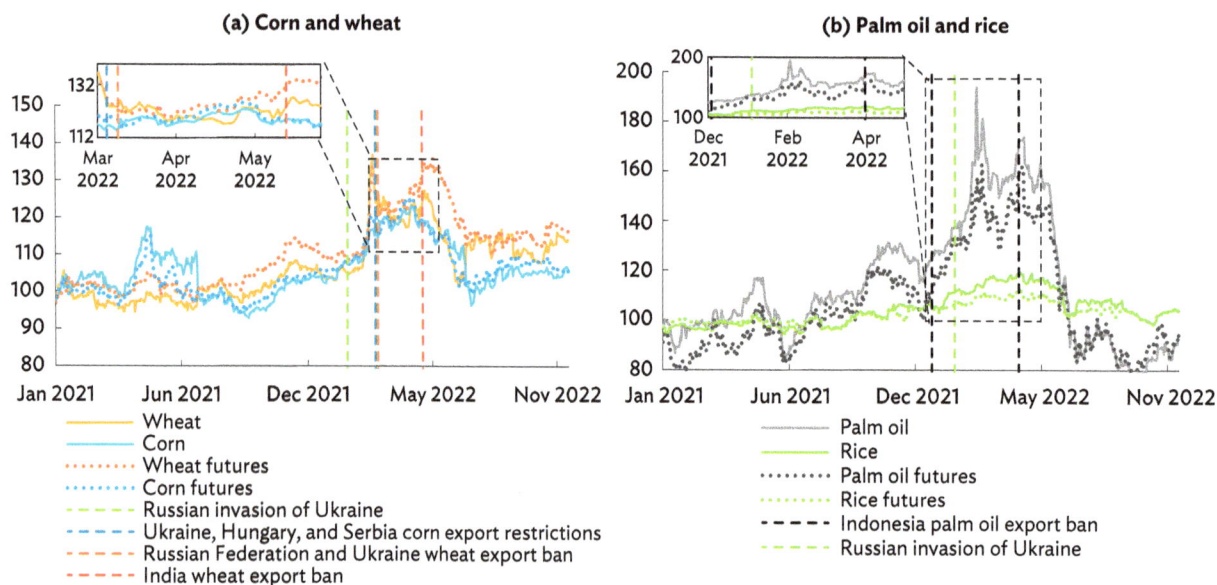

(a) Corn and wheat

- Wheat
- Corn
- ······· Wheat futures
- ······· Corn futures
- --- Russian invasion of Ukraine
- --- Ukraine, Hungary, and Serbia corn export restrictions
- --- Russian Federation and Ukraine wheat export ban
- --- India wheat export ban

(b) Palm oil and rice

- Palm oil
- Rice
- ······· Palm oil futures
- ······· Rice futures
- --- Indonesia palm oil export ban
- --- Russian invasion of Ukraine

continued on next page

Figure 2.18 *continued*

(c) Crude oil and natural gas

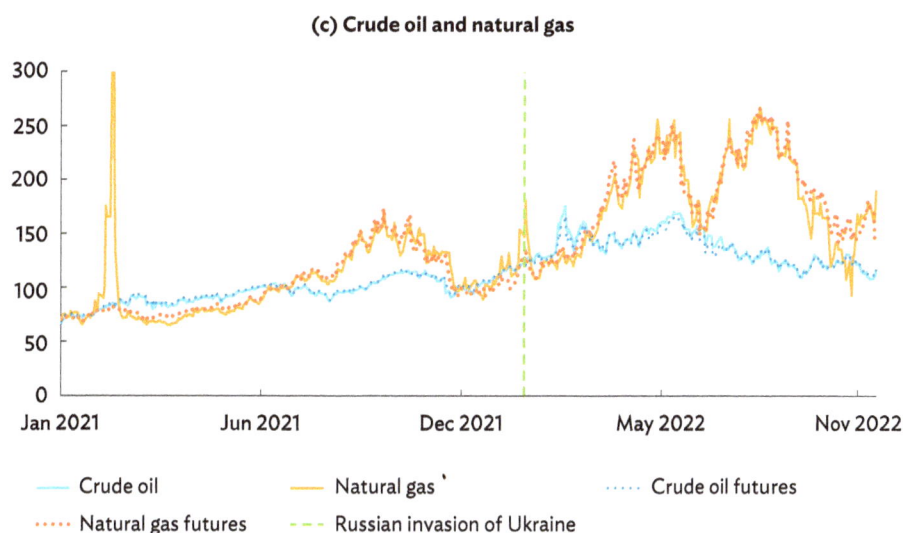

— Crude oil   — Natural gas `   ····· Crude oil futures

····· Natural gas futures   – – Russian invasion of Ukraine

Notes: Average crude oil price is computed by averaging the prices of Brent and West Texas Intermediate (WTI) crude oil. Natural gas price is the price at Henry Hub in the United States. Average corn price is computed by averaging the first-month futures prices of corn in the Dalian Commodity Exchange in the People's Republic of China (PRC) and the Chicago Board of Trade (CBOT) in the United States. Palm oil is at the price set by the Malaysian Palm Oil Board. Average prices of rice and wheat are the averages of the first-month futures prices of rice and wheat in CBOT and Zhengzhou Commodity Exchange in the PRC. The price index of natural gas reached 648.37 in February 2021. The average crude oil futures price is the average of the prices of WTI crude oil contract 4 and Brent crude oil contract 1. The natural gas futures price is the price of natural gas contract 4 at Henry Hub. The average corn futures price is the average of the fifth-month futures prices of corn in the Dalian Commodity Exchange and the second-month futures prices of corn in CBOT. Palm oil futures price is the fourth-month futures price of palm oil in the Kuala Lumpur Commodity Exchange. Rice futures price is the average of the fourth-month futures prices of rice in Zhengzhou Commodity Exchange and the second-month futures prices of rice in the CBOT. Wheat futures price is the average of the sixth-month futures prices of wheat in the Zhengzhou Commodity Exchange and the second-month futures prices of wheat in CBOT.

Sources: ADB calculations using data from Bloomberg and CEIC Data Company; and Laborde, D. and A. Mamun. Food Export & Fertilizer Restrictions Tracker. https://public.tableau.com/app/profile/laborde6680/viz/ExportRestrictionsTracker/FoodExportRestrictionsTracker (all accessed December 2022).

Figure 2.19: Number of Effective Food Trade Restrictions, 2022

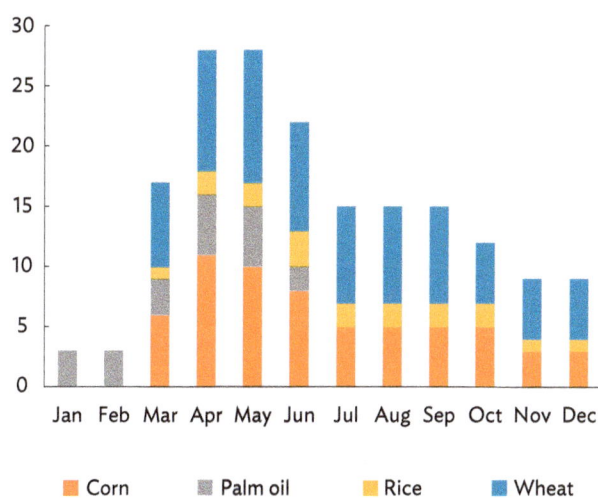

■ Corn   ■ Palm oil   ■ Rice   ■ Wheat

Source: ADB calculations using Laborde, D. and A. Mamun. Food Export & Fertilizer Restrictions Tracker. https://public.tableau.com/app/profile/laborde6680/viz/ExportRestrictionsTracker/FoodExportRestrictionsTracker (accessed January 2023).

International prices of food commodities by 30 November 2022 had almost declined to their January 2022 levels, amid better crop expectations, reopening of some port operations in the Black Sea, and the sluggish recovery of the global economy and demand. Energy commodities, however, remained high by 30 November 2022. The stronger and persistent rise in the price of energy commodities is, in a way, attributable to the inelastic supply of the energy products because of tight production capacity (EIA 2021, 2022; Konrad 2012). For natural gas, the drop in the Russian exports to Europe causes additional price pressures. Despite the downside resilience in food prices, upside and volatility risks remain, as vital inputs to the sector, such as fertilizers, depend on energy commodities, and the Russian Federation is an important supplier of nitrogen-based fertilizers. Risks of a prolonged situation and pursuant sanctions will also compound the substantial uncertainty already existing in the markets (Baffes and Nagle 2022, World Bank 2022). Futures prices are similarly affected by these recent global events (Figure 2.18).

Vulnerabilities of Asian Economies to Food and Energy Price Volatilities

Food and energy dependence. Asian economies with significant food or energy imports-to-GDP ratios are relatively more vulnerable to changes in food and energy prices. Based on 2017–2019 average trade patterns, Singapore, the Marshall Islands, Thailand, and the Republic of Korea, in that order, are the most energy import dependent economies in Asia; Kiribati, Tajikistan, Timor-Leste, and the Marshall Islands are the most food import dependent economies. Top energy-importing economies have higher import-to-GDP ratios than top food-importing economies, suggesting that they could be more affected by future price change dynamics, let alone the ameliorating effect of food price stabilization lately. Economies with significant food or energy exports-to-GDP ratios, on the other hand, are net beneficiaries. Based on 2017–2019 trade patterns, Brunei Darussalam, Azerbaijan, and Kazakhstan are the top energy-exporting economies in terms of share of GDP, while Malaysia, Cambodia, and Papua New Guinea are the top food-exporting economies. Given much higher energy export dependence, top energy-exporting economies stand to gain more than top food exporters under rising commodity prices (Figure 2.20).

Figure 2.20: Food and Energy Net Trade—Selected Asian Economies (% of GDP)

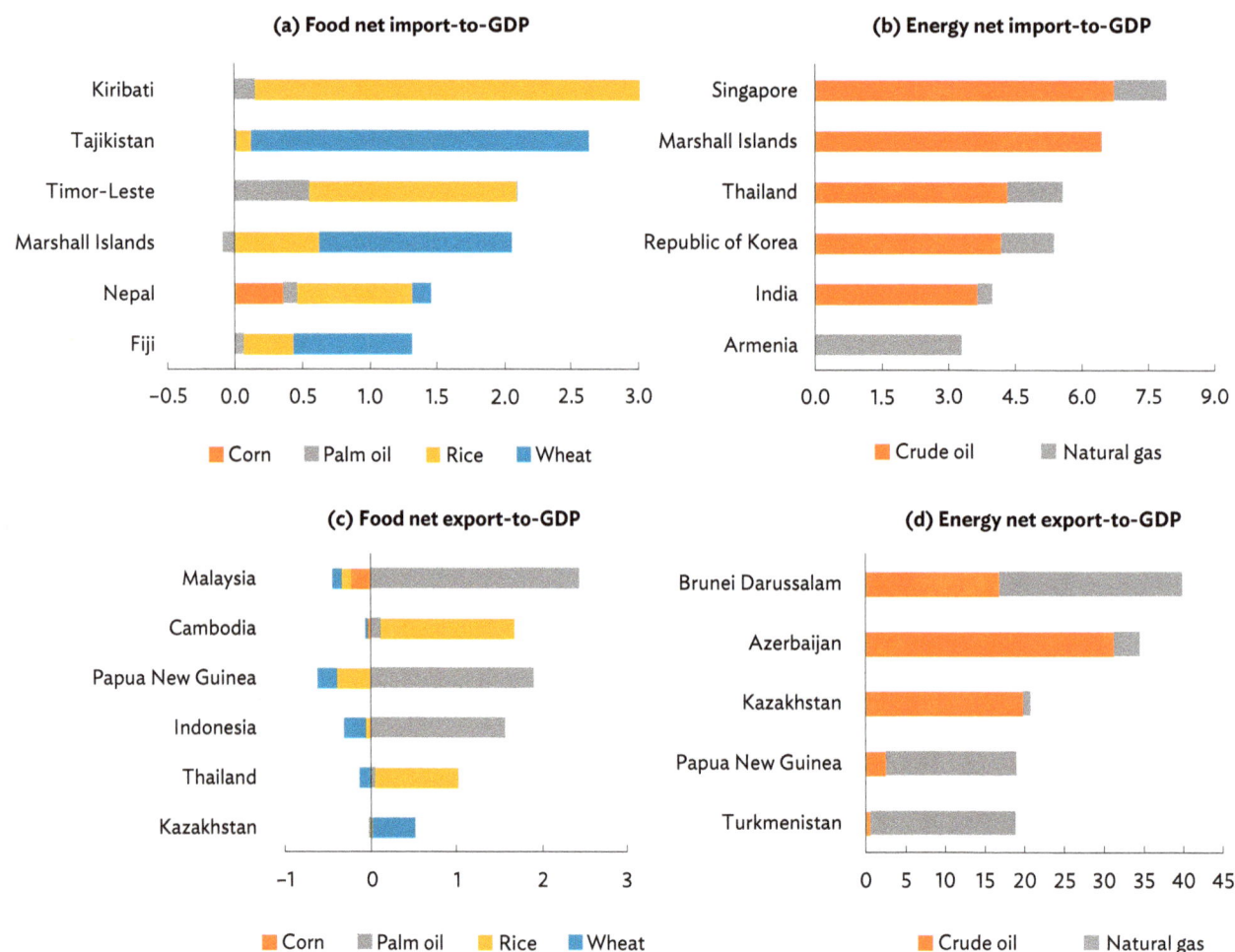

GDP = gross domestic product.

Note: Net trade-to-GDP ratio is computed using the average of 2017–2019 trade and GDP data to reflect pre-pandemic patterns.

Sources: ADB calculations using data from United Nations. Commodity Trade Database. https://comtrade.un.org; and World Bank. World Development Indicators. https://databank.worldbank.org/source/world-development-indicators (all accessed December 2022).

Foreign exchange rates volatility. Asian currencies, in general, were relatively stable in 2021. After the Russian invasion of Ukraine and the inception of monetary policy tightening in major advanced economies, however, most Asian currencies have been exposed to higher volatility risks. The currencies of the economies of South Asia, Southeast Asia, and East Asia generally weakened, while those of Central Asia and the Pacific and Oceania strengthened. Currency depreciations were highest in Sri Lanka and the Lao People's Democratic Republic since January 2022 (Figure 2.21).

Central Asian economies are closely linked to the Russian economy (Russia Briefing 2022, Wani 2022), and their currencies weakened along with the Russian currency after the Russian invasion of Ukraine and pursuant sanctions imposed by Western economies. Their currencies have recovered along with the Russian ruble. Currencies of the Pacific and Oceania economies also strengthened. For Oceania, this is mainly due to their nature as "commodity currencies," which strengthen as international commodity prices rise (FOREX.com 2021, Rampono 2022).

Food and energy price changes and weakening currencies. As international energy prices rise persistently more than food prices, energy-importing economies could be hit harder. The recent weakening of local currencies in the South Asia, Southeast Asia, and East Asia compound the pain. In addition, local currencies have depreciated in the majority of top energy-importing economies and appreciated in top food-importing economies.

Figure 2.21: Foreign Exchange Rates of Asian Economies (15 July 2021 = 100)

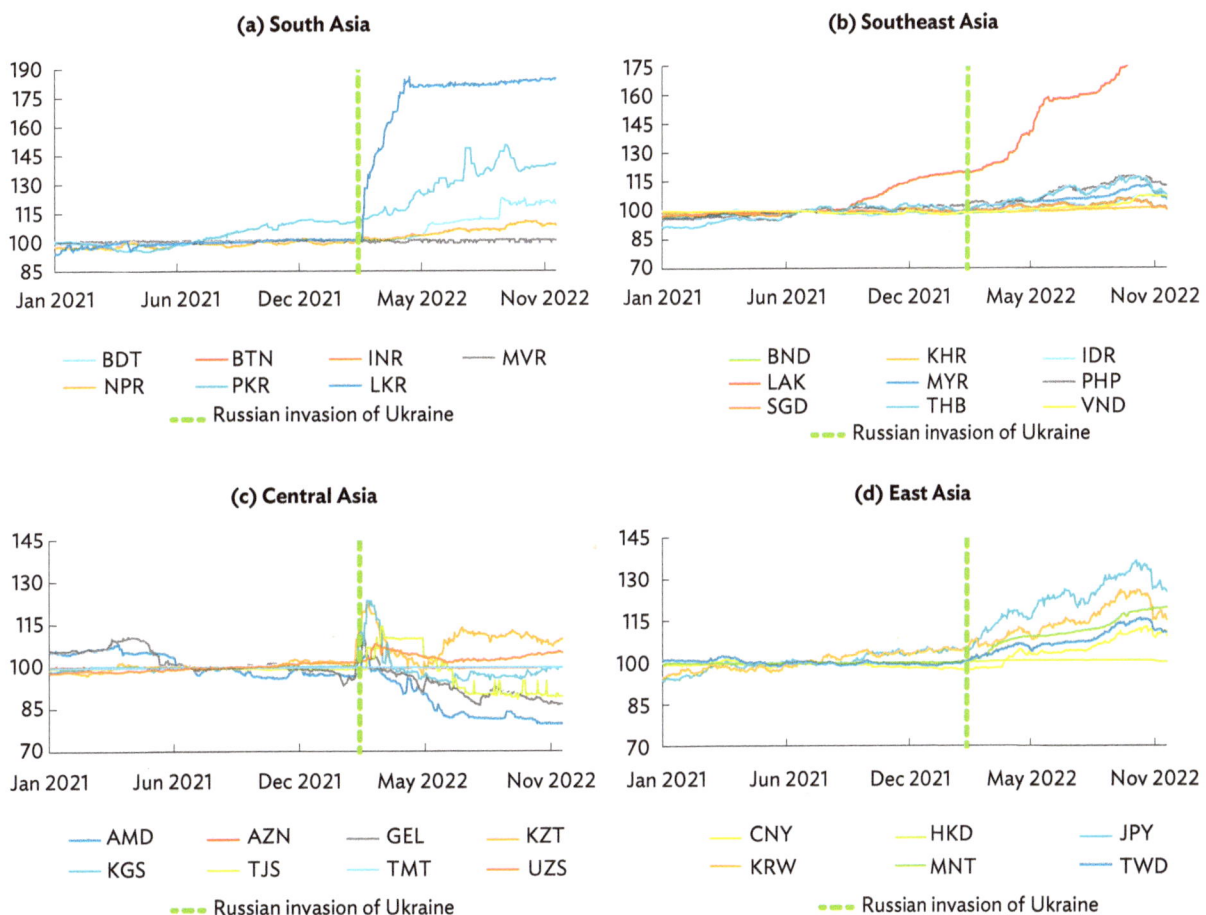

(a) South Asia

BDT — BTN — INR — MVR
NPR — PKR — LKR
--- Russian invasion of Ukraine

(b) Southeast Asia

BND — KHR — IDR
LAK — MYR — PHP
SGD — THB — VND
--- Russian invasion of Ukraine

(c) Central Asia

AMD — AZN — GEL — KZT
KGS — TJS — TMT — UZS
--- Russian invasion of Ukraine

(d) East Asia

CNY — HKD — JPY
KRW — MNT — TWD
--- Russian invasion of Ukraine

continued on next page

Figure 2.21 *continued*

(e) Pacific and Oceania

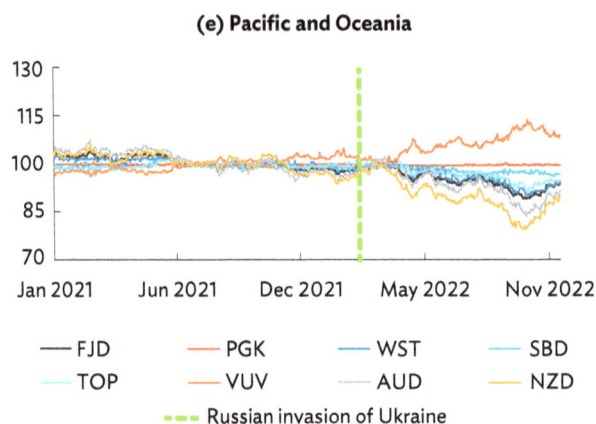

AMD = dram, AUD = Australian dollar, AZN = Azerbaijan manat, BDT = taka, BND = Brunei dollar, BTN = ngultrum, CNY = yuan, FJD = Fiji dollar, GEL = lari, HKD = Hong Kong dollar, IDR = rupiah, INR = Indian rupee, JPY = yen, KGS = som, KHR = riel, KRW = won, KZT = tenge, LAK = kip, LKR = Sri Lanka rupee, MNT = togrog, MVR = rufiyaa, MYR = ringgit, NPR = Nepalese rupee, NZD = New Zealand dollar, PGK = kina, PHP = peso, PKR = Pakistan rupee, SBD = Solomon Islands dollar, SGD = Singapore dollar, THB = baht, TJS = somoni, TMT = Turkmen manat, TOP = pa'anga; TWD = NT dollar, UZS = sum, VND = dong, VUV = vatu, WST = tala.

Note: Exchange rates are expressed as the value of the local currencies in United States dollar (100 = 15 July 2021).

Source: ADB calculations using data from Bloomberg (accessed December 2022).

The majority of Asian economies are net importers of the food and energy commodities, suggesting that the harmful effects of commodity prices could be broad. Food and energy import prices in local currency of net importers will rise further if local currencies depreciate, as is projected for Sri Lanka and Pakistan. The appreciation of local currency, on the other hand, will somehow tame import prices in local currencies of net importers, as is projected for Armenia and New Zealand (Figure 2.22).

Policy Recommendations

Prohibiting export restrictions through international cooperation. Export restrictions on food commodities, such as export licensing, export quotas, and export bans, have harmful effects on the prices and trade of such essential goods, threatening global food security and growth (Deb et al. 2021; Espitia, Rocha, and Ruta 2022). To prevent these events from aggravating food and energy crunches, international cooperation to prohibit such restrictions and for noncommercial and humanitarian purposes should be intensified.

Streamlining of the supply chain through trade facilitation and exploration of alternative transportation routes. The Russian invasion of Ukraine and the blockade of Black Sea ports have contributed to the disruption of food and energy supply chains. Whereas exploring new sources for the affected food and energy commodities is inevitable under such constraints, economies should also invest more in enhancing trade facilitation and finding alternative transportation and trading routes to smooth trade friction caused by recent global events (UNCTAD 2022).

Promoting multilateral cooperation for public stockholding. Public stockholding programs are implemented to ensure food security in an economy, especially for least developed economies. Given the limits imposed by the World Trade Organization (WTO) on public stockholding and trade-distorting support, developing economies could be exposed to potential noncompliance risks. The WTO adopted an interim solution to address the problem, but a permanent solution is imperative. Economies should discuss permanent solutions that address the problems involved in public stockholding to ensure global food security while reducing corresponding distortions to trade (Glauber and Sinha 2021).

Figure 2.22: Changes in Estimated 2022 Import Prices of Food and Energy Commodities in Local Currency—Asia and the Pacific (3 January 2022 to 30 November 2022, %)

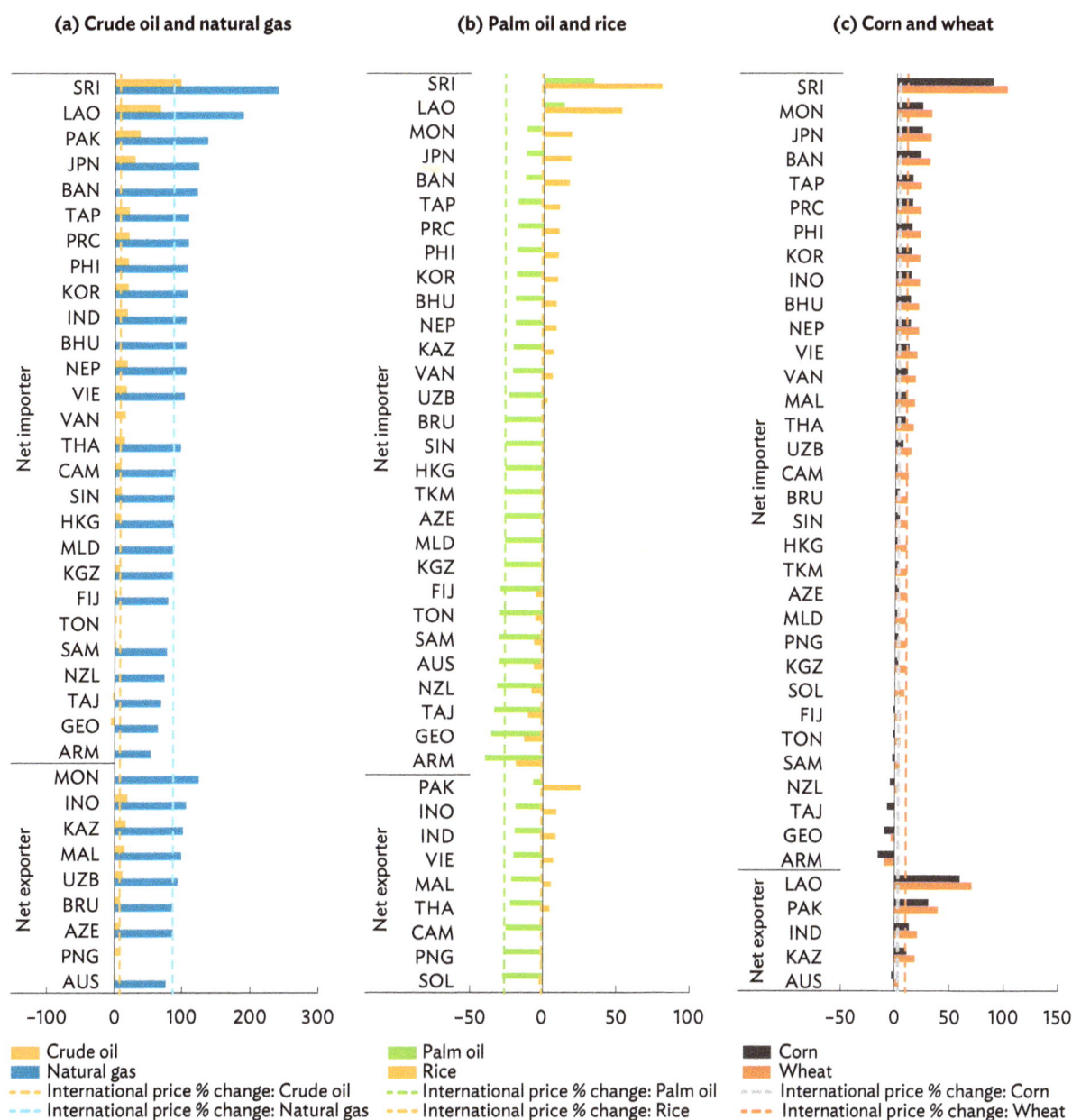

(a) Crude oil and natural gas

(b) Palm oil and rice

(c) Corn and wheat

Legend:
- Crude oil
- Natural gas
- International price % change: Crude oil
- International price % change: Natural gas
- Palm oil
- Rice
- International price % change: Palm oil
- International price % change: Rice
- Corn
- Wheat
- International price % change: Corn
- International price % change: Wheat

ARM = Armenia; AUS = Australia; AZE = Azerbaijan; BAN = Bangladesh; BHU = Bhutan; BRU = Brunei Darussalam; CAM = Cambodia; FIJ= Fiji; GEO = Georgia; HKG = Hong Kong, China; IND = India; INO = Indonesia; JPN = Japan; KAZ = Kazakhstan; KGZ = Kyrgyz Republic; KOR = Republic of Korea; LAO = Lao People's Democratic Republic; MAL = Malaysia; MLD = Maldives; MON = Mongolia; NEP = Nepal; NZL = New Zealand; PAK = Pakistan; PHI = Philippines; PNG = Papua New Guinea; PRC = People's Republic of China; SAM = Samoa; SIN = Singapore; SOL = Solomon Islands; SRI = Sri Lanka; TAJ = Tajikistan; TAP = Taipei,China; THA = Thailand; TKM = Turkmenistan; TON = Tonga; UZB = Uzbekistan; VAN = Vanuatu; VIE = Viet Nam.

Notes: To obtain the estimated 3 January 2022 and 30 November 2022 import values in US dollar of the 2019 imports, 2019 import values in US dollar for food and energy commodities were increased/decreased by the change in international prices of the goods from 31 December 2019 up to 3 January 2022 or 30 November 2022. These estimated 2022 import values in US dollars were multiplied by the foreign exchange rates of the selected Asia and Pacific economies during 3 January 2022 or 30 November 2022 to obtain the estimated 2022 import values in local currency of the 2019 imports. These two estimated 2022 import values in local currency are then utilized to calculate for the 2022 local currency import price percentage changes. Economies are classified as net importers on a bundle of goods if the sum of the import values of those goods is higher than the corresponding combined export values of those goods.

Sources: ADB calculations using data from United Nations. Commodity Trade Database. https://comtrade.un.org; Bloomberg; and CEIC (all accessed December 2022).

Providing targeted income subsidies to vulnerable groups. Low-income households will feel the high food and energy prices heavily. Supporting these vulnerable groups while letting international prices pass through domestic prices will be the more efficient and effective way to get through the crisis, instead of an across-the-board tax cut and subsidies (Amaglobeli et al. 2022).

Promoting and regulating commodity derivatives markets. Derivatives markets are used to hedge against price changes and to facilitate price discovery and trade. Providing adequate information about the derivatives market will optimize its utilization and distribute its benefits in an economy. To prevent overspeculation while nurturing the hedging functions of derivative instruments, regulations should be put in place on trading, settlement and clearing, and the transparency of market functioning and transactions must be enhanced.

Asia's Free Trade Agreement Policy

The global trade disruption and the downturn resulting from the COVID-19 pandemic have not dampened Asia and the Pacific's momentum in forging trade partnerships within and beyond the region.

Six trade agreements entered into force in 2022 (Table 2.1), four intraregional, including the historic Regional Comprehensive Economic Partnership (RCEP) agreement led by ASEAN.[27] The RCEP is the latest addition to the region's growing participation to mega regional trade agreements, following entry into force of the Comprehensive and Progressive Agreement for Trans-Pacific Partnership (CPTPP) in 2018.

While the number of newly effective Asian free trade agreements decreased in 2022 (Figure 2.23, right axis), the number of Asian economies participating in trade agreements still increased as mega regionals such as RCEP accommodated more members than bilateral deals. Asian economies have also been consistent and persistent in increasing and intensifying their participation through bilateral means. Cambodia, for example, entered into separate bilateral agreements with the PRC and the Republic of Korea in 2022, in addition to their RCEP participation.

Completing the current list of trade agreements in effect this year are bilateral deals between Bangladesh–Bhutan, India–United Arab Emirates, and the Republic of Korea–Israel. Meanwhile, more bilateral and regional trade agreements involving Asian economies are underway. To cite a few, early announcements have been issued to the WTO on the following interregional trade agreements: the EU has separate negotiations with India, Indonesia, Malaysia, the Philippines, and Thailand; European Free Trade Association with India, Kazakhstan (together with Belarus and the Russian Federation), and Viet Nam. In addition, seven agreements are being negotiated and four have been proposed or are under study.[28]

Existing trade agreements, meanwhile, are being upgraded and expanded by incorporating disciplines that go beyond market access and national treatment (Table 2.2). The evolution of these agreements comes with provisions on beyond-the-border disciplines such as trade facilitation, intellectual property rights, government procurement, competition policies, among others, while broadening and deepening the scope of goods, services, and investment liberalization commitments. Bilateral and regional trade agreements serve as more accessible platforms for economies to negotiate mutually beneficial agreements, including in areas not yet offered in mega regionals, duly

---

[27]   In May 2022, ADB released a preliminary analysis of the legal text in RCEP, comparing it with that of the CPTPP, relevant agreements of the WTO, and ASEAN+1 free trade agreements, taking into account related literature and articulating potential economic impacts (ADB 2022c).

[28]   Negotiations are also underway for (i) India–United Kingdom Free Trade Agreement (FTA) (December 2022—sixth round of negotiations); (ii) Republic of Korea–Pacific Alliance FTA (June 2022); (iii) Bangladesh–Sri Lanka FTA (June 2021); (iv) ASEAN–Canada FTA (September 2022—first round of negotiations); (v) India–Taipei,China FTA (December 2021); (vi) Canada–Indonesia Comprehensive Economic Partnership Agreement (November 2022—third round of negotiations); and (vii) Republic of Korea–Uzbekistan FTA (January 2021). FTAs that have been proposed or are under study include Bangladesh–Malaysia FTA, Georgia–Republic of Korea FTA, and Japan–Ukraine FTA.

Figure 2.23: Newly Effective Free Trade Agreements—Asia and the Pacific

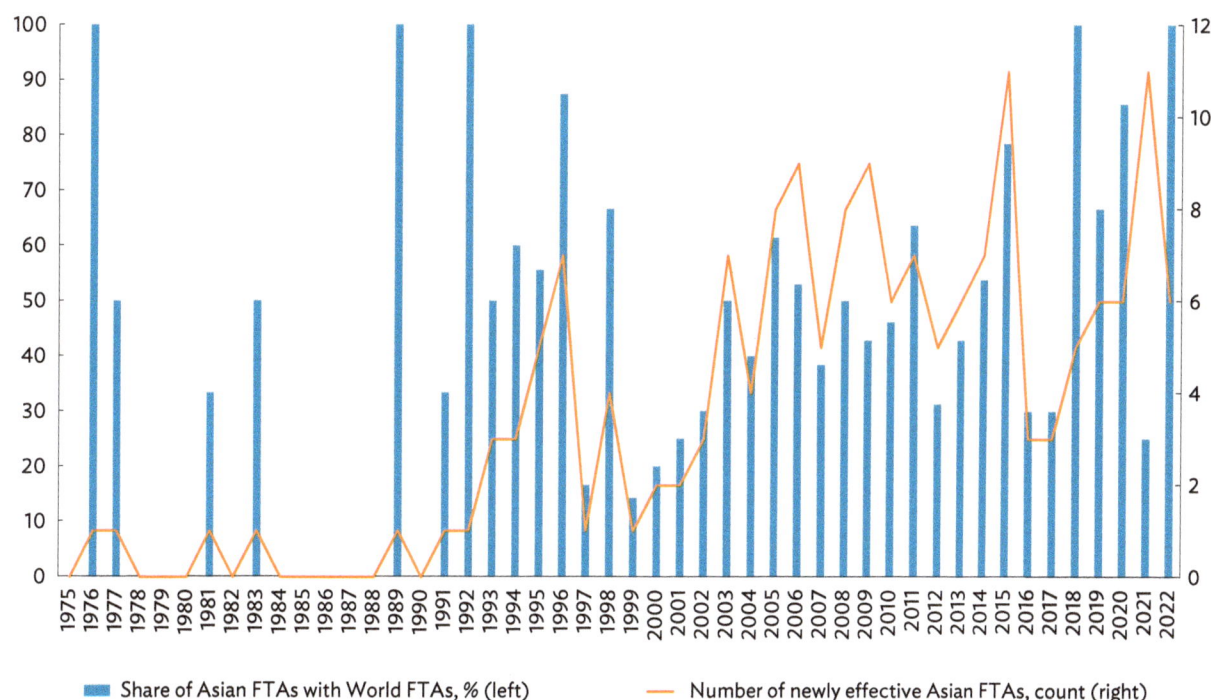

FTA = free trade agreement.

Notes: Trends for 1975–2021 derived using the the World Trade Organization's RTA Information System. The number of FTAs in 2022 derived using the Asia Regional Integration Center FTA Database.

Sources: ADB calculations using ADB data. Asia Regional Integration Center FTA Database. https://aric.adb.org/database/fta; and World Trade Organization. Regional Trade Agreement Information System. http://rtais.wto.org (both accessed December 2022).

Table 2.1: New Regional Trade Agreements in Asia and the Pacific, December 2021–December 2022

Name	Coverage	Type	Status (Date)
Intraregional			
RCEP	Goods and services	FTA	In force (1 January 2022)
Cambodia–PRC	Goods and services	FTA	In force (1 January 2022)
Bangladesh–Bhutan	Goods	PTA	In force (1 July 2022)
Cambodia–Republic of Korea	Goods and services	FTA	In force (1 December 2022)
Interregional			
India–UAE	Goods and services	CEPA	In force (1 May 2022)
Republic of Korea–Israel	Goods and services	FTA	In force (1 December 2022)
Australia–UK	Goods and services	FTA	Signed (17 December 2021)
New Zealand–UK	Goods and services	FTA	Signed (28 February 2022)
Singapore–MERCOSUR	Goods and services	FTA	Concluded (20 July 2022)

CEPA = Comprehensive Economic Partnership Agreement, FTA = free trade agreement, MERCOSUR = Mercado Común del Sur (Southern Common Market), PRC = People's Republic of China, PTA = preferential trade agreement, RCEP = Regional Comprehensive Economic Partnership, UAE = United Arab Emirates, UK = United Kingdom.

Note: Recently signed regional trade agreements in Asia and the Pacific cover December 2021 to December 2022.

Source: ADB compilation based on information available as of 25 January 2023.

considering their respective needs and state of readiness. Mega regionals could also complement these smaller agreements and the greater multilateral trading system by progressively enhancing market access and reducing trade barriers at a wider scale of participation. To this end, a noteworthy development observed recently—and to some extent attributable to the accelerated expansion of e-commerce during the pandemic—is the inclusion of e-commerce, digital trade, and data governance provisions in trade agreements, as well as the participation of Asian economies in digital economy agreements. The next section further discusses the nature of these agreements.

Digital Economy Agreements and Policy Interventions

Growing interest in digital economy agreements is a welcome reinforcement for a more secure and inclusive digital environment.

Unprecedented COVID-19 disruptions have raised the urgency for shifting to digital operations and to leverage e-commerce to keep businesses agile, boost output, and

Table 2.2: Recently Upgraded/Expanded Trade Agreements—Asia and the Pacific

Trade Agreement	Entry into Force	Recent Update	Remarks
New Zealand–People's Republic of China FTA	1 October 2008	7 April 2022	Implemented further tariff reduction or elimination; addressed compliance requirements, especially on nontariff measures; established new areas of cooperation in competition policy, e-commerce, government procurement, and environment and trade.[a]
Singapore–United Kingdom FTA	11 February 2021	14 June 2022	Entry into force of the UK–Singapore Digital Economy Agreement, which includes binding disciplines on data flows, and cooperative elements in emerging and innovative areas such as Artificial Intelligence, FinTech and RegTech, digital identities, and legal technology.[b]
Australia–Singapore FTA	28 July 2003	8 December 2020	Entry into force of the Australia–Singapore Digital Economy Agreement, which upgrades the digital trade arrangements between Australia and Singapore under the Comprehensive and Progressive Agreement on the Trans-Pacific Partnership and the Singapore–Australia Free Trade Agreement.[c]
Asia–Pacific Trade Agreement	17 June 1976	30 September 2020	Accession of Mongolia as seventh member of the APTA (UNESCAP 2020).
ASEAN–Japan Comprehensive Economic Partnership	1 December 2008	1 August 2020	Entry into force of the First Protocol to Amend the Agreement. The protocol added provisions concerning trade in services, movement of natural persons, and investment (ASEAN 2021).

ASEAN = Association of Southeast Asian Nations, FTA = free trade agreement.

Note: Recent updates report agreements with entry into force from July 2020.

[a] Government of New Zealand, Ministry of Foreign Affairs and Trade. NZ–China Free Trade Agreement. https://www.mfat.govt.nz/en/trade/free-trade-agreements/free-trade-agreements-in-force/nz-china-free-trade-agreement/.

[b] Government of Singapore, Ministry of Trade and Industry. UK–Singapore Digital Economy Agreement. https://www.mti.gov.sg/Trade/Digital-Economy-Agreements/UKSDEA.

[c] Government of Australia, Department of Foreign Affairs and Trade. Australia–Singapore Digital Economy Agreement. https://www.dfat.gov.au/trade/servicesand-digital-trade/australia-and-singapore-digitaleconomy-agreement.

Source: ADB compilation based on information available as of September 2022, including announcements from parties to the agreements.

generate employment.[29] Digital economy agreements are at the forefront of efforts to establish digital trade rules for the free flow of data across borders and contingent issues on data security, protection, and privacy, among others.

A precursor to facilitating a rules-based approach in the use of electronic means to engage in commercial activities, the United Nations Commission on International Trade Law (UNCITRAL) has enacted the Model Law of Electronic Commerce in 1996 to encourage harmonization of domestic laws and regulations on e-commerce transactions, including provisions for functional equivalence between electronic communications and paper documents.[30] Eighteen ADB economies are signatories to the UNCITRAL-Model Law of Electronic Commerce.

More recently, new generation trade agreements such as the CPTPP and the US–Mexico–Canada Agreement became templates for the design of more liberalized rules on data flows, electronic transactions, and digital trade facilitation through digital economy agreements. Table 2.3 compares digital economy agreements in Asia and the Pacific.

In 2020, a digital economy agreement between Australia and Singapore entered into force, an amendment to an existing bilateral free trade agreement and supported by memorandums of understanding to facilitate practical cooperation initiatives on data innovation, artificial intelligence, e-invoicing, e-certification for agricultural exports and imports, trade facilitation, personal data protection, and digital identity.[31]

The ASEAN Agreement on Electronic Commerce entered into force in 2021, providing a set of policies, principles, and rules to govern cross-border e-commerce in ASEAN (ASEAN 2019). The agreement is expected to facilitate aspects of e-commerce such as paperless trading, electronic authentication and electronic signatures, online consumer protection, online personal information protection, and location of computing facilities, among other things. The Singapore–New Zealand–Chile Digital Economy Partnership Agreement, signed in 2020 with the aim to harness the potential of the digital economy targeted at smaller economies, entered into force in Chile in November 2021.

The entry into force of the RCEP in 2022 included provisions on electronic commerce, which aim to promote electronic commerce among member economies, build an ecosystem of trust in the use of e-commerce, and enhance cooperation among stakeholders for its development.[32] This broadly includes transmissions of data, information, and digital products over the internet or over private electronic networks (RCEP Secretariat 2020).

The UK–Singapore Digital Economy Agreement, dubbed by the UK as the "world's most innovative trade agreement, covering the digitized trade in services and goods across the whole economy" entered into force in June 2022, building on their existing free trade agreement. The digital economy agreement's core trade areas cover open and inclusive digital markets, data flows, consumer and business safeguards, digital trading systems, financial services, and tech partnerships, among others (Government of the United Kingdom 2022).

In November 2022, the Republic of Korea and the EU launched a new digital partnership to advance cooperation on a wide array of digital issues. Initial work will be implemented on collaborative research, semiconductors, quantum technologies and high-performance computing, next generation mobile networks, artificial intelligence, online and digital platform cooperation, cybersecurity, digital identity and trust services, data-related laws and systems, digital inclusion, and digital trade principles building on the Republic of Korea–EU free trade agreement (European Commission 2022).

---

[29] Previous editions of the Asian Economic Integration Report (AEIR) extensively discussed the growing importance of the digital economy in the Asia and Pacific region. The AEIR 2021 theme chapter was on digital platforms and how they can accelerate digital transformation across the region (ADB 2021). AEIR 2022 explores the acceleration of digital services during the pandemic and the promise of regional cooperation to boost participation in digital services trade and spread its benefits evenly in developing Asia (ADB 2022b).

[30] United Nations Commission on International Trade Law (UNCITRAL). *UNCITRAL Model Law on Electronic Commerce (1996) with Additional Article 5 bis as adopted in 1998.* https://uncitral.un.org/en/texts/ecommerce/modellaw/electronic_commerce.

[31] Government of Australia, Department of Foreign Affairs and Trade. Australia–Singapore Digital Economy Agreement. https://www.dfat.gov.au/trade/services-and-digital-trade/australia-and-singapore-digital-economy-agreement.

[32] For further information on the Investment Chapter in the RCEP, refer to Box 3.2: Investment Provisions in the Regional Comprehensive Economic Partnership in Chapter 3.

Table 2.3: Selected Digital Trade Agreements in Asia and the Pacific

	Legal Framework: e-Transactions	Legal Framework: e-Transferrable Records	Electronic Authentication	Electronic Invoicing	Paperless Trading	Personal Information Protection	Cross-Border Transfer of Information	Open Government Information	Data Innovation	Cryptography Policy	Cybersecurity	Digital Inclusion
Singapore–United Kingdom Digital Economy Agreement, entered into force on 14 June 2022	Article 8.60, consistent with the United Nations Commission on International Trade Law (UNCITRAL) Model Law on Electronic Commerce 1996 or the United Nations Convention on the Use of Electronic Communications in International Contracts	Article 8.60, referenced in Article 10 of the UNCITRAL Model Law on Electronic Transferable Records of 2017	Article 8.61, covering electronic signature, electronic seals, electronic time stamps, and electronic registered delivery services	Article 8.61-A, focusing on interoperability	Article 8.61-B	Article 8.61-E	Article 8.61-F, including personal information if for the conduct of the business of a covered person	Article 8.61-H	Article 8.61-I (e.g., consumer data portability, data trusts)	Article 8.61-J	Article 8.61-L	Article 8.61-P
Regional Comprehensive Economic Partnership, entered into force on 1 January 2022	Article 12.10, consistent with the UNCITRAL Model Law on Electronic Commerce 1996 or the United Nations Convention on the Use of Electronic Communications in International Contracts	...	Article 12.6, including electronic signature	...	Article 12.5	Article 12.8	Article 12.15	...	...	...	Article 12.13	...

continued on next page

Table 2.3 continued

	Legal Framework: e-Transactions	Legal Framework: e-Transferrable Records	Electronic Authentication	Electronic Invoicing	Paperless Trading	Personal Information Protection	Cross-Border Transfer of Information	Open Government Information	Data Innovation	Cryptography Policy	Cybersecurity	Digital Inclusion
Republic of Korea–Singapore Digital Partnership Agreement,[a] concluded on 15 December 2021	Article 14.7, consistent with the UNCITRAL Model Law on Electronic Commerce 1996 or the United Nations Convention on the Use of Electronic Communications in International Contracts	Article 14.7, referenced in Article 10 of the UNCITRAL Model Law on Electronic Transferable Records of 2017	Article 14.8, including electronic signature	Article 14.10, focusing on interoperability	Article 14.12	Article 14.17	Article 14.14, including personal information if for the conduct of the business of a covered person	Article 14.26	Article 14.25	Article 14.18	Article 14.22	…
ASEAN Agreement on Electronic Commerce, entered into force on 9 September 2021	…	…	Article 7.2b, including electronic signature	…	Article 7.1	Article 7.5	Article 7.4	…	…	…	Article 8	…
Singapore–Australia Digital Economy Agreement, entered into force on 8 December 2020	Article 8, consistent with the UNCITRAL Model Law on Electronic Commerce 1996 or the United Nations Convention on the Use of Electronic Communications in International Contracts	Article 8, referenced in Article 10 of the UNCITRAL Model Law on Electronic Transferable Records of 2017	Article 9, including electronic signature	Article 10, focusing on interoperability	Article 12	Article 17	Article 23, including personal information if for the conduct of the business of a covered person	Article 27	Article 26	Article 7	Article 34	…

continued on next page

Table 2.3 continued

	Legal Framework: e-Transactions	Legal Framework: e-Transferable Records	Electronic Authentication	Electronic Invoicing	Paperless Trading	Personal Information Protection	Cross-Border Transfer of Information	Open Government Information	Data Innovation	Cryptography Policy	Cybersecurity	Digital Inclusion
Singapore–New Zealand–Chile Digital Economy Partnership Agreement, signed on 12 June 2020 * *The Republic of Korea signed on 5 October 2021 the documents to formally request to join the Digital Economy Partnership Agreement (DEPA); and Canada had exploratory discussions with DEPA members since December 2020. DEPA entered into force in Chile on 23 November 2021.*	Article 2.3, consistent with the UNCITRAL Model Law on Electronic Commerce 1996 or the United Nations Convention on the Use of Electronic Communications in International Contracts	Article 2.3, referenced in Article 10 of the UNCITRAL Model Law on Electronic Transferable Records of 2017	Article 6.9, specific to electronic signature	Article 2.5, focusing on interoperability	Article 2.2	Article 4.2	Article 4.3, including personal information if for the conduct of the business of a covered person	Article 9.5	Article 9.4	Article 3.4	Article 5.1	Article 11.1
Comprehensive and Progressive Agreement for Trans-Pacific Partnership, entered into force on 30 December 2018	Article 14.5, consistent with the UNCITRAL Model Law on Electronic Commerce 1996 or the United Nations Convention on the Use of Electronic Communications in International Contracts	...	Article 14.6, including electronic signature	...	Article 14.9	Article 14.8	Article 14.11, including personal information if for the conduct of the business of a covered person	...	...	...	Article 14.16	...

continued on next page

Table 2.3 *continued*

	Legal Framework: e-Transactions	Legal Framework: e-Transferrable Records	Electronic Authentication	Electronic Invoicing	Paperless Trading	Personal Information Protection	Cross-Border Transfer of Information	Open Government Information	Data Innovation	Cryptography Policy	Cybersecurity	Digital Inclusion
ASEAN–Australia–New Zealand Free Trade Area, entered into force in 2010	Article 4. Each Party shall maintain, or adopt as soon as practicable, domestic laws and regulations governing electronic transactions taking into account the UNCITRAL Model Law on Electronic Commerce 1996.	...	Article 5	...	Article 8	Article 7.1	...	...	...	...	...	...

... = not available, DEPA = Digital Economy Partnership Agreement.

a Based on the draft Republic of Korea–Singapore Digital Partnership Agreement uploaded by the Republic of Korea, Ministry of Trade, Industry and Energy.

Source: ADB compilation based on the legal text of the agreements and information available as of 25 July 2022.

Designing and implementing targeted policies for a digital-ready future is a complex, cross-cutting challenge. In parallel with the development of new generation agreements, digital policy interventions are proliferating—these interventions are policies and regulations imposed on the digital domain and associated technologies that can be classified into policy areas, including but not limited to data governance, content moderation, international trade, FDI, competition, registration and licensing, taxation, and other operating conditions.[33] Figure 2.24a shows a general increase in the number of digital policy interventions in seven selected Asian economies. Over 3 years, until 2022, economies had implemented 118 measures; rising above 10 interventions are the PRC (57 measures), Australia (15), and Japan (11).

Despite the disparities in numbers between the economies, there are also similarities in digital policy focus (Figure 2.24b). Australia, Japan, the PRC, and Singapore have the largest share of interventions on data governance; India, Indonesia, and the Republic of Korea have no interventions on data governance, focusing instead on taxation, foreign direct investments, and competition, respectively.[34]

Trade-Related Measures and Temporary Restrictions

Amid cascading global crises in health, food, and energy, nontariff measures imposed on the region in the form of sanitary and phytosanitary measures and technical barriers continue to peak.

Governments across the world use trade policy instruments to respond to the various economic and geopolitical challenges and pressures, both to facilitate

Figure 2.24: Digital Policy Interventions—Selected Asian Economies

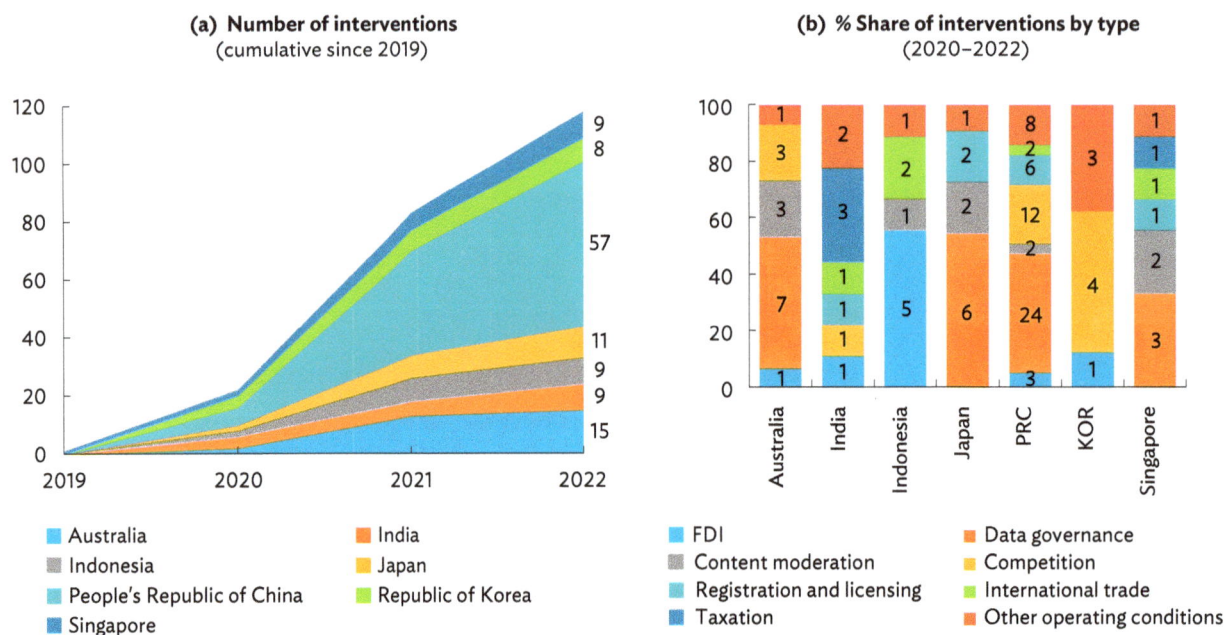

(a) **Number of interventions**
(cumulative since 2019)

(b) **% Share of interventions by type**
(2020–2022)

Legend (a):
- Australia
- India
- Indonesia
- Japan
- People's Republic of China
- Republic of Korea
- Singapore

Legend (b):
- FDI
- Content moderation
- Registration and licensing
- Taxation
- Data governance
- Competition
- International trade
- Other operating conditions

FDI = foreign direct investment, KOR = Republic of Korea, PRC = People's Republic of China.

Source: ADB calculations using data from Digital Policy Alert: https://digitalpolicyalert.org/activity-tracker (accessed August 2022).

---

[33]   See Digital Policy Alert at https://digitalpolicyalert.org/ for more information.

[34]   Additional information on digital policy interventions implemented by the economies analyzed is available in online Annex 1C: https://aric.adb.org/pdf/aeir2023_onlineannex1.pdf.

and to restrict international trade. While some of these measures have legitimate objectives,[35] such as ensuring product safety, environmental protection, or national security, it inevitably restricts trade, with negative implications for growth and sustainable development.

From less than 1% in 2000, nontariff measures in the form of sanitary and phytosanitary measures and technical barriers to trade now collectively comprise more than half of trade-related measures imposed on Asia (Figure 2.25). About 24% of nontariff measures are sanitary and phytosanitary measures, while about 29% are technical barriers to trade. Nontariff measures such as countervailing measures, safeguards, and export subsidies have been relatively constant—ranging from 500 to 700 per year.

Figure 2.25: Trade-Related Measures—Asia and the Pacific

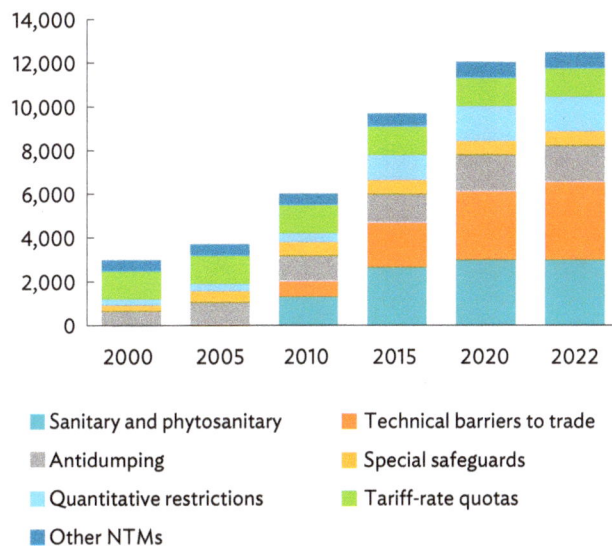

NTM = nontariff measure.

Notes: Based on cumulative number of measures in force as of the end of each year. Other nontariff measures include countervailing measures, safeguards, and export subsidies.

Source: ADB calculations using data from the World Trade Organization. Integrated Trade Intelligence Portal. https://i-tip.wto.org/goods/default.aspx (accessed July 2022).

With trade restrictions implemented during the COVID-19 pandemic still in effect, and confronted with new restrictions in response to the Russian invasion of Ukraine, the risk of maintaining defensive trade regimes remains palpable. Asia should remain steadfast in its resolve to keep markets open and to ensure stable, equitable access to necessities.

The global experience at the onset of the pandemic, in which economic uncertainties prodded some exporting economies to convert their shipments into stockpiles to secure domestic supplies, demonstrate how export restrictions can have undesirable outcomes such as greater scarcity among importing regions, and an upward drift in global commodity prices. Most recently, the escalating Russian invasion of Ukraine has severely disrupted global trade, impeding the world's post-pandemic food and energy security prospects (Box 2.3).

Analysis of trade interventions shows that 756 measures implemented from January 2020 to December 2021 were still in effect as of August 2022, and about 73% of these are considered restrictive.[36] More than 11% of Asia's 2020–2021 average total trade has been subject to restrictive interventions in 2022 (Figure 2.26a) implemented from Canada and the US (5%), Europe and the UK (2.5%), Asian economies (2.4%), and the rest of the world (1.6%).

Alongside export restrictions, several economies have also implemented import liberalization measures as in the case of necessities such as food and medical products. Liberalizing interventions implemented by Asia are shown to cover a significant portion of trade across all regions (Figure 2.26b).

---

[35] For example, technical barriers to trade establish the technical standards and regulations (e.g., packaging requirements) to ensure the quality of exports and the protection of human, animal, and/or plant health or life (WTO 1995). Sanitary and phytosanitary measures cover food safety, and animal and plant health standards to guarantee that foods are safe for human consumption and prevent the spread of diseases among plants and animals (WTO 1998).

[36] Trade interventions still in place are calculated as the total number of implemented trade interventions in 2020 and 2021 (i.e., the COVID-19 pandemic years) minus the total number of removed trade interventions implemented from 2020 to 2021.

Figure 2.26: Share of Total Trade Covered by Restrictive and Liberalizing Interventions by Region—World (%)

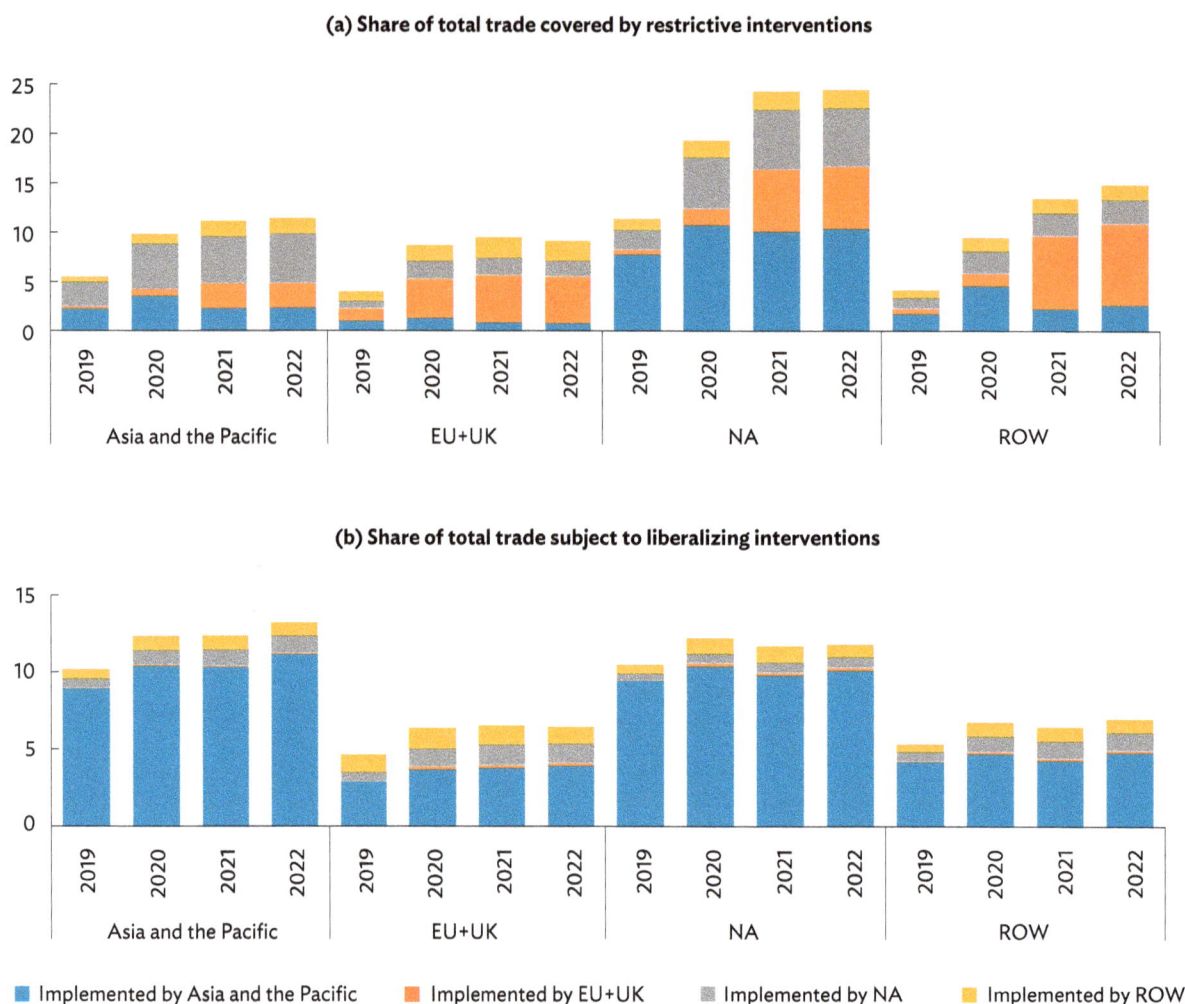

(a) Share of total trade covered by restrictive interventions

(b) Share of total trade subject to liberalizing interventions

■ Implemented by Asia and the Pacific   ■ Implemented by EU+UK   ▨ Implemented by NA   ■ Implemented by ROW

EU = European Union (27 members), NA = North America (United States and Canada), ROW = rest of the world, UK = United Kingdom.

Notes: (i) Figures for 2020 until 2022 were computed using trade interventions in effect since 2019; (ii) the Global Trade Alert (GTA) database for 2022 is yet to include measures announced in this year; (iii) GTA classifies trade measures as either restrictive or liberalizing; and (iv) the share of trade covered by trade interventions is computed using the average of total trade, i.e., the sum of exports and imports in the past 2 years.

Sources: ADB calculations using data from Global Trade Alert. https://www.globaltradealert.org/ (accessed August 2022); and UN Commodity Trade Database. https://comtrade.un.org/ (accessed August 2022).

Among subregions in Asia, Central Asia has the greatest share of total trade subject to restrictive interventions, followed by East Asia and South Asia (Figure 2.27). Restrictive measures or interventions by Europe and the UK account for the largest share of total Central Asian trade in 2021 and 2022 at 16%, while measures by the rest of the world are a distant second at about 5%. On the other hand, East Asia's total trade is largely covered by restrictive measures imposed by Canada and the US with 6%. Similarly, restrictive interventions on Asia's total trade come from Canada and the US, with about 5%, followed by the EU and the UK, at about 2.5%, and then from within Asia, at 2.4%.

Southeast Asia has the highest share of total trade covered by liberalizing measures, with about 15%, followed by East Asia and South Asia. Central Asia has the lowest share of trade benefiting from these measures, with about 4%. Across all subregions, most liberalizing measures were implemented from within the region.

Figure 2.27: Share of Total Trade Covered by Restrictive and Liberalizing Interventions by Asian Subregion (%)

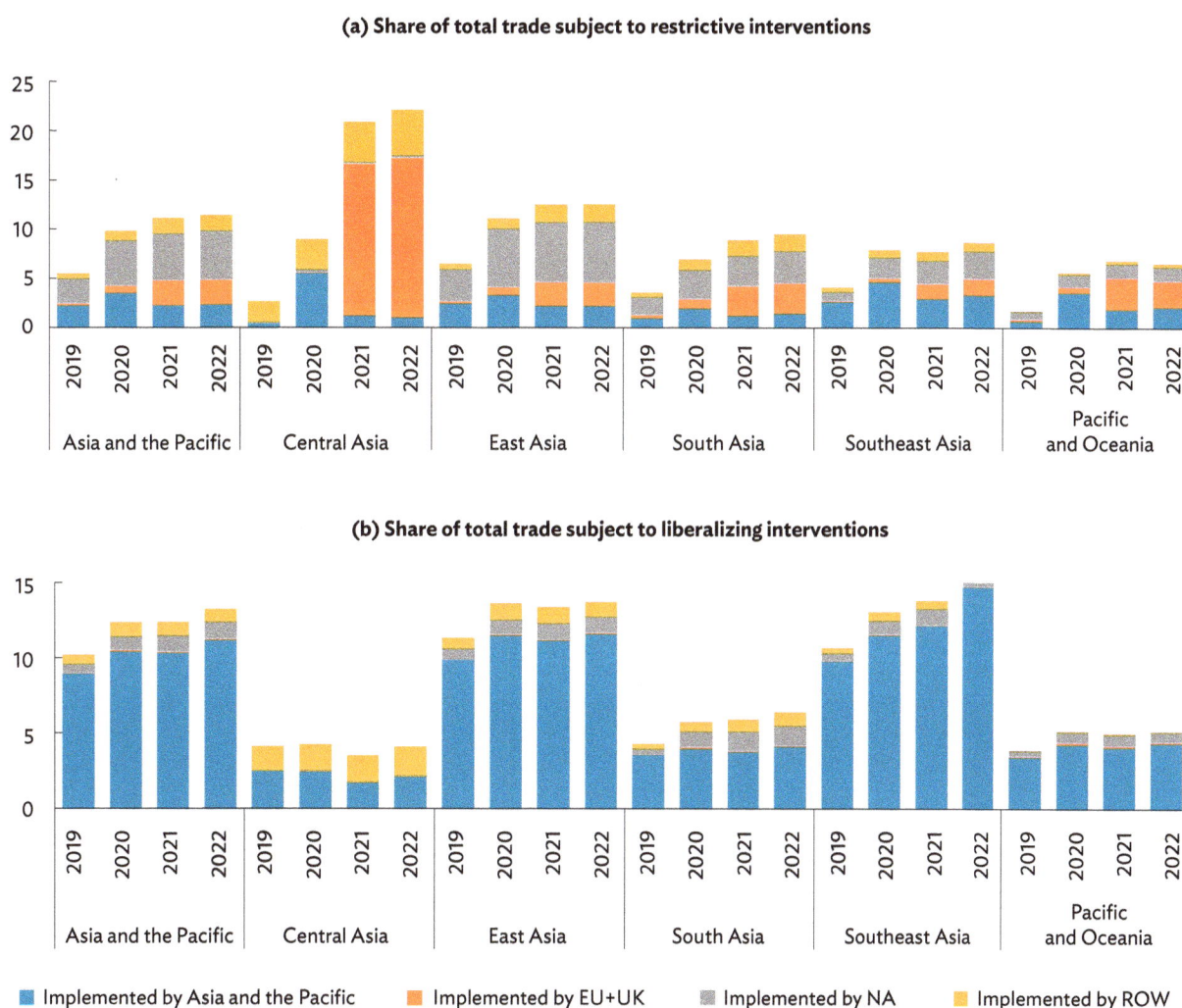

(a) Share of total trade subject to restrictive interventions

(b) Share of total trade subject to liberalizing interventions

■ Implemented by Asia and the Pacific   ■ Implemented by EU+UK   ▨ Implemented by NA   ■ Implemented by ROW

EU = European Union (27 members), NA = North America (United States and Canada), ROW = rest of the world, UK = United Kingdom.

Notes: (i) Figures for 2020 until 2022 were computed using trade interventions that were in effect since 2019; (ii) The Global Trade Alert (GTA) database for 2022 is yet to include measures announced in this year; (iii) GTA provides the classification of trade measures as either restrictive or liberalizing; and (iv) the share of trade covered by trade interventions are computed using the average of total trade, i.e., the sum of exports and imports, in the past 2 years.

Sources: ADB calculations using data from Global Trade Alert. https://www.globaltradealert.org/; and UN Commodity Trade Database. https://comtrade.un.org/ (both accessed August 2022).

Looking at the critical and essential sectors during the pandemic, more than 30% of trade in pharmaceutical products was subject to restrictive measures, most of which were attributed to EU and UK measures (Figure 2.28). More than 20% of trade in this sector was subject to liberalizing measures, a large share imposed by Canada and the US (14% of pharmaceutical trade). In contrast, restrictions on pharmaceutical products within Asia represented only 1.2% of total trade in pharmaceutical products. Keeping international markets open for trade is an essential part of economic recovery. To this end, in November 2020, the ASEAN economic ministers signed a memorandum of understanding on the implementation of nontariff measures on essential goods, calling on ASEAN member states to refrain from introducing or maintaining trade-restrictive measures on essential goods (ASEAN 2020).

In contrast, trade in of grain products (i.e., products of the milling industry, malt, and starches) has been relatively spared from restrictive measures (less than 2% of total trade) but is a significant contention of liberalizing measures mostly implemented by Asia. Similarly, measures imposed by Asia dominate the liberalizing interventions on flour (i.e., preparations of cereals, flour,

starch, or milk), covering close to 12% of total trade. Asia pushed through its liberalizing trade interventions on grain and flour, despite COVID-19 mobility restrictions; imminent shortages of farm labor; locust infestations in Africa, the Middle East, and South Asia; and dry weather in Europe and South America that disrupted yields on agricultural products (Falkendal et al. 2021).

Figure 2.28: Share of Total Trade Subject to Trade Interventions from 2019 to 2022, by Selected Commodity Group— Asia and the Pacific (%)

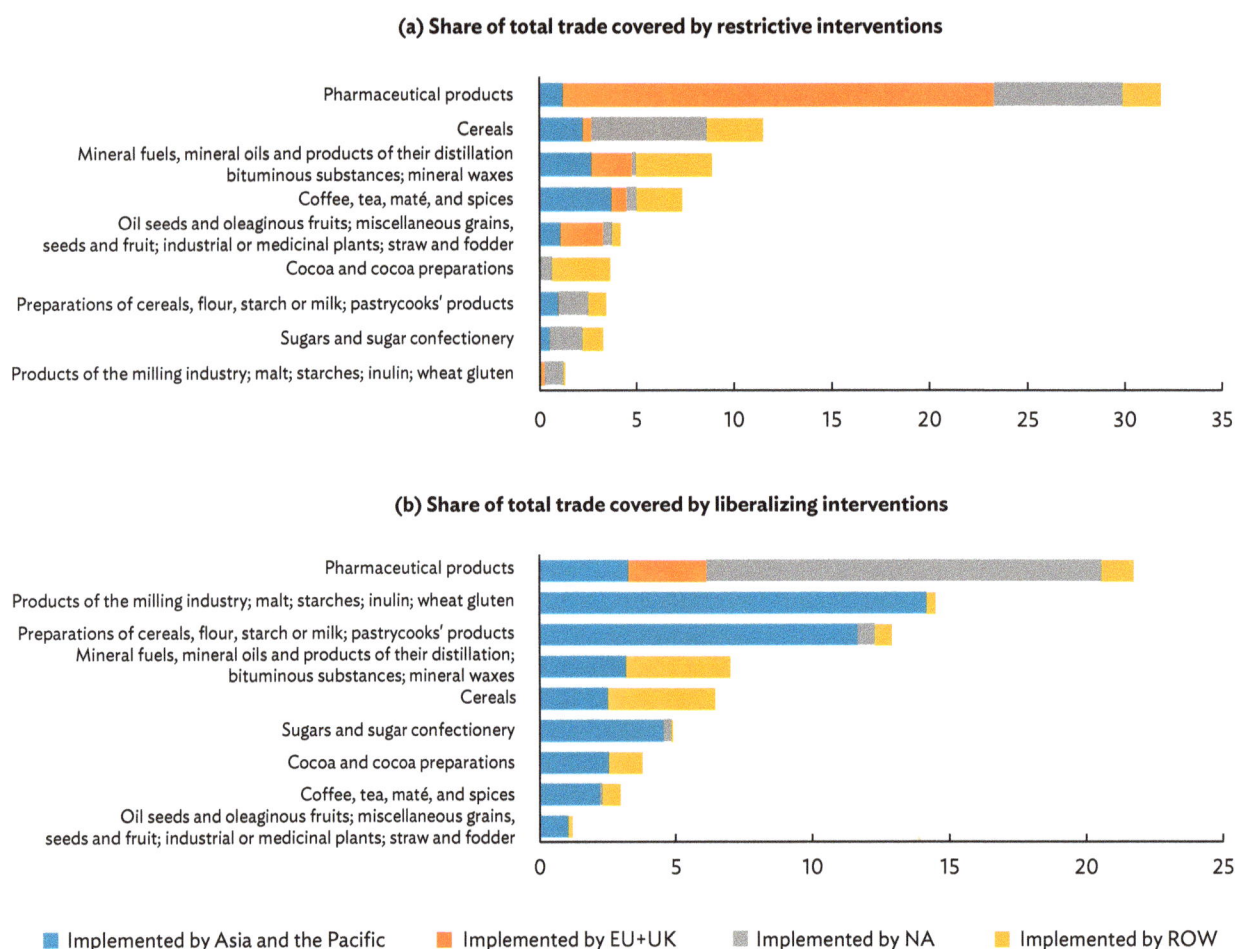

(a) Share of total trade covered by restrictive interventions

(b) Share of total trade covered by liberalizing interventions

■ Implemented by Asia and the Pacific   ■ Implemented by EU+UK   ■ Implemented by NA   ■ Implemented by ROW

EU = European Union (27 members), NA = North America (United States and Canada), ROW = rest of the world, UK = United Kingdom.

Notes: (i) Figures for 2020 until 2022 were computed using trade interventions in effect since 2019; (ii) the Global Trade Alert (GTA) database for 2022 is yet to include measures announced in this year; (iii) GTA classifies trade measures as either restrictive or liberalizing; and (iv) the share of trade covered by trade interventions are computed using the average of total trade, i.e., the sum of exports and imports, in the past 2 years.

Sources: ADB calculations using data from Global Trade Alert. https://www.globaltradealert.org/; and UN Commodity Trade Database. https://comtrade.un.org/ (both accessed August 2022).

Against challenging global economic and geopolitical environment, the outcomes of the 12th Ministerial Conference of the World Trade Organization (MC12) reflect the WTO's efforts to tackle global emergencies. Subsequently, Aid for Trade is significant in reinforcing MC12 reforms and furthering the capacity of developing economies to overcome trade-related constraints and to achieve more inclusive development.

In June 2022, MC12 gathered ministers in Geneva after almost 5 years had passed since the last meeting in Nairobi. To help governments respond to today's compounded global challenges, the conference agreed on major outcomes in response to critical issues, including landmark agreements and decisions on fisheries subsidies, WTO reform, pandemic preparedness, food security, and e-commerce (WTO 2022c):

(i)   A multilateral agreement on fisheries subsidies was adopted with new and binding provisions on members by prohibiting (a) subsidies contributing to illegal, unreported, and unregulated fishing; (b) subsidies regarding overfished stocks; and (c) subsidies for fishing in under-regulated high seas.

(ii)   Ministers launched a concrete WTO reform process, acknowledging the importance and urgency of reforming the WTO Dispute Settlement System. Discussions will be conducted about a full and well-functioning dispute settlement system accessible to all members by 2024.

(iii) A declaration was agreed on the WTO response to the pandemic and preparedness for future pandemics. WTO members agreed to implement a 5-year intellectual property waiver for COVID-19 vaccines, including its ingredients and processes, and will examine extension to therapeutics in 6 months under the WTO Agreement on Trade-Related Aspects of Intellectual Property Rights Agreement.

(iv)   The Declaration on the Emergency Response to Food Insecurity was adopted, which reaffirms the importance of not imposing WTO-inconsistent

export prohibitions or restrictions on food. Members further agreed to exempt the World Food Programme from trade-distorting measures, and to enhance the productivity, availability, affordability, and resilience of agricultural markets.

(v)   A Ministerial Decision on the Work Programme on Electronic Commerce was adopted, which extends the moratorium on customs duties on electronic transmissions until MC13.

Developing and least developed economies are poised to benefit from the MC12 outcomes through agreed agricultural reforms that are aligned with the objectives of the Doha Development Agenda, and through reinvigorated cooperation on important development issues such as food insecurity, e-commerce, and intellectual property related to the pandemic response, among others. Targeted technical assistance and capacity building programs will also be provided to advance work on enhancing the disciplines of the Agreement on Fisheries Subsidies through the WTO's new Fish Funding Mechanism to be established in cooperation with relevant international organizations such as the Food and Agriculture Organization of the United Nations and the International Fund for Agricultural Development.

MC12 developments present timely and valuable opportunities to promote more inclusive and sustained economic growth. However, complementary international assistance and cooperation beyond MC12 remain much needed by developing economies— especially the least developed and geographically challenged—to weather current trade tensions and economic uncertainties and to catch up with rapidly advancing global trends in digital trade and connectivity.

For example, the E-Commerce Capacity Building Framework launched earlier in 2022 by co-convenors of the Joint Statement Initiative on E-Commerce aims to provide a wide range of training and assistance to strengthen digital inclusion and maximize opportunities in digital trade for developing and least developed members (WTO 2022b). Similarly, the Aid for Trade initiative, which has long supported developing

Box 2.3: Trade-Restricting Measures Arising from the Russian Invasion of Ukraine

The Russian invasion of Ukraine has severely disrupted global trade and investment, impeding the world's post-pandemic food and energy security prospects. This has unleashed a new wave of protectionism as governments adopt trade-related barriers and restrictions in a bid to secure domestic stocks of food and other commodities amid shortages and rising prices.

World Trade Organization (WTO) rules allow members to impose export restrictions as a temporary measure under certain circumstances. The exception permits a WTO member to measures it considers "necessary for the protection of its essential security interests," including "in time of war or other emergency in international relations" (Article XXI, WTO General Agreement on Tariffs and Trade [GATT]). The Government of Ukraine, in its decision to impose an economic embargo with the Russian Federation and to rescind the application of WTO agreements in its relations with the Russian Federation, invoked its national security rights under, among other things, Article XXI of GATT 1994, Article XIV bis of the General Agreement on Trade in Services, and Article 73 of the WTO Agreement on Trade-Related Aspects of Intellectual Property Rights Agreement. Ukraine urged WTO members to suspend the Russian Federation's participation in the WTO (Ukraine's Mission to UNOG 2022). In response, Canada revoked the most-favored nation status of the Russian Federation and Belarus on the basis of GATT Article XXI (Government of Canada 2022). A joint statement by 14 WTO members including the European Union, Japan, and the United States, indicated that they would take action "necessary to protect our essential security interests" (US Mission 2022).

Source: ADB staff.

The Russian Federation argued that the unilateral withdrawal of most-favored-nation treatment for Russian goods and services "severely defies the fundamental WTO principle of non-discrimination" (WTO 2022a).

Export and other trade-related restrictions limit consumer choices as imported quantities decline. It may also trigger a ripple effect toward the imposition of further restrictions to include substitute goods. The number of economies that have imposed export restrictions on food supplies increased as the the Russian invasion of Ukraine ensued, according to WTO notifications. Ukraine has banned exports of agricultural commodities including barley and sugar, and has introduced export licenses for its key export goods such as wheat, corn, and sunflower oil. The Russian Federation imposed export restrictions for raw sugar, wheat, barley, and corn, among others. Argentina, Hungary, Indonesia, the Republic of Moldova, Serbia, and Türkiye announced export restrictions on products such as wheat, maize, sunflower oil, margarine, flour, and soybean oil to all trade partners, and Egypt has implemented a production license scheme for wheat producers (WTO 2022d).

The WTO's midyear report on trade-related developments covering mid-October 2021 to mid-May 2022 recorded 55 prohibitive or restrictive export measures on food, feed, fuels, and fertilizers imposed by WTO members and observers since the escalation of the invasion in late February. Of these, 15 measures have since been phased out, while 40 measures from 25 members and observers are still in place (WTO 2022e).

---

economies in building trade-related infrastructure and capacities, may also leverage digital trade by more actively addressing information and communication technology infrastructure issues and narrowing the global digital divide.[37] Through concerted efforts,

governments, multilateral institutions, and other relevant stakeholders must continue cooperating toward mitigating the negative effects of ongoing crises, while keeping pace with rapid digital trends in a still-fragile post-pandemic recovery.

---

[37]   In July 2022, ADB released a report examining the catalytic role of Aid for Trade in helping least developed, lower-middle-income, and small island developing economies narrow the digital divide and navigate the emerging trade rules in digital agreements, making trade more inclusive, resilient, and sustainable (ADB 2022a).

References

Amaglobeli, D., E. Hanedar, G. H. Hong, and C. Thévenot. 2022. Response to High Food, Energy Prices Should Focus on Most Vulnerable. International Monetary Fund Blog. 7 June. https://blogs.imf.org/2022/06/07/response-to-high-food-energy-prices-should-focus-on-most-vulnerable/.

Association of Southeast Asian Nations (ASEAN). 2019. *ASEAN Agreement on Electronic Commerce.* https://asean.org/wp-content/uploads/2021/09/ASEAN-Agreement-on-Electronic-Commerce-2019.pdf.

———. 2020. *Memorandum of Understanding on the Implementation of Non Tariff Measures (NTM) on Essential Goods under the Ha Noi Plan of Action on Strengthening ASEAN Economic Cooperation and Supply Chain Connectivity in Response to the COVID-19 Pandemic.* https://asean.org/wp-content/uploads/2021/09/5.-MOU-on-NTMs-on-Essential-Goods-for-upload.pdf.

———. 2021. Certifying Statement. First Protocol to Amend the Agreement on Comprehensive Economic Partnership among Member States of the Association of Southeast Asian Nations and Japan. https://asean.org/wp-content/uploads/2021/08/AJCEP-Prtcl-CTC.pdf.

Asian Development Bank (ADB). 2015. *Key Indicators for Asia and the Pacific 2015 46th Edition.* Manila.

———. 2021. *Asian Economic Integration Report 2021: Making Digital Platforms Work for Asia and the Pacific.* Manila.

———. 2022a. *Aid for Trade in Asia and the Pacific: Leveraging Trade and Digital Agreements for Sustainable Development.* Manila. https://www.adb.org/sites/default/files/publication/811756/aid-trade-asia-pacific-trade-digital-agreements.pdf.

———. 2022b. *Asian Economic Integration Report 2022: Advancing Digital Services Trade in Asia and the Pacific.* Manila.

———. 2022c. *The Regional Comprehensive Economic Partnership Agreement: A new paradigm in Asian regional cooperation?* Manila. https://www.adb.org/sites/default/files/publication/792516/rcep-agreement-new-paradigm-asian-cooperation.pdf.

———. Asia Regional Integration Center. Economy Groupings. https://aric.adb.org/integrationindicators/groupings.

———. Asia Regional Integration Center. Free Trade Agreements. https://aric.adb.org/fta (accessed July 2022, December 2022).

Baffes, J. and P. Nagle. 2022. Commodity Prices Surge Due to the War in Ukraine. World Bank Blogs. 5 May. https://blogs.worldbank.org/developmenttalk/commodity-prices-surge-due-war-ukraine.

Borin, A. and M. Mancini. 2019. Measuring What Matters in Global Value Chains and Value-Added Trade. *Policy Research Working Paper* No. 8804. https://openknowledge.worldbank.org/handle/10986/31533.

Centre d'Études Prospectives et d'Informations Internationales (the French Research Center in International Economics). GeoDist Database. http://www.cepii.fr/CEPII/en/cepii/cepii.asp (accessed December 2022).

CPB Netherlands Bureau for Economic Policy Analysis. World Trade Monitor. https://www.cpb.nl/en/world-trade-monitor-october-2022 (accessed January 2023).

Deb, P., J. Estafania-Flores, S. Kothari, and N. Tawk. 2021. How Trade Can Help Speed Asia's Economic Recovery. International Monetary Fund Blog. 19 November. https://blogs.imf.org/2021/11/19/how-trade-can-help-speed-asias-economic-recovery/.

Digital Policy Alert: https://digitalpolicyalert.org/activity-tracker (accessed August 2022).

Energy Information Administration (EIA). 2021. Natural Gas Explained. 2 December. https://www.eia.gov/energyexplained/natural-gas/.

———. 2022. Oil and Petroleum Products Explained - Oil Prices and Outlook. 25 February. https://www.eia.gov/energyexplained/oil-and-petroleum-products/prices-and-outlook.php.

Espitia, A., N. Rocha, and M. Ruta. 2022. How Export Restrictions Are Impacting Global Food Prices. World Bank Blogs. 6 July. https://blogs.worldbank.org/psd/how-export-restrictions-are-impacting-global-food-prices.

European Commission. 2022. Republic of Korea–European Union Digital Partnership. 28 November. https://digital-strategy.ec.europa.eu/en/library/republic-korea-european-union-digital-partnership.

Falkendal, T., C. Otto, J. Schewe, J. Jägermeyr, M. Konar, M. Kummu, B. Watkins, and M. Puma. 2021. Grain Export Restrictions During COVID-19 Risk Food Insecurity in Many Low- and Middle-Income Countries. *Nature Food*. 2. pp. 11–14.

FOREX.com. 2021. Commodity Currencies Explained. 5 May. https://www.forex.com/en/market-analysis/latest-research/commodity-currencies-explained/.

Freightos. Freightos Baltic Index (FBX): Global Container Freight Index. https://fbx.freightos.com/ (accessed January 2023).

Glauber, J. and T. Sinha. 2021. *Procuring Food Stocks Under World Trade Organization Farm Subsidy Rules: Finding a Permanent Solution.* Winnipeg: International Institute for Sustainable Development. https://www.iisd.org/system/files/2021-08/food-stocks-wto-farm-subsidy-rules.pdf.

Global Trade Alert. https://www.globaltradealert.org/ (accessed August 2022).

Government of Australia, Department of Foreign Affairs and Trade. Australia–Singapore Digital Economy Agreement. https://www.dfat.gov.au/trade/services-and-digital-trade/australia-and-singapore-digital-economy-agreement.

Government of Canada. 2022. Canada Cuts Russia and Belarus from Most-Favoured-Nation Tariff Treatment. News Release. 3 March. https://www.canada.ca/en/department-finance/news/2022/03/canada-cuts-russia-and-belarus-from-most-favoured-nation-tariff-treatment.html.

Government of New Zealand, Ministry of Foreign Affairs and Trade. NZ–China Free Trade Agreement. https://www.mfat.govt.nz/en/trade/free-trade-agreements/free-trade-agreements-in-force/nz-china-free-trade-agreement/.

Government of Singapore, Ministry of Trade and Industry. UK–Singapore Digital Economy Agreement. https://www.mti.gov.sg/Trade/Digital-Economy-Agreements/UKSDEA.

Government of the United Kingdom. 2022. *UK–Singapore Digital Economy Agreement: Final Agreement Explainer.* https://www.gov.uk/government/publications/uk-singapore-digital-economy-agreement-explainer/uk-singapore-digital-economy-agreement-final-agreement-explainer.

International Monetary Fund (IMF). Commodity Terms of Trade. https://data.imf.org/ (accessed November 2022).

———. Direction of Trade Statistics. https://data.imf.org/dot (accessed December 2022 and January 2023).

———. World Economic Outlook October 2022 Database. https://www.imf.org/en/Publications/WEO/weo-database/2022/October (accessed December 2022).

Konrad, T. 2012. The End of Elastic Oil. *Forbes.* 26 January. https://www.forbes.com/sites/tomkonrad/2012/01/26/the-end-of-elastic-oil/?sh=596997c036d6.

Laborde, D. and A. Mamun. Food Export & Fertilizer Restrictions Tracker. https://public.tableau.com/app/profile/laborde6680/viz/ExportRestrictionsTracker/FoodExportRestrictionsTracker (accessed December 2022 and January 2023).

Rampono, J. 2022. What's Driving the Australian Dollar Higher in 2022. *S Money.* 9 March. https://www.smoney.com.au/blog/whats-driving-the-australian-dollar-higher-in-2022/.

RCEP Secretariat. 2020. RCEP Agreement Chapter 12 - Electronic Commerce. https://rcepsec.org/wp-content/uploads/2020/11/Chapter-12.pdf.

Russia Briefing. 2022. European Development Bank: Economic Fallout Likely for Central Asia. 31 March. https://www.russia-briefing.com/news/european-development-bank-economic-fallout-likely-for-central-asia.html/.

Ukraine's Mission to United Nations Office at Geneva (UNOG). 2022.https://twitter.com/ukrinunog/status/1499334312755437569.

United Nations. Commodity Trade Database. https://comtrade.un.org (accessed August, November, and December 2022, and January 2023).

United Nations Conference on Trade and Development (UNCTAD). 2022. *Maritime Trade Disrupted: The War in Ukraine and Its Effects on Maritime Trade Logistics.* https://unctad.org/system/files/official-document/osginf2022d2_en.pdf.

United Nations Commission on International Trade Law (UNCITRAL). *UNCITRAL Model Law on Electronic Commerce (1996) with Additional Article 5 bis as adopted in 1998.* https://uncitral.un.org/en/texts/ecommerce/modellaw/electronic_commerce.

United Nations Economic and Social Commission for Asia and the Pacific (UNESCAP). 2020. *Mongolia Accedes to the Asia-Pacific Trade Agreement as Its Seventh Member.* https://www.unescap.org/news/mongolia-accedes-asia-pacific-trade-agreement-its-seventh-member.

US Mission. 2022. Joint Statement on Aggression by the Russian Federation Against Ukraine with the Support of Belarus: Communication from Albania; Australia; Canada; European Union; Iceland; Japan; the Republic of Korea; the Republic of Moldova; Montenegro; New Zealand; North Macedonia; Norway; the United Kingdom; and the United States. https://geneva.usmission.gov/2022/03/15/wto-members-joint-statement-on-ukraine/.

Wani, A. 2022. The Ukraine War Weighs Down on the Central Asian Republics. *Observer Research Foundation.* 13 May. https://www.orfonline.org/expert-speak/the-ukraine-war-weighs-down-on-the-central-asian-republics/.

World Bank. World Development Indicators. https://databank.worldbank.org/source/world-development-indicators (accessed December 2022).

———. 2022. Food and Energy Price Shocks from Ukraine War Could Last for Years. Press release. 26 April. https://www.worldbank.org/en/news/press-release/2022/04/26/food-and-energy-price-shocks-from-ukraine-war.

World Trade Organization (WTO). 1995. *Agreement on Technical Barriers to Trade.* https://www.wto.org/english/docs_e/legal_e/17-tbt.pdf.

———. 1998. *Understanding the WTO Agreement on Sanitary and Phytosanitary Measures.* Geneva. https://www.wto.org/english/tratop_e/sps_e/spsund_e.htm.

———. 2022a. Communication from the Russian Federation. https://docs.wto.org/dol2fe/Pages/SS/directdoc.aspx?filename=q:/WT/GC/245.pdf&Open=Tru.

———. 2022b. E-Commerce JSI co-convenors announce capacity building support. https://www.wto.org/english/tratop_e/ecom_e/jiecomcapbuild_e.htm.

———. 2022c. MC12 Outcome Document, WTO 222, adopted on 17 June 2022. https://docs.wto.org/dol2fe/Pages/SS/directdoc.aspx?filename=q:/WT/MIN22/24.pdf&Open=True.

———. 2022d. The Crisis in Ukraine: Implications of the War for Global Trade and Development. https://www.wto.org/english/res_e/booksp_e/imparctukraine422_e.pdf.

———. 2022e. WTO Members Show Restraint in Trade-Restrictive Measures Despite Economic Uncertainty. https://www.wto.org/english/news_e/news22_e/trdev_27jul22_e.htm.

———. General Agreement on Tariffs and Trade (GATT). https://www.wto.org/english/res_e/booksp_e/gatt_ai_e/art21_e.pdf.

———. Integrated Trade Intelligence Portal. https://i-tip.wto.org/goods/default.aspx (accessed July 2022).

———. Organisation for Economic Co-operation and Development (OECD). Balanced Trade in Services Dataset (BaTIS)—BPM6. https://www.wto.org/english/res_e/statis_e/trade_datasets_e.htm (accessed December 2022).

———. Regional Trade Agreement Information System. http://rtais.wto.org (accessed December 2022).

3 Cross-Border Investment

Recent Trends in Foreign Direct Investment

Inward Foreign Direct Investment

Global foreign direct investment activity saw an uptick in 2021; however, the momentum could taper off amid the growing headwinds.

After a significant dip in investment activity in 2020, global foreign direct investment (FDI) recovered strongly in 2021.[38] Based on estimates from the United Nations Conference on Trade and Development (UNCTAD), total inward FDI expanded by 64.3% in 2021 after declining by 35.0% in 2020.[39] This put FDI inflows back to pre-pandemic levels, amounting to about $1.6 trillion in 2021, nearly 7% higher than 2019 levels.

Significant merger and acquisition (M&A) deals helped boost global FDI activity. International project financing also picked up on the back of infrastructure-related stimulus packages. However, as the global economic backdrop has dimmed, global FDI may be on an unsustainable trajectory, and inflows for 2022 are expected to be more modest. The Russian invasion of

Ukraine has weighed on the global economy, causing several chokepoints in food and fuel supply. The invasion also compounds supply chain drags resulting from the pandemic flare-up in the second and third quarters (Q2 and Q3) of 2022, especially in the People's Republic of China (PRC).

Asia and the Pacific showed resilience despite the challenges, while pent-up demand and reinvested earnings drove FDI growth in developed economies.[40]

Foreign investment into Asia reached a new peak in 2021, amounting to $633.0 billion. This translates to a 19.1% expansion from the previous year (Figure 3.1). Asia's share in global inward investment slid to 40.0% in 2021 from 55.2% in 2020, as investment into economies outside Asia rebounded more dramatically. FDI into economies outside Asia reached $949.3 billion in 2021, more than double the investment receipts in 2020. Large intakes of reinvested earnings, underpinned by low financing costs and government support, were observed in developed economies, particularly the United States (US) (UNCTAD 2022a).

---

[38] For discussions on recent FDI trends, this chapter analyzes standard balance of payments data along with firm-level data by mode of entry (greenfield investment and mergers and acquisitions).

[39] The UNCTAD World Investment Report excludes the Caribbean financial centers from its total estimate. These include Anguilla, Antigua and Barbuda, Aruba, the Bahamas, Barbados, British Virgin Islands, the Cayman Islands, Curaçao, Dominica, Grenada, Montserrat, Saint Kitts and Nevis, Saint Lucia, Saint Vincent and the Grenadines, Saint Maarten, and the Turks and Caicos Islands.

[40] Asia and the Pacific consists of 49 member economies of the Asian Development Bank (ADB). The composition of economies for Central Asia, East Asia, the Pacific and Oceania, South Asia, and Southeast Asia subregions are outlined in ADB. Asia Regional Integration Center. Economy Groupings. https://aric.adb.org/integrationindicators/groupings.

**Figure 3.1: Total Inward Foreign Direct Investment—
Balance of Payments**

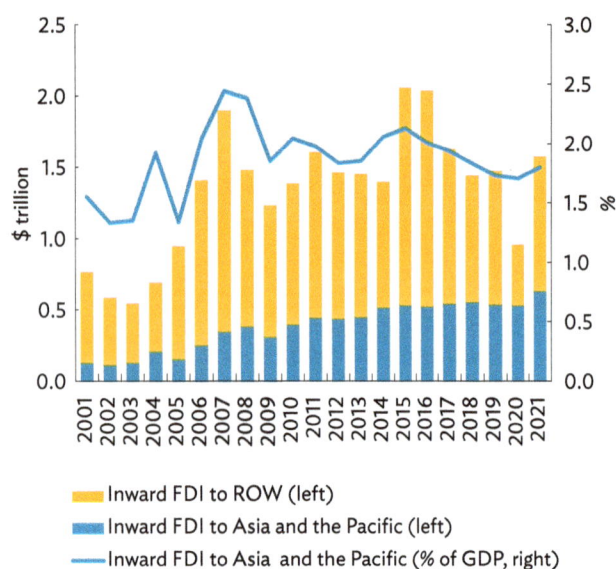

FDI = foreign direct investment, GDP = gross domestic product, ROW = rest of the world.

Sources: ADB calculations using data from ASEAN Secretariat. ASEANstats Data Portal. https://data.aseanstats.org (accessed July 2019); CEIC Data Company; Eurostat. Balance of Payments. https://ec.europa.eu/eurostat (accessed July 2022); International Monetary Fund. World Economic Outlook April 2022 database. https://www.imf.org/en/Publications/WEO/weo-database/2022/April (accessed April 2022); and United Nations Conference on Trade and Development. World Investment Report 2022 Statistical Annex Tables. https://worldinvestmentreport.unctad.org/annex-tables/ (accessed June 2022).

Large, reinvested earnings drove FDI growth in the US, making the world's largest economy the top destination for global FDI in 2021.

At the economy level, the US was the top destination globally, amassing $367.4 billion in FDI in 2021. Reinvested earnings in the economy reached $200 billion—the highest ever recorded (UNCTAD 2022a) (Table 3.1). Besides the US, other large recipients of FDI in 2021 outside of Asia are Canada ($59.7 billion), Brazil ($50.4 billion), South Africa ($40.9 billion), Mexico ($31.6 billion), and Germany ($31.3 billion).

Despite persistent lockdowns through the pandemic, the PRC was the second most attractive FDI destination globally in 2021, with receipts of $181.0 billion (up 21.2% from 2020) spurred by inflows into the services and high-tech sectors. Other developing Asian economies were also among top destinations, and investment into these economies also grew in 2021. Excluding the PRC, FDI into developing Asia, which groups 45 economies in Asia, grew 13.7% in 2021 to $398.8 billion. Among these economies, Hong Kong, China ($140.7 billion); Singapore ($99.1 billion); and India ($44.7 billion) were top destinations.

Table 3.1: Top 10 Destinations of Foreign Direct Investment—World and Asia and the Pacific ($ billion)

Global	2021	2020	Asia	2021	2020
United States	367.4	150.8	People's Republic of China	181.0	149.3
People's Republic of China	181.0	149.3	Hong Kong, China	140.7	134.7
Hong Kong, China	140.7	134.7	Singapore	99.1	75.4
Singapore	99.1	75.4	India	44.7	64.1
Canada	59.7	23.2	Australia	25.1	16.7
Brazil	50.4	28.3	Japan	24.7	10.7
India	44.7	64.1	Indonesia	20.1	18.6
South Africa	40.9	3.1	Republic of Korea	16.8	8.8
Mexico	31.6	27.9	Viet Nam	15.7	15.8
Germany	31.3	64.6	Malaysia	11.6	3.2

Source: ADB calculations using data from United Nations Conference on Trade and Development. World Investment Report 2022 Statistical Annex Tables. https://worldinvestmentreport.unctad.org/annex-tables/ (accessed June 2022).

Meanwhile, FDI in advanced Asian economies rose by 70.4% to $53.2 billion in 2021, with Australia and Japan among the top destinations. FDI inflows to Australia increased by 50.0% to $25.1 billion, while inflows to Japan more than doubled to $24.7 billion.

Global greenfield FDI and M&A deals have recovered in 2021, surpassing 2019 estimates in some regions.

Firm-level investment activity provides a detailed look into the recovery of global FDI.[41] Greenfield projects and M&A deals recovered in 2021 despite the persistence of restrictions due to the coronavirus disease (COVID-19) pandemic. Greenfield investments grew by 23.5% in 2021—reaching $891.5 billion—after contracting by 27.3% in 2020. In some regions, greenfield investments returned to pre-pandemic levels. In North America, inflows reached $339.0 billion, 40.3% higher than 2019 inflows. Meanwhile, greenfield FDI in the European Union and the United Kingdom (EU+UK) amounted to $224.5 billion, 26.3% higher than in 2020 and 9.1% higher than in 2019 (Figure 3.2a).

M&As overall grew by 17.8%, with global deal values totaling $1.1 trillion. Similarly, strong recovery in some regions propelled deal values to pre-pandemic levels. Transactions in Africa reached $22.9 billion in 2021, 35.8% higher than the 2019 estimates. North American economies also saw a large increase in M&A deals, amounting to $319.5 billion in 2021—up 37.0% from 2020 and up 7.5% from 2019 (Figure 3.2b).

Both global greenfield investment and M&As were resilient in the first half of 2022. Greenfield FDI reached $449.1 billion in the first half of 2022 (0.8% more than in the first half in 2021), while M&As logged $481.2 billion in deal values in the same period (1.6% more than in the first half of 2021).

After major setbacks due to the pandemic, greenfield investment in Asia grew modestly in 2021.[42]

After dipping in 2020, both greenfield investment and M&As in Asia recovered in 2021. Greenfield FDI in the region totaled $169.7 billion in 2021, translating to

Figure 3.2: Quarterly Global Inward Foreign Direct Investment—Firm-Level ($ billion)

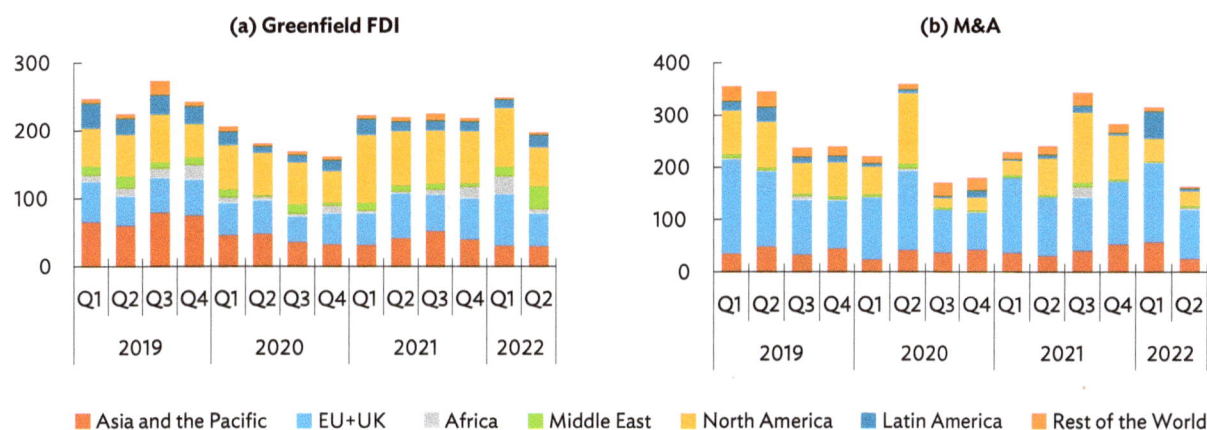

(a) Greenfield FDI

(b) M&A

Legend: Asia and the Pacific ■ EU+UK ■ Africa ■ Middle East ■ North America ■ Latin America ■ Rest of the World

EU = European Union (27 members), FDI = foreign direct investment, M&A = merger and acquisition, Q = quarter, UK = United Kingdom.

Sources: ADB calculations using data from Bureau van Dijk. Zephyr M&A Database; and Financial Times. fDi Markets.

---

[41] Firm-level estimates are computed using data from Bureau van Dijk. Zephyr M&A Database; and Financial Times. fDi Markets. The firm-level data presented in this chapter capture information on the creation of new assets (greenfield FDI) and the purchase of existing assets (M&As).

[42] The methodology for data compilation and coverage has been updated. For more information, see Box 3.1 and Chapter 8: Statistical Appendix.

a modest 0.8% growth on the previous year's inflows. While intraregional greenfield investment slid by 20.6%, significant inflows from extraregional sources cushioned the impact as investment from these economies grew by 21.3%. Meanwhile, M&A deals in Asia grew by 10.1% in 2021, reaching $167.8 billion. Intraregional transactions drove growth, posting a 20.0% increase in 2021 from $53.2 billion in 2020. Deals from economies outside Asia reached $103.9 billion—a 4.9% increase from 2020 (Figure 3.3).

Figure 3.3: Foreign Direct Investment by Mode of Entry—Asia and the Pacific, Firm-Level ($ billion)

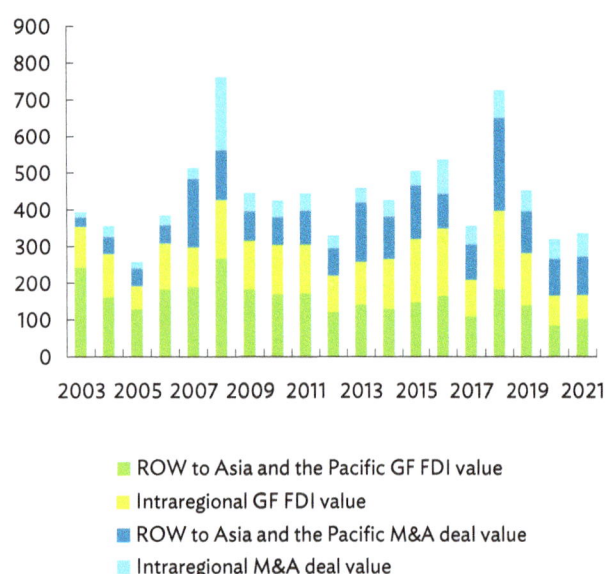

ROW to Asia and the Pacific GF FDI value
Intraregional GF FDI value
ROW to Asia and the Pacific M&A deal value
Intraregional M&A deal value

FDI = foreign direct investment, GF = greenfield, M&A = merger and acquisition, ROW = rest of the world.

Sources: ADB calculations using data from Bureau van Dijk. Zephyr M&A Database; and Financial Times. fDi Markets.

Gains in East Asian economies drove the modest growth in Asia's inward greenfield investment; however, a more strained global landscape weighed on greenfield FDI in the first half of 2022. Meanwhile, M&As in the region helped buoy recovery.

Although greenfield FDI in the region had started to recover in Q2 2021, inflows still were not near their 2019 levels as sustained bottlenecks due to the COVID-19 pandemic continued to weigh on projects and investment. Despite this, investment in the region recovered for the whole of 2021, largely due to higher inflows to East Asian economies. Greenfield investment in the subregion grew by 34.3% in 2021, equivalent to $65.4 billion. Those gains contrasted with large losses in South Asia (down 30.2%), Central Asia (down 18.8%), and the Pacific and Oceania (down 11.2%) (Figure 3.4a).

Meanwhile, M&As in Asia declined between Q4 2020 and Q2 2021 (Figure 3.4b). Despite ending 2020 down 10.0%, deals in Asia broadly returned to pre-pandemic levels in 2021, reaching $167.8 billion in value. Increased investment in the Pacific and Oceania (up 52.6%), East Asia (up 28.1%), and Southeast Asia (up 12.6%) helped offset large declines in Central Asia (down 87.7%) and South Asia (down 44.4%).

Despite an overall uptick in greenfield investments in 2021, FDI in Asia slowed in the first half of 2022. Project values reached $63.4 billion, 16.4% lower than investments in the first half of 2021. Renewed lockdowns in the PRC and global economic headwinds have weighed anew on greenfield investments. Meanwhile, M&As in the region were more resilient, as deals grew by 22.5% in the first half of 2022 to $86.6 billion.

The US was the largest source of increased FDI to Asia. FDI from the US grew by $15.3 billion between 2020 and 2021, reaching $85.3 billion. Australia also increased investments in the region, with FDI reaching $13.0 billion in 2021 from $3.9 billion in 2020. The Republic of Korea (up $7.0 billion); Taipei,China (up $6.7 billion); and Germany (up $6.3 billion) were also among top sources of increased investment in the region.

Malaysia benefited most from larger foreign investment in Asia (Table 3.2). In 2021, FDI into the economy expanded by $17.8 billion to $26.2 billion, due to recovery in greenfield investment. Investment in New Zealand also rebounded in 2021 (up $9.5 billion) after declining by $3.5 billion in 2020. The Republic of Korea (up $8.1 billion), Japan (up $8.1 billion), and the PRC (up $8.0 billion) were also top recipients of increased greenfield FDI and M&As.

Figure 3.4: Quarterly Inward Foreign Direct Investment—Asia and the Pacific, Firm-Level ($ billion)

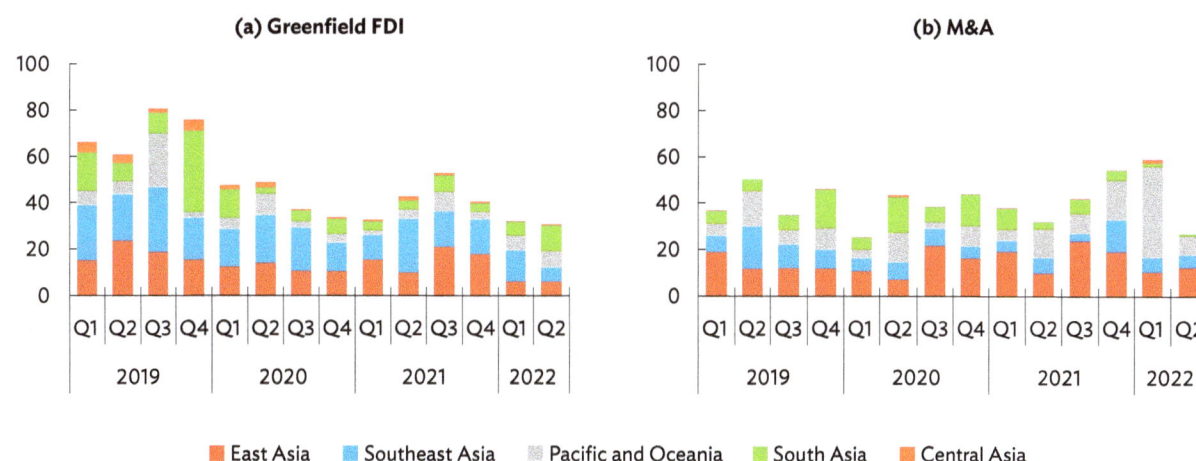

FDI = foreign direct investment, M&A = merger and acquisition, Q = quarter.

Sources: ADB calculations using data from Bureau van Dijk. Zephyr M&A Database; and Financial Times. fDi Markets.

Table 3.2: Top Recipients of Increased Foreign Direct Investment in Asia and the Pacific, Firm-Level

Destination	2021 ($ billion)	2020 ($ billion)	Change ($ billion)	Share in Asia's Total Increase in FDI (%)
Malaysia	26.2	8.5	17.8	105.8
New Zealand	14.3	4.8	9.5	56.7
Republic of Korea	13.7	5.6	8.1	48.1
Japan	28.1	20.0	8.1	48.0
People's Republic of China	63.9	55.9	8.0	47.7
Papua New Guinea	6.5	0.0	6.4	38.3
Hong Kong, China	24.5	18.5	6.0	35.7
Singapore	25.2	20.7	4.5	27.1
Thailand	5.4	2.8	2.6	15.7
Taipei,China	8.6	5.9	2.6	15.7

FDI = foreign direct investment.

Notes: Shares to Asia's total increase in FDI may read as greater than 100 since economy-level changes may be either largely positive or largely negative. When summed, all changes in the economy level would equal Asia's overall change, and the percentages would total 100%. Values are based on the sum of greenfield FDI and merger and acquisition deals.

Sources: ADB calculations using data from Bureau van Dijk. Zephyr M&A Database; and Financial Times. fDi Markets.

The manufacturing and tertiary sectors accounted for over 90% of Asia's total FDI.

FDI in Asia headed mostly toward manufacturing and the tertiary sector, with both accounting for 95% of total FDI into the region. Greenfield FDI in manufacturing accounted for 53.7% of total investment in Asia in 2021. Meanwhile, about two-thirds of Asia's M&As was in

the tertiary sector, largely consisting of service-related industries (Figure 3.5).

Greenfield FDI into Asia's manufacturing sector went primarily into the manufacture of semiconductors. Investments in this segment reached $37.4 billion in 2021, comprising 41.0% of total greenfield FDI in manufacturing that year. Electronic components received the second-largest greenfield FDI in 2021, with $19.2 billion in investments (11.3% of total greenfield FDI). As for M&As, finance and insurance-related services logged $28.3 billion worth of deals, roughly 17% of total M&As in the region. The information sector also proved to be attractive for investments, with $24.3 billion in M&As (14.5%).

Despite the increase in total values, the average project or deal size in Asia decreased by $2.2 million in 2021 (Table 3.3). While trends across sectors and modes of entry were mixed, overall estimates indicate smaller deal and project sizes. On average, greenfield projects in the region were $5.5 million smaller than in 2020, while the average M&A deal in the region was $0.8 million smaller. By sector, the value of deals and projects declined by $11.1 million in the primary sector, $8.1 million in the manufacturing sector, and $0.4 million in the tertiary sector.

Modest gains in activity generated more greenfield jobs in Asia in 2021.

While job creation and greenfield FDI have yet to return to pre-pandemic trends, 2021 saw greenfield projects in Asia increasing employment (Figure 3.6a). They created about 518,000 jobs, 18.1% more than in 2020. Much of that growth is due to greenfield projects funded from outside the region, which generated around 329,000 jobs in 2021 (up 30.7%).

The easing of pandemic-related restrictions revitalized activity in more labor-intensive sectors (Figure 3.6b). Jobs in manufacturing and the tertiary sector rebounded in 2021, with jobs generated in tertiary sectors growing by 21.9% after declining by 49.2% in 2020. Meanwhile, manufacturing-related greenfield jobs grew by 17% in 2021 after an almost 51% contraction in the previous year.

Figure 3.5: Total Inward Foreign Direct Investment to Asia and the Pacific by Sector—Firm-Level ($ billion)

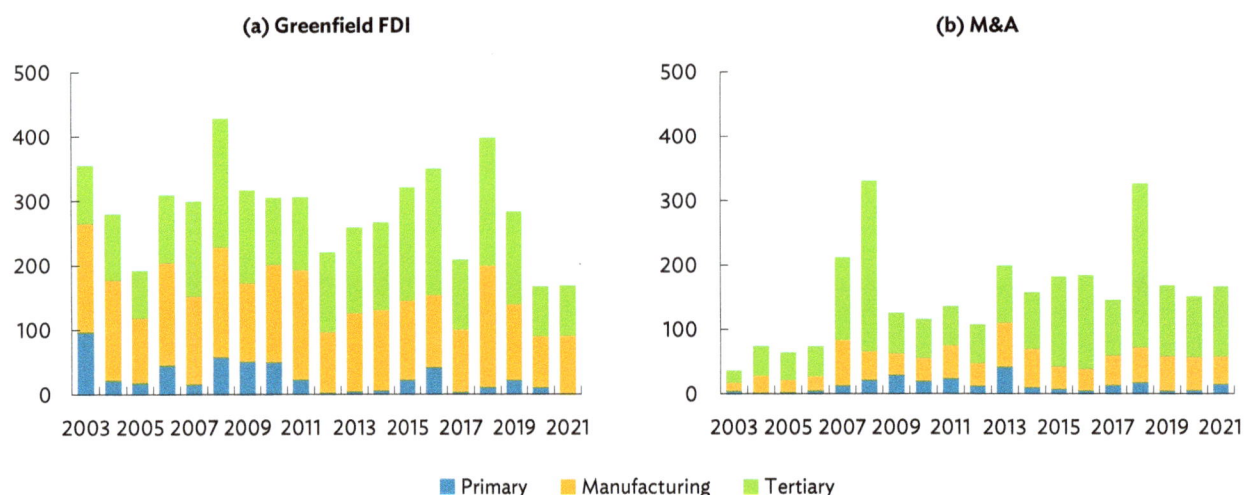

FDI = foreign direct investment, M&A = merger and acquisition.

Sources: ADB calculations using data from Bureau van Dijk. Zephyr M&A Database; and Financial Times. fDi Markets.

Table 3.3: Average Project and Deal Size by Sector—Asia and the Pacific ($ million)

| Year | GF | M&A | Total | Greenfield | | | M&A | | | Total | | |
				PRI	MFG	TER	PRI	MFG	TER	PRI	MFG	TER
2020	67.1	15.7	26.2	481.3	90.5	48.0	22.6	25.0	12.8	58.5	44.5	19.1
2021	61.6	14.9	24.1	21.9	100.0	42.9	49.3	15.7	13.3	47.3	36.4	18.7

GF = greenfield, M&A = merger and acquisition, MFG = manufacturing, PRI = primary, TER = tertiary.

Note: Average project (deal) size equals greenfield capital expenditure (M&A deal value) in Asia and the Pacific divided by number of greenfield projects (M&A deals).

Sources: ADB calculations using data from Bureau van Dijk. Zephyr M&A Database; and Financial Times. fDi Markets.

Figure 3.6: Inward Greenfield Foreign Direct Investment Job Creation—Asia and the Pacific

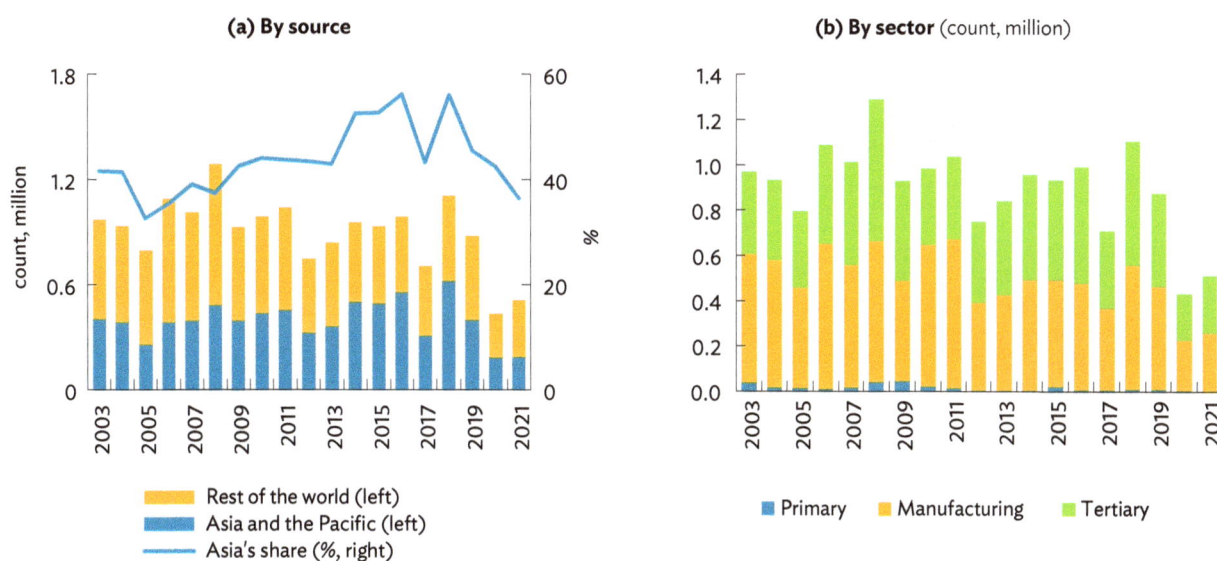

(a) **By source**

count, million

Rest of the world (left)
Asia and the Pacific (left)
Asia's share (%, right)

(b) **By sector** (count, million)

Primary   Manufacturing   Tertiary

Sources: ADB calculations using data from Bureau van Dijk. Zephyr M&A Database; and Financial Times. fDi Markets.

Intraregional investment activity continued to dip and East Asia emerged as the main source of intraregional FDI.

After a sustained 30% decline in 2020, intraregional FDI slid by just 4.7% in 2021, and amounted to $129.3 billion in 2021, based on firm-level data. Intraregional greenfield investment continued to decline, reaching only $65.4 billion in 2021—down 20.6% from 2020. Meanwhile, intraregional M&A deals saw a 20.0% growth between 2020 and 2021.

Intraregional FDI primarily came from East Asia and headed largely toward East Asia and Southeast Asia (Figure 3.7). Intraregional greenfield investment from East Asia, totaling $48.6 billion in 2021, flowed largely into East Asia ($22.8 billion) and Southeast Asia ($22.5 billion). Meanwhile, Southeast Asia injected roughly $13 billion in greenfield FDI to the region, with the majority going to Southeast Asia ($7.4 billion) and East Asia ($3.4 billion) (Figure 3.7a). East Asia was also the top source of intraregional deals in 2021, with $45.6 billion coming from the subregion (Figure 3.7b). Meanwhile, the Pacific and Oceania became the second-largest source of M&A deals in 2021, with nearly $12 billion coming from the subregion.

Foreign Investment Trends by Business Activity

Greenfield investment by business activity complements the perspective on FDI sector allocation.[43]

Together with sector classification, firm-level data from fDi Markets provide information on greenfield projects by business activity, which complement the analysis of a sector classification system. Business activity is defined as the actual function of the operation. In this case the project, not the company, is classified, allowing the identification of upstream and downstream activities in the value chain where multinationals are more actively investing. Examples of business activities include research and development (R&D), information and communication technology (ICT) and internet infrastructure, logistics, manufacturing, and technical support centers. The business activity shows how different functions are mapped out and can drive the location of a project and the sector.

[43]   fDi Markets uses a prioprietary industry classification system. Each project is classified according to its cluster, sector, sub-sector and business activity. This provides information on the different industries a firm is actively investing in.

Figure 3.7: Intraregional Foreign Direct Investment—Asia and the Pacific, Firm-Level, by Mode of Entry ($ billion)

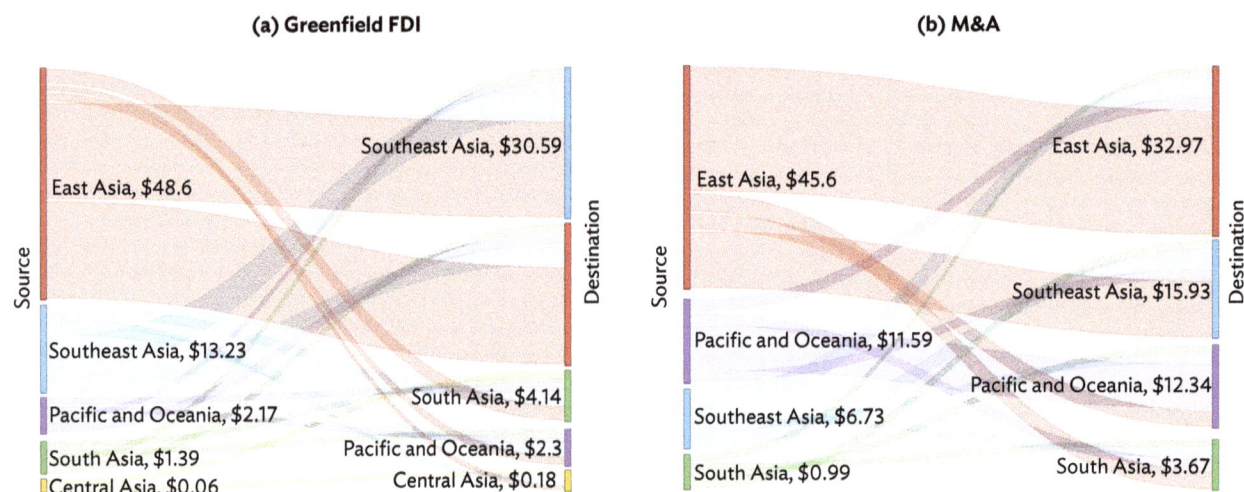

(a) Greenfield FDI

(b) M&A

FDI = foreign direct investment, M&A = merger and acquisition.

Sources: ADB calculations using data from Bureau van Dijk. Zephyr M&A Database; and Financial Times. fDi Markets.

While most greenfield investment heads toward manufacturing, recent years have seen an uptick in other business activities.

Manufacturing-related activities have historically attracted the bulk of Asia's greenfield investment, accounting on average 41% of the total between 2017 and 2021. However, recent years have seen the emergence of other business activities in inward FDI. Investment in electricity-related activities increased globally, also in Asia, representing on average 13% of the region's greenfield FDI from 2017 to 2021. Other targeted business activities by multinational firms were construction (13% on average during 2017–2021); logistics, distribution, and transportation (6%); sales, marketing, and support (5%); and business services (5%) (Figure 3.8). Among these activities, the increase in electricity investments in Asia was most notable, with average investments over the period 2017–2021 tripling ($32.4 billion) when compared with 2003–2007 ($11.6 billion). This also reflects a global trend with renewable energy investments becoming more dominant. As of 2021, renewable energy had outpaced oil and gas as the largest recipients of FDI globally.

Investment in some activities also decreased, particularly in extraction-related activities. In 2003–2007, investments in Asia's extraction activities recorded an annual average of $33.2 billion a year. This decreased to an average FDI of $3.9 billion in the last 5 years.

Trends in FDI Concentration

While global FDI has been historically concentrated, recent years have seen a gradual wider spread.

Concentration of inward FDI flows by source (or investor) economy and economic sector may be an indicator of diversification opportunities but also external vulnerabilities. The distribution of FDI sources and sector destination is generally associated with diversification of the economic base (Odusola 2018, UNESCAP 2012). This view holds that the economy's ability to attract FDI from multiple economy sources and distribute the inflows among sectors will determine the progress in advancing underdeveloped sectors that in turn can broaden the economic drivers. FDI source diversification is also linked with export market

Figure 3.8: Greenfield Investment in Asia and the Pacific, by Selected Business Activity—2003–2007 versus 2017–2021 (annual average, $ billion)

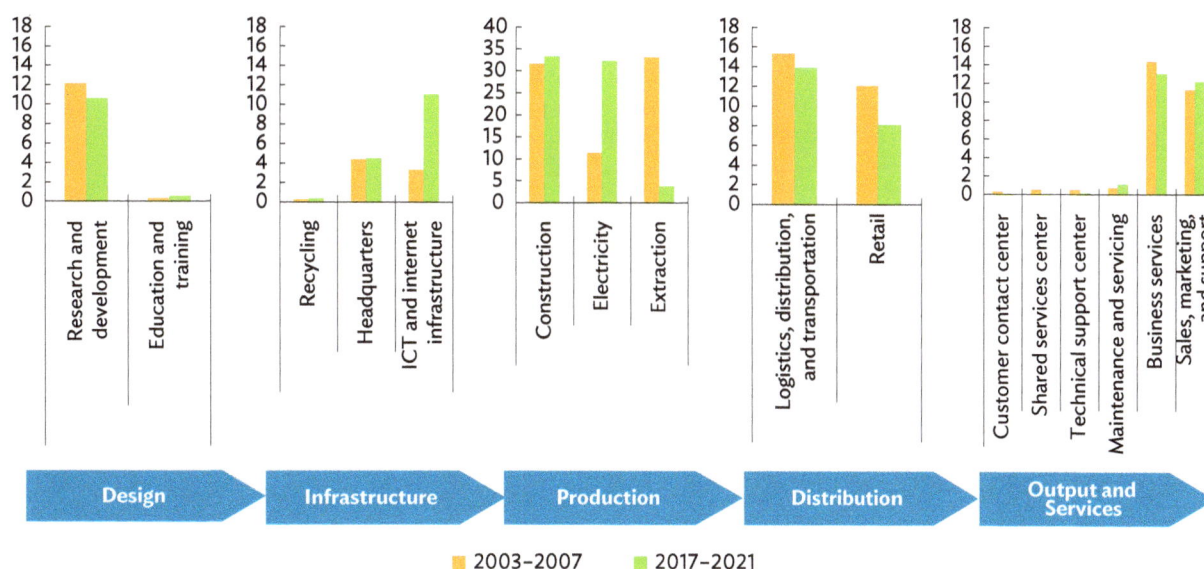

■ 2003–2007   ■ 2017–2021

ICT = information and communication technology.

Note: Excludes greenfield investment in manufacturing, which accounts for the largest investment share among business activities.

Source: ADB calculations using data from Financial Times. fDi Markets.

diversification (Pham et al. 2021; Shin 2010) and is deemed to promote resilience to external shocks (Sanghi and Johnson 2016; Shin 2010) much like the effect of cross-border bank lending source diversification (Lapid, Mercado, and Rosenkranz 2021).

Regional concentration indexes by investor show overall historically moderate to high concentration, with recent estimates pointing to a slight decline (Figure 3.9).[44] Despite concentration easing over the last 2 years, some Asian economies remain vulnerable, especially when relying on inflows from a narrow base of investors. This is the case of economies such as Armenia, Cambodia, and Uzbekistan, in contrast to more diversified economies such as the PRC, Singapore, or Viet Nam.

Global average concentration by source economy peaked at 0.293 in 2005 and has remained above 0.25 (Figure 3.9a). However, the last couple of years saw some moderation. From 2020 to 2021, bottlenecks brought about by the COVID-19 pandemic highlighted

the need to diversify investment and production bases, which may have resulted in easing concentration over those years. In 2021, concentration by source economy was lowest among Asian economies, with an average index of 0.181. This implies that Asian economies generally rely on a larger number of investment partners, and therefore may be more insulated from risk of volatile FDI flow or investor withdrawal. This was exemplified during the pandemic, as FDI into Asia remained relatively robust despite the global downturn.

Meanwhile, average global sector concentration also exhibited similar trends (Figure 3.9b). Sector concentration was elevated between 2003 and 2019, peaking at 0.341 in 2008. This indicates that some economies may be reliant on inflows to a few specific sectors and therefore more susceptible to disruptions or risks in FDI to those sectors. Sector concentration was highest in the EU+UK in 2021. Economies in the Middle East also exhibited higher measures of sector concentration that year. In Asia, sector concentration

[44] In this chapter, the measure of concentration, using the Herfindahl–Hirschman concentration index as featured in Lapid, Mercado, and Rosenkranz (2021), aims to examine the distribution of FDI inflows for a host economy by investor (economy) and economic sector. Values range from 0 to 1, with 0 indicating no concentration and 1 indicating high concentration. Based on current consensus, values larger than 0.25 already indicate a high concentration.

fluctuated between moderate and high over the years; estimates for 2021 show an elevated average of 0.251. Some Asian economies relied on investment in a less varied array of sectors, which was the case in Armenia, Cambodia, Georgia, and Fiji.

Overall, Asia's FDI concentration by investor and by sector remains moderate and relatively stable in comparison with other regions.

Figure 3.9: Foreign Direct Investment Concentration Index—Firm-Level Investment

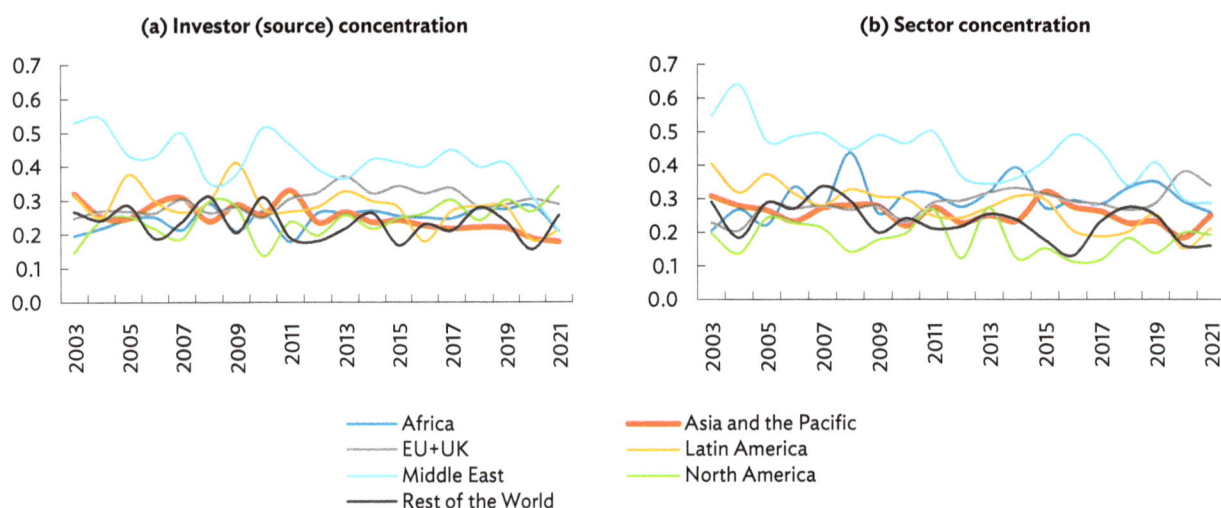

(a) Investor (source) concentration

(b) Sector concentration

Legend:
- Africa
- EU+UK
- Middle East
- Rest of the World
- Asia and the Pacific
- Latin America
- North America

EU = European Union (27 members), FDI = foreign direct investment, M&A = merger and acquisition, UK = United Kingdom.

Notes: The FDI concentration index was computed using the Herfindahl–Hirschman market concentration index, as featured in the paper by Lapid, Mercado, and Rosenkranz (2021). Values range from 0 to 1, with 0 indicating no concentration and 1 indicating high concentration. Based on current consensus, values larger than 0.25 already indicate a high concentration. Regional values are computed using the arithmetic mean of economies in each region.

Sources: ADB calculations using data from Bureau van Dijk. Zephyr M&A Database; Financial Times. fDi Markets; and Lapid, Mercado, and Rosenkranz (2021).

Box 3.1: Key Changes in Firm-Level Data Compilation

The coverage and compilation process for firm-level data were updated to better capture investment flows from multinational corporations. This updated data set was used for *Asian Economic Integration Report 2023: Trade, Investment, and Climate Change in Asia and the Pacific*. For details on the methodology and updates, see Methodological Note and Update—Firm-Level Data in Chapter 8: Statistical Appendix.

Data Coverage. Project type coverage in the firm-level data was expanded for new greenfield projects. Coverage now includes project expansions, especially those that result in new assets and jobs. Also included in the data

set is an indicator on project status (announced, opened, closed).

Sector Harmonization and Classification. The data set continues to use the North American Industry Classification System (NAICS) codes as basis for sector matching and merging. Previously, the sector classification of merger and acquisition data was converted into the proprietary classification of fDi Markets. In its current version, the greenfield classification is converted to NAICS codes first. The 2-digit NAICS codes are then used to create the 3-industry economic classification (primary, manufacturing, and tertiary).

Sources: ADB staff based on Bureau van Dijk. Zephyr M&A Database; Financial Times. fDi Markets; Government of Canada, Statistics Canada. https://www.statcan.gc.ca/en/concepts/industry; and Government of the United States, Census Bureau. https://www.census.gov/naics.

Outward Foreign Direct Investment

FDI outflows in 2021 saw renewed vigor as global outward investment reached $1.7 trillion—the highest since 2015.

Outward foreign investment recovered in 2021 after a 3-year slump, with outflows from developed economies, particularly the EU+UK and North America, driving growth (Figure 3.10). Global outward FDI reached $1.7 trillion in 2021, more than double that in 2020. Investment from Asia grew 15.3% to $551.3 billion in 2021. Meanwhile, investment from other economies almost quadrupled between 2020 and 2021, from $302.2 billion to $1.2 trillion.

The US was the largest source of global investment in 2021, with $403.1 billion in FDI flowing from the economy (Table 3.4). Germany followed, with $151.7 billion in outward investment. Among Asian economies, Japan emerged as the top source of global investment. A total of $146.8 billion flowed from Japan, 53.4% more than in 2020. This resulted in a large recovery in investment from advanced Asian economies, whose outward FDI expanded by 45.2% from 2020. The PRC came in a close second with $145.2 billion in outflows, down 5.5% from 2020.

Figure 3.10: Global Outward Foreign Direct Investment by Source—Balance of Payments

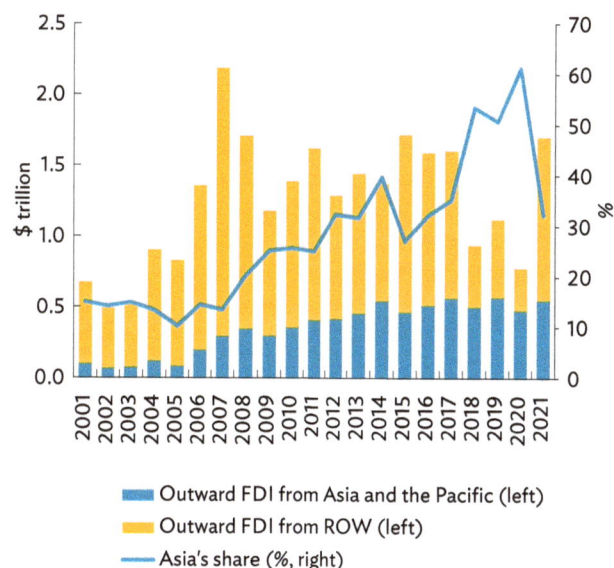

Outward FDI from Asia and the Pacific (left)
Outward FDI from ROW (left)
Asia's share (%, right)

FDI = foreign direct investment, ROW = rest of the world.

Source: United Nations Conference on Trade and Development. World Investment Report 2022 Statistical Annex Tables. https://worldinvestmentreport.unctad.org/annex-tables/ (accessed June 2022).

Outward investment from other developing Asian economies continued to grow in 2021, reaching $251.9 billion (up 15.3% from 2020). Increased FDI from economies such as the Republic of Korea (up 74.6% from 2020), Singapore (up 49.2%), and India (up 39.7%) contributed to this growth.

Table 3.4: Top 10 Sources of Foreign Direct Investment—World and Asia and the Pacific ($ billion)

Global	2021	2020	Asia and the Pacific	2021	2020
United States	403.1	234.9	Japan	146.8	95.7
Germany	151.7	60.6	People's Republic of China	145.2	153.7
Japan	146.8	95.7	Hong Kong, China	87.5	100.7
People's Republic of China	145.2	153.7	Republic of Korea	60.8	34.8
United Kingdom	107.7	-65.4	Singapore	47.4	31.8
Canada	89.9	46.5	Thailand	17.3	19.0
Hong Kong, China	87.5	100.7	India	15.5	11.1
Russian Federation	63.6	6.8	Taipei,China	10.1	11.5
Ireland	62.0	-45.0	Australia	9.2	9.9
Republic of Korea	60.8	34.8	Malaysia	4.7	2.4

Source: ADB calculations using data from United Nations Conference on Trade and Development. World Investment Report 2022 Statistical Annex Tables. https://worldinvestmentreport.unctad.org/annex-tables/ (accessed June 2022).

Outflows through greenfield investment and M&As recovered globally and in Asia.

Firm-level data also depict a vibrant backdrop for global outward investment. Outward greenfield investment recovered in most regions, with the Middle East posting the largest growth in 2021 (up 72.4%). M&As also broadly increased across regions in 2021, with deals from Africa increasing roughly tenfold to $58.3 billion in 2021.

Investment from Asia was similarly upbeat in 2021, with overall greenfield investment from the region amounting to $161.9 billion (up 6.4%) and M&A deals reaching $171.5 billion (up 8.3%). South Asia posted the highest growth in greenfield investment, with its outward FDI tripling to $13.0 billion. Meanwhile, M&A deals involving investment from Central Asia reached $493.1 million, a remarkable gain from the previous year's $0.7 million (Figure 3.11).

Asia's outward greenfield investment declined in the first half of 2022 to only $67.5 billion, almost 30% lower than in the first half of 2020. Despite this, M&As from Asian economies almost doubled between the first half of 2021 and the first half of 2022. Much of that growth came from the Pacific and Oceania, where outward deals rose to $76.8 billion in the first half of 2022, from $5.8 billion in the first half of 2021.

Despite the uptick in 2021, the dim global and political landscape in 2022 hinder investment prospects globally and in Asia.

Global and Asian FDI activity was resurgent in 2021. As the global economy started to emerge from the seemingly lasting effects of the pandemic, foreign investment started to regain strength, driven by renewed demand, government stimulus and support, and low financing costs. While investments such as in services, technology, and renewables are expected to remain robust, the effects of changes in the political and economic landscape in 2022 will likely be far-reaching.

The Russian invasion of Ukraine is expected to take a toll on FDI in 2022, compounded by reemerging surges and restrictions in relation to the COVID-19 pandemic. Investor sentiment may become more risk averse as a result, and greatly diminish global FDI flows. Global FDI inflows will likely taper in 2022 or remain flat at best.

FDI flows to Asia remained robust despite the pandemic flare-up in 2021, and the outlook for the region remains stable. Investment in the high-technology, information, manufacturing, and finance sectors remains high and will likely continue to buoy FDI. In addition, provisions for FDI in new and existing trade agreements, such as the Regional Comprehensive Economic Partnership, may complement efforts to promote investment in the region (Box 3.2).

Figure 3.11: Quarterly Outward Foreign Direct Investment—Asia and the Pacific, Firm-Level ($ billion)

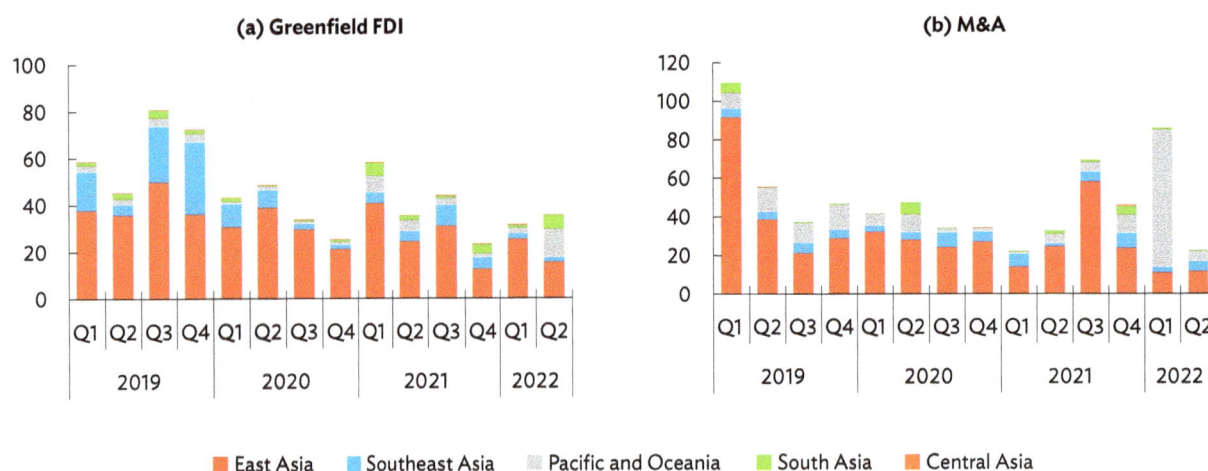

FDI = foreign direct investment, M&A = merger and acquisition, Q = quarter.

Sources: ADB calculations using data from Bureau van Dijk. Zephyr M&A Database; and Financial Times. fDi Markets.

Box 3.2: Investment Provisions in the Regional Comprehensive Economic Partnership

The Regional Comprehensive Economic Partnership (RCEP) sets standards for cooperation among 15 participants in several areas, including investment. RCEP investment provisions reflect the trend in regional trade agreements and go beyond tariff reduction. Commitments in Chapter 10 (Investment) are similar to those concluded by the Association of Southeast Asian Nations (ASEAN) Comprehensive Investment Agreement. The main difference between RCEP and the Comprehensive and Progressive Agreement for Trans-Pacific Partnership (CPTPP) concerns dispute settlement.

RCEP investment provisions cover investment liberalization, protection, and dispute settlement. RCEP provides for most favored nation and national treatment as well as fair and equitable treatment before and after foreign investment is established. It prohibits performance requirements on technology transfer or royalties, with exceptions for least developed economies. The agreement also provides protection for transfer of funds, expropriation, and compensation similar to CPTPP.

The dispute settlement provisions of RCEP and CPTPP differ significantly. RCEP has no provisions for investor-state dispute settlement (ISDS). ISDS is included in most enforced international investment agreements and free trade agreements with investment provisions. An agreement to conclude a dispute mechanism within RCEP by 2025 has been reached. Yet, RCEP includes a state-to-state dispute settlement by which investors can recur revenue to their home state if a host state fails

its investment chapter obligations. This mechanism is less robust than CPTPP, which includes provisions on consultation and negotiation, the submission of claims to arbitration under International Centre for Settlement of Investment Disputes Convention or the United Nations Commission on International Trade Law Arbitration Rules, and sets standards for the selection and conduct of arbitrators and the payment of awards.

Overall, the value added of investment liberalization in RCEP appears to be small as investors are covered by international investment agreements. The absence of an ISDS means that investors have to seek protection through the ISDS in the ASEAN Comprehensive Investment Agreement, ASEAN–Australia–New Zealand Free Trade Area, and other international investment agreements. Market access commitments in RCEP are more restrictive than in CPTPP. While all RCEP members use negative lists to state their exemptions from the investment chapter, the schedules of reservations and nonconforming measures are extensive and apply to all members. Negative lists may also change. Overall, RCEP is expected to spur investment through enhanced investment protection and market access. It also gives stronger emphasis on intellectual property rights and digital services trust mechanisms—e.g., online consumer protection, digital personal information protection, transaction transparency, paperless trading, and electronic signature acceptability in e-commerce.

Source: ADB staff based on ADB (2022b).

Policy Focus: Investment Tax Incentives in Asia and the Pacific

Investment incentives have been at the core of investment policy in emerging economies. Recent discussions about the reform of international tax rules have paid special attention to tax incentives. This section examines the main features of investment tax incentives for Asia, linkages of incentives to domestic investment laws, and other investment policy dimensions. The section is divided into four parts. First, it explores how

investment incentives are contained or covered in investment laws. Second, the discussion delves into investment tax incentives in the region, describing their main features, including those beyond special economic zones, which were the focus of previous editions of the Asian Economic Integration Report (ADB 2015). It also discusses possible implications of new global tax rules and provides sector-based discussion on the role of regulatory incentives and other incentives to enhance FDI flows, before rounding off with some policy considerations.

Domestic Investment Laws and Investment Incentives

Much like international investment regimes, domestic investment laws have been pivotal to attract and direct foreign investment.

National investment laws can increase or diminish the regulatory risks and ultimately reflect the national stance on foreign investment. Incentives, being a key feature of investment laws, are also subject to governments' discretionary power. The manner by which investment incentives are used to guide investment flows by sector, geographic location, or firm size, can respond to different criteria and considerations (James 2009). While governments use a range of targeted policies, in general investment incentives comprise tax incentives, R&D incentives, financial incentives, and regulatory incentives.[45]

Apart from incentives, investment laws also outline restrictive or facilitating investment measures by economic sector, territory, and other criteria.

A common practice in conveying to potential investors the sector restrictions is through the publication of positive and/or negative lists. The positive list includes sectors an economy promotes to foreign investors, while the negative list includes restricted sectors to foreign investment. These may or may not be stated in the national investment law.[46] In Asia, about 60% of the economies where data are available utilize a negative investment list (Hebous, Kher, and Tran 2020). The list is contained in the national investment law of only five economies (Table 3.5). None of the economies in the database indicated they would be publishing a positive list.

Recent Trends in Corporate Tax Incentives

Tax incentives are a critical component of investment regulations and among the most common policy instruments for attracting foreign investment.

Low corporate rates and incentives in the form of tax exemptions, tax allowances, tax holidays, duty exemptions, and accelerated depreciations, among other instruments, have been used to ease effective rates paid by domestic and foreign companies. Notably, tax incentives are not confined to firms operating in special economic zones. Generous tax incentives based on sector policies, geographic location, and other criteria make multinationals pay considerably lower rates.

The impact of taxes on foreign investment has long been a subject of empirical inquiry. Multinationals spend considerable resources on transfer pricing and other tax-planning techniques to minimize tax liabilities. Estimates of the elasticity of foreign investment given a change in corporate taxes range widely, although most studies suggest that the impact is significant (James 2009). More importantly, the effectiveness of incentives is linked to the environment where they are offered. A body of evidence casts doubt on the effectiveness of tax incentives as a sustainable mechanism for attracting and retaining investment. While tax incentives in theory can create new investments and economic activity, they may be also associated with lower corporate tax revenues (ADB 2022a; Kronfol and Steenbergen 2020).[47] Some evidence also suggests that tax incentives tend to be ineffective for greenfield investment as FDI is mainly motivated by access to large markets or resources (Andersen, Kett, and Uexkull 2017; Appiah-Kubi et al. 2021; Kinda 2014).

---

[45] The latter refer to administrative conditions offered by governments to foreign firms other than special fiscal (e.g., tax) or financial (e.g., subsidies) treatment (UNCTAD 2022b). Examples can include exemptions of environmental, health safety, or labor standards and stabilization clauses guaranteeing that existing regulations will not be amended to the detriment of investors.

[46] The procedural requirements can be different in putting up the positive and negative lists (European Commission 2016). In some cases, the lists are contained in other legislation or regulation and not in the national investment law itself.

[47] Estimates for a group of 109 economies indicate that a 10-percentage point increase in corporate income tax (CIT) incentives led to a decrease in CIT revenues of 0.35% of gross domestic product between 2009 and 2015 (Kronfol and Steenbergen 2020).

Table 3.5: Explicit Restrictions in Investment Laws—Selected Asia and Pacific Economies

Economy / Year of Enactment	Armenia 1994	Azerbaijan 1992	Bangladesh 1980	Cambodia 1994	China, People's Republic of 2020	Georgia 1996	Indonesia 2007	Kazakhstan 2003	Korea, Republic of 2017	Kyrgyz Republic 2003	Lao PDR 2016	Maldives 1979	Micronesia, Federated States of 1997	Mongolia 2013	Nepal 1992	Pakistan 1976	Papua New Guinea 1992	Philippines 1991	Tajikistan 2007	Timor-Leste 2017	Tonga 2016	Turkmenistan 1992	Uzbekistan 1998	Vanuatu 1998	Viet Nam 2014
Does the act prohibit investment in certain sectors/activities?	No	Yes	No	No	Yes	No	No	No	No	No	No	No	No	No	Yes	No	No	No	No	No	Yes	Yes	No	Yes	Yes
Is there a positive list (i.e., listing of sectors open to investment)?	No	No	No	No	No	No	No	No	No	No	No	No	No	No	No	No	No	No	No	No	No	No	No	No	No
a) If yes, is this included in the act?	n/a	n/a	n/a	n/a	n/a	n/a	n/a	n/a	n/a	n/a	n/a	n/a	n/a	n/a	n/a	n/a	n/a	n/a	n/a	n/a	n/a	n/a	n/a	n/a	n/a
b) If no, is it provided in a regulation or other secondary instrument?	No	n/a	n/a	n/a	n/a	n/a	n/a	n/a	n/a	n/a	n/a	n/a	n/a	n/a	n/a	n/a	n/a	n/a	n/a	n/a	n/a	n/a	n/a	n/a	n/a
Is there a negative list (i.e., listing of prohibited/restricted sectors)?	No	No	Yes	Yes	Yes	Yes	No	Yes	Yes	Yes	Yes	No	No	Yes	Yes	Yes	Yes	Yes	Yes	Yes	No	Yes	Yes	Yes	Yes
a) If yes, is it included in the act?	No	No	Yes	Yes	n/a	n/a	n/a	Yes	Yes	Yes	Yes	n/a	n/a	Yes	Yes	Yes	No	No	Yes	Yes	n/a	n/a	Yes	Yes	Yes
b) If no, is it provided in a regulation or other secondary instrument?	No	No	n/a	n/a	n/a	n/a	n/a	n/a	Yes	n/a	n/a	n/a	n/a	n/a	Yes	n/a	Yes	Yes	n/a	n/a	n/a	n/a	n/a	n/a	n/a

Legend:

Yes   No   not applicable

Lao PDR = Lao People's Democratic Republic.

Sources: Hebous, Kher, and Tran (2020); and World Bank (2020).

Corporate income tax (CIT) incentives are a significant component of investment packages.

CIT may include tax holidays, tax rate reductions, investment tax allowances, tax credits, and other instruments. Already a couple of decades ago, a sharp decline was observed in corporate tax revenue in Organisation for Economic Co-operation and Development (OECD) member economies partly due to tax competition for FDI. Industrialized economies had typically reduced CIT and designed other incentives, such as R&D incentives, to attract multinational enterprises (MNEs). More recent data suggest that CIT rates have continued to decline globally (Figure 3.12). The downward trend is evident across different regions and Asian subregions in recent decades. On average, the prevailing CIT rates in Asia tend to be lower than in the other regions.

Asia's revenue from CIT as a proportion of output is similar to other regional blocs but higher than OECD member economies (Figure 3.13). In developing Asia, CITs accounted for nearly 21% of tax revenues, in line with other developing regions and double the share in OECD economies (ADB 2022a). The region's revenue performance deteriorated marginally from about a decade earlier. Asia's average CIT revenue-to-gross domestic product ratio declined by about 30 basis points to 3.7% in 2019 from 4.0% in 2010. Of the 24 Asian economies in the sample, 10 economies saw their CIT ratios slide between 2010 and 2019.

Other incentives, beyond CIT incentives, are just as important in understanding the direction of investment policies.

Beyond CIT reductions, tax competition extends to other incentives, including indirect taxes, import duties, and tax-related financial incentives. Of the 100 economies that have adopted investment measures related to taxation over the past decade, 90 have lowered taxes, introduced new tax incentives, or made

Figure 3.12: Average Statutory Corporate Income Tax Rate by Region and Subregion, 1980–2021 (%)

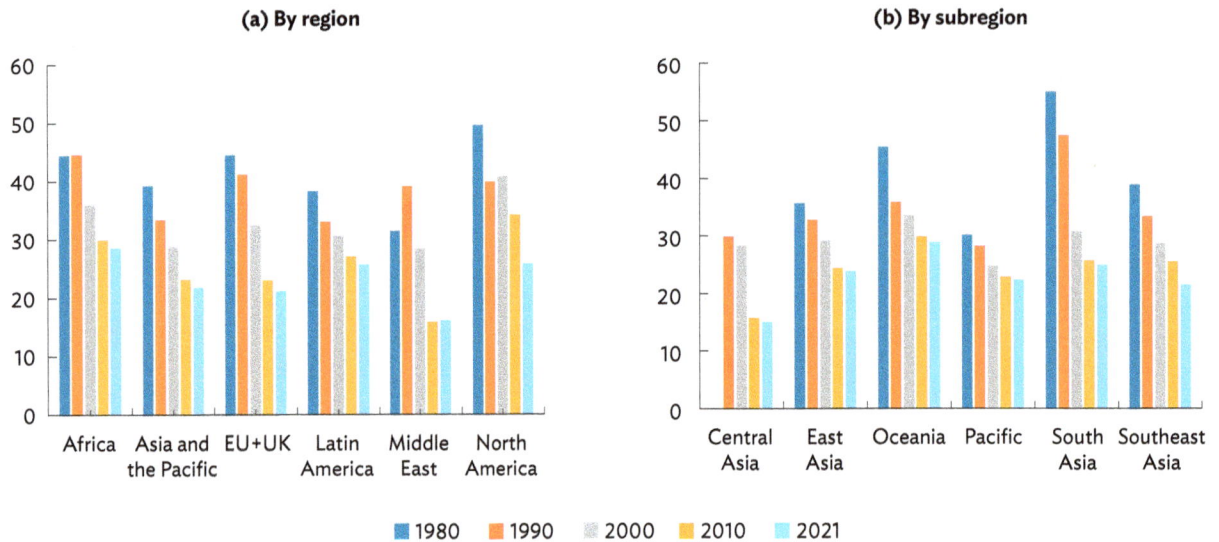

(a) By region

(b) By subregion

■ 1980 ■ 1990 ▨ 2000 ■ 2010 ■ 2021

EU = European Union (27 members), UK = United Kingdom.

Note: Data for Central Asia are not available in 1980 while the data for Kazakhstan are only for 1990.

Source: Tax Foundation. Corporate Taxes database. https://taxfoundation.org/publications/corporate-tax-rates-around-the-world/ (accessed August 2022).

Figure 3.13: Corporate Income Tax Revenue, 2010 and 2019 (% of GDP)

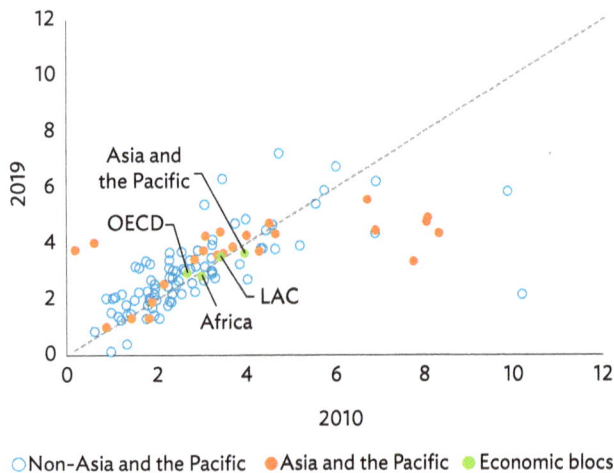

○ Non-Asia and the Pacific   ● Asia and the Pacific   ● Economic blocs

GDP = gross domestic product, LAC = Latin America and the Caribbean, OECD = Organisation for Economic Co-operation and Development.

Notes: The raw data refer to item 1200 in the database, i.e., taxes on income, profits, and capital gains of corporates. Data for economy groups refer to unweighted averages. The aggregate data for Africa, OECD, and Latin America and the Caribbean are as indicated in the source. The aggregate data for Asia and the Pacific are calculated by the authors.

Source: OECD. Global Revenue Statistics Database. https://www.oecd.org/tax/tax-policy/global-revenue-statistics-database.htm (accessed August 2022).

them more generous, bringing down the effective tax rate (UNCTAD 2022b). The use of non-CIT incentives differs in the region, even within a subregional agglomeration. In the Association of Southeast Asian Nations (ASEAN), for example, various forms of income tax holiday, capital equipment incentives, raw material and spare parts incentives, and loss carry forward are available to investors (Government of the Philippines, National Tax Research Center 2018). However, members differ in approaches to incentives for R&D, labor and training, reinvestment of earnings, and export duties.

While implementation of the new tax rules is still under discussion, economies in the region may need to review their use of investment tax incentives.

Efforts to tackle corporate tax avoidance concluded with a major reform of international tax rules.[48] The agreement aims to delimit, if not eliminate, offshore investment and tax competition on corporates and to

---

[48]   The first pillar will reallocate taxing rights estimated at more than $125 billion of profits to the market jurisdictions where consumers/users are located. The second pillar aims at reducing tax competition through a minimum corporate income tax of 15%, to be applied to multinationals with annual group consolidated revenues above €750 million.

provide tax preferences for other policy areas, such as clean energy production. The implications of these measures for investment policy in the region are still to be seen. For example, where tax incentives target MNEs with a substantial impact on jobs or physical investments, they are less likely to be affected. As a first step, assessing the effectiveness of investment tax incentives may be important for aligning to new global tax rules. Certainly, the move to limit the role of tax tools to attract investment will need a rethink in the overarching policy, including revisiting fiscal stabilization clauses with tax incentives of certain agreements and investment contracts (Lassourd, Mann, and Redhead 2021). A balance between designing an effective foreign investment policy and limiting the use of tax incentives for investment will be critical.

Investment Tax Incentives: Balancing Costs and Benefits while Addressing Redundancy

Investment tax incentives entail forgone revenues, thus should be effective in attracting the necessary investments to offset the cost.

The estimated total forgone revenue in a sample of Asian economies equals on average 2% of gross domestic product or 14% of tax revenue (Figure 3.14a). From this, the estimated forgone revenue related to CIT is on average above 2% of tax revenues, and in some economies close

Figure 3.14: Revenue Forgone in Corporate Income Tax and Investment in Selected Asia and Pacific Economies, 2019 (%)

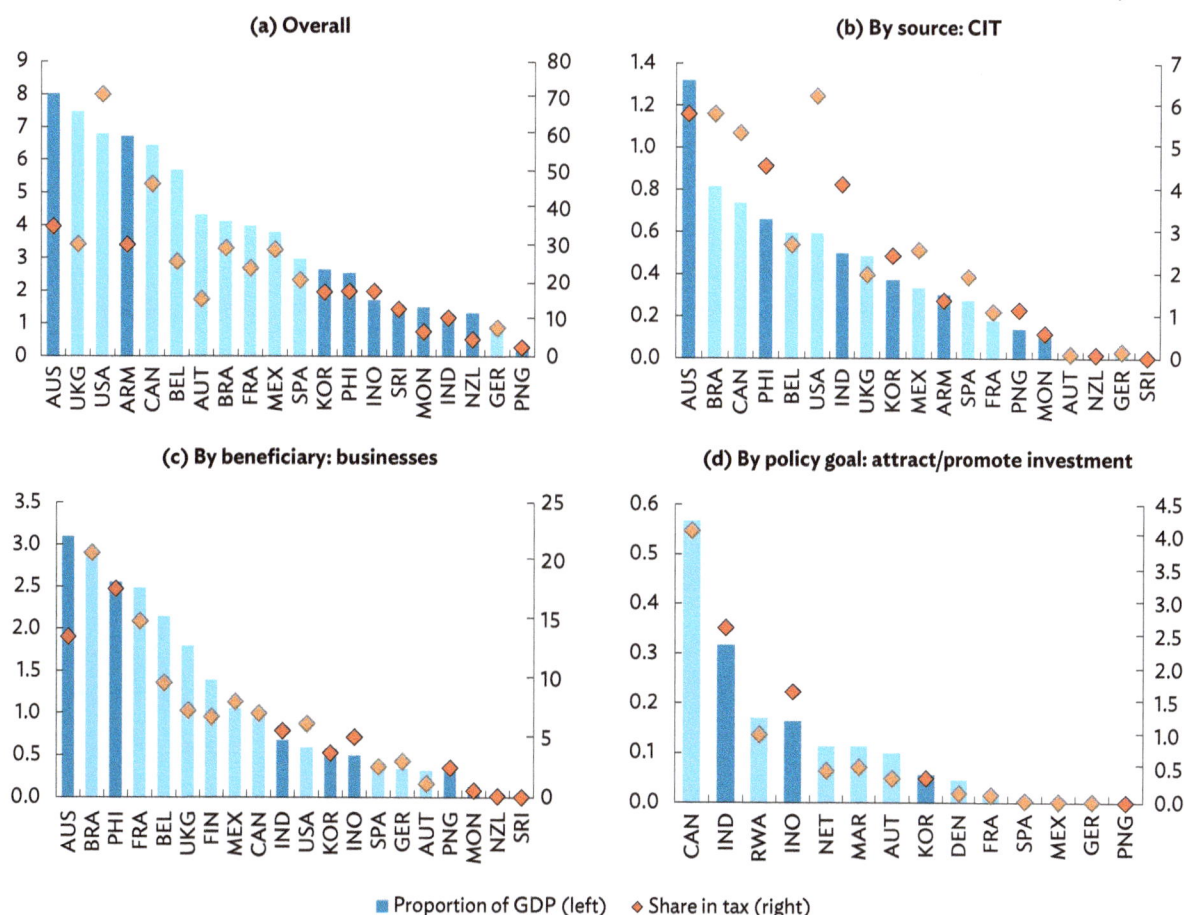

(a) Overall

(b) By source: CIT

(c) By beneficiary: businesses

(d) By policy goal: attract/promote investment

■ Proportion of GDP (left)   ◆ Share in tax (right)

ARM = Armenia, AUS = Australia, AUT = Austria, BEL = Belgium, BRA = Brazil, CAN = Canada, CIT = corporate income tax, DEN = Denmark, GDP = gross domestic product, GER = Germany, FIN = Finland, FRA = France, INO = Indonesia, IND = India, KOR = Republic of Korea, MAR = Morocco, MEX = Mexico, MON = Mongolia, NET = Netherlands, NZL = New Zealand, PHI = Philippines, PNG = Papua New Guinea, RWA = Rwanda, SPA = Spain, SRI = Sri Lanka, UKG = United Kingdom, USA = United States.

Notes: Latest available data for both revenues forgone as a percentage of GDP and tax are 2018 for India and Mongolia. The revenue forgone estimates represent the lost revenue due to items such as tax deductions, exemptions, and other tax expenditures. Estimates are based on the most recent government reports where actual data are reported. Darker bars and darker diamond markers both represent estimates for Asia and the Pacific.

Source: ADB calculations based on the Global Tax Expenditures Database. https://doi.org/10.5281/zenodo.633421 (accessed September 2022).

to 4.5% (Figure 3.14b). For economies where data are available, the estimated forgone revenues from policies to promote/attract investment are also significant (Figure 3.14d). In the context of decreasing FDI flows, scrutiny on investment incentives has increased. Incentives are expected to be nonredundant, well-targeted, and based on robust cost–benefit analyses. They are justified when they correct market inefficiencies, support new industries, assist firms during downturns, and ultimately lead to additional revenue intake. They are also more effective if the infrastructure is adequate and the overall investment policy and climate are favorable (James 2009, Kronfol and Steenbergen 2020). When poorly designed, however, they can render the tax system less efficient by narrowing the tax base, undermining competition, and signaling to investors that the investment climate is not necessarily stable. Balance is particularly important in emerging economies, where tax regimes are usually complex.

Tax expenditure provisions linked to CITs figure prominently in investment packages offered by some Asian economies.

Where information is available, CITs constitute 26.3% of the total tax expenditure provisions in Asian economies,

following 30.7% for personal income taxes (Figure 3.15a). Despite the volume of CIT-related relief measures in the region, the share of CITs in forgone revenue has remained stable after an important decline in the early 2000s (Figure 3.15b). From 2018 to 2020, the share of CITs in forgone revenue stood at about 23%. The stagnant CIT shares in tax expenditures suggest that the benefits for investors from such incentive may have become less attractive (Von Haldenwang, Redonda, and Aliu 2021).

Investment Tax Incentives in Asia

Asian economies have introduced many different tax-related investment measures in recent years.

Investment tax incentives have been commonly categorized either as CIT-based or other incentives (UNCTAD 2022b). CIT-based incentives can in turn be classified into two main categories: profit-based and expenditure (or capital investment) incentives. Profit-based incentives are based on earnings and therefore are more attractive for mobile investment, whereas expenditure investments are related to

Figure 3.15: Average Revenue Forgone by Tax Type—Selected Economies

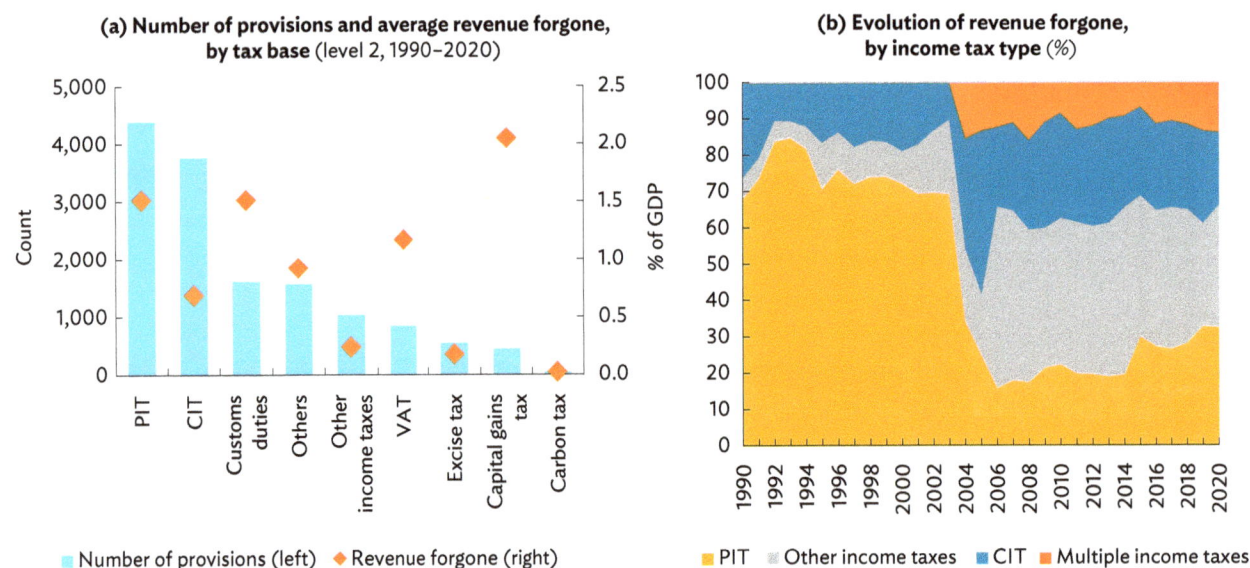

(a) Number of provisions and average revenue forgone, by tax base (level 2, 1990–2020)

(b) Evolution of revenue forgone, by income tax type (%)

■ Number of provisions (left)   ◆ Revenue forgone (right)

■ PIT   ■ Other income taxes   ■ CIT   ■ Multiple income taxes

CIT = corporate income tax, GDP = gross domestic product, PIT = personal income tax, VAT = value-added tax.

Notes: Latest available data for both revenues forgone as a percentage of GDP and tax are 2018 for Bhutan, India, and Mongolia. Estimates for panel (a) include Armenia, Australia, Bhutan, India, Indonesia, Kazakhstan, Mongolia, New Zealand, Pakistan, Papua New Guinea, the Philippines, the Republic of Korea, and Sri Lanka.

Source: ADB calculations based on Global Tax Expenditures Database. https://doi.org/10.5281/zenodo.633421 (accessed September 2022).

capital investment. CIT incentives remain the most common instrument for attracting investment. In Asia, CIT incentives accounted for 50% of all tax-related investment measures over 2011–2021 (Figure 3.16a). Of the CIT-based instruments, tax holidays are the most common in Asia, representing 47% of tax-related investment measures, followed by reduced CIT rates. Notably, developed economies have a considerably lower number of tax incentives. Comparable data on

CIT incentives for Asian economies suggest that tax exemptions and allowances are commonly used in the region, especially in Southeast Asia (Figure 3.16b). According to the OECD tax incentive classification (OECD 2022), tax exemptions remain the most widely used instrument among developing economies. Meanwhile tax allowances are often used to target qualifying capital and current expenditures.

Figure 3.16: Investment Incentives By Type, 2011–2021 (count)

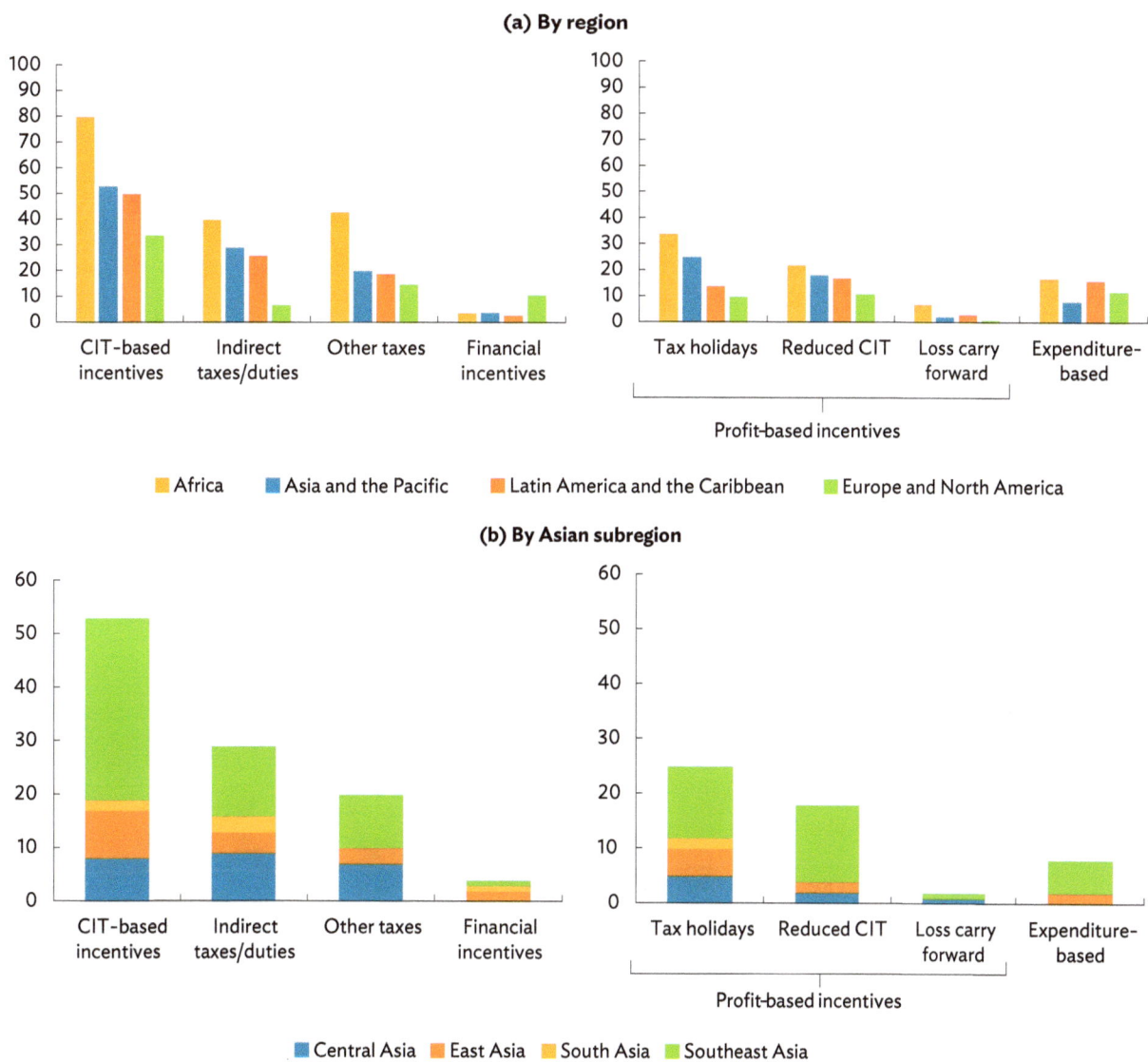

(a) By region

Africa ■ Asia and the Pacific ■ Latin America and the Caribbean ■ Europe and North America

(b) By Asian subregion

■ Central Asia ■ East Asia ■ South Asia ■ Southeast Asia

CIT = corporate income tax.

Sources: ADB calculations using data from UNCTAD and UNCTAD (2022b).

Design features of investment tax incentives determine their cost and effectiveness.

In the case of CIT rates, design features include, for example, the applicable rate, qualifying income, and time limitations. For tax exemptions, relevant design features relate to thresholds for exemptions and duration of the exemption. In the case of tax allowances of tax credits, design features may include the qualifying expenditures. Eligibility conditions are also important as they determine the beneficiary from the incentive. They may target a specific sector or industry, geographic location, ownership structure (e.g., minimum capital for domestic investors) or performance outcomes (e.g., exports, employment), among other factors.

While sector targeting remains a principle for tax incentives, these are broadly allocated.

Available information indicates that investment tax incentives in Asia are spread across most economic sectors (Table 3.6). At the same time, while most economies target specific sectors or subsectors for eligibility, tax incentives are usually broadly defined. This is the case for manufacturing, where existing incentives cover most subsectors. In contrast to negative lists, few economies specify which sectors are eligible for tax incentives.

Table 3.6: Economies Providing Investment Tax Incentives with Sector Conditions

Agri = agriculture, Lao PDR = Lao People's Democratic Republic.

Note: Blue squares indicate that the economy (y-axis) has at least one corporate income tax incentive with a sector.

Source: Celani, Dressler, and Wermenlinger (2022), based on OECD Investment Tax Incentives database, July 2021.

Special economic zones (SEZs) are special cases for the definition and granting of incentives.

SEZs are designated areas where governments facilitate investment through both tax and nontax incentives, infrastructure, and targeted sector programs. SEZs have played a key role in Asia's economic development (ADB 2015).[49] With more than 5,000 zones across the world as of 2019, SEZs have boosted the export sector, created jobs, and attracted foreign investment. SEZs also have been testing grounds for incentives and policies that have gone on to be implemented nationwide. Fiscal incentives have been considered an important feature of successful SEZs, specially for initial investments. They are useful to newly established firms, particularly in labor-intensive industries and at the lower stream of the industrial chain. They may also directly reduce production costs. However, institutional factors, such as an independent governing body and an enabling legal framework, have proved more important for investors. Lack of transparency in administration and governance of tax incentives in SEZs remains a challenge.

New Tax Rules and the Effectiveness of Investment Tax Incentives

New tax rules could offset the advantages of tax incentives for foreign investors.

The Pillar Two Model rules (also known as Global Anti-Base Erosion or GloBE rules) of the international tax agreement set agreed limits on tax competition and may limit the scope of jurisdictions to offer tax incentives (OECD 2022). While CIT rates in developing Asia are comparable to other regions and above the minimum tax rate of 15%, in practice multinationals pay considerably lower effective tax rates. In Asia, tax incentives for private investment are estimated to reduce effective tax rates on average by 8.6% (Wiedemann and Finke 2015). With the adoption of Pillar Two, eligible multinationals —those with a group consolidated revenue exceeding

€750 million—will be subject to top-up taxes in the economy where their Ultimate Parent Entity, typically the headquarters, are located. The effectiveness of the minimum tax will depend on several factors, including the determination of the effective tax rates and the extent and coverage of substance carve-outs.[50] Nevertheless, granting tax incentives to attract FDI would mean that part of this additional income would be taxed elsewhere. Indeed, under several existing tax incentive regimes, the residence economy collects tax that the source economy could have collected (Mullins 2022). Overall, the benefits of tax incentives will most likely be diminished.

Governments may therefore need to revisit their tax incentives to prevent the associated forgone revenue being taxed in another jurisdiction. They should reconsider and reform those incentives that may be inefficient. This requires a jurisdiction-specific analysis, as the impact of the GloBE rules, and policy responses, will vary between jurisdictions. Once the GloBE rules are in place, the use of investment tax incentives will still be possible, but they will need to be carefully designed and targeted (Box 3.3).

To remain attractive or to prevent MNEs from repatriating investments, developing economies may start offering other tax incentives.

New tax rules may discourage the use of CIT-related tax incentives since they are at the heart of harmful tax competition. However, they do not prevent some economies from considering other tax incentives besides corporate taxation, and outside of the new tax agreement. Measures not covered by new tax rules involve reductions in customs duties, indirect and value-added taxes, or payroll taxes. If governments change the composition of incentives without addressing key flaws on tax incentives for investment, the potential benefits of the new tax agreement for enhancing tax revenue may be limited.

---

[49]   For a comprehensive analysis on the role and impact of special economic zones in the Asia and Pacific region, see ADB (2015).

[50]   Substance carve-outs have now been replaced by the Qualified Domestic Minimum Top-Up Tax.

Box 3.3: Adapting Investment Tax Incentives to New Tax Rules

In response to the implementation of new tax rules, tax reforms need to prioritize incentives that carry the greatest risk of multinational enterprises being liable for top-up tax under the Global Anti Base Erosion (GloBE) rules.

Tax incentives are more likely to be affected where they are treated as reductions in Covered Taxes in the GloBE effective tax rate calculation. They include the majority of income-based and expenditure-based tax instruments, including preferential corporate income tax rates—through either reduced rates or exemptions—investment tax allowances or credits that seek to reduce taxable income or the tax liability on certain investments. In turn, narrowly targeted tax incentives to certain categories of income or expenditure or incentives that effectively limit tax benefits are likely to be less affected. Tax incentives targeted to specific types of income, such as intellectual property or export income, effectively limit a firm's share of total income subject to preferential tax treatment. Their impact is likely to be smaller.

Substance-based carve-outs will play a key role in determining the impact of the GloBE rules on tax incentives. If investments have high levels of substance or low levels of profit, they are to some extent less exposed to the GloBE rules. Certain refundable tax credits are generally less affected by the GloBE rules than

nonrefundable tax credits. The GloBE rules generally follow financial accounting in treating grants and qualified refundable credits as income of the recipient rather than a reduction in taxes. Accordingly, the provision of a grant or qualifying refundable tax credit will increase GloBE income instead of reducing Covered Taxes.

Tax incentives that defer tax payments into the future, such as accelerated depreciation, are generally unlikely to generate top-up taxes under the GloBE rules. Because they allow the firm to deduct these costs over a shorter period than their economic life, they lead to a reduction of taxable income in earlier years and therefore a deferral of taxation. The GloBE rules incorporate certain deferred tax adjustments so that, under a moderate tax rate and assuming no recapture is required, tax incentives such as accelerated depreciation and immediate expensing will not increase tax liability under the GloBE rules. For assets other than tangible assets, where the temporary differences last longer than 5 years, the GloBE Rules may affect the tax incentive.

Aside from the GloBE effective tax rate, the substance-based carve-out will play a key role in the use of tax incentives in a post-GloBE environment. Indeed, the top-up tax only applies to profits in excess of the substance-based carve-out.

Source: ADB staff using OECD (2022).

Fragmentation of the domestic legislation of investment incentives is a challenge for transparency and comparability.

Incentive provisions are often scattered across several laws, including the investment law, income tax law, or SEZ law. The governance structure of tax incentives usually involves several agencies and ministries, which limits transparency and accountability (Table 3.7). SEZ laws are often the primary legal framework for various incentives, including tax and land incentives. Well-defined SEZ laws could be a proxy for good incentive mechanisms, tailored to their objectives and industry policies (ADB 2015). Asian economies may need to assess their tax incentive structure more systematically

to get a good grasp of the potential impact of compliance with new international tax rules and map out the strategies on how to comply with these rules.

Incentivizing Green Investment

Incentives to attract capital for green and sustainable projects can be explored.

As stressed in the theme chapter of this report, enhancing the region's resilience to climate risks requires a steady stream of funding to adapt to and mitigate their impact. While regulatory (e.g. fines) and market-based (e.g. carbon tax) measures that deter activities related

Table 3.7: Investment Tax Incentives by Domestic Laws and Granting Authorities

(a) Legal basis of investment tax incentives, by regulating provision	Armenia	Azerbaijan	Brunei Darussalam	Cambodia	Georgia	Indonesia	Lao PDR	Thailand	(b) Granting authority of investment tax incentives	Armenia	Azerbaijan	Brunei Darussalam	Cambodia	Georgia	Indonesia	Lao PDR	Thailand
Tax Law	■				■			■	Ministry of Finance		■			■			■
Investment Law						■			Ministry of Economy		■						
SEZ Law		■				■			IPA				■			■	■
Sector Law				■		■			SEZ authority			■	■		■		
Regulations/decrees						■		■	Other ministry	■							
Other laws			■	■					Interministerial committee				■				

IPA = investment promotion agency, Lao PDR = Lao People's Democratic Republic, SEZ = special economic zone.

Source: Celani, Dressler, and Wermenlinger (2022), based on OECD Investment Tax Incentives database, July 2021.

Table 3.8: Examples of Green Incentives Used in Selected Asia and Pacific Economies

Economy	Cash Grants	Soft Loans	Tax Incentives
Australia	Yes	Yes	Yes
China, People's Republic of	Yes	No information	Yes
Fiji	No information	No information	Yes
India	Yes	Yes	Yes
Japan	Yes	No information	Yes
Korea, Republic of	Yes	No information	Yes
Singapore	Yes	No information	Yes

Legend:

Yes ■

No information ■

Note: Only seven Asian economies are included in the database.

Sources: PwC Green Taxes and Incentives Tracker. https://www.pwc.com/gx/en/services/tax/green-tax-and-incentives-tracker.html (accessed October 2022); and Watkins et al. (2018).

to carbon emissions are important, so is improving the bankability of greener projects.[51] Green incentives, defined as those that reduce harm to the environment, broadly include cash grants, soft loans, and reduction in tax liabilities. Tax incentives and cash grants are commonly used as an instrument among a sample of selected Asian economies where information is available (Table 3.8). The use of soft loans in comparison is relatively more limited.

Tax incentives have been introduced on a broad list of activities in pursuit of green goals.

Australia offers incentives for land and water conservation, mine site rehabilitation, and investment in R&D; India has reliefs for green and clean technology and infrastructure; and the Republic of Korea gives away tax credit for R&D expenses on electric vehicle batteries (Table 3.8). Separately, OECD and ASEAN Secretariat (2021) note the implementation of a green procurement initiative in Malaysia (i.e., purchasing of green products and services) together with the green technology tax incentives like the green investment tax allowance and green income tax exemptions. Several Asian economies

---

[51]   Chapter 7: Theme Chapter—Trade, Investment, and Climate Change in Asia and the Pacific discusses in detail some environmental taxation options to contain carbon emissions.

also offer fiscal incentives to promote renewable energy (Akhtar, Zahedi, and Liu 2017).[52]

Scaling up these mechanisms while maintaining fiscal discipline is nonetheless a challenge for many economies in the region. Incentives for pollution abatement as well as for R&D and investment in green technologies in the region, for instance, are still lacking (Khanna 2020). Further work is also needed to establish sound project performance monitoring frameworks, technically capable oversight institutions and project assessment standards, among others, to mainstreaming the investment support mechanisms.

The Role of Regulatory Incentives

Investment frameworks that spell openness to foreign investment encourage market competition.

A less restrictive investment environment is widely construed as a robust determinant of FDI inflows (Feng and Wang 2021; Ghosh, Syntetos, and Wang 2012; Sin and Leung 2010) even as the sensitivity can be amplified or muted by other factors (Adams 2009; Ullah and Inaba 2014). In examining the FDI-market competition nexus, the focus has been on the impact of FDI on market structure.[53] Higher competition brought about by the influx of foreign capital may yield efficiency gains for firms, facilitate technology transfer, and improve market conditions (e.g., lowering the cost of goods and services). At the same time, it can also entail easing out of local firms that cannot compete effectively with foreign entrants.[54]

In the absence of appropriate guiding policies, FDI can contribute to market concentration. Indeed, market concentration increased in developing economies in the 1990s despite inflows in greenfield investment (UNCTAD 1997). More recent empirical studies show mixed outcomes of foreign entry in local industries in Asia. The entry of foreign capital has been associated to both lower concentration (Lundin et al. 2007) and higher concentration (Singh 2011). The competitive pressure from FDI may depend on factors such as the mode of entry, investment climate, and industry-specific factors. Consistency and coherence between policies are underscored to be important in achieving competition outcomes.

As digital sectors gain importance, sustained investment and healthy market competition in sectors like telecommunications are critical.

While internet service and penetration have improved in the region, investment in this space is still insufficient in many developing Asian economies.[55] Broadband and mobile internet penetration in the region in 2020 is almost as heterogeneous as it is globally (Figure 3.17). Active mobile broadband subscriptions per 100 inhabitants range from about 0.2 to more than 10, while fixed broadband subscriptions per 100 inhabitants range from less than 12 to over 339. Price dispersion is likewise far from negligible. The extent (or lack) of competition in telecommunications, even as the market is open to foreign investors, is an issue for many economies in the region (Box 3.4).

---

[52]   Table 3.3 of Akhtar, Zahedi, and Liu (2017) lists the policy support for renewable energy in Asian economies.

[53]   Yet, the empirical literature is relatively silent on the role of market competition in attracting FDI.

[54]   Other accompanying issues related to foreign competition include the possibility of locals giving up control of key national enterprises or even sectors to nonresidents; and the risk of giving nonresidents substantial access to the residents' data and strategic infrastructure or systems. As such, while evidence suggests that FDI can support economic growth and market contestability, governments are usually wary of fully opening up their economies to foreign capital (Schmidt and Pizzetti 2019).

[55]   Examples of indicators are mobile-cellular subscriptions, individuals using the internet, fixed-broadband subscriptions, and mobile-broadband subscriptions.

Figure 3.17: Broadband and Mobile Subscriptions and Service Cost in 2020

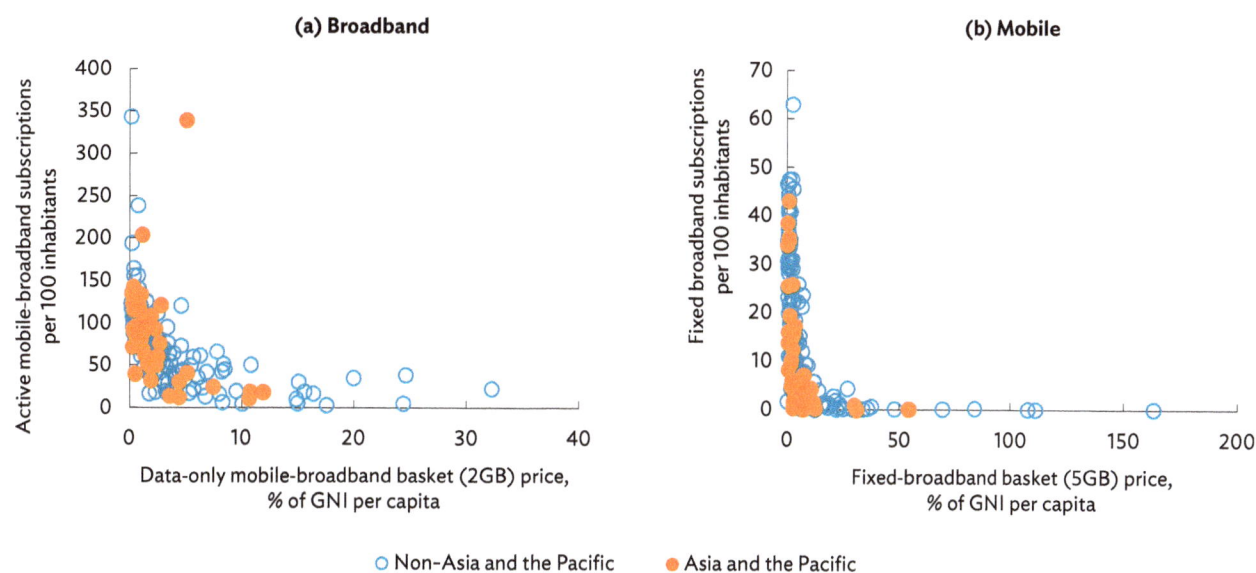

(a) Broadband

(b) Mobile

○ Non-Asia and the Pacific   ● Asia and the Pacific

GB = gigabyte, GNI = gross national income.

Source: International Telecommunication Union (ITU). ITU Statistics database. https://www.itu.int/en/ITU-D/Statistics/Pages/stat/default.aspx (accessed September 2022).

Box 3.4: Competition in the Telecommunications Sector in Asia and the Pacific

Asian telecommunications markets tend to be dominated by two or three major players even if the market is open to foreign capital. Data for India, Indonesia, the Philippines, and Thailand show that the top two service providers in both the fixed broadband and mobile internet segments account for around two-thirds of the market (box table).

Incidentally, many of the largest service providers are partly owned by one or more foreign entities.[a] This purports that foreign participation in a liberalized telecommunications market does not seem to erode the dominance of a few firms, if not reinforcing it altogether.

Mobile and Fixed Broadband Market Structures—Selected Asia and Pacific Economies

Economy	Market Share of the Top Firms	Base Data Sources
India	The top 2 firms account for 61% of the mobile phone market and 76% of the broadband market in the first quarter of 2020. The top 3 firms account for 88% of the mobile phone market and 95% of the broadband market in the first quarter of 2020.	Government of India, Department of Telecommunications (2022)
Indonesia	The top firm accounts for 85% of the fixed broadband market in 2020. The top 2 and top 3 firms account for 65% and 85%, respectively, of the mobile broadband market in 2020.	Giga, BCG, and ITU (2021)
Philippines	The top 2 firms account for 99% of the mobile phone market in the first quarter of 2022 and 80% of the broadband market in 2020.	GSMA (2022); Statista (2021)
Thailand	The top 2 firms account for 77% of the mobile phone market and 73% of the broadband market in the first quarter of 2021. The top 3 firms account for 97% of the mobile phone market space and 97% of the broadband market in the first quarter of 2021.	Rasmussen (2022)

Notes: Market share is in terms of subscribers unless otherwise indicated. The number of players in the mobile market in Thailand includes mobile virtual network operators.

[a] Annex 3a shows the limitations to foreign participation in the telecommunications sector in selected Asian economies as of 2018.

Sources: ADB compilation based on Giga, BCG, and ITU (2021); Government of India, Department of Telecommunications (2022); GSMA (2022); Rasmussen (2022); and Statista (2021).

The proliferation of mobile virtual network operators (MVNOs) could change the role of FDI in the telecommunications sector.

MVNOs, which the International Telecommunication Union (ITU) (2001) defines as those offering mobile services to end users but not having a government license to use their own radio frequency, are not necessarily new. While MVNOs have largely curated services for the business-to-consumer segment, they have now ventured into other segments and evolved toward data-centric services (Deloitte 2016; ITU 2022). In essence, MVNOs are alternative wireless service providers that buy network capacity and the right to use the network of a major mobile carrier and resell services bundled with other features, products, and contents. As they grow in importance outside of the traditional mobile network operators, MVNOs have also become attractive prospects for foreign capital.[56] To facilitate expansion, governments may consider rationalizing administrative control of entry for internet service providers and MVNOs.

Providing market entrants access to existing infrastructure can be a regulatory incentive to enhance FDI and broaden competition.[57]

Infrastructure sharing can involve sharing of nonelectronic and electronic infrastructure. The mechanism can help lower capital and operating expenditure, improve services, hasten geographic rollout, and lower prices (ITU 2017), although the risk of partner conflicts and disputes calls for a robust set of regulations. Data from the ITU show that about half of Asian economies already have a regulatory framework for infrastructure sharing, against two-thirds globally (Figure 3.18). It is noted that the scale of potential socioeconomic benefits of infrastructure sharing has led some European economies to encourage this activity (GSMA 2012, 2021).

In these conditions, policies to incentivize infrastructure sharing and cooperation between market players in the region have ample merit (Cooper et al. 2020; Situmorang, Putri, and Rahmawati 2021; Venzon 2022).[58] Kushida and Oh (2007), having examined the cases of Japan and the Republic of Korea, also underscored the value of a strong lead bureaucracy that "compartmentalized the sector, orchestrated new competitors, and micromanaged the terms of competition" under certain conditions.

Figure 3.18: Regulatory Framework for Infrastructure Sharing in the Telecommunications Sector (%)

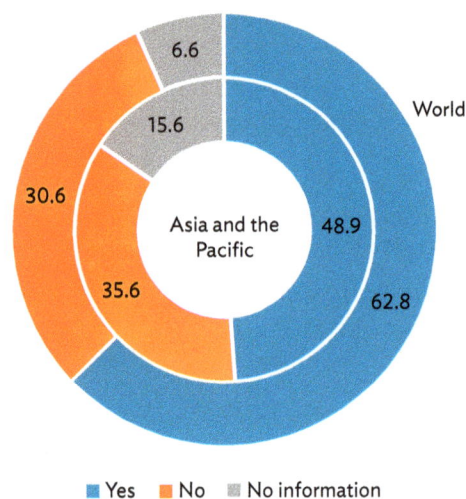

■ Yes   ■ No   ■ No information

Note: There are 196 economies with data.

Source: ADB calculations using data from the International Telecommunication Union. https://www.itu.int/en/ITU-D/Statistics/Pages/stat/default.aspx (accessed October 2022).

Additionally, the responsiveness of policies on M&As will be important in this context, considering that MVNOs rely on the strength of partnerships. As it stands, sizable M&A deals in the telecommunications space have been concluded in Indonesia, Malaysia, and Thailand

---

[56] The MVNO market is expected to grow at a rate of 7.54% from 2022 to reach a valuation of $127.1 billion in 2029, and Asia and the Pacific is forecast to account for a substantial chunk of the pie (Bridge Market Research 2021).

[57] As purported by GSMA (2012), a regulator may approve sharing, actively encourage sharing, or mandate access, but the decision should be based on the competitive impact of infrastructure sharing and in line with sound regulatory practices such as transparency, efficiency, nondiscrimination, and independence.

[58] Voluntary network sharing is argued to be a vital long-term solution to lower the risks and cost of expanding 5G coverage in remote areas (GSMA 2021), and Kushida and Oh (2007) detail the use of incentives in the telecommunications sector in Asia.

(Boghani and Dholakia 2022). In light of the cost of upgrading the systems to 5G, it is likely that similar deals could soon materialize in other parts of the region (Fitch Ratings 2022a, 2022b). Notably, some OECD economies are imposing conditions that include the divestment of spectrum or facilities (e.g., towers) as part of the approval process of mobile network operator mergers. The objective is "to open possibilities for new mobile network operators or an undertaking from the merged player to offer wholesale access obligations" while looking for ways to keep the mobile market open for a fourth player.

Policy Recommendations

Tax incentives to foreign investors are a predominant feature in Asia. With the implementation of Pillar Two and a global minimum tax, it is critical for the region to assess their investment tax incentives and introduce the necessary tax reforms accordingly. In the short term, economies can reconsider introducing new tax incentives or entering into new tax stabilization agreements and investment agreements without assessing the impact of the GloBE rules.

Economies may reconsider incentives that are treated as reductions in Covered Taxes in the GloBE rules. They include the majority of income-based and expenditure-based tax instruments including preferential CIT rates, investment tax allowances or credits. Well-targeted tax incentives to specific types of income, such as intellectual property or export income, so as tax incentives that defer tax payments, such as accelerated depreciation, are less likely to be affected by the GloBE

rules. Economies may also consider substance-based carve-outs when designing future tax incentives, as investments with high levels of economic substance, i.e., with sufficient operations in physical assets and employees, will be less affected.

Developing member economies may also consider the introduction of a Qualified Domestic Minimum Top-Up Tax to ensure they collect top-up taxes in their jurisdictions that would otherwise be collected by other jurisdictions via the other charging provisions. The Qualified Domestic Minimum Top-Up Tax mechanism can ensure increasing tax revenues without any loss of competitiveness.

Beyond tax incentives, policy makers can further explore the applicability of regulatory incentives that favor certain project or sector characteristics. One example is the introduction of MVNOs in the telecommunications sector to promote infrastructure sharing. In green energy sectors, regulatory targets and standards to promote eco-design, good waste management practices, and patent protection duration have also been effective. Such regulatory measures can promote collaboration, co-investment, and sharing of resources. To be effective, these incentives require close collaboration between regulators and the definition of clear safeguards against binding disagreements between partners.

Regional cooperation will be crucial for developing Asian economies to arrive at a well-designed incentive structure, especially in light of the increased scrutiny on the extent by which tax incentives are used. ADB's Asia Pacific Tax Hub provides an avenue to discuss policy options, direction, and sequencing for economies in the region.

References

Adams, C. 2009. *FDI Regimes and Liberalization. Presentation. Capacity Building for Sharing Success Factors for Improvement of Investment Environment.* Singapore: Asia-Pacific Economic Cooperation (APEC).

Appiah-Kubi, S. N. K., K. Malec, J. Phiri, M. Maitah, Z. Gebeltová, L. Smutka, V. Blažek, and K. Maitah. 2021. Impact of Tax Incentives on Foreign Direct Investment: Evidence from Africa. *Sustainability.* 13 (15). 8661.

Akhtar, S., K. Zahedi, and H. Liu. 2017. *Regional Cooperation for Sustainable Energy in Asia and the Pacific.* Bangkok: United Nations Economic and Social Commission for Asia and the Pacific (UNESCAP).

Andersen, M., B. Kett, and E. Uexkull. 2017. Corporate Tax Incentives and FDI in Developing Countries. In World Bank. *Global Investment Competitiveness Report 2017/2018: Foreign Investor Perspectives and Policy Implications.* Washington, DC.

Asian Development Bank (ADB). 2015. *Asian Economic Integration Report 2015: How Can Special Economic Zones Catalyze Development?* Manila.

————. 2022a. *Asian Development Outlook 2022: Mobilizing Taxes for Development.* Manila.

————. 2022b. *The Regional Comprehensive Economic Partnership Agreement: A New Paradigm in Asian Regional Cooperation?* Manila.

————. Asia Regional Integration Center. Economy Groupings. https://aric.adb.org/integrationindicators/groupings.

Association of Southeast Asian Nations (ASEAN) Secretariat. ASEANstats Data Portal. https://data.aseanstats.org (accessed July 2019).

Boghani, P. and G. Dholakia. 2022. Southeast Asia's Telcos to Look to Tower, Tech Deals as 5G Rollout Costs Add Up. Technology, Media & Telecom. *S&P Global Market Intelligence.* 12 May. https://www.spglobal.com/marketintelligence/en/news-insights/latest-news-headlines/southeast-asia-s-telcos-to-look-to-tower-tech-deals-as-5g-rollout-costs-add-up-69667006.

Bridge Market Research. 2021. *Global Mobile Virtual Network Operator (MVNO) Market—Industry Trends and Forecast to 2029.* Summary. Pune.

Celani, A., L. Dressler, and M. Wermenlinger. 2022. Building an Investment Tax Incentives Database: Methodology and Initial Findings for 36 Developing Countries. *OECD Working Papers on International Investment.* 2022/01. Paris: Organisation for Economic Co-operation and Development. (OECD) Publishing.

Cooper, G., J. Ling, W. J. Ru, and R. Irfan. 2020. Investing in Southeast Asia: Malaysia. *Herbert Smith Freehills.* 30 July. https://hsfnotes.com/malaysia/2020/07/30/investing-in-southeast-asia-malaysia.

Deloitte. 2016. Mobile Virtual Network Operators (MVNOs). Evolving Digital Realm Offers New Life for an old Model. *Flashpoint Edition.* 10. New York.

European Commission. 2016. Using 'Positive' and 'Negative' Lists. *Services and Investment in EU Trade Deals.* Brussels. https://trade.ec.europa.eu/doclib/docs/2016/april/tradoc_154427.pdf.

Eurostat. Balance of Payments. https://ec.europa.eu/eurostat (accessed July 2022).

Feng, Y. and Y. Wang. 2021. A Literature Review on the Location Determinants of FDI. *International Business Research.* 14 (4). pp. 126–126.

Fitch Ratings. 2022a. *APAC Telcos Swept Up in Consolidation Wave. Special Report.* Singapore.

———. 2022b. *APAC Telco M&A Wave to Boost Pricing Power. Special Report.* Singapore.

Ghosh, M., P. Syntetos, and W. Wang. 2012. Impact of FDI Restrictions on Inward FDI in OECD Countries. *Global Economy Journal.* 12 (3). pp. 1–26.

Giga, Boston Consulting Group (BCG), and International Telecommunication Union (ITU). 2021. Indonesia Case Study. Presentation. https://www.itu.int/en/ITU-D/Regional-Presence/AsiaPacific/Documents/Indonesia%20case%20study%5B1%5D.pdf.

Global Tax Expenditures database. https://gted.net/ (accessed September 2022).

Government of Canada, Statistics Canada. Industry Classifications. https://www.statcan.gc.ca/en/concepts/industry.

Government of India, Department of Telecommunications. 2022. Telecom Statistics India—2020. https://dot.gov.in/reportsstatistics/telecom-statistics-india-2020.

Government of the Philippines, National Tax Research Center (NTRC). 2018. Comparative Investment Incentives in ASEAN Member-Countries. *NTRC Tax Research Journal.* 30(1). Manila.

Government of the United States, Census Bureau. North American Industry Classification System. https://www.census.gov/naics/.

GSMA. 2012. *Mobile Infrastructure Sharing.* London.

———. 2021. *The Mobile Economy: Europe 2021.* London.

———. 2022. The Philippines Is a Duopoly No More: Assessing DITO's Impact on 4G and 5G Performance. Media release. 4 July.

Hebous, S., P. Kher, and T. Tran. 2020. Regulatory Risk and FDI. In World Bank. *Global Investment Competitiveness Report 2019–2020: Rebuilding Investor Confidence in Times of Uncertainty.*

International Monetary Fund (IMF). World Economic Outlook April 2021 Database. https://www.imf.org/en/Publications/WEO/weo-database/2021/April (accessed April 2022).

International Telecommunication Union (ITU). 2001. *Mobile Virtual Network Operators.* Geneva. https://www.itu.int/itunews/issue/2001/08/mvno.html.

———. 2017. Sharing Networks, Driving Growth. *ITU News Magazine.* June. Geneva.

———. 2020. The Benefits of Mobile Virtual Network Operator (MVNO) Partnerships. News. 30 April. Geneva.

———. 2022. Top 5 Trends for Mobile Virtual Network Operators (MVNOs). AI for Good. *Blog.* Geneva. https://aiforgood.itu.int/top-5-trends-for-mobile-virtual-network-operators-mvnos/.

———. ITU Statistics database. https://www.itu.int/en/ITU-D/Statistics/Pages/stat/default.aspx (accessed September 2022).

James, S. 2009. *Incentives and Investments: Evidence and Policy Implications.* Washington, DC: World Bank.

Khanna, M. 2020. Growing Green Business Investments in Asia and the Pacific: Trends and Opportunities. *ADB Sustainable Development Working Paper Series.* 72. Manila: ADB.

Kinda, T. 2014. The Quest for Non-Resource-Based FDI: Do Taxes Matter? *IMF Working Paper.* WP/14/15. Washington, DC: International Monetary Fund.

Kronfol, H. and V. Steenbergen. 2020. Evaluating the Costs and Benefits of Corporate Tax Incentives: Methodological Approaches and Policy Considerations. *Finance, Competitiveness and Innovation in Focus.* Washington, DC: World Bank.

Kushida, K. and S. Y. Oh. 2007. The Political Economies of Broadband Development in Korea and Japan. *Asian Survey.* 47 (3). pp. 481–504.

Lapid, A., R. Mercado, and P. Rosenkranz. 2021. Concentration in Asia's Cross-Border Banking: Determinants and Impacts. *ADB Economics Working Paper Series*. 636. Manila: ADB.

Lassourd, T., H. Mann, and A. Readhead. 2021. The End of Tax Incentives: How Will a Global Minimum Tax Affect Tax Incentives Regimes in Developing Countries? Analysis. 7 October. https://www.iisd.org/itn/en/2021/10/07/the-end-of-tax-incentives-how-will-a-global-minimum-tax-affect-tax-incentives-regimes-in-developing-countries-alexandra-readhead-thomas-lassourd-howard-mann.

Lundin, N., F. Sjöholm, P. He., and J. Qian. 2007. FDI, Market Structure and R&D Investments in China. *Working Paper Series*. 2007-04. Kitakyushu: The International Centre for the Study of East Asian Development.

Mullins, P. 2022. *Taxing Developing Asia's Digital Economy*. Manila: ADB.

Odusola, A. 2018. *Addressing the Foreign Direct Investment Paradox in Africa*. New York: United Nations Africa Renewal.

Organisation for Economic Co-operation and Development (OECD). 2022. Tax Incentives and the Global Minimum Corporate Tax. Reconsidering Tax Incentives after the Global Rules. Paris: OECD Publishing. https://doi.org/10.1787/25d30b96-en.

————. OECD Global Revenue Statistics Database, https://www.oecd.org/tax/tax-policy/global-revenue-statistics-database.htm (accessed August 2022).

OECD and ASEAN Secretariat. 2021. *Facilitating the Green Transition for ASEAN SMEs: A Toolkit for Policymakers*. Paris and Jakarta.

Pham, T. A, K. T. Ha, A. T. Nguyen, and Q. V. Nguyen. 2021. *2021 Viet Nam Macroeconomic Report Q1*. Ha Noi: Viet Nam Institute for Economic and Policy Research and Konrad Adenauer Stiftung.

PwC. Green Taxes and Incentives Tracker. https://www.pwc.com/gx/en/services/tax/green-tax-and-incentives-tracker.html (accessed October 2022).

Rasmussen, A. 2022. A Deep Dive into the TRUE/DTAC Merger in Thailand. *Yozzo*. 6 January. https://www.yozzo.com/insights/a-deep-dive-into-the-true-dtac-merger-in-thailand.

Sanghi, A. and D. Johnson. 2016. Deal or No Deal: Strictly Business for China in Kenya? *Policy Research Working Paper*. 7614. Washington, DC: World Bank.

Schmidt, J. and L. Pizzetti. 2019. *Foreign Direct Investment Control in Europe: Helicopter View of an Expanding Landscape*. London: Arnold & Porter Kaye Scholer LLP.

Shin, W. 2010. Openness and Diversification of Foreign Direct Investment for Export Stability Under the Global Economic Crisis: Case Study of OECD Countries. *Asia Pacific Journal of EU Studies*.

Sin, C. Y. and W. F. Leung. 2001. Impacts of FDI Liberalization on Investment Inflows. *Applied Economics Letters*. 8 (4). pp. 253–256.

Singh, J. 2011. Inward Investment and Market Structure in an Open Developing Economy: A Case of India's Manufacturing Sector. *Journal of Economics and Behavioral Studies*. 2 (6). pp. 286–297.

Situmorang, M., A. Putri, and A. Rahmawati. 2021. Indonesia: Indonesia's New Investment Regime: Telecommunication, Media, and Technologies Sector. *Mondaq*. 27 June.

Statista. 2021. *Market Share of Fixed and Mobile Broadband in the Philippines in 2020, by Service Providers*. https://www.statista.com/statistics/1194825/philippines-market-share-fixed-mobile-broadband-by-service-providers/.

Tax Foundation Corporate. Taxes database. https://taxfoundation.org/publications/corporate-tax-rates-around-the-world/ (accessed August 2022).

Ullah, M. S. and K. Inaba. 2014. Liberalization and FDI Performance: Evidence from ASEAN and SAFTA Member Countries. *Economic Structures*. 3 (6).

United Nations Conference on Trade and Development (UNCTAD). 1997. *World Investment Report 1997: Transnational Corporations, Market Structure and Competition Policy*. New York and Geneva.

————. 2022a. *World Investment Report 2022: International Tax Reforms and Sustainable Investment*. Geneva.

————. 2022b. *Corporate Income Taxes and Investment Incentives*. July 2022. Geneva.

————. World Investment Report 2022 Statistical Annex Tables. https://worldinvestmentreport.unctad.org/annex-tables/ (accessed June 2022).

United Nations Economic and Social Commission for Asia and the Pacific (UNESCAP). 2012. *Asia Pacific Trade Investment Report 2012*. Bangkok.

Venzon, C. 2022. Philippines Allows Foreigners to Own Telcos, Airlines and Railways. *Nikkei Asia*. 22 March.

Von Haldenwang, C., A. Redonda, and F. Aliu. 2021. Shedding Light on Worldwide Tax Expenditures. *GTED Flagship Report 2021*. Bonn: Global Tax Expenditures Database.

Watkins, E., M. Dornan, K. Daniell, I. van Putten, S. Pascoe, K. Hussey, J. P. Schweitzer, K. Mutafoglu, S. Withana, L. Bonduel, S. Gionfra and S. Eliaerts. 2018. *Towards Greener Taxes and Subsidies in Pacific Island Countries and Territories (PICTs)*. Nouméa: The Pacific Community.

Wiedemann, V. and K. Finke. 2015. Taxing Investments in the Asia-Pacific Region: The Importance of Cross-Border Taxation and Tax Incentives. *ZEW Discussion Papers*. 15-014. Mannheim: ZEW - Leibniz Centre for European Economic Research.

World Bank. 2020. *Global Investment Competitiveness Report 2019/2020: Rebuilding Investor Confidence in Times of Uncertainty*. Washington, DC.

Annex 3a: Foreign Direct Investment Regulatory Restrictiveness in the Telecommunications Sector

Table 3a.1: Foreign Direct Investment Regulatory Restrictiveness, Telecommunications—Selected Asian Economies, 2018

Economy	Subsector	Comment
Brunei Darussalam	Fixed and Mobile	Foreign investment in telecommunication enterprises is limited to 51% of equity ownership.
Indonesia	Fixed and Mobile	Foreign investment in fixed and mobile telecommunication services is limited to 67% of equity interest.
Malaysia	Fixed and Mobile	The Autonomous Liberalization Policy, announced in April 2012, raised FDI limits up to 70% for both NFP and NSPs; ASPs are fully open to FDI (100% foreign ownership allowed).
Philippines	Fixed and Mobile	FDI in telecommunications is limited to 40%. FDI in internet access providers is permitted without restrictions as of 2018.
Thailand	Fixed and Mobile	Foreign investment in telecommunication business is limited to 49% of equity ownership, except for Type 1 licensed business. Type 1 services include internet access services, audio text, resale of public switched telecommunications; store-and-retrieve value-added services; and international calling cards. For the purposes of the OECD FDI Regulatory restrictiveness Index, it is assumed that all fixed telecommunication services and all mobile telecommunication services (except those related to Type 1 licensed business) are subject to the foreign shareholding limitation.
Viet Nam	Fixed and Mobile	Foreign ownership in fixed telecommunications services providing network infrastructure is limited to 49%; foreign ownership in non-infrastructure telecommunications providers is limited to 65%.

ASP = application service provider, FDI = foreign direct investment, NFP = network facility provider, NSP = network service provider.

Notes: Data are as of 2018. Information on Brunei Darussalam is from the 2017 data set.

Source: Organisation for Economic Co-operation and Development. ASEAN FDI Regulatory Restrictions Database. https://qdd.oecd.org/subject.aspx?Subject=ASEAN_INDEX (accessed October 2022).

4 Financial Cooperation

Global monetary and financial conditions are tightening while capital market volatilities are rising.

Inflation has started to weigh on global economic recovery, heightening recession and stagflation risks in major advanced economies.

Persistent, high global inflation pressures are driving central banks to tighten monetary policy quicker than expected, in particular, in the United States (US). Economies in Asia and the Pacific are facing relatively benign inflation pressures due to limited exposure to grain shortages and supply chain disruptions.[59] Nevertheless, recent trends point to growing inflation pressures on regional economies as price pressures spread across broader economies from commodities to agriculture, manufacturing, and services.

Inflation rose to higher levels in most Asian economies in the second quarter (Q2) or Q3 of 2022, compared with 2021 and 2020, especially in Azerbaijan, the Lao People's Democratic Republic, Pakistan, and Sri Lanka. Excessive inflation due to rising food prices was exacerbated by rising oil and gas prices at the onset of the Russian invasion of Ukraine in February 2022 (Figure 4.1). The US Federal Reserve Bank (the Fed) began raising the federal funds rate in March 2022, the first time it has done so since December 2018 (Government of the US, Board of Governors of the Federal Reserve System 2022a). Since then, the Fed has hiked it six consecutive

times, reaching a decade high benchmark interest rate (Government of the US, Board of Governors of the Federal Reserve System 2022b, 2022c, 2022d, 2022e, 2022f, 2022g). And federal funds futures indicate the Fed's policy tightening cycle has not peaked yet—indeed, they still point to a hawkish Fed stance. The assessment of the Federal Open Market Committee participants in December 2022, indicates that the Federal funds rate would likely peak in 2023 (Figure 4.2).

Figure 4.1: Selected Commodity Prices (January 2020 = 100)

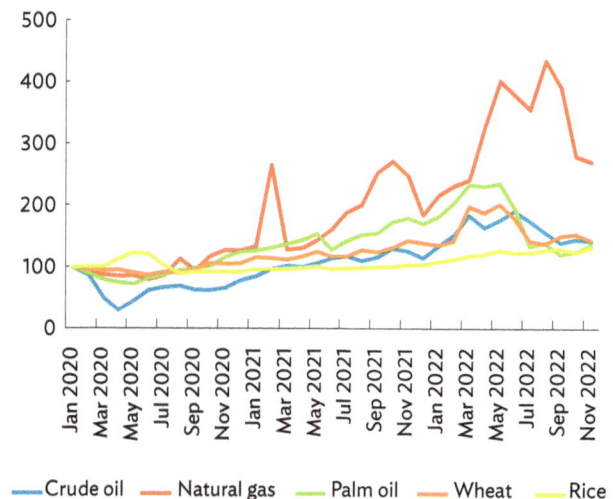

Notes: Crude oil refers to Brent crude oil. Natural gas refers to the United States Henry Hub middle spot price. Palm oil refers to the Malaysian Palm Oil Board Crude Palm Oil freight-on-board spot price. Wheat refers to the Chicago Board of Trade (CBOT) soft red winter wheat 1-month futures settlement price. Rice refers to CBOT rough rice 1-month futures settlement price.

Source: ADB calculations using data from CEIC Data Company.

---

[59] Asia and the Pacific, or Asia, refers to the 49 regional members of the Asian Development Bank (ADB), which includes Japan and Oceania (Australia and New Zealand) in addition to the 46 developing Asian economies. Subregional compositions for Central Asia, East Asia, the Pacific and Oceania, South Asia, and Southeast Asia are outlined in ADB. Asia Regional Integration Center. Economy Groupings. https://aric.adb.org/integrationindicators/groupings.

Figure 4.2: Federal Open Market Committee Participants' Assessments of Appropriate Monetary Policy (%)

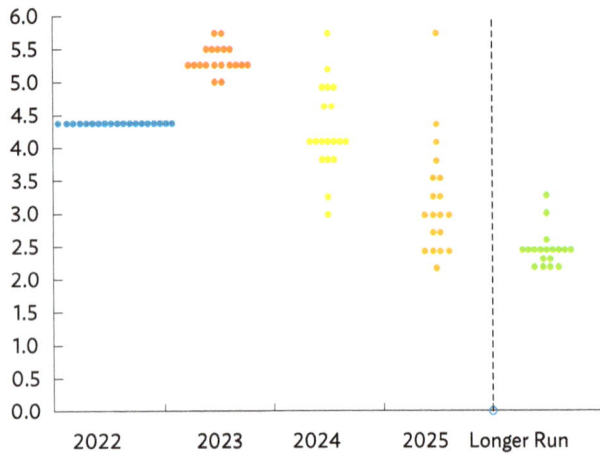

Notes:

(i) The policy rate refers to the midpoint of target range or target level for the federal funds rate.

(ii) Each shaded circle indicates the value (rounded to the nearest 1/8 percentage point) of an individual participant's judgment of the midpoint of the appropriate target range for the federal funds rate or the appropriate target level for the federal funds rate at the end of the specified calendar year or over the longer run. One participant did not submit longer-run projections for the federal funds rate.

Source: Government of the United States. Federal Reserve Board of Governors (2022h).

Global inflation pressures have prompted central banks to tighten monetary policy. The European Central Bank ended its Asset Purchase Program in June 2022 and raised all key interest rates in July 2022 (ECB 2022a and 2022b), as did other advanced economies such as Canada and the United Kingdom (Figure 4.3a). Asian economies have also started to raise key interest rates as coronavirus disease (COVID-19) inoculation rates rise and mobility restrictions loosen (Figure 4.3b). The People's Republic of China (PRC) has been the exception in easing monetary policy in 2022 amid worsening outlook in the property sector and overall sluggish economic recovery. Asian economies are increasingly concerned about domestic inflation pressures and potential capital inflow reversals stemming from narrowing interest rate differentials compared with advanced economies outside the region. However, tightening has been relatively more measured due to declining growth momentum as flagging external demand is anticipated amid sluggish global economic growth. Nevertheless, some economies in Central Asia— such as Armenia, Kazakhstan, and the Kyrgyz Republic— have increasingly widened their policy rate gap with that of the US in Q4 2022. Sri Lanka's policy rate gap has also widened amid the economic crisis (Figure 4.4). The yield

Figure 4.3: Benchmark Monetary Policy Rate (%)

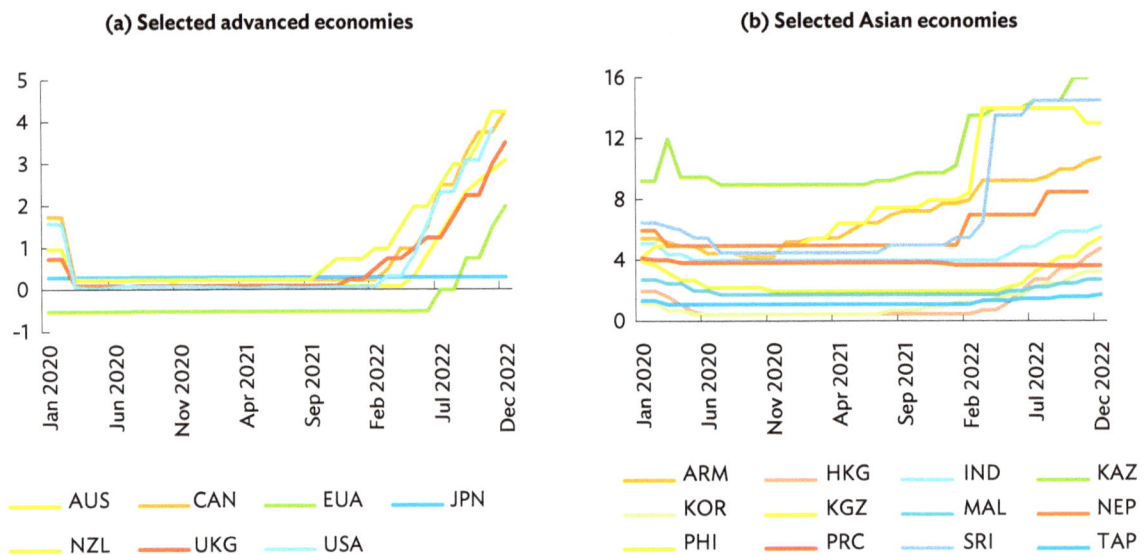

(a) Selected advanced economies

(b) Selected Asian economies

ARM = Armenia; AUS = Australia; CAN = Canada; EUA = euro area; HKG = Hong Kong, China; IND = India; JPN = Japan; KAZ = Kazakhstan; KOR = Republic of Korea; KGZ = Kyrgyz Republic; MAL = Malaysia; NEP = Nepal; NZL = New Zealand; PHI = Philippines; PRC = People's Republic of China; SRI = Sri Lanka; TAP = Taipei,China; UKG = United Kingdom; USA = United States.

Source: CEIC Data Company.

differential between the 2-year US bond and the 2-year bonds of selected Asian economies have narrowed, indeed, much narrower than the yield differential between the 10-year US bond yield and the 10-year bond yield of selected Asian economies. This also coincides with weakening local currency values in these Asian economies (Figures 4.5 and 4.6). Since the front end of the yield curve, particularly 2-year yields, is the most sensitive to changes in benchmark interest rates, this suggests that recent financial market developments are largely due to the divergent monetary policy stances of Asian economies and the US.

The synchronous global monetary policy tightening with faster-than-expected normalization of the US monetary policy has led to tighter financial conditions and heightened default risks for Asian economies, as reflected in credit default swaps (Figure 4.7). Junk bond yields in the euro area, the US, and most especially in Asia, have risen since Q2 2022 (Figure 4.8).

Figure 4.4: Policy Rate Differential with the United States Policy Rate—Selected Asian Economies (%)

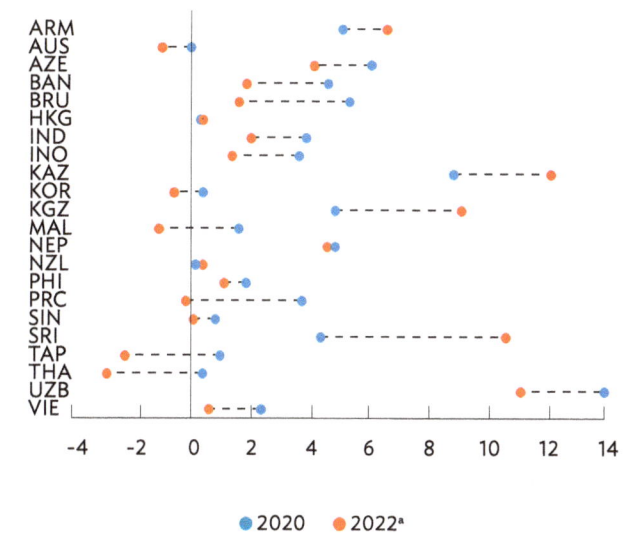

ARM = Armenia; AUS = Australia; AZE = Azerbaijan; BAN = Bangladesh; BRU = Brunei Darussalam; HKG = Hong Kong, China; IND = India; INO = Indonesia; KAZ = Kazakhstan; KOR = Republic of Korea; KGZ = Kyrgyz Republic; MAL = Malaysia; NEP = Nepal; NZL = New Zealand; PHI = Philippines; PRC = People's Republic of China; SIN = Singapore; SRI = Sri Lanka; TAP = Taipei,China; THA = Thailand; UZB = Uzbekistan; VIE = Viet Nam.

[a] As of November 2022.

Source: ADB calculations using data from CEIC Data Company.

Figure 4.5: 2-Year Bond Yields and Foreign Exchange Rate—Selected Asian Economies and the United States

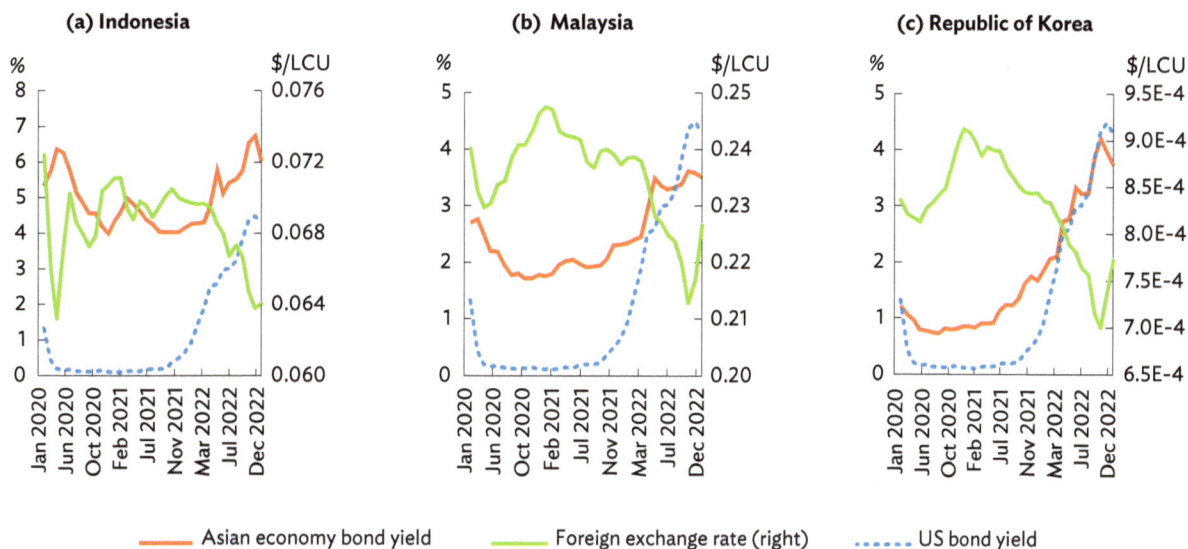

(a) Indonesia   (b) Malaysia   (c) Republic of Korea

Asian economy bond yield — Foreign exchange rate (right) ····· US bond yield

LCU = local currency unit, US = United States.

Source: ADB calculations using data from Bloomberg.

Figure 4.6: 10-Year Bond Yields and Foreign Exchange Rate—Selected Asian Economies and the United States

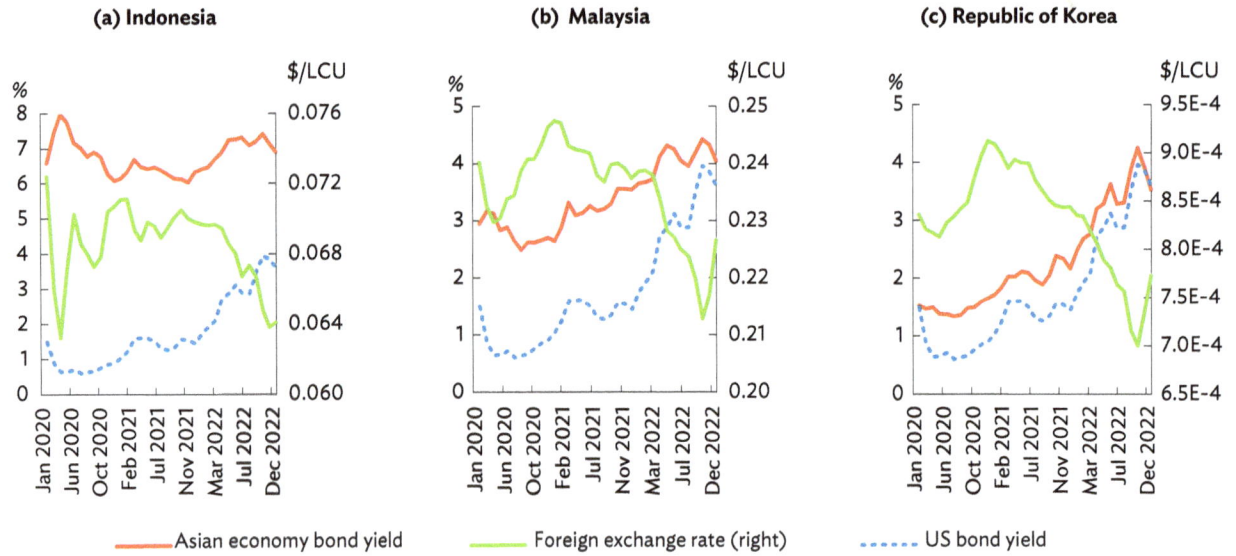

(a) Indonesia

(b) Malaysia

(c) Republic of Korea

— Asian economy bond yield   — Foreign exchange rate (right)   ····· US bond yield

LCU = local currency unit, US = United States.

Source: ADB calculations using data from Bloomberg.

Figure 4.7: Credit Default Swaps—Selected Asian Economies (2 January 2020 = 100)

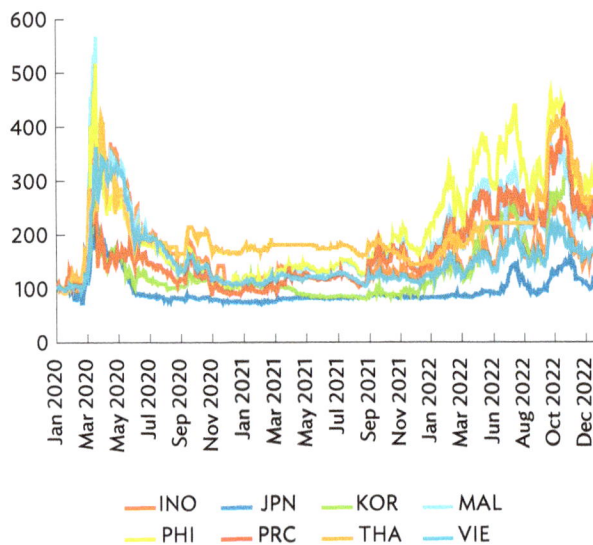

— INO   — JPN   — KOR   — MAL
— PHI   — PRC   — THA   — VIE

INO = Indonesia, JPN = Japan, KOR = Republic of Korea, MAL = Malaysia, PHI = Philippines, PRC = People's Republic of China, THA = Thailand, VIE = Viet Nam.

Notes: A credit default swap is a financial derivative that insures against the risk of default by one party. A higher index value reflects a higher spread, which is associated with higher default risk.

Source: ADB calculations using data from Bloomberg.

Figure 4.8: High Yield Indexes (%)

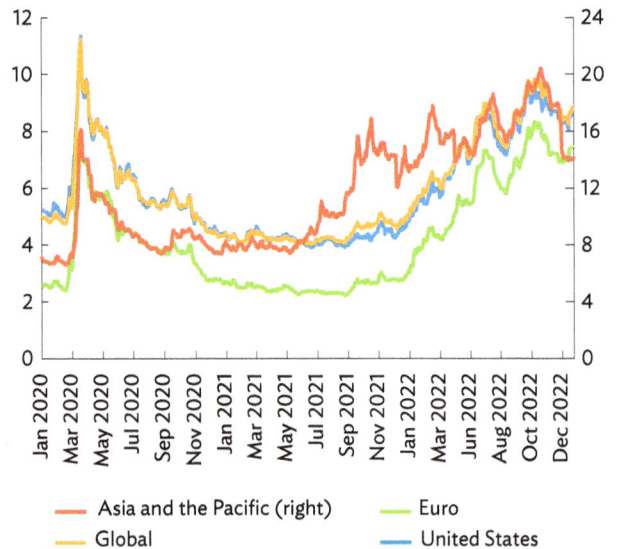

— Asia and the Pacific (right)   — Euro
— Global   — United States

ICE BofA = Intercontinental Exchange Bank of America.

Notes: Asia and the Pacific refers to the ICE BofA Asia Dollar High Yield Index. Euro refers to the ICE BofA Euro High Yield Index. Global refers to the ICE BofA Global High Yield Index. United States refers to the ICE BofA US High Yield Index.

Source: Bloomberg.

Growing uncertainty about global economic growth prospects and financial conditions is posing capital inflow reversal risks for the region, although the scale of outflows is still relatively light.

Nonresident portfolio inflows remained robust in 2021. Nonetheless, portfolio debt inflows had declined by 69% and portfolio equity inflows by 22% in December 2021 compared with December 2020 levels. This was primarily driven by a reversal in the PRC's portfolio debt flows amounting to $13.2 billion, coinciding with the strict lockdown in Shanghai during a COVID-19 outbreak. While nonresident capital inflows remained robust in 2021, nonresident portfolio inflows have declined and eventually reversed at the start of 2022. Since March 2022, nonresident portfolio inflows gradually declined. After marginally increasing in July and August 2022, it was back in the red as of September 2022, yet portfolio equity inflows has slightly recovered in November 2022. (Figure 4.9).

After the Fed began its interest rate raising cycle in March 2022, regional currencies further weakened in the first half of 2022 against the US dollar. The Sri Lanka rupee declined another 45% amid an economic crisis there; and the Japanese yen weakened, by 13%. On average, developing economies' currencies have weakened by 6.2% in 2022 (Figure 4.10).

Figure 4.9: Nonresident Portfolio Flows—Selected Asian Economies ($ billion)

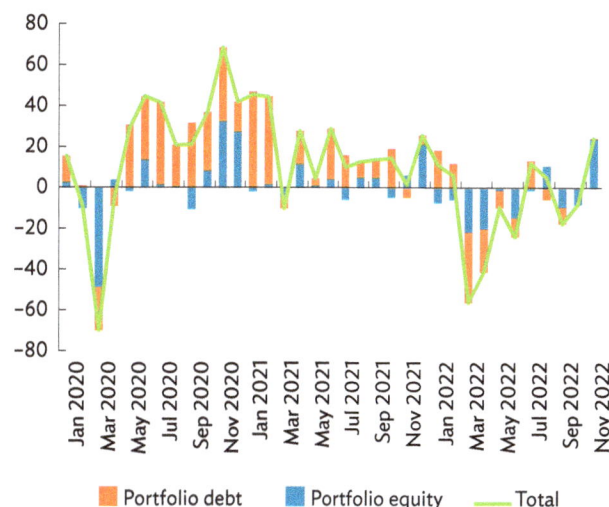

Note: The selected Asian economies are India; Indonesia; Malaysia; Mongolia; Pakistan; the People's Republic of China; the Philippines; the Republic of Korea; Sri Lanka (equity); Taipei,China (equity); Thailand; and Viet Nam (equity).

Source: ADB calculations using data from the Institute of International Finance. Monthly Emerging Markets Portfolio Flows Database. https://www.iif.com/Research/Download-Data#PortFlows (accessed December 2022).

On the policy front, safety nets were not expanding in 2022 to cope with exchange rate pressures. For example, the Fed's temporary dollar swap lines expired in 2021; in Asia, this swap line had provided $60 billion to the central banks of Australia, the Republic of Korea, and Singapore, and $30 billion to the Reserve Bank of New Zealand

Figure 4.10: Foreign Exchange Rate—Selected Asian Currencies ($/LCU)

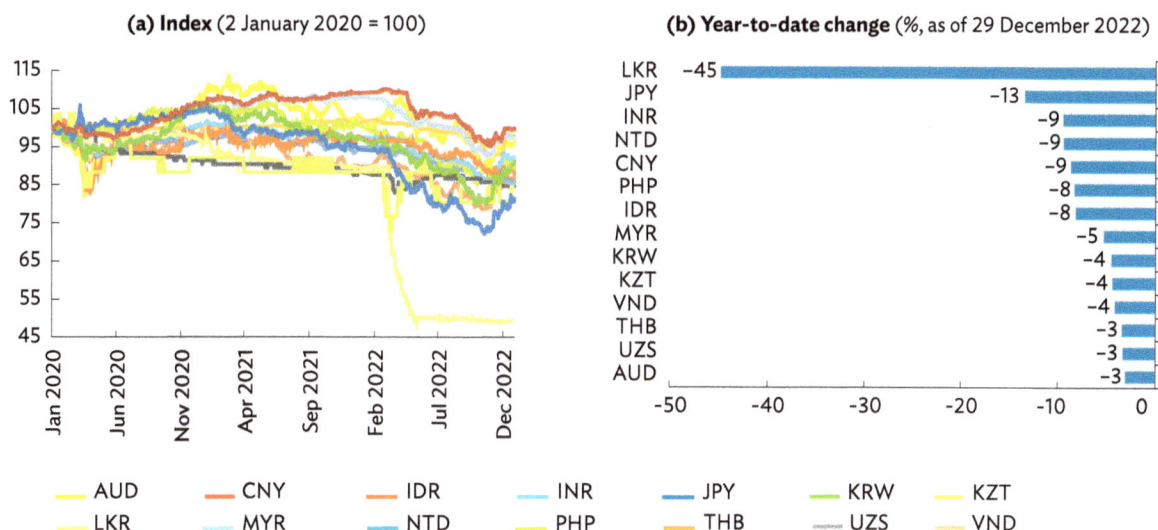

(a) Index (2 January 2020 = 100)

(b) Year-to-date change (%, as of 29 December 2022)

AUD = Australian dollar, CNY = yuan, IDR = rupiah, INR = Indian rupee, JPY = yen, KRW = won, KZT = tenge, LCU = local currency unit, LKR = Sri Lanka rupee, MYR = ringgit, NTD = NT dollar, PHP = peso, THB = baht, UZS = sum, VND = dong.

Source: ADB calculations using data from Bloomberg.

(Government of the US, Board of Governors of the Federal Reserve System 2021a). Nevertheless, some bilateral currency swap arrangements in the region were renewed, notably the currency swap arrangement between Japan and the Philippines, and Japan and India (Government of Japan, Ministry of Finance 2022a and 2022b). Bilateral swap arrangements between Australia and Indonesia, and between Indonesia and the PRC were also renewed (Government of Australia, Reserve Bank of Australia 2022; Government of the PRC, People's Bank of China 2022).

Tightening global financial market and liquidity conditions have raised capital market volatility and prompted asset price corrections across the region.

Monetary policy tightening due to globally synchronous inflation increased capital market volatility in the first half of 2022; it declined slightly in August 2022, but the volatility index started picking up again in September and October 2022 (Figure 4.11).

Figure 4.11: Volatility Index

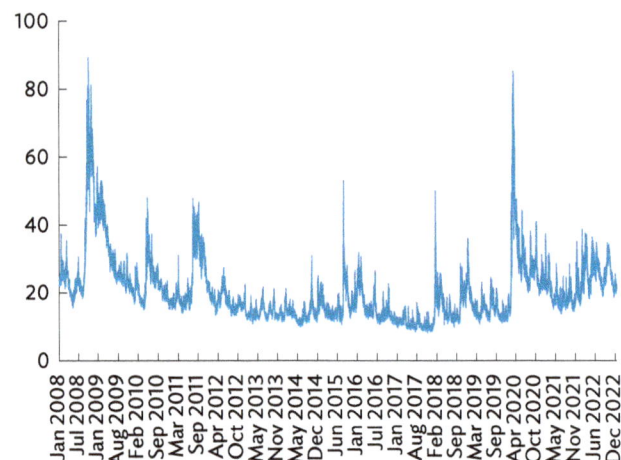

Notes: Volatility index (VIX) refers to the Chicago Board Options Exchange VIX Index's close value. High and low positions are plotted as confidence bands.

Source: Bloomberg.

Figure 4.12: Financial Stress Index

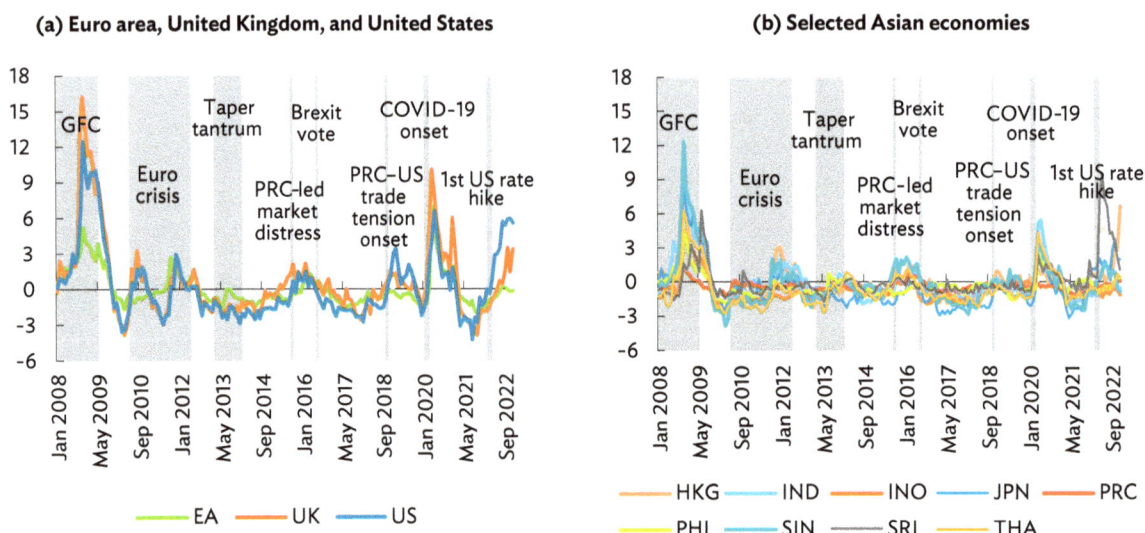

(a) Euro area, United Kingdom, and United States

(b) Selected Asian economies

COVID-19 = coronavirus disease; EA = euro area; GFC = global financial crisis; HKG = Hong Kong, China; IND = India; INO = Indonesia; JPN = Japan; PHI = Philippines; PRC = People's Republic of China; SIN = Singapore; THA = Thailand; UK = United Kingdom; US = United States.

Notes:

i.   Based on principal components analysis on data from four major finance sectors: banking, debt, equity, and foreign exchange markets.

ii.   Principal components are based on the banking sector price index, sovereign yield spreads, stock market volatility, stock price index return, and exchange market pressure index.

Sources: ADB. Asia Regional Integration Center. Financial Stress Index. https://aric.adb.org/database/fsi (accessed January 2023); and methodology by Park and Mercado (2014).

The heightened financial market risks are evident in the upward trend of the financial stress index and sovereign stripped spreads, both in advanced and emerging Asian economies (Figures 4.12 and 4.13). The financial stress index's uptick in advanced economies is more pronounced at the end of Q3 2022.

Tightening global financial market conditions and nonresident capital inflow reversals in 2022 have accelerated capital market corrections. Stock prices in the region have generally declined since the beginning of the year. Sri Lanka's stock market plunged 33%, following its announcement in April 2022 that it would suspend its debt payments. In May 2022, Sri Lanka finally defaulted on its debt payments for the first time in history. While stock prices in India, Indonesia, and Singapore increased, they declined elsewhere, and by more than 15% in Hong Kong, China; the PRC; the Republic of Korea; Sri Lanka; Taipei,China; and Viet Nam. Stock prices in Australia, Japan, Kazakhstan, and the Philippines have all gone down more than 5% (Figure 4.14).

The prices of sovereign bonds of selected Asian economies have mostly declined in 2022. Prices rose only in India and the PRC in 2022 (Figure 4.15). Sovereign bond prices diverged in 2021 and widened

further in 2022 as a broad-based search for yield by investors gradually subsided and the pace of economic recoveries in the region varied.

Figure 4.13: Sovereign Stripped Spreads (basis points)

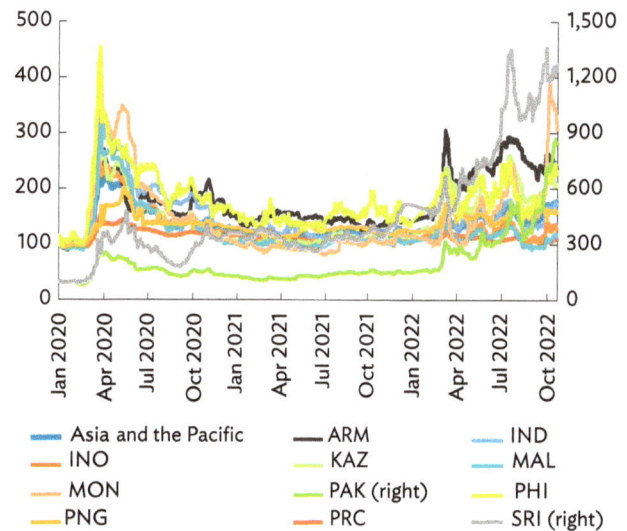

ARM = Armenia, EMBIG = Emerging Markets Bond Index Global, IND = India, INO = Indonesia, KAZ = Kazakhstan, MAL = Malaysia, MON = Mongolia, PAK = Pakistan, PHI = Philippines, PNG = Papua New Guinea, PRC = People's Republic of China, SRI = Sri Lanka.

Note: Asia and the Pacific refers to the JP Morgan EMBIG Asia Sovereign Spread.

Source: ADB calculations using data from Bloomberg.

Figure 4.14: Stock Price Index—Selected Asian Economies

(a) Index (2 January 2020 = 100)

(b) Year-to-date change (%, as of 29 December 2022)

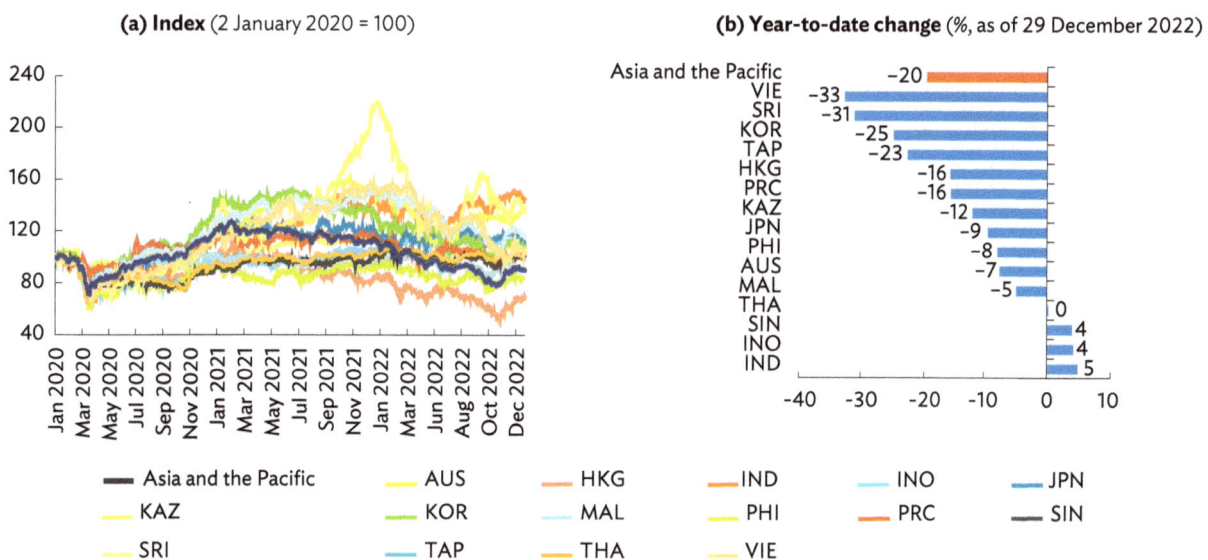

AUS = Australia; HKG = Hong Kong, China; IND = India; INO = Indonesia; JPN = Japan; KAZ = Kazakhstan; KOR = Republic of Korea; MAL = Malaysia; PHI = Philippines; PRC = People's Republic of China; SIN = Singapore; SRI = Sri Lanka; TAP = Taipei,China; THA = Thailand; and VIE = Viet Nam.

Note: Asia and the Pacific refers to the MSCI Asia Index.

Source: ADB calculations using data from Bloomberg.

Figure 4.15: Total Bond Return Index—Selected Asian Economies

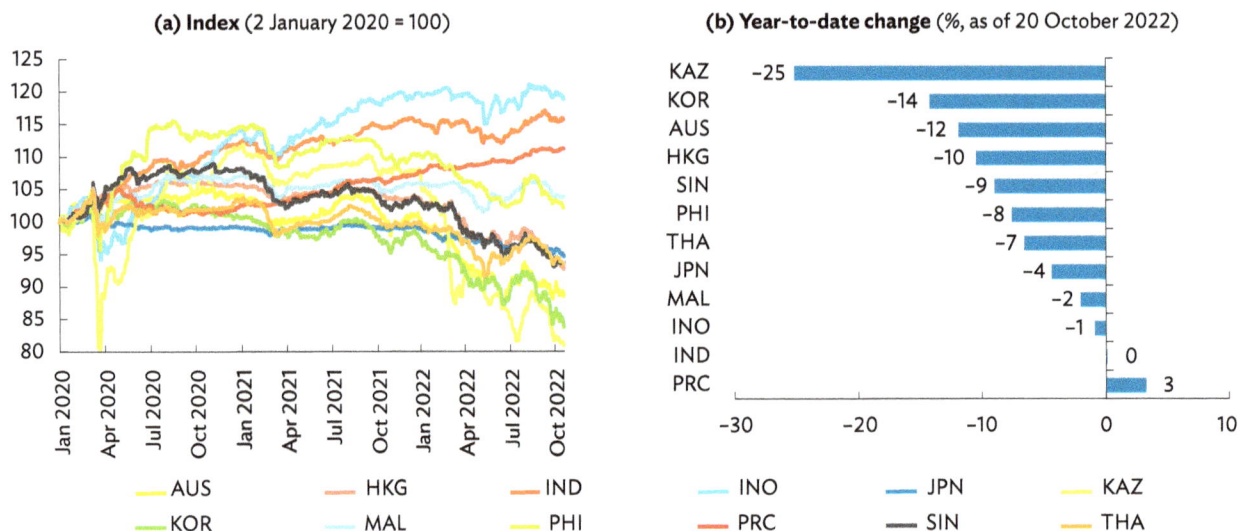

(a) Index (2 January 2020 = 100)

(b) Year-to-date change (%, as of 20 October 2022)

AUS = Australia; HKG = Hong Kong, China; IND = India; INO = Indonesia; JPN = Japan; KAZ = Kazakhstan; KOR = Republic of Korea; MAL = Malaysia; PHI = Philippines; PRC = People's Republic of China; SIN = Singapore; and THA = Thailand.

Source: ADB calculations using data from Bloomberg.

Figure 4.16: Volume of Corporate Bond Issuance and Policy Rate—Selected Asian Economies

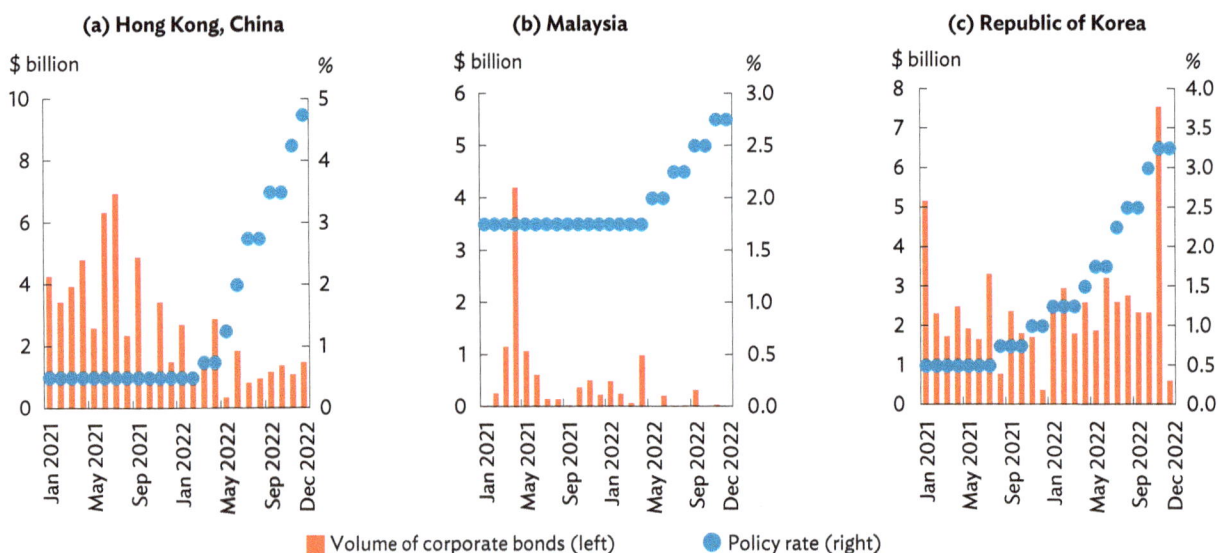

(a) Hong Kong, China

(b) Malaysia

(c) Republic of Korea

■ Volume of corporate bonds (left)   ● Policy rate (right)

Sources: ADB calculations using data from Bloomberg and CEIC Data Company.

Tightening financial market conditions raised strains in the credit market, as shown in the recent decline in volume of corporate bond issuances alongside policy rate hikes in some economies in the region (Figure 4.16).

The share of global shocks that explain the variation of equity returns in Asia increased from 20% at the onset of the COVID-19 pandemic to 26% in the most recent period (Figure 4.17). The share of regional shocks also grew from 9% at the onset of the pandemic to 11% recently. Across subregions, East Asia's equity markets witnessed a large increase in sensitivity to regional shocks during these periods. In contrast, responsiveness to global factors increased noticeably in Central Asia and South Asia. Responsiveness to regional shocks dropped in South Asia. Meanwhile, the share of domestic shocks explaining the variation of equity returns declined from 71% in the COVID-19 onset period to about 63% recently.

Figure 4.17: Variance Decomposition for Equity Returns—Asia and the Pacific (%)

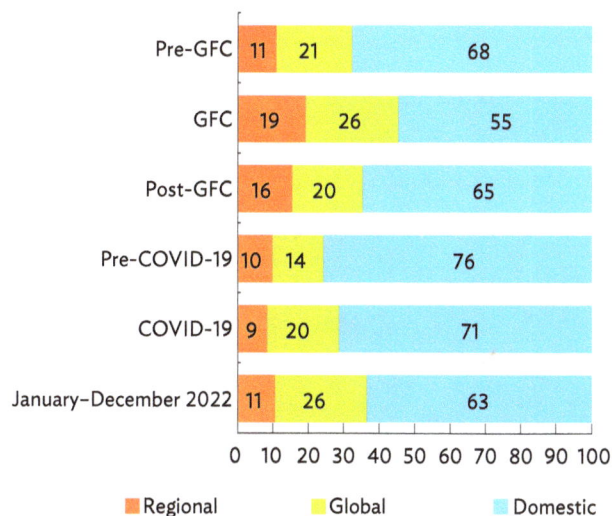

COVID-19 = coronavirus disease, GFC = global financial crisis.

Pre-GFC = January 2005 to September 2007, GFC = October 2007 to June 2009, Post-GFC = July 2009 to December 2011, Pre-COVID-19 = January 2018 to December 2019, COVID-19 = January 2020 to December 2021.

Sources: ADB calculations using data from Bloomberg; CEIC Data Company; and methodology by Lee and Park (2011).

Figure 4.18: Variance Decomposition of Bond Returns—Asia and the Pacific (%)

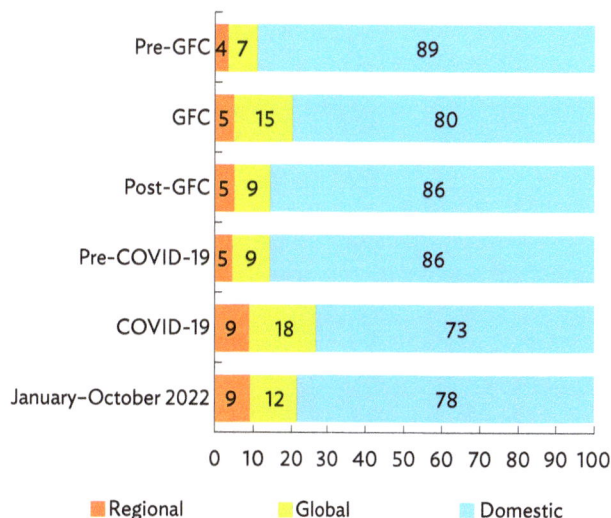

COVID-19 = coronavirus disease, GFC = global financial crisis.

Pre-GFC = January 2005 to September 2007, GFC = October 2007 to June 2009, Post-GFC = July 2009 to December 2011, Pre-COVID-19 = January 2018 to December 2019, COVID-19 = January 2020 to December 2021.

Sources: ADB calculations using data from Bloomberg; CEIC Data Company; and methodology by Lee and Park (2011).

The proportion of global shocks that explain the variation of bond returns declined to 12% in the most recent period, compared with the COVID-19 onset period, at 18%. Meanwhile the proportion of regional shocks that explained the variation of bond returns increased slightly to 9.2% from 8.9%. (Figure 4.18).

Across subregions, the increase in the share of global shocks between the COVID-19 onset period and the most recent period was highest for India, while the increase in the proportion of regional shocks was largest for Australia and New Zealand. The share of domestic shocks explaining the variation of bond returns increased from 73% in the COVID-19 onset period to 78% during the most recent period.

Rising global interest rates, weakening domestic currencies, and constrained fiscal spaces amid the pandemic might have exposed some economies in the region to increasing debt servicing costs and debt management problems.

Slow domestic economic recovery, alongside higher interest rates could make debt servicing difficult—even

more so for dollar-dominated external debts, as the US dollar continues to strengthen. The debt servicing ratio of the nonfinancial private sector had risen slightly by Q2 2022 in Hong Kong, China; the PRC; and the Republic of Korea; this ratio declined in India, Malaysia, and Thailand (Figure 4.19).

Figure 4.19: Debt Service Ratio of the Nonfinancial Private Sector (%)

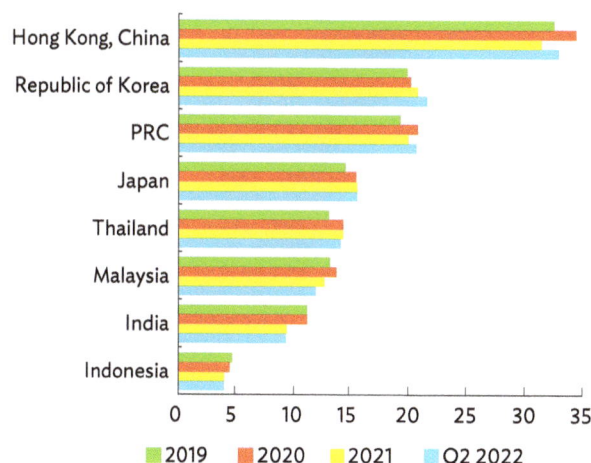

PRC = People's Republic of China, Q2 = second quarter.

Source: Haver Analytics.

As governments and corporations borrowed to weather the pandemic, total, corporate, and sovereign debt ratios increased in the region (Figure 4.20). Between 2019 and Q2 2022, changes in corporate debt ratios for Hong Kong, China; Japan; the Republic of Korea; and Singapore had been greater than 20% of gross domestic product (GDP), while the changes in the sovereign debt of Japan, the Lao People's Democratic Republic, Maldives, the Philippines, Singapore, and Sri Lanka also exceeded 20% of GDP.

As economies in the region rely heavily on bank credit for corporate financing, it adds to concerns as interest rates rise (Figure 4.21). Overall corporate financing rose

Figure 4.20: Sectoral Debt Ratio—Selected Asian Economies (% of GDP)

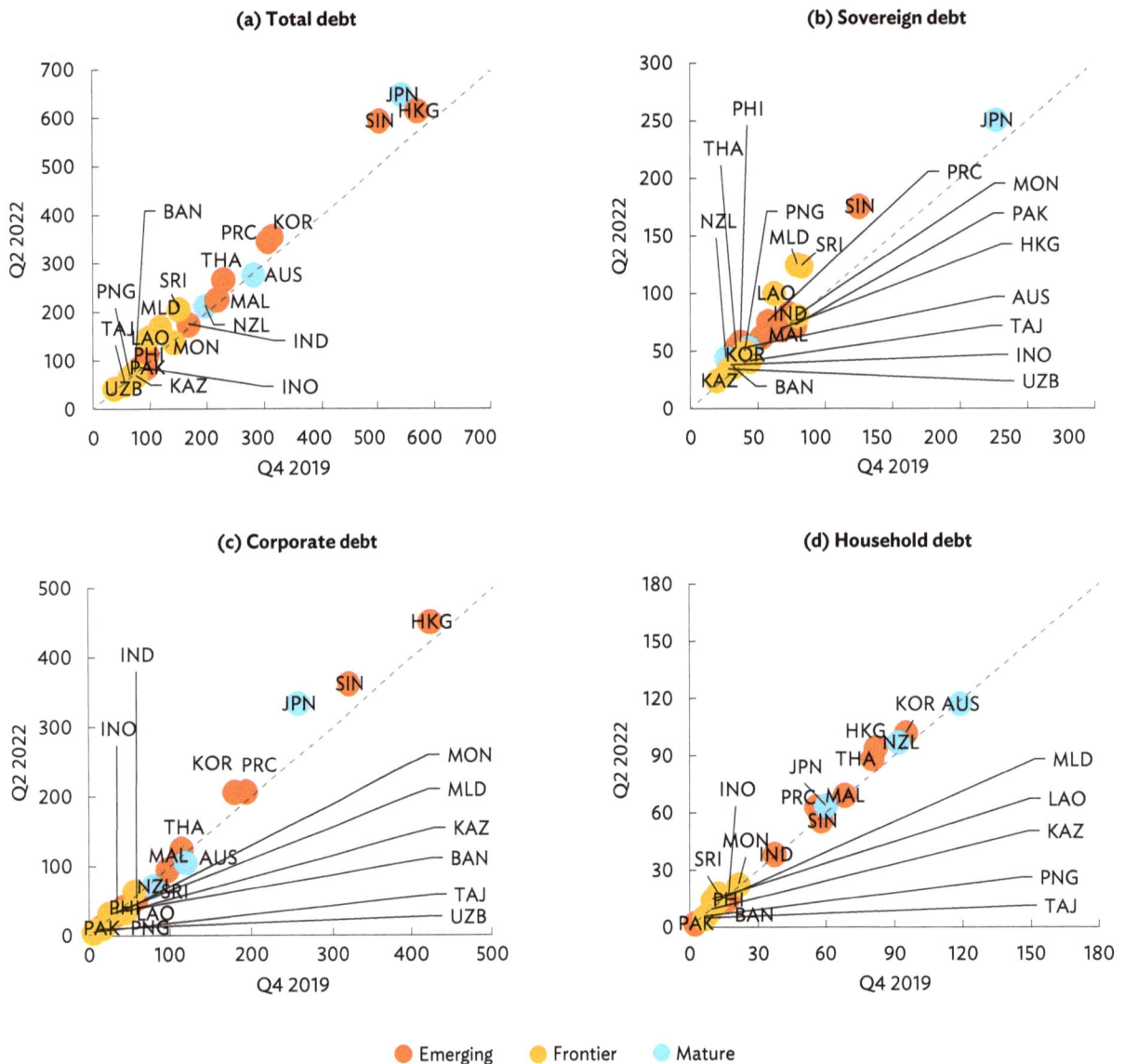

(a) Total debt

(b) Sovereign debt

(c) Corporate debt

(d) Household debt

● Emerging   ● Frontier   ● Mature

AUS = Australia; BAN = Bangladesh; GDP = gross domestic product; HKG = Hong Kong, China; IND = India; INO = Indonesia; JPN = Japan, KAZ = Kazakhstan; KOR = Republic of Korea; LAO = Lao People's Democratic Republic; MAL = Malaysia; MLD = Maldives; MON = Mongolia; NZL = New Zealand; PAK = Pakistan; PHI = Philippines; PNG = Papua New Guinea; PRC = People's Republic of China; Q = quarter; SIN = Singapore; SRI = Sri Lanka; TAJ = Tajikistan; THA = Thailand; and UZB = Uzbekistan.

Notes: Economy grouping based on Institute of International Finance definition. Emerging Asian economies include HKG, IND, INO, KOR, MAL, PAK, PHI, PRC, SIN, and THA. Frontier Asian economies include BAN, KAZ, LAO, MLD, MON, PNG, SRI, TAJ, and UZB. Mature Asian economies include AUS, JPN, and NZL.

Sources: ADB calculations using data from Institute of International Finance (IIF). Frontier Debt Monitor Database November 2022. https://www.iif.com/Research/Download-Data#DebtMonitors (accessed December 2022); and IIF. Global Debt Monitor September 2022. https://www.iif.com/Research/Capital-Flows-and-Debt/Global-Debt-Monitor (accessed October 2022).

in 2020 and 2021 due to elevated financing needs in navigating the pandemic-related business challenges, but started to decline in 2022. Comparing Q3 2021 and Q3 2022, debt, equity, and bank financing have all declined. This could reflect diminishing financing needs for companies as economies gradually return to a more normal status. But it could also be due to dwindling financing opportunities for them under the tightening financial market environment.

Figure 4.21: Corporate Financing—Emerging Asia (% of GDP)

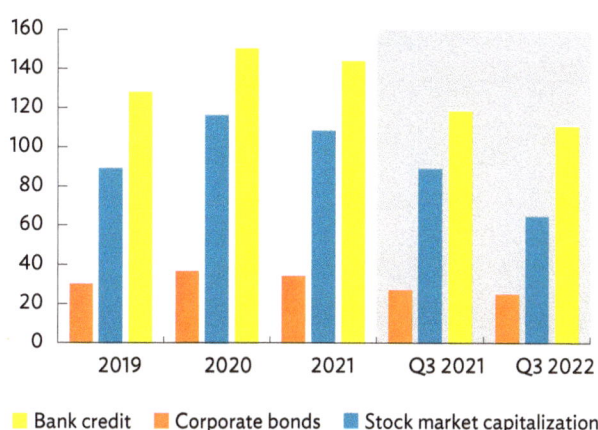

GDP = gross domestic product.

Note: Emerging Asia includes Hong Kong, China; India; Indonesia; Malaysia; the People's Republic of China; the Philippines; the Republic of Korea; Singapore; Thailand; and Viet Nam.

Sources: ADB calculations using data from ADB. AsianBondsOnline. Data Portal: Bond Market. https://asianbondsonline.adb.org/data-portal (accessed January 2023); and CEIC Data Company.

Higher corporate debt levels along with rising debt servicing costs under rising interest rates could pose risks to financial market stability as well. Should corporations be unable to make their debt payments on time, banks' asset quality could deteriorate. Bank profitability has declined based on return-on-assets and return-on-equity ratios, except in a few regional economies, such as India and the Philippines (Figures 4.22a and 4.22b). In particular, return on asset and return on equity have declined for Hong Kong, China; the PRC; the Republic of Korea; and Thailand. Nonetheless, gross interest margin and capital-to-assets ratio for these economies are staying at a relatively stable level when compared with their pre-pandemic levels (Figures 4.22c and 4.22d).

The nonperforming loan (NPL) ratio is already high in the banking sector in 2022 (Figure 4.23). For instance,

India's NPL ratio increased from 1.2% in 2019 to 5.8% by March 2022; the Philippines' from 2.0% in 2019 to 3.4% in October 2022; and the Kyrgyz Republic's from 7.6% in 2019 to 12.9% in November 2022. The NPL ratios of Cambodia; Hong Kong, China; Indonesia; Malaysia; and Viet Nam are all higher than their pre-pandemic levels. Higher interest rates and rising NPL ratios may prompt banks to be more cautious in lending, which could lead to shortages in credit for businesses, jeopardizing prospects of stronger recovery in the real sector.

Evolving financial market conditions in the region and the potential negative spillovers from inside and outside the region should be closely monitored and assessed for effective policy responses.

The variance decomposition for equity returns indicates that economies are increasingly more exposed to regional shocks. Heightened financial risk and increased capital market volatility in one part of the region could easily spread to neighboring economies. Where appropriate, central banks in the region should raise benchmark interest rates gradually to contain inflation pressures and stem the risks of capital flow reversals. The need for such measures has yet to be vetted against domestic economy status as blind monetary policy tightening could entail unintended side effects under weakening consumer sentiment and heightened corporate and household debt levels. History demonstrates that rigid foreign exchange regimes can exacerbate capital flow reversals. Economic conditions permitting, enhancing foreign exchange rate flexibility could provide a buffer to improve the stability of the domestic economy.

The Association of Southeast Asian Nations (ASEAN) plus 3 economies in the region can count on and tap the improved Chiang Mai Initiative Multilateralisation agreement when such need arises. In March 2021, members amended the agreement to increase the International Monetary Fund De-linked Portion to 40% from 30% within the total size of $240 billion (AMRO 2021). It is essential that economies in the region be made aware of the availability of this instrument, in the light of shrinking fiscal space (Ferrarini, Giugale, and Pradelli 2022). The ASEAN+3 Multi-Currency Bond

Figure 4.22: Bank Profitability Indicators—Selected Asian Economies (%)

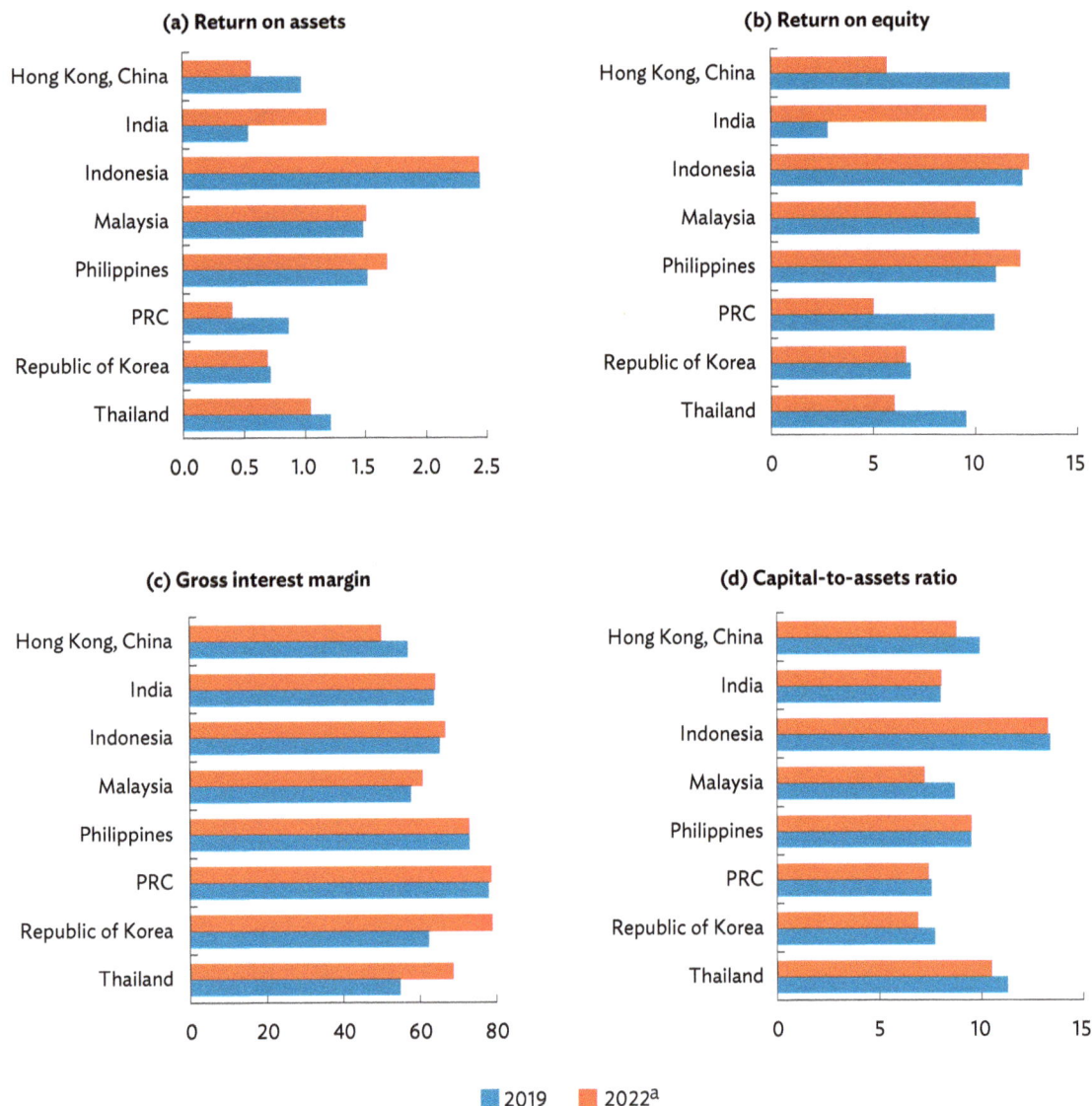

(a) Return on assets

(b) Return on equity

(c) Gross interest margin

(d) Capital-to-assets ratio

■ 2019 ■ 2022[a]

PRC = People's Republic of China.

[a] As of the first quarter (Q1) of 2022 for India and Thailand; as of Q2 2022 for Hong Kong, China; the Philippines; the PRC; and the Republic of Korea; and as of Q3 2022 for Indonesia and Malaysia.

Source: Haver Analytics.

Issuance Framework, a policy initiative under the Asian Bond Markets Initiative could promote a common bond issuance program in the region, reducing the need for non-regional foreign currency borrowing.

Higher interest rates have led to sluggish equity markets in the region, but offer an opportunity to expand local currency bond markets by broadening investor bases as yield-seeking investors might turn to high yield bonds.

Ferrarini, Giugale, and Pradelli (2022) note that thematic bonds have become a "major alternative source of funding for countries and companies ready to make commitments on the use of the proceeds." This should be considered in the development of local currency bond markets. A more in-depth discussion of sustainability and sustainability-linked bonds can be found in Chapter 7: Theme Chapter—Trade, Investment, and Climate Change in Asia and the Pacific.

Figure 4.23: Bank Nonperforming Loan Ratio—Selected Asian Economies (% of total loans)

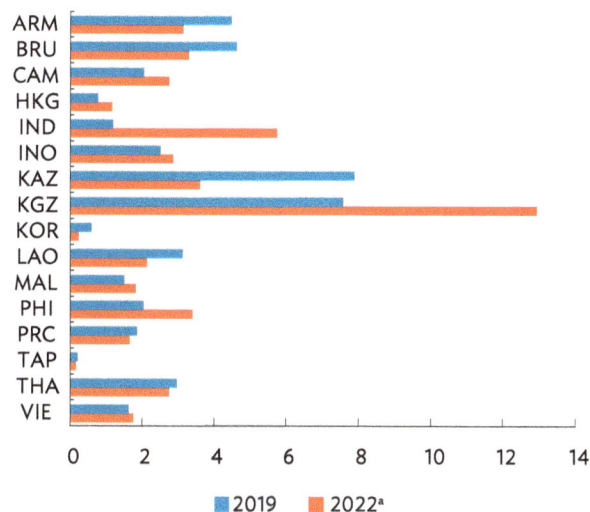

ARM = Armenia; BRU = Brunei Darussalam; CAM = Cambodia; HKG = Hong Kong, China; IND = India; INO = Indonesia; KAZ = Kazakhstan; KGZ = Kyrgyz Republic; KOR = Republic of Korea; LAO = Lao People's Democratic Republic; MAL = Malaysia; PHI = Philippines; PRC = People's Republic of China; TAP = Taipei,China; THA = Thailand; VIE = Viet Nam.

a As of March 2022 for IND; as of August 2022 for INO; as of September 2022 for BRU, CAM, HKG, LAO, PRC, THA, and VIE; as of October 2022 for KOR, PHI, and TAP; and as of November 2022 for ARM, KAZ, and KGZ.

Source: ADB calculations using data from CEIC Data Company.

Asia continues to invest more outside the region but became increasingly integrated in 2021.

Asia's total cross-border financial asset holdings reached $27 trillion as of 2021, which was significantly greater than $19 trillion reported as of the end of 2017 (Figure 4.24). Most of the region's investment holdings in 2021 were foreign direct investment (FDI) assets ($10 trillion), followed by portfolio equity ($7 trillion) and portfolio debt ($5 trillion), and then banking sector loan and deposit holdings ($4 trillion). About two-thirds of Asia's asset holdings were placed in non-regional economies, and only one-third in regional economies. Between 2017 and 2021, investment in the region grew from 33% to 36%.

The value of Asia's cross-border portfolio debt assets declined by $280 billion in 2021 from 2020 (Figure 4.25a). The $21 billion increase in the value of US bond holdings was not enough to offset the declines in portfolio debt investments from the region (-$63 billion), the European Union (EU) (-$162 billion), and the rest of the world (-$77 billion). While Asia's cross-border portfolio equity assets increased by $590 billion in 2021, this is only about half the increase

Figure 4.24: Cross-Border Assets—Asia and the Pacific

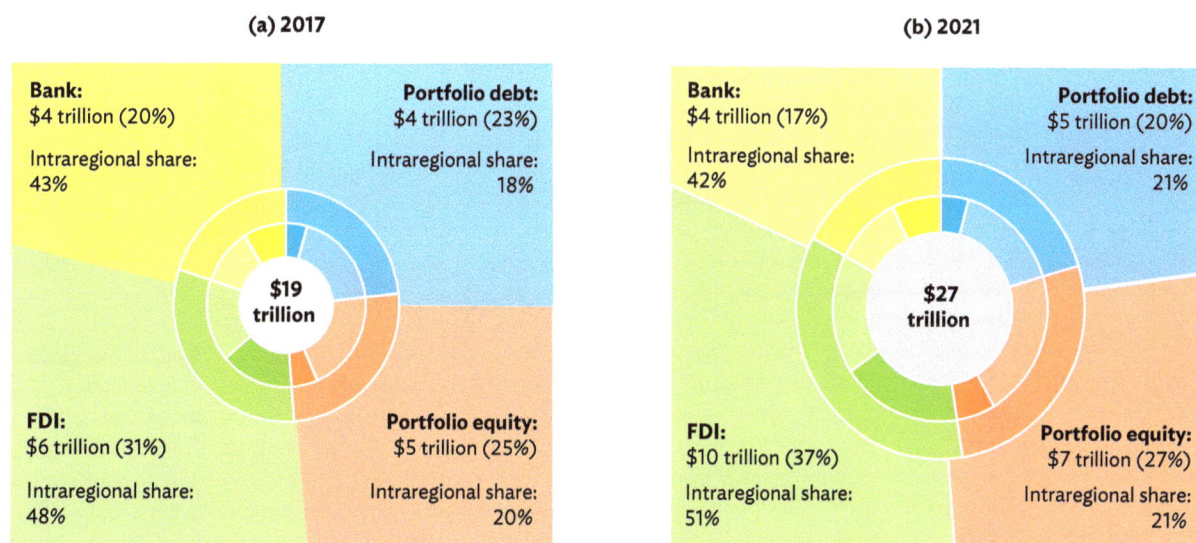

(a) 2017

Bank:
$4 trillion (20%)
Intraregional share:
43%

Portfolio debt:
$4 trillion (23%)
Intraregional share:
18%

$19 trillion

FDI:
$6 trillion (31%)
Intraregional share:
48%

Portfolio equity:
$5 trillion (25%)
Intraregional share:
20%

(b) 2021

Bank:
$4 trillion (17%)
Intraregional share:
42%

Portfolio debt:
$5 trillion (20%)
Intraregional share:
21%

$27 trillion

FDI:
$10 trillion (37%)
Intraregional share:
51%

Portfolio equity:
$7 trillion (27%)
Intraregional share:
21%

FDI = foreign direct investment.

Notes: FDI assets refer to outward FDI holdings. Bank assets (claims) are limited to loans and deposits.

Sources: ADB calculations using data from Bank for International Settlements. Locational Banking Statistics. https://www.bis.org/statistics/bankstats.htm (accessed April 2022); International Monetary Fund (IMF). Coordinated Direct Investment Survey. https://data.imf.org/cdis (accessed December 2022); and IMF. Coordinated Portfolio Investment Survey. https://data.imf.org/cpis (accessed September 2022).

in the region's portfolio equity assets in 2020 (Figure 4.25b). This was due to the reversal of equity investment to the rest of the world, from an increase of $393 billion in 2020 to a decrease of $107 billion in 2021. The increase was due to the region's investment in the EU (+$91 billion), intraregionally (+$95 billion), and in the US (+$510 billion).

In terms of cross-border banking flows, loan and deposit asset flows grew, from $51 billion in 2020 to $127 billion in 2021. Much of the increase can be attributed to the rebound in banking flows to the rest of the world and increase of intraregional banking flows. Asia's loan and deposit inflows reversed from –$33 billion in 2019 to $20 billion in 2021 as the region's intra-loan and deposit liabilities grew to $51 billion from $29 billion (Figure 4.26).

The region's total external financial liabilities also inched higher to $27 trillion in 2021, up from $21 trillion in 2017. Much of the region's liabilities were FDI ($11 trillion),

Figure 4.25: Change in Outward Portfolio Investment—Asia and the Pacific ($ billion)

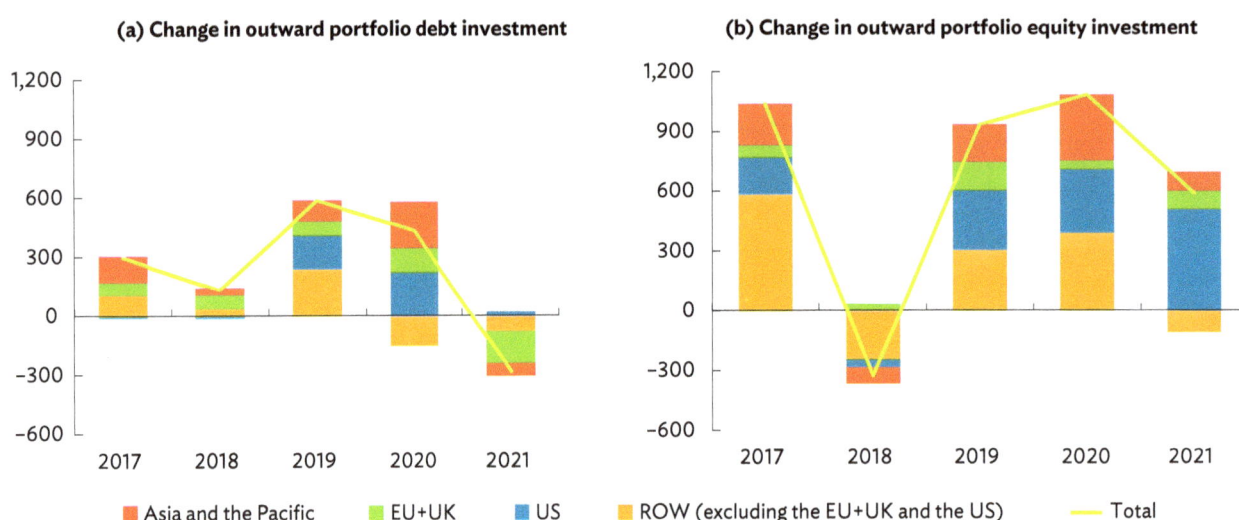

EU = European Union (27 members), ROW = rest of the world, UK = United Kingdom, US = United States.

Source: ADB calculations using data from International Monetary Fund. Coordinated Portfolio Investment Survey. https://data.imf.org/cpis (accessed September 2022).

Figure 4.26: Cross-Border Loans and Deposit Flows—Asia and the Pacific ($ billion)

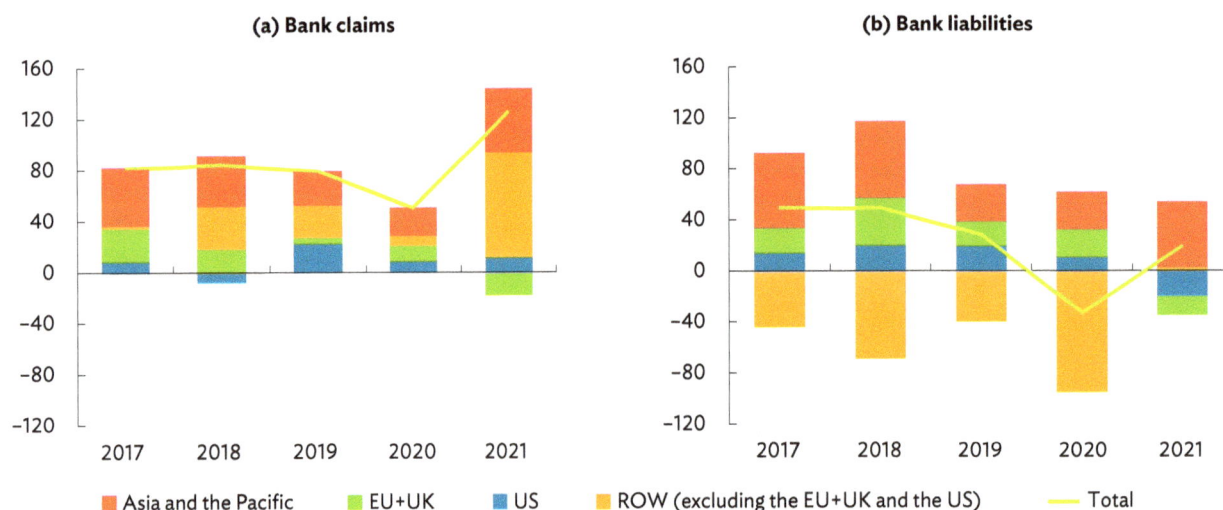

EU = European Union (27 members), ROW = rest of the world, UK = United Kingdom, US = United States.

Source: ADB calculations using data from the Bank for International Settlements. Locational Banking Statistics. https://www.bis.org/statistics/bankstats.htm (accessed April 2022).

followed by portfolio equity ($7 trillion), banking sector loan and deposit liabilities ($5 trillion), then portfolio debt ($4 trillion). As in previous years, about two-thirds of the region's external investment liabilities were held by non-regional economies and one-third by regional economies (Figure 4.27). Intraregional portfolio debt share has gradually increased to 29% in 2021 from 28% in 2017. Intraregional portfolio equity share increased to 21% from 18%, and bank loan and deposit inflow ratio increased to 38% from 37% in the same time period. The stronger regional financial integration could help recycle a greater portion of regional savings into regional investments. The growing financial interconnectedness, however, also highlights the risks of cross-border spillovers and contagion effects, which might be triggered by regional shocks and financial distress. Economies in the region could strengthen an array of safety nets, such as their international foreign exchange reserves, bilateral swap arrangements, and regional financial arrangements like the Chiang Mai Initiative Multilateralisation. Policy measures to help address the potential adverse impacts of global and regional shocks could include temporary capital flow management and foreign exchange measures, and macroprudential arrangements.

As Asia's outward portfolio debt investment declined in 2021, the portfolio debt investment into the region grew slightly, by $32 billion, with investment from the US (+$44 billion) and the EU (+$52 billion), but was offset by the decline in intraregional portfolio (–$63 billion) and investment from the rest of the world (–$0.3 billion). The portfolio equity investment into the region also grew in 2021 by $213 billion, but less than its growth in 2019 (+$864 billion) and 2020 (+$1 trillion). While the region contributed $95 billion to the growth, the EU contributed $142 billion and the US contributed $133 billion, investment into the rest of the world declined by $157 billion (Figure 4.28).

Special Topic: The Issue of Dollar Dependence in Financing and Trade Invoicing

The US dollar remains the dominant currency of the region's international investment. About 44% of the region's international asset holdings was denominated

Figure 4.27: Cross-Border Liabilities—Asia and the Pacific

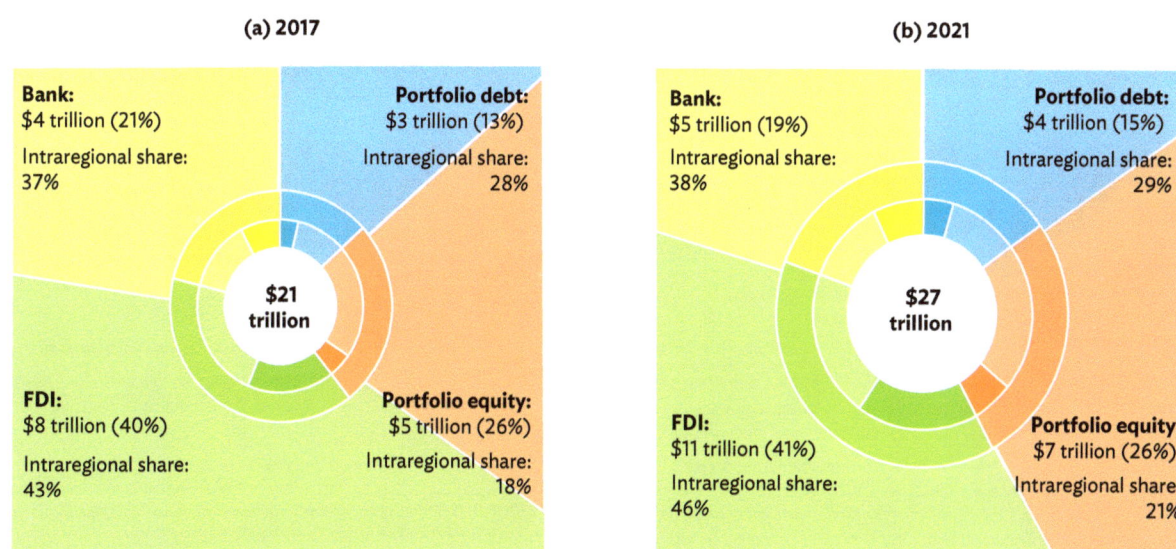

(a) 2017

Bank: $4 trillion (21%) — Intraregional share: 37%
Portfolio debt: $3 trillion (13%) — Intraregional share: 28%
FDI: $8 trillion (40%) — Intraregional share: 43%
Portfolio equity: $5 trillion (26%) — Intraregional share: 18%
$21 trillion

(b) 2021

Bank: $5 trillion (19%) — Intraregional share: 38%
Portfolio debt: $4 trillion (15%) — Intraregional share: 29%
FDI: $11 trillion (41%) — Intraregional share: 46%
Portfolio equity: $7 trillion (26%) — Intraregional share: 21%
$27 trillion

FDI = foreign direct investment.

Notes: FDI liabilities refer to inward FDI holdings. Bank liabilities are limited to loans and deposits.

Sources: ADB calculations using data from Bank for International Settlements. Locational Banking Statistics. https://www.bis.org/statistics/bankstats.htm (accessed April 2022); International Monetary Fund (IMF). Coordinated Direct Investment Survey. https://data.imf.org/cdis (accessed December 2022); and IMF. Coordinated Portfolio Investment Survey. https://data.imf.org/cpis (accessed September 2022).

Figure 4.28: Change in Inward Portfolio Investment—Asia and the Pacific ($ billion)

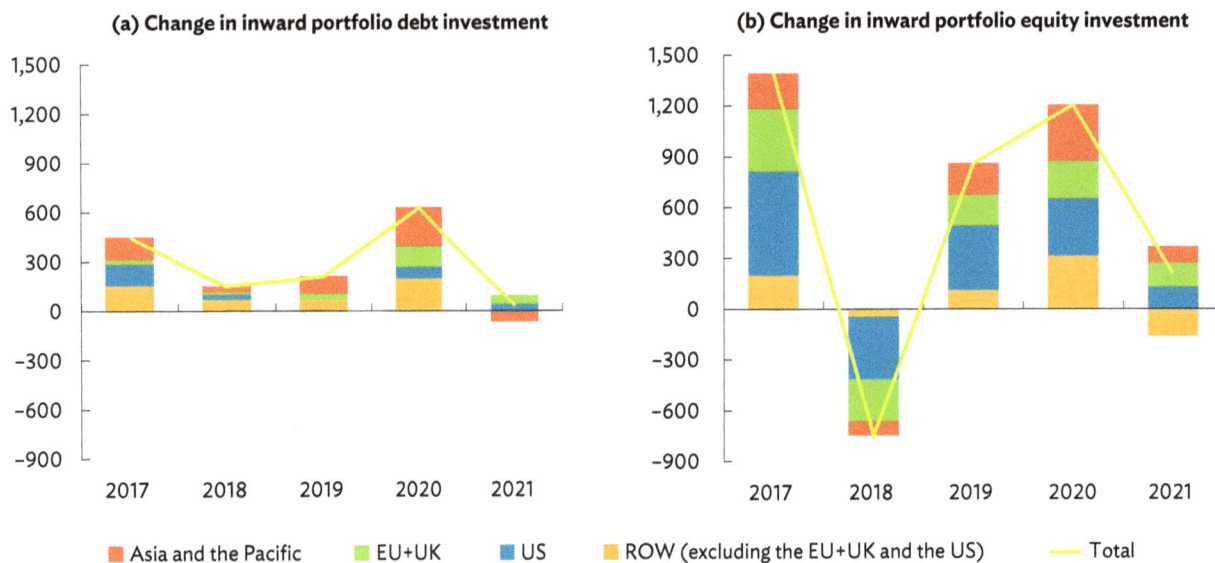

(a) Change in inward portfolio debt investment

(b) Change in inward portfolio equity investment

Asia and the Pacific   EU+UK   US   ROW (excluding the EU+UK and the US)   — Total

EU = European Union (27 members), ROW = rest of the world, UK = United Kingdom, US = United States.

Source: ADB calculations using data from International Monetary Fund. Coordinated Portfolio Investment Survey. https://data.imf.org/cpis (accessed September 2022).

Figure 4.29: Currency Composition of Asia and the Pacific's International Total Investment, 2021

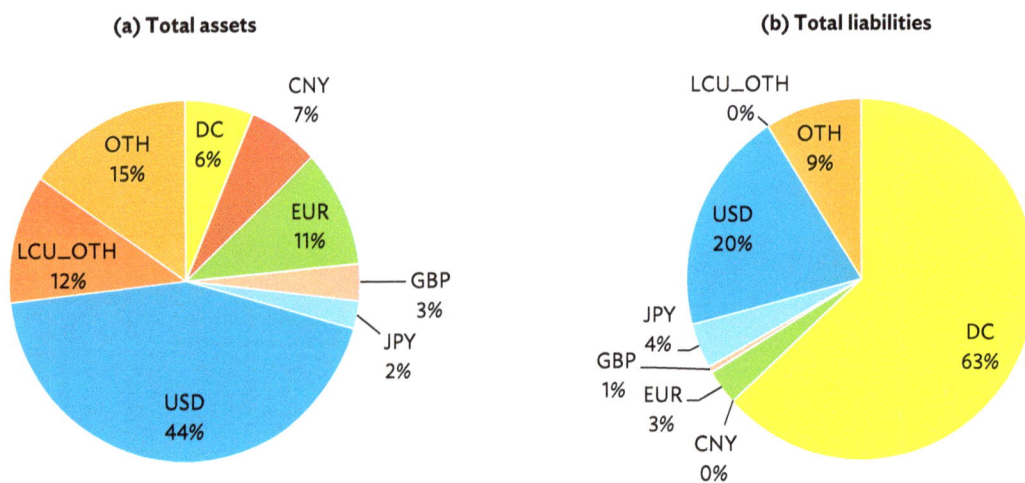

(a) Total assets

(b) Total liabilities

CNY = yuan, DC = domestic currency, EUR = euro, GBP = pound sterling, JPY = yen, LCU_OTH = regional local currency unit, OTH = other currencies, USD = United States dollar.

Notes: CNY is classified as DC for the People's Republic of China, and JPY is classified as DC for Japan. Asia and the Pacific includes Australia; Bangladesh; Hong Kong, China; India; Indonesia; Japan; Kazakhstan; Malaysia; Mongolia; New Zealand; Pakistan; the People's Republic of China; the Philippines; the Republic of Korea; Singapore; and Thailand.

Sources: ADB calculations using data from Bank for International Settlements. Locational Banking Statistics. https://www.bis.org/statistics/bankstats.htm (accessed August 2022); International Monetary Fund (IMF). Balance of Payments and International Investment Position Statistics. http://data.imf.org/IIP (accessed September 2022). IMF. Coordinated Direct Investment Survey. https://data.imf.org/cdis (accessed December 2022); IMF. Coordinated Portfolio Investment Survey. https://data.imf.org/cpis; and IMF. Currency Composition of Official Foreign Exchange Reserves. https://data.imf.org/COFER (both accessed September 2022).

in US dollar as of 2021. This was followed by other currencies (OTH) at 15%, the Asia and Pacific local currency unit (LCU_OTH) at 12%, and the euro at 11%.

In contrast, almost two-thirds of its external liabilities was dominated in domestic currencies (DC), followed by the US dollar at 20% (Figure 4.29). The region continues to have a foreign currency net asset position and local currency net liabilities position.

Across types of international investment, equity assets, which include FDI and portfolio equity, were mostly denominated in US dollars, then in other Asian currencies, as it is assumed that the currency composition of these investments closely tracks geographic positions. Equity liabilities were denominated in domestic currency as FDI and portfolio equity ownerships were denominated in the host economy's currency (Lane and Shambaugh 2007). For debt assets, which include portfolio debt and other investment, about 58% were denominated in the US dollar, followed by other currencies (14%) and the euro (12%). Similar to debt assets, 48% of debt liabilities were denominated in US dollars. This is also followed by local currencies and other currencies with a combined share of about 33% (Figure 4.30).

The dominance of the US dollar in international asset investment is a trend shared in the Latin America and the Caribbean region. In 2021, 41% of LAC's asset investments were denominated in US dollars, while 19% were denominated in other currencies and 17% were denominated in euro (Figure 4.31a). The currency composition of LAC's international liability investment is very similar to that in Asia, where 62% of liabilities were denominated in domestic currency. The US dollar comprised 27% of LAC's total liabilities and other currencies comprised 7% (Figure 4.31b).

Asia's and Latin America's international debt investment is also comparable in that more than half of their debt assets and liabilities are denominated in US dollars. Both regions' debt assets had about 60% denominated in US dollars in 2021 (Figure 4.32a). While Asia's debt liabilities had 48% denominated in US dollars, Latin America had 61% (Figure 4.32b).

Because the US dollar remains the dominant currency in the region's international investment, balance sheet effects could be more pronounced to rising interest rates and depreciating local currency values. The rising value of the US dollar will have a stronger valuation and welfare impact than other currencies.

The dominance of the US dollar in the region's asset investment has only marginally progressed, while it has trended downward in the region's liability investment since 2010. This is somewhat consistent with the

Figure 4.30: Currency Composition of Asia and the Pacific's International Debt Investment, 2021

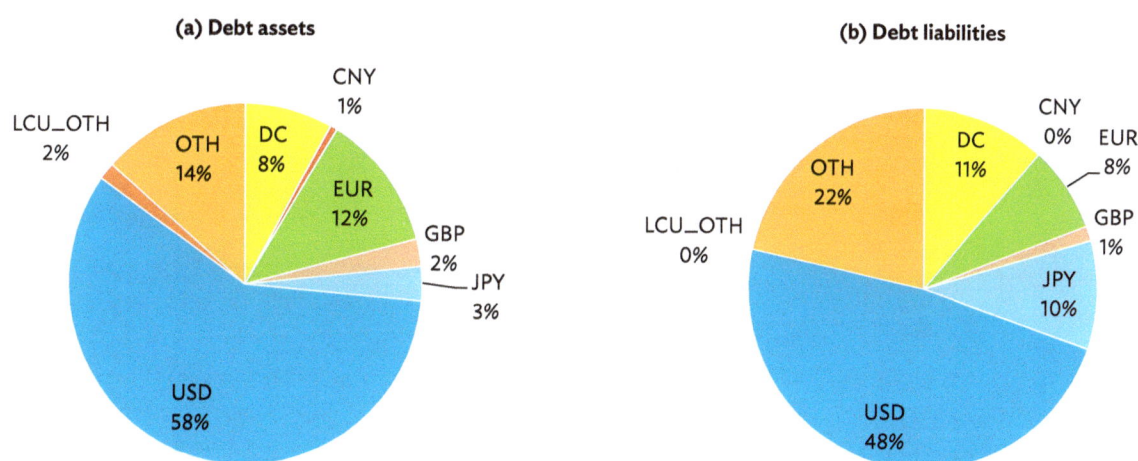

(a) Debt assets

(b) Debt liabilities

CNY = yuan, DC = domestic currency, EUR = euro, GBP = pound sterling, JPY = yen, LCU_OTH = regional local currency unit, OTH = other currencies, USD = United States dollar.

Notes: CNY is classified as DC for the People's Republic of China, and JPY is classified as DC for Japan. Asia and the Pacific includes Australia; Bangladesh; Hong Kong, China; India; Indonesia; Japan; Kazakhstan; Malaysia; Mongolia; New Zealand; Pakistan; the People's Republic of China; the Philippines; the Republic of Korea; Singapore; and Thailand.

Sources: ADB calculations using data from Bank for International Settlements. Locational Banking Statistics. https://www.bis.org/statistics/bankstats.htm (accessed August 2022); International Monetary Fund (IMF). Balance of Payments and International Investment Position Statistics. http://data.imf.org/IIP (accessed September 2022). IMF. Coordinated Direct Investment Survey. https://data.imf.org/cdis (accessed December 2022); IMF. Coordinated Portfolio Investment Survey. https://data.imf.org/cpis; and IMF. Currency Composition of Official Foreign Exchange Reserves. https://data.imf.org/COFER (both accessed September 2022).

Figure 4.31: Currency Composition of Latin America and the Caribbean's International Total Investment, 2021

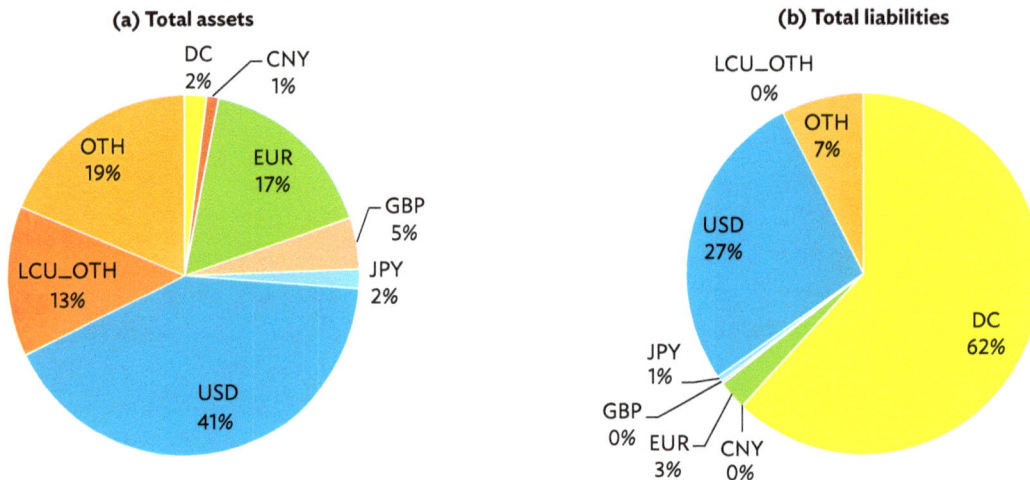

(a) Total assets

DC 2%
CNY 1%
OTH 19%
EUR 17%
GBP 5%
LCU_OTH 13%
JPY 2%
USD 41%

(b) Total liabilities

LCU_OTH 0%
OTH 7%
USD 27%
DC 62%
JPY 1%
GBP 0%
EUR 3%
CNY 0%

CNY = yuan, DC = domestic currency, EUR = euro, GBP = pound sterling, JPY = yen, LCU_OTH = regional local currency unit, OTH = other currencies, USD = United States dollar.

Note: Latin America and the Caribbean includes Aruba, Argentina, Brazil, Colombia, Costa Rica, Mexico, Peru, the Plurinational State of Bolivia, and Uruguay.

Sources: ADB calculations using data from Bank for International Settlements. Locational Banking Statistics. https://www.bis.org/statistics/bankstats.htm (accessed August 2022); International Monetary Fund (IMF). Balance of Payments and International Investment Position Statistics. http://data.imf.org/IIP (accessed September 2022). IMF. Coordinated Direct Investment Survey. https://data.imf.org/cdis (accessed December 2022); IMF. Coordinated Portfolio Investment Survey. https://data.imf.org/cpis; and IMF. Currency Composition of Official Foreign Exchange Reserves. https://data.imf.org/COFER (both accessed September 2022).

Figure 4.32: Currency Composition of Latin America and the Caribbean's International Debt Investment, 2021

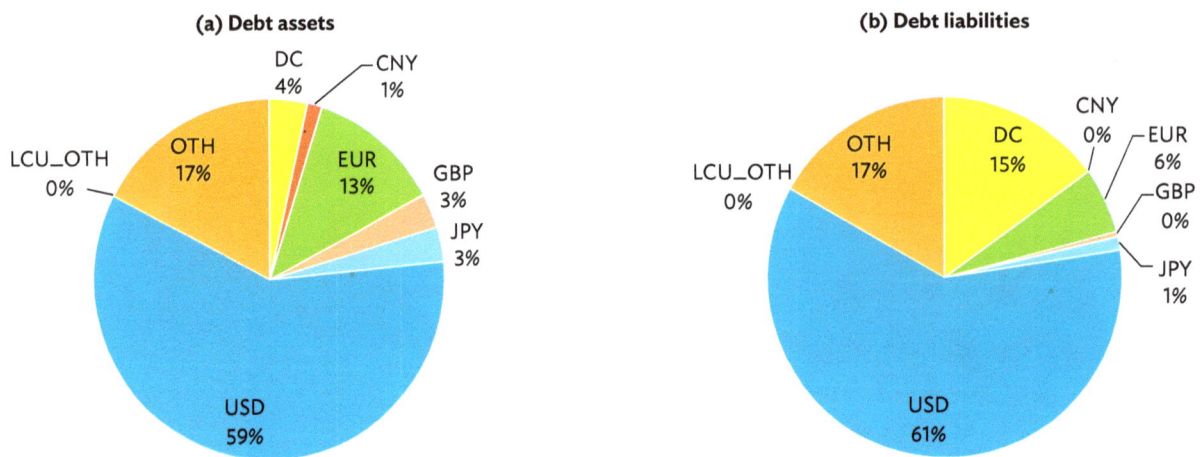

(a) Debt assets

DC 4%
CNY 1%
OTH 17%
EUR 13%
GBP 3%
LCU_OTH 0%
JPY 3%
USD 59%

(b) Debt liabilities

CNY 0%
DC 15%
EUR 6%
OTH 17%
GBP 0%
LCU_OTH 0%
JPY 1%
USD 61%

CNY = yuan, DC = domestic currency, EUR = euro, GBP = pound sterling, JPY = yen, LCU_OTH = regional local currency unit, OTH = other currencies, USD = United States dollar.

Note: Latin America and the Caribbean includes Aruba, Argentina, Brazil, Colombia, Costa Rica, Mexico, Peru, the Plurinational State of Bolivia, and Uruguay.

Sources: ADB calculations using data from Bank for International Settlements. Locational Banking Statistics. https://www.bis.org/statistics/bankstats.htm (accessed August 2022); International Monetary Fund (IMF). Balance of Payments and International Investment Position Statistics. http://data.imf.org/IIP (accessed September 2022). IMF. Coordinated Direct Investment Survey. https://data.imf.org/cdis (accessed December 2022); IMF. Coordinated Portfolio Investment Survey. https://data.imf.org/cpis; and IMF. Currency Composition of Official Foreign Exchange Reserves. https://data.imf.org/COFER (both accessed September 2022).

Figure 4.33: Currency Shares of Asia and the Pacific's International Investment Assets and Liabilities (% of total)

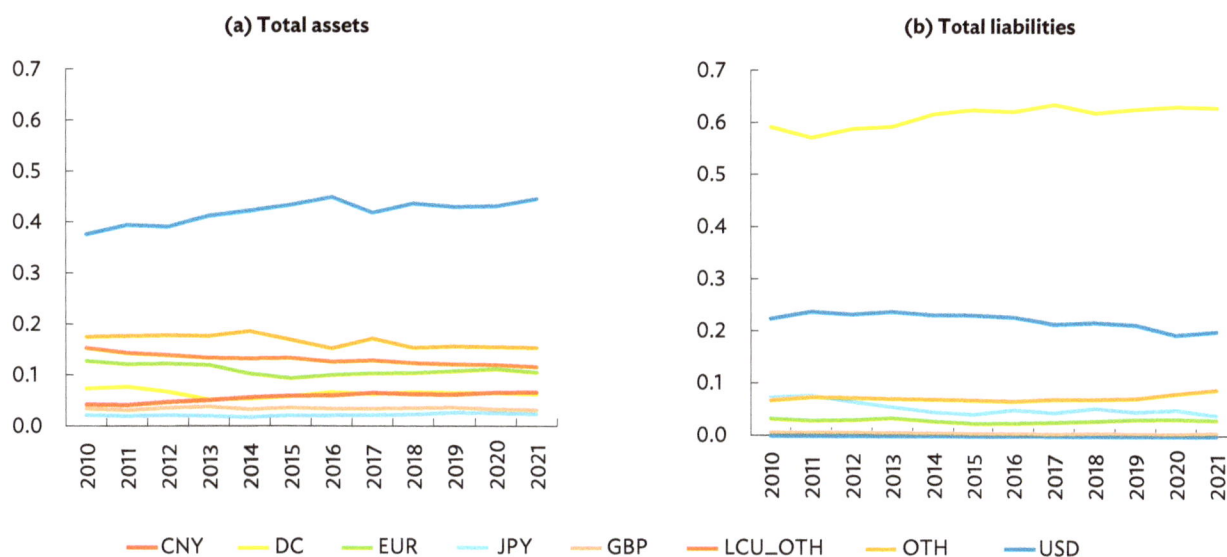

(a) Total assets

(b) Total liabilities

CNY — DC — EUR — JPY — GBP — LCU_OTH — OTH — USD

CNY = yuan, DC = domestic currency, EUR = euro, GBP = pound sterling, JPY = yen, LCU_OTH = regional local currency unit, OTH = other currencies, USD = United States dollar.

Notes: CNY is classified as DC for the People's Republic of China, and JPY is classified as DC for Japan. Asia and the Pacific includes Australia; Bangladesh; Hong Kong, China; India; Indonesia; Japan; Kazakhstan; Malaysia; Mongolia; New Zealand; Pakistan; the People's Republic of China; the Philippines; the Republic of Korea; Singapore; and Thailand.

Sources: ADB calculations using data from Bank for International Settlements. Locational Banking Statistics. https://www.bis.org/statistics/bankstats.htm (accessed August 2022); International Monetary Fund (IMF). Balance of Payments and International Investment Position Statistics. http://data.imf.org/IIP (accessed September 2022). IMF. Coordinated Direct Investment Survey. https://data.imf.org/cdis (accessed December 2022); IMF. Coordinated Portfolio Investment Survey. https://data.imf. org/cpis; and IMF. Currency Composition of Official Foreign Exchange Reserves. https://data.imf.org/COFER (both accessed September 2022).

Arslanalp, Eicheengreen, and Simpson-Bell (2022) conclusion, wherein they find a similar trend for the decline of the US dollar as a reserve asset. They also show the increasing share of the yuan and other currencies, which is also consistent with the trend in the region's choice currencies for international investment. (Figure 4.33).

Yet, the US dollar is still the preferred currency for trade invoicing. Recent data indicate that 78% of the region's merchandise goods exports were invoiced in the US dollar, although the US accounted for only about 13% of the region's merchandise exports. The merchandise imports of Asia also indicate that only 9% of total imports came from the US, but about 75% were invoiced in US dollars (Figure 4.34).

While the EU's share of trade with the US is comparable to that of the region (8% of exports and 5% of imports), the share of merchandise goods invoiced in US dollars was lower in the EU than in the region (30% of export invoices and 48% of import invoices). Figure 4.34 shows that economies in the EU are to the left of Asian economies. Meanwhile, Latin America and the Caribbean economies demonstrate larger trade shares with the US (13% of exports, 16% of imports) than Asia with equally larger share of US dollar invoices (94% of export invoices and 84% of import invoices). Dollar invoicing reliance relative to trade share, however, is most pronounced in Asia.

In the short run, the region's reliance on the US dollar may put additional inflationary pressure on the regional economies due to ballooning import prices amid a strengthening US dollar and weakening local currency environment.

Figure 4.34: Share of Trade with the United States and Trade Invoice in United States Dollar (%)

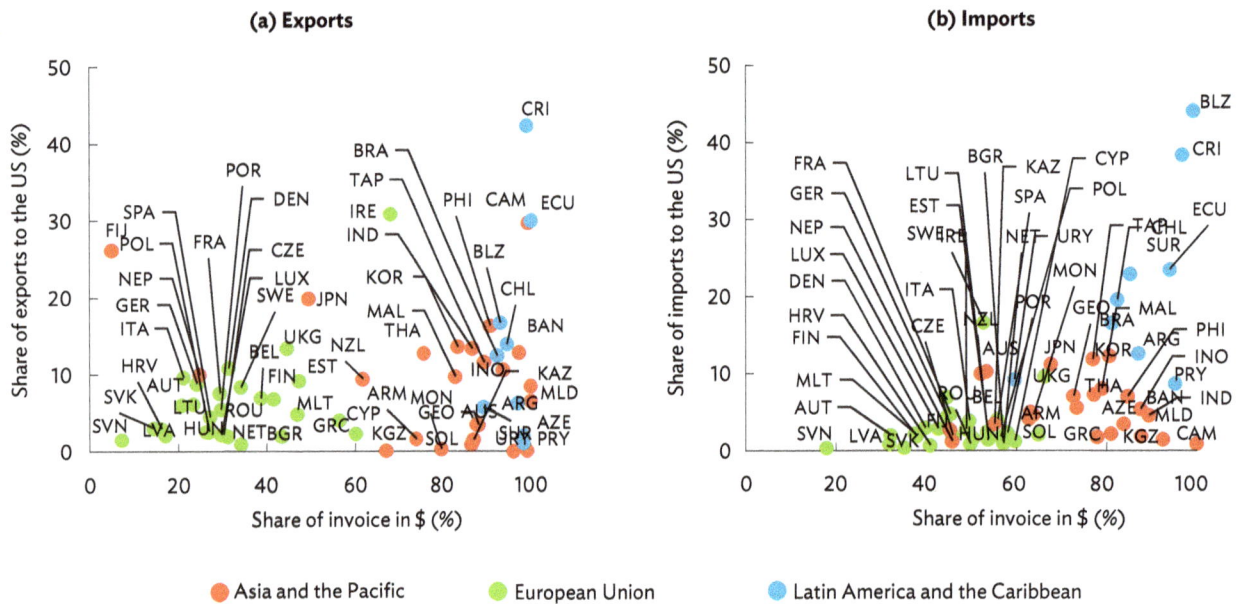

(a) Exports

(b) Imports

● Asia and the Pacific ● European Union ● Latin America and the Caribbean

ARG = Argentina; ARM = Armenia; AUS = Australia; AUT = Austria; AZE = Azerbaijan; BAN = Bangladesh; BEL = Belgium; BGR = Bulgaria; BLZ = Belize; BRA = Brazil; CAM = Cambodia; CHL = Chile; CRI = Costa Rica; CYP = Cyprus; CZE = Czech Republic; DEN = Denmark; ECU = Ecuador; EST = Estonia; FIJ = Fiji; FIN = Finland; FRA = France; GEO = Georgia; GER = Germany; GRC = Greece; HRV = Croatia; HUN = Hungary; IND = India; INO = Indonesia; IRE = Ireland; ITA = Italy; JPN = Japan; KAZ = Kazakhstan; KGZ = Kyrgyz Republic; KOR = Republic of Korea; LTU = Lithuania; LUX = Luxembourg; LVA = Latvia; MAL = Malaysia; MLD = Maldives; MLT = Malta; MON = Mongolia; NEP = Nepal; NET = Netherlands; NZL = New Zealand; PAK = Pakistan; PHI = Philippines; POL = Poland; POR = Portugal; PRY = Paraguay; ROU = Romania; SOL = Solomon Islands; SPA = Spain; SUR = Suriname; SVK = Slovak Republic; SVN = Slovenia; SWE = Sweden; TAP = Taipei,China; TIM = Timor-Leste; THA = Thailand; UKG = United Kingdom; URY = Uruguay; US = United States; UZB = Uzbekistan.

Sources: ADB calculations using data from Boz et al. (2020 and 2022); Eurostat. Extra-EU exports (imports) by Member State, shares by invoicing currency. https://ec.europa.eu/eurostat/web/international-trade-in-goods/data/main-tables; International Monetary Fund. Direction of Trade Statistics. https://data.imf.org/dot (both accessed September 2022); and domestic sources.

References

Arslanalp, S., B. Eichengreen, and C. Simpson-Bell. 2022. The Stealth Erosion of Dollar Dominance: Active Diversifiers and the Rise of Nontraditional Reserve Currencies. *IMF Working Paper.* No. 22/58. Washington, DC: International Monetary Fund (IMF).

ASEAN+3 Macroeconomic Research Office (AMRO). 2021. The Amended Chiang Mai Initiative Multilateralisation (CMIM) Comes Into Effect on 31 March 2021. Press release. 31 March. https://www.amro-asia.org/the-amended-chiang-mai-initiative-multilateralisation-cmim-comes-into-effect-on-31-march-2021.

Asian Development Bank (ADB). AsianBonds Online. Data Portal: Bond Market. https://asianbondsonline.adb.org/data-portal (accessed January 2023).

———. Asia Regional Integration Center. Economy Groupings. https://aric.adb.org/integrationindicators/groupings.

———. Asia Regional Integration Center. Financial Stress Index. https://aric.adb.org/database/fsi (accessed January 2023).

Bank for International Settlements. Locational Banking Statistics. https://www.bis.org/statistics/bankstats.htm (accessed April and August 2022).

Boz, E., C. Casas, G. Georgiadis, G. Gopinath, H. Le Mezo, A. Mehl, and T. Nguyen. 2020. Patterns in Invoicing Currency in Global Trade. *IMF Working Paper.* No. 20/126. Washington, DC: IMF.

———. 2022. Patterns in Invoicing Currency in Global Trade. *Journal of International Economics.* 136. Article 103604.

European Central Bank (ECB). 2022a. Monetary Policy Decisions. Press release. 9 June. https://www.ecb.europa.eu/press/pr/date/2022/html/ecb.mp220609~122666c272.en.html.

———. 2022b. Monetary Policy Decisions. Press release. 21 July. https://www.ecb.europa.eu/press/pr/date/2022/html/ecb.mp220721~53e5bdd317.en.html.

Eurostat. Extra-EU Exports (Imports) by Member State, Shares by Invoicing Currency. https://ec.europa.eu/eurostat/web/international-trade-in-goods/data/main-tables (accessed September 2022).

Ferrarini, B., M. M. Giugale, and J. J. Pradelli, eds. 2022. Overview and synthesis of *The Sustainability of Asia's Debt: Problems, Policies, and Practices.* Cheltenham and Northampton, MA: ADB / Edward Elgar Publishing.

Government of Australia, Reserve Bank of Australia. 2022. Renewal of Bilateral Local Currency Swap Arrangement Between the Reserve Bank of Australia and Bank Indonesia. Media release. 21 February. https://www.rba.gov.au/media-releases/2022/mr-22-04.html.

Government of Japan, Ministry of Finance. 2022a. Renewal of Bilateral Swap Arrangement between Japan and the Philippines. Joint press statement. 4 January. https://www.mof.go.jp/english/policy/international_policy/financial_cooperation_in_asia/bsa/philippines_20220104.html.

———. 2022b. Renewal of Bilateral Swap Arrangement between Japan and India. Joint press statement. 28 February. https://www.mof.go.jp/english/policy/international_policy/financial_cooperation_in_asia/bsa/india_20220228.html.

Government of the People's Republic of China, People's Bank of China (PBC). 2022. PBC and Bank Indonesia Renew Bilateral Currency Swap Agreement. Press release. 27 January. http://www.pbc.gov.cn/en/3688110/3688172/4437084/4461712/index.html.

Government of the United States (US), Board of Governors of the Federal Reserve System. 2021a. Federal Reserve Announces the Extension of Its Temporary US Dollar Liquidity Swap Lines with Nine Central Banks through December 31, 2021. Press release. 16 June. Washington, DC. https://www.federalreserve.gov/newsevents/pressreleases/monetary20210616c.htm.

——. 2021b. Foreign and International Monetary Authorities (FIMA) Repo Facility. Washington, DC. https://www.federalreserve.gov/monetarypolicy/fima-repo-facility.htm.

——. 2022a. Federal Reserve Issues Federal Open Market Committee (FOMC) Statement. 15–16 March. https://www.federalreserve.gov/monetarypolicy/files/monetary20220316a1.pdf.

——. 2022b. Federal Reserve Issues FOMC Statement. 4 May. https://www.federalreserve.gov/monetarypolicy/files/monetary20220504a1.pdf.

——. 2022c. Federal Reserve Issues FOMC Statement. 15 June. https://www.federalreserve.gov/monetarypolicy/files/monetary20220615a1.pdf.

——. 2022d. Federal Reserve Issues FOMC Statement. 27 July. https://www.federalreserve.gov/monetarypolicy/files/monetary20220727a1.pdf.

——. 2022e. Federal Reserve Issues FOMC Statement. 21 September. https://www.federalreserve.gov/monetarypolicy/files/monetary20220921a1.pdf.

——. 2022f. Federal Reserve Issues FOMC Statement. 2 November. https://www.federalreserve.gov/monetarypolicy/files/monetary20221102a1.pdf.

——. 2022g. Federal Reserve Issues FOMC Statement. 14 December. https://www.federalreserve.gov/monetarypolicy/files/monetary20221214a1.pdf.

——. 2022h. Summary of Economic Projections. FOMC Meeting. Washington, DC. 13–14 December.

Institute of International Finance. Frontier Debt Monitor Database November 2022. https://www.iif.com/Research/Download-Data#DebtMonitors (accessed December 2022).

——. Global Debt Monitor September 2022. https://www.iif.com/Research/Capital-Flows-and-Debt/Global-Debt-Monitor (accessed October 2022).

——. Monthly Emerging Markets (EM) Portfolio Flows Database. https://www.iif.com/Research/Download-Data#PortFlows (accessed October 2022).

International Monetary Fund. Balance of Payments and International Investment Position Statistics. https://data.imf.org/IIP (accessed September 2022).

——. Coordinated Direct Investment Survey. https://data.imf.org/CDIS (accessed December 2022).

——. Coordinated Portfolio Investment Survey. https://data.imf.org/CPIS (accessed September 2022).

——. Currency Composition of Official Foreign Exchange Reserves. https://data.imf.org/COFER (accessed September 2022).

——. Direction of Trade Statistics. https://data.imf.org/DOT (accessed September 2022).

Lane, P. and J. C. Shambaugh. 2007. Financial Exchange Rates and International Currency Exposures. Paper presented at the 8th Jacques Polak Annual Research Conference. Washington, DC. 15–16 November.

Lee, J. W. and C. Y. Park. 2011. Financial Integration in Emerging Asia: Challenges and Prospects. *Asian Economic Policy Review.* 6 (2). pp. 176–198.

Park, C. Y. and R. Mercado. 2014. Determinants of Financial Stress in Emerging Market Economies. *Journal of Banking and Finance.* 45. pp 199–224.

5 Movement of People

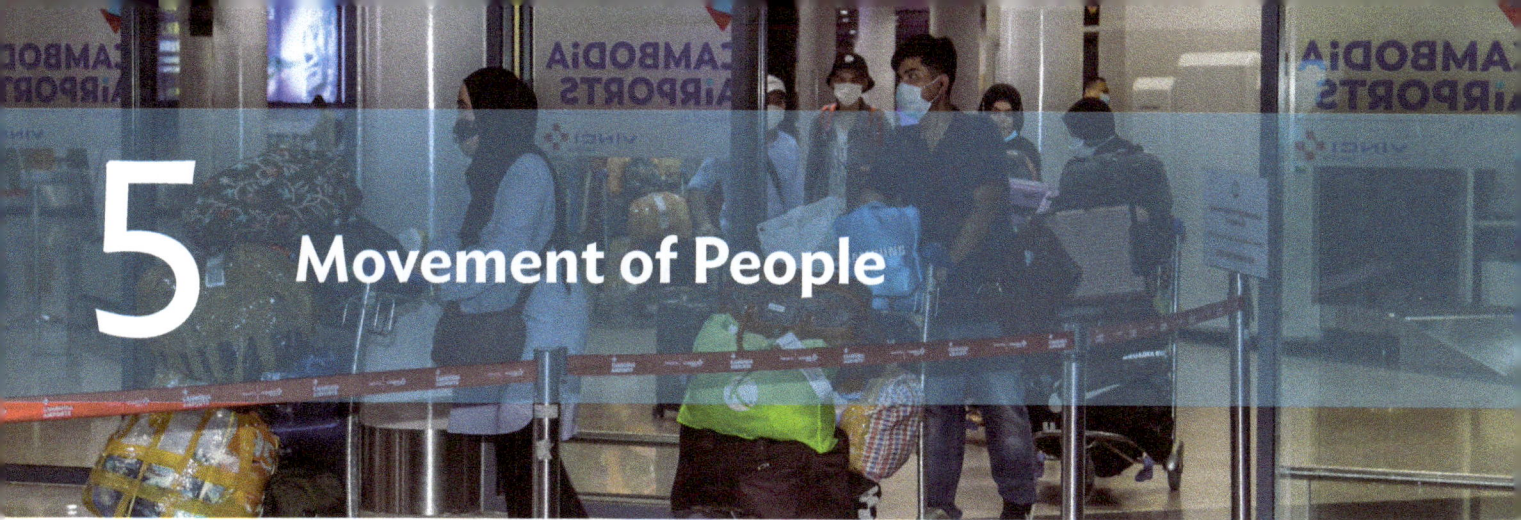

Migration

International Migration, the Continued Effects of COVID-19, and Emerging Global Shocks

The coronavirus disease (COVID-19) pandemic and new global shocks continue to roil international migration dynamics as more economies open their borders and ease travel requirements.

The widespread administration of vaccine programs has enabled major migrant host economies to begin rolling back restrictions on human mobility in 2022. As vaccination rates picked up, blanket travel restrictions evolved into conditional entry requirements, and eventually most major extraregional hosts of migrants from Asia and the Pacific began relaxing entry protocols.[60] Stringent entry requirements were lifted or replaced with proof of vaccination, negative COVID-19 test results before entry, and/or completion of conditional quarantine mandates imposed on emigrant workers. International travel has since resumed, with 73.7% of airports and close to 60% of land and water borders fully operational by December 2022 (Figure 5.1).

The top extraregional host economies of Asian migrants are in the Middle East, North America, and Europe

(Table 5.1). These hosts were home to 125.6 million migrants in 2020, 40.6% of them from Asia. As of 31 December 2022, these economies accounted for 30.1% of COVID-19 cases and 30.9% of COVID-19 deaths globally. The United States (US) remains the top destination of migrants globally, including those from Asia. Between 1990 and 2020, Asian migrants in the US had nearly tripled, from 4.5 million to 12.5 million. Despite registering the highest shares of COVID-19 cases and deaths, the US remains the priority destination of migrants, with its health infrastructure and the availability and ease of access to COVID-19 vaccines.[61] Canada's various migration pathways also make it attractive

Figure 5.1: Status of International Points of Entry—Global (as of December 2022)

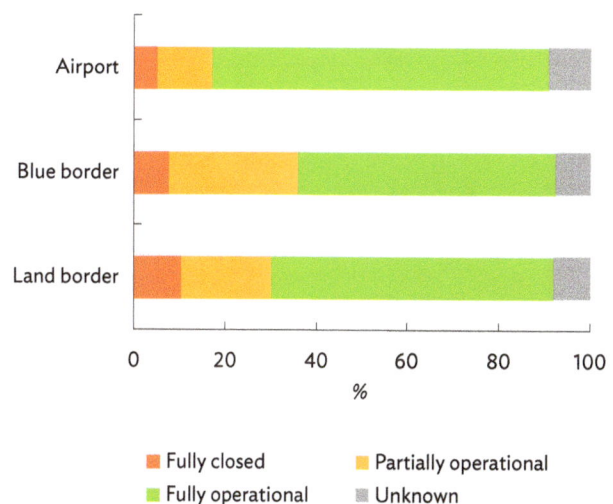

Source: International Organization for Migration. COVID-19 Mobility Impacts. https://migration.iom.int/ (accessed December 2022).

---

[60] Asia and the Pacific, or Asia, consists of the 49 regional member economies of the Asian Development Bank (ADB). The composition of economies for Central Asia, East Asia, the Pacific and Oceania, South Asia, and Southeast Asia are outlined in ADB. Asia Regional Integration Center. Economy Groupings. https://aric.adb.org/integrationindicators/groupings.

[61] When the administration of President Joe Biden took over, it immediately sought to reverse immigration restrictions imposed by former President Donald Trump, including lifting restrictions that drastically reduced the number of visas issued by the US (Krogstad and Gonzalez-Barrera 2022).

to Asian migrants—the stock of Asian migrants in Canada had increased 3.3 times between 1990 and 2020. Migrants from top-sending economies such as India, the People's Republic of China (PRC), the Philippines, the Republic of Korea, and Viet Nam comprised 74.3% of Asian migrants in North American economies in 2020.

Work opportunities in the Middle East continue to appeal to migrant workers, especially those from South Asia. At least 60% of Asian migrants were in Saudi Arabia and the United Arab Emirates in 2020. Germany, the second-largest migrant host economy in the world, hosted 2.4 million migrants from the Asian region in 2020 and has been actively seeking skilled migrant workers, even those from outside the European Union (EU), to address its worsening labor shortage (Reuters 2022). Many of these host economies had already lifted COVID-19 travel requirements as part of their national strategy "to live with the COVID-19 virus."

In 2021, signs of global economic recovery were apparent despite the persistence of COVID-19 and the emergence of its new variants. Powered by expansionary fiscal and accommodative monetary policies, global gross domestic product (GDP) gained rapidly, growing 5.5%–6.0% for the year as the world emerged from the lockdown-induced recession of 2020. The trajectory of events, however,

drastically changed with the Russian invasion of Ukraine, global inflation, and rising interest rates, subduing consumer demand and tightening labor markets in 2022.

Outbound migration from Asia continued amid evolving external risks in a pandemic environment.

Accounting for 1 of 3 global migrants, the pattern of outmigration from Asia to major host economies hardly changed. Between 2015 and 2020, the stock of Asian migrants in major regional destinations increased— North America (up 3.0%), Europe (up 10.5%), and the Middle East (up 17.3%) (Figure 5.2).

Among the top migrant-sending economies in the region, 7 suffered GDP contractions in 2020, ranging from –0.9% for Pakistan to 9.5% for the Philippines (ADB 2022). These top migrant-sending Asian economies accounted for 15.8% (104.1 million) of global COVID-19 cases and 13.9% (0.9 million) of global COVID-19 deaths. The economies also had generally stricter responses to the pandemic, based on the stringency index, policies for contact tracing, face coverings, and vaccine roll-out relative to the Asian and global averages (Table 5.2).

Table 5.1: Top Extraregional Host Economies of Asia and Pacific Migrants

	Stock of migrants, in million (share of migrants from Asia and the Pacific)	COVID-19 cases per thousand population (share of global total)	COVID-19 deaths per thousand population (share of global total)
United States	50.6 (24.7%)	297.8 (15.3%)	3.2 (16.3%)
Germany	15.6 (15.7%)	448.2 (5.7%)	1.9 (2.4%)
Saudi Arabia	13.5 (69.9%)	22.7 (0.1%)	0.3 (0.1%)
Russian Federation	11.6 (58.5%)	148.5 (3.3%)	2.7 (5.8%)
United Kingdom	9.4 (30.5%)	357.5 (3.7%)	3.2 (3.2%)
United Arab Emirates	8.7 (75.9%)	110.9 (0.2%)	0.2 (0.04%)
Canada	8.0 (41.6%)	117.2 (0.7%)	1.3 (0.7%)
Kuwait	3.1 (72.3%)	155.3 (0.1%)	0.6 (0.04%)
Iran	2.8 (97.6%)	85.4 (1.1%)	1.6 (2.2%)
Oman	2.4 (88.2%)	87.2 (0.1%)	1.0 (0.1%)
Top 10 hosts	125.6 (40.6%)	243.7 (30.1%)	2.5 (30.9%)

COVID-19 = coronavirus disease.

Note: Data are as of 31 December 2022; global COVID-19 cases totaled 660,300,641 while global COVID-19 deaths totaled 6,689,977.

Sources: ADB calculations using data from United Nations Department of Economic and Social Affairs, Population Division. International Migrant Stock 2020. https://www.un.org/development/desa/pd/content/international-migrant-stock (accessed May 2022); and Mathieu et al. (2020).

Figure 5.2: Migration to and from Asia and the Pacific, by Region, 1990–2020 (million)

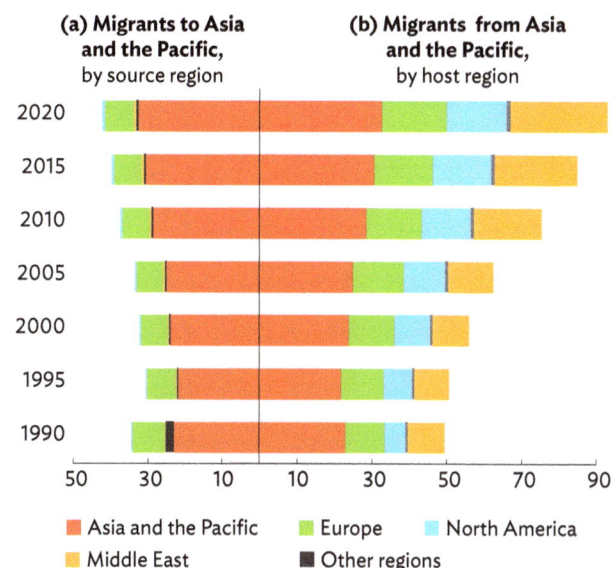

(a) Migrants to Asia and the Pacific, by source region

(b) Migrants from Asia and the Pacific, by host region

■ Asia and the Pacific   ■ Europe   ■ North America
■ Middle East   ■ Other regions

Source: ADB calculations using data from United Nations Department of Economic and Social Affairs, Population Division. International Migrant Stock 2020. https://www.un.org/development/desa/pd/content/international-migrant-stock (accessed May 2022).

For major Asian emigrants, outbound migration was one way to secure income flow, especially with their origin economy in dire straits. In the Philippines, over 300,000 overseas Filipino workers had returned by December 2020, at a time when local unemployment reached its highest level in decades—a survey by International Organization for Migration indicated that 48% of these returnees had remigration plans, given difficulty finding income-earning opportunities in the local labor market (Kang and Latoja 2022).[62] In some major migrant-sending economies, there were massive repatriation activities just as local outputs were contracting significantly. As vaccines became available and borders opened in the Middle East, migrants began to gradually return in 2021 (Figure 5.3). Granted that migrant outflows remain way below 2019 levels, the numbers have improved. In Indonesia and Pakistan, the share of outmigrants in 2022 exceeded the 2019 level. This gradual recovery in the pace of migration helped facilitate remittances to the migrant-sending economies

Table 5.2: Top 10 Migrant Sending Economies in Asia and the Pacific and COVID-19 Indexes

	Stock of Outmigrants (million, per '000 population)	COVID-19 Cases (million, share of global total)	COVID-19 Death (per '000, share of global total)	Containment and Health Index (0-100)
India	17.9 (12.6)	44.1 (6.8%)	530.7 (7.9%)	44.4
PRC	10.5 (7.3)	1.9 (0.3%)	5.2 (0.1%)	78.0
Bangladesh	7.4 (43.2)	2.0 (0.3%)	29.4 (0.4%)	28.0
Pakistan	6.3 (26.8)	1.6 (0.2%)	30.6 (0.5%)	49.9
Philippines	6.1 (52.7)	4.1 (0.6%)	65.4 (1.0%)	41.3
Indonesia	4.6 (16.7)	6.7 (1.0%)	160.6 (2.4%)	48.0
Kazakhstan	4.2 (216.7)	1.5 (0.2%)	19.1 (0.3%)	19.1
Viet Nam	3.4 (34.5)	11.5 (1.7%)	43.2 (0.6%)	39.9
Nepal	2.6 (85.1)	1.0 (0.2%)	12.0 (0.2%)	35.4
Republic of Korea	2.2 (42.5)	29.1 (4.4%)	32.2 (0.5%)	34.5
Asia and the Pacific	93.0 (21.5)	177.2 (26.8%)	1,197.4 (17.9%)	32.1

COVID-19 = coronavirus disease 2019, PRC = People's Republic of China.

Notes: Data are as of 31 December 2022; global COVID-19 cases totaled 660,300,641 and global COVID-19 deaths, 6,689,977. The Containment and Health Index builds on the stringency index, using its nine indicators plus testing policy, extent of contact tracing, polices to wear face coverings, and policies around vaccine roll-out. A higher score indicates a stricter response (100 = strictest response).

Sources: ADB calculations using data from United Nations Department of Economic and Social Affairs, Population Division. International Migrant Stock 2020. https://www.un.org/development/desa/pd/content/international-migrant-stock (accessed May 2022); and Mathieu et al. (2020).

[62] This figure refers to the number of overseas Filipino workers repatriated through efforts of the Department of Foreign Affairs of the Philippines.

burdened by the pandemic-induced recession and inflicted by the variants of COVID-19 and the slow rollout of vaccines.

Figure 5.3: Outflow of Migrants from Selected Asian Economies (% share of 2019 level)

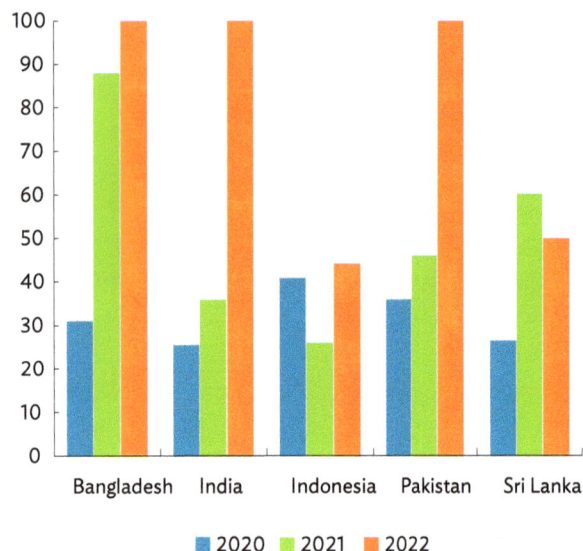

Sources: Government of Bangladesh, Bureau of Manpower, Employment, and Training. http://www.old.bmet.gov.bd/BMET/stattisticalDataAction; Government of India, Ministry of External Affairs. Performance Smartboard. http://meadashboard.gov.in/indicators/15; Government of Pakistan, Bureau of Emigration and Overseas Employment. https://beoe.gov.pk/reports-and-statistics (all accessed January 2023); and Kikkawa et al. (2022).

Despite aggravated labor market conditions for migrants due to the Russian invasion of Ukraine, Central Asia experienced large inflows of migration and money transfers as more Russian skilled workers and businesses relocated to the subregion.

The Russian invasion of Ukraine in February 2022 unleashed a torrent of sudden changes that would impact global trade flows, inflate commodity prices, alter growth estimates, and escalate tensions along some borders. It also increased demand for humanitarian assistance for affected migrants.[63] With 6.7 million

Central Asian migrants in the Russian Federation, sanctions imposed on that economy immediately affected labor market dynamics, as many Central Asian workers returned to their origin economies. Migrants faced financial difficulties and either lost their jobs, took shorter work hours, or took another job to maintain the same support provided to families back home (Hashimova 2022, Najibullah 2022, Al Jazeera 2022).

Meanwhile, Russian workers and entrepreneurs have been relocating to Central Asia since the Russian invasion of Ukraine, improving the manpower landscape in the subregion. Armenia recorded a 50% year-on-year increase in the number of information technology (IT) workers on account of Russian technology firms moving their staff abroad (Borak 2022). The ease of doing business has attracted Russian businesses and entrepreneurs to Armenia as well as to Georgia and Azerbaijan (Mgdesyan 2022). The relocation of Russian skilled workers (managers and IT specialists) has been a boon for Kazakhstan and Uzbekistan—government officials in Tashkent even expedited work and residency permits, tax benefits, and housing and child-care assistance as it anticipated the inflow of around 100,000 Russian IT specialists (Najibullah 2022, Tomas 2022).

New trends are emerging in job opportunities for Asian migrant workers as major developed host economies pursue post-pandemic goals.

The pandemic wiped out a decade's progress in employment rates among immigrants, but it also showcased the depth of migrants' contributions to their host economies and shed light on the range of skills and professions of workers deemed essential in a crisis (OECD 2020). For instance, 13% of essential workers in the EU are immigrants while 30% of doctors and 27% of farm workers in the US are foreign-born (Foresti 2020).

---

[63]   One month into the Russian invasion of Ukraine, "some 13 million people are estimated to be stranded in affected areas or unable to leave due to heightened security risks, destruction of bridges and roads, as well as lack of resources or information on where to find safety and accommodation" (Billing 2022).

Other key occupations, such as work in construction and mining, food service and processing, and domestic care are performed mostly by migrants. Amid the decline in migrant flows, the pandemic led to a dramatic structural transformation of the labor market and has underscored the dependence of these destination economies on migrant workers (TASS 2021).

On the demand side, a shift toward skilled workers seems to be occurring in the demand for migrant labor in host economies to complement strategic economic focus toward technology, automation, and other high-value industries. Compared with 2019, there was a slightly higher percentage of employed highly skilled migrants in Germany, Saudi Arabia, Spain, the US, and the United Arab Emirates (Figure 5.3a). Among intraregional host economies, however, results were mixed—the share of highly skilled migrants was higher in Australia, the Philippines, and Thailand; but lower for Malaysia and Viet Nam (Figure 5.3b). Saudi Arabia launched its Skills Verification Program in 2021 as part of its Vision 2030 to keep the inflow of foreign labor aligned with the manpower development needs of the economy and to reduce the inflow of unskilled migrant labor (Abujaleel 2021). Germany, which put into force the Immigration Act for Skilled Workers in March 2020, is further simplifying procedures to accelerate the inflow of migrant labor into the economy—it needs 400,000 annually to mitigate the labor impact of its aging population (Government of Germany Federal Office for Migration and Refugees 2021; Look 2022).

Labor shortages in some host economies underscore the importance of migrant labor in several key industries (Canadian Manufacturing 2022, Child 2021, Ivanova 2022, Riley 2022). Within Asia, shortages in migrant labor were also reported by Australia, Malaysia, New Zealand, the Republic of Korea, Thailand, and Viet Nam (Nguyen 2021; Lee 2022; Lee, Latiff, and Chu 2022; Thaiger 2022). These shortages threatened to derail economic recovery and were costing firms in forgone output and sales contracts. The combination of changes in migration policies to accommodate the inflow of more migrant workers in answer to the labor shortage and rising demand for more skilled workers suggest more

job opportunities are available and augurs well for Asian migrants (Figure 5.4).

Figure 5.5 illustrates how migrant flows are faring in select developed host economies. In some economies, it might take a while before pre-pandemic migration levels are reached as labor markets, migration policy, and economic targets evolve in both sending and host economies. In the US, work visas issued to Asian migrants had been on a massive decline relative to 2019—they were 32% lower in 2020 and 68.2% in 2021. The work visa ban impacted US technology firms, which disproportionately employ migrant workers, mostly from South Asia (Wiessner 2020). The relocation of US firms hiring mostly migrant workers to other economies such as Canada and the PRC also caused labor market pain (Lee 2020). In Canada, travel restrictions have produced a backlog in the inventory of migration applications. Invitations to apply via federal high-skilled streams were also paused to help manage the processing of applications inventory. This could account for the declining trend in the total number of visas issued under the Temporary Foreign Worker Program—relative to 2019, total visas issued under the program declined by 14.2% in 2020 and 37.7% in 2021. In the United Kingdom (UK), migrants from Asia and Oceania (particularly from Australia, New Zealand, and India) were found to have high-skilled jobs working as teachers, IT specialists, doctors and nurses, and managers, in stark contrast to the low-skilled jobs held by migrants from the new EU-accession economies (Fernandez-Reino and Rienzo 2022). UK work visas issued to Asian migrants fell 43.5% in 2020 but rebounded 58.9% in 2021. Work visas issued by New Zealand grew 14.3% in 2021 after initially falling 23.1% in 2020. In August 2022, the New Zealand government introduced temporary changes in immigration rules to accelerate the inflow of foreign workers and help plug labor market gaps, including providing median wage exemptions to crucial sectors through sector agreements, temporarily doubling numbers under the Working Holiday Scheme, and extending visas for 6 months to migrant workers already in the economy (Mint 2022). The government also announced changes to make it easier for health workers to migrate, including fast tracking and covering

Figure 5.4: Distribution of Employed Migrants in Major Host Economies by Level of Skills (% of total)

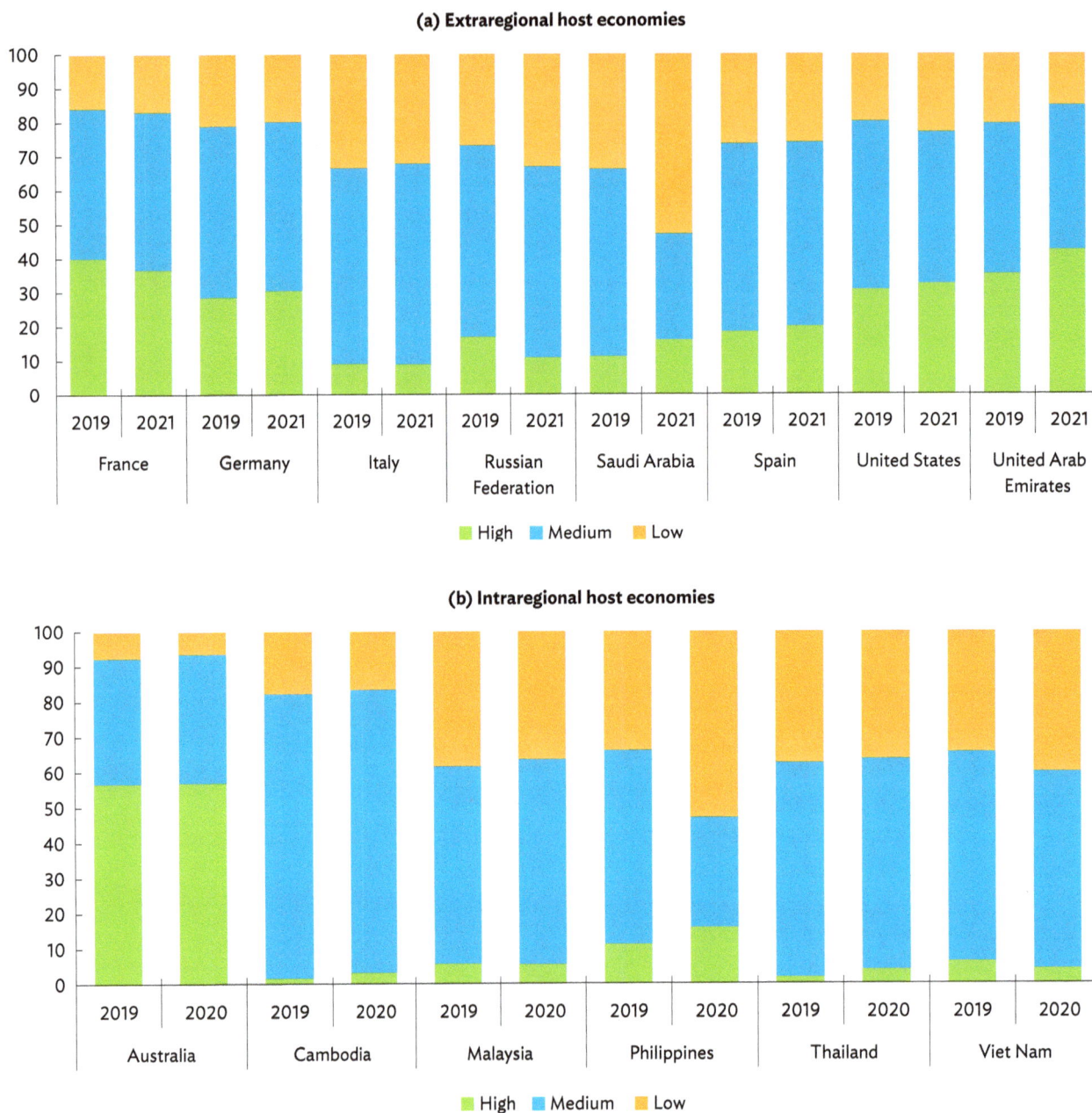

(a) Extraregional host economies

High   Medium   Low

(b) Intraregional host economies

High   Medium   Low

Sources: ADB calculations using data from Government of Saudi Arabia, General Authority for Statistics. Labor Force. https://www.stats.gov.sa/en/814; Government of the United Arab Emirates, Federal Competitiveness and Statistics Centre. Statistics. https://fcsc.gov.ae/en-us/Pages/Statistics/Statistics.aspx; International Labour Organization (ILO). ILOSTAT Database. International Standard Classification of Occupations. https://ilostat.ilo.org/resources/concepts-and-definitions/classification-occupation; and ILO. ILOSTAT Database. Data. https://ilostat.ilo.org/data (all accessed November 2022).

NZ$10,000 of an overseas nurses' registration cost, as well as other health-care worker training and national and international recruitment drives, and setting up a

dedicated immigration support service to make it easier for workers to move to New Zealand (Witton 2022).[64]

---

[64]   New Zealand requires internationally qualified nurses to complete a competency assessment program that takes 8 weeks and costs $10,000 before they can work in New Zealand. Similar courses in the UK and Australia have changed to help internationally qualified nurses to register in less time and at lower cost (Bhatia 2022).

Figure 5.5: Visas Issued to Asian Migrants in Select Migrant Host Economies (thousand)

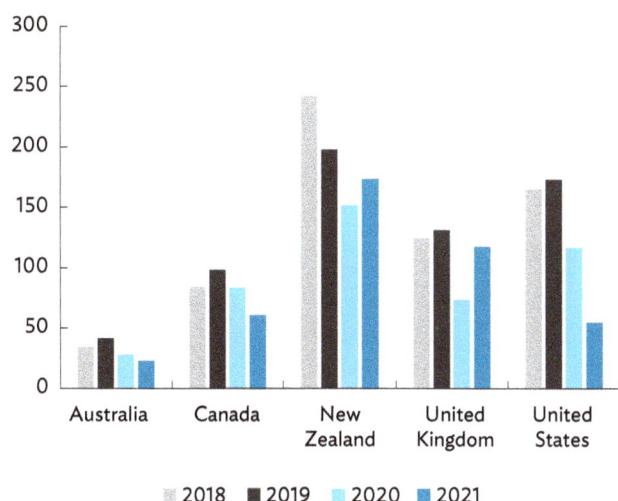

Notes: Australia data refer to visas issued under the Temporary Skill Shortage and Temporary (Work) Skilled Visa programs; Canada data refer to Temporary Foreign Worker Program Work Permit holders; New Zealand data refer to work visas issued; United Kingdom data refer to work visas issued to Asian migrants; and United States data refer to total first and second half visas granted to migrants from Asia and the Pacific.

Sources: ADB calculations using data from Government of Australia, Department of Home Affairs. Visa Statistics. https://www.homeaffairs.gov.au/research-and-statistics/statistics/visa-statistics; Government of Canada, Employment and Social Development Canada. Temporary Foreign Worker Program 2021 Q1-2022Q3. https://open.canada.ca/data/en/dataset/e8745429-21e7-4a73-b3f5-90a779b78d1e; Government of the United Kingdom, Home Office. Immigration Statistics. https://www.gov.uk/government/collections/immigration-statistics-quarterly-release; Government of the United States, Department of State, Bureau of Consular Affairs. Visa Statistics. https://travel.state.gov/content/travel/en/legal/visa-law0/visa-statistics.html (all accessed July 2022).

In Australia, the pandemic caused temporary visa holders to leave their jobs in aged care, agriculture, construction, and hospitality, causing a skills shortage which disrupted the Australian workforce (Croft 2021). Responding to its economic and labor market needs, the skills stream of Australia's migration program has focused on granting visas to migrants with the capacity to drive economic growth and investment, particularly to applicants under the employer-sponsored scheme and the business, innovation, and investment program. Under the Temporary Skill Shortage program, total visas

granted in fiscal year 2020–2021 had declined 18.5% and were only 56.2% of the pre-pandemic total. The slow return of migrant workers to Australia may have been caused by pandemic border policies that left "a lingering level of uncertainty among potential skilled migrants" (Wright 2022). With unemployment at a 48-year low of 3.5%, business groups have called for an increase in the migration cap from 160,000 per year to 200,000 annually for the next 2 years to ease the labor shortage and help boost Australia's relative advantage in data science and digital technology (Read 2022).

Developments in Migration Governance and Implications for Asia

Improved migration governance could foster inclusive and sustainable economic recovery in the region.

The pandemic may have changed the immediate context of migration, but it has not changed the underlying beneficial reality of international migration for economies of origin and destination, or for migrants and their families (Newland 2020). Supporting the Global Compact for Safe, Orderly and Regular Migration (GCM), adopted in 2018, through its six policy dimensions—migrant rights; whole-of-government and evidence-based policies; cooperation and partnerships; socioeconomic well-being; mobility dimensions of crises; and safe, orderly, and regular migration—means that more economies will work together to implement the GCM's objectives which, in turn, will help them move beyond the crisis and generate the essential building blocks of global recovery.[65]

However, the GCM is a nonbinding document and therefore needs economies that would champion its overarching goal of international cooperation and the sharing of best practices on international migration in all its dimensions. To this end, the United Nations identified

---

[65]   The GCM, prepared under the auspices of the United Nations, is the first intergovernmentally negotiated agreement covering all dimensions of international migration in a holistic and comprehensive manner. It (i) supports international cooperation on the governance of international migration, (ii) provides participating economies with a comprehensive menu of policy options to address international migration issues, and (iii) gives participating economies the freedom to pursue implementation based on their own migration realities and capacities (United Nations. Global Compact for Migration. https://www.un.org/en/migration2022/global-compact-for-migration).

six economies in Asia as GCM champion economies since 2018—Bangladesh, Cambodia, Indonesia, Nepal, the Philippines, and Thailand (IOM 2021).

Figure 5.6 illustrates policy progress on GCM goals. In Asia, only 36% of participating economies meet policy requirements to support the GCM and 23% partially meet them. By comparison, at least three-quarters of Organisation for Economic Co-operation and Development (OECD) economies meet the requirements. Significant data gaps also exist; in the OECD, no policy status information exists on 10.5% of its economies, and in Asia, on 36%. These gaps underscore the need for improving data collection related to migration and for facilitating better communication among participating economies. The Philippines took a step in this direction in 2018, when it began compiling survey-based baseline information on domestic and international migration of its citizens to eventually standardize and harmonize migration data (Philippine News Agency 2022). The recently established Department of Migrant Workers also provides an online portal for registration and employment opportunities for a more comprehensive management of Filipino migrant data.

Policy status in top host economies of migrants from Asia is diverse in support of the GCM (Table 5.3). Most notable among these economies is the absence of information from the US and the United Arab Emirates, host to 20.6% of Asian migrants. Other reporting top host economies fully meet policies to support the sixth dimension of the GCM, but more work needs to be done to promote migrant rights, socioeconomic well-being, and mobility in crises, for both extraregional and intraregional host economies. The region will also benefit from improved better sharing of policies and best practices, especially since intraregional migration in Asia is a considerable share of the total.

Despite economies championing GCM goals, enhanced participation among signatory economies remains a challenge (Ratha 2021). The perceived impact of (im)migration on citizens, especially as it affects jobs and earnings—amid loud anti-immigrant sentiment and xenophobia, especially during the pandemic—seems to drown out the established benefits of migration to societies in destination economies. The lack of external sources of financing to support public spending on migrant populations is another obstacle, given a debt

Figure 5.6: Status of Policies to Facilitate Orderly, Safe, Regular, and Responsible Migration and Mobility of People, 2021

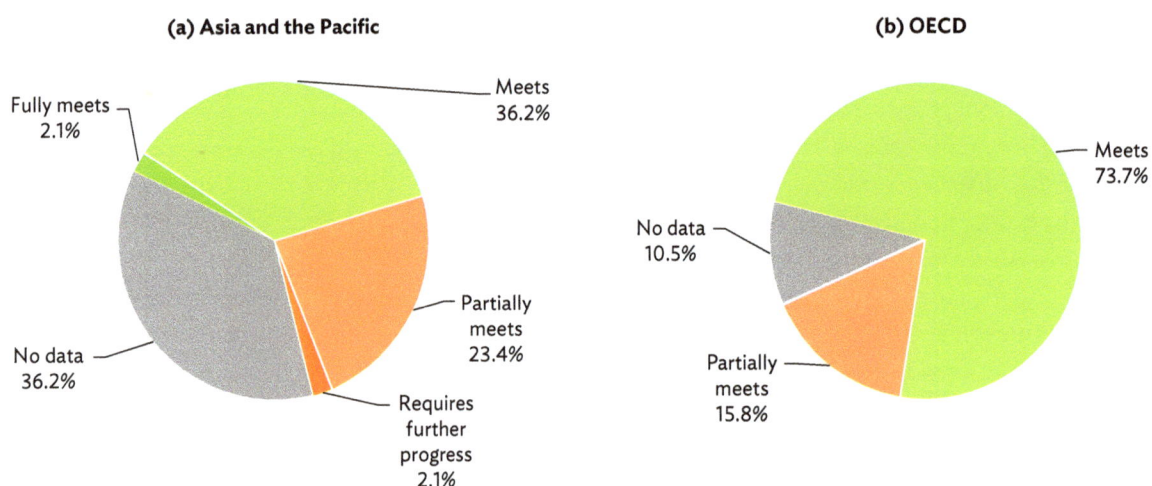

(a) Asia and the Pacific

Fully meets 2.1%
Meets 36.2%
Partially meets 23.4%
Requires further progress 2.1%
No data 36.2%

(b) OECD

Meets 73.7%
Partially meets 15.8%
No data 10.5%

OECD = Organisation for Economic Co-operation and Development.

Source: ADB calculations using data from United Nations Department of Economic and Social Affairs, Population Division and International Organization for Migration (2021).

overhang in many economies. Likewise, constrained economic recovery in developed migrant host economies is a hurdle, even though the international community is counting on these to lead migration governance.

Now more than ever, international migration needs vigorous global partnerships for effective governance. To rally support for migration policies at the national level, it is instructive to integrate migration policies into development and governance policies at the local level, where the drivers and effects of migration are strongly felt (Riallant 2017). Doing so would allow local and regional authorities to funnel their expertise and knowledge into national policy, making for more responsive and relevant national migration policies that are implementable, measurable, and can be sustainably monitored at the local level. This approach would be particularly useful in anchoring the environmental and climate dimensions of the international migration governance agenda. Although most people displaced or migrating as a result of climate impacts are staying within their economies of origin, the accelerating trend of global displacement related to climate impacts is increasing cross-border movements as well. Mainstreaming discussion of how climate and environmental factors

Table 5.3: Status of Policies to Facilitate the Global Compact on Migration in Major Migrant Host Economies

Host Economies	Overall Summary	Migrant Rights	Whole-of-Government/ Evidence-Based Policies	Cooperation and Partnerships	Socioeconomic Well-Being	Mobility Dimensions of Crises	Safe, Orderly, and Regular Migration
United States	No data	No data	No data	No data	No data	No data	No data
Saudi Arabia	Meets	Partially meets	Fully meets	Meets	Fully meets	Fully meets	Fully meets
Russian Federation	Meets	Partially meets	Fully meets	Fully meets	Partially meets	Requires further progress	Fully meets
UAE	No data	No data	No data	No data	No data	No data	No data
Canada	Meets	Meets	Fully meets	Fully meets	Fully meets	Fully meets	Fully meets
UK	Meets	Meets	Fully meets	Fully meets	Meets	Fully meets	Fully meets
Iran	No data	No data	No data	No data	No data	No data	No data
Germany	Meets	Meets	Fully meets	Fully meets	Fully meets	Meets	Fully meets
Kuwait	Partially meets	Partially meets	Meets	Fully meets	Fully meets	Partially meets	Fully meets
Oman	Partially meets	Partially meets	Fully meets	Partially meets	Requires further progress	Fully meets	Fully meets
India	Partially meets	Requires further progress	Fully meets	Fully meets	Fully meets	Requires further progress	Requires further progress
Australia	Meets	Meets	Fully meets	Fully meets	Fully meets	Meets	Fully meets
Thailand	Meets	Meets	Fully meets	Fully meets	Fully meets	Fully meets	Fully meets
Malaysia	No data	No data	No data	No data	No data	No data	No data
Pakistan	No data	No data	No data	No data	No data	No data	No data
Hong Kong, China	No data	No data	No data	No data	No data	No data	No data
Singapore	No data	No data	No data	No data	No data	No data	No data
Japan	Meets	Meets	Fully meets	Fully meets	Fully meets	Fully meets	Fully meets
Bangladesh	Partially meets	Requires further progress	Fully meets	Fully meets	Fully meets	Requires further progress	Partially meets
Republic of Korea	No data	No data	No data	No data	No data	No data	No data

Top extraregional hosts: United States through Oman. Top intraregional hosts: India through Republic of Korea.

Legend:

Fully meets — (green)   Partially meets — (orange)   No data — (gray)
Meets — (light green)   Requires further progress — (yellow)

UAE = United Arab Emirates, UK = United Kingdom.

Source: ADB calculations using data from United Nations, Department of Economic and Social Affairs, Population Division and International Organization for Migration (2021).

are reinforcing push factors for global migration will not only benefit migration-focused policy process, but also reinforce the role of migrants as positive contributors to climate change mitigation and adaptation.

Since the pandemic, additional reforms and initiatives have been implemented to improve migrants' access to labor markets, social protection, and basic services. In late 2020, Saudi Arabia launched a labor reform initiative to ease out of the "kafala" system and place greater emphasis on job mobility and the contractual relationship between employers and foreign employees (Shadmand et al. 2020).[66] Under this reform, employees could choose and change jobs more easily, while employers will benefit from a more mobile and flexible labor force that could respond better to the diversification objectives of Saudi Arabia (IOM 2020). Qatar has also initiated reforms to protect and improve workers' conditions and guarantee their rights, provide training programs to promote innovation, and prepare the workforce for modern digital transformation (The Peninsula 2022).

In Southeast Asia, Singapore and the Philippines signed the Joint Communique on the Recruitment of Filipino Healthcare Workers in September 2022 for the continued deployment of Filipino health workers to Singapore, and to promote greater bilateral cooperation in the field of health care (Parrocha 2022). Nongovernment organizations in Thailand have initiated a program to develop Thai language and computer literacy skills among migrant workers to improve their quality of life and ensure migrant workers have proper access to welfare and assistance while working in Thailand (Pattaya Mail 2022). In Central Asia, Uzbeks going abroad for temporary work were granted 20% discounts on tickets for the National Railway Company

and the National Air Company. This included a partial reimbursement of the transport cost up to SUM300,000 once a year (United Nations Network on Migration 2020). The Government of Uzbekistan also removed the state monopoly in employment of citizens abroad and allowed private employment agencies to participate in job selection, recruitment, and information and consulting services in employment. It also established a social protection fund for migrant workers during emergencies such as injury, lost documents, financial need, deportation, among others.

Migration is a vital human experience in search of better opportunities and a fundamental reality. Transitioning from the ravages of the pandemic calls for a better narrative to make the case for practical and sustainable approaches to international migration governance (Foresti, Rajah, and Bither 2022). Developing the skills and talents of global migrants is essential to achieve economic and social aspirations while reinforcing the contribution of migration to development. More importantly, migration governance should articulate the urgency of providing and promoting legal pathways to migration, without which the relevance of skill levels and job opportunities is diluted. At the national level, innovative attempts at digitalizing key migrant services and the growth of online services in employment administration must be maintained and reviewed for sustainable enhancement (Kikkawa et al. 2022). Stronger cooperation and collaboration between origin and destination economies could help usher in bilateral and regional labor agreements. This could lower costs of migration, help standardize deployment of health and safety protocols, create more thorough licensing and monitoring of recruitment agencies, and help control irregular migration.

---

[66]   Kafala is a sponsorship system that regulates the relationship between employers and migrant workers and is common in Saudi Arabia, Jordan, Lebanon, and most Arab gulf economies (Robinson 2021). The labor reform initiative of Saudi Arabia, which will eventually replace the "kafala" system, was passed via Resolution No. 51848/1442 of the Minister of Human Resources and Social Development and became effective on 14 March 2021.

Remittances

Growth in global remittance inflows leaped 9.9% in 2021 to $781.1 billion, from a 1.5% contraction in 2020. In a display of resilience, inflows to Asia increased 3.4% to $325.5 billion in 2021, and are estimated to grow 4.7% to $340.7 billion in 2022.

Amid ongoing economic strain caused by the COVID-19 pandemic, global remittance inflows rebounded in 2021, growing by a new record 9.9% in 2021, its highest since 2011 (Figure 5.7). This resilience of inflows underscores migrants' commitment to supporting their families and communities (over 800 million beneficiaries globally), enabled by a strong pickup in economic activity and employment in major host economies, which implemented massive fiscal stimulus programs and accommodative monetary policy (Ratha et al. 2022a). For instance, the American Rescue Plan helped job creation and migrant workers' incomes and strengthened income flows to recipient economies primarily dependent on US-based remittance outflows, such as in Asia and Latin America and the Caribbean.

After a dip of 1.9% in 2020, remittance inflows to Asia rebounded by 3.4% in 2021, reaching $325.5 billion, as noted. A combination of factors, both external and domestic, underpinned the recovery of remittance inflows in 2021, even as the pandemic entered its second year. Easing of COVID-19 curbs and better-than-expected economic recovery in several major hosts in North America, the Middle East, and Europe in 2021 helped revive labor demand and supported the emigration of migrant workers who had returned to their home economies in 2020 (Ratha et al. 2022a). A new record high of $340.7 billion in inflows into Asia is estimated in 2022 as the demand for outmigrant labor from the region is expected to remain robust among high-income economies (Ratha et al. 2022b).

As an important source of external finance for the region, on average, remittances are 43% the size of foreign direct investment (FDI) and at least 10 times the size of official development assistance in 2010–2020 (Figure 5.7a). Since 2019, remittance inflows had also overtaken tourism receipts as the second-largest type of financial inflow into the region. A ray of hope in macroeconomic scenarios in developed host economies alongside fiscal support enabled migrants from Asia to

Figure 5.7: Remittance Inflows to Asia and the Pacific, and the World

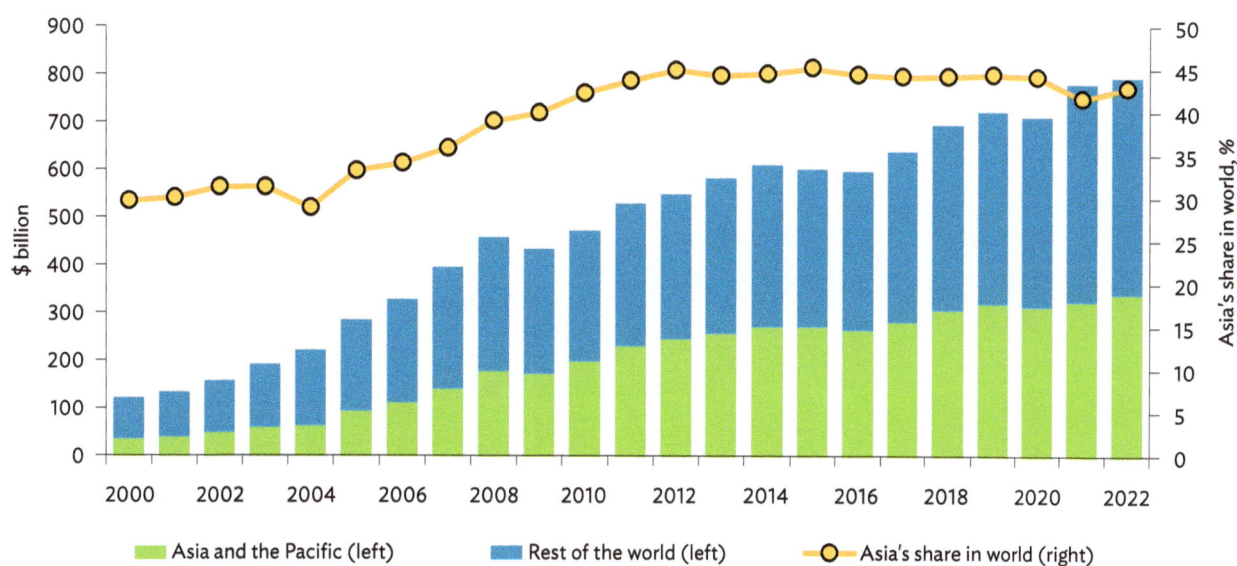

Note: Data for 2022 are estimates.

Source: ADB calculations using data from the Global Knowledge Partnership on Migration and Development (KNOMAD) Remittances Data. http://www.knomad.org/data/remittances (accessed December 2022).

remit more in 2021. Remittances to the region bolster financial resilience for the poorest of the poor and build financial independence (IFAD 2018).

The share of remittance inflows relative to other external flows differs across regions (Figure 5.8). In Latin America and the Caribbean, remittances benefited from better performance and employment numbers in the US (where 57.3% of outmigrants from Latin America and

the Caribbean reside). Additionally, migrants' altruistic response to the ongoing effects of COVID-19 impacts and adverse impact of hurricanes caused remittance flows to grow to their highest in 2021, both in relative (25.0%) and nominal level terms ($26.4 billion). These financial flows from migrants have also become key external resources against the backdrop of the weak investments. As a proportion of FDI, Latin America and the Caribbean's share of remittances rose from 22% in

Figure 5.8: Financial Flows in Selected Regions ($ billion)

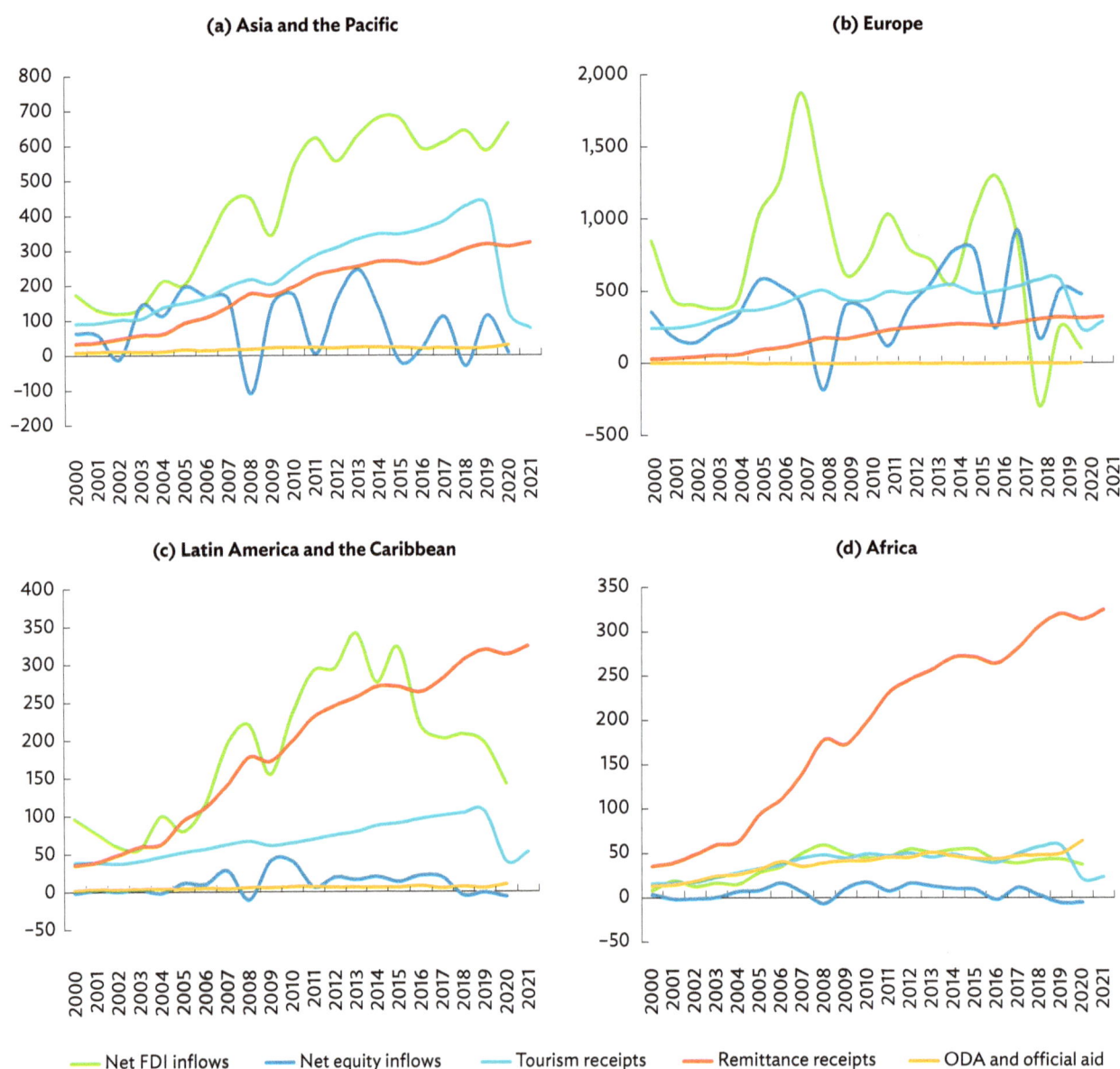

(a) Asia and the Pacific

(b) Europe

(c) Latin America and the Caribbean

(d) Africa

Net FDI inflows   Net equity inflows   Tourism receipts   Remittance receipts   ODA and official aid

FDI = foreign direct investment, ODA = official development assistance.

Sources: ADB calculations using data from the Global Knowledge Partnership on Migration and Development (KNOMAD). Remittances Data. http://www.knomad.org/data/remittances; and World Bank. World Development Indicators. https://databank.worldbank.org/source/world-development-indicators (both accessed December 2022).

2010–2012 to 49% in 2019. During the first year of the pandemic, in 2020, remittance inflows were 72% the size of FDI. Remittances are an essential source of foreign exchange reserves particularly for economies in Latin America and the Caribbean with current account deficits and where these flows account for at least a quarter of GDP, such as El Salvador (26.4%), Honduras (25.5%), and Jamaica (24.0%).

In contrast, remittance inflows to Europe trail tourism receipts and portfolio inflows (Figure 5.7c). In 2020, remittance inflows to Europe ($174.7 billion) were 64% higher than FDI, which suffered a 58.2% decline over the previous year. As economic momentum and energy prices improved, remittance inflows to Europe increased $17.3 billion in 2021 over 2020, led by flows to France and Germany, which make up 27% of total remittances to the region. In Africa, remittance inflows, which totaled $84.0 billion in 2020, are the region's key source of external finance and has exceeded FDI inflows since 2010 (Figure 5.7d). Compared with other regions, Africa registered the second-highest growth in remittances in 2021 (14.4%), riding on the economic recovery in the US and Europe (Mdoe 2021). The additional $12.1 billion in inflows—of which 68% were from Egypt, Nigeria, and Morocco—made for essential cover for the dip in the region's investments and tourism receipts (Table 5.4). In 2022, remittance inflows are foreseen to continue to grow in Asia, Latin America and the Caribbean, and Africa. Inflows to Asia will continue to benefit from robust migrant outflows and bilateral labor arrangements

with key host economies, while sustained strong growth in the US labor market will continue to be the dominant element supporting inflows to Latin America and the Caribbean. Inflows to Africa will moderate but remain positive as the region navigates the impact of the external environment on food production and prices, and the effect of a slowdown in the euro area, a major source of remittance, on the incomes of African migrants (Ratha et al. 2022b).

Remittance Flows to Asian Subregions Amid External Shocks

Remittance inflows to Asian subregions improved in 2021, except in East Asia and Oceania. In 2022, the Russian invasion of Ukraine led to large, unexpected money transfers into Central Asia.

About 47.7% of total remittances to Asia flowed to South Asia, defying the pandemic odds for the second year in a row. Inflows to the subregion grew 6.7% in 2021, fueled primarily by inflows to India and Pakistan (Table 5.5). In the US, real sector improvement, vaccine availability, and wage hikes, benefited many South Asian migrants, many of whom are highly skilled and enjoy higher-income jobs (Ratha et al. 2022a). Remittances from the Middle East to South Asia also improved in 2021 as migrant flows were revived to near pre-pandemic levels. After a minute contraction in 2020, remittance flows to India grew 7.5%

Table 5.4: Remittance Inflows by Recipient Region

Region	Share of Total 2021	Remittance Inflows ($ billion) 2021	Remittance Inflows ($ billion) 2022e	Growth 2021	Growth 2022e	Level Change ($ billion) 2021	Level Change ($ billion) 2022e
Asia and the Pacific	41.7%	325.5	340.7	3.4%	4.7%	10.8	15.3
Europe	24.6%	192.0	176.7	9.9%	−8.0%	17.3	−15.3
Latin America and the Caribbean	16.8%	131.3	143.5	26.0%	9.3%	27.1	12.2
Middle East	3.2%	25.2	23.4	9.9%	−6.9%	2.3	−1.7
North America	1.0%	7.7	6.3	3.4%	−17.9%	0.3	−1.4
Africa	12.3%	96.2	100.2	14.4%	4.2%	12.1	4.1

e = estimate.

Source: ADB calculations using data from Global Knowledge Partnership on Migration and Development (KNOMAD). Remittances Data. http://www.knomad.org/data/remittances (accessed December 2022).

in 2021 to $89.4 billion, spurred as migrants responded strongly to the massive COVID-19 infections and deaths due to the Delta variant. Flows to Bhutan, on the other hand, declined sharply by 30.9% in 2021 from a high of 47.3% in 2020.

Remittance flows are essential to easing external account pressures, as in Pakistan and Sri Lanka (Box 5.1). Pakistan was able to sustain its double-digit growth in inflows in 2021—20.0% in 2021 and 17.2% in 2020, as government incentives continued to influence formal remittance flows. Bhutan and Sri Lanka saw remittances contract sharply in 2021. Embroiled in economic woes in recent years, the Sri Lankan economy suffers high levels of public debt, high deficits, and high macroeconomic volatility (Weerakoon, Kumar, and Dime 2019).

Remittance inflows to Southeast Asia improved to $78.3 billion in 2021 and reversed a 3.0% contraction in 2020 with 3.4% growth in 2021. Higher inflows to the Philippines, Thailand, and Viet Nam more than compensated for the decline in flows to other economies in the subregion. All three economies are recipients of remittances from the US and are anticipated to account for 88.8% of the $3.0 billion additional inflows to the subregion in 2022 (Ratha et al. 2022b). The Philippines, in particular, received about 40% of its 2021 inflows from the US (Ratha et al. 2022a).

Led by robust inflows to Fiji, Samoa, and Tonga, the Pacific experienced double-digit growth (36.5%) in 2021 for the second year in a row. Economies in the Pacific are dependent on remittances more than any other region in the world. In absolute terms, remittance inflows are small, around $1 billion. However, remittances are the third most important source of external financial resources to the subregion, after official development assistance and FDI. In Tonga, Samoa, and the Marshall Islands, remittances are at least 12% of GDP (Figure 5.8b). And although most of the Pacific economies receive the least amount of remittance inflows, these are nonetheless significant in per capita terms—in Tonga and Samoa, for instance, remittance per capita was 30%-50% of GDP per capita in nominal terms (Figure 5.8c). Remittance inflows to Oceania and East Asia continued to drop. Remittances to the PRC, the second-largest recipient economy in 2021, declined 10.9% to $53 billion in 2021, relative to $59.5 billion in 2020.

Central Asia rebounded with a strong double-digit growth (25.0%) in 2021 after inflows contracted by 10.8% in 2020. Inflows rose by $4.2 billion to $21 billion in 2021 as higher inflows went to the Uzbekistan (up $2.2 billion), Tajikistan (up $0.7 billion), and Georgia (up $0.5 billion) and to a lesser extent, the Kyrgyz Republic (up $0.4 billion), Armenia (up $0.3 billion), and Azerbaijan (up $0.1 billion). In 2021, higher energy prices boosted recovery in the

Table 5.5: Remittance Inflows by Recipient Subregions

Region	Share of Total, 2021	Remittance Inflows ($ billion)		Growth		Level Change ($ billion)	
		2021	2022e	2021	2022e	2021	2022e
South Asia	48.2%	157.0	162.5	6.7%	3.5%	9.9	5.5
Southeast Asia	24.1%	78.3	81.4	3.4%	3.9%	2.6	3.0
East Asia	20.6%	67.0	65.2	−8.0%	−2.6%	−5.8	−1.7
Central Asia	6.5%	21.0	29.7	25.0%	41.5%	4.2	8.7
Oceania	0.3%	0.9	0.8	−29.6%	−18.9%	−0.4	−0.2
Pacific	0.4%	1.2	1.1	36.5%	−5.9%	0.3	8.7
Asia and the Pacific	100%	325.5	340.7	3.4%	4.7%	10.8	15.3

e = estimate.

Source: ADB calculations using data from Global Knowledge Partnership on Migration and Development (KNOMAD). Remittances Data. http://www.knomad.org/data/remittances (accessed May 2022).

Box 5.1: Economic Crisis and Remittance Inflows: The Cases of Sri Lanka and Pakistan

Sri Lanka is currently reeling from an economic crisis driven primarily by years of fiscal and balance of payment deficits, linked to low revenue collection, restrictive trade regime, and sluggish tourism industry. In addition to external financing from India, it also sought the assistance of the International Monetary Fund (IMF) for possible bailout measures.[a]

Pakistan is also under duress. In July, it reached an initial agreement with the IMF to replenish its foreign currency reserves, a resumption of the bailout package originally signed in 2019.[b] Owing to soaring energy prices and an elevated import bill, the economy is experiencing a huge current account deficit, reaching as high as $17.4 billion from fiscal year 2022 (4.6% of gross domestic product [GDP]) from $2.82 (0.8% of GDP) in the last fiscal year according to the State Bank of Pakistan.

After remittances put in a robust performance amid the pandemic—showing 5.8% growth in 2020 ($7.1 billion), remittance inflows to Sri Lanka (6.5% of GDP and a major source of foreign exchange reserves), plunged 22.7% year-on-year in 2021 ($5.5 billion) and 51.6% in January–June 2022 (box figure 1). The sharp decline resulted mainly from a dive in the official foreign exchange rate that triggered the prevalence of informal remittance channels (box figure 2). Remittances to Pakistan (9% of GDP), on the other hand, grew 20% in 2021 ($31.1 billion), following a 17.2% growth in 2020 ($26.1 billion), propelled by government incentives and a strong response from migrants to the pandemic. For the first half of 2022, remittances to Pakistan managed to grow 0.6%.

1: Monthly Remittance Inflows (year-on-year, %)

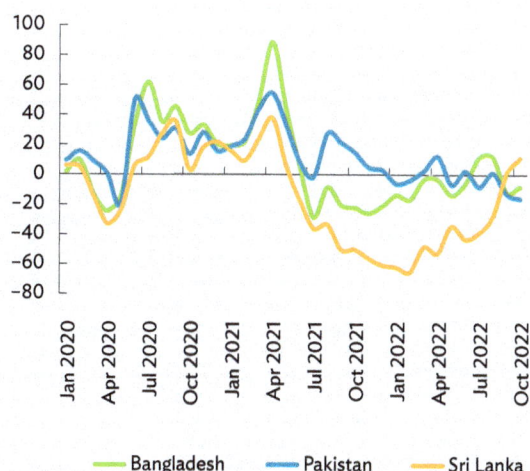

2: Selected South Asian Currencies (16 June 2020 = 100)

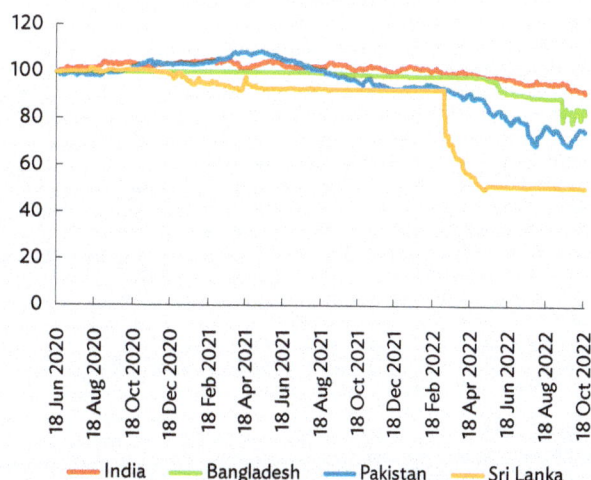

Sources: ADB calculations using data from CEIC Data Company; Government of Bangladesh, Bangladesh Bank. Open Data Initiative. https://www.bb.org.bd/en/index.php/econdata/index; Government of Pakistan, State Bank of Pakistan. Economic Data. https://www.sbp.org.pk/ecodata/index2.asp; and Government of Sri Lanka, Central Bank of Sri Lanka. Economic Indicators. https://www.cbsl.gov.lk/en/statistics/economic-indicators (all accessed December 2022).

Since the onset of the pandemic, governments have offered incentives to encourage migrant workers to send remittances through formal channels. Pakistan launched the Sohni Dharti Remittance Program in 2021, which awards cash-convertible points for every remittance transaction made. Prior to this, the Roshan Digital Account enabled nonresident Pakistanis to digitally open bank accounts in Pakistan.[c]

In Sri Lanka, the Central Bank of Sri Lanka offered an additional SLRs for each dollar remitted in December 2021, on top of the SLRs2 per US dollar given earlier in December 2020, under the "Incentive Scheme on Inward Workers' Remittances" program. Aside from this, the central bank has also borne the transaction costs of migrant remittances, up to a certain limit, starting in February 2022.

continued on next page

Box 5.1 continued

However, the policy effects were diluted by capital control and changes in foreign exchange policies that have widened the gap between official and unofficial foreign exchange rates. The official exchange rate pegged between SLRs200–SLRs203 per US dollar resulted in a huge disparity in the exchange rate offered by the central bank and the black/kerb market, estimated to be more than SLRs25 per US dollar, from July to November 2021 (Weeraratne 2021). This prompted migrant workers to use informal channels known as the "hawala" system, which offer more attractive rates. This also led to a steeper decline in formal remittances (Shivani and Ritzema 1999).[d]

The intensifying economic distress of migrants' families further drove migrant workers to seek higher returns to their foreign exchange in the parallel market.

The opposite is happening in Pakistan, however, with government incentives and policy measures working effectively to attract remittances. However, this does not imply the absence of informal channels. In fact, remittances coursed through informal channels are estimated at around $7 billion–$8 billion per year as they offer better terms on the rate and transaction fees (Siddiqui 2020).

[a] Discussions between IMF and Sri Lanka are under way as of 31 July, after the IMF concluded its visit on 30 June 2022, with a view of reaching a staff-level agreement and Executive Board approval.

[b] International Monetary Fund. World Economic Outlook October 2022 Database. https://www.imf.org/en/Publications/WEO/weo-database/2022/October (accessed December 2022).

[c] Government of Pakistan, State Bank of Pakistan. Roshan Digital Account https://www.sbp.org.pk/rda/index.html; and Government of Pakistan, State Bank of Pakistan. Sohni Dharti Remittance Program. https://www.sbp.org.pk/sohnidharti/index.html.

[d] Shivani and Ritzema (1999) argue that about 13% of total remittances to Sri Lanka are leaked through the "hawala" system. But this share seems to have grown in the recent past, according to former deputy governor of the Central Bank of Sri Lanka. Jayamaha (2006) noted that 30%–40% of remittances were coursed through informal institutional channels.

Sources: ADB staff using Jayamaha (2006); Shivani and Ritzema (1999); Siddiqui (2020); and Weeraratne (2021).

Russian Federation and resulted in increased demand for highly skilled migrants in the oil and education sectors, as well as low-skilled migrants in agriculture and construction. Reentry was also allowed to 300,000 migrant workers and Tajikistan and Uzbekistan (Ratha et al. 2021). These developments benefited cross-border labor mobility and influenced remittance flows.

Remittances are important to several economies in Central Asia, in volume (Uzbekistan is among the top 10 remittance recipient economies) and as a share of GDP, such as in Armenia, Georgia, the Kyrgyz Republic, Tajikistan, and Uzbekistan (Figures 5.9a and 5.9b). Since the Russian invasion of Ukraine in 2022, Central Asia has experienced large inflows of Russian nationals and

Figure 5.9: Top 10 Remittance Recipient Economies in Asia and the Pacific

(a) $ billion

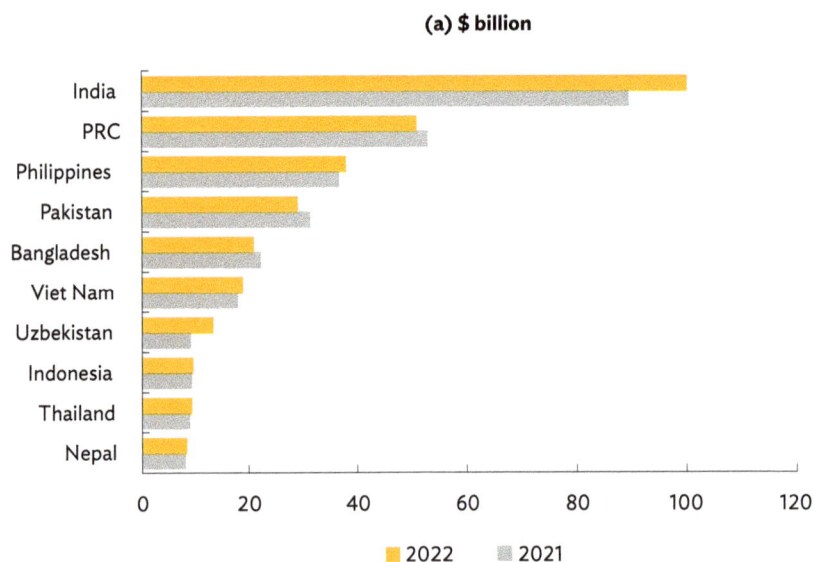

continued on next page

Figure 5.9 continued

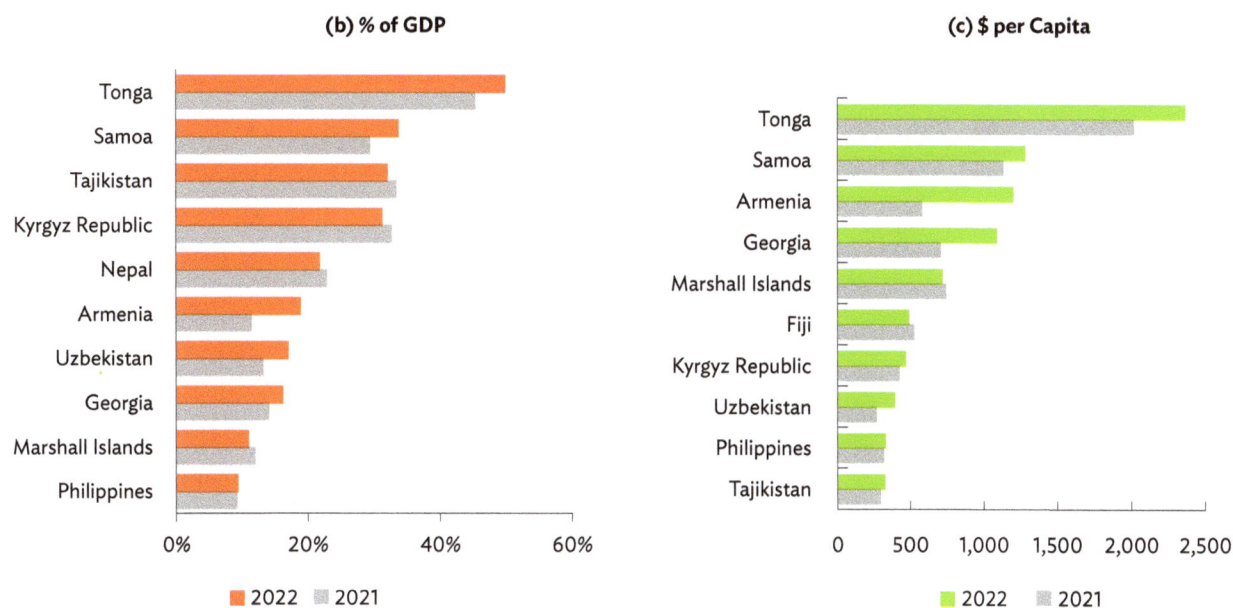

(b) % of GDP

(c) $ per Capita

PRC = People's Republic of China.

Sources: Global Knowledge Partnership on Migration and Development (KNOMAD). Remittances Data. http://www.knomad.org/data/remittances; International Monetary Fund. World Economic Outlook October 2022 Database. https://www.imf.org/en/Publications/WEO/weo-database/2022/October (both accessed December 2022); and United Nations Department of Economic and Social Affairs, Population Division. (2022).

related money transfers into the subregion (Box 5.2). Inflows to the subregion are estimated to gallop to 41.5% in 2022 as conscription activities of the Russian Federation increase the demand for labor from Central Asia while the subregion itself is benefiting from money transfers related to the relocation of Russian businesses and skilled workers (Ratha et al. 2022b).

High inflation and interest rate hikes could lead to a significant delay in economic recovery in major migrant host economies in 2022 and onward. The Russian invasion of Ukraine adds more uncertainty to the outlook for remittance inflows to Asia.

Asia has been resolute in its efforts to move out of the pandemic's shadow and advance toward a stronger, more resilient new normal. An increasing number of economies have reopened borders and have either eliminated or eased COVID-19 restrictions. In the

process, the region has benefited from mobility-driven economic activities that primed the wheels of economic recovery. Remittance inflows have also been resilient despite the obstacles related to the pandemic. However, these gains have been eclipsed by the Russian invasion of Ukraine, which fueled rising food and gas prices, and monetary tightening in advanced economies (ADB 2022).

The redlining issue of high inflation has important implications for most economies in the region. Growth prospects for developing Asia have been revised downward to 4.2% (from 4.3%) in 2022 and 4.0% (from 4.9%) in 2023 while the regional inflation forecast was adjusted to 4.4% in 2022 and 4.2% in 2023. Prolonged season of soaring prices could thus lead to reduced real wages and loss of employment opportunities for migrants in major host economies. They could also threaten the consumption and savings possibilities for remittance-dependent households in the region. Amid rising inflationary pressures across the world, its

Box 5.2: The Impact of the Russian Invasion of Ukraine on Money Transfers to Central Asia

Central Asian economies were immediately impacted by the Russian invasion of Ukraine. Within 2 months of the invasion, money transfers, which include remittances, into Kazakhstan contracted 20.0% and 13.2% in February and March 2022 (box figure 1).[a] Year-on-year monthly inflows to the Kyrgyz Republic fell 28.4% in March 2022 while flows from the Russian Federation dipped 33.2%. However, by April 2022, year-on-year growth indicated some unusually high rates of money transfers (box figure 2). Money transfers from the Russian Federation to

Armenia nearly doubled and had at least quadrupled by June. Meanwhile, on average, monthly transfers to Georgia have gone up fourfold from April to August. In Kazakhstan, money transfers from the Russian Federation have grown by an average of no less than 700% (year-on-year) within the same period—inflows in April ($40.4 million) were at least 2.5 times the 2021 level, and peaked to $66.9 million in June. Money transfers from the Russian Federation have also been robust in the Kyrgyz Republic, Tajikistan, and Uzbekistan where the demand for migrant labor is rising (Usov 2022).

1: Monthly Money Transfers to Central Asian Economies (year-on-year growth, %)

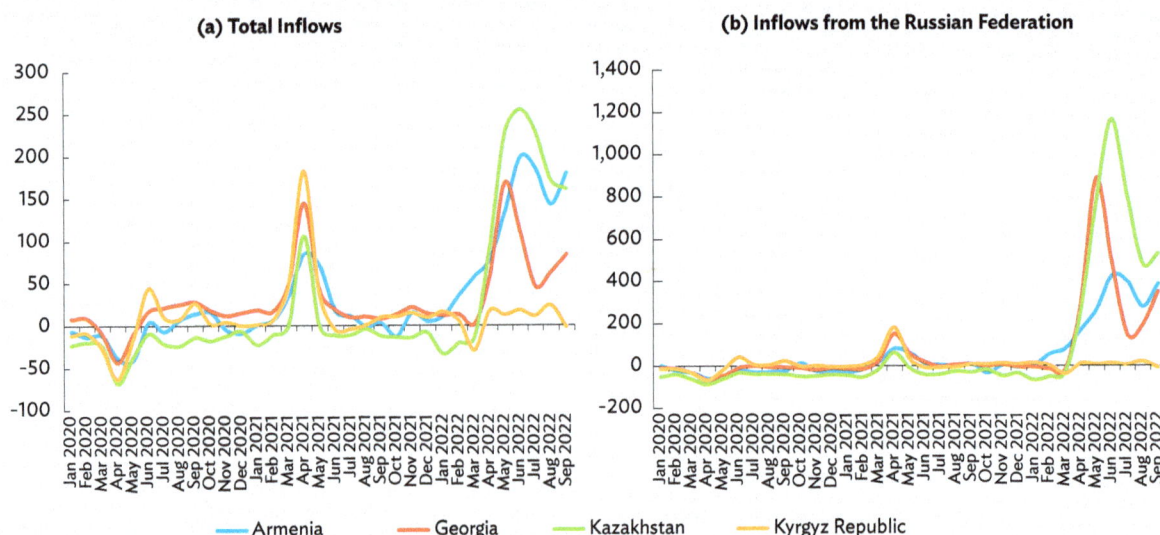

(a) Total Inflows

(b) Inflows from the Russian Federation

— Armenia   — Georgia   — Kazakhstan   — Kyrgyz Republic

Sources: ADB calculations using data from the Government of Armenia, Central Bank of Armenia. External Sector Statistics. https://www.cba.am/en/SitePages/statexternalsector.aspx; Government of Georgia, National Bank of Georgia. Statistics Data. https://nbg.gov.ge/en/statistics/statistics-data; Government of Kazakhstan, National Bank of Kazakhstan. Statistics. https://www.nationalbank.kz/en/page/statistika; and the Government of the Kyrgyz Republic, National Bank of the Kyrgyz Republic. External Sector of the Economy. https://www.nbkr.kg/index1.jsp?item=128&lang=ENG (all accessed December 2022).

According to relevant central bank figures, Armenia received about 40% of its annual money transfers from the Russian Federation in 2021. However, the share in the second quarter of 2022 significantly rose to 66% due to a large inflow of Russian nationals into Armenia and related funds transferred from the Russian Federation (see figure). This is also the case for Georgia and Kazakhstan where the share increased to 50%–60% from about 20% in 2021. In the Kyrgyz Republic, majority of the inflows have been from the Russian Federation.

Meanwhile, sanctions on the Russian Federation have affected international payment systems. Cards by Visa and Mastercard issued in the Russian Federation no longer work abroad and the MIR card is used in its stead. MIR bank cards are also issued by 10 economies that accept

them, including Armenia, Kazakhstan, the Kyrgyz Republic, Tajikistan, Uzbekistan, and Viet Nam (Bunina 2022). In the Kyrgyz Republic, Russian nationals have been transferring or bringing large amounts of rubles in and then cashing them out as US dollars, causing a 7%–10% deficit of the currency to requirements (Imanaliyeva 2022). Although the National Bank of the Kyrgyz Republic had banned companies from taking dollars out of the economy, no such prohibition is in place for individuals.

Inflows of Russians to most Central Asian economies are expected to benefit the volume of money transfers accompanying the relocation of Russian-speaking families and enterprises. Households seeking to obtain international payment cards are placing their foreign currency savings in Central Asia while Russian businesses

continued on next page

Box 5.2 continued

are attracted to special economic zones in Central Asia, such as Uzbekistan's IT Park, which appeal to digital nomads and exporters of information technology services. Hence, despite the huge uncertainty stemming from the Russian invasion of Ukraine, it appears Central Asian economies are regaining their footing. High revenues from the exports of hydrocarbon, gas, and oil are benefiting Azerbaijan, Kazakhstan, Turkmenistan, and Uzbekistan (ADB 2022). Kazakhstan and the Kyrgyz Republic are also benefiting from reexports of computers to the Russian Federation. ADB's growth forecast for Central Asia is 4.8% in 2022 and 4.2% in 2023. The European Bank for Reconstruction and Development (EBRD 2022) has also set optimistic growth rates for the subregion— 4.3% in 2022 and 4.9% in 2023.

2: Source of Money Transfers to Selected Central Asian Economies (% of total)

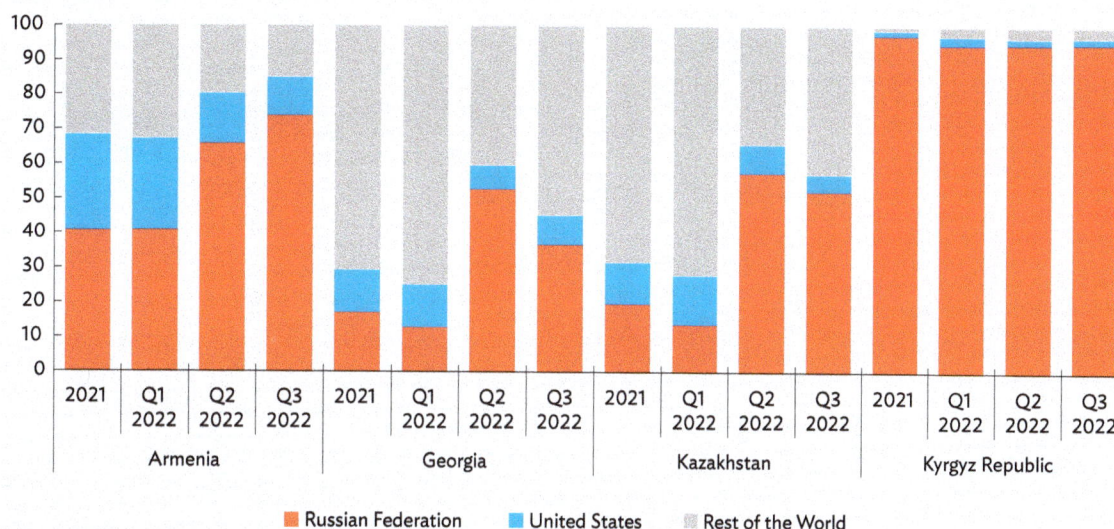

Q = quarter.

Sources: ADB calculations using data from the Government of Armenia, Central Bank of Armenia. External Sector Statistics. https://www.cba.am/en/SitePages/statexternalsector.aspx; Government of Georgia, National Bank of Georgia. Statistics Data. https://nbg.gov.ge/en/statistics/statistics-data; Government of Kazakhstan, National Bank of Kazakhstan. Statistics. https://www.nationalbank.kz/en/page/statistika; and the Government of the Kyrgyz Republic, National Bank of the Kyrgyz Republic. External Sector of the Economy. https://www.nbkr.kg/index1.jsp?item=128&lang=ENG (all accessed December 2022).

a   According to the Balance of Payments and International Investment Position Manual (IMF 2010), remittances mainly consist of all current transfers between residents and nonresidents; and net earnings of nonresident workers. In general, being present for 1 year or more in a territory or intending to do is sufficient to qualify as being a resident. Short trips to other economies do not lead to a change of residence.

Sources: ADB staff using ADB (2022); Bunina (2022); EBRD (2022); Imanaliyeva (2022); IMF (2010); and Usov (2022).

implication for remittances is increasingly important as they are significant external sources of income in many economies in developing Asia.

Given the current high-price environment and tight financial conditions, the continuing COVID-19 pandemic, policy uncertainty, and a slowdown in global growth, the outlook for remittances shows moderation in 2022 as spikes in prices erode wages, and pandemic-related support programs end in host economies (IFAD 2022). Meanwhile, strong job growth in the US and renewed demand for migrant labor in other developed host economies will help boost the growth of remittance flows to the region.

Harnessing Remittance Resilience through Vigorous Policy Approach

Better remittance infrastructure and greater use of technology/digital channels help reduce average cost of remittances to achieve the relevant Sustainable Development Goal (SDG) and promote financial inclusion.

As a lifeline to many families, bringing down the cost of remitting money will benefit migrants and their beneficiaries and encourage use of formal remittance channels. Indeed, reducing the price to remit to 3% is an SDG. According to the World Bank (2022), cutting existing remittance prices by at least 5 percentage points could save up to $16 billion a year, and for migrants from lower middle-income economies, cutting remittance fees by even 2 percentage points could translate into $12 billion of annual savings.

As of the second quarter (Q) of 2022, the average cost of sending $200 anywhere in the world was 6.0% of the remittance amount, double the SDG target (Figure 5.10a). The rate was lower in Asia, at 5.0%, but subregional variations can be significant. For instance, rates in the Pacific have been historically higher than the global rate and nearly twice the regional average. Remittance costs in Central Asia (until Q4 2021) and South Asia are lower than other subregions.

The majority of formal remittances are over-the-counter, cash-in/cash-out transactions, which are the costliest in most regions relative to other transfer channels (Figure 5.10b). Cash remittances sent through banks were lowest in Central Asia (5.6%), but rates for money sent through money transfer operators are lowest in South Asia (3.8%). Although cash sent through these operators costs less than when sent through banks, it usually comes with various additional fees across various stages of the transfer until the local currency cash equivalent is received by the intended household beneficiary from the nearest branch, which is often not near at all (Aneja and Etter 2021).

In 2020 (and 2021), lockdowns and social distancing rules hindered mobility and thus personal transactions, including through informal channels.[67] This boosted the use of digitalized remittance channels, which lifted the capture of formal remittance data. Digitalization is less costly than cash transfers and has reinforced the adoption of mobile money, the most affordable among payment instruments, averaging 2.6% in Asia and 3.5% globally, as of Q2 2022.

Advancing knowledge transfer on digital financial platforms could help sustain the momentum of digital usage among migrant senders and simultaneously advance the financial inclusion of migrants and their families. One example is the regional electronic know-your-customer initiative of the Reserve Banks of Australia and New Zealand which would allow digital verification of clients in the entire Pacific and more customers into the fold of banking services in economies where access to personal documents might be limited or nonexistent (Pinczewski and Capal 2022). Promoting greater transparency, such as making publicly available up-to-the-minute comparison tables indicating the cheapest way to send money from one economy to another, could also help lower remittance costs.

Changes in the legal and regulatory environment governing the remittance market could contribute to interoperability of cross-border remittances and further promote formal remittance channels.

The legal and regulatory environment surrounding remittances must be brought up to speed with industry changes. Outdated regulatory barriers on both sending and receiving ends result in higher and less transparent costs for the 2 billion transactions a year—most amounting to just $200–$300 each (IFAD 2018).

---

[67] For less accessible communities or people remitting relatively small amounts on a regular basis, informal channels such as the "hawala" system, which are commonly used in Bangladesh and Pakistan, may be cost-effective in the sense that funds are sent through unregulated large networks. However, informal channels can be used as a conduit for criminal activity and distort the true picture of recipient economies' balance of payments, which, in turn, could harm credit ratings and make it harder and more expensive to finance the kinds of large-scale initiatives needed by these economies to develop (Aneja and Etter 2021).

Figure 5.10: Average Total Cost of Remitting $200 (% of transaction amount)

(a) Quarterly trend

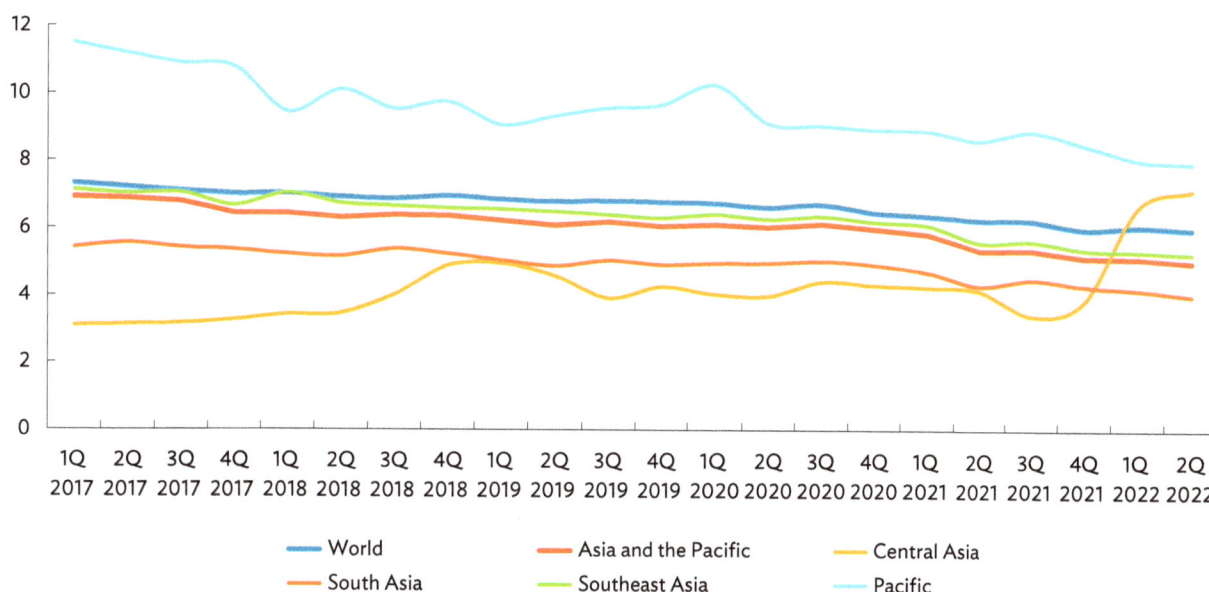

Legend: World, Asia and the Pacific, Central Asia, South Asia, Southeast Asia, Pacific

(b) By service provider and payment instrument, Q2 2022

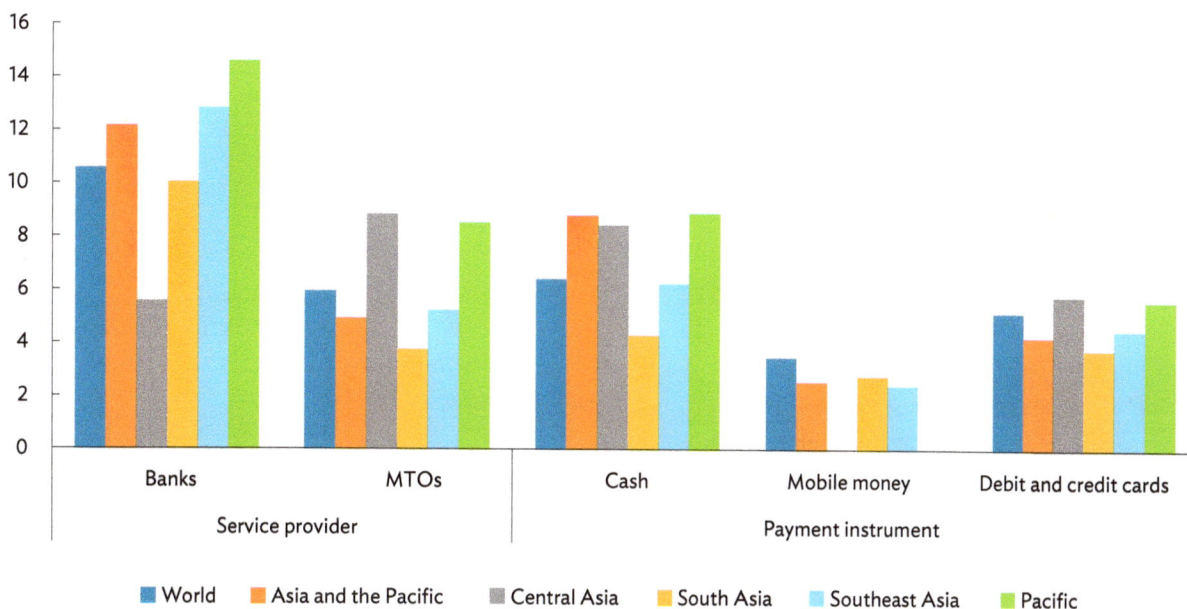

Legend: World, Asia and the Pacific, Central Asia, South Asia, Southeast Asia, Pacific

MTO = money transfer operator, Q = quarter.

Source: ADB calculations using data from World Bank. Remittance Prices Worldwide. https://remittanceprices.worldbank.org/ (accessed August 2022).

Remittance families generally spent about 70% of remittances on basic needs, leaving about 30% that could be saved and invested in asset-building or income-generating activities to help families establish livelihoods and begin securing their future. However, access to financial services is key, and many families, especially in rural areas, cannot save, borrow, and invest money through formal financial services.

Reducing regulatory barriers and onboarding banks could reduce the gaps in converting remittances into savings and investment instruments. Regulators and private sector companies need to make more joint efforts to harmonize legal and regulatory frameworks between economies to support digitalization and the birth of new remittance-linked financial products. While it is true that financial inclusion has improved from 68.5% in 2017 to 76.2% in 2021, the reality remains that a substantial majority of remittance-receiving families are mostly in rural areas outside the envelope of financial inclusion.[68]

The remittance environment also depends on the level of infrastructure that serves as good foundation for advancing interoperability possibilities. To this end, Australia, Japan, and the US have partnered in funding the construction of a new undersea cable in the Federated States of Micronesia, Kiribati, and Nauru to enhance internet connectivity (Australian Infrastructure Financing Facility for the Pacific 2021).

Financial products and green investments to mobilize remittance flows could promote resilience among beneficiary households and communities and improve welfare.

Remittance inflows have improved the quality of life of household beneficiaries, especially in developing economies. Although about 70% of remittances are spent on consumption needs, many remittance-receiving families consistently demonstrate a commitment to save and/or invest given the opportunity, using channels they understand and trust.[69] Whatever savings these families might have are often not sufficiently invested in productive sectors that could generate revenue streams for themselves and their immediate communities. Clearly, these gaps suggest that programs on financial literacy could be ramped up to advance the cause of financial inclusions. Greater engagement of players in the financial services industry could also bridge the gap and assist families in converting their savings into investment products that could be the first step in wealth creation. Promoting entrepreneurship using diaspora savings

could have far-reaching impact in generating sustainable livelihood and contributing to community development (Ahamed 2022).

Advancing the digitalization of remittances could also make it possible to link remittance inflows into a wider suite of financial services such as savings, credit, insurance, investments, and pensions, something that is difficult to accomplish for as long as most remittances are cash-based (Aneja and Etter 2021). In Bangladesh, the government in late 2019 implemented a compulsory insurance system for migrants. Under this policy, the Wage Earners' Welfare Board provides a 50% premium of Tk500 for coverage of Tk200,000. This is also equivalent to 20% premium for a coverage of Tk500,000. The government also completed the Bangladesh Migration Crisis Operational Framework, which articulates the roles of various agencies in assisting the more than 12 million migrants in host economies during periods of emergency and crises (United Nations Network on Migration 2021).

Tourism

International Tourism Trends

Asia is showing strong recovery although international tourist arrivals remain well below those of 2019.

After being turned upside down by the COVID-19 pandemic in 2020, the global tourism sector is on the path of gradual recovery. The pace of recovery in 2021 was weak, with global tourism arrivals only 30.4% of the 2019 level (UNWTO 2022a). The pace has since picked up, fueled by the easing of COVID-19-related border restrictions, supported by improved vaccine administration, and strong pent-up demand in

---

[68]   Data refer to the percentage of the population aged 15 and older who report having an account at any type of financial institution or using a money mobile service based on the World Bank. Global Financial Inclusion Database. https://databank.worldbank.org/source/global-financial-inclusion# (accessed December 2022).

[69]   Global Forums on Remittances, Investment and Development. Topic: Remittance Families and Development. https://gfrid.org/topics/remittance-families-and-development.

Europe, the Americas, and the Middle East. As a result, international tourist arrivals to major regions were 513.5 million from January to August of 2022, at least twice the 201.2 million in the same period in 2021.

By region, Asia recorded a bullish year-on-year growth in tourist arrivals (398.8%) during the first 8 months of 2022 (Figure 5.11a). However, even if cumulative arrivals to the region were five times the volume during the same months in 2021, the flow of tourists from January to August (35.3 million) was only about 10.3% of the pre-pandemic figure of 343.4 million in 2019 (Figure 5.11b). In comparison, Europe's year-on-year growth (149.7%) propelled the region to reach 50.9% of its pre-pandemic tourist arrival figure, while arrivals to the Middle East have achieved 51.4% of pre-pandemic arrivals traffic.

While tourist arrivals to Asia are trending upward, subregions vary. Data in Q3 2022 indicate an upswing for all subregions, with robust year-on-year growth rates ranging from 119.4% in Central Asia to 1148.5% for Southeast Asia, highlighting the role of easier travel

requirements and open borders in recovering tourism arrivals (Figure 5.12). Despite this high year-on-year growth, arrivals to Southeast Asia were only 15% of pre-pandemic levels. Within the first 9 months of 2022, arrivals to Central Asia, and South Asia were about 50% of 2019 levels. In East Asia, the recovery of tourism will be a long road, given the restrictive travel-related policies of some economies in the region. The PRC, which until recently, maintained its grip on zero-COVID policy, by far the most stringent approach, and had resulted in severe curtailment of international travel for Chinese tourists and a huge loss to global tourism, especially for PRC-dependent tourism markets (Li et al. 2022).[70] Chinese travelers spent about $255 billion in international tourism in 2019, and outbound travel restrictions since the pandemic began have resulted in a global slump in tourism activities catering to the Chinese market (Kotoky 2022). Hong Kong, China's maintenance of restrictions, such as quarantine and testing in some jurisdictions, has starved the economy of tourists, slowing its recovery attempts and making it a relative laggard to other subregions (Riordan et al. 2022).

Figure 5.11: International Tourist Arrivals

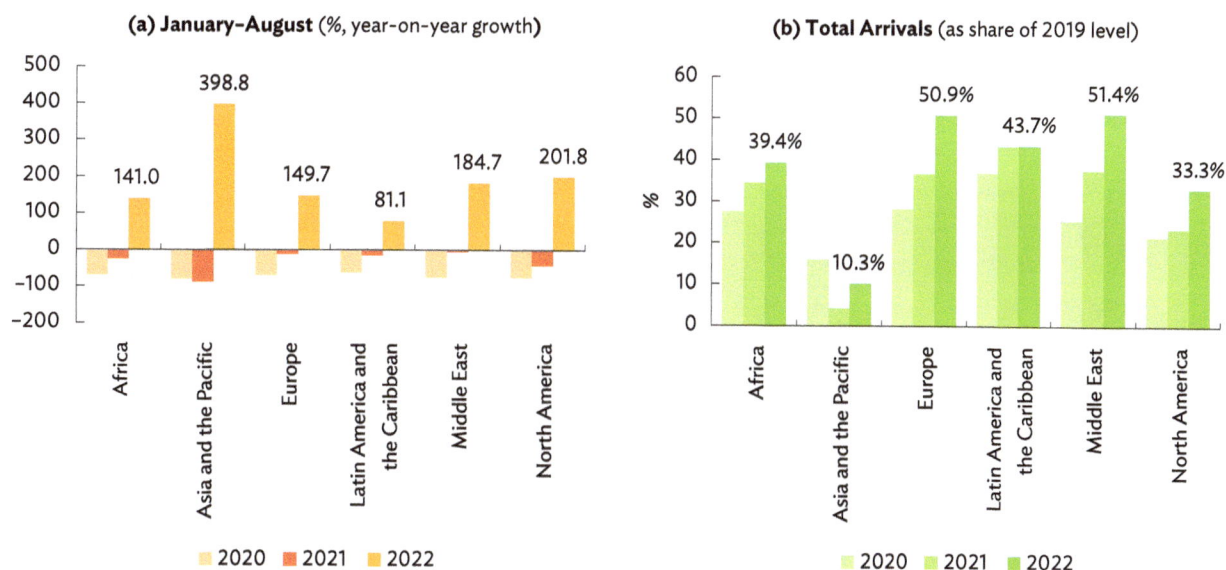

(a) January–August (%, year-on-year growth)

(b) Total Arrivals (as share of 2019 level)

Source: ADB calculations using data from United Nations World Tourism Organization. Tourism Recovery Tracker. https://www.unwto.org/tourism-data/unwto-tourism-recovery-tracker (accessed December 2022).

[70] On 7 December 2022, the PRC government unveiled a broad easing of its strict zero-COVID policy. Key changes include the following: (i) for intra-PRC regional travel, PCR tests and health codes will no longer be checked; (ii) quarantine and isolation will be allowed from home; and (iii) in high-risk areas, lockdowns will be lifted if no new case is found on the fifth day (Che, Chien, and Stevenson 2022).

Figure 5.12: Monthly Tourist Arrivals by Asian Subregions
(January 2019 = 100)

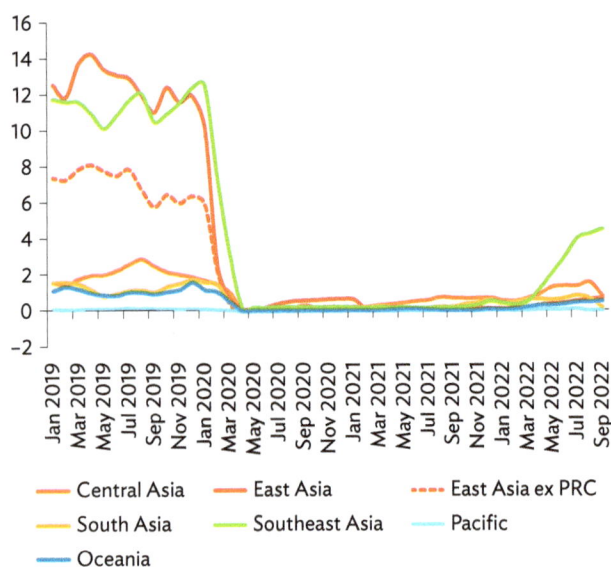

ex PRC = excluding People's Republic of China.

Source: ADB calculations using data from United Nations World Tourism Organization. Tourism Data Dashboard. https://www.unwto.org/tourism-data/unwto-tourism-dashboard (accessed December 2022).

The variation in pace of recovery is due to differences in national policies to reopen borders while being mindful of health and hygiene. For instance, nearly all Southeast Asian economies have eased COVID-19-related travel restrictions to reopen the travel industry while adopting precautionary measures (such as high vaccination rate, directives for COVID-19 infection, greater safety, and hygiene standards) and guidelines to help people live with the COVID-19 virus. Singapore, for instance, has eased various COVID-19 community measures including relaxing limits on social gathering group sizes as part of the nationwide approach to learn to live with the COVID-19 virus, while simultaneously enforcing vaccination-differentiated safety management and related health measures to complement its open-border strategies (Tan 2022).

Tourism receipts reflect tourist arrivals. International tourism receipts improved to $621.0 billion in 2021 from a low of $548 billion in 2020 (UNWTO 2022a). However, this is only 42% of the $1.5 trillion of 2019 (Figure 5.13a). Similarly, in Asia, recovery in tourism receipts lagged in 2021—$95.3 billion of tourism

earnings for the region were only 19.7% of the 2019 level and 58.0% of 2020 (Figure 5.13b). Europe recorded the most improvement in nominal terms, with 27.6% growth over 2020, 55.1% of the pre-pandemic level.

International tourism receipts peaked in 2019 across most of the Asian subregions (East Asia and the Pacific peaked in 2018) and plunged afterward (Figure 5.13c). Receipts contracted in 2020 and 2021 due to pandemic-related factors (with the exception of Central Asia's 70% growth in 2021). In 2021, tourism receipts to Central Asia, South Asia, and Oceania were at least one-third of the 2019 level. For the rest of the subregions, recovering tourism earnings will require more than just reopening borders and relaxing travel protocols. The blow to international tourism in 2020–2021 was the most severe since 2000 (Box 5.3).

The setback to tourism during the pandemic has hurt overall economies and external sectors, although recovery is underway. COVID-19 slashed tourism's total contribution to global GDP by 54.9% in 2020 (for $4.9 trillion in GDP loss), while recovering some ground in 2021 (Table 5.6) (WTTC 2022). In Asia, tourism's contribution to GDP likewise plunged in 2020, reaching 52% of the 2019 level in 2021. Indeed, while all subregions are inching toward the 2019 level, some are doing so faster than the others. For example, tourism's contribution to GDP in 2021 for Central Asia was 49% of the 2019 level, 36% for Southeast Asia, and 32% for the Pacific.

Export revenue from tourism activities declined steeply in 2020—the region's total export revenues from international tourism fell 71.2% in 2020 and 36.3% in 2021. Across subregions, the pandemic hurt three subregions the most—Central Asia, the Pacific, and Southeast Asia. In these subregions, export revenues from tourism in 2020 were just one-fifth of the pre-pandemic level. In 2021, Central Asia recovered to about one-third of its 2019 export revenue levels, but Southeast Asia and the Pacific were still struggling, with revenues equal to less than 10% of what they were before the pandemic struck.

Figure 5.13: International Tourism Receipts ($ billion)

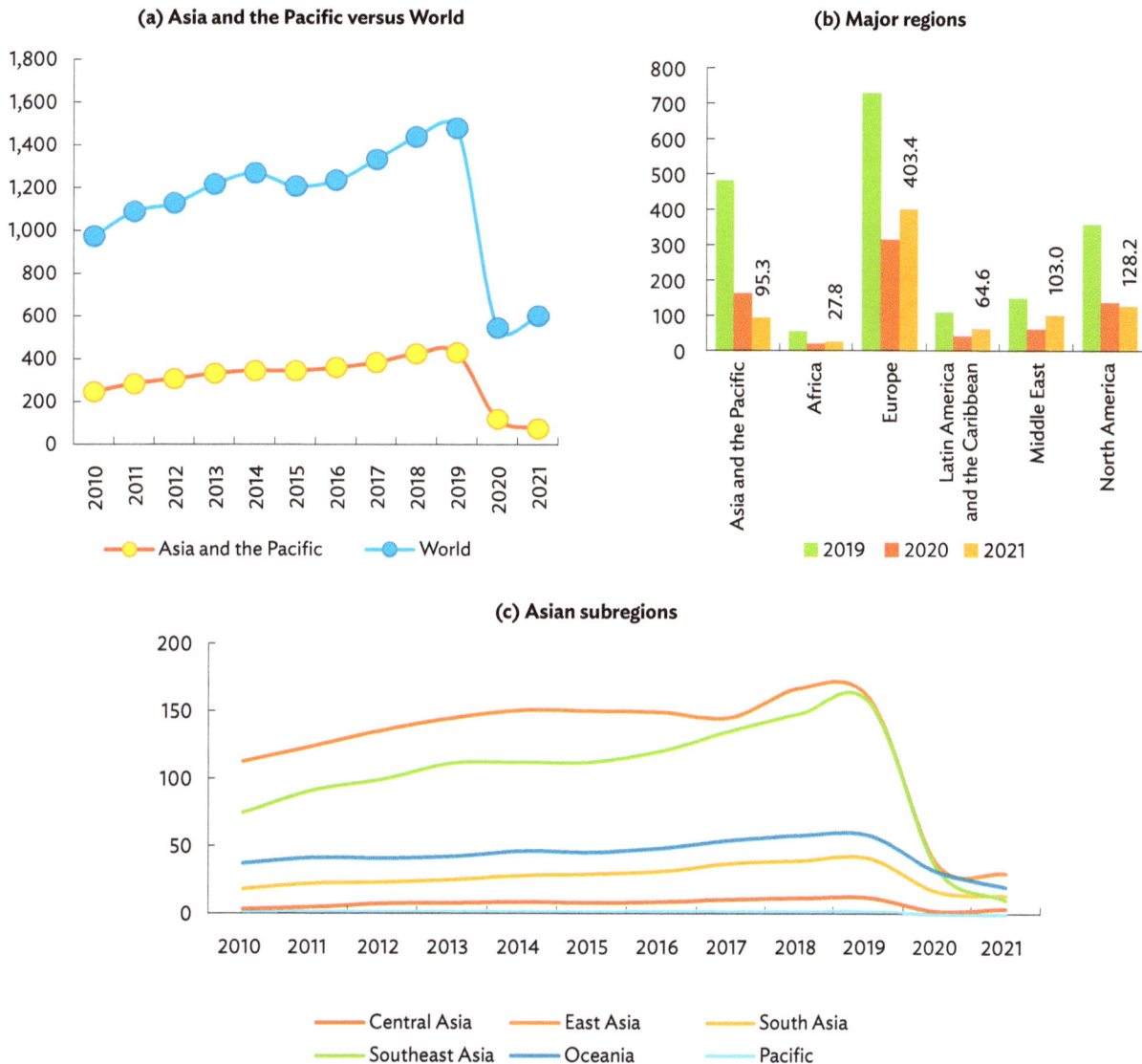

(a) Asia and the Pacific versus World

(b) Major regions

(c) Asian subregions

Source: ADB calculations using data from United Nations World Tourism Organization. UNWTO Tourism Data Dashboard. https://www.unwto.org/tourism-data/unwto-tourism-dashboard (accessed November 2022).

The recovery of tourist arrivals in Asia is trending behind other regions due to the slow opening of borders, staggered reopening policies, and the slow pace of vaccinations.

Asia's cautious stance on reopening borders and its comparatively more restrictive travel policies have caused the region to lag behind the global average. The region has been relatively careful in reopening borders. In Q1 2021, about 33.6% of Asian destinations were not accessible compared with only 11% of destinations in the rest of the world (Figure 5.14). By Q2 2022, although the proportion of closed destinations in Asia declined to 16.8%, it was still higher than the 0.6% for the rest of the world. As more economies began eliminating most (if not all) of COVID-19 entry requirements, the share of closed destinations declined further to 1.8% by Q4 2022 for Asian destinations.

Asian economies also planned for a staggered reopening, with some opening in phases or parts of their jurisdictions. For example, Thailand followed phased

Table 5.6: International Tourism: Export Revenues and Contribution to Gross Domestic Product—Asia and the Pacific

Asian Subregions	Export Revenue from Tourism ($ billion)			Export Revenue from Tourism (as share of 2019 level)		Total Contribution to GDP ($ billion)		
	2019	2020	2021	2020	2021	2019	2020	2021
Central Asia	12.6	2.5	4.3	19.9%	33.8%	22.0	7.7	10.7
East Asia	160.9	38.1	30.3	23.7%	18.8%	2,079.9	923.8	1,081.8
Oceania	41.9	17.3	13.9	41.2%	33.3%	180.1	106.5	98.7
Pacific	157.6	34.7	10.8	22.0%	6.8%	2.9	1.1	0.9
South Asia	58.5	31.9	20.2	54.5%	34.5%	255.6	148.6	204.6
Southeast Asia	2.2	0.4	0.1	16.9%	3.5%	395.6	137.9	143.2
Asia and the Pacific	433.8	124.9	79.5	28.8%	18.3%	2,936.1	1,325.5	1,539.9

GDP = gross domestic product.

Note: Export revenue from tourism refers to the sum of international receipts from passenger travel items and transport items.

Sources: United Nations World Tourism Organization (UNWTO 2022a); UNWTO. Tourism Data Dashboard. https://www.unwto.org/tourism-data/unwto-tourism-dashboard; World Bank. World Development Indicators. https://databank.worldbank.org/source/world-development-indicators (both accessed November 2022); and World Travel and Tourism Council. Economic Impact Reports. https://wttc.org/Research/Economic-Impact.

Box 5.3: The Sharpest Downturn in International Tourism Since 2000

Global tourism enjoyed a decade of brisk uninterrupted growth from 2010 to 2019, after weathering different crises in 2000–2009 that had constrained the flow of international tourists (box figure).

The attacks on the World Trade Center in New York City on 11 September 2001 shocked the world and had considerable impact on aviation and travel protocols. Although no airline in the United States (US) immediately failed, within 4 years, employment in the US airline industry had fallen by 28% as 150,000 jobs were lost; every major US international carrier filed for bankruptcy protection (except American Airlines); and it was not until 2005 that available airline seats reached pre-9/11 peak levels (Clark 2007, US Department of Transportation, Bureau of Transportation Statistics 2021). Despite the ensuing geopolitical ramifications of 9/11, international tourist arrivals grew 2.7% to 702.4 million in 2002 as growth in other regions eclipsed the decline in tourist flows in North America. In Asia, arrivals climbed 9.0% to 116.1 million in 2002.

Meanwhile, in 2002, the bombings in Bali, Indonesia caused a steep drop in tourism in Indonesia (11.2%) and in the Asian region (8.9%). The severe acute respiratory syndrome (SARS) viral outbreak in late 2002–2003 impacted the People's Republic of China and Hong Kong, China most severely (Cherry 2004, Little 2020). The advice of the World Health Organization was to postpone nonessential travel to affected economies, hitting Asian tourism, which had the most infected areas (ADB 2003).

An empirical study by Kuo et al. (2008) revealed that in advanced economies, infectious diseases had statistically insignificant effect on tourism flows. But in developing economies, especially where such diseases tend to be more prevalent and health infrastructure lags, the magnitude and statistical significance is much greater. For SARS, a 10% increase in the number of confirmed infections led to a decline of about 8% in international tourist arrivals to developing economies—almost twice as much as the average impact on all economies.

The global financial crisis in the second half of 2008 that caused a drop in business and consumer confidence led to a global recession that moved international tourist arrivals into negative territory in the second half of 2008 after a 5% increase in the first half (UNWTO 2009). As a result, global arrivals in 2008 increased 1.7% year-on-year while tourist arrivals to Asia rose 0.9%. In 2009, the impact of the global financial crisis on tourism manifested as a 4.2% contraction in international arrivals (–2.0% in Asia). Displaying resilience, tourism rebounded in 2010, with 76.7 million additional arrivals over 2009, or growth equivalent to 8.7% (11.7% growth for Asia). International receipts were also estimated to have increased by about 5%–6% in real terms.

From 2010 to 2019, international tourist arrivals rose by an annual average of 4.9%. About 1.5 billion tourist arrivals were recorded in 2019. During this period, global tourism was riding high and mighty: it created 1 in every 10 jobs;

continued on next page

Box 5.3 continued

earned $1.7 trillion in export revenues; and generated $3.5 trillion in direct tourism GDP (UNWTO 2020). It was not until the first quarter of 2020, that the COVID-19 outbreak and subsequent restrictions on travel and domestic mobility turned the global tourism sector on its head. All of the previous crises that the global tourism economy encountered and surpassed seemed to be "minor bumps on the road" compared with the wrath of the coronavirus pandemic (World Economic Forum 2022). Labeled as "the worst year in tourism history" by the United Nations World Tourism Organization

(UNWTO), the pandemic slashed international arrivals by 1 billion, put 100 million–120 million direct tourism jobs at risk, disproportionately diminished the employment of informal and migrant workers (particularly women and youth) and risked compromising the progress of the UN Sustainable Development Goads (Goretti et al. 2021). As a result of travel and mobility restrictions, the estimated loss in export revenues was $1.3 trillion, more than 11 times the loss recorded during the 2009 global economic crisis (UNWTO 2021).

International Tourist Arrivals and Growth Rates—Asia and the Pacific versus the World

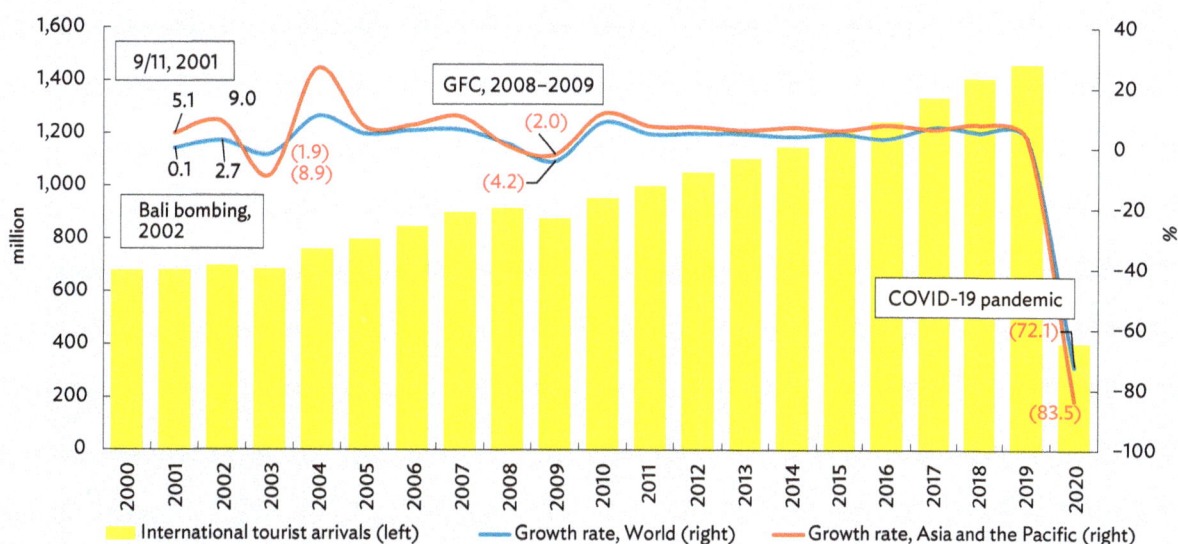

GFC = global financial crisis.

Note: Numbers in parentheses are negative.

Sources: ADB calculations using data from United Nations World Tourism Organization (UNWTO 2004). Tourism Barometer. https://www.unwto.org/; UNWTO. Tourism Statistics. https://www.e-unwto.org/toc/unwtotfb/current (accessed August 2022); UNWTO (2004); and World Bank. World Development Indicators. https://databank.worldbank.org/ (all accessed August 2022).

Sources: ADB staff compilation using ADB (2003); Cherry (2004); Clark (2007); Goretti et al. (2021); Kuo et al. (2008); Little (2020); US Department of Transportation, Bureau of Transportation Statistics (2021); UNWTO (2009, 2021, 2022b); and World Economic Forum (2022).

reopening between July 2021, when they announced the Phuket Sandbox, and July 2022, when they removed the Thailand Pass registration scheme. These initiatives led to a record an eightfold increase in average monthly arrivals, from 56,159 in June–December 2021 to 457,740 in January–July 2022.[71] Australia, which shut its borders from March 2020, began to welcome tourists only from

21 February 2022. Since then, monthly arrivals have been growing at an average rate of 25.4%, quadrupling from February (90,460) to September (371,850). Japan's decision to finally allow independent inbound tourism from 11 October 2022 immediately caused a surge in travel demand, especially for the cherry blossom season in 2023. As of January 2023, 99 economies

---

[71] UNWTO. Tourism Data Dashboard. Global and Regional Tourism Performance. https://www.unwto.org/tourism-data/global-and-regional-tourism-performance (accessed October 2022).

Figure 5.14: International Travel Restrictions (% of total)

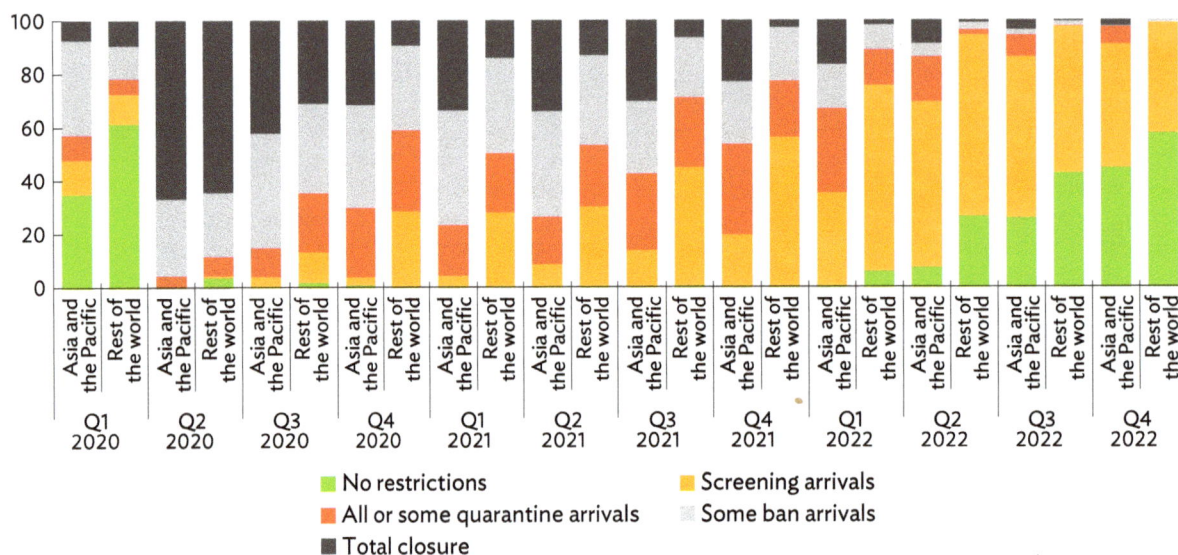

Q = quarter.

Source: ADB calculations using data from University of Oxford, Blavatnik School of Government. Oxford COVID-19 Government Response Tracker Database. https://github.com/OxCGRT/covid-policy-tracker/tree/master/data/timeseries (accessed October 2022). In Hale et al. (2021).

(of which 34% are in Europe; 13% in Asia) are without any COVID-19 restrictions.[72] These restriction-free economies accounted for 31% of arrivals and 23% of tourism receipts volume in 2019.

The time and pace of the rollout of COVID-19 vaccination programs was an important factor in reopening the borders and restoring travel confidence for the tourism industry.[73] In major regions where about 70% of the population have received complete COVID-19 and booster vaccination, empirical results show that lower COVID-19 infection and death rates have helped to enhance tourism recovery (Okafor and Yan 2022) (Figure 5.15a). Trends in international arrivals to these regions in the first half of 2022 indicate that the tourism economy in these regions is clearly poised for take-off.

In Asia, that path to recovery is nuanced and, in some subregions, laden with obstacles. Higher vaccination

coverage does not immediately lead to higher probability of tourism recovery, as domestic COVID-19 containment policies and travelers' perceptions of health, safety, and hygiene are equally important determinants to boost cross-border mobility. In East Asia, for example, about 90% of the population have been vaccinated, but its COVID-19 restrictions remain stricter than in other subregions (Figure 5.15b). In Southeast Asia, where travel restrictions have been considerably relaxed, the percentage of the population fully vaccinated against COVID-19 ranges from a low of 60% in Timor-Leste to as high as 100% in Brunei Darussalam—82% in Malaysia; 63% in the Philippines; 75% in Thailand (Figure 5.16). The subregion was the most visited region during January–July 2022, followed by Central Asia. Meanwhile, for the Pacific, other than an uneven pace of vaccination, the region suffers from lack of transport competitiveness to kickstart a tourism recovery in the aftermath of the pandemic (Park et al. 2021).

---

[72]   UNWTO. Tourism Recovery Tracker. https://www.unwto.org/tourism-data/unwto-tourism-recovery-tracker (accessed November 2022).

[73]   The direct effects of the COVID-19 vaccine rollout on tourism recovery efforts have not yet been definitively established in literature. The key factors that could determine the successful outcomes from vaccination rollout programs include varying degrees of vaccine hesitancy, uneven distribution and/or limited availability of vaccines (especially in developing economies), and different levels of efficacies of different vaccines. This implies that high vaccination coverage alone may not be enough for the tourism sector to rebound, but that the number of vaccinated people per million population must significantly outpace the number of COVID-19 deaths per million.

Figure 5.15: COVID-19 Vaccination Profile by Region (% of the population)

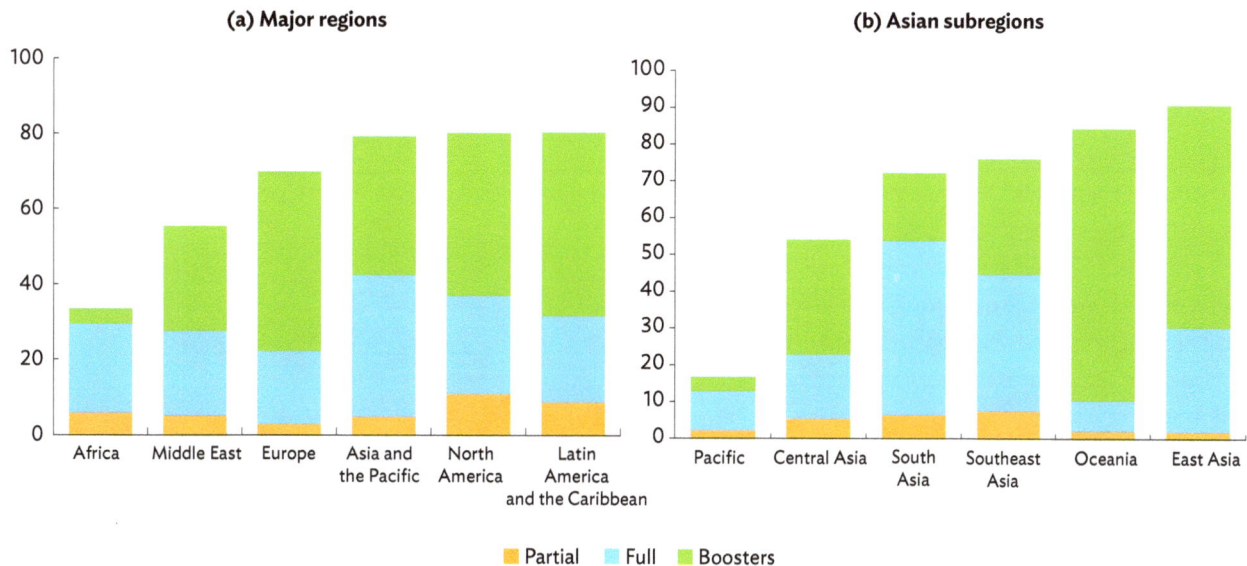

(a) Major regions

(b) Asian subregions

Partial   Full   Boosters

Note: Latest available data are used at the economy level.

Source: ADB calculations using data from CEIC Data Company.

Figure 5.16: Fully Vaccinated Persons and COVID-19 Cases (% of population)

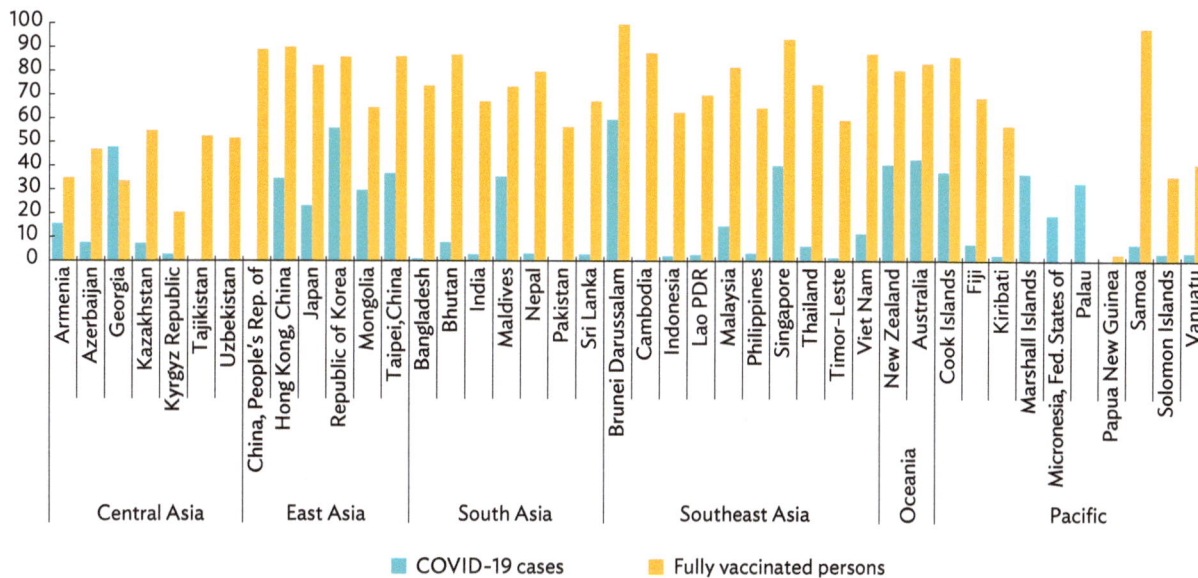

COVID-19 cases   Fully vaccinated persons

COVID-19 = coronavirus disease, Lao PDR = Lao People's Democratic Republic.

Source: ADB calculations using data from Mathieu et al. (2020).

Status of Tourism's Rebound Efforts and Experts' Outlook on Recovery

Pressures from external risks are dampening recovery momentum. Experts foresee the rebound of international tourism to 2019 levels by 2024.

The estimated global economic slowdown, rising inflation and interest rates, and the Russian invasion of Ukraine have brought additional downside risks to tourism and increased uncertainty on the return of confidence to global travel (UNWTO 2022a, 2022c). The invasion represents a downside risk for tourism even for Asia. Pre-pandemic travel patterns suggest that

Asia accounted for one-third (33.1%) of the Russian outbound tourism market. The loss of inbound tourists from the Russian Federation will affect the PRC, some Central Asian economies, and Thailand—in 2019, around half of Asia-bound travelers from the Russian Federation visited Kazakhstan, Georgia, Azerbaijan, and Thailand (Figure 5.17). In the case of Ukraine, its outbound travelers are mostly Europe-bound—only 2.6% visited Asia. The longer-term impact of the Russian invasion of Ukraine would be through the effects of airspace restrictions and rising oil prices which, in turn, could impact airfares and stall the recovery of international travel (Figure 5.18).

Tourism recovery is also affected by rising oil prices, which is making travel expensive. Airlines, which have just started to return to normal operations, are under pressure from soaring jet fuel prices—in Asia, jet fuel prices are up 73.3% year-on-year (Figure 5.16).[74] This affects the ability of airlines to offer competitive airfares and a range of flights they can operate (Bowerman 2022). In addition, consumer travel plans will be more discerning,[75] amid reduced purchasing

Figure 5.17: Outbound Tourism from the Russian Federation and Ukraine, 2019

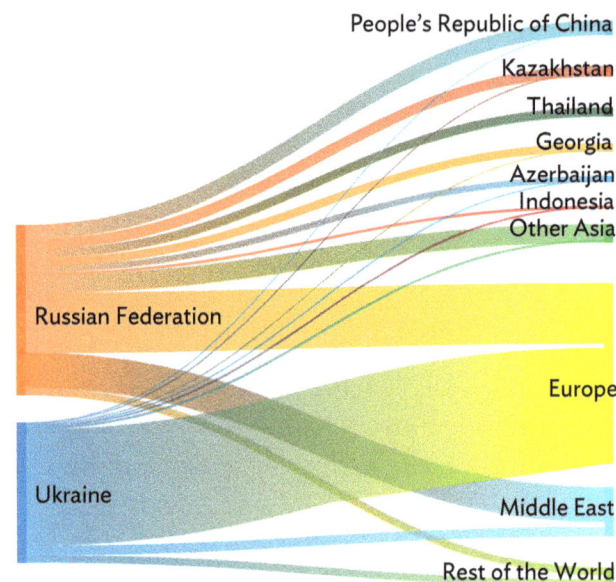

Source: ADB calculations using data from United Nations World Tourism Organization. Tourism Satellite Accounts. http://statistics.unwto.org (accessed December 2022).

Figure 5.18: Crude Oil and Jet Fuel Price Indexes

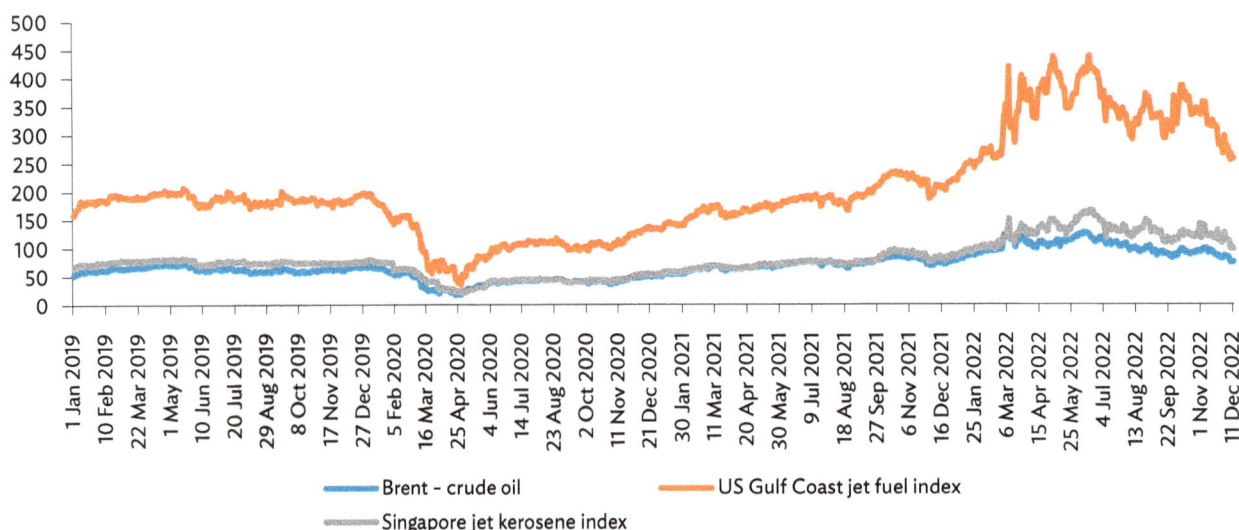

Source: ADB calculations using data from Bloomberg.

---

[74]   Based on average Singapore jet kerosene spot prices from January to November 2021 and for the same months in 2022, data accessed from Bloomberg.

[75]   A survey in the United Kingdom indicated that the rising cost of living, rising cost of fuel, and personal finances are the top three constraints to taking an overnight trip (Visit Britain 2022).

power and discretionary incomes due to rising interest rates and inflation arising from supply chain disruption since the pandemic.

Results of the United Nations World Tourism Organization (UNWTO) Confidence Index survey conducted for the UNWTO Panel of Experts in September 2022 revealed that 78% see better prospects for 2022. About 27% of experts see a potential return of international arrivals to 2019 levels in 2023 (down from 48% in the May 2022 survey), while 61% believe it will occur in 2024 or later.[76] Globally, improvements in the economic environment, reining in high prices, and continuous easing of travel restrictions will help boost the recovery of global tourism (Figure 5.19).

Figure 5.19: Barriers to Recovery of Global Tourism

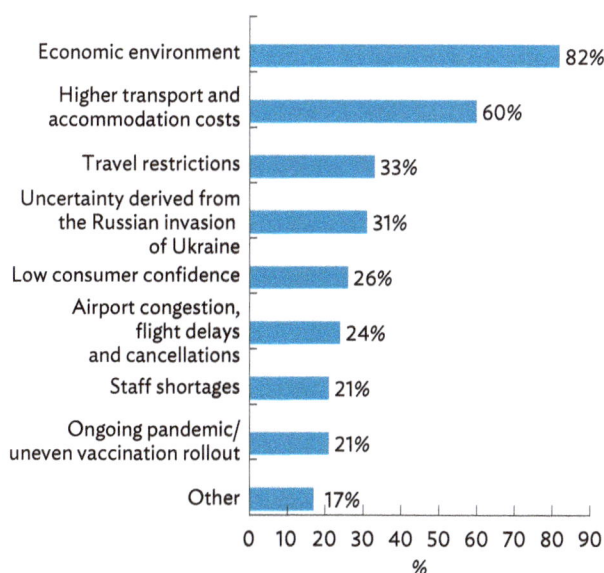

Note: Data were published in September 2022.
Source: UNWTO (2022a).

In Asia, the easing/removal of travel restrictions and accelerated vaccination rollout to further control the pandemic will benefit ongoing tourism recovery efforts in the region. A survey by AirAsia Philippines (2022) of 1,605 respondents indicated that 60% are willing to travel domestically and at least 50% are willing to travel internationally in case travel restrictions are further relaxed. Meanwhile, travel sentiment remains robust

among Europeans, with 58% planning to travel at least twice despite rising inflation, the Russian invasion of Ukraine, and the ongoing pandemic (European Travel Commission 2022).

Meanwhile, the World Travel and Tourism Council estimates an annual average growth rate of 5.8% from 2022 to 2032 in international tourism versus the 2.7% increase in global GDP, and the creation of 126 million new jobs within the next decade (WTTC 2022). The travel and tourism industry's portion of GDP is forecast to reach $8.4 trillion in 2022 and $9.6 trillion in 2023 globally, marking the return to its pre-pandemic level. Tourism jobs are projected to recover to 324 million in 2023. In Asia, travel and tourism's contribution to GDP is set to hit $2.7 trillion in 2022, before returning to the 2019 level in 2023. Ultimately, the pace and expanse of the tourism recovery will depend on how cross-economy policy responses develop as the pandemic evolves (Goretti et al. 2021).

Essential Focus Areas for Sustainable Tourism Recovery

In Asia, a proper reboot of the tourism economy requires addressing the challenges facing the sector even before the pandemic.

Even before COVID-19, the region's tourism sector was facing several challenges. These included a narrow source market, over-tourism, infrastructure and connectivity, informal economy, and a lack of data collection and analysis across tourism value chain activities. Several tourism-dependent economies also entered the pandemic "with limited fiscal space, weak public sector balance sheets, inadequate external buffers, and foreign exchange revenues concentrated in tourism," which made managing the extreme repercussion of the pandemic severely challenging (Goretti et al. 2021). Post-pandemic recovery in Asia will need policy options that build sustainability and resilience. While some of these can be developed at the domestic level, others need greater regional cooperation to address the prolonged challenges.

---

[76]   In UNWTO (2022b), it was forecast that 55% to 70% of international arrivals will reach pre-pandemic levels in 2022.

Expand tourism markets by recalibrating approaches to economic partnerships and forging diverse ties outside of traditional sources of international visitors.

Tourism-dependent economies must build strategic partnerships and explore new source markets other than their traditional ones. Tourism in Asia is driven highly by arrivals from East Asian economies—in 2019, 47.0% of total tourist arrivals to Asia were from Hong Kong, China (87.4 million); the People's Republic of China (70.3 million); the Republic of Korea (23.3 million); Taipei,China (16.5 million); Japan (15.5 million); and Mongolia (2.1 million) (Figure 5.20). These five economies were also among the top intraregional source markets and accounted for 59.5% of intra-Asian travelers in 2019. Leading extraregional visitors to Asia include the US (14.6 million), the Russian Federation (11.9 million), the UK (7.2 million), Germany (4.5 million), and France (3.8 million). With the onset of COVID-19 in 2020, arrivals from the top source markets of intra-Asian tourism saw a year-on-year drop of 93.2% (200.2 million). The same from the leading extra-Asian markets fell by 90.9% (34.1 million), showing relatively lesser vulnerability when compared with Asian travelers.

While Asia must capitalize on its traditional source market of neighboring economies, it should also explore ways to attract more international tourists from non-regional markets. Outbound tourism may remain subdued in the coming year as the PRC remains relatively closed to overseas leisure travel even when many economies are open to PRC travelers. To compensate for the revenue loss from fewer PRC tourists, Asian economies should work to restore traveler confidence from existing source markets. They can build partnerships with local brands of the source economies to generate familiarity and instill confidence and can secure sustainable destination labels for tourist spots and hotels to convince people to travel.

The region should also pay attention to alternative market sources and cooperate on common or compatible travel standards. Adopting best practices that include accelerating the pace of vaccination can contribute to more effective tourism recovery. Better coordination and communication toward harmonized travel protocols can expedite efforts to reinvigorate tourism. For instance, there have been

Figure 5.20: Source Markets for Inbound Tourism in Asia and the Pacific, 2019

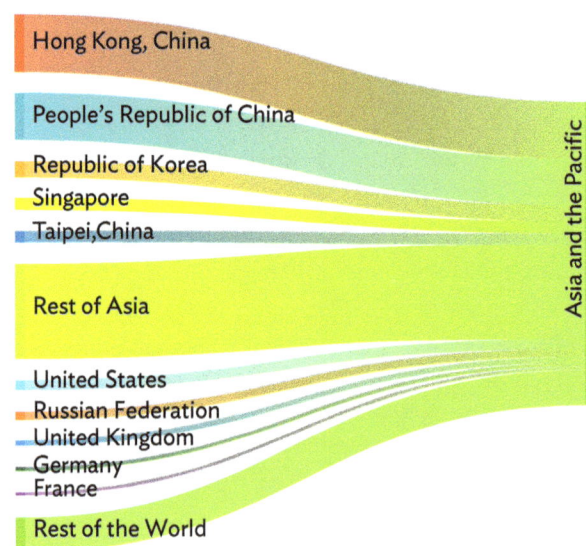

Source: ADB calculations using data from United Nations World Tourism Organization. Tourism Satellite Accounts. http://statistics.unwto.org (accessed December 2022).

discussions of an Association of Southeast Asian Nations (ASEAN)-recognized digital vaccination certificate, but 3 years into the pandemic, such a mutually recognized health measure, which would have been an ideal take-off point for harmonization of related travel protocols within the subregion, has yet to come into existence. In addition, the economic effects of the travel shutdown on jobs, businesses, and livelihood have all contributed to the reduced financial capacity to travel, in addition to the different perceptions about health risks and travel safety. Hence, despite the loud volume of so-called revenge travel and pent-up demand, predicting travel flows remains an exercise of uncertain possibilities (Bowerman 2022).

Government and destination management organizations should enhance partnerships to help restructure the sector to lure new kinds of travelers. As more borders reopen and work arrangements become more flexible, governments can benefit from leveraging this new normal and work with industry players and other stakeholders to better capture this newly emerging market segment. Thailand, a leading tourism economy in Asia, is riding the potential of the new normal with its systematic shift from mass tourism to more higher value-added tourism using the DASH Program (Box 5.4).

Box 5.4: Thailand's Tourism Transformation Approach: DASH Model

Thailand was the most visited destination in Southeast Asia until the coronavirus disease (COVID-19) pandemic hammered its tourism industry. From an annual average of 37.9 million visitors in 2017–2019, arrivals plunged 82.3% to 6.7 million in 2020 and 0.4 million in 2021.

Realizing the immense vulnerability to its tourism sector to external global health shocks, mobility restrictions, and limited source markets, Thailand has embarked on a strategic, multipronged approach to revitalize and transform its tourism industry toward a stronger and sustainable, more responsible, more digital, and more inclusive tourism.

Using a "DASH" model to underpin its transformative goals and action plans, Thailand intends to boost **domestic travel** by focusing on both tourists and tourism operators; **accelerate demand** by diversifying its source markets and targeting high-income segments; **shape supply** toward quality and sustainable income for all sectors by focusing on responsible tourism and digitalization; and **healing** the Thai economy through tourism by leveraging the 5Fs (food, film, fashion, festival, and fight) and 4Ms (music, museum, master, and meta).

The DASH model, focused on a domestic tourism transformation, is targeting 160 million trips and B656 billion from specific segments for innovative travel experiences—including "workcation," "staycation," wellness, sports, and responsible tourism. In international tourism, Thailand is looking to achieve an immediate target of 10 million international tourists and revenues of B625 billion by the end of 2022, in light of formally recognizing COVID-19 as an endemic virus and fully lifting entry requirements related to the pandemic from 1 October 2022 (Tourism Authority of Thailand 2022a).

This diversification approach is banking on strong intraregional ties, especially in the Association of Southeast Asian Nations (ASEAN)—in 2019, 79.2% of international visitors to Thailand were intraregional, of which 35.4% were from ASEAN economies. Recent bilateral initiatives include working with India and the Republic of Korea, as well as with Canada, Saudi Arabia, and Türkiye to boost bilateral tourism flow (Tourism Authority of Thailand 2022b, 2022c, 2022d, 2022e, 2022f). Meanwhile, the "Amazing Thailand Workplace Paradise" campaign is marketed to entice remote workers from long-haul international markets. A long-term resident visa of up to 10 years (and extendable) has been introduced for high-net-worth foreigners to live and do business in Thailand, with the view of attracting 1 million visa holders under the scheme and generating B1 trillion in investments and real property sales in the next 5 years. On the other hand, the short haul international segment is targeting leisure travelers, students, and digital nomads. To push sustainability across the tourism value chain, tourism enterprises are encouraged to adopt the bio-circular-green model into their regular operations, such as adopting the use of renewable energy in accommodation infrastructures.

International tourism receipts accounted for 11% of gross domestic product (GDP) ($59.7 billion) in 2019 but plunged to $5.1 billion (or 1% of GDP) in 2021. The pickup in arrivals during the first three quarters of 2022 offer the possibility that travel receipts have begun recovery and will continue to do so well into 2023/2024. As Thailand continues to drive investments in infrastructure and facilities supporting tourism, and induces encouraging GDP growth, one could look forward to the return of a vibrant tourism industry as a key contributor to growth in the short and medium term.

Sources: ADB staff using Tourism Authority of Thailand (2022a , 2022b, 2022c, 2022d, 2022e, 2022f).

Managing volumes of tourist inflow must be in line with the goals of protecting and preserving heritage and cultural sites and the environment.

Targeting high arrival numbers was the pre-pandemic norm of the Asian tourism strategy, backed by the premise that more visitors would lead to more tourism revenues. But this strategy compromised the areas of tourism management tasked with assessing tourist inflows against the costs of hosting too many visitors. Mass tourism, which is associated with over-tourism, ensued in many go-to places in Asia. Too many visitors in each place and time undermine the tourism experience by focusing on tourism's natural assets and aggravating problems of pollution, sewage, and wastewater management, environmental degradation, and even caused the destruction of some important cultural and heritage sites. Examples of destinations that fell prey to over-tourism include Boracay in the Philippines, Maya Bay in Thailand, and Sipadan Island in Malaysia. Mass tourism could also result in the gentrification of tourist-heavy neighborhoods, which raise the cost of living to the point that even the locals could be forced to relocate.

Tourists are motivated to visit Asian destinations primarily because of the local landscapes, biodiversity, heritage, and cultures, making it imperative to retain and preserve as much natural resources while adapting to the changing social, environmental, and climatic conditions (The ASEAN Post 2018). Incentivizing measures to help distribute tourism traffic throughout the year could reduce the potential for hordes of tourists to chafe against environmentally friendly tourism action plans. Destinations could have caps on visitor numbers during peak season and instead offer discounted rates at other times of the year. A destination could also temporarily close to allow for some of the environmental damage caused by mass tourism to be repaired.

Fortify investments in tourism infrastructure and harness (digitalization) technology to promote sustainability and evidence-based policy making.

Mobility and connectivity are fundamental drivers of a sustainable and inclusive tourism sector. Post COVID-19, transport, hygiene, health care, and internet connectivity assume great importance in travelers' choices of tourist destination. Investments in this infrastructure are thus essential to improve tourism readiness for Asian destinations. For example, in ASEAN, while the number of passenger arrivals grew by an annual average of 9.5% from 2008 to 2019, the international aircraft traffic increased 7% annually over the same period. These trends must be studied alongside gateway development plans to ensure there are enough airports and means of transport to support tourism growth. At the subregional

level, these types of investment needs will vary. For instance, Central Asia, with its nascent tourism sector, stands to benefit from rapid investments in all modes of transport to boost connectivity.[77]

Further investments in the physical and technological infrastructure are necessary to enhance the competitiveness of Asian tourism. Greater public–private engagement should be encouraged to facilitate a shift toward digitally enabled self-guided tourism that may not require group travel. With greater digitalization, governments should work with small and medium-sized enterprises to enable them to embrace digital tools and capabilities to increase the resilience of their business operation. Reskilling and training of tourism employees will be crucial to adjust to the new normal, while mitigating adverse impact of job loss in the sector. Accordingly, governments, private players, and tourists should work together to create transparency and enable data flow among tourist sending and receiving destinations.

Contribute to promoting tourism's social safety structure by addressing informality in employment.

The informal segment is an integral part of the nature of Asian tourism. This is because most tourism work and businesses are seasonal, and the regulations and enforcement of laws related to legal hiring and remuneration practices are often weak. Most tourism workers are employed on a part-time or occasional basis, or as an additional job, and the sector is characterized by high turnover and limited access to social safety nets (Goretti et al. 2021).

Some economies employ migrants in their tourism industry, particularly lower-wage workers from neighboring economies or workers from rural areas within the same economy. In Australia, for instance, migrants employed in the tourism and hospitality

---

[77]   Among the recent initiatives in Central Asia to address the connectivity issue while promoting collaboration to deepen tourism and cultural linkages is the opening of regular flights on the Almaty–Yerevan route, providing impetus to the development of mutual tourism between Kazakhstan and Armenia (Kazinform 2022). Meanwhile, India has expressed its willingness to cooperate, invest, and build connectivity within Central Asia (Schulz 2022).

industry are one of the largest users of temporary work visas. In Thailand, it is estimated that a fifth of workers in the hospitality sector come from the low-wage Southeast Asian economies. In ASEAN, nearly 97% of unemployed migrants in tourism have no access to their host economy's social safety nets (Goretti et al. 2021). Strong bilateral and regional cooperation are necessary to address tourism informality in the region.

Refocusing on resilience, inclusivity, and innovation (creative transformation) will boost industry strength and generate quality tourism products.

The pandemic has invited a rethink of medium- and long-term tourism strategies. The crisis thus brings with it the opportunity to align the tourism sector toward a more resilient, human-centered future (ILO 2021). Economies must redesign their tourism models, while creating opportunities for diversification within and beyond the industry, through policy support and structural reforms. There's no standard template to reinvigorate each tourism economy. The road to recovery will differ, just as the new normal for international tourism will be unique for each economy. Asian destinations must shift their messaging from the traditional sun-sea-and-sand type of tourism to one that is more interactive, environment-friendly, and engages the local community. Trends indicate a growing demand for formerly niche tourism products involving nature, heritage, and cultural experiences such as ecotourism, mountain tourism, food and wine tourism, health tourism, farm tourism, spiritual tourism, and even senior citizen tourism.

Regional cooperation remains crucial to accelerate tourism recovery.

The global tourism industry has endured the intense pressure of rebirth and transformation. With the pandemic in its third year, regional cooperation among economies remains of great relevance for recovery and sustainability. ASEAN has always paid great attention to promoting intraregional tourism as its policy priority. It has developed the ASEAN Tourism Forum, a cooperative regional effort to promote the ASEAN region as one tourist destination, and has also endorsed the ASEAN declaration on digital tourism to use digital means to improve the competitiveness of the sector. It has also signed the ASEAN–EU Comprehensive Air Transport Agreement, the world's first bloc-to-bloc air transport agreement that allows airlines of ASEAN and the EU to fly any number of passenger and cargo services between both regions. Not only will this arrangement enhance passenger and air cargo traffic, it will also provide cooperation between ASEAN and the EU in areas such as aviation safety, air traffic management, consumer protection, and environmental and social issues (Government of Singapore, Ministry of Transport 2022). Meanwhile, the Government of Cambodia, the host of the 40th ASEAN Tourism Forum, called on tourism ministers and health institutions of ASEAN member states to develop a common ASEAN-wide system for the certification of full vaccination—a vaccination passport or digital health pass—for the region and to gradually ease travel restrictions while providing the highest level of vigilance (Phnom Penh Post 2022).

The enthusiasm of regional cooperation also finds its way in how tourism transformation is approached at the national or bilateral level. One example is the Philippines, which has recently embarked on a series of initiatives to reinforce its bilateral and regional ties with major tourism partners while boosting relations with new markets (Rocamora 2022). It has renewed its tourism cooperation with Brunei Darussalam and Thailand for 2022–2028 and is crafting a new tourism cooperation agreement with Malaysia to revive arrivals which had declined by 10.2% between 2015 and 2019. A joint working group to implement tourism cooperation programs with the Republic of Korea is also expected to restore the volume of arrivals. As part of its market diversification efforts, potential partnerships are being explored with Israel and the EU, while discussions with Japan aim to foster deeper bilateral relations in the travel and tourism segment.

The pandemic has provided many interesting lessons and opened areas of vulnerabilities. While much can be resolved by multifaceted national policies, addressing complex challenges of concentrated source markets, inadequate transport and internet connectivity, and regulating environment degradation will require regional cooperation. This will enable pooling of resources and development of commensurate cross-border rules for sustainable and resilient movement of people across borders.

References

Abujaleel, B. 2021. Saudi Arabia: New Skills Verification Program for Foreign Workers. *WTW.* 8 April. https://www.wtwco.com/en-US/Insights/2021/04/saudi-arabia-new-skills-verification-program-for-foreign-workers.

Ahamed, A. 2022. Business of Remittances Should Not Be Limited to Ensuring Funds Reach Recipients. *Gulf News.* 16 June. https://gulfnews.com/business/analysis/business-of-remittances-should-not-be-limited-to-ensuring-funds-reach-recipients-1.88624145.

AirAsia Philippines. 2022. 7 Out of 10 Filipinos Pushing through with Air Travel in 2022, AirAsia Survey Shows. 13 January. https://newsroom.airasia.com/news/2022/1/13/7-out-of-10-filipinos-pushing-through-with-air-travel-in-2022-airasia-survey-shows.

Al Jazeera. 2022. Far from Putin's Russia, Tajikistan's People Feel Sanctions Pain. 7 March. https://www.aljazeera.com/economy/2022/3/7/far-from-putins-russia-tajikistans-people-feel-sanctions-pain.

Aneja, A. and B. Etter. 2021. The Pandemic May Change Remittances—for the Better. *Foreign Policy.* 8 February. https://foreignpolicy.com/2021/02/08/the-pandemic-may-change-remittances-for-the-better.

The ASEAN Post. 2018. Identifying Threats to Tourism. 18 November. https://theaseanpost.com/article/identifying-threats-tourism.

Asian Development Bank (ADB). 2003. *Asian Development Outlook 2003 Update.* Manila. https://www.adb.org/sites/default/files/publication/30245/ado-2003-update.pdf.

———. 2022. *Asian Development Outlook 2022 Update: Entrepreneurship in the Digital Age.* Manila. https://www.adb.org/sites/default/files/publication/825166/ado2022-update.pdf.

———. Asia Regional Integration Center. Economy Groupings. https://aric.adb.org/integrationindicators/groupings.

Australian Infrastructure Financing Facility for the Pacific. 2021. Improving East Micronesia Telecommunications Connectivity. 13 December. https://www.aiffp.gov.au/news/improving-east-micronesia-telecommunications-connectivity.

Bhatia, R. 2022. International Nurses Coming to NZ Hampered by Entry Course, Research Shows. *Stuff.* 4 August. https://www.stuff.co.nz/pou-tiaki/300653949/international-nurses-coming-to-nz-hampered-by-entry-course-research-shows.

Billing, K. L. 2022. A Month Since the Start of the War, Almost a Quarter of Ukraine's Population are Displaced. *Briefing Notes.* 25 March. Geneva: United Nations High Commissioner for Refugees. https://www.unhcr.org/news/briefing/2022/3/623da5894/month-since-start-war-quarter-ukraines-population-displaced.html.

Borak, M. 2022. Fleeing Putin, Russian Tech Workers Find a Home in Armenia. 20 July. *Rest of World.* https://restofworld.org/2022/russian-tech-workers-armenia/.

Bowerman, G. 2022. Six Challenges for Reviving Tourism in South East Asia. *Asia Media Centre.* 1 March. https://www.asiamediacentre.org.nz/features/six-challenges-for-reviving-tourism-in-south-east-asia.

Bunina, M. 2022. What Is Russia's 'MIR' Payment System? *Russia Beyond.* 10 March. https://www.rbth.com/business/334833-russian-mir-payment-system-card.

Canadian Manufacturing. 2022. CFIB Says that Quebec's Small Businesses Are Losing Nearly $11B Annually to Labour Shortages. 22 August. https://www.canadianmanufacturing.com/manufacturing/cfib-says-that-quebecs-small-businesses-are-losing-nearly-11b-annually-to-labour-shortages-284526/.

Che, C., A. C. Chien, and A. Stevenson. 2022. What Has Changed About China's 'Zero Covid' Policy. *New York Times*. 7 December. https://www.nytimes.com/2022/12/07/world/asia/china-zero-covid-changes.html.

Cherry, J. 2004. The Chronology of the 2002–2003 SARS Mini Pandemic. *Paediatric Respiratory Reviews*. 5 (4). pp. 262–269.

Child, D. 2021. 'Unprecedented Exodus': Why Are Migrant Workers Leaving the UK? *Al Jazeera*. 15 January. https://www.aljazeera.com/news/2021/1/15/uk-twin-pandemic-and-brexit-crises-prompt-unprecedented-exodus.

Clark, A. 2007. US Airline Emerges From Post-9/11 Bankruptcy. *The Guardian*. 1 June. https://www.theguardian.com/business/2007/jun/01/theairlineindustry.travel.

Croft, L. 2021. COVID-19 Creating Skills Shortages in the Australian Workforce. *Lawyers Weekly*. 16 August. https://www.lawyersweekly.com.au/biglaw/32214-covid-19-creating-skills-shortages-in-the-australian-workforce.

European Bank for Reconstruction and Development (EBRD). 2022. *Regional Economic Prospects*. September. London.

European Travel Commission. 2022. Many Europeans Planning Multiple Holidays Despite Concerns Around Increasing Travel Costs. 16 June. https://etc-corporate.org/news/many-europeans-planning-multiple-holidays-despite-concerns-around-increasing-travel-costs/.

Fernandez-Reino, M. and C. Reinzo. 2022. Migrants in the UK Labor Market: An Overview. Oxford: The Migration Observatory at the University of Oxford. https://migrationobservatory.ox.ac.uk/resources/briefings/migrants-in-the-uk-labour-market-an-overview/.

Foresti, M. 2020. Less Gratitude, Please. How COVID-19 Reveals the Need for Migration Reform. *Brookings*. 22 May. https://www.brookings.edu/blog/future-development/2020/05/22/less-gratitude-please-how-covid-19-reveals-the-need-for-migration-reform/.

Foresti, M., C. Rajah, and J. Bither. 2022. What International Migration Policy Must Address. Interview by A. Rinderspacher. *Robert Bosch Stiftung*. 13 May. https://www.bosch-stiftung.de/en/what-international-migration-policy-must-address.

Global Forums on Remittances, Investment and Development. Topic: Remittance Families and Development. https://gfrid.org/topics/remittance-families-and-development.

Global Knowledge Partnership for Migration and Development (KNOMAD). Remittances Data. https://knomad.org/data/remittances (accessed May and December 2022).

Goretti, M., L. Y. Leigh, A. Babii, S. Cevik, S. Kaendera, D. V. Muir, S. Nadeem, and G. Salinas. 2021. Tourism in the Post-Pandemic World: Economic Challenges and Opportunities for Asia-Pacific and the Western Hemisphere. *Departmental Paper*. No. 2021/002. Washington, DC: IMF.

Government of Armenia, Central Bank of Armenia. External Sector Statistics. https://www.cba.am/en/SitePages/statexternalsector.aspx (accessed December 2022).

Government of Australia, Department of Home Affairs. Visa Statistics. https://www.homeaffairs.gov.au/research-and-statistics/statistics/visa-statistics (accessed July 2022).

Government of Bangladesh, Bangladesh Bank. Open Data Initiative. https://www.bb.org.bd/en/index.php/econdata/index (accessed December 2022).

Government of Bangladesh, Bureau of Manpower, Employment, and Training. http://www.old.bmet.gov.bd/BMET/stattisticalDataAction (accessed January 2023).

Government of Canada, Employment and Social Development Canada. Temporary Foreign Worker Program 2021Q1-2022Q3. https://open.canada.ca/data/en/dataset/e8745429-21e7-4a73-b3f5-90a779b78d1e (accessed July 2022).

Government of Georgia, National Bank of Georgia. Statistics Data. https://nbg.gov.ge/en/statistics/statistics-data (accessed December 2022).

Government of Germany, Federal Office for Migration and Refugees. 2021. Skilled Immigration Act for Qualified Professionals. 1 March. https://www.bamf.de/SharedDocs/Meldungen/EN/2021/210301-am-fachkraefteeinwanderungsgesetz.html.

Government of India, Ministry of External Affairs. Performance Smartboard. http://meadashboard.gov.in/indicators/15 (accessed January 2023).

Government of Kazakhstan, National Bank of Kazakhstan. Statistics. https://www.nationalbank.kz/en/page/statistika (accessed December 2022).

Government of the Kyrgyz Republic, National Bank of the Kyrgyz Republic. External Sector of the Economy. https://www.nbkr.kg/index1.jsp?item=128&lang=ENG (accessed December 2022).

Government of Pakistan, Bureau of Emigration and Overseas Employment. https://beoe.gov.pk/reports-and-statistics (accessed January 2023).

Government of Pakistan, State Bank of Pakistan. Economic Data. https://www.sbp.org.pk/ecodata/index2.asp (accessed December 2022).

———. Roshan Digital Account. https://www.sbp.org.pk/rda/index.html.

———. Sohni Dharti Remittance Program. https://www.sbp.org.pk/sohnidharti/index.html.

Government of Saudi Arabia, General Authority for Statistics. https://www.stats.gov.sa/en/814 (accessed 2 November 2022).

Government of Singapore, Ministry of Transport. 2022. ASEAN and the European Union Sign Comprehensive Air Transport Agreement. Press release. 17 October. https://www.mot.gov.sg/news/details/asean-and-the-european-union-sign-comprehensive-air-transport-agreement.

Government of Sri Lanka, Central Bank of Sri Lanka. Economic Indicators. https://www.cbsl.gov.lk/en/statistics/economic-indicators (accessed December 2022).

Government of the United Arab Emirates, Federal Competitiveness and Statistics Centre. Statistics. https://fcsc.gov.ae/en-us/Pages/Statistics/Statistics.aspx (accessed 2 November 2022).

Government of the United Kingdom, Home Office. Immigration Statistics. https://www.gov.uk/government/collections/immigration-statistics-quarterly-release (accessed July 2022).

Government of the United States, Department of State, Bureau of Consular Affairs. Visa Statistics. https://travel.state.gov/content/travel/en/legal/visa-law0/visa-statistics.html (accessed July 2022).

Government of the United States, Department of Transportation, Bureau of Transportation Statistics. 2021. *Twenty Years Later, How Does Post-9/11 Air Travel Compare to the Disruptions of COVID-19?* https://www.bts.gov/data-spotlight/twenty-years-later-how-does-post-911-air-travel-compare-disruptions-covid-19.

Hashimova, U. 2022. Are Central Asian Migrant Workers Ready to Leave Russia? *The Diplomat.* 13 April. https://thediplomat.com/2022/04/are-central-asian-migrant-workers-ready-to-leave-russia/.

Imanaliyeva, A. 2022. Kyrgyzstan: Where Have All the Dollars Gone? *Eurasianet.* 28 July. https://eurasianet.org/kyrgyzstan-where-have-all-the-dollars-gone.

International Fund for Agricultural Development (IFAD). 2018. Remittances to the Asia-Pacific Region Reach $256 Billion Helping Millions of Families to Build a Better Future. Press release. 7 May. https://www.ifad.org/en/web/latest/-/news/remittances-to-the-asia-pacific-region-reach-us-256-billion-helping-millions-of-families-to-build-a-better-future.

_____. 2022. Global Remittances Flows Expected to Reach US$5.4 Trillion by 2030 Spurred on by Digitalization. Press release. 16 June. https://www.ifad.org/en/web/latest/-/global-remittances-flows-expected-to-reach-us-5.4-trillion-by-2030-spurred-on-by-digitalization.

International Labour Organization (ILO). 2021. ILO Research Highlights Massive COVID-19 Impact on Tourism Employment in Asia and the Pacific. Press release. 18 November. https://www.ilo.org/asia/media-centre/news/WCMS_827494/lang--en/index.htm.

———. ILOSTAT Database. Data. https://ilostat.ilo.org/data (accessed 2 November 2022).

———. ILOSTAT Database. International Standard Classification of Occupations. https://ilostat.ilo.org/resources/concepts-and-definitions/classification-occupation.

International Monetary Fund (IMF). 2010. *Balance of Payments and International Investment Position Manual, Sixth Edition.* Washington, DC. https://www.imf.org/en/Publications/Manuals-Guides/Issues/2016/12/31/Balance-of-Payments-Manual-Sixth-Edition-22588.

———. World Economic Outlook October 2022 Database. https://www.imf.org/en/Publications/WEO/weo-database/2022/October (accessed December 2022).

International Organization for Migration (IOM). 2020. IOM Welcomes the Launch of Labour Reforms in the Kingdom of Saudi Arabia. *Press release.* 5 November. https://www.iom.int/news/iom-welcomes-launch-labour-reforms-kingdom-saudi-arabia.

———. 2021. Cooperation Key to Ensuring Rights-Based Migration in Asia-Pacific. *Statement of the United Nations Regional Network on Migration for Asia and the Pacific on International Migrants Day.* https://www.iom.int/news/cooperation-key-ensuring-rights-based-migration-asia-pacific.

———. COVID-19 Mobility Impacts. https://migration.iom.int/ (accessed December 2022).

Ivanova, I. 2022. America's Labor Shortage Is Actually an Immigrant Shortage. *CBS News.* 8 April. https://www.cbsnews.com/news/immigration-jobs-workers-labor-shortage/.

Jayamaha, R. 2006. Moving from Informal to Formal in the Provision of Remittances. Speech for Global Payments Week. Sydney. 3–6 October. https://www.bis.org/review/r070115g.pdf.

Kang, J. W. and M. C. G. Latoja. 2022. COVID-19 and Overseas Filipino Workers: Return Migration and Reintegration into the Home Country—the Philippine Case. *ADB Southeast Asia Working Paper Series.* No. 21. Manila: ADB.

Kazinform. 2022. Kazakhstan, Armenia Discuss Economic and Inter-Regional Cooperation. 26 August. https://www.inform.kz/en/kazakhstan-armenia-discuss-economic-and-inter-regional-cooperation_a3971565.

Kikkawa, A., R. Gaspar, K. Kim, and P. Sirivunnabood. 2022. COVID-19 and the Deployment of Labor Migrants from Asia: Lessons Learned and Ways Forward. *ADB Briefs.* No. 223. Manila: ADB. https://www.adb.org/sites/default/files/publication/835626/adb-brief-223-covid19-deployment-labor-migrants-asia.pdf.

Kotoky, A. 2022. China's Covid Stance Has Created a $280 Billion Black Hole for Global Tourism. *Bloomberg.* 4 March. https://www.bloomberg.com/news/features/2022-03-03/china-s-covid-stance-has-created-a-280-billion-black-hole-for-global-tourism.

Krogstad, J. M. and A. Gonzalez-Barrera. 2022. Key Facts About U.S. Immigration Policies and Biden's Proposed Changes. *Pew Research Center*. 11 January. https://www.pewresearch.org/fact-tank/2022/01/11/key-facts-about-u-s-immigration-policies-and-bidens-proposed-changes/.

Kuo, H., C. Chen, W. Tseng, L. Ju, and B. Huang. 2008. Assessing Impacts of SARS and Avian Flu on International Tourism Demand to Asia. *Tourism Management*. 29 (5). pp. 917–928.

Lee, H-J. 2022. Korea's Farms Hit Hard as Pandemic Leads to Foreign Worker Shortage. *The Korea Times*. 19 April. https://www.koreatimes.co.kr/www/nation/2022/04/177_327614.html.

Lee, N. 2020. Experts Warn the U.S. Work Visa Ban Will Be China's Gain in the Long Run. *CNBC News*. 31 July. https://www.cnbc.com/2020/07/31/work-visa-ban-how-it-impacts-the-us-economy.html.

Lee, L., R. Latiff, and M. M. Chu. 2022. Malaysia Firms Turn Down Orders as Migrant Labour Shortage Hits. *Reuters*. 13 June. https://www.reuters.com/article/malaysia-labour-shortage-idAFKBN2NU014.

Li, D., L. Yi, T. C. Lee, and Y. Xu. 2022. Why Is Mainland China Sticking with "Zero-COVID" Policy? *S&P Global Market Intelligence*. 27 June. https://ihsmarkit.com/research-analysis/why-mainland-china-sticking-zerocovid-policy.html.

Little, B. 2020. SARS Pandemic: How the Virus Spread Around the World in 2003. *History*. 30 January. https://www.history.com/news/sars-outbreak-china-lessons.

Look, C. 2022. Germany Needs Immigration of 400,000 Workers Per Year, FDP Says. *Bloomberg*. 21 January. https://www.bloomberg.com/news/articles/2022-01-21/germany-needs-immigration-of-400-000-workers-per-year-fdp-says.

Mathieu, E., H. Ritchie, L. Rodés-Guirao, C. Appel, C. Giattino, J. Hasell, B. Macdonald, S. Dattani, D. Beltekian, E. Ortiz-Ospina, and M. Roser. 2020. Coronavirus Pandemic (COVID-19). *Our World In Data*. https://ourworldindata.org/coronavirus.

Mdoe, G. 2021. How Remittances Play Central Role in Africa's Development. *The Exchange Africa*. 1 December. https://theexchange.africa/countries/tanzania/how-remittances-play-central-role-in-africas-development.

Mgdesyan, A. 2022. Armenia Anticipates an Influx of Russian Businesses, Capital. 10 March. *Eurasianet*. https://eurasianet.org/armenia-anticipates-influx-of-russian-businesses-capital.

Mint. 2022. New Zealand Relaxes Immigration Rules: Visa Extension, Special Scheme Limit Hike. 22 August. https://www.livemint.com/news/world/new-zealand-relaxes-immigration-rules-visa-extension-special-scheme-limit-hike-11661152586244.html.

Najibullah, F. 2022. Russian Émigrés in Central Asia: While Some Settle Into New Lives, Others Await Change in the Kremlin. *Radio Free Europe*. 4 June. https://www.rferl.org/a/russian-emigres-central-asia-ukraine-war/31883254.html.

Newland, K. 2020. Will International Migration Governance Survive the COVID-19 Pandemic? *Policy Brief*. Washington, DC: Migration Policy Institute. https://www.migrationpolicy.org/sites/default/files/publications/globalcompact-migration-governance-pandemic-final.pdf.

Nguyen, V. 2021. Businesses Struggle with Labour Shortage Following the Big Exodus of Migrant Workers. *Viet Nam News*. 18 October. https://vietnamnews.vn/economy/1060825/businesses-struggle-with-labour-shortage-following-the-big-exodus-of-migrant-workers.html.

Okafor, L. and E. Yan. 2022. Covid-19 Vaccines, Rules, Deaths, and Tourism Recovery. *Annals of Tourism Research*. 95. Article 103424. https://www.ncbi.nlm.nih.gov/pmc/articles/PMC9110313/pdf/main.pdf.

Organisation for Economic Co-operation and Development (OECD). 2020. COVID-19 Crisis Puts Migration and Progress on Integration at Risk. 19 October. https://www.oecd.org/migration/covid-19-crisis-puts-migration-and-progress-on-integration-at-risk.htm.

Park, C. Y., K. Kim, M. Helble, and S. Roth. 2021. Getting Ready for the COVID-19 Vaccine Rollout. *ADB Briefs*. No. 166. Manila: ADB. https://www.adb.org/sites/default/files/publication/678541/adb-brief-166-getting-ready-covid-19-vaccine-rollout.pdf.

Parrocha, A. 2022. PH, Singapore Ink Deal on Recruitment of Healthcare Workers. *Philippine News Agency*. 7 September. https://www.pna.gov.ph/articles/1183116.

Pattaya Mail. 2022. NGOs Launch Thai Language Program for Migrant Workers. 20 September. https://www.pattayamail.com/pattayamail/ngos-launch-thai-language-program-for-migrant-workers-410894.

The Peninsula. 2022. Arab Meet Recognizes Qatar's Reforms to Improve Workers' Conditions. 22 September. https://thepeninsulaqatar.com/article/22/09/2022/arab-meet-recognises-qatars-reforms-to-improve-workers-conditions.

Philippine News Agency. 2022. Philippines Makes Headway in Addressing Data Gaps in Migration. 19 May. https://www.pna.gov.ph/articles/1174836.

Phnom Penh Post. 2022. ASEAN Tourism Forum Puts Focus on Regenerating Travel in the Region. 26 January. https://phnompenhpost.com/national/asean-tourism-forum-puts-focus-regenerating-travel-region.

Pinczewski, J. and J. Capal. 2022. Three Ways to Reduce Pacific Remittance Costs. *DevPolicyBlog*. 24 June. Canberra: Development Policy Centre. https://devpolicy.org/three-ways-to-reduce-pacific-remittance-costs-20220624/.

Ratha, D. 2021. Staying the Course on Global Governance of Migration Through the COVID-19 and Economic Crises. *International Migration*. 59 (1). pp. 285–288. https://www.ncbi.nlm.nih.gov/pmc/articles/PMC8014625/pdf/IMIG-59-285.pdf.

Ratha, D., E. J. Kim, S. Plaza, G. Seshan, E. J. Riordan, and V. Chandra. 2021. Recovery: COVID-19 Crisis Through a Migration Lens. *Migration and Development Brief*. 35. Washington, DC: KNOMAD–World Bank.

Ratha, D., E. J. Kim, S. Plaza, E. J. Riordan, and V. Chandra. 2022a. A War in a Pandemic: Implications of the Russian Invasion of Ukraine and the COVID-19 Crisis on Global Governance of Migration and Remittance Flows. *Migration and Development Brief*. 36. Washington, DC: KNOMAD–World Bank.

Ratha, D., V. Chandra, E. J. Kim, B. Pradhan, E. J. Riordan, M. Vezmar, and S. Plaza. 2022b. Remittances Brave Global Headwinds, Special Focus: Climate Migration. *Migration and Development Brief*. 37. Washington, DC: KNOMAD–World Bank.

Read, M. 2022. Skilled Migrants Needed to Plug Tech Gaps: Productivity Commission. *Australia Financial Review*. 23 August. https://www.afr.com/politics/skilled-migrants-needed-to-plug-tech-gaps-productivity-commission-20220822-p5bbsr.

Reuters. 2022. Germany Plans Immigration Reforms to Attract Foreign Workers. 20 July. https://www.reuters.com/world/europe/germany-plans-immigration-reforms-attract-foreign-workers-2022-07-20/.

Riallant, C. 2017. Ensuring Migration Benefits Development. *IOM Blog*. 21 September. Geneva: IOM. https://weblog.iom.int/ensuring-migration-benefits-development.

Riley, J. L. 2022. Immigrants Can Help Relieve the Labor Shortage. *Wall Street Journal*. 16 August. https://www.wsj.com/articles/immigrants-can-help-relieve-the-labor-shortage-unemployment-workers-job-openings-migrants-staffing-inflation-border-11660685996.

Riordan, P., A. Lin, K. Inagaki, and C. Davies. 2022. Covid Restrictions Stymie Tourism Revival in Japan and Much of Asia. *Financial Times*. 17 August. https://www.ft.com/content/5f6a889c-023e-4df0-ac8b-923fe95f97e2.

Robinson, K. 2021. What Is the Kafala System? *Council on Foreign Relations*. https://www.cfr.org/backgrounder/what-kafala-system.

Rocamora, J. A. L. 2022. 1st 100 Days: Bringing Back Tourism Jobs; Promoting PH Beyond Fun. *Philippine News Agency*. 7 October. https://www.pna.gov.ph/articles/1185566.

Schulz, D. 2022. How India Can Broaden Its Relationships with Central Asia. *The Diplomat*. 10 December. https://thediplomat.com/2022/12/how-india-can-broaden-its-relationships-with-central-asia.

Shadmand, S. L., B. K. Biesenthal, J. S. Beaumont, and O. Gidalevitz. 2020. Saudi Arabia Introduces Significant Labor Reforms. *Society for Human Resource Management*. 11 December. https://www.shrm.org/resourcesandtools/hr-topics/global-hr/pages/saudi-arabia-labor-reform-initiative.aspx.

Shivani, P. and T. Ritzema. 1999. Migrant Worker Remittances, Micro-Finance and the Informal Economy: Prospects and Issues. *Social Finance Unit Working Paper*. No. 21. Geneva: International Labour Office. https://www.ilo.org/wcmsp5/groups/public/---ed_emp/documents/publication/wcms_117997.pdf.

Siddiqui, S. 2020. State Bank of Pakistan Raises Margins on Remittances. *Pakistan Tribune*. 16 April. https://tribune.com.pk/story/2198927/state-bank-pakistan-raises-margins-remittances.

Tan, L. 2022. Singapore's Endemic Community Measures, Effective 26 April: Group & Capacity Limits, Booster Shots, and More. *Human Resources Online*. 25 April. https://www.humanresourcesonline.net/singapore-s-general-endemic-measures-effective-26-april-group-capacity-limits-booster-shots-and-more.

TASS. 2021. Pandemic Reveals Dependence of Certain Countries on High-Qualified Migrants, Say Experts. 25 August. https://tass.com/society/1330077.

Thaiger. 2022. Pandemic Creates Labour Shortages in Thailand. 17 January. https://thethaiger.com/news/national/pandemic-creates-labour-shortages-in-thailand.

Tomas, J. P. 2022. Huawei Moves Russian Staff to Central Asia: Report. *RCI Wireless News*. 6 September. https://www.rcrwireless.com/20220906/5g/huawei-moves-russian-staff-central-asia-report.

Tourism Authority of Thailand (TAT). 2022a. 'Visit Thailand Year 2022: Amazing New Chapters' Envisioned Thai Tourism Transformation. Press release. 11 February. https://www.tatnews.org/2022/02/visit-thailand-year-2022-amazing-new-chapters-envisioned-thai-tourism-transformation/.

———. 2022b. TAT Stages Amazing Thailand Fest 2022 in New Delhi. Press release. 26 November. https://www.tatnews.org/2022/11/tat-stages-amazing-thailand-fest-2022-in-new-delhi/.

———. 2022c. TAT Launches New High-End Travel Deal for Luxury-Minded South Korean Travellers. Press release. 30 November. https://www.tatnews.org/2022/11/tat-launches-new-high-end-travel-deal-for-luxury-minded-south-korean-travellers/.

———. 2022d. Amazing Thailand Fest 2022 in Saudi Arabia Strengthens Saudi-Thai Tourism Cooperation. Press release. 2 December. https://www.tatnews.org/2022/12/amazing-thailand-fest-2022-in-saudi-arabia-strengthens-saudi-thai-tourism-cooperation/.

———. 2022e. Bangkok Welcomes Air Canada's Seasonal Non-Stop Flight from Vancouver. Press release. 3 December. https://www.tatnews.org/2022/12/bangkok-welcomes-air-canadas-seasonal-non-stop-flight-from-vancouver/.

———. 2022f. 'Amazing Thailand' Roadshow to Istanbul Highlights TAT's Aim to Grow Türkiye Market to Thailand. Press release. 7 December. https://www.tatnews.org/2022/12/amazing-thailand-roadshow-to-istanbul-highlights-tats-aim-to-grow-turkiye-market-to-thailand/.

United Nations. Global Compact for Migration. https://www.un.org/en/migration2022/global-compact-for-migration.

United Nations Department of Economic and Social Affairs, Population Division. 2022. *World Population Prospects 2022: Summary of Results*. New York.

———. International Migrant Stock 2020. https://www.un.org/development/desa/pd/content/international-migrant-stock (accessed May 2022).

United Nations Department of Economic and Social Affairs, Population Division and International Organization for Migration. 2021. SDG Indicator 10.7.2 Number of Countries with Migration Policies to Facilitate Orderly, Safe, Regular, and Responsible Migration and Mobility of People: Country Data. https://www.un.org/development/desa/pd/data/sdg-indicator-1072-migration-policies.

United Nations Network on Migration. 2020. *Uzbekistan–GCM Voluntary National Report (Regional Review: Europe and North America)*. Grand-Saconnex. https://migrationnetwork.un.org/resources/uzbekistan-gcm-voluntary-national-report-regional-review-europe-and-north-america.

———. 2021. *Bangladesh–GCM Voluntary National Report (Regional Review: Asia and the Pacific)*. Grand-Saconnex https://migrationnetwork.un.org/resources/bangladesh-gcm-voluntary-national-report-regional-review-asia-and-pacific.

United Nations World Tourism Organization (UNWTO). 2004. World Tourism Barometer. 2 (3).

———. 2009. World Tourism Barometer. 7 (3).

———. 2020. Impact Assessment of the COVID-19 Outbreak on International Tourism. 9 March. https://www.unwto.org/impact-assessment-of-the-covid-19-outbreak-on-international-tourism.

———. 2021. 2020: Worst Year in Tourism History with 1 Billion Fewer International Arrivals. News release. 28 January. https://www.unwto.org/news/2020-worst-year-in-tourism-history-with-1-billion-fewer-international-arrivals.

———. 2022a. World Tourism Barometer. 20 (5).

———. 2022b. World Tourism Barometer. 20 (3).

———. 2022c. Impact of the Russian Offensive in Ukraine on International Tourism. *Impact Assessment*. Issue 4. https://www.unwto.org/impact-russian-offensive-in-ukraine-on-tourism.

———. Tourism Data Dashboard. https://www.unwto.org/tourism-data/unwto-tourism-dashboard (accessed November and December 2022).

———. Tourism Data Dashboard. Global and Regional Tourism Performance. https://www.unwto.org/tourism-data/global-and-regional-tourism-performance (accessed October 2022).

———. Tourism Recovery Tracker. https://www.unwto.org/tourism-data/unwto-tourism-recovery-tracker (accessed November and December 2022).

———. Tourism Satellite Accounts. http://statistics.unwto.org (accessed December 2022).

———. Tourism Statistics. https://www.e-unwto.org/toc/unwtotfb/current (accessed August 2022).

University of Oxford, Blavatnik School of Government. Oxford COVID-19 Government Response Tracker Database. https://github.com/OxCGRT/covid-policy-tracker/tree/master/data/timeseries (accessed October 2022). In Hale, T, N. Angrist, R. Goldszmidt, B. Kira, A. Petherick, T. Phillips, S. Webster, E. Cameron-Blake, L. Hallas, S.

Majumdar, and H. Tatlow. 2021. A Global Panel Database of Pandemic Policies (Oxford COVID-19 Government Response Tracker). *Nature Human Behaviour*. https://doi.org/10.1038/s41562-021-01079-8.

Usov, A. 2022. Central Asia Shows Strong Resilience to Geopolitical Turmoil. *European Bank for Reconstruction and Development*. 28 September. https://www.ebrd.com/news/2022/central-asia-shows-great-resilience-to-geopolitical-turmoil-.html.

Visit Britain. 2022. *Domestic Sentiment Tracker*. August. https://www.visitbritain.org/sites/default/files/vb-corporate/2022-08-17_domestic_sentiment_tracker_report_-_august_release.pdf.

Weerakoon, D., U. Kumar, and R. Dime. 2019. Sri Lanka's Macroeconomic Challenges: A Tale of Two Deficits. *ADB South Asia Working Paper Series*. No. 63. Manila: ADB. https://www.adb.org/sites/default/files/publication/493451/swp-063-sri-lanka-macroeconomic-challenges-two-deficits.pdf.

Weeraratne, B. 2021. Black, White and Grey Markets: The Dynamics of Foreign Exchange and Remittances in Sri Lanka. *Talking Economics*. Colombo: Institute of Policy Studies of Sri Lanka. https://www.ips.lk/talkingeconomics/2021/12/17/black-white-and-grey-markets-the-dynamics-of-foreign-exchange-and-remittances-in-sri-lanka.

Wiessner, D. 2020. Trump Administration Unveils Rule to Limit Work Visas for Skilled Foreign Laborers. *Reuters*. 7 October. https://www.reuters.com/article/us-usa-labor-visas-idUSKBN26R3AY.

Witton, B. 2022. Health Minister Andrew Little Announces Plan to Boost Health Worker Numbers Amid 'Extreme Pressures'. *Stuff*. 1 August. https://www.stuff.co.nz/national/health/129439230/health-minister-andrew-little-announces-plan-to-boost-health-worker-numbers-amid-extreme-pressures.

World Bank. 2022. Remittances to Reach $630 billion in 2022 with Record Flows into Ukraine. Press release. 11 May. https://www.worldbank.org/en/news/press-release/2022/05/11/remittances-to-reach-630-billion-in-2022-with-record-flows-into-ukraine.

————. Global Financial Inclusion Database. https://databank.worldbank.org/source/global-financial-inclusion# (accessed December 2022).

————. Remittance Prices Worldwide. https://remittanceprices.worldbank.org/ (accessed August and November 2022).

————. World Development Indicators. https://databank.worldbank.org/source/world-development-indicators (accessed August, November, and December 2022).

World Economic Forum. 2022. *This Is the Impact of COVID-19 on the Travel Sector*. 25 January. Geneva. https://www.weforum.org/agenda/2022/01/global-travel-tourism-pandemic-covid-19/.

World Travel and Tourism Council (WTTC). 2022. Travel & Tourism Sector Expected to Create Nearly 126 Million New Jobs within the Next Decade. Press release. 21 April. https://wttc.org/news-article/travel-and-tourism-sector-expected-to-create-nearly-126-million-new-jobs-within-the-next-decade.

————. Economic Impact Reports. https://wttc.org/research/economic-impact.

Wright, S. 2022. Australia's Most In-Demand Professions Revealed, But Migrants Wary of Returning. *The Sydney Morning Herald*. 22 August. https://www.smh.com.au/politics/federal/australia-s-most-in-demand-professions-revealed-but-migrants-wary-of-returning-20220821-p5bbho.html.

6 Updates on Subregional Cooperation Initiatives

Subregional cooperation initiatives in Asia and the Pacific generally seek greater cooperation and economic integration in transport and trade; access to global value chains, markets, and tourism, along with economic corridor and shared resource development.[78] They are wide in variety and include subregional initiatives that are led and monitored by the Asian Development Bank (ADB) such as the Central Asia Regional Economic Cooperation (CAREC) Program, the Greater Mekong Subregion (GMS) Program, and the South Asia Subregional Economic Cooperation (SASEC) Program. Government-led subregional programs include the Indonesia–Malaysia–Thailand Growth Triangle (IMT-GT), the Brunei Darussalam–Indonesia–Malaysia–Philippines East ASEAN Growth Area (BIMP-EAGA), the South Asian Association for Regional Cooperation (SAARC), the Bay of Bengal Initiative for Multi-Sectoral Technical and Economic Cooperation (BIMSTEC), and the Pacific Islands Forum.

This chapter begins with a difference from previous reports, highlighting estimates from the Asia-Pacific Regional Cooperation and Integration Index (ARCII), a measure of the progress of subregional initiative , with a focus on intrasubregional integration (ie. integration among members of the subregional initiative). It then examines how they have progressed over the past year, particularly through and recovering from the coronavirus disease (COVID-19) pandemic, as well as geopolitical tensions from the Russian invasion of Ukraine in

February 2022, which has added to global supply chain disruptions, pushing up energy prices and contributing to high inflation, food shortages, financial turmoil, and reduced remittances. Economies at the local and regional levels continue to make significant efforts to foster resilient economic growth and socioeconomic stability amid these challenges. The discussions also highlight ADB's contribution to promoting subregional cooperation through inclusive and sustainable cross-border development.

Integration Index Estimates for Subregional Initiatives

ARCII estimates show most of the subregional initiatives gaining traction from 2006 to 2020 (Figure 6.1). Initiatives and programs comprising economies from Southeast Asia, exhibited the highest levels of intrasubregional integration. They also indicate consistent improvement over time. Starting from a low base for performance in 2006, the CAREC initiative show considerable improvement up to 2019. The COVID-19 pandemic did not shock regional integration trends as much as had been expected, with just a few initiatives, including SASEC and SAARC, reporting lower intrasubregional integration estimates in 2020 over the previous year, while the overall regional trend remained stable.

---

[78] Asia and the Pacific, or Asia, consists of the 49 regional member economies of the Asian Development Bank (ADB). The composition of economies for Central Asia, East Asia, the Pacific and Oceania, South Asia, and Southeast Asia are outlined in ADB. Asia Regional Integration Center. Economy Groupings. https://aric.adb.org/integrationindicators/groupings.

Figure 6.1: Overall Integration Indexes, by Subregional Initiative

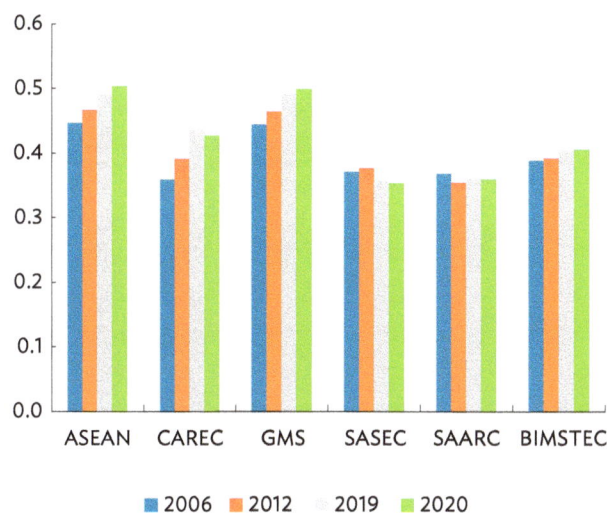

ASEAN = Association of Southeast Asian Nations, BIMSTEC = Bay of Bengal Initiative for Multi-Sectoral Technical and Economic Cooperation, CAREC = Central Asia Regional Economic Cooperation, GMS = Greater Mekong Subregion, SAARC = South Asian Association for Regional Cooperation, SASEC = South Asia Subregional Economic Cooperation.

Notes: Based on the Asia-Pacific Regional Cooperation and Integration Index (ARCII) estimates. The bars reflect intrasubregional integration.

Source: ADB. Asia Regional Integration Center. ARCII Database. https://aric.adb.org/database/arcii (accessed December 2022).

The extent of regional cooperation and integration within subregional initiatives varies across the eight dimensions of the ARCII (Figure 6.2). The largest gaps are observed in trade and investment, infrastructure and connectivity, and institutional arrangements. Economies in ASEAN and GMS are the most integrated among members in these dimensions. While SAARC and SASEC were the least integrated in 2020, their performance in some dimensions, including environmental cooperation in SASEC, does not fall too far behind other subregional initiatives.

Overall, an increase in intrasubregional integration is apparent in most subregional initiatives. The improvement is most prominent in CAREC, which posted a 19.1% increase in the overall index from 2006 and 2020. The mild shock to regional integration brought about by the COVID-19 pandemic is mostly seen in regional value chain, people and social integration, and infrastructure and connectivity, which slightly declined across many subregional initiatives from 2019 to 2020. However, over the same period, all subregional initiatives became more integrated infrastructure and connectivity in technology and digital connectivity.

Figure 6.2: Dimensional Estimates by Subregional Initiative, 2020

Subregional Initiative	Trade and Investment	Money and Finance	Regional Value Chain	Infrastructure and Connectivity	People and Social Integration	Institutional Arrangements	Technology and Digital Connectivity	Environmental Cooperation	% Change in Overall ARCII (2006/2020)
ASEAN	0.24	0.49	0.63	0.68	0.51	0.71	0.48	0.36	▲ 12.93
CAREC	0.13	0.33	0.60	0.45	0.44	0.60	0.47	0.30	▲ 19.14
GMS	0.29	0.35	0.64	0.63	0.51	0.79	0.48	0.35	▲ 12.51
SASEC	0.18	0.33	0.53	0.33	0.38	0.40	0.33	0.32	▼ −4.47
SAARC	0.21	0.29	0.51	0.42	0.34	0.54	0.32	0.24	▼ −2.16
BIMSTEC	0.19	0.33	0.60	0.49	0.43	0.59	0.33	0.29	▲ 4.78

ARCII = Asia-Pacific Regional Cooperation and Integration Index, ASEAN = Association of Southeast Asian Nations, BIMSTEC = Bay of Bengal Initiative for Multi-Sectoral Technical and Economic Cooperation, CAREC = Central Asia Regional Economic Cooperation, GMS = Greater Mekong Subregion, SAARC = South Asian Association for Regional Cooperation, SASEC = South Asia Subregional Economic Cooperation.

Note: The bars reflect intrasubregional integration.

Source ADB. Asia Regional Integration Center. Asia-Pacific Regional Cooperation and Integration Database. https://aric.adb.org/database/arcii (accessed December 2022).

Spider charts showing the ARCII estimates of subregional integration for each of the subregional initiatives are presented in Annex 6a.

Central Asia Regional Economic Cooperation Program[79]

The Central Asia Regional Economic Cooperation (CAREC) Program is a partnership of 11 countries (Afghanistan, Azerbaijan, the People's Republic of China [PRC], Georgia, Kazakhstan, the Kyrgyz Republic, Mongolia, Pakistan, Tajikistan, Turkmenistan, and Uzbekistan) working together with support from development partners to accelerate

growth and reduce poverty in the subregion.[80] The CAREC 2030 strategy fosters an open and inclusive cooperation platform to help connect people, policies, and projects for shared and sustainable development.[81] Building on more than 20 years of progress in transport, energy, and trade connectivity (Table 6.1), CAREC is expanding cooperation into new areas—including economic and financial stability, agriculture and water, and human development, as well as cross-cutting themes of digital connectivity, gender equality, and climate change mitigation and adaptation. Strengthening regional cooperation and integration among CAREC member countries is key to mitigating the impact of the pandemic and the Russian invasion of Ukraine, and for setting the path for a green, sustainable, and inclusive recovery.

Table 6.1: Selected Economic Indicators, 2021—Central Asia Regional Economic Cooperation Program

	Population (million)	Nominal GDP ($ billion)	GDP Growth (2017–2021, average, %)	GDP per Capita (current prices, $)	Trade Openness (total trade, % of GDP)
Afghanistan	40.1	19.9	1.5	497	31.4
Azerbaijan	10.3	54.6	1.1	5,296	62.1
China, People's Republic of	1,425.9	16,579.1	6.0	11,627	36.5
Georgia	3.8	18.7	3.7	4,976	76.7
Kazakhstan	19.2	197.1	2.8	10,268	51.7
Kyrgyz Republic	6.5	8.5	1.7	1,308	84.6
Mongolia	3.3	15.8	3.1	4,723	102.0
Pakistan	231.4	348.2	3.7	1,505	29.0
Tajikistan	9.8	8.8	7.1	897	66.0
Turkmenistan	6.3	62.2	0.8	9,808	21.5
Uzbekistan	34.1	69.2	5.0	2,030	54.8
CAREC	**1,790.7**	**17,382.2**	**5.9**	**9,707**	**36.7**

CAREC = Central Asia Regional Economic Cooperation, GDP = gross domestic product.

Notes: CAREC's average GDP growth rate is weighted using nominal GDP. Average GDP growth data for Afghanistan is 2016–2020. Total trade refers to the sum of exports and imports. ADB placed on hold its assistance in Afghanistan, effective 15 August 2021 (ADB. 2021f. ADB Statement on Afghanistan. News release. 10 November. https://www.adb.org/news/adb-statement-afghanistan). The data on Afghanistan were collected from international sources.

Sources: ADB calculations using data from ADB. Asian Development Outlook database for GDP growth; and Haver Analytics, Inc. for nominal GDP, population, and trade.

---

[79]   Contributed by the CAREC Secretariat including staff from the Regional Cooperation and Operations Coordination Division of the Central and West Asia Department and Public Management, Financial Sector, and Regional Cooperation Division of East Asia Department, ADB.

[80]   ADB placed on hold its assistance in Afghanistan effective 15 August 2021. (ADB. 2021f. ADB Statement on Afghanistan. News release. 10 November. https://www.adb.org/news/adb-statement-afghanistan). The data and information on Afghanistan were collected from international sources.

[81]   The CAREC 2030 strategy focuses on five operational clusters: (i) economic and financial stability; (ii) trade, tourism, and economic corridors; (iii) infrastructure and economic connectivity; (iv) agriculture and water; and (v) human development.

Overview

Investments continue to grow and help CAREC countries mitigate impacts from the COVID-19 pandemic and the Russian invasion of Ukraine.

As of June 2022, CAREC investments reached $45.7 billion and covered 246 regional projects (distributed across all CAREC countries), increasing from $41.1 billion in June 2021. Of the total, more than $16.9 billion was financed by ADB, $19.4 billion by other development partners, and $9 billion by CAREC governments (Figure 6.3). Transport has the biggest share, at about 71% of these investments, or more than $32 billion; energy accounts for 22%, or more than $10 billion; and trade accounts for 3%, or $1.4 billion (Figure 6.4). Although majority of CAREC investments are focused on these traditional support sectors, it is diversifying, including into agriculture and tourism.

Performance and Progress over the Past Year

Implementation of CAREC 2030 is being strengthened for a resilient post-pandemic recovery and to improve socioeconomic stability.

In 2022, the COVID-19 pandemic still poses threats to global and regional growth. In addition, the Russian invasion of Ukraine induced a series of international sanctions against the Russian Federation and adversely affected all countries in the region. ADB's Building Resilience with Active Countercyclical Expenditures (BRACE) program is helping CAREC countries mitigate the social and economic impacts of the pandemic and the Russian invasion of Ukraine. ADB has provided four BRACE programs to CAREC countries— the Kyrgyz Republic, Pakistan, Tajikistan, and Uzbekistan— totaling $2.1 billion in loans and grants. These provide (i) food security, price stability, and business support; (ii) direct social assistance; and (iii) social protection and employment support, in particular, strengthening the support for the poor and vulnerable groups and

Figure 6.3: Investments by Funding Source—Central Asia Regional Economic Cooperation Program (as of 30 June 2022, $ billion)

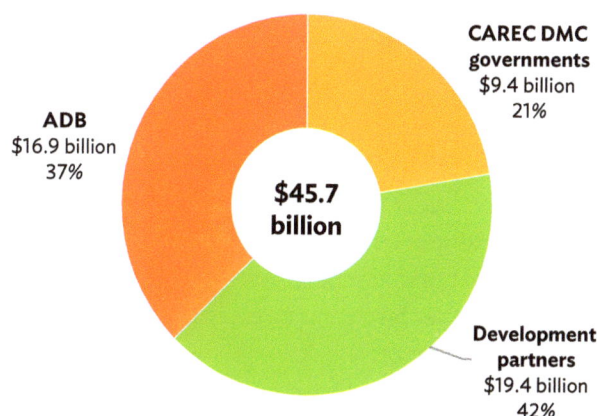

ADB = Asian Development Bank, CAREC = Central Asia Regional Economic Cooperation, DMC = developing member country.

Source: ADB. 2022a. CAREC Program Portfolio. Unpublished.

Figure 6.4: Investments by Sector—Central Asia Regional Economic Cooperation Program ($ billion)

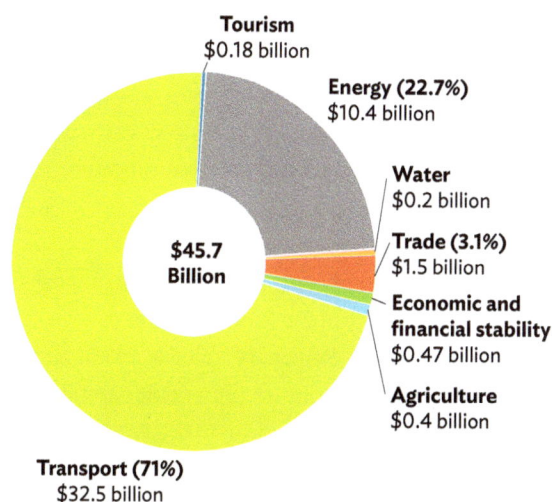

CAREC = Central Asia Regional Economic Cooperation.

Source: ADB. 2022a. CAREC Program Portfolio. Unpublished.

improving economic resilience, including upgrading skills of returned migrants to seek alternative destination countries, and of small and medium-sized enterprises (SMEs) that manufacture for export markets. The CAREC secretariat has undertaken several key knowledge works to provide policy recommendations for CAREC countries to address new challenges through regional cooperation including a CAREC Post-Pandemic Framework for a Green, Sustainable and Inclusive Recovery; a Regional Cooperation Framework for Agricultural Development and Food Security in the CAREC Region; and a Scoping Study on Supporting Regional Actions to Address Climate Change as a Cross-Cutting Theme under CAREC 2030.

Taking advantage of the improved COVID-19 situation and the relaxing of travel restrictions in the region, the CAREC secretariat strengthened contacts and links with CAREC countries by organizing events with virtual and physical participation.

Economic and Financial Stability. The cluster continues its mandate of promoting policy dialogue on important economic and financial stability issues in CAREC, as well as regional learning on macroeconomic policy coordination. In October 2022, a high-level policy dialogue was co-organized virtually with the International Monetary Fund and the World Bank under the theme of Dealing with Risks and Vulnerabilities: Tightening Global Financial Conditions Amid Post-Pandemic Recovery and Geopolitical Conflict. Senior government officials including central bank governors, vice-governors, and finance ministers attended, and presentations highlighted the emerging risks and vulnerabilities to financial stability in the region amid tightening global financial conditions, with discussions on policy measures to mitigate risks in CAREC countries from the Russian invasion of Ukraine. A study on the CAREC Regional Capital Market Landscape recommended a road map for enhancing capital market development, including a forum on the structure of capital market regulators and identifying pilot projects and studies in improving capital market development in areas such as bond and equity markets, legal and regulatory harmonization, capacity building, standard setting, cross-listing, and mutual and multilateral recognition. Technical assistance supporting the CAREC Regional Capital Markets Regulators Forum was approved in August 2022.

Trade, Tourism, and Economic Corridors. Progress has been notable in implementing international trade agreements, aligning with international standards, and accelerating digital trade among CAREC members. Azerbaijan and Uzbekistan advanced their efforts

in World Trade Organization (WTO) working party discussions, while Turkmenistan was granted acceding country status in February 2022 and began its accession work program in July 2022. CAREC members are on track for implementing commitments under the WTO Trade Facilitation Agreement, with the PRC and Georgia having implemented them all. In September 2022, the CAREC Forum on Developing Sustainable Economic Zones and the Roundtable on Supply Chain Connectivity and Resilient Border Operations were organized in Mongolia and virtually. Tailored in-country activities on sanitary and phytosanitary measures were conducted in Azerbaijan, Mongolia, Pakistan, and Uzbekistan from March to July 2022. CAREC countries continue to promote e-commerce and accelerate digital trade, with Pakistan launching an e-commerce portal in 2022, and Uzbekistan and the PRC exchanging electronic phytosanitary certificates through the International Plant Protection Convention's ePhyto solution. Turkmenistan acceded to the UN Framework Agreement on Facilitation of Cross-Border Paperless Trade in Asia and the Pacific in May 2022, Mongolia in July 2022, and Tajikistan in December 2022, joining Azerbaijan and the PRC as parties to the treaty.

Efforts continue to support CAREC countries' interest to pursue free trade agreements. A report on the feasibility of a CAREC-wide free trade agreement was presented in August 2022, and phased implementation of capacity building activities is actively being undertaken through various blended learning techniques and modern approaches. A webinar series on e-commerce was organized in May 2022, and two studies assessing the regulatory framework and infrastructure of developing e-commerce ecosystems were completed in 2022. The CAREC Trade Information Portal was updated in August 2022. As part of the dissemination plan, the quarterly newsletter *CAREC Trade Insights and News* was launched in 2022 and is published quarterly. Several key studies and events were completed in 2022, including (i) a flagship study on Progress in Trade Facilitation in CAREC Countries: A 10-Year Corridor Performance Measurement and Monitoring Perspective; (ii) the CAREC Digital Trade Forum; and (iii) the 20th Year of Customs Cooperation Committee.

In **tourism**, initiatives and activities in 2022 under the CAREC Tourism Strategy 2030 and its accompanying Regional Tourism Investment Framework 2021–2025 included development of the CAREC tourism portal (set to be launched in the first quarter of 2023) as a regional tool for sharing and consolidating tourism-related information and generating opportunities for the private sector. A report assessing tourism infrastructure, services, and project prioritization for tourism investments is being finalized. A pilot study on the Assessment of Common Health and Safety Protocols and Standards in Kazakhstan and the Kyrgyz Republic has been completed. The pilot aims to improve existing health and safety protocols and measures, develop capacities of stakeholders, and harmonize a regional accommodation classification system, with virtual and physical training sessions conducted in both countries. The pilot supports development of a travel bubble under the Almaty–Bishkek Economic Corridor (ABEC) and will help establish the Almaty–Issyk Kul tourism cluster. It is a concept that can be replicated in other CAREC countries. Further capacity building on sustainable tourism development has also been conducted in 2022, along with convening the Tourism Working Group, which has discussed next steps for implementing the tourism strategy.

CAREC countries have achieved notable progress on **economic corridor** development (ECD), promoting it as a national development strategy to strengthen economic links and drive trade through cross-border cooperation and achieve wider economic benefits. Two CAREC initiatives have produced substantive results. The already mentioned ABEC saw the first ABEC-supported project approved by ADB to strengthen regional health security. Other ADB-supported projects include Preparing the Modern Agriculture Wholesale Market Development Project, the Issyk-Kul Lake Environmental Management for Sustainable Tourism Project, and the ABEC Regional Improvement of Border Services Project. Urban air quality measuring devices were deployed in Bishkek and Almaty, while the road map for Shymkent–Tashkent–Khujand Economic Corridor development is also making notable progress, with pre-feasibility studies on an International Center for Industrial Cooperation between Kazakhstan and Uzbekistan, and a Trade and Logistics

Center in Sughd Oblast of Tajikistan being finalized. An ADB-supported study on an ECD framework and operational guidelines has been completed, providing guidance to ECD operations for ADB and its developing member economies, reflecting wider economic benefits and capturing the diversity of regions in Central Asia.

Infrastructure and Economic Connectivity. In the transport sector, most planned events and knowledge products were completed in a timely manner and continued to support capacity development of government ministries and relevant authorities. With COVID-19-related restrictions generally more relaxed across CAREC countries, the 19th Transport Sector Coordinating Committee Meeting, and the 6th Railway Working Group Meeting were conducted physically on 17–20 October 2022. Training workshops on road safety and road asset management systems took place virtually. The transport sector also produced key knowledge products, such as *Road Asset Management System and Performance-Based Road Maintenance Contracts in the CAREC Region*, and *The Situation of Railways in CAREC Countries and Opportunities for Investment, Commercialization, and Reform*. The *CAREC Road Safety Engineering Manual 5: Star Ratings for Road Safety Audit* and the *CAREC Road Safety Report Card* were published in June and July 2022. Other key knowledge products on aviation and cross-border transport and logistics are underway, including the *Aviation Freight Study, the Low-Cost Carriers Study*, and *Developers' Guide on Planning and Design of Logistics Centers*. The ongoing CAREC Regional Improvement of Border Services projects in Pakistan, Mongolia, and the Kyrgyz Republic continue to support cross-border trade expansion in the CAREC region.

In the **energy** sector, phase 1 activities under the CAREC Energy Strategy 2030 were completed. The Energy Sector Coordinating Committee (ESCC) endorsed a plan to establish a CAREC Green Energy Alliance to be the region's first targeted financing vehicle for green energy projects and launched the first regionwide energy efficiency campaign. The ESCC launched a 24/7 tool for policy makers—the *CAREC Energy Reform Atlas*—which aims to support decision makers in resolving the typical dilemmas in energy sector reform. The ESCC also laid foundation for a new Regional Transmission

Cooperation Association as a body to establish regional grid enhancement plans and execute future cross-border projects. Another 2030 flagship deliverable—the *CAREC Energy Outlook 2030* was endorsed and officially published in December 2022 and will attract much-needed investment. The first CAREC Women-in-Energy Program was launched. It includes an action plan and a new CAREC energy web platform (www.carecenergy.org) targeted at improving women's employability, visibility, and education in the energy sector. The program's visibility received a significant boost as the new online energy platform led to organizations and development partners expressing significant interest in joining the program.

A **CAREC Regional Infrastructure Projects Enabling Facility** is being conceptualized under ADB-supported technical assistance. It aims to reduce regional infrastructure financing gaps and strengthen the capacity of CAREC member countries to develop regional infrastructure projects. These include project preparation and readiness, initial design, and the application of appropriate financial solutions including bankable projects for investment opportunities catalyzed by private sector and public–private partnership financing. An ADB-supported transaction technical assistance facility, operational from November 2021 with initial funding of $1.4 million, is supporting ADB in preparing regional infrastructure projects. Structured finance and cofinance experts have been engaged to help the CAREC secretariat deliver the required outputs. The enabling facility concept is a work in progress; consultations with ADB's internal counterparts, development partners, potential donors, and CAREC stakeholders took place in 2022.

Agriculture and Water. Steady progress has been made in this cluster. For **agriculture**, a recently concluded technical assistance succeeded in aligning national food safety regulations in compliance with international food safety standards for Azerbaijan, Kazakhstan, the Kyrgyz Republic, Tajikistan, Turkmenistan, and Uzbekistan. Technical training was also provided to establish national future actions, such as providing knowledge support in this area, and to explore country-specific lending opportunities to improve food safety laboratories

and related infrastructure, in accordance with the preferences and priorities identified by CAREC member countries. The CAREC secretariat has completed work on the Cooperation Framework for Agricultural Development and Food Security in the CAREC Region to address deepening challenges exacerbated by the pandemic and the Russian invasion of Ukraine. The framework prioritizes activities that foster agriculture modernization and improve food security in the region, and was prepared in consultation with CAREC member countries. It served as a key deliverable for the CAREC Ministerial Conference in November 2022.

In the **water** sector, efforts continue to expand the geographic scope of the pillar framework on water sector cooperation into more CAREC countries (e.g., Azerbaijan and Georgia), and identify pipeline projects in fostering climate-resilient and productive water systems and sustainable water resources management in the region from an initial five Central Asian countries in 2021. Activities in 2022 to facilitate these included five national consultations and a regional consultation workshop in November to identify synergies with ongoing and pipeline projects and to develop a short list of potential projects for more detailed project design and possible funding in 2023. The second policy dialogue on Sustainable Water Governance in Central Asia was held virtually on 27 April 2022, and ADB presented findings of an analytical report, *Water Footprint Analysis of Central Asia,* which outlined policy recommendations for mitigating climate change challenges through sustainable water management practices. Knowledge events on related topics were also carried out in 2022, in alignment with a study by the CAREC Institute entitled *Water Infrastructure in Central Asia: Promoting Sustainable Financing and Private Capital Participation.*

Human Development. Good progress has been made in implementing the CAREC Health Strategy 2030. Consultations on the implementation of the strategy started in the second quarter of 2022 with agreement from interested CAREC countries (e.g., Georgia) in incorporating regional approaches in their national health strategies. A Regional Investment Framework (2022–2026) is being finalized following consultations and country feedback during the 2nd Meeting of the CAREC

Working Group on Health in October 2022 in Georgia. A series of regional webinars in 2022 focused on *Covid Vaccine Hesitancy and Behavior Change Communication, Strengthening Health Supply Chain Management and Regional Collaborative Procurement,* and *Practical Epidemiology for COVID-19.* These were conceptualized in coordination with CAREC member countries. A webinar series on *Digital Health and Regional Collaboration among Drug Regulatory Authorities* has started in December 2022. In addition, support to piloting a regional health security dashboard was explored. The updated CAREC health subsite provides an overview of key milestones in the CAREC health work.[82]

In **education**, $2 million of ADB technical assistance was approved in October 2021 to support regional cooperation on skills development in CAREC countries. This was intended to spearhead support for CAREC member countries' ongoing standardization and harmonization of technical and vocational education and training (TVET) and higher education by developing a regional database and labor market information system on skills needs, regional job search and placement, and collaborations in cross-border higher education and TVET. The inception meeting and a roundtable were held in June 2022 in Tbilisi, Georgia. The focus was on key developments, challenges, and opportunities for collaboration on skills development in the CAREC region. Two policy papers facilitating CAREC countries' policy formulation on education cooperation were reviewed by CAREC countries. They included a systematic assessment of existing relevant skills and utilizable skills in CAREC countries, and looking at how well skills development systems function in CAREC countries, particularly on higher education and TVET. ADB is working with partners interested in developing the CAREC University Consortium Network to serve as a platform for consultations among academic stakeholders and as an exchange mechanism for collaborative initiatives in the region.

CAREC has laid the groundwork to advance **cross-cutting themes** in its 2030 strategy. On **gender**,

ADB is implementing technical assistance to promote gender equality as a specific measure in the CAREC Gender Strategy 2030. An inaugural expert group meeting and a CAREC Women's Empowerment Forum were held in August 2022, where representatives discussed strategy implementation issues, agreed on the working mechanism, and shared experiences in promoting women's economic and social empowerment. Preparatory work is underway to develop a regional gender action plan in collaboration with potential partners, to generate investment opportunities for regional cooperation projects, promoting women participation and gender equality, and facilitating knowledge sharing and cross learning. A CAREC Gender web page was launched on LinkedIn and Facebook to promote the CAREC Gender Strategy 2030. In addition, concept notes about a CAREC businesswomen forum and other regional pilot activities are being developed in consultation with the Regional Gender Expert Group.

Information and communication technology (ICT) has become a crucial tool for connectivity since the onset of the COVID-19 pandemic. Various activities are being undertaken to implement the CAREC Digital Strategy 2030. The CAREC Digital Strategy 2030 portal was created on the CAREC website to promote it. The CAREC Digital Strategy Steering Committee held its first meeting in October 2022. The CAREC program is supporting the development of the startup ecosystem in the region to mitigate the economic impact of the COVID-19 pandemic and facilitate economic revival. Initiatives are being implemented under a virtual startup ecosystem hub, which will engage relevant stakeholders to promote networking and knowledge exchange. These include the launch of the CAREC Startup Map[83] and the CAREC Innovation Network to encourage cross-country cooperation and collaboration between entrepreneurs and stakeholders active in the region. As part of hosting open innovation challenges, the secretariat concluded the CAREC University Startup Generator challenge in which more than 100 students developed their startup ideas.

---

[82] CAREC. Health. https://www.carecprogram.org/?page_id=19337.

[83] CAREC Startup Ecosystem. https://www.startupcarec.org/ (accessed November 2022).

Prospects

ADB will continue supporting sustainable and resilient economic growth in CAREC.

The Russian invasion of Ukraine led to more aggressive monetary tightening in advanced economies, while COVID-19 lockdowns in the PRC worsened regional economic prospects. CAREC countries are all affected by the Russian invasion of Ukraine in varying degrees. In the September 2022 edition of the *Asian Development Outlook Update,* growth projections for the Caucasus and Central Asia were revised upward from 3.6% to 3.9% for 2022 and from 4.0% to 4.2% for 2023, mainly reflecting the sharp increase in inbound money transfers to some countries due to a large influx of foreign visitors relocating their businesses from the sanctioned Russian Federation (ADB 2022b). However, growth prospects across the CAREC region remain uncertain and may decelerate in the coming months amid the uncertain geopolitical environment and possible renewed COVID-19 outbreaks. In addition, climate change and its impact on agriculture, the environment, and health remain a long-term risk to the region's economy.

Consistent with CAREC 2030, the priority agenda for 2022 aims to facilitate a green, sustainable, and inclusive post-pandemic recovery by restructuring economic paradigms to balance visions of growth and development with attention to pressing issues. These include development of (i) the CAREC Post-Pandemic Framework for Green, Sustainable and Inclusive Recovery, which provides analysis on and policy recommendations in overcoming old and new challenges for a green, sustainable, and inclusive recovery in the region; (ii) a systematic regional approach to the climate agenda by informing the climate change issues with recommended policies and instruments, including regional cooperation in addressing climate issues in CAREC countries; and (iii) a cooperation framework for agricultural development and food security in the CAREC region by introducing modern agricultural technologies to adapt to and mitigate climate change effects for improved agricultural productivity, modernizing sanitary and phytosanitary measures and food quality systems, improving customs administration to facilitate trade

of agriculture products, and developing agricultural extention services and food value chains to improve availability, affordability, and stability of food supply.

Policy Challenges

CAREC needs to strengthen the implementation of existing strategies to achieve tangible results and increase visibility on the ground.

Since the adoption of CAREC 2030 Strategy in 2017, CAREC has renewed strategies in its traditional sectors (e.g., transport, energy, trade), and formulated strategies in the new sectors and thematic areas (e.g., tourism, gender, health, ICT) under its five operational clusters. Strengthening the implementation of existing CAREC strategies remains a priority for boosting people-centered development to facilitate resilient recovery and inclusive growth. It also remains a challenge given that prolonged pandemic conditions have made full physical interaction among CAREC stakeholders difficult in the short term. Progress in implementing existing strategies is slow, as most of the physical events had to be either postponed or replaced with virtual ones. Networks among CAREC countries are a struggle without face-to-face contact, affecting the momentum of implementing these strategies, particularly in new sectors, as regular contact among CAREC stakeholders remain crucial for implementation.

To mitigate these challenges, the CAREC secretariat has strengthened the implementation of the CAREC Digital Strategy 2030 by promoting the utilization of ICT tools and online platforms to improve the efficiency of online communication. This includes the establishment of a CAREC Innovation Network that connects key startup stakeholders in the region to foster engagement and collaboration among CAREC countries and develop the region's startup ecosystem. The secretariat has also upscaled its communications, in close collaboration with ADB's Department of Communications through various measures to reflect the tangible achievement of CAREC and benefits to local communities, including through proactive interviewing with local beneficiaries of CAREC projects, and other measures.

Greater Mekong Subregion Program[84]

Cambodia, the PRC (Yunnan Province and Guangxi Zhuang Autonomous Region), the Lao People's Democratic Republic (Lao PDR), Myanmar, Thailand, and Viet Nam are the six members of the Greater Mekong Subregion (GMS) Program.[85] ADB houses the GMS central secretariat. The GMS has created an interconnected subregion that continues to see improved economic growth amid enhanced connectivity and competitiveness. Since the program's 1992 launch, 122 investment projects and 236 technical assistance projects amounting to a total of $30.2 billion have been approved. Of this amount, ADB contributed $14.1 billion, GMS governments $6.6 billion, and other development partners/the private sector $9.5 billion.

Overview

Growth rebounded for most GMS members in 2021 as COVID-19 vaccination coverage increased and mobility restrictions were eased.

For countries whose growth bounced back, recovery was underpinned by solid export performance and stronger domestic consumption and/or investment for some. For GMS as a whole, growth rebounded to 4.2% in 2021 from 0.3% in 2020 (Table 6.2).

New challenges emerged in the external environment that may dampen recovery.

Geopolitical tensions from the prolonged Russian invasion of Ukraine pushed up commodity prices and led to tightening monetary policy in advanced economies. These add to existing risk that a more deadly COVID-19 variant may emerge, and uncertainty brought about by rapid technological change. Nonetheless, the correct mix and timing of policy responses can overcome these challenges. The reopening of tourism, an important sector in some GMS countries, will support economic recovery.

Performance and Progress over the Past Year

The program has achieved impressive outcomes in its efforts to build community, connectivity, and competitiveness.

Connectivity in particular has been dramatically enhanced by 12,500 kilometers (km) of new or upgraded roads and more than 1,000 km of railway lines. Over 3,000 megawatts of electricity have been generated, and over 2,700 km of transmission and distribution lines now provide electricity to close to 165,000 new households.

Table 6.2: Selected Economic Indicators, 2021—Greater Mekong Subregion

	Nominal GDP ($ billion)	GDP Growth and Trend (2017 to 2021, average, %)		GDP Growth (%, y-o-y)	GDP per Capita (current prices, $)	Inflation (%, y-o-y)	Merchandise Export Growth (%)
Cambodia	26	4.3	↓	3.0	1,586	2.9	1.6
Guangxi ZAR, PRC	384	6.2	↑	7.5	7,618	0.9	15.4
Yunnan Province, PRC	421	7.6	↓	7.3	8,978	0.2	20.9
Lao PDR	19	3.9	↓	2.3	2,498	3.7	25.8
Myanmar	65	3.2	↓	-5.9	1,211	3.6	-7.0
Thailand	506	1.2	↓	1.5	7,066	1.2	19.2
Viet Nam	366	5.3	↓	2.6	3,757	1.8	18.9
GMS	**1,787**	**4.6**	↓	**4.2**	**5,192**	**1.2**	**17.8**

GDP = gross domestic product, GMS = Greater Mekong Subregion, Guangxi ZAR = Guangxi Zhuang Autonomous Region, Lao PDR = Lao People's Democratic Republic, PRC = People's Republic of China, y-o-y = year-on-year.

Sources: ADB calculations using data from ADB. Asian Development Outlook database for GDP growth and inflation; CEIC Data Company for Guangxi ZAR and Yunnan Province, PRC; and Haver Analytics, Inc. for nominal GDP, population, and trade.

---

[84]   Contributed by GMS Secretariat, Southeast Asia Department, ADB.

[85]   ADB has temporarily put on hold sovereign project disbursements and new contracts in Myanmar effective 1 February 2021. ADB is closely monitoring the situation in Myanmar and remains committed to supporting its people.

The GMS Economic Cooperation Program Strategic Framework 2030 (GMS 2030), which sets the program's direction and priorities was endorsed by GMS leaders in 2021 (ADB 2021a). The new strategy is guided by the program's vision of developing a more integrated, prosperous, sustainable, and inclusive subregion. GMS 2030 supports the new mission statement for the GMS Program, which aims to further expand community, connectivity, and competitiveness while promoting environmental sustainability and resilience; enhanced internal and external integration; and inclusivity.

The GMS Regional Investment Framework (RIF), a medium-term pipeline of priority investment and technical assistance projects, operationalizes GMS strategic thrusts and priorities. The RIF's 2022 *Fourth Progress Report,* which is the last update of the RIF 2022, mentions a total of 120 investment and 85 technical assistance projects requiring financing of $77.6 billion. A new 3-year rolling pipeline of projects under RIF 2023–2025 was developed and completed in line with the principles of the GMS 2030. Standards for project inclusion in the new pipeline were raised with respect to project readiness, economic and social returns, and adherence to good environmental and social practices and project management standards that increase the attractiveness of initiatives to development partners and the private sector.

GMS countries cooperate in important projects and/or activities in priority GMS sectors that support its three pillars.

Pillar 1: Community

Health and Other Human Resources Development. The GMS Health Cooperation Working Group continues to implement the GMS Health Cooperation Strategy 2019–2023, which has three pillars: (i) strengthening national health systems to tackle transnational health threats and address health security as a regional public good; (ii) responding to the health challenges and health impacts because of connectivity and mobility; and (iii) health workforce development (ADB 2019).

In 2021, the $5 million technical assistance program, Supporting Enhanced COVID-19 Vaccination and

Post-COVID-19 Health Security Response in Southeast Asia, assisted countries in vaccine rollout and delivery, supporting pillar 1 of the strategy (ADB 2021b). In February 2022, ADB further supplemented COVID-19-related assistance to Cambodia with the approval of a $95 million Asia Pacific Vaccine Access Facility loan intended for the purchase of safe and effective COVID-19 vaccines.

Under pillar 2, a proposed ADB project will improve access to health services for migrant workers in selected GMS border areas through social infrastructure development and support for health financing. The project showcases the comparative advantage of ADB in the GMS, building on ongoing support for health security, migrant population health, communicable disease control, and the strengthening of health systems. The GMS Secretariat also organized the Mekong Dialogue on Labor Mobility in May 2022 to share knowledge and good practices for a post-COVID-19 recovery and better migration management. The initiative looked at addressing the impacts of labor mobility and strengthening border health systems as part of improving regional health security in the subregion.

Another priority in the GMS Health Cooperation Strategy is One Health. A One Health response takes a unified approach to environmental, animal, and human health and their interactions, and to upgrading cross-border cooperation instruments. The Strengthening Regional Health Cooperation in the GMS project supports the promotion and implementation of collaborative, interdisciplinary, and cross-sectoral One Health responses to public threats. In June 2021, a GMS regional meeting discussed One Health systems and policies in the GMS. A follow-up meeting in April 2022 dealt with operationalizing and integrating One Health approaches for a green and sustainable post-COVID-19 recovery in the subregion. The project is also funding assessments to strengthen reporting systems on public health emergencies of international concern.

Environment. Environmental sustainability and robust response to climate change is a key priority for the GMS Program. The Core Environment Program Strategic Framework and Action Plan 2018–2022 aims to mainstream sound environment management and climate resilience across priority sectors to improve the development impact and sustainability of the GMS Program. The GMS Working Group on Environment will complete a new GMS 2030-aligned strategy in 2023.

An additional grant amounting to $2 million was approved in 2021 to support green and resilient COVID-19 recovery in selected GMS countries through the GMS Climate Change and Environmental Sustainability Program (CCESP). The additional grant will finance CCESP's work on policy support, institutional and technical capacity building, and field demonstrations. Demonstrations will be used to pilot climate action practices, innovative technologies, and financing instruments. These demonstrations could eventually be scaled up or lead to wider investments across GMS countries.

In June 2022, a workshop promoted a deeper understanding among GMS stakeholders and implementing partners about CCESP's activities. The workshop discussed how to develop demonstration proposals, sought to identify and encourage innovative ideas and demonstration proposals, and share how they will be selected.

The GMS Working Group in Environment met in October 2022 to discuss key challenges and possible solutions in the light of the UN Biodiversity Conference (COP15-Part 1) and the UN Climate Change Conference (COP26), and prepared for the COP27 and COP15-Part 2 international meetings. The working group discussed national and subregional climate resilience and post-2020 biodiversity conservation frameworks and actions in the GMS in the context of COPs and COVID-19. Group participants agreed on priority actions for regional cooperation under the CCESP to improve climate and disaster resilience, and biodiversity conservation in the GMS.

Pillar 2: Connectivity

Energy. GMS 2030 emphasizes stronger promotion of regional cross-border power trade, establishing regional technical and regulatory conditions for developing

regional markets, and expanding investments in clean and renewable energies with a greater role for the private sector. In support of GMS 2030, GMS countries are working together to achieve greater integration of renewable energies in countries' energy development plans. In July 2021, ADB approved a technical assistance for knowledge and support—Accelerating the Clean Energy Transition in Southeast Asia—to help countries in the subregion accelerate their transition to cleaner, climate-friendly forms of energy.

In July 2022, GMS member countries convened the final meeting of the GMS Regional Power Trade Coordination Committee, a landmark meeting signaling its evolution into the GMS Energy Transition Taskforce. The taskforce has an expanded mandate to accelerate the clean energy transition in addition to its continued focus on power trade expansion. That mandate includes a multi-country pilot project and activities across three other workstreams: renewable energy and energy storage, energy efficiency, and green finance.

Cross-Border Transport Connectivity. Transport infrastructure remains the backbone of the GMS Program. The RIF 2022 mentions 68 transport investment projects with financing worth $65.8 billion, or 85% of the total RIF value. For the new RIF 2023–2025, transport projects remain the bulk of GMS investments, at 46% of their estimated value.

Innovation in the railway subsector is being sought as part of GMS 2030, given that it is the most energy-efficient and environmentally friendly mode of transportation. Through the framework of the Greater Mekong Railway Association, GMS countries are pursuing various priority railway links: the Vientiane–Boten Railway (416 km, valued at $5.8 billion) and the Yuxi–Mohan Railway (517 km, valued at $8 billion) that make up the Lao PDR–PRC (Vientiane–Kunming) Highspeed Rail Project #5 priority link (operations launched in December 2021). In the first half of 2022, the priority link transported 3.27 million passengers (2.86 million in the PRC and 410,000 in the Lao PDR) and 4.03 million tons of goods, including 647,000 tons of cross-border goods. It implemented efficient trade facilitation by reducing clearance time to 5 hours compared with 24 hours by road—in part because of high road demand. The significant GMS investment projects are part of the bigger Kunming–Singapore railway or the Pan–Asia railway Network, which is a network of railways connecting the PRC and all contiguous Southeast Asia.

Pillar 3: Competitiveness

Agriculture. The GMS Sustainable Agriculture and Food Security Program, an ADB regional technical assistance, continues to help GMS countries with greening their supply chains, improving food safety and quality, and tackling key climate change challenges to agriculture. The program supports the GMS 2030 aim to raise food safety and quality standards for expanding exports and encouraging climate- and environment-friendly production practices along the value chain, as well as efforts to sustain natural assets with a focus on small-scale farmers and micro, small, and medium-sized agro-enterprises. In 2021, $1.75 million in additional funding was approved to promote inter-subregional cooperation and the COVID-19 response and recovery of food systems in the GMS. In 2022, the program stepped up preparation of five pilot demonstrations and value chain studies, all aimed at addressing systemic vulnerabilities and risks in agri-food value chains while adding stricter cross-border trade regulations by introducing internationally recognized digital traceability standards and approaches in the subregion.

The June 2022 meeting of the GMS Working Group on Agriculture focused on adaptations in the context of climate change and used the water–food–energy nexus as a key analytical lens/approach to facilitate discussion. Group members agreed to five priority actions that will serve as guide for the transition to long-lasting food security and sustainable agriculture practices in the subregion.

The GMS Cross-Border Livestock Health and Value Chains Project, planned for Cambodia, the Lao PDR, and Viet Nam, will promote regional cooperation and health security. The project aims to reduce transboundary animal diseases, food safety, and zoonotic disease risk; and improve climate change adaptation, resilience of livestock value chains, and COVID-19 responses.

Tourism. GMS countries started to reopen to international travelers in late 2021, while considerable reductions in travel restrictions or requirements by the first half of 2022 allowed for the increase in tourist arrivals and generated receipts.

GMS countries' continued COVID-19 response and recovery efforts for the tourism sector were supported by the GMS Tourism COVID Recovery Communications Plan and accompanying Tool Kit prepared and implemented by the GMS Tourism Working Group. These guided the dissemination of accurate and engaging information to support a safe, resilient, and sustainable GMS tourism recovery.

Many ongoing and proposed ADB-assisted projects are promoting resiliency, sustainability, and inclusion in the GMS tourism sector. These include (i) GMS Tourism Infrastructure for Inclusive Growth Projects ($220 million); (ii) Guangxi Li River Comprehensive Ecological Rehabilitation Project ($371 million); (iii) ADB Frontier Fund—a nonsovereign investment fund that will invest in growth-oriented tourism-related SMEs in Southeast Asia (emphasizing the Lao PDR and Cambodia) and the Pacific ($28 million); (iv) Urban Environment Improvement Investment Project ($33 million); (v) Hoa Binh Tourism Infrastructure Development Project ($75 million); and (vi) Lao Cai Sustainable Urban and Infrastructure Development Project ($86 million).

Urban Development. GMS 2030 priority directions for urban development include building resilience of cities to future pandemics over the medium term (through the enhanced use of digital technologies, among others) and in the long term develop livable cities that combine gray, green, and blue infrastructure and strategies for a holistic development. Recently approved GMS RIF projects supporting these directions include (i) Guangxi Regional Cooperation and Integration Promotion Investment Program–Tranche 3 (October 2021, $326.7 million); and (ii) Livable Cities Investment Project (Cambodia, November 2021, $196.1 million).

Bavet, Kampot, and Poipet were chosen as sites for the Livable Cities Project in Cambodia because they have potential to service cross-border trade (Bavet for

Viet Nam–Cambodia border trade and Poipet for Thailand–Cambodia trade), and opportunities to promote tourism (Kampot). The project will provide improved infrastructure (wastewater and solid waste management services, and urban stormwater drainage systems) and support capacity development that will strengthen the institutional capacity of municipal administration in operations and the maintenance of public services to facilitate sustainable and economic growth over the long term.

The GMS Urban Development Working Group met in February 2022 to discuss emerging ICT and digital solutions. Water service providers were also presented with new, transformative opportunities for more efficient water management, and for improved customer services. This will support GMS economies in building resilience of cities. The working group also agreed to take steps toward developing a new GMS Urban Development Strategic Framework (2023–2030).

Prospects and Policy Challenges

Substantial funds are required for countries to take advantage of rapid changes in technology (especially through digitalization) and ensure that commitments to a green and inclusive growth are met.

Some countries have yet to recover from the heavy public spending needed to combat the COVID-19 pandemic. Moreover, current tight monetary conditions to combat inflation do not favor attempts to raise funds.

To help GMS countries overcome these challenges and to meet GMS 2030 priorities for improving competitiveness, member countries agreed to establish the GMS Trade and Investment Task Force. The task force promotes trade and investment facilitation among members and external parties, which will enable open, fair, and nondiscriminatory business environments to flourish, and so help jumpstart GMS economies and sustain recovery.

An initial scoping study (September 2021–February 2022) took stock of progress in trade and investment facilitation in GMS (ADB 2022d). The study also identified areas of improvement to better facilitate trade and investment in the subregion and mapped out short- and long-term interventions. The task force was established in March 2022 and its 2-year work plan was approved in its first meeting on 28 October 2022. One of the main agreements was for the task force to focus work on a "digital supply chain" and the need to consult and coordinate activities with relevant GMS working groups and committees and the private sector.

Strengthening collaborative arrangements is one of the best options GMS countries have to tackle current policy challenges. Work with other regional cooperation and integration programs like ASEAN will ensure that GMS actions complement the wider regional agenda. Establishing the GMS Trade and Investment Task Force is consistent with the GMS 2030's collaborative approach that embraces private sector solutions to leverage expertise and financing.

Brunei Darussalam–Indonesia–Malaysia–Philippines East ASEAN Growth Area and Indonesia–Malaysia–Thailand Growth Triangle[86]

The Brunei Darussalam–Indonesia–Malaysia–Philippines East ASEAN Growth Area, or BIMP-EAGA, is a cooperation initiative established in 1994 to spur development in remote and less-developed areas in the four participating Southeast Asian countries. BIMP-EAGA cooperation is anchored on five strategic pillars: connectivity, food basket, tourism, environment, and sociocultural and education. Thanks to strong ownership and commitment, as demonstrated by the financial, human and technical resources put in by member governments, BIMP-EAGA has helped support more balanced and inclusive growth in the subregion, boosting

---

[86]   Contributed by Regional Cooperation and Operations Coordination Division, Southeast Asia Department, ADB.

trade, tourism and infrastructure investments, and contributing to regional economic integration in the ASEAN Economic Community. ADB has been a development partner of BIMP–EAGA since 1996 and the program's Regional Development Advisor since 2003.

The Indonesia–Malaysia–Thailand Growth Triangle (IMT-GT) was established a year earlier than BIMP-EAGA in 1993. The IMT-GT consists of the 10 provinces of Sumatra, Indonesia; 8 states in peninsular Malaysia; and 14 provinces in southern Thailand. Malaysia is in the process of including a further three states, thus encompassing the entire peninsula. The goals of the IMT-GT program are similar to BIMP-EAGA: to accelerate economic growth and transformation in its member states, especially those with less developed areas along coastal and border areas. The program's aspiration is to leverage underlying economic complementarities, comparative advantages, geographic proximity, and the close historical, cultural, and linguistic ties of its member provinces and states.

Overview

Even as the COVID-19 pandemic continued to present an array of challenges to both BIMP-EAGA's and IMT-GT's development agenda, its targets remain on track.

A 2022 midterm review found some BIMP-EAGA sectors exceeding goals, thanks to well-defined project management mechanisms and planning. Connectivity remains a cornerstone of BIMP-EAGA cooperation, and 88 priority infrastructure projects with the combined $24.23 billion are helping to generate cross-border activities, promote access to markets, reduce trade and transport costs, and facilitate growth between neighboring production, export, and consumption points. Despite the challenges of COVID-19, about one-third (27) of the priority projects have been completed. A further 10 projects were due for completion in 2022, with 8 large-scale infrastructure projects having completed phases, and a remaining 43 projects in different stages of implementation.

In IMT-GT, amid finalizing the Implementation Blueprint 2022–2026, the second such 5-year plan, officials are taking stock and strategizing initiatives to alleviate some of the devastation from the COVID-19 pandemic. Tourism, arguably the most economically devastated segment, is the bellwether for the services sector. It has been earmarked as a key subsector for focused recovery with several key IMT-GT activities planned in 2023–2025: the Visit IMT-GT 2023 year to mark its 30th anniversary, preparation of a regional Tourism Recovery Communication Tool Kit and mobilization of the ASEAN Post Pandemic Tourism Recovery Plan. Over the longer term, the implementation blueprint centers on efforts to restart some $39 billion worth of priority projects comprising quality infrastructure and software.

Performance and Progress over the Past Year

The pace of the recovery varied across the countries in the BIMP-EAGA and IMT-GT subregions.

In 2020 and 2021, fiscal policy helped cushion the impact of COVID-19 and a robust recovery in domestic demand supported economic growth. Commodity exporters—Indonesia and Malaysia stand out—benefited from rising commodity prices, and tourism showed some recovery signs in 2021. Inflation was relatively low and driven largely by the continuing economic recovery and elevated energy and commodity prices. Recovery was ongoing in 2022 but new challenges cast a shadow over the path for both the BIMP-EAGA and IMT-GT subregions. Weaker growth in key export markets, challenges following the Russian invasion of Ukraine, disruptions in trade supply chains, more aggressive monetary tightening in advanced economies, and the movement of energy and food prices will underpin the growth momentum in the BIMP-EAGA and IMT-GT subregions.

While COVID-19 reduced trade and production in BIMP–EAGA, direct foreign and domestic investments continued to rise (Chapter 3), helping to boost economic recovery as the subregion continued to build on its achievements in improving connectivity, strengthening trade and supply chains, and promoting inclusive growth.

At their annual ministerial meeting in 2022, BIMP-EAGA leaders expressed appreciation for ADB's cooperation, including support for the COVID-19 response, transport and energy projects, analytical work on border areas and special economic zone development, promotion of green recovery, support for the tourism revival, the protection of marine ecosystems, and the provision of capacity-building opportunities for government officials. ADB support to BIMP-EAGA countries included $875 million through the Asia Pacific Vaccine Access Facility to help the Philippines and Indonesia procure and deliver safe and effective vaccines, and $3 billion in quick-disbursing loans to support their COVID-19 response.

New challenges during the pandemic also intensified the need for timely and innovative knowledge solutions. ADB provided key knowledge work to support special economic zones and the subregion's economic corridors. Recommendations from member states were instrumental in the expansion of IMT-GT to encompass the entire Peninsular Malaysia by including the states of Johor, Pahang, and Terengganu—expanding IMT-GT so that it now borders Singapore. In turn, a new economic corridor was added to the existing five corridors. Economic Corridor 6 is envisaged to stretch from the eastern seaboard of Thailand, across the flank of the east coast of Malaysia to Singapore, connect with the Riau Islands and Batam and Bintan, reaching land again at Pekanbaru in Sumatra.

Progress in Subregional Connectivity. Despite the pandemic, priority infrastructure projects were completed in 2020 and 2021 at BIMP-EAGA, including the Temburong Bridge (Sultan Haji Omar Ali Saifuddien Bridge) in Brunei Darussalam, the Manado–Bitung Link (Toll Road) in Indonesia, the LNG ISO Tank Export Facilities in Bintulu Port in Malaysia, the Juwata International Airport (Tarakan) in Indonesia, Mukah Airport (Sarawak) in Malaysia, and the General Santos Astropolis Airport in the Philippines. The road projects are expected to reduce costs and travel time and lead to greater efficiencies and competitiveness; the ports will contribute to maritime connectivity; the liquefied natural gas export facility will serve as a pioneering ASEAN port exporting alternative and renewable energy sources; and the airports will improve access to tourist destinations and the movement of cargo.

In the energy sector, completed projects include the enclave interconnections in North Kalimantan in Indonesia for the Tidang Pale–Malinau Segment of the Tanjung Redep–Malinau Transmission, and the Mindanao Transmission Backbone Upgrading in the Philippines.

ADB's road projects in BIMP-EAGA countries include the Improving Growth Corridors in Mindanao Road Sector Project in the Philippines, which will upgrade 300 kilometers of national roads, where implementation is ongoing. Another planned ADB road project is the National Roads Development Project in Kalimantan, Indonesia, which is slated for approval later in 2024. The project will improve regional connectivity by rehabilitating and upgrading 280 km of road sections in North and East Kalimantan, with road safety and biodiversity designs included. As part of its support of Sulawesi following the 2018 earthquake and tsunami, ADB is providing about $110 million for the rehabilitation and reconstruction of three seaports, and the rehabilitation and upgrade of the Mutiara Sis Al Jufri Airport in Palu.

Working groups across sectors in IMT-GT achieved consistent progress over 2021–2022, despite the challenge of meeting virtually. The Working Group for Transport Connectivity has 22 ongoing projects including 17 priority connectivity projects and 5 others. The working group also added three new priority connectivity projects.

Prospects

The two subregional programs, as building blocks of ASEAN integration, are aligning recovery and resilience measures with the ASEAN Comprehensive Recovery.

With ADB's support, BIMP-EAGA is preparing to refine its long-term plans and goals, based on the results of a midterm review of the BIMP-EAGA Vision 2025, to ensure that work remains relevant and responsive to the challenges and opportunities beyond the pandemic. For IMT-GT, ADB provided support for the preparation of the IMT-GT Implementation Blueprint 2022–2026 by engaging local consultants, providing technical inputs, thematic studies, and helping with technical editing. ADB will support the blueprint through the preparation of national strategic action plans that will be linked to the respective national plans.

Amid the pandemic, BIMP-EAGA leaders recognized the need for stronger border cooperation to sustain trade and ensure that supply chains remain open. Accordingly, increased cooperation in monitoring and inspection of goods under the One Borneo Quarantine Initiative helps safeguard the opening of borders to trade and to enhance protection from pests and diseases.

BIMP–EAGA has aligned its measures with the ASEAN Comprehensive Recovery Framework's broad strategies, given the subregion's role in ASEAN integration. This includes aligning the BIMP-EAGA Tourism Recovery Framework with the ASEAN Post Pandemic Recovery Plan. For its part, ADB has supported development of the BIMP-EAGA Tourism Recovery Communications Plan and Tool Kit, which is aligned with the ASEAN Post Pandemic Tourism Recovery Plan. ADB has also organized workshops to provide officials of national tourism organizations with focal points from BIMP-EAGA, with foundational tools in strategic communications planning customized to the needs of the subregion's tourism recovery.

In addition to tourism, IMT-GT ministers in 2022 endorsed the recommendations of the implementation blueprint. The recommendations covered the expansion of the additional economic corridor, Economic Corridor 6, and discussed agriculture commodity improvements and leveraging quality infrastructure to support sustainable urban development. The blueprint calls for member countries to develop their own strategic action plans to identify synergies between respective national strategies with regional cooperation and integration development strategies.

Policy Challenges

Greater energy access and reliability is needed to drive BIMP-EAGA's recovery and future economic development.

The signing of the Sabah–Sarawak Power Interconnection Power Exchange Agreement between SESCO, a subsidiary of Sarawak Energy Bhd, and Sabah Electricity Sdn Bhd, will pave the way for establishing the Borneo Grid and the ASEAN Power Grid. The Sabah–Sarawak project also complements the Trans Borneo Power Grid Sarawak–West Kalimantan Interconnection Project, both of which are vital to the ASEAN Power Grid project. ADB is also helping Indonesia build a cross-border high-voltage transmission line and substation linking the West Kalimantan grid with that of Sarawak, Malaysia, which is another important component in the Trans Borneo Power Grid for enabling power trading between BIMP–EAGA countries.

For IMT-GT, the absence of respective explicit national strategies for subregional cooperation discourages in-country stakeholders from making long-term investment commitments in the subregion. Hence, there is an urgent need for individual strategic subregional cooperation action plans to guide systematic involvement of public and private stakeholders in IMT-GT and help them navigate the complex subregional institutional setup and engagement processes.

Bay of Bengal Initiative for Multi-Sectoral Technical and Economic Cooperation[87]

ADB's role in advancing regional cooperation and integration in South Asia and Southeast Asia through its support for the Bay of Bengal Initiative for Multi-Sectoral Technical and Economic Cooperation (BIMSTEC) and its member states is evolving and expanding. Early focus on research in transport connectivity has widened to cover institutional strengthening and regional policy dialogue

---

[87]   Contributed by Thiam Hee Ng, director, Regional Cooperation and Operations Coordination Division (SARC), South Asia Department; Dongxiang Li, lead regional cooperation specialist, SARC; Lani Garnace, economics officer, SARC; and John Mercurio, ADB consultant, SARC.

on a range of areas, including trade, tourism, financing, and people-to-people exchange. ADB-supported studies are helping shape policies and programs. Institutional strengthening and regional policy dialogue activities have progressively equipped BIMSTEC with the capacity and knowledge to plan, implement, and monitor these policies and programs.

Overview

Regional cooperation and integration is at the heart of ADB's partnership with BIMSTEC.

ADB's work with BIMSTEC began in 2005 when the bank began offering technical and financial assistance. ADB collaborates closely with the BIMSTEC secretariat to advance economic cooperation and integration in South Asia and Southeast Asia through (i) research and knowledge outreach; (ii) institutional strengthening; and (iii) regional policy dialogues. ADB also supports BIMSTEC member states through technical assistance projects and project financing under GMS and South Asia Subregional Economic Cooperation (SASEC) programs.

BIMSTEC is a regional organization of seven member states in the littoral and adjacent areas of the Bay of Bengal, which constitute a contiguous region. This subregional organization was formed on 6 June 1997 through the Bangkok Declaration.[88] Member states include five from South Asia (Bangladesh, Bhutan, India, Nepal, Sri Lanka) and two from Southeast Asia (Myanmar and Thailand).[89] The BIMSTEC subregion is home to around 1.8 billion people, about 22% of the global population and has a combined GDP of $4.3 trillion (Table 6.3). Its secretariat was established in Dhaka in 2014.

The economic bloc was formed by four member states with the acronym "BIST-EC" (Bangladesh, India, Sri Lanka, and Thailand Economic Cooperation). Following the inclusion of Myanmar in December 1997, the group was renamed "BIMST-EC" (Bangladesh, India, Myanmar, Sri Lanka, and Thailand Economic Cooperation). The grouping took its current name with the admission of Nepal and Bhutan at the Sixth Ministerial Meeting in 2004.

BIMSTEC constitutes a bridge between South Asia and Southeast Asia and reinforces relations among these countries. The group has also established a platform

Table 6.3: Selected Economic Indicators, 2021—Bay of Bengal Initiative for Multi-Sectoral Technical and Economic Cooperation

	Population (million)	Nominal GDP ($ billion)	GDP Growth (%, 2017–2021, average)	GDP per Capita (current prices, $)	Trade Openness (total trade, % of GDP)
Bangladesh	169.4	416.3	6.4	2,457.9	25.6
Bhutan	0.8	2.4	1.5	3,140.9	170.4
India	1,407.6	3,176.3	3.8	2,256.6	30.4
Myanmar	53.8	65.2	3.2	1,211.2	45.4
Nepal	30.0	35.8	5.0	1,193.5	49.2
Sri Lanka	21.8	89.0	1.8	4,086.6	30.1
Thailand	71.6	505.9	1.2	7,065.6	105.4
BIMSTEC	**1,754.9**	**4,290.9**	**3.7**	**2,445.1**	**39.2**

BIMSTEC = Bay of Bengal Initiative for Multi-Sectoral Technical and Economic Cooperation, GDP = gross domestic product, IMF = International Monetary Fund.

Note: BIMSTEC average GDP growth rate is weighted using nominal GDP. Nominal GDP figures are based on IMF staff estimates.

Sources: ADB calculations using data from ADB. Asian Development Outlook database for GDP growth; and Haver Analytics, Inc. for nominal GDP, population, and trade.

---

[88]   BIMSTEC. 1997. *Declaration on the Establishment of Bangladesh–India–Sri Lanka–Thailand Economic Cooperation.* Bangkok.

[89]   ADB has temporarily put on hold sovereign project disbursements and new contracts in Myanmar effective 1 February 2021. ADB is closely monitoring the situation in Myanmar and remains committed to supporting its people.

for intraregional cooperation between SAARC and ASEAN members. For this reason, ADB's support to BIMSTEC is bolstered by the GMS and SASEC programs. The BIMSTEC Charter, signed by leaders of member states in Sri Lanka at the 5th BIMSTEC Summit in March 2022, mandates the organization to cooperate with international and regional organizations that have similar aims and purposes. It directs BIMSTEC member states to "cooperate more effectively in joint efforts that are supportive of and complementary to national development plans of the Member States which result in tangible benefits to the people in raising their living standards, including through generating employment and improving transportation and communication infrastructure" (BIMSTEC 2022).

Performance and Progress over the Past Year

ADB's role in advancing economic cooperation and integration in South Asia and Southeast Asia through BIMSTEC is evolving and expanding.

The early years of the partnership focused on research in transport connectivity. But this has gradually widened to cover institutional strengthening and regional policy dialogue on a wider range of areas, including trade, tourism, financing, and people-to-people exchange. ADB-supported studies are helping shape economic cooperation and integration policies and programs (ADB 2008, 2018a). Institutional strengthening and regional policy dialogue activities have progressively equipped BIMSTEC with the capacity and knowledge to plan, implement, and monitor these policies and programs. Recently, ADB responded quickly to a BIMSTEC request to prepare studies to tap opportunities for member states on tourism, trade facilitation, and transport infrastructure financing. Its reports are being finalized for publication.

Tourism Development. ADB, prompted by the collapse of tourism due to the COVID-19 pandemic, assisted BIMSTEC with the *Leveraging Thematic Circuits for BIMSTEC Tourism Development* study. In analyzing ways to revive tourism, the study provides valuable inputs needed to draw up a comprehensive strategy on developing tourism in the subregion. Recommendations include improving tourism infrastructure, stimulating the sustainable development of themes for tourists to follow (the so-called thematic circuits), using marketing and branding, and putting a focus on developing human resources for meeting public and private sector tourism development needs.

Trade Facilitation. The BIMSTEC Trade Facilitation Strategic Framework 2030 was prepared to respond to BIMSTEC's call for promoting intraregional trade by reducing nontariff barriers. It identifies nontariff barriers to trade in the subregion and provides a structured approach to enhancing trade facilitation. This effort has four main components: (i) soft infrastructure, including the promotion of increased remote processing and clearances, automation, and the rationalization of documentation; (ii) hard infrastructure, including developing land border facilities, inland clearance container depots, dry ports, and testing laboratories; (iii) logistics, including promoting advanced logistical applications and strengthening linkages between national single windows and port community systems; and (iv) building institutional capacity and promoting mutual cooperation among member states to facilitate transfer of technical skills.

Transport Connectivity. The ADB-supported BIMSTEC Master Plan for Transport Connectivity was adopted in March 2022. The document is the first of its kind to be adopted by BIMSTEC leaders and contains a comprehensive 10-year strategy and action plan to improve transport linkages in the subregion. Since the leaders of member states called for its immediate implementation, ADB is now poised to help implement 141 flagship projects to improve transport connectivity in the Bay of Bengal at an estimated cost of $47 billion. These projects cover eight operational areas: (i) roads and road transport; (ii) railways and rail transport; (iii) ports and maritime transport; (iv) inland water transport; (v) civil aviation and airports; (vi) multimodal and intermodal transport; (vii) trade facilitation; and (viii) human resources development (ADB 2022e). They will be monitored against strategic goals over the 10 years of the plan.

Transport Connectivity Financing. ADB supported a study on *Financing for Transport Connectivity Infrastructure* to fill financing gaps of projects included in the master plan. The study assesses the financing landscape for infrastructure in the subregion and analyzes the various modes for financing transport infrastructure, including public–private partnerships. Its recommendations include ensuring adequate enablers for the strategy, planning, coordination, and implementation of projects. Formulating standard contractual agreements and harmonizing technical standards for use in regional projects are also recommended, as is setting up a BIMSTEC regional fund to address funding challenges and to better control project preparation and implementation timelines.

Policy Dialogues and Capacity Building. Success in providing just-in-time responses to BIMSTEC's knowledge needs is built on sound policy dialogues with representatives from member states. As in previous years, ADB supported important events organized by the BIMSTEC secretariat, including the BIMSTEC Transport Connectivity Working Group meetings that served as the main channel for policy discussions leading to the formulation of the master plan. Knowledge sharing has also played a huge part in the success of the ADB-BIMSTEC partnership. Although sidelined by the pandemic, training and capacity-building activities remained on top of ADB–BIMSTEC partnership initiatives. In 2021, the BIMSTEC secretariat and ADB agreed to follow a revised list of training activities focused on strengthening the capacities of the secretariat and member states to promote cooperation and integration.

Prospects

The BIMSTEC Charter stipulates the group's objectives, principles, and organizational setup and arrangements to accelerate economic growth and social progress.

The month before BIMSTEC heads of government signed the charter at their March 2022 summit, ADB and the secretariat specified their cooperation arrangements through a memorandum of understanding (MOU), the secretariat's first MOU with an international organization. Under the MOU, ADB will help BIMSTEC in planning and managing projects and programs by providing technical and financial assistance for information exchange, knowledge products formulation, policy dialogue, knowledge sharing, and institutional development.

An area where BIMSTEC requested significant focus is ADB's support for the BIMSTEC Master Plan for Transport Connectivity. Using the SASEC forum and the network of ADB resident missions, ADB is taking stock of the status of transport projects and formulating a 3-year rolling action plan. ADB will help the secretariat organize a workshop in 2023 to discuss the initial progress and arrangements for its implementation, including the financing arrangements for some of the projects.

ADB will also continue to support regional policy dialogues, knowledge sharing, and capacity building. Facilitation of knowledge exchange and dialogues with ASEAN, UNESCAP, and other international organizations will constitute an important engagement. And as to the direct engagement with BIMSTEC secretariat, the first ADB-supported institutional development activity on team building, leadership, and emotional intelligence was held in Dhaka in April 2022 for secretariat officials and staff.

Policy Challenges

Progress in BIMSTEC can be accelerated by tackling the challenges of enormous and unmet resource requirements, improving institutional capacity, and removing system constraints.

The group's ambitious economic and social advancement agenda has already achieved much good progress in areas such as transport connectivity and trade through the efforts of BIMSTEC member states and the support of development partners.

The February 2022 MOU provides a great opportunity for ADB and BIMSTEC to work together more closely to accelerate economic cooperation and integration, particularly in the broad areas of transport connectivity, trade facilitation, energy, environment and climate change, tourism development, and infrastructure financing.

The subregion's geographic contiguity, abundant natural and human resources, rich historical linkages, and common cultural heritage present great potential for BIMSTEC to promote cooperation and integration in areas identified in the agreement. ADB welcomes the convergence of BIMSTEC's development agenda and ADB's strategic priorities. With the BIMSTEC Charter's statement of renewed commitment to the cause of promoting peace, prosperity, and sustainable development, ADB is committed to accelerating and expanding support to BIMSTEC under Strategy 2030 and through the GMS and SASEC programs to achieve a prosperous, sustainable, resilient, and inclusive Bay of Bengal region.

South Asia Subregional Economic Cooperation[90]

The ADB-supported South Asia Subregional Economic Cooperation (SASEC) program is a partnership of seven countries (Bangladesh, Bhutan, India, Maldives, Myanmar, Nepal, and Sri Lanka) that aims to improve economic cooperation and address development challenges in the subregion.[91] ADB is lead financier, secretariat, and development partner, financing investments and technical assistance. By 2022, SASEC has built a portfolio of 77 projects amounting to almost $18 billion, with the largest share of investments made for connectivity infrastructure. SASEC members are now undertaking a strategic refocusing of the program through a reorientation of the SASEC Vision (ADB 2017), including adding climate, pandemic, and disaster resilience as an operational priority and new initiatives across areas of cooperation. Institutional improvements, the establishment of a SASEC secretariat within the subregion, and a mechanism for deeper sectoral focus are also being pursued.

Overview

In 2022, SASEC pushed forward with strategic refocusing of the program to support the post COVID-19 green and resilient recovery efforts of its member countries.

Bangladesh, Bhutan, India, and Nepal established SASEC in 2001 to strengthen subregional economic cooperation and address development challenges such as persistent poverty and demographic expansion (Table 6.4). Maldives and Sri Lanka joined in 2014 followed by Myanmar in 2017, expanding opportunities to enhance cross-border connectivity, intraregional trade, and regional cooperation and integration.

In 2021, ADB committed $1.26 billion in regional cooperation and integration assistance for three multisector projects, one transport, and one energy project. It was on track to commit $1.81 billion for 13 projects in 2022.[92] Robust growth in GDP per capita in Bangladesh, India, and Maldives in 2021 (ranging from 6% to 26%) will continue in 2022–2023 for these countries; however, low growth or declines in GDP per capita in Sri Lanka and Myanmar in 2021 are expected to deepen poverty in these countries.

By 31 October 2022, 77 projects ($17.56 billion) had been financed along with $199.68 million in 143 technical assistance grants. Investments in infrastructure connectivity accounted for the largest share (44 projects, $12.32 billion), with power generation, transmission, and cross-border electricity trade next (16 projects, $2.92 billion). Investments in economic corridor development and/or multisector projects (8 projects worth $1.94 billion), trade facilitation (5 projects worth $328.15 million), ICT (2 projects worth $20.80 million), and health (2 projects worth $25.92 million), constituted the remainder (Figure 6.5). ADB committed about $10.31 billion in investments ($6.94 billion from ordinary capital resources and $3.37 billion in concessional finance), while SASEC members and cofinanciers contributed over $7.25 billion.

---

[90]   Contributed by Thiam Hee Ng, director, SARC; Tadateru Hayashi, principal economist, SARC; Pia Reyes, senior regional cooperation officer, SARC; Esnerjames Fernandez, associate regional cooperation officer, SARC; Jesusito Tranquilino, ADB consultant, SARC; and Leticia de Leon, ADB consultant, SARC.

[91]   ADB has temporarily put on hold sovereign project disbursements and new contracts in Myanmar effective 1 February 2021. ADB is closely monitoring the situation in Myanmar and remains committed to supporting its people.

[92]   Consisting of four transport projects, two trade facilitation program loans, one clean energy project, four multisector corridor development projects, and two health projects.

Table 6.4: Selected Economic Indicators, 2021—South Asia Subregional Economic Cooperation

Economy	Population (million)	Nominal GDP ($ billion)	GDP Growth (%, 2017–2021, average)	GDP per Capita (current prices, $)	Trade Openness (total trade, % of GDP)
Bangladesh	169.4	416.3	6.4	2,457.9	25.6
Bhutan	0.8	2.4	1.5	3,140.9	170.4
India	1,407.6	3,176.3	3.8	2,256.6	30.4
Maldives	0.5	5.2	6.1	9,979.7	52.4
Myanmar	53.8	65.2	3.2	1,211.2	45.4
Nepal	30.0	35.8	5.0	1,193.5	49.2
Sri Lanka	21.8	89.0	1.8	4,086.6	39.9
SASEC	**1,683.8**	**3,790.2**	**4.1**	**2,250.9**	**30.6**

GDP = gross domestic product, SASEC = South Asia Subregional Economic Cooperation.

Note: SASEC average GDP growth rate is weighted using nominal GDP, based on International Monetary Fund staff estimates.

Sources: ADB calculations using data from ADB. Asian Development Outlook database for GDP growth; and Haver Analytics, Inc. for nominal GDP, population, and trade.

Figure 6.5: Total Portfolio By Sector—South Asia Subregional Economic Cooperation, 2001–2022
(as of 31 October 2022)

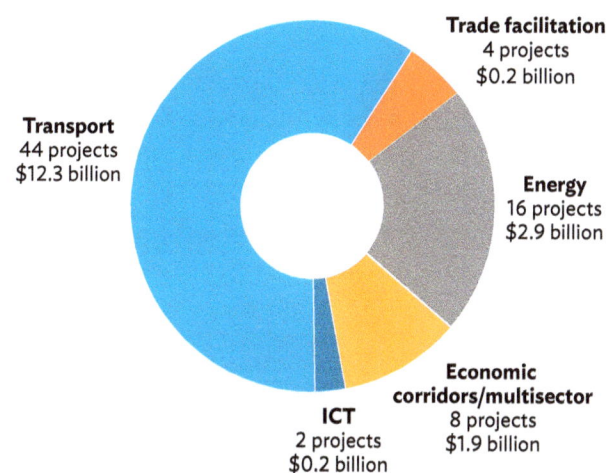

Transport
44 projects
$12.3 billion

Trade facilitation
4 projects
$0.2 billion

Energy
16 projects
$2.9 billion

Economic corridors/multisector
8 projects
$1.9 billion

ICT
2 projects
$0.2 billion

ICT = information and communication technology.

Source: ADB estimates and ADB 2022c.

SASEC knowledge initiatives tackle trade constraints discussed in SASEC Vision and Operational Plan documents (ADB 2016, 2017). These and added complications from pandemic-induced supply chain disruptions, provide the basis for a strategic refocusing, aligned with the subregion's targets for the Sustainable Development Goals (SDGs).[93] ADB has completed studies on advancing maritime sector cooperation, strengthening tourism cooperation mechanisms, and promoting safe mobility and better road asset management. Route initiative studies have identified issues that hamper cross-border flows and solutions that will create highly facilitated trade corridors (HFTCs).[94] Supply chain mapping studies explored how to harness complementarities between SASEC corridors and actions to strengthen value chains. A scoping study on One Health, initiated by the climate, pandemic, and disaster resilience operational priority, looked at improving health security through harmonized policy and project interventions.[95]

---

[93] Also to better align with ADB's Strategy 2030 (ADB 2018b).

[94] HFTCs are economic trade routes that enhance trade and transit efficiency in the region and can generate demonstration effect leading to adoption of similar facilitation measures in other cross-border corridors and lead to better regional integration. Crucial elements of HFTCs include (i) full implementation of WTO Trade Facilitation Agreement measures, (ii) systems interoperability, (iii) developing testing and certification facilities and progressing to mutual recognition, (iv) seamless cross-border transport operations, and (v) coordinated border infrastructure development.

[95] One Health is a United Nations' initiative to forge close collaboration between human and animal health measures to address the risk of spread of zoonotic diseases. The SASEC scoping study looked at potential regional-level interventions such as disease surveillance systems to enable seamless information sharing and monitoring between countries.

Updates to the Action Plan on SASEC Initiatives 2022–2024 reflect revised SASEC priorities under the SASEC Operational Plan 2016–2025 (ADB 2016) and its 2019 revamp (ADB 2020a). Project tables featuring the SASEC operational priorities are now to be updated quarterly and made available in real time on the SASEC website.[96]

Performance and Progress over the Past Year

The two-pronged approach for strategic reorientation of the SASEC program was endorsed at virtual meetings of SASEC nodal officials and working groups in June 2022. The new climate, pandemic, and disaster resilience operational priority includes strengthening regional health security through the One Health Approach. Proposed new initiatives to realign priorities include (i) promoting HFTCs, (ii) ramping up maritime cooperation, and (iii) implementing the tourism program.

The second approach, institutional enhancement, involves regularizing SASEC finance minister meetings, strengthening subregional and national institutional arrangements for SASEC, and establishing a SASEC secretariat. Subgroups will be formed for more focused discussions on sector-specific or other issues and actions. The identified subgroups cover (i) food regulators' forum; (ii) tourism; (iii) supply chain development; (iv) road/rail, maritime, and inland waterways; and (v) a business forum.

Transport. In 2021, ADB provided $400 million for the Dhaka–Sylhet Corridor Road Investment project tranche 1, which will improve the efficiency, connectivity, and safety of this international corridor. The SASEC program will continue to prioritize enhancing multimodal linkages between port gateways and landlocked areas, including improving Nepal's transit trade access to Indian ports. Maritime investments and further knowledge work will arise from recommendations of the completed maritime cooperation studies discussed at SASEC meetings in June 2022. These studies looked into improving port

facilities, port approaches, and hinterland connectivity infrastructure, as well as developing cruise passenger terminals and adopting environmental management system for ports, among others. The road safety and asset management study findings will support the incorporation of road safety and performance standards in future road project designs. All these efforts contribute to the realization of a safe, efficient, and seamless movement of cargo and passenger traffic between intermodal transport systems along key trade routes.

Trade Facilitation. In addition to expediting cargo clearance and promoting efficient compliance management, SASEC will focus on addressing trade barriers and border facilities issues to achieve a more efficient trade logistics experience in the subregion, as provided under the SASEC Trade Facilitation Framework for 2014 to 2018 (ADB 2014), and extended to 2025 under the SASEC Operational Plan. The Customs Subgroup has advanced national and subregional projects (e.g., electronic data exchanges, transit automation, capacity building), and adopted measures to help customs administrations better handle trade disruptions. SASEC mechanisms will be used to improve border infrastructure. The Bangladesh SASEC Integrated Trade Facilitation Sector Development program, with an ADB commitment of $143 million in 2022, will support customs modernization, upgrade cargo transshipment, and improve infrastructure at key border crossings. Moreover, SASEC cross-border route studies will guide actions in HFTCs, such as upgrading certification facilities and streamlining transport operations to improve trade and transit efficiency, aligning operations toward better regional integration.[97]

Energy. Developing connectivity for regional power trade remains SASEC's priority for the energy sector. ADB committed an additional $60 million in 2021 for strengthening Nepal's transmission system. While the SASEC Regional Power Trade Framework Agreement has not been finalized, bilateral power trade arrangements continue to advance. This will eventually lead to facilitation of transmission corridor access and more competitive pricing of traded power. The SASEC Cross-Border Power Trade Working Group will oversee this and firm up the priority

---

96   South Asia Subregional Economic Cooperation. http://www.sasec.asia/.

97   Along the (i) Kolkata–Dhaka, and (ii) Kathmandu–Kakarvitta–Panitanki–Phulbari–Bangalbandha–Chattogram/Mongla routes.

regional transmission and generation pipeline by updating the SASEC power master plan. In line with ADB's new Energy Policy, SASEC countries have agreed to emphasize renewable clean energy, but have stressed the need for long-term low-cost financing for transition to cleaner energy. The program will implement a Green Fuel Development initiative, which will examine and share clean energy technology through a new regional technical assistance program.

Economic Corridor Development. Comprehensive development plans were prepared from 2018 for sections of India's East Coast Economic Corridor in SASEC Corridor 2, outlining linkages between production networks and ports along the east coast, combined with a business-friendly policy framework. The India Northeast Region Corridor study expands the earlier Vision Study to develop Assam as India's expressway to ASEAN. In Bangladesh, both the Southwest and Northeast corridor studies identify multimodal transport spines that would link to gateways and markets in India, Bhutan, and Nepal, spurring industrial growth. The India studies, covering master planning for selected corridor nodes, have led to an ADB commitment of $797 million for four multisector/economic corridor development projects in 2021–2022 (as of 30 June 2022). These projects aim to enhance transport connectivity and facilitate industrial development in line with the recommendations of various studies.

Prospects

The refocusing and realignment of SASEC priorities are reflected in the Action Plan on SASEC Initiatives 2022–2024, which can be used as a tool to monitor the progress of shortlisted projects and programs and to devise actions to follow up on various knowledge initiatives for better program coordination and effectiveness. These aim to move the program forward.

The One Health approach includes knowledge-sharing events to trigger policy discussions on how the SASEC platform could better address regional health security issues. A regional One Health working group has been formed with planned activities that include bridging the information gap and building a regionwide early warning system about health threats.

In transport, the maritime subgroup will focus on priority port logistics and infrastructure investments to be pursued. In trade facilitation, HFTC implementation may be initiated through national working groups to develop consensus on customs interventions/trade protocols and through-transport mechanisms for each corridor. Moreover, the SASEC Food Regulators' Forum will address sanitary and phytosanitary and technical barriers to trade and harmonize regulations and standards with a view to improving regional trade in food products.

To support economic corridors, the supply chain development subgroup will discuss findings of mapping studies to improve production linkages for priority sectors within and between SASEC corridors. The tourism subgroup will develop strategies for joint marketing and promotion of unique travel circuits while looking at easing border travel constraints. And the proposed SASEC Business Forum will facilitate public–private dialogue on key subregional issues and coalesce private sector positions on improving the business environment.

Also, the establishment of the SASEC secretariat in the subregion will enable more effective coordination among development partners operating in all member states. The SASEC secretariat can help better synchronize the SASEC-related programs of development partners and promote deeper understanding of the synergies and impacts of initiatives.

Policy Challenges

Wide-ranging institutional enhancement, while geared to meet the strategic reorientation of the SASEC program, will need stronger ownership from member countries. The program will also require more effective resource mobilization to support its strategic goals.

SASEC member countries have shown strong ownership of the SASEC program, having generally endorsed the proposed institutional enhancements during the meetings of the working groups and nodal officials in June 2022. However, they would demonstrate stronger commitment to the program by organizing requisite national coordination bodies and building internal mechanisms for focal agencies to work more closely with the subgroups and forums that will be established under the program. A subgroup tasked to implement the economic corridor approach will require multisectoral engagement.

Moreover, creating the planned institutions, conducting new studies, and revising the SASEC Vision will all require additional resources. Given that the pandemic has strained member countries' fiscal positions, there is some urgency in improving resource mobilization for the program. With that in mind, the formation of the SASEC Business Forum is a way to generate wider private sector buy-in for SASEC initiatives.

South Asian Association for Regional Cooperation[98]

The South Asian Association for Regional Cooperation (SAARC), founded in 1985, was established to promote collective social, economic, and cultural progress of its eight member states in South Asia: Afghanistan,[99] Bangladesh,

Bhutan, India, Maldives, Nepal, Pakistan, and Sri Lanka. ADB commenced dialogue with the SAARC secretariat in 2003. ADB and the secretariat signed an MOU on 12 April 2004 to establish a cooperative relationship with a view to promoting regional cooperation among the SAARC member states. The first SAARC summit was held in Dhaka, Bangladesh in 1985. The association's secretariat was established in Kathmandu on 16 January 1987.

Overview

The COVID-19 pandemic affected the normal functioning of SAARC, just as it did for other subregions. However, ADB has helped by extending significant assistance to the SAARC secretariat in several areas.

Several important areas of cooperation under SAARC include trade, transport, energy, climate change, poverty alleviation, and agriculture. SAARC has established several technical committees, working groups, and other mechanisms to pursue its goals. Since the MOU in 2004, ADB has extended its support in research and knowledge

Table 6.5: Selected Economic Indicators, 2021—South Asian Association for Regional Cooperation

Member states	Population (million)	Nominal GDP ($ billion)	GDP Growth (%, 2017–2021, average)	GDP per Capita (current prices, $)	Trade Openness (total trade, % of GDP)
Afghanistan	40.1	20.1	1.3	502.2	31.1
Bangladesh	169.4	416.3	6.4	2,457.9	25.6
Bhutan	0.8	2.4	1.5	3,140.9	170.4
India	1,407.6	3,176.3	3.8	2,256.6	30.4
Maldives	0.5	5.2	6.1	9,979.7	52.4
Nepal	30.0	35.8	5.0	1,193.5	49.2
Pakistan	231.4	348.2	3.7	1,504.9	29.0
Sri Lanka	21.8	89.0	1.8	4,086.6	30.1
SAARC	**1,901.5**	**4,093.4**	**4.0**	**2,152.7**	**30.0**

GDP = gross domestic product, SAARC = South Asian Association for Regional Cooperation.

Notes: Average GDP growth rate for Afghanistan covers until 2020. SAARC average GDP growth rate is weighted using nominal GDP. Nominal GDP figures are based on International Monetary Fund staff estimates. ADB placed on hold its assistance in Afghanistan, effective 15 August 2021 (ADB. 2021f. ADB Statement on Afghanistan. News release. 10 November. https://www.adb.org/news/adb-statement-afghanistan). The data and information on Afghanistan were collected from international sources.

Sources: ADB calculations using data from ADB. Asian Development Outlook database for GDP growth; and Haver Analytics, Inc. for nominal GDP, population, and trade.

---

[98]   Contributed by Thiam Hee Ng, director, SARC; Dongxiang Lee, lead regional cooperation specialist, SARC; Lani Garnace, economics officer, SARC; and Subash Sharma, ADB consultant, SARC.

[99]   ADB placed on hold its assistance in Afghanistan, effective 15 August 2021 (ADB. 2021f. ADB Statement on Afghanistan. News release. 10 November. https://www.adb.org/news/adb-statement-afghanistan). The data and information on Afghanistan were collected from international sources.

dissemination, capacity building and institution strengthening, and regional policy dialogue. With ADB support, SAARC has been able to conduct various studies. These include a Regional Economic Integration Study (Phases I and II); the SAARC Regional Multimodal Transport Study (SRMTS); a study for the SAARC Agreement on Trade in Services; and *Climate Risks in the SAARC Region: Ways to Address the Social, Economic and Environmental Challenges*. Table 6.5 presents some most recent economic indicators for SAARC member states.

The objectives of SAARC as enshrined in its Charter[100] signed on 8 December 1985 are to (i) promote the welfare of the people of South Asia and to improve their quality of life; (ii) accelerate economic growth, social progress, and cultural development in the region and to provide all individuals the opportunity to live in dignity and to realize their full potential; (iii) promote and strengthen collective self-reliance among the countries of South Asia; (iv) contribute to mutual trust, understanding, and appreciation of one another's problems; (v) promote active collaboration and mutual assistance in the economic, social, cultural, technical, and scientific fields; (vi) strengthen cooperation with other developing countries; (vii) strengthen cooperation among themselves in international forums on matters of common interest; and (viii) cooperate with international and regional organizations with similar objectives.

The meetings of the heads of state or government of the SAARC countries are the highest decision-making authority of the group. The summits are held biennially and are hosted by the member state chairing the association, with that responsibility rotating in alphabetical order. Nepal is the current chair, having hosted the 18th meeting in Kathmandu in November 2014.

Performance and Progress over the Past Year

In June 2020, ADB approved a regional technical assistance project, Strengthening the Implementation of Regional Cooperation and Integration Initiatives of the South Asian Association for Regional Cooperation, in the amount of $800,000. Endorsed by member states in September 2021, it is now being implemented. It covers areas such as regional economic integration, financial cooperation, transport connectivity, trade facilitation, climate change, and poverty alleviation.

Financial Cooperation. Informal meetings of SAARC finance ministers are held every year on the sidelines of ADB annual meetings. Sixteen have been held. Economic Recovery from COVID-19: Towards Inclusive and Resilient Growth was the theme of the last one, which took place on 5 May 2021. The next informal meeting will be held in May 2023.

Transport Connectivity. The SRMTS was conducted with the support of ADB. Member states have taken actions necessary for implementing prioritized recommendations identified in the study. At the 14th SAARC Summit in 2007, governments called for the SRMTS to be extended to all member states. The next summit in Nepal in 2014 saw leaders stress the need to link South Asia with contiguous regions, including Central Asia and beyond, by all modes of connectivity. The Third SAARC–ADB Special Meeting on Regional Economic Integration, in 2017, invited member states to put forward proposals for updating the SRMTS to the SAARC secretariat and follow up on the study's recommendations. Accordingly, the SRMTS is now being updated with the financial and technical assistance of ADB. An inception report and country-specific questionnaires have been circulated among all member states through the SAARC secretariat.

Energy Cooperation. ADB has extended support for the energy sector in SAARC in recent years. In this regard, the Capacity Building Training Program on HVDC Transmission Systems was organized on 14–18 February 2022. Similarly, another Capacity Building Training Program on Cross Border Electricity Trade among SAARC Countries was organized by ADB on 17–26 May 2022. A SAARC Council of Experts of Energy Regulators (Electricity) is functioning with the financial and technical assistance of ADB and has held four meetings, with a fifth scheduled for 2023.

---

[100] SAARC Charter. https://saarc-sec.org/index.php/about-saarc/saarc-charter.

Trade Facilitation. ADB is also undertaking a study to promote intraregional trade by harmonizing the 8-digit Harmonized System tariff lines of all SAARC member states. It comes at the request of the SAARC secretariat and member states. An inception report and questionnaire were prepared and forwarded through the SAARC secretariat for member states to take action.

Regional Economic Integration in SAARC. ADB assisted SAARC in conducting the *Regional Economic Integration Study*. Foreign secretaries of member states had approved the second phase of the study in 2014. Subsequently, through four meetings of representatives from the Ministries of Commerce and Finance, the SAARC members have identified seven recommendations for priority action. These are (i) the reduction/removal of nontariff barriers and para-tariff barriers; (ii) energy cooperation; (iii) trade facilitation measures; (iv) investment cooperation; (v) a reduction of products in sensitive lists; (vi) the SAARC Agreement on Trade in Services; and (vii) improvements in connectivity (rail, road, air, maritime) among member states.

The fifth meeting of the Representatives of the Ministries of Commerce and Finance of the SAARC Member States is expected to be held in 2023. The theme of the Fifth Meeting would be "Reduction/ Removal of NTMs/PTBs."

Poverty Alleviation. ADB has also agreed to assist SAARC in contextualizing the SDGs and the Post-2015 Development Agenda for the SAARC region and to revisit the 2004 SAARC Plan of Action on Poverty Alleviation, as mandated by the SAARC leaders.

ADB will help identify common priority SDGs to appropriately contextualize them for the SAARC region; monitor the progress of key performance indicators; suggest mid-course correction; review the progress and revisit the 2004 poverty alleviation action plan; and prepare a concept paper for deliberation during the Consultative Workshop on Contextualization of SDGs in SAARC. Members of the SAARC Inter-Governmental Expert Group on Poverty Alleviation will attend the

workshop along with other relevant authorities/experts from member states.

Other Areas. As part of its technical assistance to SAARC, ADB has also provided for the conduct of other analytical studies and the organization of knowledge-sharing and capacity-building activities related to COVID-19, agriculture, food security, and other topics that the SAARC secretariat may request it look into.

Prospects

SAARC-ADB activities are likely to pick up in the coming months.

The current focus is on accelerating the implementation of agreed activities. The actions include (i) updating and extending the SRMTS, including adding a chapter on connecting South Asia with Central Asia; (ii) conducting a study on harmonization of 8-digit HS codes; (iii) conducting special meetings on the Regional Economic Integration Study (Phase II); (iv) holding the 17th Informal Meeting of SAARC Finance Ministers on the sidelines of ADB's 56th annual meeting; (v) holding an intergovernmental expert meeting on climate change; (vi) holding a consultative workshop on the contextualization of SDGs in SAARC; and (vii) assisting other projects requested by SAARC, such as technical support to the SAARC Energy Center for the creation and management of a database of regional regulatory functions and trade.

Policy Challenges

Considerable scope exists for the timely implementation of activities agreed through various SAARC mechanisms. This is brought to the attention of the SAARC secretariat at meetings and bilateral consultations between ADB and SAARC. ADB has expressed its commitment to assist SAARC in different areas of cooperation, particularly toward the passage of a South Asia Economic Union.[101] Holding the long-pending 19th

---

[101]   To assist SAARC in its journey towards South Asian Economic Union, the next phase of the study, "Next Steps to South Asian Economic Union - Regional Economic Integration Study (Phase-II)" has been conducted with the support of ADB. SAARC has already implemented initial steps such as SAARC Preferential Trading Arrangement (SAPTA) and South Asian Free Trade Area (SAFTA) for this purpose.

SAARC Summit, set to take place in Islamabad, Pakistan would invigorate the SAARC process.

The objectives of SAARC are aligned with those of other regional groupings such as BIMSTEC, CAREC, and SASEC. Intraregional connectivity, trade facilitation, assisting the power trade, and tackling climate change are among the initiatives SAARC has in common with other subregional organizations in South Asia and Central Asia. Since many SAARC member states are also in these regional groupings, it is important to enhance dialogue between them to promote synergies and complementarities. The efforts of all economic cooperation and integration initiatives in South Asia should focus on collaboration in critical areas such as transport, energy, trade, and finance for the benefit of the people living in South Asia. ADB can play a significant role in sharing best practices and study results across regional organizations with a view to deepening their impact.

The Pacific: Regionalism to Support Resilience[102]

ADB's work in the Pacific is helping to build and sustain resilience in the subregion, including through connectivity, subregional trade, and development of regional public goods. This work is aligned with the goals and priorities of the Pacific Islands Forum, whose 2050 Strategy for the Blue Pacific Continent seeks to employ regional mechanisms to build security, inclusive growth, and resilience. Regional cooperation and mechanisms are instrumental in broadening the reach of ADB support, collaboration, and knowledge work throughout the Pacific. Regional financing and technical assistance, in particular, are helping developing member countries respond to and recover from the impacts of climate change and disasters.

Overview

ADB's regional strategic framework for the Pacific seeks to build and support resilience in the subregion, including through connectivity, subregional trade,

and the development of regional public goods, and is closely aligned with the goals and priorities of the Pacific Islands Forum—the principal regional platform—which works toward building security, inclusive growth, and resilience. Regional cooperation and mechanisms are instrumental in broadening the reach of ADB support, collaboration, and knowledge work throughout the Pacific, and in addressing many of the challenges facing ADB developing member countries, such as small size, remoteness, limited capacity and weak institutions, and vulnerability to climate change and disasters caused by natural hazards.

Guided by ADB's corporate regional cooperation and integration operational plan, operations in the Pacific continue to focus on improving connectivity (air, land, and maritime) and trade, and enhancing regional public goods that bring shared benefits and development outcomes to many of ADB's developing member countries in the Pacific. In 2022 alone, ADB approved $86.4 million in regional investment loans and grants, and $51.6 million in regional technical assistance (including co-financing).

Supporting Resilience for the Blue Pacific Continent

ADB's regional strategic framework, the Pacific Approach 2021–2025, articulates the goal of building and supporting resilience across its 14 Pacific developing member countries. The approach puts a focus on preparing for and responding to shocks, delivering sustainable services, and supporting inclusive growth. It also highlights the importance of supporting regional cooperation and integration initiatives that deepen collaboration among Pacific countries, including coordinating with regional organizations; exploring and developing regional investment and technical assistance projects; working across Pacific developing member countries on topics of mutual interest; and supporting regional policy studies and dialogue.

The Pacific Approach aligns with the aims of the Pacific Islands Forum. The Forum aims to achieve "a resilient Pacific Region of peace, harmony, security, social

---

102   Contributed by Rosalind McKenzie, principal operations coordination specialist (fragile situations), Social Sectors and Public Sector Management Division (PASP), Pacific Department; and Cara Tinio, associate economics officer, PASP.

inclusion, and prosperity, that ensures all Pacific peoples can lead free, healthy, and productive lives" (Pacific Islands Forum 2022). It promotes political dialogue and decision-making among its 18 members (which include ADB's 14 Pacific developing member countries) and collaboration with international agencies. The Forum also represents its members' interests in other international settings. Its secretariat facilitates dialogue and coordinates implementation of regional policies and initiatives. The Council of Regional Organisations of the Pacific (CROP), a high-level multisectoral advisory body, helps facilitate policy formulation at national, regional, and international levels.

In July 2022, Forum members approved the 2050 Strategy for the Blue Pacific Continent, their framework to realize a collective vision for the Pacific. The strategy outlines the following thematic areas: (i) political leadership and regionalism; (ii) people-centered development; (iii) peace and security; (iv) resource and economic development; (v) climate change and disasters; (vi) ocean and environment; and (vii) technology and connectivity. Regional cooperation and integration runs through many action points in these strategic pathways and is recognized as key to enabling access to affordable and quality social services, ensuring that ocean-based natural resources are used sustainably, strengthening resilience to climate change and disaster risk, promoting connectivity, and accelerating economic growth.

ADB is an observer in the Forum and supports its development objectives through regional operations. ADB has collaborated with CROP member agencies, including the Secretariat of the Pacific Regional Environment Programme and the University of the South Pacific (USP), to establish a platform for capacity building and knowledge transfer on environmental and social sustainability (ADB 2020d). It has helped organize and cosponsor regional knowledge events such as the 2015–2017 Pacific Update Conferences with USP and other partners, and workshops on managing fisheries revenues with the Forum Fisheries Agency and the Pacific Financial Technical Assistance Centre. ADB has also engaged in technical collaborations with the Pacific Community to build the subregion's statistical capacity.

Its ongoing work with USP is helping expand access to higher education through projects to improve regional university campuses and learning programs, including distance learning (ADB 2012).

ADB supports regional digital and transport connectivity and trade for economic development. Outside of collaborations with CROP member agencies, ADB also supports the Forum through its regional programming (Figures 6.6 and 6.7). For instance, it helps enhance resilient and sustainable connectivity and accelerate economic growth in the Pacific through investment projects that are improving the flow of goods and services, a crucial step for these geographically remote, highly dispersed, and heavily import-dependent economies. ADB has enhanced internet connectivity in Tonga, Samoa, and Palau by linking them to the international submarine cable network and is pursuing similar investments in the Cook Islands and Kiribati. Further, it developed major seaports in the Cook Islands, Papua New Guinea, and Vanuatu, among others, with ongoing investments continuing to enhance the safety, security, and sustainability of Apia Port in Samoa and upgrade Nuku'alofa Port in Tonga. Port improvements in Tonga will allow deployment of larger vessels, reduce shipping and import–export costs, and encourage regional trade to neighboring states, with connecting shipping routes such as the Cook Islands, Samoa, and main trading partners. A 2022 investment in Tuvalu will simultaneously strengthen domestic shipping and make travel between Fiji, Kiribati, and Tuvalu safer and more convenient, contributing to better subregional business and trade and helping maintain cultural linkages (ADB 2022f). ADB also extended an innovative loan to Fiji Airways, the subregion's largest airline, to help sustain its business during the disruptions arising from the COVID-19 pandemic and subsequently ramp up its flight operations (ADB 2020b); and expects to support additional sea and/or airport connectivity projects in the Cook Islands, Fiji, Papua New Guinea, Solomon Islands, and Tonga before 2025.

ADB is also helping governments strengthen their capacity and readiness to safely reopen borders to tourists. This includes approval of a 2022 investment to enhance safety measures at Fiji's Nadi International

Airport, an important Pacific gateway, and a COVID-19 testing facility for asymptomatic tourism- and travel-related testing and disease control (ADB 2022g). This builds on ADB's experience implementing similar improvements in the Cook Islands in 2021. These projects will provide critical assistance toward reinvigorating regional and international tourism in the Pacific, a key economic growth driver that was virtually shut down by the COVID-19 pandemic.

Figure 6.6: ADB Regional Investment in the Pacific— Loans and Grants, 2010–2022

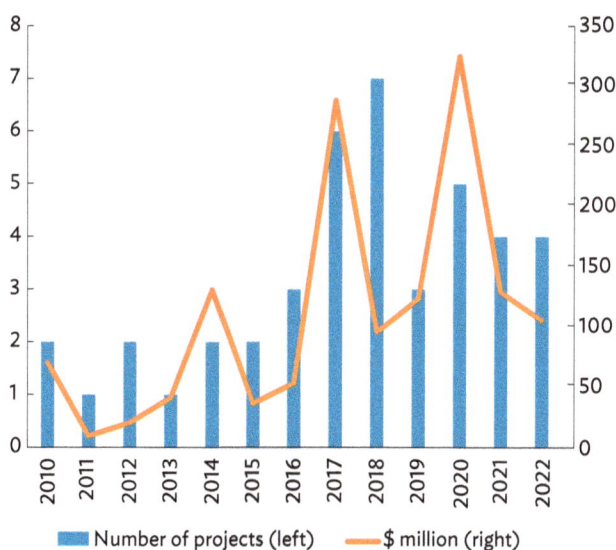

Number of projects (left) $ million (right)

Source: Asian Development Bank.

ADB builds regional public goods by addressing regional health challenges. ADB continued to bolster the emerging recovery and resilience of the Pacific subregion by approving additional financing in 2021 of its regional program strengthening systems for effective coverage of new vaccines, approved in 2018, to include COVID-19 vaccines (ADB 2021c; Tinio et al. 2022). Helping the governments of Samoa, Tonga, Tuvalu, and Vanuatu prepare to receive and roll out COVID-19 vaccines contributes to safer subregional travel, tourism, and trade, and aligns with the Forum's focus on people-centered development. ADB expects to extend this regional vaccine coverage support in the subregion.

Figure 6.7: ADB Regional Investment in the Pacific— Loans and Grants by Sector, 2010–2022 (number)

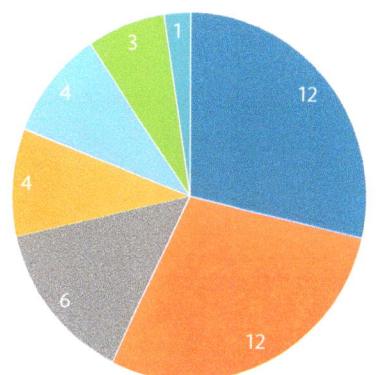

Public sector management   Energy
Transport   Health
ICT   Finance
Education

ICT = information and communication technology.

Source: Asian Development Bank.

Policy-based operations help strengthen resilience. ADB's Pacific developing member countries are island states that are small and/or facing the challenges of fragile situations with limited institutional capacities. Policy-based mechanisms therefore are integral to fostering key reforms and promoting regionalism in these economies. Support to the Cook Islands, for example, is helping to implement quarantine-free travel arrangements and reforms that improve labor mobility and competition in the telecommunications sector (ADB 2021d, 2021e). In addition, ADB approved a policy-based grant in 2022 to Samoa to strengthen foreign investment and establish an online credit registry that will bring regional benefits to the subregion (ADB 2022h).

Regional technical assistance is a key channel for support to the Pacific. Since January 2020, ADB has funded over $38 million in regional technical assistance projects in the Pacific, enabling robust training and capacity building for developing member countries in support of several of the Forum's 2050 Strategy focus areas. Current technical assistance is, among others, strengthening education, gender, and social protection development outcomes; building gender-responsive judicial systems; developing health sectors and COVID-19 responses; creating solutions for climate and disaster resilience; supporting analysis of exclusive economic zones; establishing a regional network of energy regulators; and developing regional financial integration systems and instruments.

Promoting Climate Change Agenda as a Cross-Cutting Theme

Strengthening CAREC Cooperation in Promoting Climate Change Agenda

Climate change is a defining challenge for global development in the 21st century. The CAREC region contributes to and is increasingly affected by climate change effects. CAREC countries are increasingly associated with key challenges related to climate change, including high energy intensity with renewable energy accounting for a small share in overall energy mix, and are highly exposed and vulnerable to disasters such as earthquakes, floods and droughts, and an increasing scarcity of water resources to support the sizable population working in agriculture and husbandry. All these affect socioeconomic development—including human health, poverty, and inequality—and create potential fragility and conflict in the region. The CAREC 2030 has envisioned these challenges by aligning closely with the Sustainable Development Goals and the 21st Conference of the Parties to the United Nations Framework Convention on Climate Change (COP21). Climate change is thus identified as a theme that cuts across all five operational clusters of CAREC 2030.

ADB has set an ambitious climate finance target of $100 billion from 2019 to 2030, to effectively finance climate mitigation and adaptation efforts in its developing member countries to reduce greenhouse gas emissions, and so contribute to low-carbon economic growth. This also cascades in CAREC operations, with 60% of projects required to contribute to climate change mitigation and adaptation. ADB is helping CAREC countries undertake initiatives and actions to promote the climate change

agenda across CAREC's operational clusters. These include

(i)   Conceptualization of a CAREC Green Energy Alliance as a new financing vehicle to support energy efficiency projects and renewable energy projects. The Alliance provides a virtual platform for a marketplace of projects and supports the preparation of high-quality investment-ready projects.

(ii) Strengthening regional cooperation on disaster risk management by developing a disaster risk transfer facility in the CAREC region to support collaboration among member countries on disaster risk financing and help governments make informed decisions on disaster risk management.

(iii) Promoting green and resilient transport connectivity, such as upgrading the railway lines by electrifying rail sections and incorporating climate-resilient components in all road rehabilitation projects in CAREC countries.

(iv) Promoting cooperation in transboundary water resources management and integrated urban development by designing and applying a water sector cooperation framework to foster climate-resilient and productive water systems and sustainable water resources management in the region.

(v)   Strengthening the implementation of the new CAREC digital strategy to promote e-commerce through digitalizing sanitary and phytosanitary measures, customs services, and other processes.

Developing A Climate Change Action Plan in BIMSTEC

ADB would also like to expand the cooperation to other important areas such as energy, environment and climate change, and people-to-people exchange. Following a request from BIMSTEC, ADB is preparing the BIMSTEC grid interconnection master plan to provide a framework to enhance power grid connectivity across member states. The plan focuses on developing interconnecting transmission line infrastructure to facilitate power trade among BIMSTEC countries and enhance energy cooperation and gradual evolution to market-based power trade. Likewise, the recently completed BIMSTEC tourism study may also be upgraded to set out a holistic regional strategy and plans that encompass infrastructure, marketing and branding, capacity building, skills development, and the like, while covering key thematic circuits in the region. Input from member states and private sector stakeholders are being sought. This holds tremendous potential for development. ADB could also work with BIMSTEC to develop an action plan for climate change, disaster risk management, and environmental conservation.

Review of Climate Change Initiatives in the SAARC Region

In response to SAARC's request, ADB is also making efforts to review the implementation of the Thimphu Statement on Climate Change, develop a road map for implementing the study on climate risks in the SAARC region, and suggest a way forward. ADB has agreed to assist in organizing a meeting of the SAARC Inter-Governmental Expert Group on Climate Change for this purpose and to advise on measures for effective implementation of the Thimphu statement and the Dhaka Declaration and SAARC Action Plan on Climate Change through all SAARC member states, as well as regionally.

Regional Action to Address Climate Change and Disaster Risk in the Pacific

The Pacific is one of the most vulnerable regions of the world to the impacts of extreme weather events and natural hazards. Over 2018–2021, the *World Risk Report* consistently ranked five ADB Pacific developing member countries within the 20 countries most exposed to risk, with Vanuatu the most exposed throughout this period. The Pacific economies' narrow output bases, limited implementation capacities, and distance from global supply chains make reconstruction,

rehabilitation, and recovery particularly challenging. This is compounded by the increasing frequency and intensity of extreme weather events and natural hazards brought on by climate change.

The Forum's 2050 Strategy highlights the need to strengthen investments in research on climate change and disaster risk, and to cooperate and collaborate regionally to build the capacity to tackle the impacts of climate events and disasters. Given the significant cost of building resilience, it also identifies increasing access to climate finance as a priority.

ADB is helping its Pacific developing member countries improve preparedness for climate change and disaster risks not only by climate-proofing investment projects, but also through regional mechanisms that provide financing and better equip governments to design and implement policies for climate change adaptation and disaster risk mitigation. The Pacific Disaster Resilience Program is a regional facility that (i) supports disaster preparedness actions in participating developing member countries, and (ii) provides fast-disbursing financing following declaration of a state of national disaster or emergency (ADB 2020c). The quick-financing feature has helped expedite the provision of emergency and early recovery needs in the wake of disasters, and the recent expansion of coverage to include health emergencies allowed participating countries to access the facility when community transmission of COVID-19 broke out (Government of Samoa 2022). The first three phases of the program have drawn the participation of 10 Pacific developing member countries, with the fourth round of facility replenishment for five countries expected in 2023.

Further, regional technical assistance is helping all 14 Pacific developing member countries develop climate-resilient investment pathways through better access to climate change information for strategic decision-making, enhancements to planning and policy development processes to better adapt to climate change, and direct support to projects and programs with a focus on upstream inputs and partnership-building (ADB 2020e). It is also supporting clean energy technologies to help Pacific economies reduce their carbon emissions and adapt to climate change impacts.

Finally, in support of access to ocean and climate financing, ADB's Blue Pacific Finance Hub is working to leverage $500 million in new investments in ocean-climate action (coastal resilience and ocean-based mitigation); sustainable and climate-resilient seafood; and circular economy for marine pollution control (ADB 2022i). The hub provides grant and technical assistance funding to support Pacific developing member countries in building an enabling environment for a sustainable blue economy; developing a pipeline of ocean projects; and matching prepared projects to funding.

References

Asian Development Bank (ADB). Asia Regional Integration Center. Economy Groupings. https://aric.adb.org/integrationindicators/groupings.

———. Fiji: Enhancing COVID-19 Preparedness for Tourism Recovery. https://www.adb.org/projects/55172-001/main (accessed August 2022).

———. Projects. https://www.adb.org/projects (accessed July–August 2022).

———. Regional: Accelerating the Clean Energy Transition in Southeast Asia. https://www.adb.org/projects/55124-001/main.

———. 2008. BIMSTEC Transport Infrastructure and Logistics Study. Manila.

———. 2011. *Regional Technical Assistance for Support to Building Capacity for Statistics in the Pacific.* Manila.

———. 2012. *Report and Recommendation of the President to the Board of Directors: Proposed Multitranche Financing Facility: Higher Education in the Pacific Investment Program.* Manila.

———. 2014. *South Asia Subregional Economic Cooperation Trade Facilitation Strategic Framework 2014–2018.* Manila.

———. 2016. *South Asia Subregional Economic Cooperation Operational Plan 2016–2025.* Manila.

———. 2017. *SASEC Powering Asia in the 21st Century.* Manila.

———. 2018a. *Updating and Enhancement of the BIMSTEC Transport Infrastructure and Logistics Study.* Manila.

———. 2018b. *Strategy 2030: Achieving a Prosperous, Inclusive, Resilient, and Sustainable Asia and the Pacific.* Manila.

———. 2019. *Greater Mekong Subregion Health Cooperation Strategy, 2019–2023.* Manila.

———. 2020a. *South Asia Subregional Economic Cooperation Operational Plan 2016–2025 Update.* Manila.

———. 2020b. *Fiji Airways COVID-19 Liquidity Support Facility.* Manila.

———. 2020c. *Pacific Disaster Resilience Program (Phase 3).* Manila.

———. 2020d. *Technical Assistance for Sustainable Capacity Development for Safeguards in the Pacific—Phase 1.* Manila.

———. 2020e. *Technical Assistance for Support to Climate Resilient Investment Pathways in the Pacific.* Manila.

———. 2021a. *The Greater Mekong Subregion Economic Cooperation Program Strategic Framework 2030.* Manila.

———. 2021b. *The Greater Mekong Subregion COVID-19 Response and Recovery Plan 2021–2023.* Manila.

———. 2021c. *Report and Recommendation of the President to the Board of Directors: Regional: Systems Strengthening for Effective Coverage of New Vaccines in the Pacific Project under the Asia Pacific Vaccine Access Facility (Additional Financing).* Manila.

———. 2021d. *Cook Islands: Supporting Sustainable Economic Recovery Program.* Manila.

———. 2021e. *Cook Islands: Supporting Safe Recovery of Travel and Tourism.* Manila.

——. 2021f. ADB Statement on Afghanistan. News release. 10 November. https://www.adb.org/news/adb-statement-afghanistan.

——. 2022a. CAREC Program Portfolio. Unpublished.

——. 2022b. *Asian Development Outlook Update*: September. Manila

——. 2022c. *SASEC Project Portfolio 30 June 2022*.

——. 2022d. *Scoping Study: Enhancing Collaboration in Trade And Investment Under the GMS Program*. Unpublished Report.

——. 2022e. *BIMSTEC Master Plan for Transport Connectivity*. Manila.

——. 2022f. *Report and Recommendation of the President to the Board of Directors: Proposed Grant for Tuvalu: Strengthening Domestic Shipping Project*. Manila.

——. 2022g. *Report and Recommendation of the President to the Board of Directors: Proposed Grant for Fiji: Enhancing COVID-19 Preparedness for Tourism Recovery*. Manila.

——. 2022h. *Report and Recommendation of the President to the Board of Directors: Proposed Programmatic Approach and Policy-Based Grant for Subprogram 1 Independent State of Samoa: Strengthening Macroeconomic Resilience Program*. Manila.

——. 2022i. Technical Assistance for Support to Blue Pacific Finance Hub: Investing in Resilient Ocean Ecosystems and Economies (working title). Manila.

Australian National University (College of Asia and the Pacific), Crawford School of Public Policy Development Policy Centre. *Pacific Update*. Canberra. https://devpolicy.crawford.anu.edu.au/pacific-update (accessed August 2022).

BIMSTEC. 2022. BIMSTEC Charter. Colombo.

Bündnis Entwicklung Hilft. *WorldRiskReport*. Berlin (4 years: 2018–2021).

Government of Samoa. 2022. ADB Provides $10 Million Grant to Help Samoa Manage COVID-19. News Release. 25 April.

Pacific Islands Forum. The Pacific Islands Forum. https://www.forumsec.org/who-we-arepacific-islands-forum/ (accessed July 2022).

——. Pacific Islands Forum Secretariat. https://www.forumsec.org/pacific-islands-forum-secretariat/ (accessed July 2022).

——. Council of Regional Organisations of the Pacific. https://www.forumsec.org/council-of-regional-organisations-of-the-pacific/ (accessed July 2022).

——. 2022. *2050 Strategy for the Blue Pacific Continent*. https://www.forumsec.org/wp-content/uploads/2022/07/PIFS-2050-Strategy-WEB-11July2022.pdf.

South Asia Subregional Economic Cooperation (SASEC). http://www.sasec.asia/.

——. 2014. *South Asia Subregional Economic Cooperation Trade Facilitation Strategic Framework 2014–2018*. Manila.

Tinio, C., I. Mikkelsen-Lopez, K. Lam, R. Patagan, and R. Rabanal. 2022. The Pacific: Leveraging Regional Reach for Broader COVID-19 Vaccine Coverage. In *Asian Economic Integration Report 2022: Advancing Digital Services Trade in Asia and the Pacific*. Manila: ADB.

Annex 6a: Subregional Integration Indexes

(a) Central Asia Regional Economic Cooperation Program

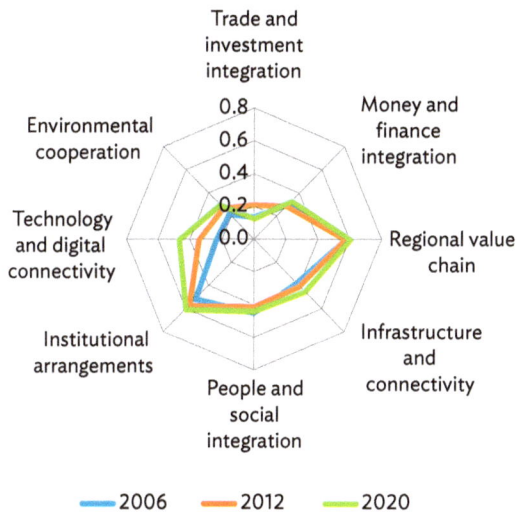

2006   2012   2020

(b) Greater Mekong Subregion Program

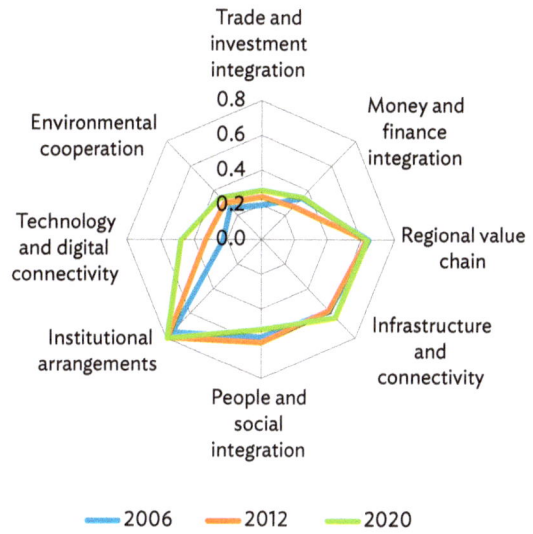

2006   2012   2020

(c) South Asia Subregional Economic Cooperation (SASEC)

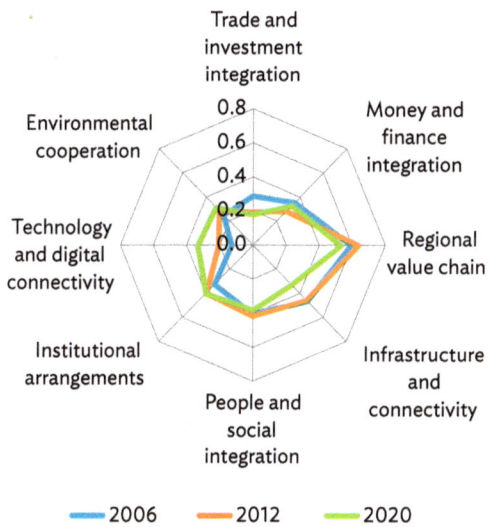

2006   2012   2020

(d) South Asian Association for Regional Cooperation (SAARC)

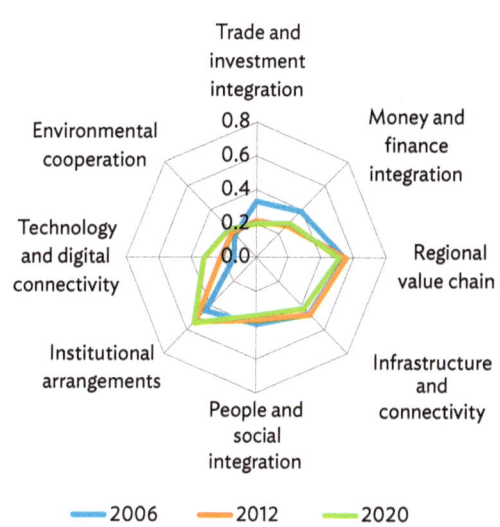

2006   2012   2020

(e) Bay of Bengal Initiative for Multi-Sectoral Technical and Economic Cooperation (BIMSTEC)

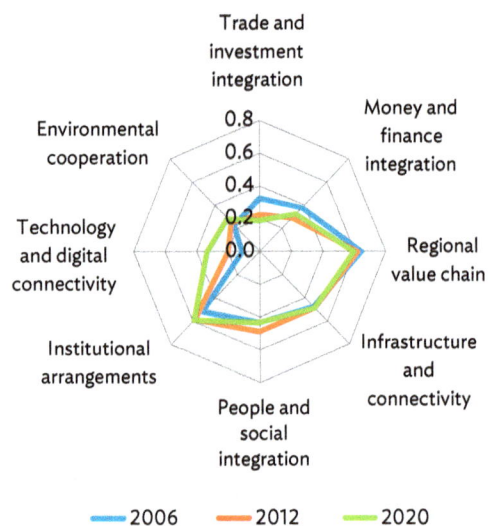

Notes: Estimates represent integration within the subregional initiative. Higher values denote greater integration.

Source: ADB. Asia Regional Integration Center. Asia-Pacific Regional Cooperation and Integration Database. https://aric.adb.org/database/arcii (accessed December 2022).

7 THEME CHAPTER
Trade, Investment, and Climate Change in Asia and the Pacific

Introduction

Asia and the Pacific is on the frontline of climate change, with the region subjected to more extreme weather events and many people working and living in low-lying coastal cities.[103] Asia is experiencing the highest temperatures in the last 30 years, with average temperatures in 2021 reaching 0.86°C above the 1981–2010 average, and 2020 the warmest year on record since 1900 (WMO 2022). Extreme precipitation events such as storms, floods, and landslides, which led to over 48 million people directly affected and 4,000 lives lost in 2021 in the region, are becoming more frequent (WMO 2022). Almost 40% of disasters worldwide have occurred in Asia, much higher than just over 20% each in Africa and the Americas (Figure 7.1). Southeast Asia, East Asia, and South Asia are the most affected subregions. The Pacific is increasingly affected by rising sea levels as many Pacific island countries are low-lying or just a few feet above sea level.

Rising temperatures from climate change present significant economic risks in Asia. Various estimation exercises present diverse economic impact assessments depending on the methodologies employed. Common to those exercises, however, is that Asia is expected to suffer larger economic losses than the world average from rising temperatures. Only developed Asian economies will experience economic losses below the world average. It is therefore crucial that Asian economies address these challenges.

Figure 7.1: Number of Disasters, 2000–2021

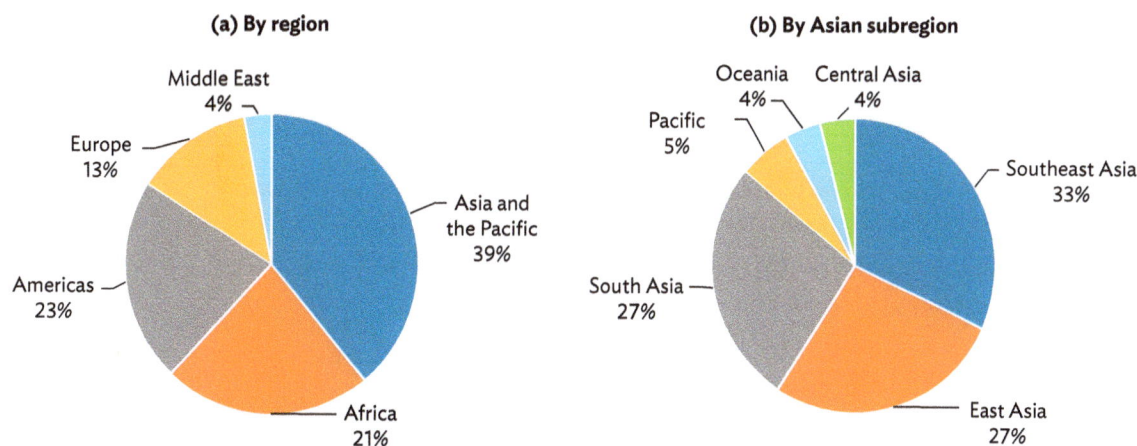

(a) By region

Middle East 4%
Europe 13%
Americas 23%
Africa 21%
Asia and the Pacific 39%

(b) By Asian subregion

Oceania 4%
Central Asia 4%
Pacific 5%
Southeast Asia 33%
South Asia 27%
East Asia 27%

Notes: Disaster includes natural occurrences like animal accident, drought, earthquake, epidemic, extreme temperature, flood, glacial lake outburst, insect infestation, landslide, mass movement (dry), storm, volcanic activity, and wildfire. Americas include Latin America and North America.

Source: ADB calculations using data from Centre for Research on the Epidemiology of Disasters - CRED. EM-DAT The International Disaster Database. http://www.emdat.be (accessed January 2023).

[103] Unless otherwise specified, Asia and the Pacific, or Asia, refers to the the 49 regional members of Asian Development Bank (ADB). List of economies is available at ADB. Asia Regional Integration Center. Economy Groupings. https://aric.adb.org/integrationindicators/groupings.

Higher frequency of extreme weather events in Asia will affect economic activities, particularly trade and investment. Trade and investment have played an outsized role in the economic development of the region. Many of its economies have relied on exports and foreign direct investments (FDI) as engines of economic growth (Stiglitz 1996; World Bank 1993). The region accounts for 35% of world trade in 2020, up by 10 percentage points from 10 years ago, and a third of global FDI in 2019. [104] Without climate change mitigation and adaptation efforts globally, potential disruptions to transportation and production will hamper Asia's trade and FDI performances, and hence its economic growth.

Asia also sits at the center of global production networks. Besides the traditional manufacturing powerhouses, many developing economies in the region—such as Cambodia, the Lao People's Democratic Republic, and Viet Nam—are increasing their participation in global value chains (ADB 2021a). The coronavirus disease (COVID-19) pandemic alerted the world to the fragility of global supply chains. Similarly, any disruptions to production procedures either upstream or downstream due to extreme weather events caused by climate change will impede economic activities in the region. Such events can cause production losses, while rising temperatures and increasing water scarcity can affect agricultural productivity (ADB 2021b).

The region's experience with severe earthquakes and floods portends a gamut of impacts of climate change-related disasters. The disruption to infrastructure from flooding provides insights into the negative effects of climate change. The March 2011 earthquake in Japan, for example, damaged the nuclear power plant in Fukushima. Although its impacts were mainly local with the four most affected prefectures contributing less than 5% of Japan's gross domestic product (GDP), the disaster decreased real

GDP growth in Japan by 0.47 percentage points due to industrial linkages between the prefecture and other regions, which is substantial considering Japan's average growth of about 0.6% during 2000–2010. [105] Similarly, the floods in northern Thailand in July 2011 inundated seven industrial parks and affected 800 companies (Haraguchi and Lall 2015). Damages and economic losses caused by tropical cyclones to some of the Pacific island countries over the past decade also attest to the severe impact of climate change. Recent floods in Pakistan, which affected 33 million people and brought enormous damage to infrastructure and agriculture, are a devastating reminder of part of the region's acute vulnerability to climate change.

Asia is a large contributor to global carbon dioxide (CO_2) emissions. The region alone is now responsible for about half of global annual CO_2 emissions. Asia's outsized contribution to climate change is a byproduct of its economic success, which has led the region into a crucial dilemma: how to balance potential trade-offs between economic growth and environmental costs. Many studies have examined the relationship between economic growth and environmental outcomes. The environmental Kuznets curve posits an inverse-U shaped relationship between per capita income and environmental quality. However, this relationship is not so easy to interpret as these two variables are highly endogenous and related to other factors (Copeland and Taylor 2004).

Trade and investment play a critical role in Asia's economic growth and development and can significantly affect climate change by influencing how much is produced, what is produced, and how goods and services are produced (given technology's effect on the emission intensity of production) and transacted.

---

[104]   Based on the Direction of Trade Statistics of the International Monetary Fund and United Nations Conference on Trade and Development's World Investment Report 2022 Statistical Annex Tables.

[105]   What is more pertinent are the linkages the firms in these prefectures had with the rest of Japan. A study by Carvalho et al. (2021) shows that the negative impact of the earthquake was propagated through the network, affecting not only the customers and suppliers or affected firms, but even their customers (i.e., customers' customers) and their suppliers (i.e., suppliers' suppliers).

The Trade/Investment and Climate Change Nexus

A Conceptual Framework

This theme chapter examines the impact of trade and investment on climate change using a framework that decomposes main drivers into economic scale, industrial structure, and technological advancement. Carbon emissions from Asia can increase as production and trade expand (economic scale) and the share of carbon intensive industries and exports increases (industrial structure), and decrease as production becomes less emission-intensive (technological advancement).

- *Economic scale effect* examines how carbon emissions will increase when production "scales" up or increases, without any changes in the technology (e.g., emission intensity) or industrial composition. This occurs as the economy's production increases along with economic growth (furthered by trade and investment), which in the case of Asia has been supported by exports and integration into the global economy.

- *Industrial structure effect* examines how the economy's share of production in carbon intensive sectors changes, keeping the economic size and the technology level constant. This can be driven by specialization in trade and FDI in carbon intensive industries. FDI may be attracted by less stringent environmental policies and regulations.

- *Technological advancement effect* captures the change in the emission intensity of production holding the scale and industrial structure of the economy constant. Emission intensities can decline when the businesses adopt new technology (such as decarbonization) or employ environmental goods and services to lower carbon emissions per unit of output.

A gap between the private and the social cost of carbon emissions is a challenge for climate policy. As a global public "bad," climate change poses a fundamental problem in that its costs or benefits are not captured in market prices (Nordhaus 2018). The public good is being depleted because the private cost of carbon emissions does not fully reflect the overall social cost. Indeed, firms have the incentive and capacity to increase emissions for their own benefit, generating negative externalities without any compensation mechanism. The social cost of carbon is a crucial metric for understanding these impacts. In essence, the social cost of carbon encapsulates the cost of damages created by one extra ton of CO_2 emissions (Nordhaus 1992). It reflects the multiple economic and human welfare outcomes affected by climate change, such as lower agricultural yields, rising sea levels, and decline in human productivity and health. By providing a standardized measure to weigh the benefits of climate mitigation against its costs, the social cost of carbon can provide a price signal for carbon intensive goods, services, and processes; induce firms to adopt low carbon technologies; and encourage innovation in cleaner sectors.

Narrowing the gap between the private and the social cost of carbon emissions is essential. While multiple forms of carbon pricing instruments exist, they all aim to create a price signal for greenhouse gas (GHG) emissions. In practice, initiatives can be classified into two main groups. Enforcement mechanisms, on the one hand, are conducted through regulations and administrative measures by setting emissions standards and pollution limits as are often called "command and control." Market-based mechanisms, on the other hand, use price signals in inducing less carbon-emitting production and consumption activities. For example, carbon taxes could be levied on fossil fuel producers in proportion to the carbon content of their products. Emission trading systems aim to establish limits on carbon emissions and enable trading of units or define a baseline and reduce emissions below it and are a prominent market-based mechanism. Bilateral agreements, regional alliances, and other instruments are also increasingly used in international carbon trading under Article 6 of the Paris Agreement. There is potential to further strengthen them in the region, to the extent that market-based mechanisms can facilitate trade in carbon assets, establish common standards and guidelines, and increase technology transfer and diffusion.

The chapter discusses policy recommendations to ensure that trade and investment activities become part of climate solutions. Economies can promote "green trade," of low carbon intensive products and environmental goods and services. Strengthening environmental regulations could help reduce CO_2 emissions through both industrial structure and technique effects by inducing more investments in clean industries and technologies. Regional and international cooperation should supplement domestic efforts. Some of the focus can be on ensuring that investment and trade agreements support national environmental and climate policies, or on promoting new models of cooperation.

There are two important points the chapter does not consider. First, a complicated nexus exists between climate change and trade and investment, and that relationship can be bidirectional: that is, trade and investment can contribute to climate change, but climate change can also impact trade and investment. The chapter focuses on how trade and investment could contribute to climate change and its solutions, leaving the latter to other studies such as simulations and modeling by WTO (2022) and Brenton and Chemutai (2021).

Second, the chapter starts from the premise that trade is not only beneficial for economic development but also can be part of the climate change solution. According to literature, the gains from trade— efficiency, price reductions, product variety—can outweigh the environmental costs (Shapiro 2016). Antweiler, Copeland, and Taylor (2001) show that trade openness is beneficial to the environment if the technique effect is greater than the composition and scale effects. Indeed, higher income from increased trade can enable economies to import technologies for production that are less polluting. Meanwhile, Managi, Hibiki, and Tsurumi (2009) concluded that trade openness can have a negative impact on CO_2 emissions in nonindustrialized economies where the

scale and composition effects played the dominant role. While some climate activists propose curtailing trade and economic activities so that less resources are used and emissions reduced,[106] this may not consider the crucial roles played by power generation, transportation, industrial production, construction, and trade, which significantly affect people's welfare. Making a value judgment on economic growth versus environmental protection is beyond the scope of this chapter.

Emissions from Production, Demand, and Trade[107]

Asia's CO_2 Emissions Embodied in Production and Demand

Asia's CO_2 emissions embodied in production and demand both increased over time. According to the estimation using the CO_2 emissions embodied in international trade (TECO$_2$) data set of the Organisation for Economic Co-operation and Development (OECD) described in Box 7.1, Asia's CO_2 emissions embodied in both production and consumption have almost tripled since 1995, with the former rising faster than the latter (Figure 7.2). This largely reflects the region's rapid economic growth and expansion of economic size, which has involved heavy resources consumption and manufacturing and production of goods. Asia's fast incorporation into global value chains during the process of industrialization, while contributing to economic growth and prosperity, has contributed to this byproduct. This suggests that the adoption of emissions-mitigating production technologies that could have lowered the carbon intensity of production (i.e., CO_2 emissions per unit of output) may have been insufficient to offset the economic scale and industrial structure effects for the region. Meanwhile, Asia's CO_2 emissions embodied in consumption has not grown as much as its production side has, leading to net CO_2 emissions embodied

---

[106]   The argument put forward by activists can be captured under the "degrowth" movement. The World Economic Forum provides a good explanation of the degrowth movement. See Masterson (2022).

[107]   In this section, Asia refers to the 20 Asian economies with available data in Organisation for Economic Co-operation and Development's (OECD) carbon dioxide emissions embodied in international trade (TECO$_2$) data set. Asia is broken down into the following subregions: Central Asia (Kazakhstan); developed Asia (Australia, Japan, and New Zealand); East Asia (Hong Kong, China; the People's Republic of China; the Republic of Korea; and Taipei,China); South Asia (Bangladesh, India, and Pakistan); and Southeast Asia (Brunei Darussalam, Cambodia, Indonesia, the Lao People's Democratic Republic, Malaysia, the Philippines, Singapore, Thailand, and Viet Nam).

in exports to the rest of the world. In 2019, Asia's production-based CO_2 emissions were 17.2 giga tonnes, and after exporting 4.5 giga tonnes and importing 3.5 giga tonnes, the region ended up consuming 16.2 giga tonnes of CO_2 emissions.

On the other hand, the rest of the world's CO_2 emissions embodied in production and demand have been relatively stable. After gradually increasing until 2008, CO_2 emissions embodied in production and consumption in the rest of the world stabilized and even declined slightly afterward.

Asia has consistently been a net exporter of CO_2 emissions while the rest of the world has been a net importer. In Figure 7.2, the gap between production-based CO_2 emissions and demand-based CO_2 emissions is the net export or import position of CO_2 emissions for the respective regions. The size of the gap for Asia and the rest of the world is exactly the same by definition. Net exports from Asia (and net imports to the rest of the world) increased significantly in the 2000s but has been relatively stable since 2008.

Figure 7.2: Production- and Demand-Based Carbon Emissions—Asia versus Non-Asia (giga tonnes CO_2)

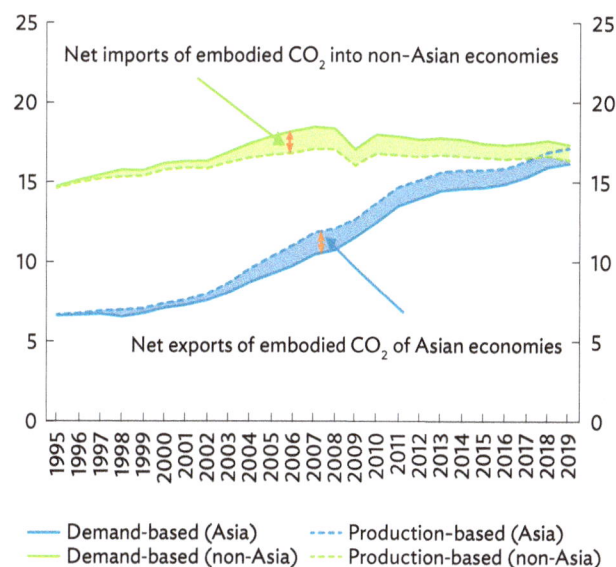

CO_2 = carbon dioxide.

Note: The shaded areas in the graph represent the absolute difference between production-based (CO_2 emissions based on production, i.e., emitted by economies) and demand-based (CO_2 emissions embodied in domestic final demand, i.e., consumed by economies) CO_2 emissions.

Source: ADB calculations using data from Organisation for Economic Co-operation and Development. Carbon dioxide emissions embodied in international trade ($TECO_2$) data set.

Box 7.1: Carbon Dioxide Emissions Embodied in International Trade Data Set

The carbon dioxide (CO_2) emissions embodied in international trade data set of the Organisation for Economic Co-operation and Development (OECD) covers those embodied in international trade and domestic final demand. This data set explicitly defines types of emissions based on three allocation methods: territorial-based emissions accounting, production-based emissions accounting, and final demand-based emissions accounting. This data set is novel in that it covers gaps in the International Energy Agency's CO_2 database for all economies to account for CO_2 emissions from fuel combustion, includes CO_2 emissions from fuel combustion by nonresident household and industries, and provides estimates of CO_2 intensity for each bilateral trade relationship.

OECD's Inter-Country Input–Output data are broken down between 66 economies and the rest of the world on an annual time series from 1995 to 2019 for 45 industries

(25 industry aggregates). In 2018, these 66 economies cover 92.9% of global gross domestic product, 71.0% of population, 91.4% of exports, 89.2% of imports, and of 89.8% of production-based CO_2 emissions from fossil fuels.

Methodology

To estimate CO_2 emissions embodied in international trade and final demand, the same input–output analysis methodologies used to calculate indicators of Trade in Value Added and Trade in Employment are applied.

Territory-based emissions are based on the International Energy Agency's CO_2 emissions from fuel combustion data set, which covers 46 unique fuel products, 34 unique flows from combustion sectors, and 138 individual economies matching the target economies in the OECD Inter-Country Input–Output database.

Source: OECD. Carbon Dioxide Emissions Embodied in International Trade. https://www.oecd.org/sti/ind/carbondioxideemissionsembodiedininternationaltrade.htm (accessed November 2022).

Asia's persistent position as a net CO$_2$ emissions exporter reflects the region's role as a major provider of products to serve global demand. Consumption demand in advanced economies might have not been met without Asia's rapid expansion of production capacity, which also increased CO$_2$ emissions as a byproduct. This global imbalance between production and demand of CO$_2$ emissions, including both consumption and investment between economies and regions, also underlies global discussions on resource transfer and appropriate compensation mechanisms for reducing the CO$_2$ emissions embodied in production.

The region's economic structure relying more on the manufacturing sector than on the primary and services sectors also partly explains Asia's high CO$_2$ emissions embodied in production. Asia's manufacturing share of gross domestic product (GDP) exceeds 20%, which is much higher than 11% for the United States (US) and 15% for the European Union (EU) (Figure 7.3). The heavy reliance on industrial inputs for the manufacture of goods, with the share of industrial inputs out of total imports at about 60%, also contributes to Asia's large contribution to CO$_2$ emissions (Figure 7.4). The effect of this factor is likely to diminish as more Asian economies develop and transition to more services-driven and digital economies.

Asia's CO$_2$ Emissions Embodied in Trade

CO$_2$ emissions embodied in Asia's exports and imports have also increased over time. In line with production, the region's CO$_2$ emissions embodied in exports have also increased. Relative to other regions, Asia's CO$_2$ emissions embodied in gross exports increased significantly from 1995 to 2019 (Figure 7.5a). Since the 2010s, however, the increasing trend has moderated. The CO$_2$ emissions embodied in exports can come from domestic sources or foreign industries upstream in the production chain. The total CO$_2$ emissions in gross exports have risen from 1,516 million tonnes to more than 4,506 million tonnes over 20 years—almost a threefold increase. The emissions embodied in exports from Europe and North America have stayed relatively constant over the last 2 decades with the overall trend decreasing, especially since 2008–2009.

Figure 7.3: Gross Domestic Product by Economic Activity (% of GDP)

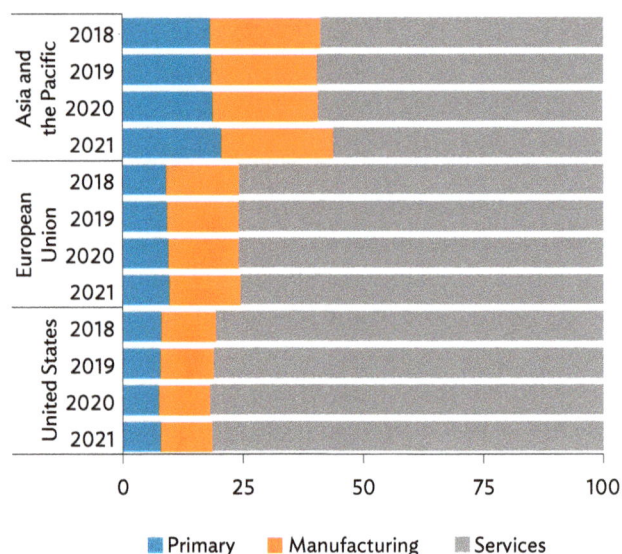

GDP = gross domestic product.

Note: Weighted using gross national income.

Sources: ADB calculations using data from World Bank. World Development Indicators. https://datatopics.worldbank.org/world-development-indicators/ (accessed December 2022); and domestic sources.

Figure 7.4: Share of Industrial Inputs in Total Imports— Asia and the Pacific, European Union, United States (%)

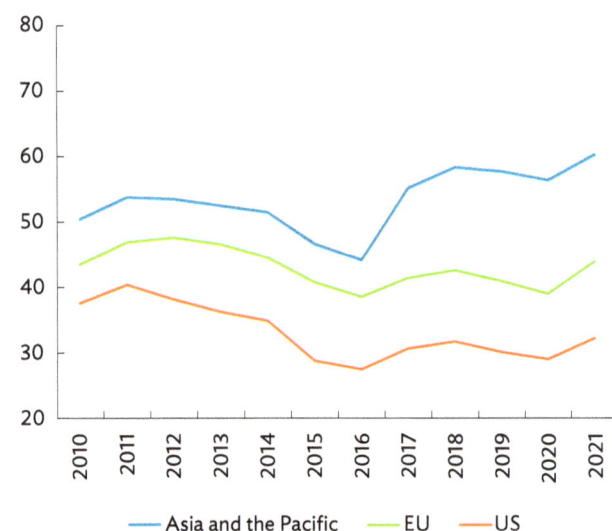

EU = European Union (27 members), US = United States.

Notes: Industrial inputs consist of food and beverages (primary and processed, mainly for industry), industrial supplies not elsewhere classified, and fuel and lubricants, based on Broad Economic Categories commodity classification. Values expressed as percentage of the region's total merchandise goods imports.

Source: ADB calculations using United Nations. Commodity Trade Database. https://comtrade.un.org (accessed December 2022).

The embodied CO$_2$ emissions in Asia's exports surpassed Europe's in 2003, led by East Asia. East Asia (excluding Japan) dominates the share of CO$_2$ emissions embodied in exports, comprising 56.3% of Asia's total CO$_2$ emissions in 2019 (Figure 7.5b). CO$_2$ emissions embodied in exports from East Asia increased from 797 million tonnes in 1995 to 2.5 billion tonnes in 2019. In this subregion, the People's Republic of China (PRC) has the highest CO$_2$ emissions from gross exports, which have steadily increased over the years. Southeast Asia has the next highest, comprising 22.1% of Asia's total CO$_2$ emissions. The CO$_2$ emissions embodied in exports from South Asia also increased substantially over the same period, by about fivefold. Export-related CO$_2$ emissions from developed Asia (Australia, Japan, and New Zealand) have increased more slowly than the rest of the region.

A similar pattern is seen in CO$_2$ emissions embodied in Asia's imports. Europe had the highest total CO$_2$ emissions embodied in its gross imports until 2011, when Asia overtook the region (Figure 7.6a). At this point, the embodied CO$_2$ emissions in Asia's and Europe's imports were about 3,300 million tonnes. Since 2011, the CO$_2$ emissions in Asia's imports continued to rise, having more than doubled over the last 25 years.

In the region, East Asia has the highest CO$_2$ emissions embodied in its gross imports. The subregion comprises 46.3% of Asia's total embodied CO$_2$ emissions in gross imports in 2019 (Figure 7.6b). East Asia's share is dominated by the PRC, which has the highest CO$_2$ emissions embodied in gross imports. Southeast Asia has the next highest CO$_2$ emissions, comprising 23.9% of Asia's total CO$_2$ emissions embodied in gross imports in 2019. The gap between Asia's CO$_2$ emissions embodied in gross exports and gross imports represents the region's net CO$_2$ emissions exports, which is tantamount to the gap between production and demand-based CO$_2$ emissions that was discussed in relation to Figure 7.2.

The increasing CO$_2$ emissions embodied in Asia's exports and imports partly reflect the growing importance of regional value chains. A sizable portion of CO$_2$ emissions in Asia's exports and imports are going to or coming from within the region. In 2019, the embodied CO$_2$ emissions in East Asia's exports primarily went to economies within its own subregion (433 million tonnes) and other Asian subregions (730 million tonnes) (Figure 7.7). This was driven mainly by the PRC's major role in regional value chains. Southeast Asia and developed Asia have the next highest CO$_2$ emissions going to Asian destinations (at 604 million tonnes and 296 million tonnes). CO$_2$ emissions to foreign destinations, especially the EU and the US, are relatively low.

Figure 7.5: Embodied Carbon Emissions in Exports (million tonnes)

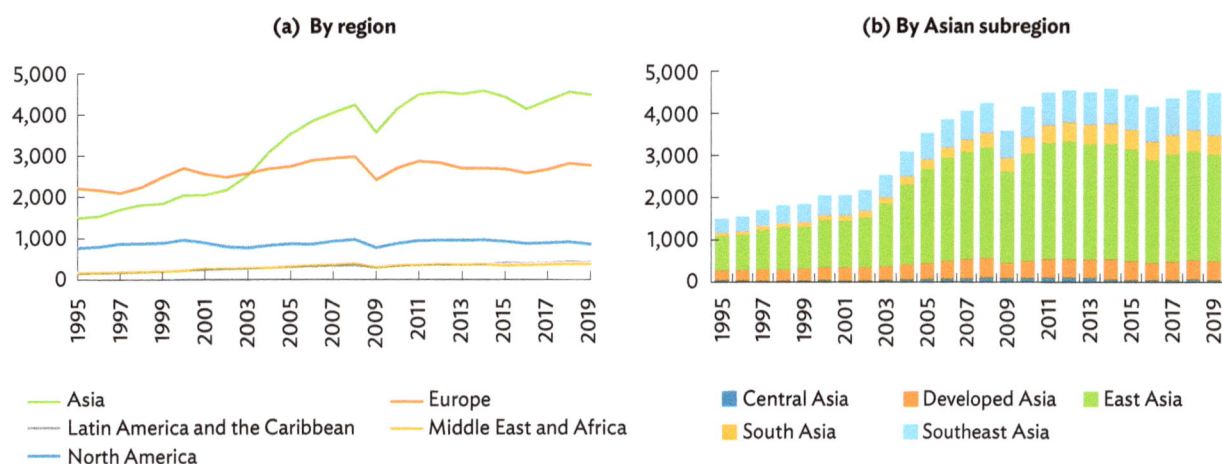

Notes: Developed Asia includes Australia, Japan, and New Zealand. East Asia excludes Japan.

Source: ADB calculations using data from Organisation for Economic Co-operation and Development. Carbon dioxide emissions embodied in international trade (TECO$_2$) data set.

Figure 7.6: Embodied Carbon Emissions in Imports (million tonnes)

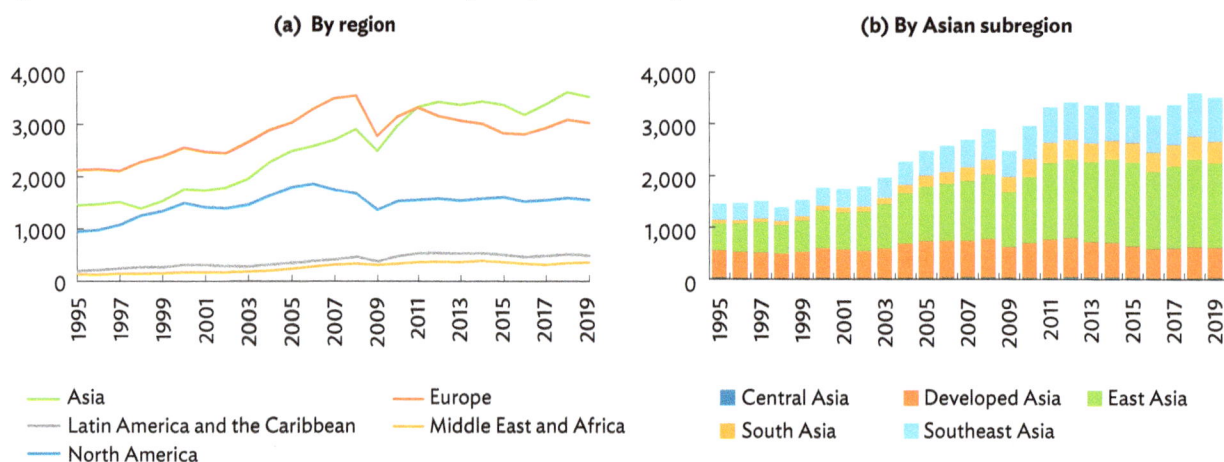

(a) By region

(b) By Asian subregion

Notes: Developed Asia includes Australia, Japan, and New Zealand. East Asia excludes Japan.

Source: ADB calculations using data from Organisation for Economic Co-operation and Development. Carbon dioxide emissions embodied in international trade (TECO$_2$) data set.

Figure 7.7: Asian Subregions' Carbon Emissions Embodied in Exports by Destination, 2019 (million tonnes)

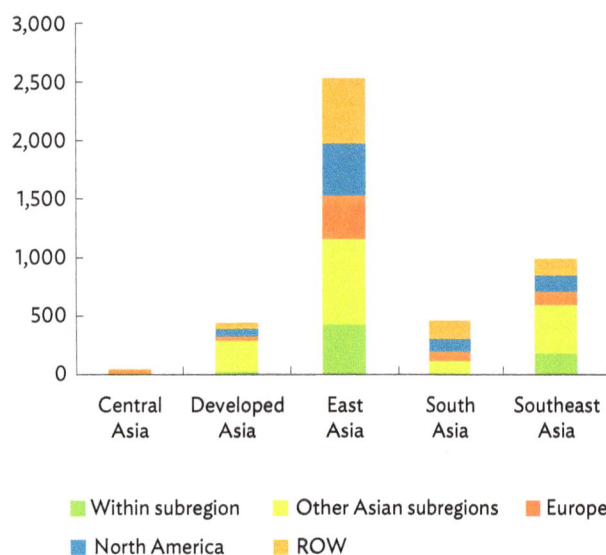

ROW = rest of the world.

Notes: Developed Asia includes Australia, Japan, and New Zealand. East Asia excludes Japan.

Source: ADB calculations using data from Organisation for Economic Co-operation and Development. Carbon dioxide emissions embodied in international trade (TECO$_2$) data set.

Similarly, a large portion of Asia's CO$_2$ emissions embodied in imports came from Asian sources in 2019 (Figure 7.8). East Asia has the highest CO$_2$ emissions embodied in gross imports from within Asia, followed

by Southeast Asia and developed Asia—which includes Australia, Japan, and New Zealand. This again is attributable to well-developed regional value chains in the East Asia and Southeast Asia subregions and the region at large.

Figure 7.8: Asian Subregions' Carbon Emissions Embodied in Imports by Source, 2019 (million tonnes)

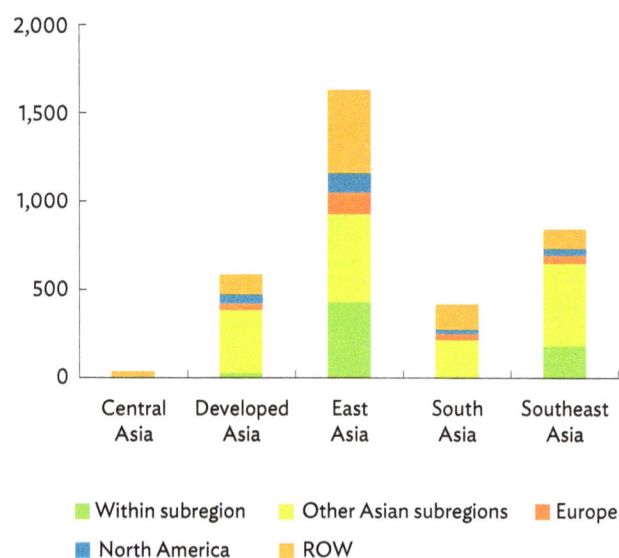

ROW = rest of the world.

Notes: Developed Asia includes Australia, Japan, and New Zealand. East Asia excludes Japan.

Source: ADB calculations using data from Organisation for Economic Co-operation and Development. Carbon dioxide emissions embodied in international trade (TECO$_2$) data set.

Asia's CO$_2$ Emissions Balance versus Other Regions

The gap between domestic production and demand is international trade, which also moves CO$_2$ across borders. Just as an economy's demand is not expected to balance with its own supply of products, CO$_2$ emissions from its production will generally not equal CO$_2$ emissions embodied in its consumption. This is primarily a consequence of the international division of labor and the gains from specialization and trade. The discrepancy between production-based CO$_2$ emissions and demand-based CO$_2$ emissions displayed in Figure 7.2 thus should not be referred to as carbon leakage unless it reflects production shifts caused by regulatory discrepancies. The pollution haven hypothesis posits that companies move production to economies with laxer environmental regulations.

Many Asian economies have a positive CO$_2$ balance with developed economies in Europe, North America, and within the region (Figure 7.9). A positive CO$_2$ balance means the economy has more CO$_2$ emissions in its production than in its consumption—i.e., it is a net exporter of carbon emissions. On average, the PRC is the largest net exporter of CO$_2$ emissions to North America (161.5 million tonnes), Europe (6.5 million tonnes), and Japan (73.2 million tonnes) over the period 2014–2019. As the PRC exports many final products to these destinations, it comes as no surprise that it has such a large positive CO$_2$ balance with these trade partners.

It turns out that many Asian economies also have a negative CO$_2$ balance with the PRC, i.e., they are net importers of CO$_2$ emissions from the PRC (Figure 7.10). Among Asian economies, Japan and India are the largest net importers of CO$_2$ emissions from the PRC, reflecting

Figure 7.9: Average Annual Net Carbon Emissions Balance by Major Trade Partners, 2014–2019—Asian Economies (million tonnes)

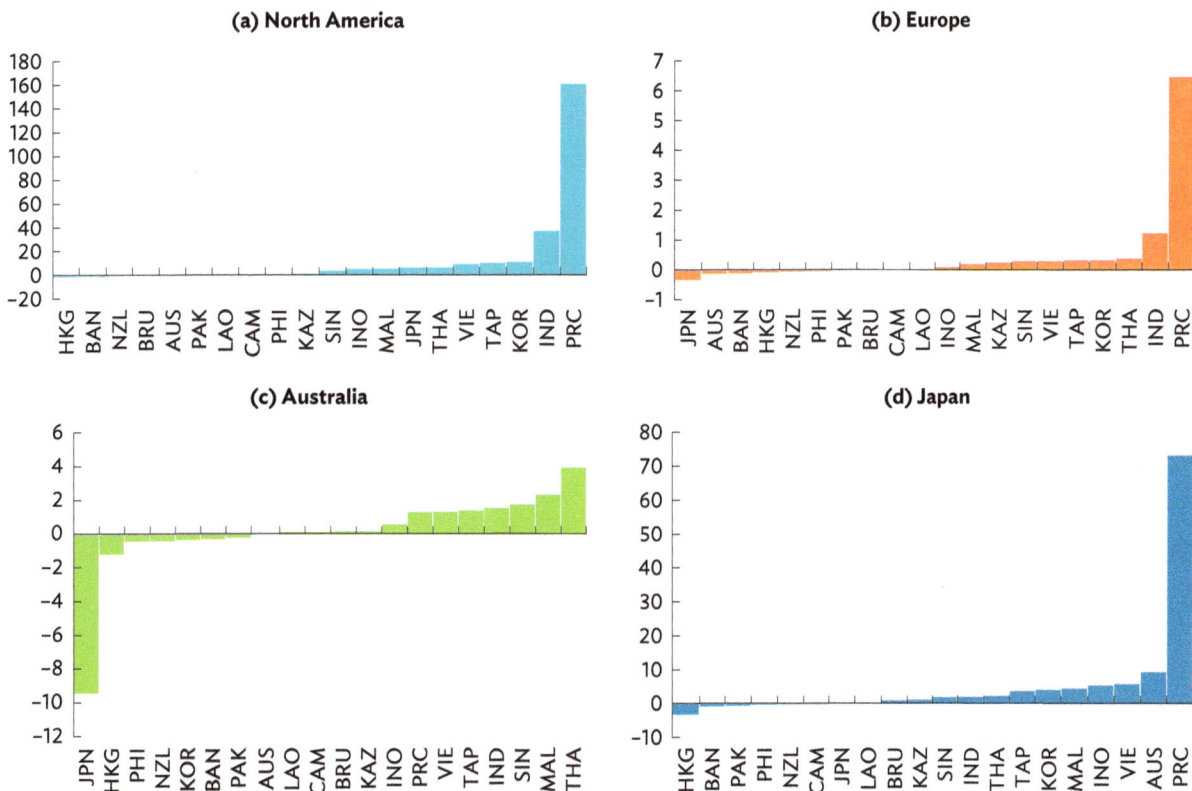

AUS = Australia; BAN = Bangladesh; BRU = Brunei Darussalam; CAM = Cambodia; CO$_2$ = carbon dioxide; HKG = Hong Kong, China; IND = India; INO = Indonesia; JPN = Japan; KAZ = Kazakhstan; KOR = Republic of Korea; LAO = Lao People's Democratic Republic; MAL = Malaysia; NZL = New Zealand; PAK = Pakistan; PHI = Philippines; PRC = People's Republic of China; SIN = Singapore; TAP = Taipei,China; THA = Thailand; VIE = Viet Nam.

Notes: The average net CO$_2$ balance is taken between 2014 and 2019. A positive CO$_2$ balance means the economy has more CO$_2$ emissions in its production than consumption, i.e., it is a net exporter of carbon emissions.

Source: ADB calculations using data from Organisation for Economic Co-operation and Development. Carbon dioxide emissions embodied in international trade (TECO$_2$) data set.

their trade deficits with the PRC. In contrast, Kazakhstan; Singapore; and Taipei,China are still net exporters with the PRC, with Taipei,China the largest due to its role as a supplier of semiconductor and electrical parts.

Figure 7.10: Net Carbon Emission Balance with the People's Republic of China, 2014–2019 (million tonnes)

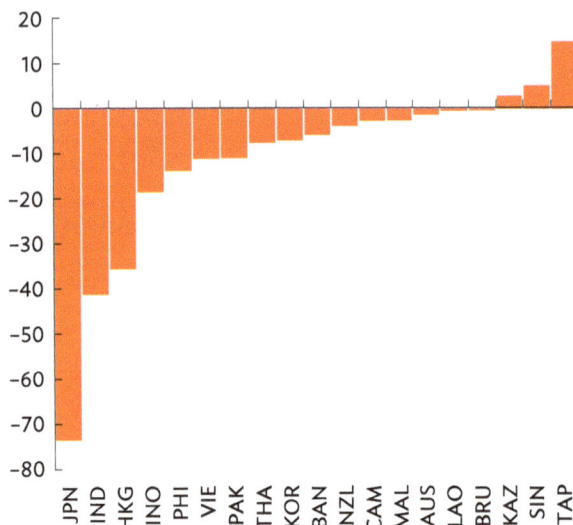

AUS = Australia; BAN = Bangladesh; BRU = Brunei Darussalam; CAM = Cambodia; CO$_2$ = carbon dioxide; HKG = Hong Kong, China; IND = India; INO = Indonesia; JPN = Japan; KAZ = Kazakhstan; KOR = Republic of Korea; LAO = Lao People's Democratic Republic; MAL = Malaysia; NZL = New Zealand; PAK = Pakistan; PHI = Philippines; SIN = Singapore; TAP = Taipei,China; THA = Thailand; VIE = Viet Nam.

Notes: The average net CO$_2$ balance is taken between 2014 and 2019. A positive CO$_2$ balance means the economy has more CO$_2$ emissions in its production than consumption, i.e., it is a net exporter of carbon emissions.

Source: ADB calculations using data from Organisation for Economic Co-operation and Development. Carbon dioxide emissions embodied in international trade (TECO$_2$) data set.

Impact of Industrial Structure and Technique

Emission Intensity of Production

The emissions intensity of an economy reflects both industrial structure and technological advancement effect and is a crucial factor characterizing the pathway toward net-zero goals. Even with a large production base (economic scale effect), an economy's industrial structure can include large shares of relatively fewer carbon intensive sectors to achieve a less carbon intensive industry profile (industrial structure effect), and it can also reduce carbon emissions in a specific sector if it has low emissions per unit of production in that sector

(technological advancement effect). A low emission intensity can be achieved by adopting more sustainable production processes, using fewer carbon intensive energy sources, and adopting decarbonization technologies such as carbon sequestration. Barrows and Ollivier (2021) show that Indian firms increased their CO$_2$ emissions growth when foreign demand grew but also were able to decrease their emissions growth by lowering emission intensity through fuel switching and technological upgrades.

Production has become cleaner over the past 2 decades in all regions. This could be a result of better technology, stricter environmental regulations (to control pollution of businesses), and growing environmental consciousness. Production-based CO$_2$ emissions relative to GDP—also called the emission factor—have decreased globally (Figure 7.11). While North America had the highest CO$_2$ emission factor at the start of the century, it has since declined steeply from 414 tonnes per million US dollars in 2000 to 243 tonnes per million US dollars in 2019. In 2003, Asia overtook North America and had the highest emission factor since then.

Figure 7.11: Production Carbon Emission Factor by Region (tonnes CO$_2$ per $ million)

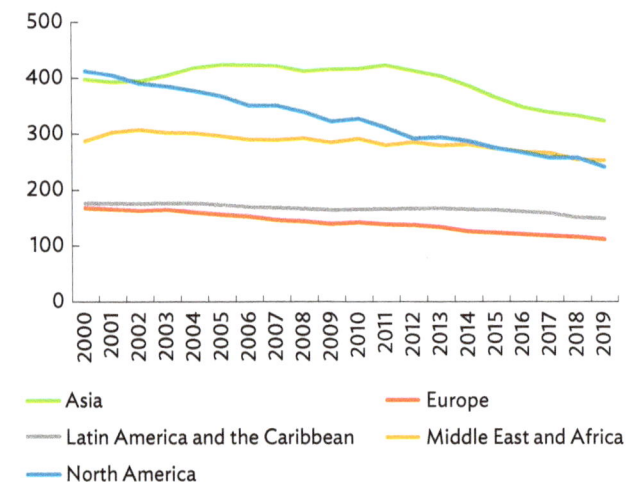

CO$_2$ = carbon dioxide, GDP = gross domestic product.

Notes: The production carbon emission factor shows an economy's intensity of CO$_2$ emissions, in tonne CO$_2$ per $ million of GDP. It is calculated by dividing an economy's production-based carbon emissions by its GDP (purchasing power parity) at constant 2017 $. Regionwide aggregates are computed by dividing the regional sum of emissions across economies by the regional GDP.

Sources: ADB calculations using data from Organisation for Economic Co-operation and Development. Carbon dioxide emissions embodied in international trade (TECO$_2$) data set; and World Bank. World Development Indicators. https://databank.worldbank.org/source/world-development-indicators (accessed January 2023).

The decline of Asia's emission factor is driven largely by Central Asia and East Asia (Figure 7.12). The fall is a consequence of strong GDP growth accompanied by a gradual reduction in annual CO_2 emissions over the years. Rising income also tends to be associated with the growth of the services sector of an economy and likely enables an economy to adopt greener technologies or enforce stricter environmental regulations. South Asia and Southeast Asia had a relatively stable emission factor over the past 2 decades. Compared with 2000, their latest emission factor is lower—by about 7%. For developed Asia, it is close to 28%.

Emissions Intensity of Trade

In a similar pattern to the emission factor described in the previous section, the carbon emission intensity of Asia's exports and imports also has been decreasing over the past 2 decades. The carbon emission intensity of exports, or the CO_2 emissions per export value, has been decreasing globally (Figure 7.13). In general, the carbon emission intensity of exports declined in all regions and by 2019 reached 635 tonnes of CO_2 per million US dollars in Asia, 391 tonnes per million US dollars in North America, and 387 tonnes per million US dollars in Europe. Since 2002, Asia has the highest average carbon emission intensity of exports globally.

Figure 7.12: Production Carbon Emission Factor by Asian Subregions (tonnes CO_2 per $ million)

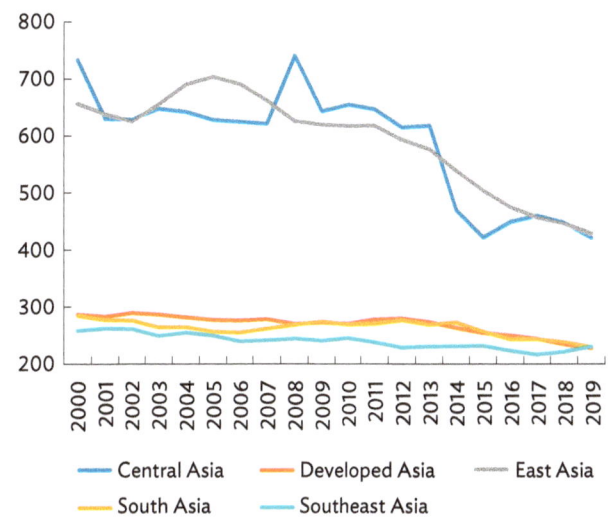

CO_2 = carbon dioxide, GDP = gross domestic product.

Notes: The production carbon emission factor shows an economy's intensity of CO_2 emissions, in tonne CO_2 per $ million of GDP. It is calculated by dividing an economy's production-based carbon emissions by its GDP (purchasing power parity) at constant 2017 $. Subregional aggregates are computed by dividing the subregional sum of emissions across economies by the subregional GDP.

Sources: ADB calculations using data from Organisation for Economic Co-operation and Development. Carbon dioxide emissions embodied in international trade (TECO$_2$) data set; and World Bank. World Development Indicators. https://databank.worldbank.org/source/world-development-indicators (accessed January 2023).

High CO_2 intensity in Asian exports and imports is partly due to the high shares of traded products coming from carbon intensive industries. Figures 7.14a and 7.14c show industries covered in OECD's TECO$_2$

Figure 7.13: Carbon Emissions Intensity of Gross Exports and Imports, by Region (tonnes CO_2 per $ million)

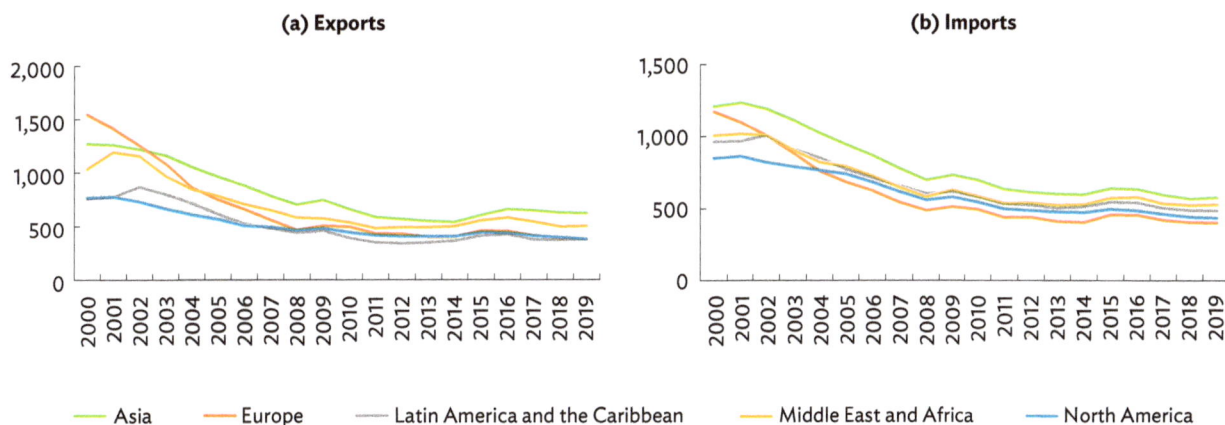

CO_2 = carbon dioxide.

Note: Emission intensity of exports (imports) are CO_2 emissions per export (import) value.

Source: ADB calculations using data from Organisation for Economic Co-operation and Development. Carbon dioxide emissions embodied in international trade (TECO$_2$) data set.

data categorized into sectors that are either most carbon intensive, more carbon intensive, or less carbon intensive. In 2018, the share of carbon intensive exports from Asia was 62.3%, while for the EU and the United Kingdom (EU+UK), it was 40.2%, and for North America 37.3%. Meanwhile, the share of carbon intensive imports in Asia was 58.8%,

which is also higher than the shares of the EU+UK and North America (Figures 7.14b and 7.14d). The bias toward carbon intensive sectors in Asia's exports and imports partly reflects the region's industrial structure of production, with higher dependence on the manufacturing sector relative to the primary and services sectors.

Figure 7.14: Carbon Emissions Intensity per Industry and Trade Shares per Region, 2018

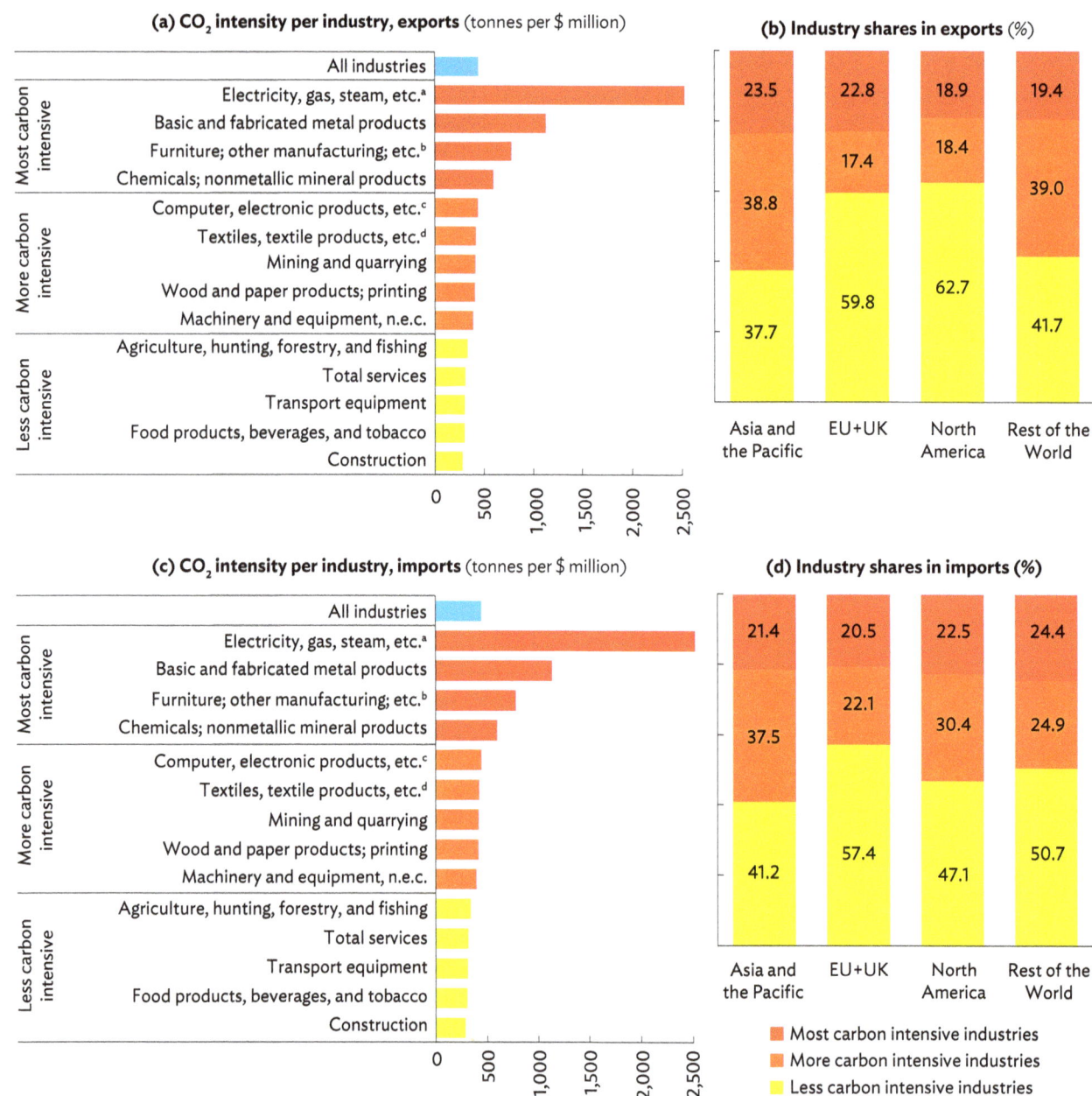

(a) CO_2 intensity per industry, exports (tonnes per $ million)

(b) Industry shares in exports (%)

(c) CO_2 intensity per industry, imports (tonnes per $ million)

(d) Industry shares in imports (%)

Most carbon intensive industries
More carbon intensive industries
Less carbon intensive industries

CO_2 = carbon dioxide, EU = European Union (27 members), n.e.c. = not elsewhere classified, UK = United Kingdom.

[a] Includes air conditioning and water supply; sewerage, waste management and remediation activities.
[b] Includes repair and installation.
[c] Includes optical products and electrical equipment.
[d] Includes leather and footwear.

Source: Kang, Gapay, and Quizon (2022) using data from Organisation for Economic Co-operation and Development. OECDstat: Carbon dioxide emissions embodied in international trade (TECO$_2$) data set. https://stats.oecd.org (accessed December 2021).

The emission intensity of Asia's exports in most carbon intensive sectors is generally higher than in other regions. As seen in Figure 7.15, in the most carbon-intensive sectors many Asian economies have higher CO_2 emission intensity than in the US and EU economies, led by the utility sector (electricity, gas, steam and air conditioning; sewerage, waste management and remediation activities). However, some Asian economies have lower emission intensity than developed economies, even in carbon intensive sectors. For example, utilities in Japan, Singapore, and Thailand recorded lower carbon emission intensity compared with both the world average and the levels in the US and several EU economies in 2018. Likewise, Brunei Darussalam and Cambodia showed lower emission intensity than the US, Canada, and some other EU economies in basic metals and fabricated metal products. This heterogeneous pattern of sectoral carbon intensity across economies is also seen for chemicals and nonmetallic mineral products (Figure 7.15).

Figure 7.15: Carbon Emissions Embodied in Exports By Sector, 2018 (tonnes per $ million)

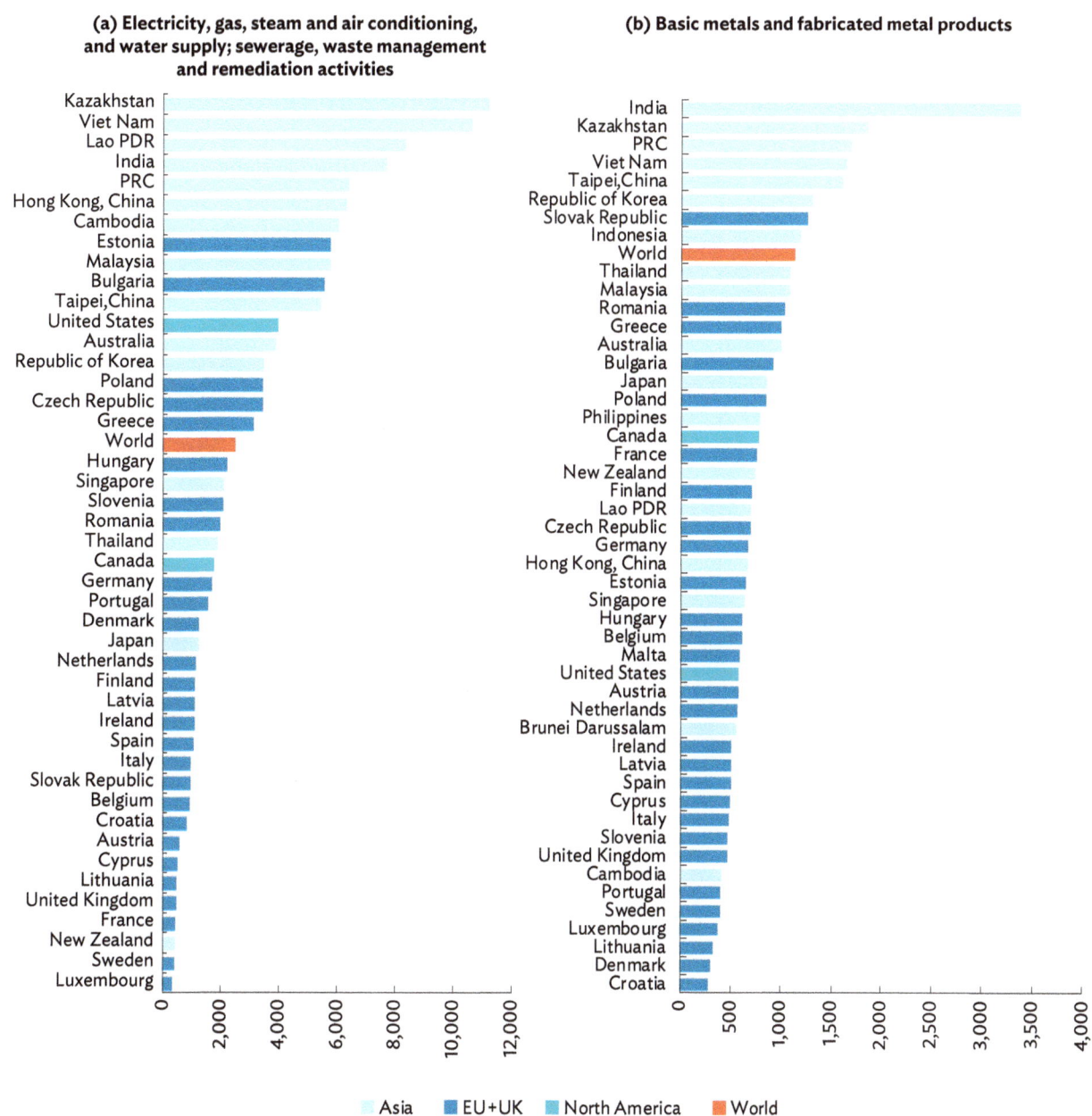

(a) Electricity, gas, steam and air conditioning, and water supply; sewerage, waste management and remediation activities

(b) Basic metals and fabricated metal products

Asia   EU+UK   North America   World

continued on next page

Figure 7.15 *continued*

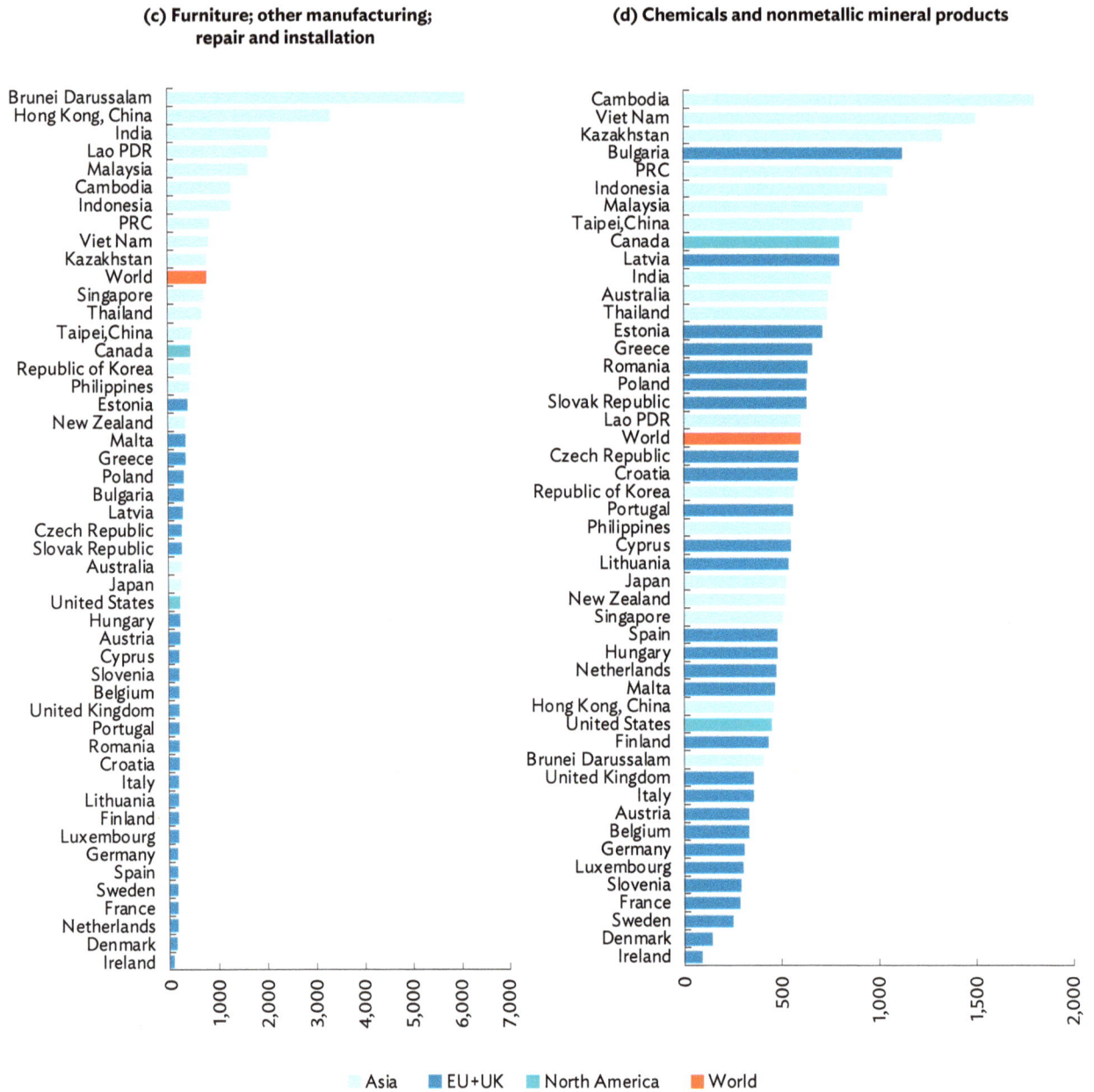

(c) Furniture; other manufacturing; repair and installation

(d) Chemicals and nonmetallic mineral products

Asia   ■ EU+UK   ■ North America   ■ World

EU = European Union (27 members), Lao PDR = Lao People's Democratic Republic, PRC = People's Republic of China, UK = United Kingdom.

Source: Kang, Gapay, and Quizon (2022) using data from Organisation for Economic Co-operation and Development. OECDstat: Carbon dioxide emissions embodied in international trade (TECO$_2$) data set. https://stats.oecd.org (accessed December 2021).

The ranking of the economies in each industry shows that there is no consistent pattern in the relative positions of their emission intensities. The carbon emission intensity of an industry can differ because of the energy sources used in production and the production technology itself. Some economies can have higher carbon emission intensity in one industry than another as a result of the status of technological development, which reflects each sector's production capability and an economy's capacity to reduce emissions in that sector.

Foreign Direct Investment Impact on Environmental Outcomes[108]

Multiple Channels to Define

The nexus between FDI and climate change involves multiple channels and requires thorough assessment. The economic benefits and costs of FDI inflows in terms of economic growth, productivity spillovers, technology transfer, and employment have been well studied (Haskel, Pereira, and Slaughter 2007; Iwasaki and Tokunaga 2016; Liu and Wang 2003; Meyer and Sinani 2009; Nair-Reichert and Weinhold 2001; Newman et al. 2015; Ning, Wang, and Li 2016; Xu and Sheng 2012). Still, there is little consensus on the relationship between FDI and climate change. Most of the literature focuses attention on (i) the relationship between FDI flows and environmental regulations, and (ii) the environmental impacts of FDI on host economies (Cole, Elliott, and Zhang 2017; Dean, Lovely, and Wang 2009; Demena and Afesorgbor 2020; Erdogan 2014; Pazienza 2014).

Today, there is not a common definition of green FDI used by governments and market participants. Typically, green or low-carbon FDI refers to the transfer of technologies, practices, or products such that their own and related operations, and use of their products and services, generate significantly lower GHG emissions (UNCTAD 2010). As such, green FDI may include goods in renewable energy (including solar, wind, biomass, hydroelectric, geothermal, marine, and other renewable power generation), recycling activities and low-carbon technology manufacturing. More comprehensive definitions combine two components to define green FDI, including (i) FDI in environmental goods and services, and (ii) FDI in environmental-damage mitigation processes (Golub, Kauffmann, and Yeres 2011). For the latter, the identification of environmental damage mitigation processes can be challenging. Identifying investments that promote cleaner and more

efficient technologies requires detailed and comparable information on emissions at the economy, sector, and process level, which are needed to create a common benchmark. FDI in capital equipment to reduce carbon use in the production of goods can be considered as part of investment in environmental-damage mitigation processes.

To address this gap, we construct a measure of "carbon intensive" or "non-carbon intensive" FDI based on the pollution intensity of industries. We define carbon intensive industries as those whose CO_2 emissions are above the median carbon emissions across industries in a given year (Box 7.2). For each economy, industries are classified as "non-carbon intensive" or "carbon intensive" as a function of the average carbon emissions of that industry each year. As a robustness check, alternative definitions of carbon intensive FDI were used, with similar results. We consider time invariant sectoral classifications, definitions of the median for the major sectoral groups (primary, manufacturing, services) and classifications based on pollution abatement by industry (Bialek and Weichenrieder 2021).

Trends of Carbon and Non-Carbon Intensive FDI

Trends for greenfield FDI flows suggest that Asia hosts a greater share of FDI from carbon intensive industries than any other region. On average, Asia accounted for 33.1% of inward carbon intensive FDI flows from 2008 to 2016 (Figure 7.16a). This is followed by North America (29.7%) and Europe (22.5%). Shares of carbon intensive industries do not seem to change substantially over time. For non-carbon intensive industries, Europe accounts for nearly half of global FDI inflows from 2008 to 2016 (Figure 7.16b). Asia is the second most important destination for investments in non-carbon intensive industries, making up about 20% of the investments for the period. The share of non-carbon

---

[108]   For this section, Asia and the Pacific, or Asia, excludes Oceania (Australia and New Zealand) given the different effect these economies would have compared with the rest of Asian economies.

Box 7.2: Classification of Carbon Intensive and Non-Carbon Intensive Industries

The classification of industries by carbon dioxide (CO_2) emissions is important for assessing how foreign direct investment (FDI) impacts the profile of carbon emissions in home (sending) and host (recipient) economies. For the purposes of this chapter, industries are classified into two categories (carbon intensive and non-carbon intensive) according to the relative level of carbon emissions of each industry and year.

World Input-Output Database figures are used to identify CO_2 emissions by industry and year. The database covers 43 economies for 56 sectors classified according to the International Standard Industrial Classification (ISIC), Revision 4. Out of 56 industries, 7 are used in this study. These are further classified into broader categories representing "manufacturing," "information and communication," and "financial and insurance activities," based on the ISIC of All Economic Activities, Revision 4.

One step further classifies these broad categories into sectors: agriculture, industry, and services. To classify the industry, category, and sector as carbon intensive, the level of CO_2 emissions is evaluated around the median. The

median of CO_2 emissions is based on the industry and year.

The box figure shows the sectoral composition of carbon intensive industries FDI in 2008 and in 2016 for global greenfield investment. Manufacturing accounts for the largest share of FDI for both carbon intensive and non-carbon intensive industries. In 2008, mining and quarrying accounted for the second-largest share of carbon intensive FDI, followed by electricity, gas, and water supply. Meanwhile, electricity, gas, and water supply, as well as real estate sectors make up the largest share of FDI in non-carbon intensive industries. Overall, the sectoral composition of FDI remained stable from 2008 to 2016. For the major sectoral classification, manufacturing accounts for sizable FDI over both time periods, with a growing share of investments in tertiary sectors.

As a robustness test, alternative classifications of carbon and non-carbon intensive industries were adopted. Results under alternative classifications are mostly consistent with the findings presented in this section.[a]

Composition of Carbon and Non-Carbon Intensive Industry FDI (%)

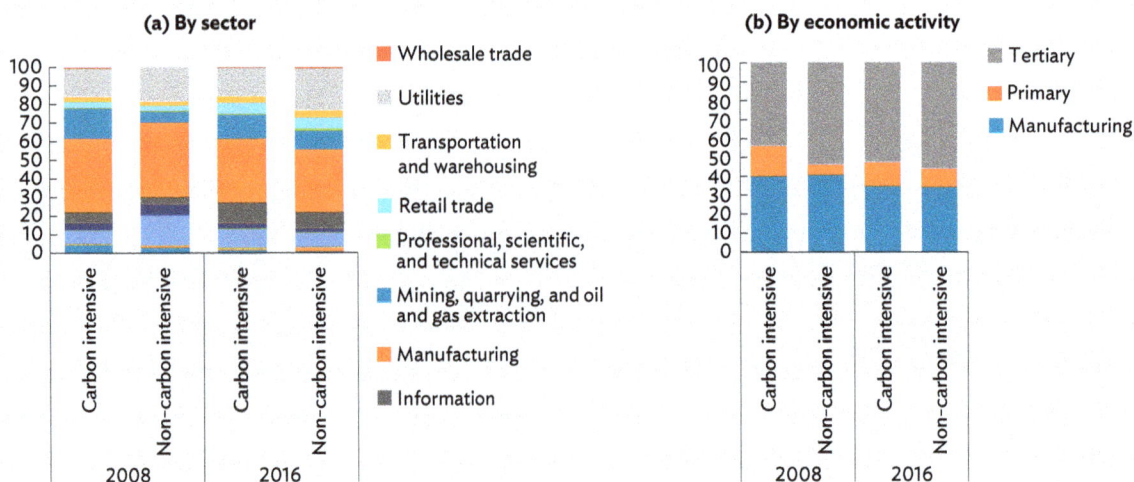

(a) By sector

Legend: Wholesale trade; Utilities; Transportation and warehousing; Retail trade; Professional, scientific, and technical services; Mining, quarrying, and oil and gas extraction; Manufacturing; Information

(b) By economic activity

Legend: Tertiary; Primary; Manufacturing

FDI = foreign direct investment.

Sources: ADB calculations using data from Financial Times. fDI Markets; Groningen Growth and Development Centre. World Input-Output Database (WIOD). https://www.rug.nl/ggdc/valuechain/wiod/?lang=en (accessed November 2022); and WIOD methodology based on Timmer et al. (2015).

[a] Several definitions of carbon and non-carbon intensive industries were considered for the analysis, yielding similar results. First, an industry is defined as carbon intensive if emissions are above the median of the 2-digit Nomenclature of Economic Activities industries for the pooled data set (time invariant). Second, a similar definition is considered but the median is determined each year (time variant). Third, an industry was defined as carbon intensive if carbon emissions are above the median of a major sectoral group (primary/manufacturing/services). Fourth, a similar definition using major sectoral groups is used but the median is defined each year. Last, we employ the classification of Bialek and Weichenrieder (2021) who used pollution abatement as their basis for their classification. This classification is also time invariant.

Source: ADB staff.

intensive FDI to Asia has also increased over the years. FDI from non-carbon intensive sources represented 7.3% of Asia's total greenfield investment, above North America (4.4%) and below Europe (20.6%).

Nevertheless, the share of inward FDI in highly carbon intensive industries relative to non-carbon intensive industries remains moderate in Asia. An estimation of the ratio of inward investment in the top 25% (top quartile) carbon intensive industries over the bottom 25% (bottom quartile) underscores regional differences. From 2011 to 2016, Asia's average ratio of investment in carbon to non-carbon intensive industries (29.3) remained within the global average, higher than Europe, but lower than other regions. While the concentration of greenfield FDI in manufacturing and less energy efficient industries could influence the overall outcomes, regional differences also reflect the large heterogeneity in carbon emissions across industries and economies.

By Asian subregion, East Asia received the largest share of carbon intensive FDI for Asia from 2008 to 2016 (Figure 7.17). On average, carbon intensive industry FDI flows to East Asia account for 42.8% of the region's total, followed by Southeast Asia (33.5%). In recent years, increasing participation of FDI from carbon intensive

industries is observed for Central Asia. Investments on non-carbon intensive industries have been dominated by East Asia and Southeast Asia, which together account for three-fourths of the region's investment. The ratio of inward FDI in the top and bottom carbon intensive industries (by quartile) depicts a more uniform picture across Asian subregions. From 2011 to 2016, the average ratio of investment in carbon to non-carbon intensive industries for Central Asia (30.8), East Asia (26.7), South Asia (37.4), and Southeast Asia (34.4) was relatively similar and stable over time although the annual fluctuation could be affected by some large investments made in extractive industries for a particular year.

Jobs created by greenfield FDI are mostly concentrated in carbon intensive industries. Following the pattern for capital expenditure on greenfield projects, Asia accounts for the largest share (44.3%) of jobs created by FDI in carbon intensive industries from 2008 to 2016, followed by Europe (27.4%) and North America (25.1%) (Figure 7.18a). For non-carbon intensive industries, Europe is dominant with 53.9% of job creation (Figure 7.18b), followed by Asia (28.6%), where the share has gradually increased. Still, FDI in carbon intensive industries remains the largest source of job creation for all regions.

Figure 7.16: Carbon Intensive and Non-Carbon Intensive Foreign Direct Investment by Host Region ($ billion)

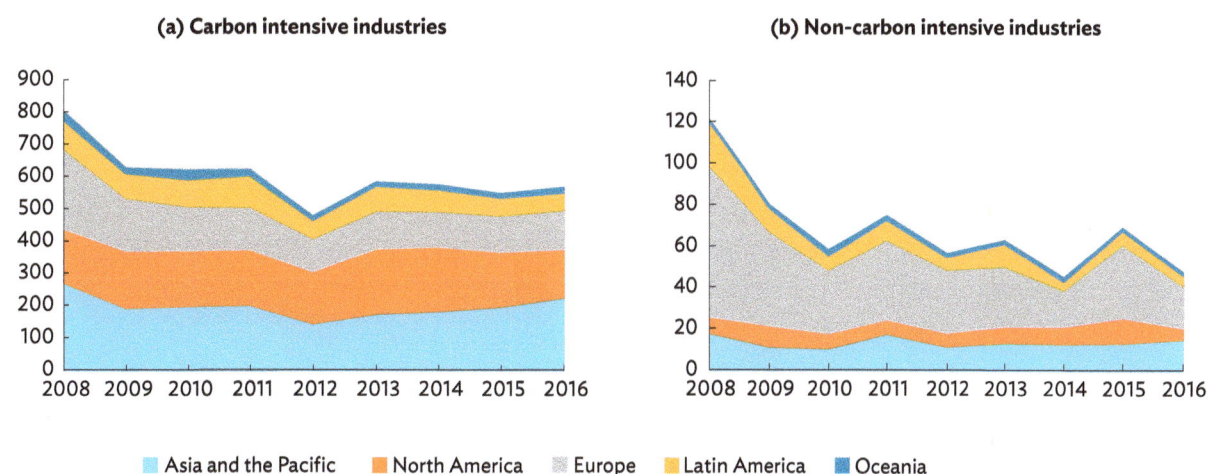

(a) Carbon intensive industries

(b) Non-carbon intensive industries

Legend: Asia and the Pacific | North America | Europe | Latin America | Oceania

FDI = foreign direct investment.

Notes: Figure shows share of FDI by geographic location of destination economy from 2008 to 2016. The left panel shows the shares for carbon intensive industries while the right panel shows the share for non-carbon intensive industries. The graph does not include data from Africa and the Middle East.

Sources: ADB calculations using data from Financial Times. fDI Markets; and Groningen Growth and Development Centre. World Input-Output Database. https://www.rug.nl/ggdc/valuechain/wiod/?lang=en (accessed November 2022); and methodology based on Timmer et al. (2015).

Figure 7.17: Carbon Intensive and Non-Carbon Intensive Foreign Direct Investment by Asian Subregions ($ billion)

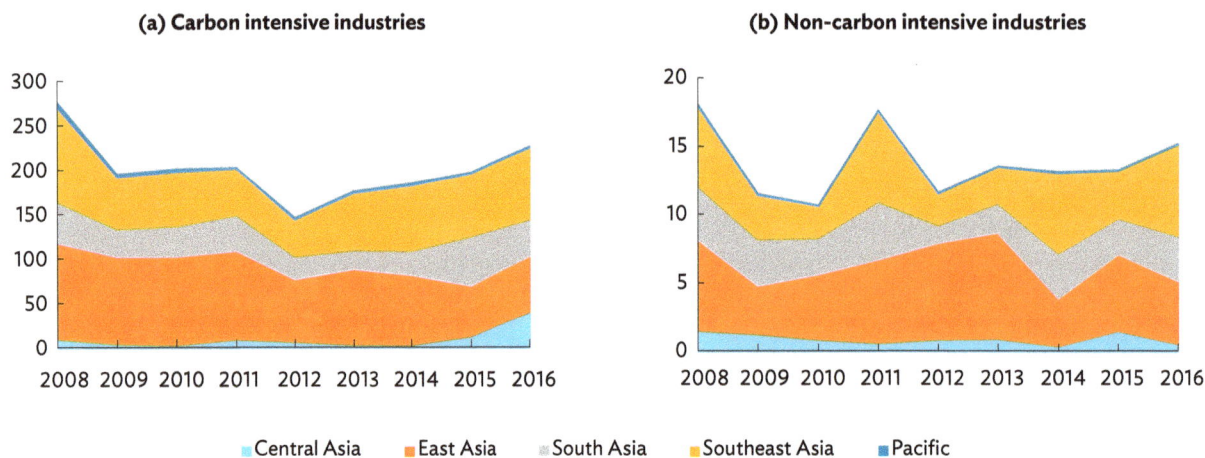

(a) Carbon intensive industries

(b) Non-carbon intensive industries

Central Asia   East Asia   South Asia   Southeast Asia   Pacific

FDI = foreign direct investment.

Notes: Figure shows share of FDI flowing to Asia and the Pacific by Asian subregion from 2008 to 2016. The left panel shows the shares for carbon intensive industries while the right panel shows the share for non-carbon intensive industries.

Sources: ADB calculations using data from Financial Times. fDI Markets; and Groningen Growth and Development Centre. World Input-Output Database. https://www.rug.nl/ggdc/valuechain/wiod/?lang=en (accessed November 2022); and methodology based on Timmer et al. (2015).

Figure 7.18: Job Creation in Greenfield Foreign Direct Investment for Carbon Intensive and Non-Carbon Intensive Industries (%)

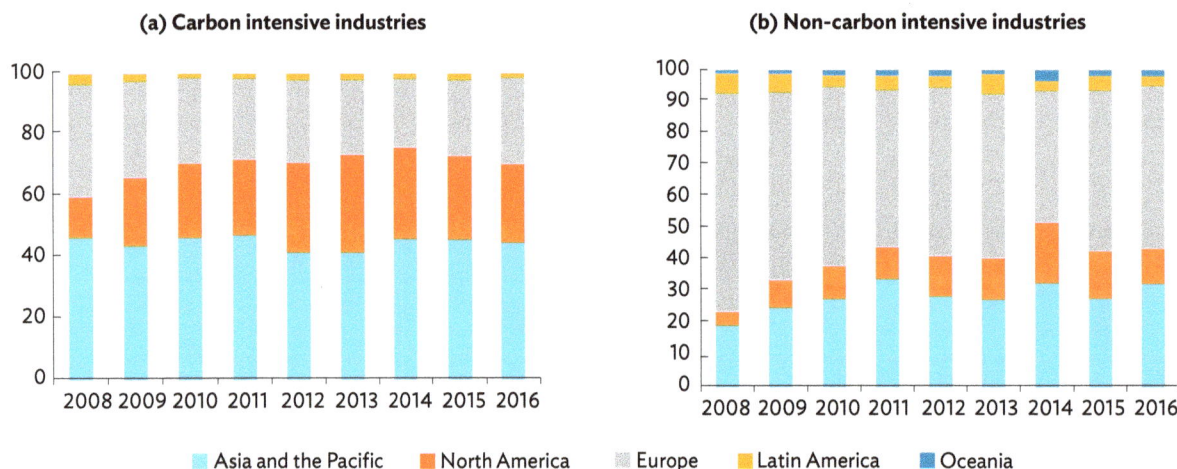

(a) Carbon intensive industries

(b) Non-carbon intensive industries

Asia and the Pacific   North America   Europe   Latin America   Oceania

Notes: Figure shows share of job creation by geographic location of destination economy from 2008 to 2016. The left panel shows the shares for carbon intensive industries while the right panel shows the share for non-carbon intensive industries. The graph does not include data from Africa and the Middle East.

Sources: ADB calculations using data from Financial Times. fDI Markets; and Groningen Growth and Development Centre. World Input-Output Database. https://www.rug.nl/ggdc/valuechain/wiod/?lang=en (accessed November 2022); and methodology based on Timmer et al. (2015).

Asia's FDI in carbon intensive industries is more reliant on intraregional sources. A glance at FDI flows to Asia by investor region shows that intraregional flows (Asian economies investing in Asia) account for the largest share (44.9%) of carbon intensive industry investments in the region (Figure 7.19a). North America

represented, on average, 28.5% of Asia inward investment in carbon intensive industries, whereas the share from Europe fell from 25.8% in 2008 to 15.9% in 2016. For non-carbon intensive industries, European economies account for a substantial majority of FDI flows into Asia (Figure 7.19b). Asian investors account on average for

11.7% of Asia's inward investment in non-carbon intensive industries, but the share had increased to 31.5% by 2016, and most likely increased further after. Much like trade, FDI in Asia reflects patterns of specialization with a focus on manufacturing and other carbon intensive industries. There also exists room for strengthening policy efforts in fostering FDI in less carbon intensive industries. Policies in the form of investment incentives (fiscal, financial), easing foreign investment restrictions in less polluting industries, and targeted investment promotion strategies could be effective in directing investments toward greener industries.

Asia's FDI in environmental goods and services is growing. Regional estimates on the share of FDI in environmental goods, based on the classification system of the Asia-Pacific Economic Cooperation (APEC), suggest that the volume remains smaller than for other industries (Figure 7.20a). However, investment into these sectors has increased in most regions. Asia's estimated share of FDI in environmental goods and services grew from 3.4% 2005 to 11.4% for greenfield investment, with a clear uptick in recent years. Estimates for mergers and acquisitions are about the same magnitude (10%), with higher fluctuation across years. A breakdown of the most important environmental

goods and services highlights the major role of renewable energy investments (Figure 7.20b). Between 2005 and 2021, an average 41.6% of FDI in environmental goods and services in Asia was destined to solar electric power and 20.5% to wind electric power.

FDI and Environmental Regulations

Environmental standards can be a factor for multinationals when locating subsidiaries. Studies have shown that regions with lax environmental regulations may have a comparative advantage in pollution intensive production, thereby attracting FDI to polluting industries from economies with more stringent environmental regulations (Millimet and Roy 2016; Motta and Thisse 1994; Ranocchia and Lambertini 2021; Xing and Kolstad 2002). This phenomenon is known as the pollution haven hypothesis. At the same time, some foreign firms may prefer to relocate to an economy with higher environmental standards if such a move raises its rival domestic firm's costs by more than its own (Dijkstra, Matthew, and Mukherjee 2011) or to prevent entry by a domestic competitor. Elliott and Zhou (2013) refer to this effect as environmental regulation induced FDI. The effect on outward investment is also

Figure 7.19: Sources of Greenfield Foreign Direct Investment for Asia and the Pacific (%)

(a) Carbon intensive industries

(b) Non-carbon intensive industries

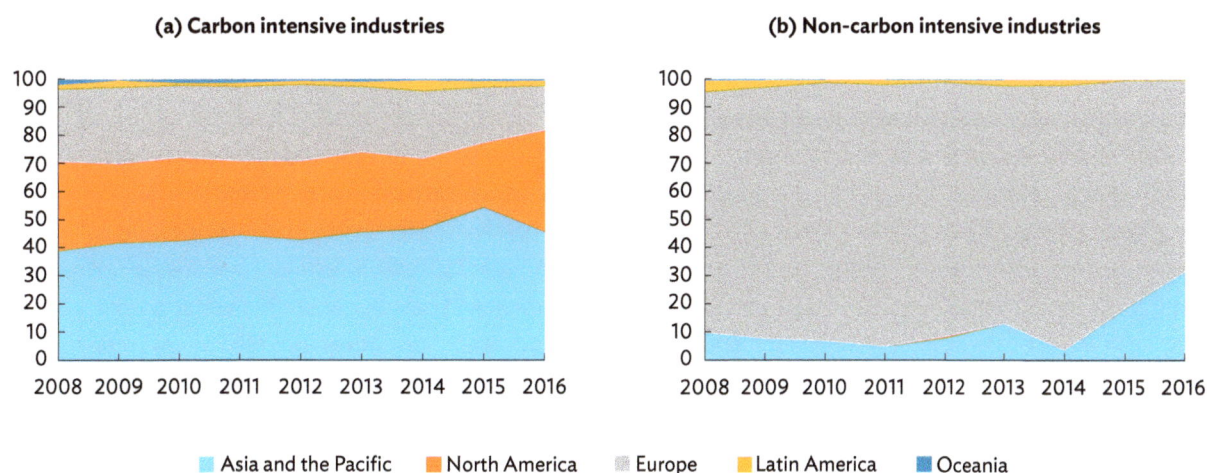

Asia and the Pacific   North America   Europe   Latin America   Oceania

FDI = foreign direct investment.

Notes: Figure shows the composition of investor source for FDI flowing into Asia and the Pacific from 2008 to 2016. The left panel shows the shares for carbon intensive industries while the right panel shows the share for non-carbon intensive industries. The graph does not include data from Africa and the Middle East.

Sources: ADB calculations using data from Financial Times. fDI Markets; Groningen Growth and Development Centre. World Input-Output Database (WIOD). https://www.rug.nl/ggdc/valuechain/wiod/?lang=en (accessed November 2022); and WIOD methodology based on Timmer et al. (2015).

Figure 7.20: Estimated Greenfield Foreign Direct Investment toward Environmental Goods and Services (3-year moving averages)

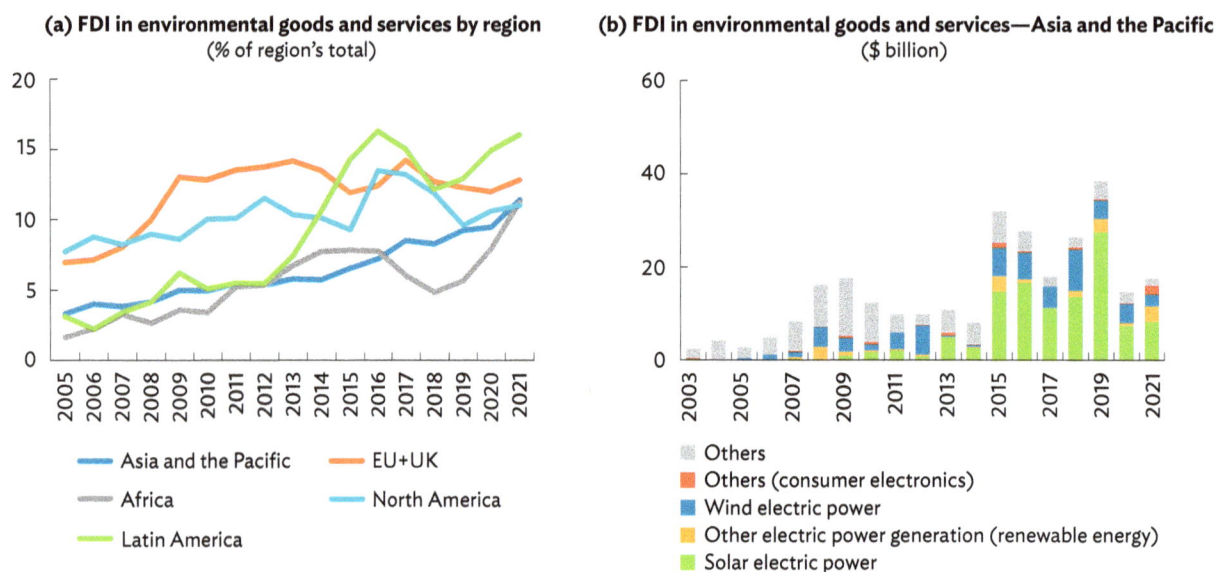

(a) FDI in environmental goods and services by region
(% of region's total)

Asia and the Pacific • EU+UK • Africa • North America • Latin America

(b) FDI in environmental goods and services—Asia and the Pacific
($ billion)

Others • Others (consumer electronics) • Wind electric power • Other electric power generation (renewable energy) • Solar electric power

EU = European Union (27 members), FDI = foreign direct investment, M&A = merger and acquisition, UK = United Kingdom.

Notes: Estimates for firm-level FDI into environmental goods and services were based on the list of environmental goods from the Asia-Pacific Economic Cooperation (APEC), which uses the Harmonized System codes and includes goods. To reflect investment in potential environmental services or sectors, codes listed in the APEC list were matched with the International Standard Industrial Classification of All Economic Activities using a concordance key from the Organisation for Economic Co-operation and Development and then to the North American Industry Classification System. The complete list of sectors for both greenfield and M&A FDI is in Chapter 8: Statistical Appendix.

Sources: ADB calculations using data from Bureau van Dijk. Zephyr M&A Database; and Financial Times. fDi Markets.

ambiguous. Local regulations could lead a firm to increase or reduce its investment in both the home economy and in the economy where environmental standards are less stringent (Eskeland and Harrison 2003). Other drivers, including institutional factors, industries, and investor characteristics are also important.

To untangle this nexus, empirical analyses have studied the channels that link investment and environmental outcomes. These include the impact of environmental costs on FDI location, evidence on the pollution haven hypothesis, and the impact of FDI on domestic environmental policies (Cole, Elliott, and Zhang 2017; Erdogan 2014; Rezza 2015). How environmental regulations are measured influences whether these linkages are supported. More recently, the benefits of FDI on domestic environmental standards have been explored. This perspective, also known as the pollution

halo effect, is based on the notion that FDI can benefit the local environment around the site of investment (Wei, Ding, and Konwar 2022).[109] The pollution halo effect encompasses policy options that encourage the diffusion of clean technologies through FDI. This can take shape as environmental spillovers from foreign to local firms that drive rapid reductions in CO_2 emissions.

Measures of environmental regulations and environmental performance are wide-ranging. Commonly used regulatory measures include environmental levies, investment in industrial pollution treatment and pollution abatement projects, the number of administrative cases filed by environmental authorities, and the number of public servants working in environmental protection agencies (Bu et al. 2013; Pan et al. 2020; Zhang and Fu 2008). Cross-economy indicators suggest that environmental enforcement is related to

---

[109]   Wei, Ding, and Konwar (2022) find that 40 articles on the environmental performance of FDI in the People's Republic of China support the pollution halo effect, and argue that FDI leads to better environmental performance through a pollution abatement effect, but not through enhancements in green total factor productivity.

environmental stringency, subject to some regional differences (Figure 7.21). Measures of environmental policy are also important at the domestic level. These include, for example, participation in international environmental treaties or carbon emission systems (Shao, Yu, and Chen 2022; Xu, Wu, and Shi 2021; Yu and Li 2020) or the use of environmental regulation policy tools. Certain province-level regulations also have been used to identify causal effects of environmental regulations on FDI flows.[110] Likewise, several measures of environmental performance have been used, from air pollutants and quality emissions (CO_2, sulfur dioxide [SO_2], PM10, and PM2.5) (Cole, Elliott, and Zhang 2017; Liu and Zhang 2022; Wang and Chen 2014; Yang et al. 2021). Other studies have focused on energy consumption, energy intensity, and environmental total factor productivity as indicators of environmental performance (Bu et al. 2013; Elliott, Sun, and Chen 2013; Hübler and Keller 2010; Xie, Yuan, and Huang 2017; Zhou et al. 2019). While a broad number of indicators have been proposed, no single measure can reflect all aspects of environmental regulation or performance.

Is the Region a Pollution Haven for FDI?

While evidence is wide-ranging, most studies support the presence of a pollution haven effect in Asia. Economies like Japan and the Republic of Korea have strict, well-enforced environmental regulations, while environmental stringency and enforcement is considerably weaker in parts of developing Asia. Most evidence from the PRC favors the pollution haven hypothesis, as FDI inflows tend to be located in the PRC regions with weaker environmental regulations (Cheng, Li, and Liu 2018; He 2006; Lin and Sun 2016; Zhang and Fu 2008) and tougher regulations reduce the probability of entry of foreign enterprises (Li, Lin, and Wang 2022). Some research suggests little effect from environmental regulations on FDI, as in Japan (Elliott and Shimamoto 2008) or even an increase in inward FDI following stricter regulations (Shao, Yu, and Chen 2022).

Figure 7.21: Correlation of Stringency and Enforcement of Environmental Regulations

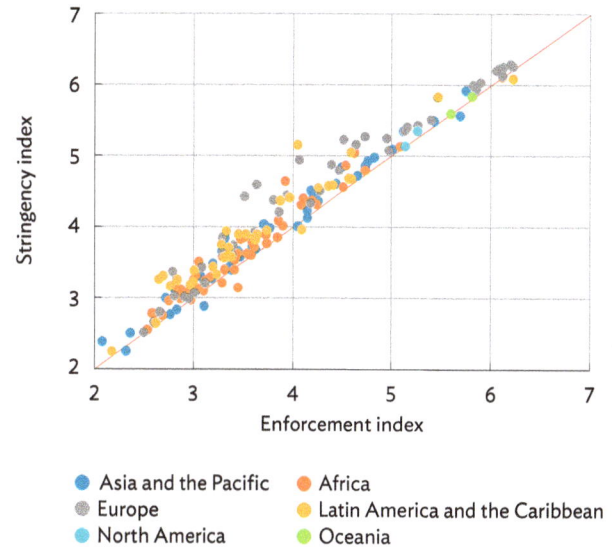

Notes: Data correspond to the latest available year. Red line represents the 45-degree line. Based on the survey data of World Economic Forum (WEF) on stringency of environmental regulations (EOSQ160) and enforcement of environmental regulations (EOSQ161) in 2018. The index covers 134 economies and 16,658 respondent firms.

Source: WEF. Environmental indicators in the WEF Executive Survey.

Evidence of the pollution haven hypothesis for Asia's outward investment is more mixed. While increasing environmental stringency in home economies could lead to FDI relocation or firm exit, the evidence for Asia is limited (Greaney, Li, and Tu 2017; Kirkpatrick and Shimamoto 2008). More recent studies find a positive effect on the probability of foreign firms to stay once environmental regulations are tightened (Shao, Yu, and Chen 2022; Tai and Yan 2022).

These findings suggest that multinationals may respond differently to increasing environmental stringency. For example, firms with higher motivation or environmental capabilities may invest more in environmentally stringent locations (Javorcik 2004; Meyer and Sinani 2009). Export-oriented FDI is also more sensitive to environmental regulations than local market-oriented FDI (Tang and Tan 2015). FDI can facilitate both a "race to the bottom" and a "race to the top" (Patala et al. 2021; Ullah et al. 2022).

---

[110] A popular regulation to study in the PRC is the Two Control Zone policy and its impact on firm location. For example, Cai et al. (2016) use the Two Control Zone policy, where the PRC government in 1998 assigned certain provinces to be acid rain and sulfur dioxide (SO_2) pollution control areas, as a natural experiment in which assigned regions can be thought of as being more strictly regulated. They find that the implementation of the policy led to reduced FDI into the more strictly regulated regions.

Environmental Impact of FDI into Asia

The relationship between FDI and the environment is characterized by both positive and negative externalities. FDI into Asia has led to greater environmental degradation and carbon emissions (Behera and Dash 2017; Borga et al. 2022). In India, a 1% increase in inward FDI may have increased CO_2 emissions by 0.86% from 1980 to 2003 (Acharyya 2009). This is consistent with impact assessments in the Association of Southeast Asian Nation (ASEAN) economies, where inward FDI is associated with an overall increase in CO_2 emissions (Baek 2016; Tang and Tan 2015). FDI is also associated with lower environmental standards in SO_2 emissions, air quality, and industrial waste (Cole, Elliott, and Zhang 2011; Liu and Zhang 2022). Other studies have found mixed results or some beneficial effects of FDI on the environment (Jiang et al. 2018; Liu, Hao, and Gao 2017; Zhang and Zhou 2016).

Foreign investment can support cleaner production processes and green technological development. The benefits of FDI for promoting green technological innovation and energy efficiency in the region have been documented (Chen et al. 2014; Li et al. 2016, 2017; Piperopoulos, Wu, and Wang 2018). One example of cleaner production is the use of desulfurization equipment in coal-fired power-generating units. While costlier than normal production processes, using such equipment can generate energy more efficiently and emit less emissions. Evidence suggests that foreign investment largely increases usage of desulfurization in the energy sector (Huang et al. 2019). The environmental impact of the PRC's FDI has often been discussed particularly in the context of the Belt and Road Initiative (Box 7.3).

Box 7.3: Outbound Foreign Direct Investment of the People's Republic of China and the Belt and Road Initiative

The Belt and Road Initiative (BRI) of the People's Republic of China (PRC) provides an example of outbound foreign direct investment policy that is increasingly linked to the climate change agenda. Economic motives for the BRI are to absorb some of the PRC's productive capacity, create regional production chains, and increase energy security. Its impact on economic growth and social and environmental outcomes continues to be widely discussed (Khan et al. 2020; Liu et al. 2020; Mahadevan and Sun 2020; Tian et al. 2019).

Some environmental concerns over the BRI are related to high energy consumption for construction and maintenance of infrastructure projects, mostly from fossil fuels (Zhang et al. 2017). The effect on carbon emissions in host economies has been the subject of discussion. Early assessments suggest that the BRI could lead to a modest increase in global carbon emissions in host economies. The PRC benefits from outsourcing part of its production abroad, while host economies absorb this production and related emissions (Maliszewska and van der Mensbrugghe 2019).

More recently, some assessments suggest that the BRI also can contribute to improving the environmental quality of economies that have received investments (Cao, Teng, and Zhang 2021). Indeed, economies with lower environmental quality could have benefited from technology transfers and more stringent environmental regulations. The launch of the PRC's pilot emissions trading scheme may also have accelerated the transfer of carbon intensive production activities abroad and increased the scale of investments in economies where PRC firms have an affiliate (Yu, Cai, and Sun 2021). Other studies suggest that the impact of the PRC's outward foreign direct investment on green total factor productivity has been positive, with a larger effect on economies with stronger institutions (Wu et al. 2020).

Overall, there is wider awareness of these assessments, and the PRC has worked toward integrating green development and environmental protection into its BRI projects. A Coalition for Green Development on the Belt and Road was proposed in 2017 to this effect, considering the complexities of measuring the environmental impact and implementation of transnational infrastructure. Efforts in host economies to better identify bankable projects and incorporate environmental impact assessments also contribute to better environmental outcomes of BRI projects.

Source: Cole, Elliott, and Zhang (2022).

FDI and Energy Transition in Asia

FDI can be a vehicle for more efficient energy consumption, energy intensity, and transfer of energy-saving technologies. FDI in and from Asia has been found to reduce energy intensity and carbon emissions. While a positive link between FDI and energy consumption is not uncommon (Azam et al. 2015; Mudakkar et al. 2013), recent evidence from the PRC and Bangladesh suggests that FDI has boosted renewable power generation (Ahmad et al. 2019; Murshed et al. 2022; Tiwari, Nasreen, and Anwar 2022). As a result of investments in more efficient and cleaner energy sources, FDI has had an impact on plant energy intensity. Evidence for Indonesia shows that foreign ownership increased energy usage while reducing plant energy intensity (Brucal, Javorcik, and Love 2019). Evidence also shows how FDI inflows can improve energy efficiency, as measured by total factor energy efficiency (Ren, Hao, and Wu 2022) and promote regional convergence in energy efficiency (Zhao, Zhang, and Li 2019). These examples also highlight that positive spillovers from FDI on energy are related to the institutional context of the host economies, with more positive effects in high income economies (Dong, Gong, and Zhao 2012). From an energy efficiency perspective, policies to encourage even access to FDI can improve overall efficiency and reduce regional efficiency differences.

Environmental spillovers from FDI can be realized through the adoption of more advanced technologies and better management practices. For example, cleaner production partnerships through FDI have been effective. Hong Kong, China and the Guangdong region successfully introduced cleaner production technologies, by promoting management systems to improve energy efficiency and reduce effluent discharges and production costs (Jiao et al. 2020). Environmental technologies can also be transferred back to the home economy through outward investment, a process referred to as reverse green technology spillovers (Liu et al. 2021; Ren, Hao, and Wu 2022).

While the potential for positive environmental spillovers is large, they may not materialize in the short term. As a short-term strategy for Asia to meet net-zero goals, encouraging FDI in the renewable energy sector may be important. Active investment policies to redirect FDI toward renewables could be part of the region's strategy to meet climate goals. This may offset the negative impact of FDI on other environmental outcomes. It also takes into account the positive impact that FDI may have on energy intensity.

Challenges in Greening Trade and Investment

Pathways toward Cleaner Production and International Trade

Asia needs to intensify national and international efforts to expand energy efficient and emission reducing production capacity and trade. In the short-term, carbon intensity of production and trade could be lowered further by engaging cleaner technologies, where knowledge transfer through regional and international cooperation can play a crucial role. In the mid-to-long term, moving up the value ladder by accelerating industrial transformation into high-end, high value-added manufacturing and services would not only contribute to economic growth but sustainable development. Potential carbon leakage due to heterogeneity in environmental regulations and carbon pricing mechanisms may not be the main source of cross-border CO_2 emission imbalances, but it still calls for stronger multilateral and regional policy cooperation.

Trade and investment need to be part of the climate solution. Trade and investment, while moving goods and services and production capacities across borders, can bring clean technologies and the know-how embedded in them. Insufficient regulatory harmonization and international cooperation, however, could get in the way of streamlining cross-border economic transactions of green technologies and increasing interoperability in key areas for trade such as certification and emissions accounting systems. Lack of price signals for CO_2 emissions also remains a major barrier to providing strong incentives to reduce carbon emissions.

A reduction in emission intensity can be brought about by adopting green technologies to abate carbon emissions. Economies can adopt these technologies through two channels—trade of environmental goods and services, and technology transfer from foreign investment and firms. This can bring down the cost of adopting new green technologies and drive innovation as reflected in the decline in solar photovoltaic panel and wind energy costs (Figure 7.24).

Current Status and Main Challenges

Trade in environmental goods and services have been increasing since 2005. Asia's imports, using the APEC list of environmental goods, have been increasing over the years, and the region has consistently accounted for about 40%–45% of the global imports (Figure 7.22). The Asia total for imports of environmental goods increased from $137 billion in 2006 to $235 billion in 2019, reflecting a rising trend in consumption of environmental goods in the region. As the PRC and the Republic of Korea increased production of these goods, the share of the region's exports has also increased from below 40% in 2006 to almost 50% in 2020. Yet, it is striking that the total value of environmental goods imports and exports globally has remained consistent at about $530 billion in the

last 5 years. As for services trade, using a definition by Sauvage and Timiliotis (2017), as applied in Figure 7.23, the share of environmental services exports in total services exports increased from just under 8% in 2010 to almost 12% in 2020. Similar growth in environmental services imports is also observed. Most of this is driven by the EU economies, with Asia and the Pacific capturing only about 1.7% of services exports and about 1.4% of services imports in the last decade. As a result, the region's share of total environmental services trade has been decreasing and this is in contrast to growth in trade from the EU, non-EU, and North American economies. Most of the environmental services trade in Asia is from Japan, the Republic of Korea, and Singapore.

The price of solar modules has been declining in the top five producing economies, not only in the developed economies—Germany, Japan, and the US—but also in developing Asian economies such as the PRC and the Republic of Korea (Figure 7.24). Indeed, prices of solar modules are converging to below $1 per watt. Trade can enable the spread of low-cost renewable energy and foreign firms can bring these technologies when they enter new markets. Environmental goods such as solar panels and wind turbines can increase the use of green technology, and this can significantly reduce an economy's emission intensity.

Figure 7.22: Total Environmental Goods Imports and Exports by Region ($ billion)

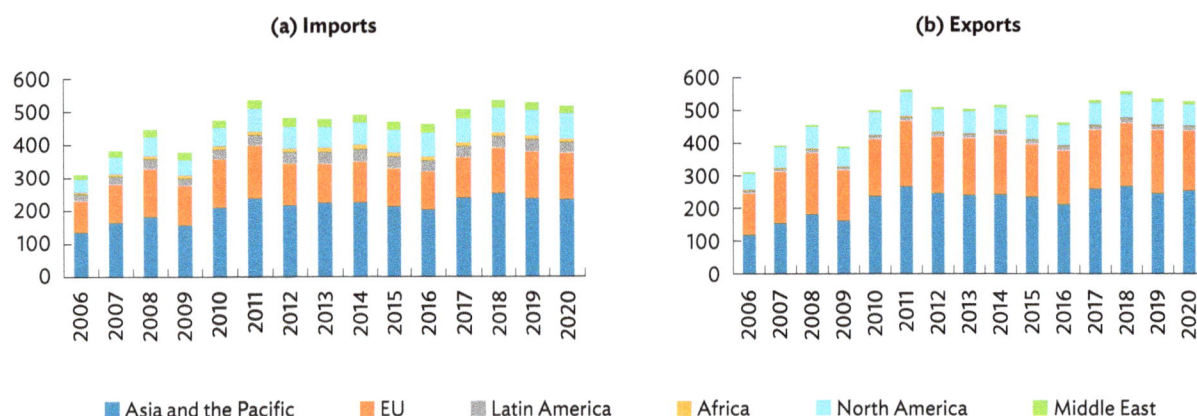

EU = European Union (27 members).

Note: Environmental goods are defined according to the Asia-Pacific Economic Cooperation (APEC) List of Environmental Goods.

Source: ADB calculations using United Nations. Commodity Trade Database. https://comtrade.un.org (accessed August 2022).

Figure 7.23: Share of Regional Environmental Services in Total Imports and Exports (%)

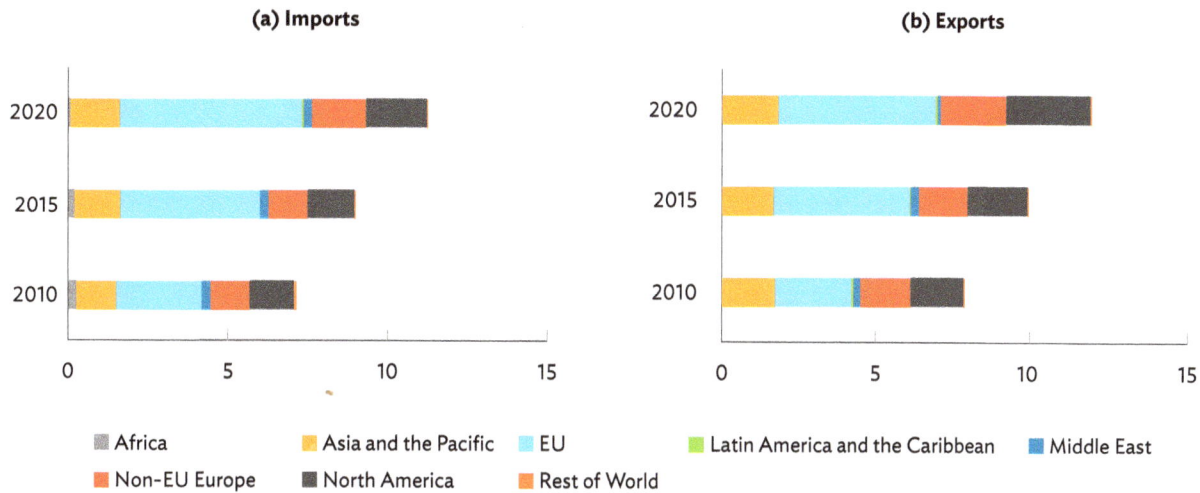

(a) Imports

(b) Exports

Legend: Africa · Asia and the Pacific · EU · Latin America and the Caribbean · Middle East · Non-EU Europe · North America · Rest of World

EU = European Union (27 members).

Note: Environmental services are defined according to the list in Annex 2 of Sauvage and Timiliotis (2017).

Source: ADB calculations using data from World Trade Organization. Statistics on trade in commercial services. https://www.wto.org/english/res_e/statis_e/tradeserv_stat_e.htm (accessed August 2022).

Figure 7.24: Price of Solar Modules in the Top Producing Economies ($ per watt)

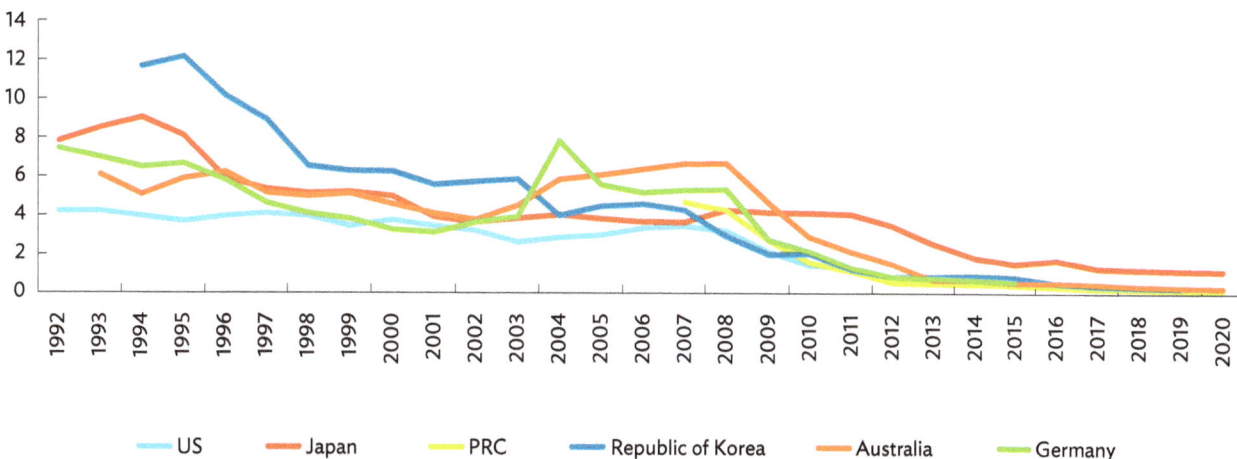

Legend: US · Japan · PRC · Republic of Korea · Australia · Germany

PRC = People's Republic of China, US = United States.

Sources: International Energy Agency Photovoltaic Power Systems Programme (IEA PVPS). National Survey Reports of PV Power Application: Solar Module Prices. https://iea-pvps.org/national-survey-reports/ (accessed November 2022); International Energy Agency Photovoltaic Power Systems Programme (2021); Taghizadeh-Hesary, Yoshino, and Inagaki (2018); and Organisation for Economic Co-operation and Development. OECDstat: Exchange Rates. https://stats.oecd.org/ (accessed November 2022).

Despite the benefit of encouraging more trade in environmental goods, efforts at the international level have stalled and trade barriers remain. Discussions on liberalizing trade in environmental goods and services began in 2001 at the World Trade Organization (WTO) Doha Round and was formalized in 2014 when a group of WTO members started negotiations for the Environmental Goods Agreement. Little has been achieved on this front besides some regional progress through the APEC Vladivostok Declaration on environmental goods, where APEC members agreed to a 5% limit on tariffs on 54 environmental goods by 2015. This commitment, however, is voluntary and unenforceable. More importantly, high income economies already have low import tariffs on these environmental goods compared with lower middle income and low income economies. In the area of services, negotiations are particularly challenging given the difficulty of defining "environmental," which remains ambiguous (Sauvage and Timiliotis 2017).

Asymmetric information about environmental attributes of products and the environmental impacts of enterprises has led to a rise in eco-labeling and certification. Consumers can encourage greening of businesses by rewarding environmentally responsible firms and products. Demand for environmentally friendly products has grown and is expected to increase. However, the institutional frameworks to respond to this demand are still nascent in many Asian economies. Standards and national labeling programs, based on established environmental benefits and with robust verification schemes, transparent standard-setting processes, and scientific validation are relatively recent. Mandatory labeling and information schemes, which have been shown to increase awareness and influence consumer preferences, are uneven across the region. And many small and medium-sized enterprises (SMEs) have limited technical, financial, and organizational capacity to transform their products and processes into more environmentally sound ones to obtain an eco-label.

Export-oriented firms in Asia are seeking certification for their products as an international trade strategy. Supply chain pressures have also been effective in driving green business development. Market demand for environmental goods, services, and technologies from downstream buyers or businesses is growing. Multinational firms are implementing stricter global environmental standards and promoting greener business practices. This has led many upstream businesses in Asia to adopt high-quality environmental management systems. One indicator of this is the rising share of ISO 14001 certificates issued to companies in

Asia, particularly in the PRC (Figures 7.25a and 7.25b), which aim to ensure that companies have a framework for environmental management and control. Some governments have also encouraged green supply chain management through public procurement policies that incentivize domestic SMEs to adopt greener practices.

While more firms in Asia are obtaining certification, the certification needs to involve a broader scope of firms and facilitate green trade. In 2020, Asia had 63% of all businesses with ISO 14001 certificates globally and over 50% of sites where business activities are supported by the certificate (Figure 7.25c). Much of the growth in Asia is in the PRC and to a lesser extent in Japan (Khanna 2020). Notwithstanding this progress, the growing number of ISO 14001 businesses in Asia may not fully reflect the pace of greening businesses since the certificate is voluntary and requires large, fixed costs.[111] Thus, the certificates are best used as a supplementary metric in assessing a firm's environmental management. Moreover, while product certification can be a valuable tool for green trade, it can also be a barrier. Product certification can be costly and increase the regulatory burden on supply chain participants.

Climate change provisions are increasingly important in trade agreements, but further progress can be achieved. The number and level of detail of environmental provisions in regional trade agreements (RTAs) notified to the WTO has increased significantly over the years. According to the TRade and ENvironment Database, and as shown in Figure 7.26a, the average number of environmental provisions included in preferential trade agreements increased dramatically from 2 in 1990 to 87 in 2018. However, Figure 7.26b shows that chapters on environment and climate change are limited in comparison to those dedicated to trade facilitation reforms, with the highest share reported in the Pacific and Oceania, reflecting the vulnerability of the subregion to climate change risks and disasters. While explicit provisions on climate change in RTAs have increased, these are still fewer—and tend to be less detailed—than other types of environmental

---

[111] The costs of an ISO 14001 certification involve staff training, collection of information of past and current activities, consultant and certification fees, and a dedicated staff to ensure compliance.

Figure 7.25: Environment-Related Certifications by Region and in Asia and the Pacific

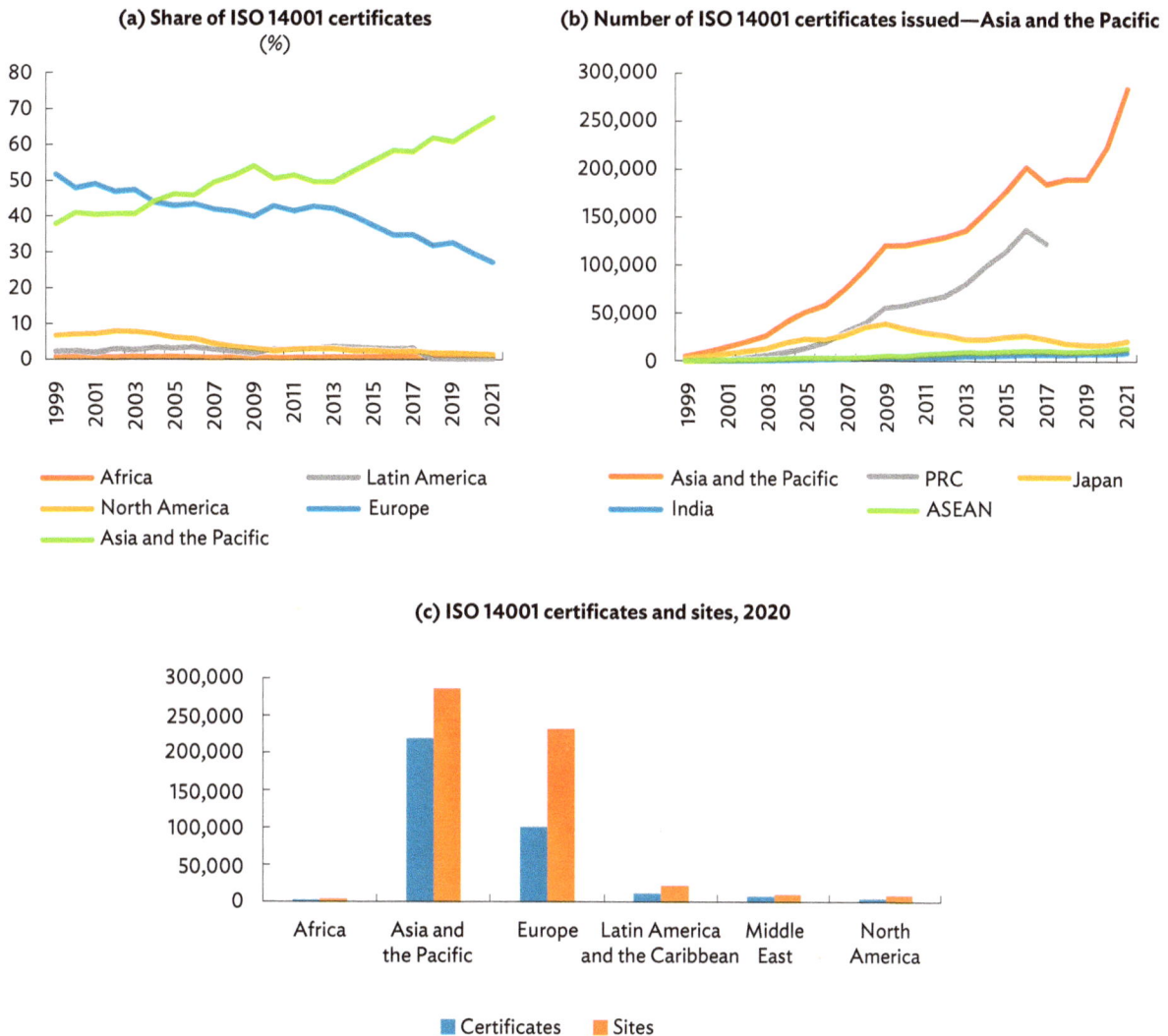

(a) Share of ISO 14001 certificates (%)

(b) Number of ISO 14001 certificates issued—Asia and the Pacific

Legend (a): Africa, North America, Asia and the Pacific, Latin America, Europe

Legend (b): Asia and the Pacific, India, PRC, ASEAN, Japan

(c) ISO 14001 certificates and sites, 2020

Legend (c): Certificates, Sites

Categories: Africa, Asia and the Pacific, Europe, Latin America and the Caribbean, Middle East, North America

ASEAN = Association of Southeast Asian Nations, ISO = International Organization for Standardization, PRC = People's Republic of China.

Notes:

(i) ISO 14001 sets out the criteria for an environmental management system and can be certified to. It maps out a framework that a company or organization can follow to set up an effective environmental management system.

(ii) "Certificates" are the documents issued by ISO when the business demonstrates conformity to the standard. "Sites" are the locations where the business carries out the activity.

Source: ISO. Committee 09: ISO Survey of Certifications to Management System Standards—Full Results. https://isotc.iso.org/livelink/livelink?func=ll&objId=18808772&objAction=browse&viewType=1ISO survey (accessed October 2022).

provisions (WTO 2021). Explicit provisions on climate change are usually complemented by provisions on renewable and alternative energy, the transition to a low emission economy, and institutional arrangements to ensure implementation. Although empirical evidence on the environmental effectiveness of climate change provisions in RTAs is scarce, research suggests that environmental provisions in RTAs reduce emissions

(Baghdadi, Martinez-Zarzoso, and Zitouna 2013; Martinez-Zarzoso and Oueslati 2018).

Asia's international investment agreements contain fewer environmental and climate-change related references than other regions. Less than 10% of bilateral investment treaties in Asia contain environmental and climate-related references

Figure 7.26: Preferential Trade Agreements and Environmental Provisions

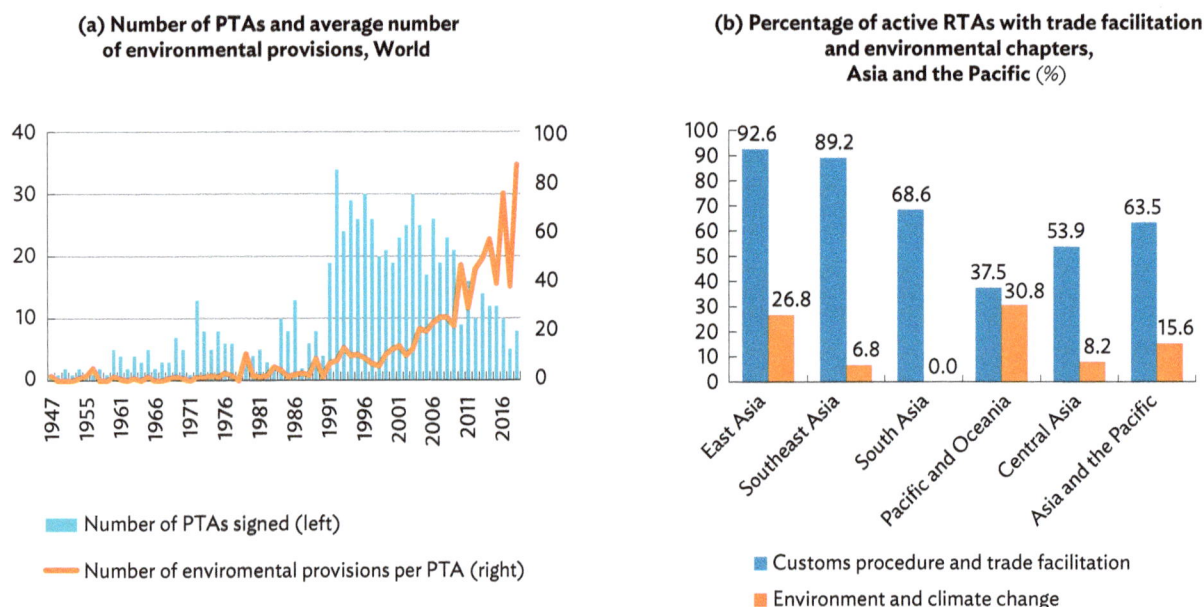

(a) Number of PTAs and average number of environmental provisions, World

- Number of PTAs signed (left)
- Number of enviromental provisions per PTA (right)

(b) Percentage of active RTAs with trade facilitation and environmental chapters, Asia and the Pacific (%)

East Asia: 92.6, 26.8
Southeast Asia: 89.2, 6.8
South Asia: 68.6, 0.0
Pacific and Oceania: 37.5, 30.8
Central Asia: 53.9, 8.2
Asia and the Pacific: 63.5, 15.6

- Customs procedure and trade facilitation
- Environment and climate change

PTA = preferential trade agreement, RTA = regional trade agreement.

Sources: ADB. Asia Regional Integration Center. Free Trade Agreement Database. https://aric.adb.org/database/fta (accessed May 2022); Brandi et al. (2020); Kim et al. (2022); and World Trade Organization. Regional Trade Agreements Database. https://rtais.wto.org/UI/PublicMaintainRTAHome.aspx (accessed May 2022).

(Figure 7.27a). Most of them reserve policy space for environmental regulation and greater environmental cooperation. Other regions show a similar pattern, except for North America. The contrast between Asian regional agreements with investment provisions is stark, as nearly half of them have incorporated climate-related references whether in Asia or in other regions (Figure 7.27b).[112] While intraregional investment agreements in Asia tend to contain fewer environmental references than extraregional ones, agreements incorporating climate measures have been increasing since the early 2000s. India, Japan, Singapore, Azerbaijan, the PRC, and the Republic of Korea have the highest shares of agreements with environmental elements, while Australia relies more on trade agreements to conduct climate policy.

There is growing momentum on the use of carbon pricing instruments to reduce GHG emissions cost-effectively and achieve net-zero targets, however, the region has yet to seize the momentum fully. Worldwide, a total of 68 carbon taxes and emissions trading schemes (ETSs) are operating and three more are scheduled for implementation (World Bank 2022). In Asia and the Pacific, there are six economy-wide direct carbon pricing initiatives that are being implemented. Japan and Singapore employ a carbon tax while Kazakhstan, New Zealand, the Republic of Korea, and the PRC have launched an emissions trading scheme (ETS) (Figure 7.28). In addition, Viet Nam and Indonesia are making significant progress in introducing a carbon price in their jurisdictions (Pangetsu 2022). Despite this progress, several challenges remain for the adoption of effective carbon pricing mechanisms. Carbon taxes may

[112] In this chapter, international investment agreements refer to both bilateral investment treaties (BITs) and regional trade agreements or treaties including investment chapters or investment provisions.

Figure 7.27: International Investment Agreements with Environmental Reference, by Region and Treaty Element
(% share of total)

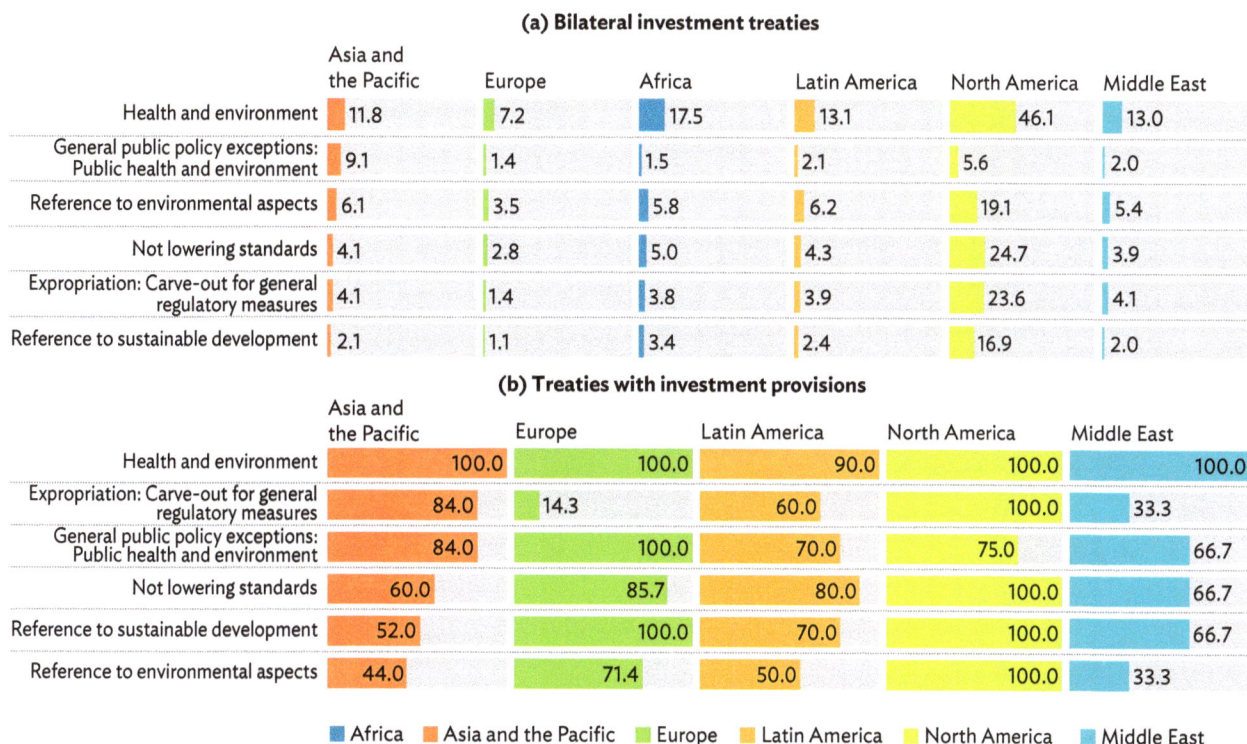

(a) Bilateral investment treaties

	Asia and the Pacific	Europe	Africa	Latin America	North America	Middle East
Health and environment	11.8	7.2	17.5	13.1	46.1	13.0
General public policy exceptions: Public health and environment	9.1	1.4	1.5	2.1	5.6	2.0
Reference to environmental aspects	6.1	3.5	5.8	6.2	19.1	5.4
Not lowering standards	4.1	2.8	5.0	4.3	24.7	3.9
Expropriation: Carve-out for general regulatory measures	4.1	1.4	3.8	3.9	23.6	4.1
Reference to sustainable development	2.1	1.1	3.4	2.4	16.9	2.0

(b) Treaties with investment provisions

	Asia and the Pacific	Europe	Latin America	North America	Middle East
Health and environment	100.0	100.0	90.0	100.0	100.0
Expropriation: Carve-out for general regulatory measures	84.0	14.3	60.0	100.0	33.3
General public policy exceptions: Public health and environment	84.0	100.0	70.0	75.0	66.7
Not lowering standards	60.0	85.7	80.0	100.0	66.7
Reference to sustainable development	52.0	100.0	70.0	100.0	66.7
Reference to environmental aspects	44.0	71.4	50.0	100.0	33.3

■ Africa ■ Asia and the Pacific ■ Europe ■ Latin America ■ North America ■ Middle East

Source: ADB calculations using data from United Nations Conference on Trade and Development (UNCTAD). Investment Policy Hub: International Investment Agreements Navigator. https://investmentpolicy.unctad.org/international-investment-agreements (accessed May 2022).

lack public or political support, have less predictable impacts, and disproportionately affect certain industries or income groups. Cross-border mechanisms are likely to raise trade tensions. On the ETS front, the absence of consistent monitoring and accounting rules, concerns about the quality of carbon credits and environmental integrity in some carbon markets, lack of involvement of local stakeholders, and perverse incentives to lower emission reduction targets are some of the challenges to expanding and implementing the Paris agreement.

How Can Trade and Investment Policies Be Integrated with Climate Action?

Trade and FDI in Asia contribute to CO$_2$ emissions through economic scale, industrial structure, and technological advancement effects. Asian economies are now confronted by the effects of climate change. Economies thus should make trade and investment policies "climate smart" or "climate sensitive" to ensure that trade and FDI can be part of the solution rather than the problem. All else equal, Asia will generate more CO$_2$ emissions and contribute to climate change due to the scale of economic growth and development. It may be more important to consider how economies can tilt the balance toward greener industries and more sustainable production practices. Ultimately, economies are confronted to consider how changes in the relative prices of goods, services, and technology can make production techniques greener.

Policy makers in Asia can focus on four policy areas that support climate action in the context of trade, investment, and climate change:

(i)   Promote trade in environmental goods and services;

Figure 7.28: Carbon Pricing Initiatives Implemented in Asia and the Pacific

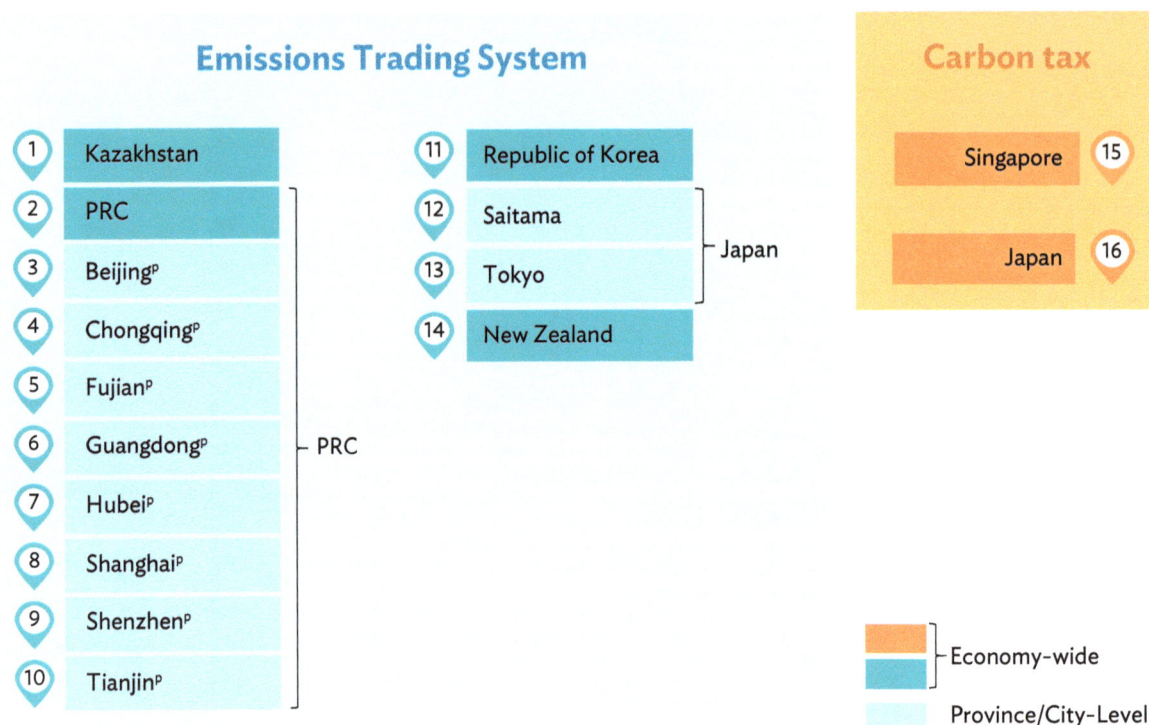

p = pilot, PRC = People's Republic of China.

Note: As of April 2022.

Sources: Duggal (2022); and World Bank. Carbon Pricing Dashboard. https://carbonpricingdashboard.worldbank.org/map_data (accessed January 2023).

(ii)   Nurture green businesses;

(iii) Enhance bilateral, regional, and international regulatory cooperation; and

(iv)   Develop carbon pricing mechanisms (carbon tax, emission trading system, and border carbon adjustment).

Promoting Trade in Environmental Goods and Services

A reduction in emission intensity can be brought about by adopting green technologies to abate carbon emissions. Economies can adopt such technologies through two possible channels—trade in environmental goods and services, and technology transfer from foreign investment and firms. That this can bring down the cost of adopting new green technologies and drive innovation is reflected in the decline in solar photovoltaic panel and wind energy costs (Figure 7.24).

Efforts at the international level should be reinforced to lower trade barriers on environmental goods and services. In a simple partial equilibrium study, De Melo and Solleder (2022) show that import volumes by low-income economies can rise by 5.8% if tariff rates on the APEC list of environmental goods are halved and by 14.7% if tariffs are fully eliminated. In addition, environmental services such as sanitation, environmental protection, engineering, and scientific services are crucial inputs to climate mitigation efforts. For instance, even with lower cost solar panels, their placement and installation will still require firms to pay for engineering consulting services that may be scarce and expensive. APEC leaders have recently reaffirmed their commitments to freer trade of environmental services during the 2021 APEC Ministerial Meeting. Noting that "these services are now more important than ever to prevent, protect against and remedy environmental degradation" (APEC 2021a), the ministers endorsed the Reference List of Environmental and Environmentally Related Services based on the CPC

2.1 classification (APEC 2021b). However, encouraging trade of environmental goods will require going beyond the list of environmental goods and services that receive some form of preferential treatment.

Expanding the list of environmental goods and services based on a global value chain approach is critical to promote greener trade. The APEC list of environmental goods is the only negotiated list of environmental goods. Used as the basis for WTO negotiations on the Environmental Goods Agreement, it consists of only 54 products at the HS-6 product code level and broadly corresponds to three categories: renewable energy production, environmental monitoring analysis and assessment, and waste management and systems.[113] There are few or no goods to manage energy efficiency and resource efficiency. APEC has considered adding 21 new environmental goods to the list (APEC 2021c), but adoption remains voluntary among members. Further efforts are therefore needed to expand the list by adopting a global value chain approach that takes into account not only final goods but also raw materials, services and intermediate inputs, including waste and recycling (APEC 2021c).

Agreeing on a common definition of environmental goods is challenging. The list-based approach followed by APEC and the WTO has some limitations and challenges (Aisbett et al. 2022). The approach crucially relies on readily observable physical characteristics of goods and depends on there being unambiguous alignment between such physical characteristics and environmental impact (for example, solar panels or wind turbine components). Defining the product at the broad HS 6-digit level code invariably leads to the inclusion of both environmental and nongreen goods, or could include dual-use goods (such as tanks that store fossil fuels or green hydrogen) that are economy- and context-specific. Given also that green technologies are rapidly

changing, what may be agreed to be "environmentally preferred" and considered appropriate for inclusion in the list may not stay relevant in the future. Finally, the current lists of goods are mostly industrial goods of interest to advanced industrial economies and producing economies such as the PRC and do not include sustainable agricultural goods that might be more useful to developing economies.

An alternative to a list-based approach is to follow a general definition of an environmental good. The OECD and Eurostat (the Statistical Office of the European Communities) have developed a general definition of an environmental industry that includes activities to limit or reduce environmental damage to water, air and soil, and technologies, products, and services that preclude environmental risks or minimize pollution (OECD and Eurostat 1999).[114] The definitional approach also has its limitations, in particular being based on the process and production methods (PPMs) of the good, which does not leave identifiable characteristics on the product itself and can be burdensome to prove.

In overcoming negotiating challenges, in the short term, economies may consider a combination of different options as a way forward for the liberalization of trade in environmental goods.

- **Unilateral liberalization.** Since liberalization of trade in environmental goods provides dual wins, jurisdictions can undertake it without the need for reciprocal treatment, as a priority over negotiating delays in an attempt to extract concessions from trading partners. A unilateral approach allows lists of environmental goods to be tailored to the specific circumstances of the liberalizer, and of being easier to amend in light of ongoing technological change. As an illustration, the UK has adopted this approach,

[113] The WTO Environmental Goods Agreement negotiations have identified between 300 and 400 potential HS6 product categories and 10 sectors for preferential liberalization, but negotiations have stalled.

[114] The full definition of an environmental industry by the OECD and Eurostat is "activities which produce goods and services to measure, prevent, limit, minimise or correct environmental damage to water, air and soil as well as problems related to waste, noise and eco systems. Clean technologies, processes, products and services which reduce environmental risks and minimise pollution and material use are also considered part of the environmental industry" (OECD and Eurostat 1999).

eliminating tariffs on over 100 environmental goods since leaving the EU. A successful implementation of unilateral liberalization is nevertheless conditional on the capacity of the implementing economy to conduct adequate life cycle or process and production method-based assessments. In the longer run, it will also be important to ensure consistency (or at a minimum, interoperability) with the approaches of trading partners in the application of other forms of trade and climate governance, including certification schemes.

- **Deep regulatory collaboration** with a relatively small group of like-minded jurisdictions for the development of common definitions of environmental goods or emission accounting systems, can help overcome the downsides to unilateral approaches and reduce nontariff barriers (NTBs). This could involve anything from the detailed assessment of proposed environmental goods, as is the case in the Agreement on Climate Change, Trade and Sustainability, through to codevelopment of embedded emissions accounting frameworks and agreed definitions of environmental goods, as is being discussed for the Australia–Singapore Green Economy Agreement (Steenblik and Droege 2019). Regulatory collaboration is particularly important to reduce the potential for embedded emissions accounting systems and certification schemes to become significant NTBs if not developed collaboratively to maximize consistency and interoperability.

- **Targeted collaboration** on specific groups of goods associated to the net-zero transition, in the line of the APEC Scoping Study on New and Emerging Environmental Goods provides a valid way forward. This could be supplemented with more complex and rigorous approaches to specific goods that are of high importance but have important process and production method considerations, such as for example, hydrogen and derivatives. Different ways of making hydrogen and ammonia have dramatically different emissions implications—with some so polluting that the life-cycle implications are on par

or worse than the fossil fuels they replace. The EU has previously recommended certification to identify environmental goods in this sort of situation.

Nurturing Green Businesses

With better access to green technologies, goods, and services, it will be less costly for businesses to be less carbon intensive. The environmental market in Asia is growing and there are more businesses adopting systems for environmental management and resource-use efficiency and reducing the environmental impact of their production (Khanna 2020). To facilitate this trend, policy makers could employ both regulatory measures and market-based mechanisms. It is important to consider the advantages and disadvantages of regulatory approaches such as environmental laws, regulations and standards, and market-based mechanisms such as emission trading systems and carbon taxes. The section below examines some of these aspects. Regulatory measures could often expand trade opportunities and enhance interoperability but can also impose trade barriers at the same time. Important factors in adopting carbon-reducing mechanisms include their flexibility, level of ambition, and comparability with other economic mechanisms. Some evidence suggest market-based mechanisms are more likely to meet these criteria better. They could allow companies to plan ahead their production and emissions paths and envisage more ambitious goals for climate action via voluntary actions and cooperation.[115]

Regulation and Policy Incentives

Environmental laws and regulations have been effective in regulating pollution and inducing a switch to renewables and other less-polluting inputs. Renewable energy standards, tax credits, and low-cost financing led to growth in renewable energy use in developed economies. A combination of stringent regulations, encouraging environmental self-regulation among firms, and providing regulatory relief and

---

[115]   One concern with the use of regulatory approaches rather than market-based mechanisms is the difficulty to quantify the implicit cost resulting from the regulations. While some methodologies have been developed in this direction (Dang and Mourougane [2014] present a literature review), these costs are notoriously variable and difficult to estimate.

public recognition for such efforts has been effective for greening businesses in developed economies. Typically, regulations tend to be of the command and control type, which limit incentives for pollution abatement and innovation in green technologies. Other mechanisms, such as performance-based standards, market-based instruments, and responsible business systems have been more effective in promoting energy transition. Increasing public scrutiny, public disclosure programs, and other nonregulatory mechanisms have also encouraged companies to improve environmental performance (ADB 2020a).

Innovation to design new technologies that lower pollution and increase resource efficiency will be key. Many economies in the region need to catch up with innovation through adoption and adaptation of existing green technologies and indigenous technology development. Research and development policy incentives to innovate in the environmental sectors, curbing policy distortions on free trade in clean technologies, and removing subsidies on fossil fuels can help accelerate the pace of green technology innovation. Stringent but flexible environmental regulations can also induce innovation and increase competitiveness.

Certification can be critical to make trade greener and inform how products contribute to mitigating environmental or climate change challenges. The fundamental motivation for certification is to correct information failures for consumers regarding the attributes of a certain product. They are particularly prevalent where process and production methods endow the product with attributes that are difficult or impossible to verify based on the characteristics of the final product. Market participants can include private buyers with supply chain decarbonization commitments, investors with "green investment" requirements, and governments seeking to ensure that markets deliver particular policy objectives such as emissions targets through regulatory and/or incentive schemes. The case of hydrogen is an example of recent progress in developing certification (Box 7.4).

While certification can be an important tool to help facilitate green trade, it also has substantial potential to become an NTB. The balance between trade facilitation and trade inhibition depends on good design choices and targeted regulatory collaboration. While product certification can be valuable in facilitating green trade, it also has potential costs. Obtaining certification inevitably places a regulatory burden on supply chain participants, ultimately increasing costs for consumers. This burden can become large enough that certain suppliers are unable to service markets, and certification becomes an NTB to trade. To avoid unnecessary costs, several aspects need to be considered in certification design and implementation.

Box 7.4: Certification and Net-Zero Goals: The Case of Hydrogen

Hydrogen is the most prominent example of a product for which certification schemes to support trade are under development. Accurate and reliable certification of climate mitigation credentials for such products is particularly important because hydrogen production can be very polluting. Whether derived directly from fossil fuels or by electrolysis using electricity with high embedded emissions, replacing fossil fuels with dirty hydrogen products can be as bad, or worse, than business as usual (Longden et al. 2022). On the other hand, genuine renewable hydrogen with clean supply chains can be a major tool in efforts

to mitigate climate change (IRENA 2021). Certification can support other regulatory and policy efforts such as preferential liberalization of environmental goods.

For hydrogen certification, a requirement that renewable electricity needs to meet European Union (EU) Renewable Energy Directive II (RED II) may be challenging to translate to non-EU jurisdictions. Refining evolving European certification schemes requires particular care to ensure that RED II equivalence is applied in ways that do not introduce biased or arbitrary barriers based on producer geographic location.

Source: Aisbett et al. (2022).

Certification scheme design includes decisions in multiple dimensions. These criteria include boundaries of what processes and scope will be included in environmental accounting; whether the scheme will certify that a product has cleared a threshold or the quality of information about the product; whether the public or private sector will run the scheme; whether it will be mandatory or voluntary; and whether certification will be required to be performed by a third party. Table 7.1 compares these features across several schemes. The following sections describe each design feature with further examples.

A certification scheme with lower regulatory burden is preferable. In a competitive market, regulatory compliance costs will be passed on to consumers, raising the costs of the energy transition. Furthermore, if a scheme has a high regulatory burden, then some producers may be excluded. This is likely to disproportionately affect small producers and producers in economies that lack existing regulatory infrastructure. While private/voluntary certification schemes can cause market access problems for some producers, public/mandatory schemes are more likely to constitute a technical barrier to trade in the eyes of global trade rules. A balance and some degree of flexibility in how supply

Table 7.1: Examples of Low-Emissions or Green Certification Schemes

Scheme Owner	Product(s)	Supply Chain Coverage	Public/Private	Threshold/ Information	Mandatory/ Voluntary	Third Party?
CertifHy Phase II	Hydrogen	Well-to-gate (factory)	Public–private	Threshold	Voluntary	Third party
Government of Australia	Hydrogen	Well-to-gate (factory)	Public	Information	Voluntary	Third party
Government of the People's Republic of China	Hydrogen	Cradle-to-gate (factory)	Public	Threshold	Voluntary	Third party
Vietnam Green Label Scheme (Huyen 2016)	Paper, laptops, batteries, printers, ceramic building materials, hair care products, soap, architectural coating products, laundry detergent, dishwashing detergent, shopping bags, food packaging, fluorescent lightbulbs, printer cartridges	Cradle-to-grave	Public	Threshold	Voluntary	Third party
Philippine Energy Labeling Program (Government of the Philippines, Department of Energy 2022)	Energy-consuming products, including refrigeration systems, air conditioners, and televisual and lighting products	Cradle-to-gate	Public	Information	Voluntary	Third party
Japan Eco Mark (Eco Mark Office 2022; Huong 2016)	511 product categories, including office equipment, furniture, electric products, construction materials, household items and services	Cradle-to-grave	Public–private	Threshold	Voluntary	Third party
Korean Eco-Labelling Program (Huong 2016)	165 product categories, including office equipment, furniture, electric products, construction materials, household items, and automobile-related goods	Cradle-to-grave	Public	Threshold	Voluntary	Third party
Government of the Republic of Korea (Proposed) (Stangarone 2021)	Hydrogen	Well-to-gate (factory)	Public	Threshold	Voluntary	Third party

Source: Aisbett et al. (2022).

chain participants prove they meet scheme requirements is inherent to avoiding implicit discrimination.

Mandatory certification is more likely as national emissions commitments become more stringent. Following the European example, jurisdictions may use tradable certificates to track progress toward emission reduction goals. Only certificates recognized by jurisdictional regulations will contribute toward official emissions goals. The EU Renewable Energy Directive II (RED II) represents one such scenario, where hydrogen guarantee of origin certificates will be used as a mechanism to track progress toward emission reduction goals (Barth et al. 2019). The Republic of Korea's Renewable Portfolio Standard Scheme, pursuant to its 2012 Renewable Energy Act, is emerging and is expected to help the economy reach its 2050 Carbon Neutrality Scenario (Seol, Kim, and Lee 2022).

Multiple certification schemes can be costly in the long term. If different markets use different and noninteroperable certification systems, supply chain participants may face higher regulatory burdens (Daugbjerg 2012). Issues arising from multiple certification schemes are not merely theoretical. Numerous certification schemes for hydrogen and its derivatives are emerging in jurisdictions that are aiming to be either producers or consumers of these products, with many being developed by industry associations. The multidimensional design choices discussed previously illustrate the vast potential for rules of different schemes to diverge. As of now, there is little chance of a uniform global hydrogen standard or certification scheme in the short to medium term.

Development finance institutions and multilateral development banks will have a key role to play in catalyzing sustainable finance in Asia to support green businesses—particularly in developing economies. Given their convening power and experience, these institutions can help to develop

---

Box 7.5: Innovative Approaches to Climate Financing and Catalyzing Private Sector Investments

Multilateral development banks and bilateral partners will have to be innovative to encourage more private sector participation in climate financing.

The Asian Development Bank (ADB) is partnering with the private sector to catalyze more climate financing in two initiatives. The first is Project Regeneration, a partnership with Singapore's sovereign wealth fund Temasek, HSBC, and Clifford Capital Holdings. Project Regeneration aims to solve critical bankability issues by addressing policy and regulatory constraints and source concessional financing for sustainable infrastructure. Its initial focus on Indonesia and Viet Nam is to mobilize private sector capital for renewable energy, water and waste, and sustainable transport projects. The second initiative is the Climate Innovation and Development Fund, a $25 million blended finance facility supported by ADB, the Bloomberg Family Foundation, and the Goldman Sachs Charitable Gift Fund. It will support the clean energy transition in South Asia and Southeast Asia, initially focusing on India and Indonesia.

Another innovative scheme is the Energy Transition Mechanism (ETM), which ADB is piloting in Southeast

Asia to accelerate the move out of coal to clean energy. The ETM was launched in November 2021 at COP26 to create scalable and collaborative investment facilities for energy transition. It has three goals: the early retirement of coal-fired power plants; scaling up clean, renewable energy solutions; and ensuring the transition is just and affordable. Concessional funds can mobilize large amounts of private financing, creating a pool of low-cost capital to retire or repurpose coal plants. It can simultaneously unleash new investment in clean energy, the electricity grid, and energy storage. Economy-specific ETM funds will be supported by donor funds and capital from private institutional investors, international finance institutions, and other public or private sources. Feasibility studies have been conducted for Indonesia, the Philippines, and Viet Nam to develop optimal business models and transaction structures. Once scaled up, ETM has potential to be the largest carbon reduction model in the world. For example, if 50% of coal power plants can be retired over the next 10–15 years in Indonesia, the Philippines, and Viet Nam, then 200 million tonnes of carbon dioxide emissions per year will be removed—equivalent to taking 61 million cars off the road.

Source: ADB staff based on ADB (2021c); ADB. Energy Transition Mechanism. https://www.adb.org/what-we-do/energy-transition-mechanism-etm (accessed August 2022).

investable projects, reassure investors, and use their financial resources to reduce risks for other investors. Furthermore, they can initiate innovative approaches that could help to attract private investors and broaden the investor base (Box 7.5).

Bilateral, Regional, and International Cooperation

Leveraging on national efforts to cultivate the ground for environmental goods and services production and trade through technological development and streamlined procedures, regional cooperation is essential for the development of a green and sustainable trading system. Facilitating trade in environmental goods, ensuring interoperability and regulatory coherence, and fostering green investments are key areas for action.

While Asia's regional trade agreements (RTAs) are gradually embracing environmental provisions, more efforts should be made to strengthen their coverage and depth, to contribute more to making trade greener and reducing CO_2 emissions (Abman, Lundberg, and Ruta 2021; Baghdadi, Martinez-Zarzoso, and Zitouna 2013; Brandi et al. 2020; Martinez-Zarzoso and

Oueslati 2018). Exploring new innovative avenues for international cooperation including through the green economy agreements will also help forge focused and deep collaborative arrangements in addressing common climate challenges. International investment agreements can also promote climate action by affecting investment decisions. However, many international investment agreements by Asian economies have yet to mainstream climate change related issues. As investment frameworks become more ambitious in climate policy, policy makers may consider introducing substantive standards on environmental protection and access to investor–state dispute mechanisms in climate-related cases. New generation international investment agreements could also consider facilitating market access and investment facilitation in green industries.

Breaking through the Barriers

Interoperability of certification systems could be a pathway to lowering regulatory burden and facilitating trade conditional on consistent accounting of embedded emissions (Box 7.6). Embedded emissions—emissions over the supply chain or parts thereof—are a central part of certification aimed at supporting net-zero transition. Alignment

---

Box 7.6: Toward Consistent Methodologies for the Calculation of Embedded Emissions

Consistent methodologies for the calculation of embedded emissions are an important step toward interoperability. Where methodologies for calculating emissions within each module can be considered equivalent across certification schemes, emissions estimates from supply chain modules across jurisdictions can be combined to calculate the total embedded emissions within the certification scheme boundary. Basing modules on national carbon accounting methodologies is consistent with the modular approach and could support cross-border supply chain embedded emissions calculations (Reeve and Aisbett 2022).

Jurisdictions including Australia, Singapore, and the European Union are currently investigating or developing public embedded emissions accounting frameworks. These can provide the embedded emissions accounting basis for both public and private certification schemes in these jurisdictions, and so support the interoperability of schemes within jurisdictions. Regulatory collaboration to align these frameworks across jurisdictions can further enhance interoperability. Examples of where such collaboration is either happening or planned include the Australia–Singapore Green Economy Agreement, the Joint US–EU Statement on Trade in Steel and Aluminum, and the International Partnership for the Hydrogen Economy.

Source: Aisbett et al. (2022).

of embedded emissions accounting boundaries is a fundamental requirement if certification schemes are to be interoperable. Interoperability can best be supported by taking a modular approach to boundary definition for embedded emissions accounting (White et al. 2021). The modular approach means that embedded emissions are calculated for the distinct "modules" comprising the supply chain. The total embedded emissions for any chosen certification scheme boundary are then calculated by adding the emissions from the relevant modules.

Mutual recognition agreements (MRAs) for conformity assessments can facilitate access to markets. MRAs for conformity assessment should be differentiated from the mutual recognition principle/automatic mutual recognition.[116] Automatic mutual recognition implies that the certification system in a first jurisdiction is also recognized in its entirety as valid in a second jurisdiction, and vice versa. In this case, goods or service providers do not have to register or certify again beyond their home jurisdiction. For example, if there was a mutual recognition for low-emissions hydrogen certification between Bhutan and the Republic of Korea, hydrogen certified as low emissions in Bhutan could be marketed and sold as such in the Republic of Korea and vice versa. MRAs are government-to-government agreements that can be used when full equivalence (mutual recognition) or other forms of interoperability cannot be achieved. MRAs establish procedures that enable parties to recognize each other's competent conformity assessment bodies and to accept their results for regulatory purposes (NIST 2020). While specific MRAs among Asian economies for environmental goods are still very early in development, experiences from Europe's Implementation of Mutual Recognition Agreements on conformity assessment and the Protocol on European Conformity Assessment Document and from the US for other types of products, could provide useful examples (EU 1998; NIST 2020). Even when

certification systems are not interoperable, MRAs can significantly decrease regulatory burdens by allowing a single verification by a given conformity assessment body to provide the information required for multiple certification schemes.[117]

The Important Role of Trade Agreements

Regional trade agreements can foster greener trade through various channels, including environmental, climate change mitigation, and trade facilitation provisions. The drastic increase in environmental provisions in regional trade agreements over the last 3 decades (Figure 7.30) contributed to removing barriers to climate-friendly goods and services, and facilitating the adoption of green technologies. Complemented by provisions on alternative energy or net-zero transition goals, trade agreements also outline other areas for climate mitigation. Trade facilitation efforts supported by relevant trade agreement chapters can also reduce waiting time at ports and border-crossing points, thereby reducing transport congestion and GHG emissions from idle vehicles. Policy reforms, such as increased transparency, simplified customs procedures, and improved border agency coordination, offer the opportunity to lower GHG emissions by reducing delays at the border, particularly at land borders. Delays or slow movement of vehicles crossing borders can significantly increase air pollution. For example, the California-Baja California land border crossing is reported to result in an average of 457 metric tonnes of CO_2 emissions each day, equivalent to consumption of more than 51,400 gallons of gasoline (NBC San Diego 2021). Computer modeling, estimating emissions from trucks at the US–Mexico border in 2015, found that the improved efficiency of customs and inspection processes can lower GHG emission by 31%–36%. Emissions go up significantly when the traffic volumes go up at the border (Reyna et al. 2016).

---

[116]   The EU Commission states on its website that "the mutual recognition principle should not be mistaken for mutual recognition agreements that facilitate access to markets between the EU and non-EU economies" (European Commission. Single Market and Standards: Mutual Recognition of Goods. https://single-market-economy.ec.europa.eu/single-market/goods/free-movement-sectors/mutual-recognition-goods_en).

[117]   Certification systems are interoperable when at least some of the information from one scheme can be used toward meeting the requirements of another.

Among the trade facilitation measures in the WTO Agreement, digital trade facilitation has the highest potential impact in mitigating carbon emissions. The indicative impact of trade facilitation measures on climate change is summarized in Annex 7a.[118] This highlights the importance of accelerating the digitalization of trade. Digital trade facilitation measures, or paperless trade, can limit transportation for physical delivery and lower time and transaction costs, thereby reducing GHG emissions. Duval and Hardy (2021) estimate that going paperless could eliminate between 9 million and 23 million tonnes of CO_2 emissions annually in Asia and the Pacific. These estimates, however, do not account for other indirect CO_2 emissions from the electricity used to maintain the servers needed for paperless trade. In addition, the saving of 23 million tonnes of CO_2 emissions, while large, is still miniscule compared with the 17 billion tonnes of CO_2 annual emissions by Asia. Most importantly, the overall impact of trade facilitation on CO_2 emissions remains unclear as gross trade volumes will increase while the emission intensity of trade will decline.[119]

More efforts are needed to strengthen the RTAs' greening function through broader and deeper commitments to climate action. While RTAs have increasingly acknowledged the importance of environmental sustainability, environmental provisions are limited in scope and depth for developing Asian economies. Climate change provisions in Asian RTAs have increased from 0 in 2002 to 61 in 2022 (34% of RTAs involving Asian economies).[120] Looking ahead, expanding their coverage and depth, including on implementation and enforcement matters, will be useful to ensure their effectiveness in achieving climate goals.

Economies could also consider incorporating a separate chapter in RTAs on climate change and the environment instead of having various provisions scattered across multiple chapters to enhance the transparency and clarity of commitments.

Environment chapters in trade and economic partnership agreements have been a feature of many so-called deep trade agreements (DTAs). Globally, 274 such agreements and 84 involving Asian economies contain environment chapters.[121] These chapters in DTAs differ from so-called joint statements of intent, a more general, entry level form of collaboration. Environment chapters in DTAs have standing in international law and are more binding and detailed than joint statements of intent. The downside is that substantially greater government resources are required to negotiate them. In practice, however, many of the provisions in the environment chapters of DTAs are declaratory. Environment chapters in modern DTAs also address the goal of expanding consumer rights and social welfare obligations on exporters. However, the emphasis on constraint rather than creation limits the usefulness of many existing DTAs as tools for an international green industrial policy (Aisbett 2022). Another initiative is the Agreement on Climate Change, Trade and Sustainability, whose negotiating parties include Fiji and New Zealand. Despite the title, this is a relatively traditional trade agreement approach focusing on tariff elimination on environmental goods and services, disciplining fossil fuel subsidies through trade mechanisms, and establishing voluntary eco-labeling guidelines. These three objectives sit comfortably within the scope of DTAs as they do not emphasize shared supply chains or novel technologies/industries.

---

[118]   The relative ranking of measures reported in Annex 7a only provides a cursory preview into the whole trade facilitation and climate change scenario. This qualitative assessment is not based on quantitative estimates of the absolute intensive and extensive impact of these measures and should therefore not be taken as the be-all and end-all. A comprehensive economic modeling is needed to evaluate and capture the complex relationships and dynamic effects of trade facilitation on climate change through trade.

[119]   Empirical studies have found that further trade liberalization can increase GHG emissions. Using a comprehensive panel data, Managi (2004) derived an elasticity of 0.579 on the impact of trade liberalization to GHG emissions. Similarly, Corong (2008) showed that a tariff reduction imposed by the Philippines brought an increase of 0.12% in carbon emissions. By reducing trade costs, trade facilitation can potentially have a similar impact as tariff elimination. A simulation conducted by ADB and UNESCAP find that full implementation of both binding and nonbinding measures of the WTO Trade Facilitation Agreement reduces trade costs by 7% (ADB 2021d). Trade facilitation will also have implications for export participation of economies (Lee, Rocha, and Ruta 2021).

[120]   ADB calculation based on the TRade and ENvironment Database, including 14 variables on climate change.

[121]   Computed based on data from World Bank. Deep Trade Agreements: Data, Tools, and Analysis. https://datatopics.worldbank.org/dta/ (accessed September 2022). Asia includes Australia; Bangladesh; Brunei Darussalam; India; Indonesia; Japan; Malaysia; New Zealand; the Philippines; Singapore; the Republic of Korea; Taipei,China; Thailand; and Viet Nam.

Change through International Investment

Economies in the region are slowly committing to improving their investment policy frameworks in response to climate change. International investment agreements (IIAs) are now seen as policy tools for guiding climate policy in foreign investment. In the absence of specific environmental provisions in IIAs, the gradual introduction of references related to climate change underpins the growing need to fill the gap for states and investors. Climate-related litigation is also on the rise, stressing the need for aligning IIAs with net-zero commitments. Over 100 investor–state dispute settlement cases involved fossil fuel industries, many of them involving large awards (UNCTAD 2022). However, the current framework is not yet well aligned with the decarbonization agenda. Existing treaties may divert investments toward climate-risky projects by providing insurance against possible government climate action and by dissuading governments to take climate action in the first place (Aisbett et al. 2018). Also, emission-intensive investments are more prone to seek protection through IIAs.

While environmental and climate dimensions in new generation investment agreements are more common, their scope remains limited. Many trade agreements and investment chapters in recent free trade agreements contain environmental provisions describing formal commitments and cooperation to enforce environmental laws (Monteiro 2016).[122] In IIAs, references are often made to reserving policy space for environmental regulation, expropriation, not lowering environmental standards to attract investment, environmental disputes and investor–state dispute settlement, environmental impact assessments, and support for environmental cooperation. To the extent that governments adequately incorporate these aspects in investment provisions, they can make commitments more binding in the wake of the Paris Agreement. In the case of Asia, such aspects are concentrated in a few provisions, which often grant extensive rights to the investors (Figure 7.29). Empirical analysis based on ADB's IIA database suggests that the inclusion of environmental references in bilateral investment treaties (BITs) could have a positive effect on FDI flows, particularly in non-carbon intensive industries (Box 7.7).

Figure 7.29: International Investment Agreements with Environmental Reference, by Provision

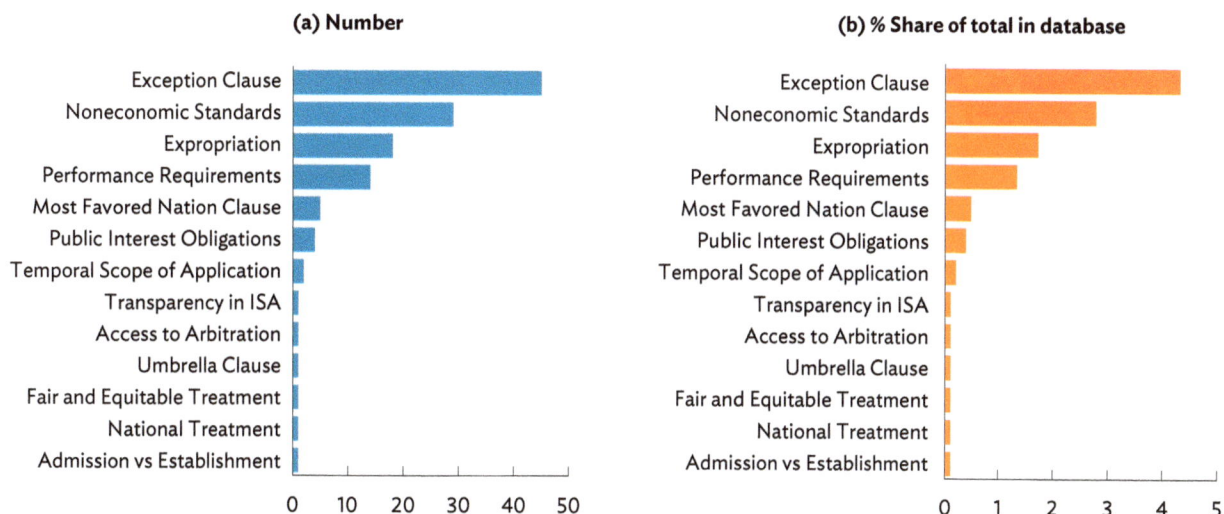

(a) Number

(b) % Share of total in database

BIT = bilateral investment treaty, ISA = investor–state arbitration.

Note: The total number of BITs in ADB's database on international investment agreements is 1,044.

Source: ADB calculations using data from ADB. International Investment Agreement Database. https://aric.adb.org/database/iias (accessed May 2022).

[122]   Recent instruments such as Norway's Model Bilateral Investment Treaty or the Japan–Switzerland Free Trade Agreement contain detailed preambular language, a general exception clause, and a right to regulate clause, which express a commitment to replace sustainable development at the core of international investment law.

Box 7.7: Assessing the Investment Effects of Environmental and Climate Change Elements of International Investment Agreements

Analysis on the effects of climate change and environmental-related provisions in international investment agreements is relatively recent. While literature on the role of the agreements has suggested some positive impact on foreign direct investment (FDI) flows (Busse, Königer, and Nunnenkamp 2010; Neumayer and Spess 2005), some studies suggest the effect is comparable to regional and preferential trade agreements (Heid and Vozzo 2020; Kox and Rojas-Romagosa 2020). Recent work also explores the causal effect of investment regimes on foreign direct investment (FDI) flows (Bhagwat, Brogaard, and Julio 2021; Falvey and Foster-McGregor 2017; Strezhnev 2018). Most of these studies, however, focus on the aggregate impact of international investment agreements on FDI.

We explore this question through a difference-in-difference approach to assess the role of newly enforced agreements, including environmental elements. We use FDI firm-level data from fDi Markets and Zephyr, and textual analysis from investment provisions in ADB's International Investment Agreement database for Asia and the Pacific, which includes bilateral investment treaties (BITs) and investment chapters in regional trade agreements. A treatment variable is defined for BITs that were terminated and replaced by a new BIT including environmental references (box figure 1). An initial comparison of average green FDI flows in the treated and control groups suggests an increase around the time of the signing of the new treated BITs (box figure 2).

1: Pretreatment and Posttreatment Periods of Treated Economy-Pairs

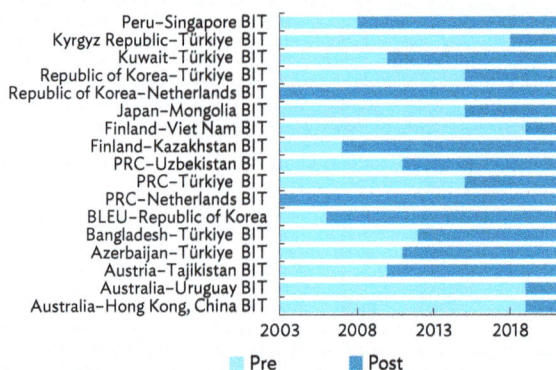

2: Average FDI Flows (Logged), by Treated and Control Groups

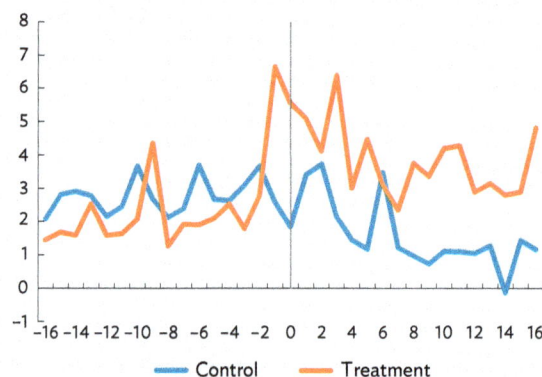

BIT = bilateral investment treaty, BLEU = Belgium–Luxembourg Economic Union, FDI = foreign direct investment, PRC = People's Republic of China.

Notes: Time period for treated and control group readjusted, with the treatment year being set to time = 0. For treatment group, green FDI flows were averaged across economy-pairs before and after the treatment year. The same procedure is applied for the control group.

Source: Avendano et al. (2022).

Our estimation method draws from the recent literature using a difference-in-difference model to tease out a causal impact of BITs, expressed as:

$$FDI_{ijt} = a_{ij} + b_t + \delta Env\_BIT_{ijt} + \beta \mathbf{X}_{ijt} + \epsilon_{ijt}$$

Where FDI_{ijt} pertains to the log + 1 of FDI flows by entry mode (M&A and greenfield) and type (total FDI and non-carbon intensive FDI as previously defined in this chapter) from economy i to economy j, a_{ij} corresponds to panel fixed effects (i.e., reporter, partner), b_t corresponds to the time fixed effects, and Env_BIT_{ijt} is the treatment variable, which takes the value of 1 if a terminated BIT is replaced with a BIT with environmental reference and 0 (control

group) otherwise. The control group is defined by economy-pair observations involving at least one BIT member where no change in policy (i.e., inclusion of environmental elements in BIT) was observed.[a] Meanwhile, $\mathbf{X}$ pertains to a vector of additional control variables, with the set akin to Falvey and Foster-McGregor (2017). In particular, a measure of bilateral economic size (i.e., $\ln(GDP_{it} + GDP_{jt})$), and a dummy for preferential trade agreement is included. Multilateral resistance is captured through the inclusion of time-varying fixed effects (e.g., reporter-year, partner-year). As an alternative and sensitivity check, multilateral resistance terms as introduced in Baier and Bergstrand (2009) were also applied.

continued on next page

Box 7.7 continued

Results shown in the table suggest that the inclusion of climate change and environmental elements in BITs has a moderate but positive effect on FDI flows. Baseline results for the full sample suggest that the effect of new environmental elements in BITs is positive and significant for total FDI and green FDI. For individual economies, the inclusion of environmental elements in BITs has a positive effect for Australia; Hong Kong, China; the Republic of Korea; and Viet Nam, particularly for green FDI inflows. Notably, environmental elements in international investment agreements for these economies are typically not included in the preamble but in specific provisions, such as expropriation and performance requirements.

Effects (not shown) are similar for the case of outward green FDI flows.

Our analysis also indicates that the modernization of BIT provisions could be a viable reform path for some economies to uphold climate and environmental objectives. Bilateral action may be faster in bringing reforms and could be complemented by other multilateral reform processes (UNCTAD 2022). Ultimately, no one-size-fits-all model exists for an environmental provision in international investment agreements. Economies need to carefully assess their situation when deciding the type of investment agreement reform needed for effective climate mitigation.

BITs with Environmental Content and FDI Flows: Difference-in-Difference Estimates

Treatment Effect	Total FDI			Green FDI			Observations
	(1)	(2)	(3)	(4)	(5)	(6)	
	Ln(Total FDI)	Ln(M&A Deals)	Ln(Greenfield Capital Expenditure)	Ln(Total FDI)	Ln(M&A Deals)	Ln(Greenfield Capital Expenditure)	
Full sample							
SE not clustered at economy-pair level	0.255**	0.415***	0.182	0.231***	0.141***	0.138**	23,217
	(0.114)	(0.107)	(0.117)	(0.065)	(0.051)	(0.058)	
R-squared	0.566	0.438	0.546	0.559	0.453	0.529	
Reporter-year FE	Yes	Yes	Yes	Yes	Yes	Yes	
Partner-year FE	Yes	Yes	Yes	Yes	Yes	Yes	
SE clustered at economy-pair level	0.255	0.415	0.182	0.231	0.141	0.138	23,217
	(0.261)	(0.257)	(0.253)	(0.171)	(0.121)	(0.159)	
R-squared	0.566	0.438	0.546	0.559	0.453	0.529	
Reporter-year FE	Yes	Yes	Yes	Yes	Yes	Yes	
Partner-year FE	Yes	Yes	Yes	Yes	Yes	Yes	
Narrow sample*, all flows							
All standard errors clustered at the economy-pair level							
BB-MR FE*	0.635	0.983**	0.589	0.697*	0.443*	0.525	9,376
	(0.506)	(0.404)	(0.515)	(0.379)	(0.238)	(0.349)	
R-squared	0.311	0.247	0.295	0.270	0.249	0.226	
Economy-year FE	0.273	0.237	0.247	0.254	0.117	0.173	9,376
	(0.450)	(0.428)	(0.451)	(0.296)	(0.202)	(0.280)	
R-squared	0.644	0.568	0.626	0.664	0.595	0.631	
Narrow sample*, by type of flow and for selected Asian economies							
All standard errors clustered at the economy-pair level							
Inflows in Asia							
Republic of Korea	-0.771	0.477	-0.884	-1.056	0.408**	-1.345	890
	(1.063)	(0.807)	(1.029)	(1.314)	(0.188)	(1.401)	

continued on next page

Box 7.7 continued

Narrow sample*, by type of flow and for selected Asian economies							
All standard errors clustered at the economy-pair level							
Inflows in Asia							
Australia	0.127	1.010*	0.266	0.415***	0.323**	0.496***	342
	(0.280)	(0.570)	(0.206)	(0.139)	(0.151)	(0.156)	
Hong Kong, China	-0.307	-0.110	-1.402	2.341***	2.159***	-0.160	208
	(0.857)	(0.509)	(1.079)	(0.287)	(0.269)	(0.246)	
Uzbekistan	-0.294	-0.285*	-0.249	0.094	-0.056	0.089	436
	(0.314)	(0.142)	(0.310)	(0.126)	(0.099)	(0.116)	
Viet Nam	1.206***	0.507*	0.398	0.935***	0.749***	0.327**	493
	(0.214)	(0.275)	(0.244)	(0.138)	(0.142)	(0.147)	
Partner FE	Yes	Yes	Yes	Yes	Yes	Yes	
Time FE	Yes	Yes	Yes	Yes	Yes	Yes	

BB-MR = Baier and Bergstrand multilateral resistance term, BIT = bilateral investment treaty, FDI = foreign direct investment, FE = fixed effect, M&A = merger and acquisition, SE = standard error, *** $p<0.01$, ** $p<0.05$, * $p<0.1$.

Notes: The independent variable reported in the table represents treatment effects for the full and narrow samples, where treatment variable takes the value of 1 if a terminated BIT is replaced with a BIT with environmental references and 0 otherwise. Full sample includes all BIT pairs, while narrow sample includes economy-pairs of BITs with at least one of the Asian economies in the treatment group. Following Falvey and Foster-McGregor (2017), other independent variables included are bilateral economic size and a dummy for preferential trade agreement (not reported).

Sources: ADB calculations using data from United Nations Conference on Trade and Development. Investment Policy Hub: International Investment Agreements Navigator. https://investmentpolicy.unctad.org/international-investment-agreements. Bureau van Dijk. Zephyr M&A Database; and Financial Times. fDi Markets (all accessed August 2022).

[a] For example, as the new Republic of Korea–Türkiye BIT includes environmental elements, observations are assigned to treatment group, whereas observations for other unchanged BITs involving these two economies are assigned to the control group.

Source: Avendano et al. (2022).

Looking ahead, governments should consider a more ambitious approach in embracing new investment agreements. A model agreement or "opt-in" mechanism—a multilateral agreement where economies can flexibly join to modify old agreements—including substantive standards on environmental protection and climate change should be part of the reforms to existing agreements. The use of exceptions for climate policy measures and damage or compensation caps to discourage carbon-intensive investments should also be considered. Besides regulatory measures, Asian agreements could expand to cover other areas to support climate mitigation policies, including market access for climate investment and investment facilitation in green industries (OECD 2022).

New Modes of Cooperation

Beyond standard trade and investment agreements, new modalities of international cooperation are emerging to encourage environmental protection. A wave of novel international green economy collaborations covers topics such as the identification, certification, and liberalization of green products. Current examples range from joint statements of intent to memorandums of understanding, joint-funded research projects, and negotiations of comprehensive international agreements. These international green economy collaborations (known as IGECs) are better understood as international green industrial policy than as deep trade agreements (Aisbett et al. 2022).

The need for international green industrial policies can be an important driver of IGECs. Such policy initiatives (often referred to as GIPs) are increasingly popular for tackling challenges beyond green goods certification and liberalization. One way to understand green industrial policies is through their function in solving market failures that inhibit the emergence and growth of green technologies and industries. While domestic GIP has much to contribute, it is limited by the fact that many industries comprise regional and global value chains (World Bank 2020). This, in turn, means that many of the relevant market failures are international in nature.

Memorandums of understanding (MOUs) and joint statements of intent (JSIs) are entry level forms of international green economy collaboration. MOUs and JSIs are low cost in terms of bureaucratic resources and low risk as they generally are not legally binding (Munoz 2021; Talmon 2021). They can be a stepping stone toward more ambitious collaboration such as legally binding agreements. The 2021 Japan–Australia partnership on decarbonization through technology is an example of JSI. Both economies are leading proponents of international collaboration on the green economy.[123] In typical content, JSIs outline the industries, technologies or supply chains of focus, forms of collaboration, and relationship to other regulation and governance (Munoz 2021). Joint research and development are a popular component, making innovation a key part of collaboration. In some cases, such as in the EU, JSI can also include deep regulatory collaboration commitments. While JSIs have advantages, they also are limited in what they achieve. As official public statements, they serve as signaling devices to both industry and other jurisdictions, although the strength of that signal is limited by the low cost of reneging on the statements.

Green economy agreements (known as GEA) offer an innovative, promising avenue for cross-border collaboration to tackle climate change. New and more practical approaches are looming and policy makers can consider these for strengthening

their climate policy. GEAs offer the possibility of combining green industrial policy objectives with the depth, commitment, and legal standing of deep trade agreements. A prominent example is the proposed Singapore–Australia GEA (Box 7.8). The Singapore–Australia GEA is undoubtedly a piece of international green industrial policy as emphasized also in the Joint Vision Statement. Its vision speaks to one of the drivers of international green economy collaboration: the need for deep regulatory collaboration. It also focuses on doing business and trading in environmental goods and services across borders. While these elements are more consistent with traditional DTAs, they are substantially more ambitious than most (Laurens, Brandi, and Morin 2022). To be more successful, GEAs require significant institutional resources and capacity. Applying this in the context of ADB's developing member economies might require a modified approach that accommodates resource constraints and allows flexibility and learning.

Carbon Pricing Mechanisms

Carbon Tax and Carbon Markets

Carbon pricing is an integral component of the broader climate policy architecture that can help economies reduce emissions cost-effectively. Embodied commonly in tax and carbon markets and in adjustments to prices at borders, carbon pricing helps internalize the external costs of GHG emissions, thereby incorporating climate costs into production and consumption decisions. Carbon pricing can disincentivize the use of fossil fuels, making deployment of renewables more attractive. It can generate revenue for green recovery and growth and promote diffusion of advanced low carbon technologies (ADB 2021c). Crucially, it can also support the energy transition, foster regional cooperation, improve energy security, and reduce vulnerability to international energy price shocks (ADB 2022). There is robust evidence that carbon pricing instruments have been effective at promoting

---

123   Government of Australia, Department of Industry, Science and Resources. Japan–Australia Partnership on Decarbonisation through Technology. https://www.minister.industry.gov.au/ministers/taylor/media-releases/japan-australia-partnership-decarbonisation-through-technology.

Box 7.8: Singapore–Australia Green Economy Agreement

The text below is an excerpt from a joint media release on the Singapore–Australia Green Economy Agreement (GEA), with bold emphasis by authors to highlight Green Industrial Policy elements that are typically not found in deep trade agreements (DTAs), "while the italics highlight" more traditional DTA aspects.

October 2021

Our vision is to enhance the livelihood of our communities whilst **transitioning to greener economies and addressing the challenges of climate change.**

The GEA will deliver on this vision by reducing barriers to the trade in environmental goods and services; fostering convergence on regulations and standards; **exploring new opportunities in green growth sectors;** *adopting environmental measures that facilitate trade and investment in a manner consistent with existing international trade and investment obligations;* **and ensuring our smooth and inclusive transition into a green economy that creates good jobs for our people.**

We envisage an agreement that is practical, ambitious, and **innovative, where technologies catalyze business and commercial opportunities, intergovernmental and public-private partnerships implement new cooperative projects, pathfinder initiatives scale up to benefit the broader region, and effective solutions assist us [to] achieve our ambition of net zero emissions as soon as possible.**

Our joint work will result in practical applications and benefits to the real economy and workforce. They aim to **accelerate the adoption of low-carbon and green technologies, low-carbon and renewable energy, and decarbonized production processes. Our industry consultations and pilot proof of concept projects will ensure the GEA supports job creation, supply chains, and market development in green sectors. Drawing on cutting-edge knowledge,** *the GEA will improve the compatibility of our systems to ease doing business and trading in environmental goods and services across our borders.*

Source: Government of Singapore, Green Economy Agreement (2021).

---

low-cost emission reductions.[124] Carbon pricing is also associated with higher labor productivity, health outcomes, and material conditions. There is a broad landscape of carbon pricing instruments, and carbon taxes and emissions trading schemes (ETSs) are the two most common direct pricing instruments alongside baseline-and-crediting mechanisms (Box 7.9).

The momentum seems to have been maintained during the COVID-19 pandemic in the economies that considered and planned carbon pricing instruments before the pandemic. It is also worth noting that the carbon pricing mechanisms were largely resilient to suppressed economic activities during the pandemic, with several economies increasing

their carbon tax rates and adopting more ambitious trajectories. Many economies in Asia made an ETS their choice of direct carbon pricing instrument. ETSs may be more attractive as they are more flexible in design, making it easier to accommodate political economy considerations, and they are inherently countercyclical, in that the demand and price of allowances will fall during recessions, just when regulated firms need relief. ETS design can retain industry support by allocating a portion of the emission permits free of charge and accommodating industrial interests in a tailored allocation formula. The allocations are expected to be phased out over the long term.

---

[124]   Intergovernmental Panel on Climate Change. Sixth Assessment Report of Working Group III, Mitigation of Climate, Chapter 13.6.3.

Box 7.9: The Landscape of Carbon Pricing Instruments

Carbon taxes and emissions trading schemes (ETSs) are the two most common direct pricing instruments. Both are "flexible" policy instruments since they give regulated entities different options. A carbon tax will require businesses to pay a tax on their carbon emissions or will act as an incentive for them to reduce emissions. The effect of an ETS will depend on its design: regulated entities will have to submit permits equivalent to their emissions, which can either be bought or allocated for free, under a certain cap or threshold. Carbon trading allows buyers and sellers to exchange allowances and carbon credits for a price. When used as an instrument for compliance, buyers use carbon markets to source more cost-effective emission reductions. The key difference between these two instruments is that under a carbon tax the price of emissions is fixed but the quantity is not. In an ETS, the quantity of emissions is fixed but the price is not. However, designing the system well can be more important than the choice between systems.

Baseline-and-crediting mechanism is another way of pricing carbon as it puts a price on the emission reduction by setting a baseline for emissions and issuing credits only after emission reductions have been verified below the predetermined baseline. These can be developed on a national basis, such as the China Certified Emission Reductions or include the use of international carbon crediting mechanisms such as under Article 6 of the Paris Agreement. Independent standards used by companies and other organizations for voluntary purposes are also based on baseline-and-crediting. Baseline-and-crediting mechanisms are typically used to create flexibility for domestic or international emissions trading systems or for organizations' voluntary greenhouse gas emission offset purposes.

Source: Duggal (2022).

Border Adjustment Mechanism

Border carbon adjustment (BCA) can take many forms as an environmental trade policy, depending on the sectors it considers, the scope of emissions it covers, the appropriate price level, and the adjustment mechanism. It is based on the premise that an unintended consequence of introducing carbon pricing could be carbon leakage given its impact on trade and investment. For instance, if carbon pricing is introduced in a jurisdiction without coordination with trading partners, it could lead to higher production costs for domestic producers, and may make it difficult for them to compete with imports that are not subject to carbon pricing. One possible outcome is that more of the local demand will be met through more emission-intensive imports, which would result in higher emissions. Internationally coordinated and agreed approaches for introducing carbon pricing, particularly for emission-intensive trade-exposed sectors, offer the most effective solutions for addressing carbon leakage concerns.

The EU is the closest toward implementing a BCA through its Carbon Border Adjustment Mechanism (CBAM). Other economies—Canada, the US, and the UK—are also contemplating to implement or are exploring a BCA.[125] The CBAM will impose a carbon price on imports of emissions-intensive and trade-exposed goods to ensure that they have a similar carbon price to domestically produced products.[126] While the exact CBAM implementation details need to be finalized and there are issues about its design and compatibility with WTO rules (Marcu, Mehling, and Cosbey 2020), the European Council has approved the mechanism (Box 7.10). Bellora and Fontagne (2022) show that although the CBAM could succeed in reducing carbon leakage, the EU would lose competitiveness in its export markets while downstream industries could be subject to higher intermediate costs.

---

[125] Cosbey, Bernstein, and Stiebert (2021) present a closer discussion of the different BCAs discussed in Canada and the US.

[126] In the European Commission's initial proposal, the CBAM will at first cover these five emissions-intensive and trade-exposed sectors: cement, aluminum, fertilizers, electricity generation, and iron and steel. The commission selected these sectors because they have a high risk of carbon leakage and high carbon emissions. The administrative feasibility of covering the sectors in the CBAM from the start of implementation was also taken into account. Hydrogen and a limited number of downstream products were later added in the proposal.

Box 7.10: The Process of Implementing the European Union's Carbon Border Adjustment Mechanism

The European Union (EU) target is to reduce its carbon emissions by 55% in 2030 from 1990 and become climate-neutral by 2050. One of its main instruments for achieving this is the Emission Trading Scheme (ETS). Emission-intensive trade-exposed sectors are included in the EU ETS but receive free allocation of emission permits. As the EU increases its climate actions, it is seeking to phase out free permits and introduce a carbon border adjustment mechanism (CBAM).

After several rounds of negotiations, the European Council on 15 March 2022 agreed to a general approach. The CBAM, while meant to complement the EU ETS, was formulated to combat carbon leakage and ensure that imports have a similar carbon price as domestically produced products. Through the CBAM, the EU also aspires to catalyze and incentivize climate action globally. On 13 December 2022, the European Council and the European Parliament reached a provisional agreement,

postponing the CBAM transition period to 1 October 2023 from the earlier expected start date of 1 January 2023. Both institutions need to confirm and formally adopt the agreement before it becomes final.

The EU plans to implement the CBAM in two stages. First, the CBAM will be introduced from October 2023 with reporting and monitoring obligations only for importers in a transition period that will last until 2025. Then from 2026, the CBAM will be fully applied, with price adjustments on imported products. The CBAM will be phased in gradually in parallel with the gradual phase out of free allowances under the revised EU ETS (European Council 2022). The CBAM will initially include cement, aluminum, fertilizers, electric, and iron and steel as well as hydrogen, some precursors, and a limited number of downstream products. Indirect emissions would also be considered for inclusion, under certain conditions.

Sources: Duggal (2022); and Tan, Tayag, and Quizon (2022).

The CBAM's relevance, effectiveness, and potential impact need careful calibration. The introduction of the CBAM may cause problems for developing economies. An UNCTAD (2021) study finds that introduction of the CBAM could alter trade patterns in favor of economies where production is relatively carbon efficient and reduce export from developing economies in favor of developed economies with less carbon intensive production. Economies where emissions-intensive and trade-exposed products have a large share of exports will be particularly exposed. In addition, economies would be more vulnerable in adapting to the CBAM if they rely on the EU as an export market and if they do not have the capacity to track and report production-related carbon emissions. Economies with limited capacity to adjust to a low-carbon paradigm may also be at higher risk of economic impact from the CBAM. A risk index can be constructed based on the exposure and vulnerability of the economies to the CBAM. Simulation results in a dynamic computable general equilibrium model-based estimation suggest that the CBAM could widen the gap between developed and developing economies in GDP and welfare, worsening

the unequal income and welfare distributions between rich and poor economies (He, Zhai, and Ma 2022).

The mechanism also has potential to conflict with the principle of voluntary mitigation efforts. The principle of "common but differentiated responsibilities and respective capabilities," established with the UN Framework Convention on Climate Change, has underpinned the voluntary nature of nationally determined contributions, which embody efforts by each economy to reduce national emissions and adapt to the impacts of climate change (Zhang 2021). The CBAM mechanism currently under contemplation risks departing from this key principle, with significant implications for climate-related global discussions in the future.

Some questions on operational details still remain. These include (i) the lack of consideration for the breadth and depth of environmental regulations implemented by exporting economies apart from the carbon pricing mechanism, (ii) the inadequacy of economy-wide border adjustment levies in differentiating the heterogeneity of the carbon intensity of production at the firm level, and (iii) the inability to properly internalize the global social cost of emissions—the global public "bads"—into the production cost or sales price, given the bilateral nature of different adjustment levies.

Questions also arise about whether a BCA mechanism can be imposed unilaterally and be compatible with WTO rules. One view is that a BCA is considered WTO compatible as the jurisdiction utilizes a BCA mechanism to charge an import fee on foreign producers at the border. However, the jurisdiction might also consider keeping free allowances or providing export rebates to safeguard domestic producers against competitive disadvantage in domestic or foreign markets, raising concerns about compliance with WTO rules. Recycling CBAM revenues to help those developing economies subject to CBAM imposition could help avoid such controversies and support their transition into green economies through technological development and green investment.

The scope of CBAM needs to be carefully vetted. Given uncertainties associated with the relevance and efficiency in mitigating carbon leakages, the sectoral coverage of CBAM needs to be minimized, with a scientific and enforceable implementation structure in place until its effectiveness can be sufficiently verified. This is also important so as not to stoke welfare-degenerating retaliatory responses from the trading partners of CBAM-imposing economies. At the same time, discussion and concerted efforts to achieve global solutions as the first best option should intensify to minimize the risks that a unilateral adjustment mechanism could spread and prevail.

The Asian region retains low overall risk and vulnerability to the CBAM given its relatively small share of trade with the EU, yet certain subregions or economies may be relatively more affected. Based on estimated composite index of exposure and vulnerability to CBAM, Africa, the Middle East, and non-EU Europe have the highest potential risk for the EU's CBAM adoption as they have stronger trade linkages with the EU, particularly in carbon intensive goods (Tan, Tayag, and Quizon 2022).[127] However, Asia has relatively higher levels of CO_2 emissions, which could make its products more likely to be subjected to the CBAM in the future. It also has more economies with lower statistical capacity, making it more difficult to trace and trade CO_2 emissions. Certain Asian subregions are more exposed in that they trade more carbon intensive goods with the EU (such as Central Asia due mostly to high exports of aluminum and fertilizer to the EU) or they may struggle to adapt to CBAM implementation (such as the Pacific and South Asia due to the absence of carbon emission reducing mechanisms and low statistical capacity to measure and report emissions). Examining individual indicators compiled also reveals that while some economies may be weaker than others in the same indicator, their risk may derive from different sources. Some economies are more exposed in iron and steel or aluminum exports to the EU, while others are more vulnerable as they lack statistical infrastructure or environmental data (Annex 7c provides more details).

Efforts should be made to mitigate the potential that CBAM reduces exports and hurts domestic economies. Asian economies need to be closely monitoring developments given the looming possibility that some regions and advanced economies are likely to adopt the CBAM. Presently, the main risks to CBAM are from the importance of EU trade to domestic economy and reliance on the EU for emission-intensive and trade-exposed exports. Technical and financial support can be provided to increase the productive capacity of other sectors to reduce the reliance on emission-intensive and trade-exposed sectors. Diversification of export destinations would also help mitigate risk exposure to the introduction of CBAM by specific trading partners. Finally, technical assistance and capacity building through international cooperation and collaboration are needed to help economies implement carbon pricing and increase their statistical capacity. Detailed implementation arrangements and its future evolution

---

[127] Following Eicke et al. (2021), Tan, Tayag, and Quizon (2022) used 19 indicators across four dimensions to compute for the composite risk index: (i) exposure to CBAM; (ii) reliance on trade with the EU; (iii) emission levels and lack of decarbonization efforts; and (iv) statistical capacity to measure, report, and verify emissions. Annex 7c provides the methodology and detailed results.

of CBAM yet remain to be seen.[128] In the long term, however, the region needs to explore ways to transform the challenges of the changing trade environment into opportunities by increasing green investments and embracing cleaner production technologies.

Benefits of International Carbon Markets in Addressing Potential Cross-Border Carbon Leakages

A global approach presents multiple benefits and can more effectively support carbon emission reductions. An international framework on cross-border carbon measures or a global carbon pricing mechanism can be considered first-best solutions to address existing deficiencies in unilateral approaches. To the extent that BCAs bring domestic benefits at the expense of other economies, and partial measures do not necessarily prevent carbon leakage, more comprehensive methods can be considered. Within global approaches, consideration of environmental effectiveness, costs, and feasibility for implementation are important. For international emissions trading, theoretically a top-down approach through a global cap-and-trade system still offers the best outcome for reducing carbon emissions. Nevertheless, bottom–up approaches by means of decentralized efforts for establishing ETS remain a plausible alternative, and can be building blocks for supporting the eventual establishment of a global carbon market.

Bottom–up approaches to support the development of international carbon markets has proven more effective. Intermediate architectures through direct and indirect linking can be a cornerstone of an international climate policy framework. Compared with a fragmented approach, direct or indirect linking of ETSs can reduce mitigation costs by fostering partial or full convergence in carbon prices and improve efficiency and performance. Analysis of the economic effects of direct and indirect linking of ETS suggests that the greater the difference in carbon prices across regions, the greater the gains from linking (Dellink et al. 2014).[129] Linking can also reduce carbon leakage. For this, it is important to assess the tradeoffs between direct and indirect approaches and the conditions in which linking can lead to price convergence (Flachsland, Marschinski, and Edenhofer 2009; Grull and Taschini 2012). Recent research shown in Box 7.11 also suggests potential benefits of international carbon markets for the region.

Design features will continue to be important for implementing a multilateral or global carbon pricing mechanism. In the case of scaling up cap-and-trade systems via linking, features include identifying the setting and trajectory of emission cap levels, ceilings for permit prices, the sectors covered, and the rules on banking in and borrowing of emission allowances. Some features are important for attaining certain outcomes. Experience suggests that the banking of allowances in ETS systems can make them more welfare-improving than other schemes (Kuusela and Lintunen 2020). Information requirements for setting such programs can also be important. They include data on historical emissions, projections on future emissions under different scenarios, estimates for the technical feasibility of reductions in covered and uncovered sectors, and estimates on marginal abatement cost curves. Economies in the region should also continue to work toward improving systems for monitoring, reporting, and verifying emissions.[130]

---

[128]   One hypothetical scenario for the mechanism is it becomes widely adopted by the region's trading partners and its industrial coverage expands.

[129]   Estimates also suggest that indirect linking could bring substantial benefits. Allowing developed economies to meet up to 50% of their domestic commitments through the use of offsets would trigger major carbon price convergence (Dellink et al. 2014).

[130]   Several initiatives aim at enhancing facility-level monitoring, reporting and verification in ASEAN. Examples are provided in Government of Japan, Ministry of Environment. Activities for the ASEAN Region. https://www.env.go.jp/earth/ondanka/pasti/en/activity/asean.html and European Union. Enhanced Regional EU-ASEAN Dialogue Instrument (E-READI). https://www.eeas.europa.eu/eeas/enhanced-regional-eu-asean-dialogue-instrument-e-readi_en (both accessed January 2023).

Box 7.11: Reaching Net Zero through an International Carbon Market: Evidence for Asia and the Pacific

Kim et al. (2022) use a recursive computable general equilibrium model to simulate the effects of the net-zero transition on several economic indicators under various scenarios. Computable general equilibrium models are grounded in economic theory and calibrated with real-world economic data to capture interdependencies between different parts of the economy through a set of equations. The recursive-dynamic model employed by the authors computes equilibriums period-by-period by solving these equations. Different scenarios are compared with a baseline or business-as-usual scenario to investigate the economic effects of the net-zero transition between 2022 and 2050. In particular, the adoption of an international carbon market in conjunction with carbon pricing (the Orderly Net Zero Transition scenario) is examined in the study. Under this scenario, the adoption of an international carbon market in Asia means that economies can make carbon credit transactions, while the differentiated carbon prices follow those suggested by the International Energy Agency to reach the net-zero target (IEA 2021).

Change in Greenhouse Gas Emissions by Scenario, 2022–2050 (% difference from business-as-usual)

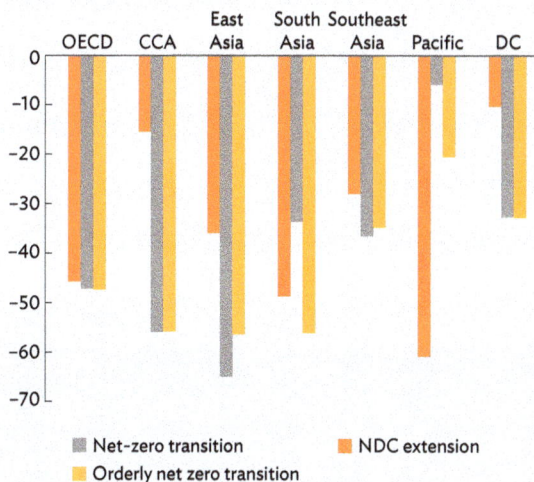

CCA = Caucasus and Central Asia, DC = developed countries, NDC = nationally determined contributions, OECD = Organisation for Economic Co-operation and Development.

Source: Kim et al. (2022).

Overall, the authors find that achieving targets on nationally determined contributions and net zero would induce limited costs in real gross domestic product (GDP)

in comparison with the sizable reduction in greenhouse gas (GHG) emissions in developing Asian economies. Among Asian subregions, the Orderly Net Zero Transition scenario would produce the largest benefits in GHG emission reduction in East Asia, Central Asia, and South Asia. In 2022–2050, emissions would be less than half of the business-as-usual baseline in these three subregions. GHG emission reductions would be over 30% from the baseline in Southeast Asia and around 20% in the Pacific under the same scenario. However, the Pacific is the only subregion where the Orderly Net Zero Transition scenario would generate economic gains, as real GDP is estimated to increase by 0.17% relative to the baseline. Real GDP would decline between 2022 and 2050 in all other Asia and Pacific subregions, ranging from –0.63% to –3.37% relative to the business-as-usual scenario, with East Asia and Southeast Asia recording the smallest drops (–1.59% and –0.63%).

In most subregions, the study shows that allowing international carbon trading among Asian economies would help reduce the costs (in real GDP) resulting from the adoption of differentiated carbon pricing. Economic losses in real GDP in Asian developing economies would therefore be modest in comparison to the substantial reductions in GHG emissions achieved through carbon pricing and the introduction of an international carbon market.

In addition to the findings of Kim et al. (2022), it can be shown that reducing GHG emissions would bring substantial economic and human benefits such as avoided crop yield losses and premature deaths. Results derived from the World Induced Technical Change Hybrid (WITCH) model, which relies on a macroeconomic structure that considers the energy sector and models carbon mitigation policy alternatives for major GHGs, demonstrates this (Emmerling et al. 2022). Simulations show that 400,000 premature deaths a year would be avoided by 2050 through air pollution reduction under the most ambitious scenarios, with carbon budgets of less than 1,360 giga tonnes of CO_2 between 2020 and 2100. These deaths would be mostly avoided in the PRC and India. The Accelerated Net Zero scenario, which assumes Global Net Zero with a carbon budget of 1,150 giga tonnes of CO_2 between 2020 and 2100, would result in a further 300,000 avoided deaths by 2030. This scenario would also avoid damages that account for up to 40% of GDP in India and South Asia, and up to 30% in Southeast Asia and Indonesia. Overall, the WITCH model reveals that the costs of mitigation are considerably lower than the benefits resulting from climate action.

Source: Kim et al. (2022).

Significant momentum has been created to operationalize international carbon markets, primarily due to the adoption of Article 6 Rules. Article 6 of the Paris Agreement lays the foundation for international carbon markets and can be a key element of the broader climate policy toolbox that economies in the region can deploy to accelerate climate action.[131] Article 6 includes two market-based approaches, with Article 6.2 being a bilateral or multilateral bottom-up approach to market mechanisms, an Article 6.4 whereas 6.4 is a top-down centrally government mechanism under the United Nations Framework Convention on Climate Change (UNFCCC). Article 6.2 provides an accounting framework for managing cooperative approaches that lead to a transfer of internationally transferred mitigation outcomes. It allows economies to sell extra carbon emission reductions they have achieved compared with their target. Article 6.2 covers, among other mechanisms, emission trading between states, linking of ETSs or agreed baseline-and-crediting mechanisms.[132] Article 6.4, on the other hand, creates a new mechanism with a governance structure subject to centralized oversight, similar to the Clean Development Mechanism (CDM). Looking ahead, Article 6.4 will take up CDM modalities and adopt elements of the CDM if parties and international regulators are willing to do so (ADB 2020b; Duggal 2022).

International cooperation under Article 6 has the potential to reduce the total implementation cost of nationally determined contributions by more than $250 billion per year in 2030 (Edmonds et al. 2019).

International carbon markets are gradually introducing innovative and more flexible instruments. As new mechanisms under Article 6 take shape, economies in the region will need support to take full advantage of these opportunities. For example, Switzerland recently signed bilateral agreements with

Thailand, Vanuatu, and other emerging economies for Article 6 trading.[133] Under such schemes, host economies receive financial support from buyer economies to invest in climate mitigation activities, generating internationally transferred mitigation outcomes that count in the buyer economies' nationally determined contributions. Projects in host economies involve, for example, introducing sustainable agricultural practices or securing electricity access through renewable energy. Sweden and Nepal have signed an MOU to cooperate under the Mobilizing Article 6 Trading Structures Program (GGGI 2022). These bilateral agreements, particularly under Article 6.2, will become increasingly common, while the centralized mechanism under Article 6.4 may require more time to put in place the necessary rules and infrastructure for carbon credits.[134]

Voluntary Carbon Markets (VCMs) provide an opportunity to enhance climate action and efforts to harmonize standards and core principles in the VCM are ongoing. There is a growing momentum to take advantage of the voluntary carbon market with an increase in voluntary commitment from the private sector to achieve net-zero targets. However, challenges remain in the VCM, in particular with regard to establishing credible baselines or counterfactual scenarios in the absence of investment through carbon finance. Technical assistance and capacity building may be needed to understand different types of carbon markets and the technical options and key issues in their implementation.

One key area for harmonization is the assessment of offset units. For example, the Integrity Council for the Voluntary Carbon Market (Integrity Council) is working to set global threshold standards for carbon credits.[135] Another important goal will be to ensure that the design features of the VCM are compatible with the international regulatory framework under

---

[131]   ADB (2020b) provides a complete analysis of Article 6 of the Paris Agreement.

[132]   See Box 7.9 for a description of ETS (or cap and trade) and baseline-and-credit (or offsetting) mechanisms.

[133]   Switzerland Federal Office for the Environment. Bilateral Agreements on Emission Reductions and Carbon Storage Abroad. https://www.bafu.admin.ch/bafu/en/home/topics/climate/info-specialists/climate--international-affairs/staatsvertraege-umsetzung-klimauebereinkommen-von-paris-artikel6.html (accessed June 2022)

[134]   UNFCCC. Article 6.4 Supervisory Body. https://unfccc.int/process-and-meetings/bodies/constituted-bodies/article-64-supervisory-body (accessed June 2022).

[135]   ICVCM. The Integrity Council for the Voluntary Carbon Market. https://icvcm.org/ (accessed June 2022).

Article 6, domestic carbon pricing policies as well as nationally determined contributions implementation plans and long-term strategies. One approach provided by standards for the voluntary market is the separation between "adjusted units" and "support units." Adjusted units would be subject to authorization by the host economy and an adjustment of the host economy's emissions balance to reflect the export of mitigation outcomes. Support units imply a financial assistance for mitigation activity in the host economy that supports reducing emissions and the achievement of the host economy's nationally determined contributions targets. Discussions at the UNFCCC (COP27) meeting resulted in a non-adjusted unit for Article 6.4 (mitigation contribution A6.4 emission reduction).

Regional carbon market alliances can be critical for limiting the potential of emission leakage and perceptions of competitive distortions. With a broad landscape of carbon market instruments and new approaches emerging under Article 6, opportunities for regional collaboration are increasing. A regional carbon market for both ETS and international carbon markets can bring various benefits, from improving liquidity and facilitating trade of carbon assets to increasing transparency and efficiency through common standards.

This is particularly the case when ETSs of two or more jurisdictions are linked, allowing them to trade carbon allowances. Linking the ETSs can increase the liquidity of a carbon market, offer regulated entities additional abatement opportunities, and reduce the cost of achieving the combined emissions caps of the linked ETSs. A notable example is the linking between the California and Quebec ETS. Where full linking is not feasible, governments may choose more indirect forms of linking. Indirect linking occurs, for instance, when allowing carbon credits for flexibility for compliance buyers from one standard or mechanism in several ETSs. Regional carbon market alliances outside of ETS linking—such as the Eastern African and West African Alliances on Carbon Markets and Climate Finance—can also foster a regional approach to international carbon markets and increase capacity to access climate finance for implementing nationally determined contributions. This regional approach may also be suitable for selected industries, such as international aviation, where a single global mechanism is essential for avoiding competitive distortions.

Background Papers

Aisbett, E., W. Cheng, B. Jones, W. Raynal, and L. White. 2022. Trade and Climate: Lessons from the Past and Ways Forward. Background Paper for the *Asian Economic Integration Report 2023* Theme Chapter on "Trade, Investment, and Climate Change in Asia and the Pacific." Manuscript.

Avendano, R., C. Park, S. Tan, and L. Tolin. 2022. Environmental Elements in International Investment Agreements and FDI Flows in Asia and the Pacific. Background Paper for the *Asian Economic Integration Report 2023* Theme Chapter on "Trade, Investment, and Climate Change in Asia and the Pacific." Manuscript.

Cole, M. A., R. J. Elliott, and L. Zhang. 2022. A Review of FDI and the Environment in Asia Literature: Are There Lessons for Climate Change Mitigation Strategies? Background Paper for the *Asian Economic Integration Report 2023* Theme Chapter on "Trade, Investment, and Climate Change in Asia and the Pacific." Manuscript.

Duggal, V. K. 2022. *The Role of Carbon Pricing.* Background Paper for the *Asian Economic Integration Report 2023* Theme Chapter on "Trade, Investment, and Climate Change in Asia and the Pacific." Manuscript.

Ehlers, T. and J. La Rosa. 2022. Sustainable Finance in Asia. Background Paper for the *Asian Economic Integration Report 2023* Theme Chapter on "Trade, Investment, and Climate Change in Asia and the Pacific." Manuscript.

Kang, J., J. Gapay, and K. Quizon. 2022. Factors Affecting Carbon Dioxide Emissions Embodied on Trade. Background Paper for the *Asian Economic Integration Report 2023* Theme Chapter on "Trade, Investment, and Climate Change in Asia and the Pacific." Manuscript.

Kim, K., S. Basu-Das, and Z. Ardaniel. 2022. Trade Facilitation and Climate Change Nexus. Background Paper for the *Asian Economic Integration Report 2023* Theme Chapter on "Trade, Investment, and Climate Change in Asia and the Pacific." Manuscript.

Tan, S., M. Tayag, and K. Quizon. 2022. Asia's Exposure and Vulnerability to EU's Carbon Border Adjustment Mechanism. Background Paper for the *Asian Economic Integration Report 2023* Theme Chapter on "Trade, Investment, and Climate Change in Asia and the Pacific." Manuscript.

References

Abman, R., C. Lundberg, and M. Ruta. 2021. The Effectiveness of Environmental Provisions in Regional Trade Agreements. *Policy Research Working Paper*. 9601. Washington, DC: World Bank.

Acharyya, J. 2009. FDI, Growth and the Environment: Evidence from India On CO_2 Emission During the Last Two Decades. *Journal of Economic Development*. 34 (1). pp. 43–58.

Ahmad, M., Z. Y. Zhao, A. Rehman, M. Shahzad, and H. Li. 2019. Revealing Long- and Short-Run Empirical Interactions among Foreign Direct Investment, Renewable Power Generation, and CO_2 Emissions in China. *Environmental Science and Pollution Research*. 26 (22). pp. 220–245.

Aisbett, E. 2022. International Green Economy Collaborations. Paper presented at Applied Energy Symposium. 5-8 July. Cambridge: Massachusetts Institute of Technology.

Aisbett, E., B. Choudhury, O. de Schutter, F. J. Gardia, J. Harrison, and S. Hong. 2018. *Rethinking International Investment Governance: Principles for the 21st Century*. New York: Columbia University.

Antweiler, W., B. R. Copeland, and M. S. Taylor. 2001. Is Free Trade Good for the Environment? *American Economic Review*. 91 (4). pp. 877–908.

Asian Development Bank (ADB). 2020a. *Growing Green Business Investments in Asia and the Pacific: Trends and Opportunities*. Manila.

———. 2020b. *Decoding Article 6 of the Paris Agreement Version II*. Manila.

———. 2021a. *Global Value Chain Development Report 2021: Beyond Production*. Manila.

———. 2021b. *Asian Development Outlook 2021 Update: Transforming Agriculture in Asia*. Manila.

———. 2021c. *Carbon Pricing for Green Recovery and Growth*. November. Manila.

———.2021d. *Asia-Pacific Trade Facilitation Report 2021: Supply Chains of Critical Goods Amid the COVID-19 Pandemic—Disruptions, Recovery, and Resilience*. Manila.

———. 2022. *Carbon Pricing for Energy Transition and Decarbonization*. Manila.

———. Asia Regional Integration Center. Free Trade Agreement Database. https://aric.adb.org/database/fta (accessed May 2022).

———. Asia Regional Integration Center. International Investment Agreement Database. https://aric.adb.org/database/iias (accessed May 2022).

Asia-Pacific Economic Cooperation (APEC). 2021a. 2021 APEC Ministerial Meeting. 9 November. https://www.apec.org/meeting-papers/annual-ministerial-meetings/2021/2021-apec-ministerial-meeting.

———. 2021b. 2021 APEC Ministerial Meeting: Annex 2—Reference List of Environmental and Environmentally Related Services. https://www.apec.org/meeting-papers/annual-ministerial-meetings/2021/2021-apec-ministerial-meeting/annex-2---reference-list-of-environmental-and-environmentally-related-services.

———. 2021c. ADB, Partners to Set Up New Platform to Catalyze Investments in Sustainable Infrastructure in Asia. News Release. 30 September. https://www.adb.org/news/adb-partners-new-platform-catalyze-investments-sustainable-infrastructure-asia.

———. 2021d. *Scoping Study on New and Emerging Environmental Goods*. Singapore.

Azam, M., A. Q. Khan, K. Zaman, and M. Ahmad. 2015. Factors Determining Energy Consumption: Evidence from Indonesia, Malaysia and Thailand. *Renewable and Sustainable Energy Reviews*. 42. pp. 1123–1131.

Baek, J. 2016. A New Look at the FDI–Income–Energy–Environment Nexus: Dynamic Panel Data Analysis of ASEAN. *Energy Policy.* 91. pp. 22–27.

Baghdadi, L., I. Martínez-Zarzoso, and H. Zitouna. 2013. Are RTA Agreements with Environmental Provisions Reducing Emissions? *Journal of International Economics.* 90 (2). pp. 378–390.

Baier, S. L. and J. H. Bergstrand. 2009. Bonus Vetus OLS: A Simple Method for Approximating International Trade-Cost Effects Using the Gravity Equation. *Journal of International Economics.* 77 (1). pp. 77-85.

Barrows, G. and H. Ollivier. 2021. Foreign Demand, Developing Economy Exports, and CO_2 Emissions: Firm-Level Evidence from India. *Journal of Development Economics.* 149. 102587.

Barth, F., T. Winkel, W. Vanhoudt, A. Kuronen, M. Lehtovaara, M. Altmann, and P. Schmidt. 2019. Towards a Dual Hydrogen Certification System for Guarantees of Origin and for the Certification of Renewable Hydrogen in Transport and for Heating & Cooling: Final Report of Phase 2.

Behera, S. R. and D. P. Dash. 2017. The Effect Of Urbanization, Energy Consumption, and Foreign Direct Investment on the Carbon Dioxide Emission in the SSEA (South and Southeast Asian) Region. *Renewable and Sustainable Energy Reviews.* 70. pp. 96-106.

Bellora, C. and L. Fontagne. 2022. EU in Search of a WTO-Compatible Carbon Border Adjustment Mechanism. Unpublished.

Bhagwat, V., J. Brogaard, and B. Julio. 2021. A BIT Goes a Long Way: Bilateral Investment Treaties and Cross-border Mergers. *Journal of Financial Economics.* 140 (2). pp. 514–538.

Bialek, S., and A. J. Weichenrieder. 2021. Do Stringent Environmental Policies Deter FDI? M&A versus Greenfield. *Environmental & Resource Economics.* 80 (3). pp. 603–636.

Borga, M., A. Pegoue, M. G. M. Legoff, A. S. Rodelgo, D. Entaltsev, and K. Egesa. 2022. Measuring Carbon Emissions of Foreign Direct Investment in Host Economies. *IMF Working Paper.* 22/86. Washington, DC: International Monetary Fund.

Brandi, C., J. Schwab, A. Berger, and J. F. Morin. 2020. Do Environmental Provisions in Trade Agreements Make Exports from Developing Countries Greener? *World Development.* 129 (104899).

Brenton, P. and V. Chemutai. 2021. *The Trade and Climate Change Nexus: The Urgency and Opportunities for Developing Countries.* Washington, DC: World Bank.

Brucal, A., B. Javorcik, and I. Love. 2019. Good for the Environment, Good for Business: Foreign acquisitions and Energy Intensity. *Journal of International Economics.* 121. 103247.

Bu, M., Z. Liu, M. Wagner, and X. Yu. 2013. Corporate Social Responsibility and the Pollution Haven Hypothesis: Evidence from Multinationals' Investment Decisions in China. *Asia-Pacific Journal of Accounting and Economics.* 20 (1). pp. 85–99.

Busse, M., J. Königer, and P. Nunnenkamp. 2010. FDI Promotion through Bilateral Investment Treaties: More Than a Bit? *Review of World Economics.* 146 (1). pp. 14–177.

Cai, X., Y. Lu, M. Wu, and L. Yu. 2016. Does Environmental Regulation Drive Away Inbound Foreign Direct Investment? Evidence from a Quasi-Natural Experiment in China. *Journal of Development Economics.* 123. pp. 73–85.

Cao, X., C. Teng, and J. Zhang. 2021. Impact of the Belt and Road Initiative on Environmental Quality in Countries along the Routes. *Chinese Journal of Population, Resources And Environment.* 19 (4). pp. 344–351.

Carvalho, V. M., M. Nirei, Y. U. Saito, and A. Tahbaz-Salehi. 2021. Supply Chain Disruptions: Evidence from the Great East Japan Earthquake. *The Quarterly Journal of Economics.* 136 (2). pp. 1255-1321.

Centre for Research on the Epidemiology of Disasters - CRED. EM-DAT The International Disaster Database. http://www.emdat.be (accessed January 2023).

Chen, Q., M. Maung, Y. Shi, and C. Wilson. 2014. Foreign Direct Investment Concessions and Environmental Levies in China. *International Review of Financial Analysis.* 36. pp. 241–250.

Cheng, Z., L. Li, and J. Liu. 2018. The Spatial Correlation and Interaction between Environmental Regulation and Foreign Direct Investment. *Journal of Regulatory Economics.* 54 (2). pp. 124–146.

Cole, M. A., R. J. Elliott, and J. Zhang. 2011. Growth, Foreign Direct Investment, and the Environment: Evidence from Chinese Cities. *Journal of Regional Science.* 51 (1). pp. 121–138.

———. 2017. Foreign Direct Investment and the Environment. *Annual Review of Environment and Resources.* 42. pp. 465–487.

Copeland, B. R. and M. S. Taylor. 1994. North-South Trade and the Environment. *The Quarterly Journal of Economics.* 109 (3). pp. 755–787.

———. 2004. Trade, Growth, and the Environment. *Journal of Economic Literature.* 42 (1). pp. 7–71.

———. 2022. Globalization and Environment. In G. Gopinath, E. Helpman, and K. Rogoff, eds. *Handbook of International Economics,* Volume 5. North Holland.

Corong, E. L. 2008. Tariff Reductions, Carbon Emissions, and Poverty: An Economy-Wide Assessment of the Philippines. *ASEAN Economic Bulletin.* 25. pp. 20–31.

Cosbey, A., M. Bernstein, and S. Stiebert. 2021. *Enabling Climate Ambition: Border Carbon Adjustment in Canada and Abroad.* International Institute for Sustainable Development and Clean Prosperity.

Dang, T. and A. Mourougane. 2014. Estimating Shadow Prices of Pollution in OECD Economies. *OECD Green Growth Papers.* No. 2014-02. Paris: OECD Publishing.

Daugbjerg, C. 2012. The World Trade Organization and Organic Food Trade: Potential for Restricting Protectionism? *Organic Agriculture.* 2 (1).

Dean, J. M., M. E. Lovely, and H. Wang. 2009. Are Foreign Investors Attracted to Weak Environmental Regulations? Evaluating the Evidence from China. *Journal of Development Economics.* 90 (1). pp. 1–13.

Dellink, R., S. Jamet, J. Chateau, and R. Duval. 2014. Towards Global Carbon Pricing: Direct and Indirect Linking of Carbon Markets. *OECD Journal: Economic Studies.* 2013 (1). pp. 209–234.

De Melo J., and J. M. Solleder. 2022. Towards an Environmental Goods Agreement Style (EGAST) Agenda to Improve the Regime Complex for Climate Change. In M. Jakob, ed. *Handbook on Trade Policy and Climate Change.* Cheltenham and Massachusetts: Edward Elgar Publishing Limited.

Demena, B. A. and S. K. Afesorgbor. 2020. The Effect of FDI on Environmental Emissions: Evidence from a Meta-Analysis. *Energy Policy.* 138 (111192).

Dijkstra, B. R., A. J. Mathew, and A. Mukherjee. 2011. Environmental Regulation: An Incentive for Foreign Direct Investment. *Review of International Economics.* 19 (3). pp. 568–578.

Dong, B., J. Gong, and X. Zhao. 2012. FDI and Environmental Regulation: Pollution Haven or a Race to the Top? *Journal of Regulatory Economics.* 41 (2). pp. 216–237.

Duval, Y. and Hardy, S. 2021. A Primer on Quantifying the Environmental Benefits of Cross-Border Paperless Trade Facilitation. *ARTNeT Working Paper Series.* 206. Bangkok: Asia-Pacific Research and Training Network on Trade.

Eco Mark Office. 2022. Japan Eco Mark Certification Criteria. Japan Environment Association. https://www.ecomark.jp/nintei/index_en.html.

Edmonds, J., D. Forrister, L. Clarke, S. de Clara, and C. Munnings. 2019. *The Economic Potential of Article 6 of the Paris Agreement and Implementation Challenges*. Washington, DC: International Emissions Trading Association, University of Maryland, and Carbon Pricing Leadership Coalition.

Eicke, L., S. Weko, M. Apergi, and A. Marian. 2021. Pulling Up the Carbon Ladder? Decarbonization, Dependence, and Third-Country Risks from the European Carbon Border Adjustment Mechanism. *Energy Research & Social Science*. 80 (102240).

Elliott, R. J. and K. Shimamoto. 2008. Are ASEAN Countries Havens for Japanese Pollution-intensive Industry? *World Economy*. 31 (2). pp. 236–254.

Elliott, R. J. and Y. Zhou. 2013. Environmental Regulation Induced Foreign Direct Investment. *Environmental and Resource Economics*. 55 (1). pp. 141–158.

Elliott, R. J., P. Sun, and S. Chen. 2013. Energy Intensity and Foreign Direct Investment: A Chinese City-Level Study. *Energy Economics*. 40. pp. 484–494.

Erdogan, A. M. 2014. Foreign Direct Investment and Environmental Regulations: A Survey. *Journal of Economic Surveys*. 28 (5). pp. 943–955.

Emmerling, J. L. A. Reis, L. Drouet, D. Raitzer, and M. Pradhananga. 2022. What a Net Zero Transition Means for Asia and the World. Presentation. Manila. October.

Eskeland, G. S. and A. E. Harrison. 2003. Moving to Greener Pastures? Multinationals and the Pollution Haven Hypothesis. *Journal of Development Economics*. 70 (1). pp. 1–23.

European Commission. Single Market and Standards: Mutual Recognition of Goods. https://single-market-economy.ec.europa.eu/single-market/goods/free-movement-sectors/mutual-recognition-goods_en.

European Council. 2022. EU Climate Action: Provisional Agreement Reached on Carbon Border Adjustment Mechanism (CBAM). Press Release. 13 December. https://www.consilium.europa.eu/en/press/press-releases/2022/12/13/eu-climate-action-provisional-agreement-reached-on-carbon-border-adjustment-mechanism-cbam/.

European Union. Enhanced Regional EU-ASEAN Dialogue Instrument (E-READI). https://www.eeas.europa.eu/eeas/enhanced-regional-eu-asean-dialogue-instrument-e-readi_en (accessed January 2023).

———. 1998. *Implementation of Mutual Recognition Agreements on Conformity Assessment (MRA) and Protocol on European Conformity Assessment (PECA)*. European Commission Docs Room. https://ec.europa.eu/docsroom/documents/6417.

Falvey, R. and N. Foster-McGregor. 2017. North-South Foreign Direct Investment and Bilateral Investment Treaties. *The World Economy*. 41 (1). pp. 2–28.

Flachsland, C., R. Marschinski, and O. Edenhofer. 2009. Global Trading versus Linking: Architectures for International Emissions Trading. *Energy Policy*. 37. pp. 1637–1647.

Global Green Growth Institute (GGGI). 2022. GGGI Facilitates Memorandum of Understanding between Nepal and Sweden for Bilateral Cooperation under Article 6 of the Paris Agreement. Press release. 1 June. https://gggi.org/gggi-facilitates-memorandum-of-understanding-between-nepal-and-sweden-for-bilateral-cooperation-under-article-6-of-the-paris-agreement/.

Golub, S. S., C. Kauffmann and P. Yeres. 2011. Defining and Measuring Green FDI: An Exploratory Review of Existing Work and Evidence. *OECD Working Papers on International Investment*. 2011/02. Paris: OECD Publishing.

Gordon, K. and J. Pohl. 2011. Environmental Concerns in International Investment Agreements: A Survey. OECD Working Papers on International Investment. 2011/01. Paris: OECD Publishing.

Government of Australia, Department of Industry, Science and Resources. Japan–Australia Partnership on Decarbonisation through Technology. https://www.minister.industry.gov.au/ministers/taylor/media-releases/japan-australia-partnership-decarbonisation-through-technology.

Government of Japan, Ministry of Environment. Activities for the ASEAN Region. https://www.env.go.jp/earth/ondanka/pasti/en/activity/asean.html (accessed January 2023).

Government of the Philippines, Department of Energy. 2022. *Philippine Energy Labeling Program: Related Laws, Issuances and Implementing Guidelines.* https://www.doe.gov.ph/pelp?q=pelp/related-laws-issuances-and-implementing-guidelines&withshield=1.

Government of Singapore, Green Economy Agreement. 2021. Joint Media Release on the Singapore Australia Green Economy Agreement. Media release. 21 October. https://www.gea.gov.sg/resources/media-centre/joint-media-release.

Greaney, T. M., Y. Li, and D. Tu. 2017. Pollution Control and Foreign Firms' Exit Behavior in China. *Journal of Asian Economics.* 48. pp. 148–159.

Grull, G. and L. Taschini. 2012. Linking Emission Trading Schemes: A Short Note. *Economics of Energy and Environmental Policy.* 1 (3).

Haraguchi, M. and U. Lall. 2015. Flood Risks and Impacts: A Case Study of Thailand's Floods in 2011 and Research Questions for Supply Chain Decision Making. *International Journal of Disaster Risk Reduction.* 14 (3). pp. 256–272.

Haskel, J. E., S. C. Pereira, and M. J. Slaughter. 2007. Does Inward Foreign Direct Investment Boost the Productivity of Domestic Firms? *The Review of Economics and Statistics.* 89 (3). pp. 482–496.

He, J. 2006. Pollution Haven Hypothesis and Environmental Impacts of Foreign Direct Investment: The Case of Industrial Emission of Sulfur Dioxide (SO_2) in Chinese Provinces. *Ecological Economics.* 60 (1). pp. 228–245.

He, X., F. Zhai, and J. Ma. 2022. *The Global Impact of a Carbon Border Adjustment Mechanism: A Quantitative Assessment.* March. https://www.bu.edu/gdp/files/2022/03/TF-WP-001-FIN.pdf.

Heid, B. and I. Vozzo. 2020. The International Trade Effects of Bilateral Investment Treaties. *Economics Letters.* 196 (109569).

Huang, Y., Y. Zhang, L. Lin, and G. Wan. 2019. Foreign Direct Investment and Cleaner Production Choice: Evidence from Chinese Coal-Fired Power Generating Enterprises. *Journal of Cleaner Production.* 212. pp. 766–778.

Hübler, M. and A. Keller. 2010. Energy Savings via FDI? Empirical Evidence from Developing Countries. *Environment and Development Economics.* 15 (1). pp. 59–80.

Huong, N. 2016. *SWOT Analysis of Vietnam Green Label Program Report: Project "Stimulating the Demand and Supply of Sustainable Products Through Sustainable Public Procurement and Ecolabelling."* Ha Noi.

Huyen, P. A. 2016. Vietnam Green Label and Green Public Procurement. Presented at the International Symposium and Expert Meeting. https://www.env.go.jp/policy/hozen/green/kokusai_platform/2016symposium/03_Vietnam.pdf.

International Energy Agency (IEA). 2021. Net Zero by 2050: *A Roadmap for the Global Energy Sector.* https://www.iea.org/reports/net-zero-by-2050.

International Energy Agency Photovoltaic Power Systems Programme (IEA PPSP). 2021. *Snapshots of Global PV Markets 2021.* Rheine.

International Organization for Standardization (ISO). Committee 09: ISO Survey of Certifications to Management System Standards—Full Results. https://isotc.iso.org/livelink/livelink?func=ll&objId=18808772&objAction=browse&viewType=1ISO survey (accessed October 2022).

International Renewable Energy Agency (IRENA). 2021. *Green Hydrogen Supply: A Guide to Policy Making*. Abu Dhabi.

Iwasaki, I. and M. Tokunaga. 2016. Technology Transfer and Spillovers from FDI in Transition Economies: A Meta-Analysis. *Journal of Comparative Economics*. 44 (4). pp. 1086–1114.

Javorcik, B. S. 2004. Does Foreign Direct Investment Increase the Productivity of Domestic Firms? In Search of Spillovers through Backward Linkages. *American Economic Review*. 94 (3). pp. 605–627.

Jiang, L., H. F. Zhou, L. Bai, and P. Zhou. 2018. Does Foreign Direct Investment Drive Environmental Degradation in China? An Empirical Study Based on Air Quality Index from a Spatial Perspective. *Journal of Cleaner Production*. 176. pp. 864–872.

Jiao, Y., C. Ji, S. Yang, G. Yang, M. Su, and H. Fan. 2020. Home Governments Facilitate Cleaner Operations of Outward Foreign Direct Investment: A Case Study of a Cleaner Production Partnership Programme. *Journal of Cleaner Production*. 265 (121914).

Khan, A., Y. Chenggang, S. Bano, and J. Hussain. 2020. The Empirical Relationship between Environmental Degradation, Economic Growth, and Social Well-Being in Belt and Road Initiative Countries. *Environmental Science and Pollution Research*. 27 (24). pp. 30800–30814.

Khanna, M. 2020. Growing Green Business Investment in Asia and the Pacific: Trends and Opportunities. *ADB Sustainable Development Working Paper Series*. 72. Manila: ADB.

Kim, Y., T. Y. Jung, J. Moon, J. Kim, and G. Estrada. 2022. Costs and Benefits of Low Carbon Transition in Asia. Background Paper for *Asian Development Outlook 2023* Theme Chapter. Manuscript.

Kirkpatrick, C. and K. Shimamoto. 2008. The Effect of Environmental Regulation on the Locational Choice of Japanese Foreign Direct Investment. *Applied Economics*. 40 (11). pp. 1399–1409.

Kox, H. L. and H. Rojas-Romagosa. 2020. How Trade and Investment Agreements Affect Bilateral Foreign Direct Investment: Results from a Structural Gravity Model. *The World Economy*. 43 (12).

Kuusela, O. P. and J. Lintunen. 2020. A Cap-and-Trade Commitment Policy with Allowance Banking. *Environmental and Resource Economics*. 75 (3). pp. 421–455.

Laurens, N., C. Brandi, and J. F. Morin. 2022. Climate and Trade Policies: From Silos to Integration. *Climate Policy*. 22 (2). pp. 248–253.

Lee, W., N. Rocha, and M. Ruta. 2021. Trade Facilitation Provisions in Preferential Trade Agreements. *Policy Research Papers*. Washington, DC: World Bank.

Li, J., R. Strange, L. Ning, and D. Sutherland. 2016. Outward Foreign Direct Investment and Domestic Innovation Performance: Evidence from China. *International Business Review*. 25 (5). pp. 1010–1019.

Li, Y., F. Lin, and W. Wang. 2022. Environmental Regulation and Inward Foreign Direct Investment: Evidence from the Eleventh Five-Year Plan in China. *Journal of Economic Surveys*. 36 (3). pp. 684–707.

Lin, L. and W. Sun. 2016. Location Choice of FDI Firms and Environmental Regulation Reforms in China. *Journal of Regulatory Economics*. 50 (2). pp. 207–232.

Li, L., X. Liu, D. Yuan, and M. Yu. 2017. Does Outward FDI Generate Higher Productivity for Emerging Economy MNEs? Micro-Level Evidence from Chinese Manufacturing Firms. *International Business Review*. 26 (5). pp. 839–854.

Liu, X. and C. Wang. 2003. Does Foreign Direct Investment Facilitate Technological Progress? Evidence from Chinese Industries. *Research Policy.* 32 (6). pp. 945–953.

Liu, H., Y. Wang, J. Jiang, and P. Wu. 2020. How Green Is the "Belt and Road Initiative"?—Evidence from Chinese OFDI in the Energy Sector. *Energy Policy.* 145. 111709.

Liu, L., Z. Zhao, M. Zhang, C. Zhou, and D. Zhou. 2021. The Effects of Environmental Regulation on Outward Foreign Direct Investment's Reverse Green Technology Spillover: Crowding Out or Facilitation? *Journal of Cleaner Production.* 284. 124689.

Liu, S. and P. Zhang. 2022. Foreign Direct Investment and Air Pollution in China: Evidence from the Global Financial Crisis. The Developing Economies. 60 (1). pp. 30–61.

Liu, Y., Y. Hao, and Y. Gao. 2017. The Environmental Consequences of Domestic and Foreign Investment: Evidence from China. *Energy Policy.* 108. pp. 271–280.

Longden, T., F. J. Beck, F. Jotzo, R. Andrews, and M. Prasad. 2022. 'Clean' Hydrogen? – Comparing the Emissions and Costs of Fossil Fuel Versus Renewable Electricity Based Hydrogen. *Applied Energy.* 306, Part B (118145).

Mahadevan, R. and Y. Sun. 2020. Effects of Foreign Direct Investment on Carbon Emissions: Evidence from China and its Belt and Road Countries. *Journal of Environmental Management.* 276. 111321.

Maliszewska, M. and D. van der Mensbrugghe. 2019. The Belt and Road Initiative: Economic, Poverty and Environmental Impacts. *Policy Research Working Papers.* 8814. Washington, DC: World Bank.

Managi, S. 2004. Trade Liberalization and the Environment: Carbon Dioxide for 1960–1999. *Economics Bulletin.* 17 (1). pp. 1–5.

Managi, S., A. Hibiki, and T. Tsurumi. 2009. Does Trade Openness Improve Environmental Quality? *Journal of Environmental Economics and Management.* 58 (3). pp. 346–363.

Marcu, A., M. Mehling, and A. Cosbey. 2020. Border Carbon Adjustments in the EU Issues and Options. *ERCST Roundtable on Climate Change and Sustainable Transition.* 30 September.

Martínez-Zarzoso, I. and W. Oueslati. 2018. Do Deep and Comprehensive Regional Trade Agreements Help in Reducing Air Pollution? *International Environmental Agreements: Politics, Law and Economics.* 18 (6). pp. 743–777.

Masterson, V. 2022. Degrowth – What's Behind the Economic Theory and Why Does It Matter Right Now?. World Economic Forum. https://www.weforum.org/agenda/2022/06/what-is-degrowth-economics-climate-change/.

Meyer, K. E. and E. Sinani. 2009. When and Where Does Foreign Direct Investment Generate Positive Spillovers? A Meta-Analysis. *Journal of International Business Studies.* 40 (7). pp. 1075–1094.

Millimet, D. L. and J. Roy. 2016. Empirical Tests of the Pollution Haven Hypothesis When Environmental Regulation Is Endogenous. *Journal of Applied Econometrics.* 31 (4). pp. 652–677.

Monteiro, J.-A. 2016. Typology of Environment-Related Provisions in Regional Trade Agreements. *Staff Working Paper:* No. ERSD-2016-13. Geneva: World Trade Organization.

Motta, M. and J. F. Thisse. 1994. Does Environmental Dumping Lead to Delocation? *European Economic Review.* 38 (3–4). pp. 563–576.

Mudakkar, S. R., K. Zaman, H. Shakir, M. Arif, I. Naseem, and L. Naz. 2013. Determinants of Energy Consumption Function in SAARC Countries: Balancing the Odds. *Renewable and Sustainable Energy Reviews.* 28. pp. 566–574.

Munoz, E. 2021. What Is a Memorandum of Understanding (MOU)? *LegalVision*. 6 October. https://legalvision.com.au/memorandum-of-understanding/.

Murshed, M., M. Elheddad, R. Ahmed, M. Bassim, and E. T. Than. 2022. Foreign Direct Investments, Renewable Electricity Output, and Ecological Footprints: Do Financial Globalization Facilitate Renewable Energy Transition And Environmental Welfare In Bangladesh? *Asia-Pacific Financial Markets*. 29 (1). pp. 33–78.

Nair-Reichert, U. and D. Weinhold. 2001. Causality Tests for Cross-Country Panels: A New look at FDI and Economic Growth in Developing Countries. *Oxford Bulletin of Economics and Statistics*. 63 (2). pp. 153–171.

National Institute of Standards and Technology (NIST). 2020. *Mutual Recognition Agreements for Conformity Assessment of Telecommunications Equipment*. https://www.nist.gov/mutual-recognition-agreements-mras.

NBC San Diego. 2021. Delays at Border Crossings Cost San Diego–Tijuana Region Billions: SANDAG Study. 27 February. https://www.nbcsandiego.com/news/local/delays-at-border-crossings-cost-san-diego-tijuana-region-billions-sandag-study/2533918/.

Neumayer, E. and L. Spess. 2005. Do Bilateral Investment Treaties Increase Foreign Direct Investment to Developing Countries? *World Development*. 33 (10). pp. 1567–1585.

Newman, C., J. Rand, T. Talbot, and F. Tarp. 2015. Technology Transfers, Foreign Investment and Productivity Spillovers. *European Economic Review*. 76. pp. 168–187.

Ning, L., F. Wang, and J. Li. 2016. Urban Innovation, Regional Externalities of Foreign Direct Investment and Industrial Agglomeration: Evidence from Chinese Cities. *Research Policy*. 45 (4). pp. 830–843.

Nordhaus, W. 1992. An Optimal Transition Path for Controlling Greenhouse Gases. *Science*. 258 (5058). pp. 1315–1319.

———. 2018. Projections and Uncertainties about Climate Change in an Era of Minimal Climate Policies. *American Economic Journal: Economic Policy*. 10 (3). pp. 333–360.

Organisation for Economic Co-operation and Development (OECD). OECDstat: Carbon dioxide emissions embodied in international trade (TECO$_2$) data set. https://stats.oecd.org (accessed December 2021).

———. Exchange Rates. https://stats.oecd.org/ (accessed November 2022).

———. 2022. *Investment Treaties and Climate Change: Background Note for November 2022 Meeting*. Geneva.

OECD and Eurostat 1999. *The Environmental Goods and Services Industry: Manual for Data Collection and Analysis*. Paris: OECD Library. https://read.oecd-ilibrary.org/industry-and-services/the-environmental-goods-and-services-industry_9789264173651-en#page1.

Pan, X., S. Guo, C. Han, M. Wang, J. Song, and X. Liao. 2020. Influence of FDI Quality on Energy Efficiency in China based on Seemingly Unrelated Regression Method. *Energy*. 192 (116463).

Pangestu, M. E. 2022. Carbon Pricing Leadership Coalition Report 2021-2022. World Bank Blogs. 25 May. https://blogs.worldbank.org/voices/carbon-pricing-leadership-coalition-report-2021-2022.

Patala, S., J. K. Juntunen, S. Lundan, and T. Ritvala. 2021. Multinational Energy Utilities in the Energy Transition: A Configurational Study of the Drivers of FDI in Renewables. *Journal of International Business Studies*. 52 (5). pp. 930–950.

Pazienza, P. 2014. *The Relationship between FDI and the Natural Environment: Facts, Evidence and Prospects.* New York: Springer.

Piperopoulos, P., J. Wu, and C. Wang. 2018. Outward FDI, Location Choices and Innovation Performance of Emerging Market Enterprises. *Research Policy.* 47 (1). pp. 232–240.

Ranocchia, C. and L. Lambertini. 2021. Porter Hypothesis vs Pollution Haven Hypothesis: Can There Be Environmental Policies Getting Two Eggs in One Basket? *Environmental and Resource Economics.* 78 (1). pp. 177–199.

Reeve, A. and E. Aisbett. 2022. National Accounting Systems as a Foundation for Embedded Emissions Accounting in Trade-Related Climate Policies. *Journal of Cleaner Production.* 371 (133678).

Ren, S., Y. Hao, and H. Wu. 2022. The Role of Outward Foreign Direct Investment (OFDI) on Green Total Factor Energy Efficiency: Does Institutional Quality Matter? Evidence from China. *Resources Policy.* 76. 102587.

Reyna, J., S. Vadlamani, M. Chester, and Y. Lou. 2016. Reducing Emissions at Land Border Crossings through Queue Reduction and Expedited Security Processing. *Transportation Research Part D: Transport and Environment.* 49. pp. 219–30. https://doi.org/10.1016/j.trd.2016.09.006.

Rezza, A. 2015. A Meta-Analysis of FDI and Environmental Regulations. *Environment and Development Economics.* 20 (2). 185–208.

Sauvage, J. and C. Timiliotis. 2017. Trade in Services Related to the Environment. *OECD Trade and Environment Working Papers.* 2017/02. Paris: OECD Publishing.

Seol, T. K., Y. S. Kim, and S. P. Lee. 2022. The Renewable Energy Law Review: South Korea. *The Law Reviews.* July.

Shao, W., X. Yu, and Z. Chen. 2022. Does the Carbon Emission Trading Policy Promote Foreign Direct Investment?: A Quasi-Experiment From China. *Frontiers in Environmental Science.* 9 (798438).

Shapiro, J. S. 2016. Trade Costs, CO_2, and the Environment. *American Economic Journal: Economic Policy.* 8 (4). pp. 220–254.

Stangarone, T. 2021. South Korean Efforts to Transition to a Hydrogen Economy. *Clean Technologies and Environmental Policy.* 23 (2). pp. 509–516.

Steenblik, R. and S. Droege. 2019. Time to ACCTS? Five countries announce new initiative on trade and climate change. *Insight.* 25 September. https://www.iisd.org/articles/insight/time-accts-five-countries-announce-new-initiative-trade-and-climate-change.

Stiglitz, Joseph. 1996. Some Lessons from the East Asian Miracle. The *World Bank Research Observer.* 11 (2). pp. 151–177.

Strezhnev, A. 2018. Essays on Causal Inference and the International Investment Regime. PhD dissertation. Harvard University.

Taghizadeh-Hesary, F., N. Yoshino, and Y. Inagaki. 2018. Empirical Analysis of Factors Influencing Price of Solar Modules. *ADBI Working Paper Series. No.* 836. Tokyo: Asian Development Bank Institute.

Tai, L. and L. Yan. 2022. The Impact of Environmental Regulation on Foreign Firms' Exit: From the Perspective of Competition. *Environmental Science and Pollution Research.* 29 (11). pp. 15539–15550.

Talmon, S. 2021. Germany Directs Attention to Questions Surrounding Non-Legally Binding International Agreements. *German Practice in International Law.* 21 May. https://gpil.jura.uni-bonn.de/2021/05/germany-directs-attention-to-questions-surrounding-non-legally-binding-international-agreements/.

Tang, C. F. and B. W. Tan. 2015. The Impact of Energy Consumption, Income and Foreign Direct Investment on Carbon Dioxide Emissions in Vietnam. *Energy.* 79. pp. 447–454.

Tian, X., Y. Hu, H. Yin, Y. Geng, and R. Bleischwitz. 2019. Trade Impacts of China's Belt and Road Initiative: From Resource and Environmental Perspectives. *Resources, Conservation and Recycling.* 150. 104430.

Timmer, M. P., E. Dietzenbacher, B. Los, R. Stehrer, and G. J. de Vries. 2015. An Illustrated User Guide to the World Input–Output Database: The Case of Global Automotive Production. *Review of International Economics.* 23. pp. 575–605.

Tiwari, A. K., S. Nasreen, and M. A. Anwar. 2022. Impact of Equity Market Development on Renewable Energy Consumption: Do the Role of FDI, Trade Openness, and Economic Growth Matter in Asian Economies? *Journal of Cleaner Production.* 334 (130244).

Ullah, A., X. Zhao, M. Abdul Kamal, and J. Zheng. 2022. Environmental Regulations and Inward FDI in China: Fresh Evidence from the Asymmetric Autoregressive Distributed Lag Approach. *International Journal of Finance and Economics.* 27 (1). pp. 1340–1356.

United Nations. Commodity Trade Database. https://comtrade.un.org (accessed December 2022).

United Nations Conference on Trade and Development (UNCTAD). 2004. *Key Terms and Concepts in International Investment Agreements: A Glossary.* Geneva.

———. 2010. *World Investment Report 2010: Investing in a Low-Carbon Economy.* Geneva.

———. 2021. *A European Union Carbon Border Adjustment Mechanism: Implications for Developing Countries.* Geneva.

———. 2022. Treaty-based Investor–State Dispute Settlement Cases and Climate Action. *IIA Issues Note.* No. 4. September. Geneva.

———. Investment Policy Hub: International Investment Agreements Navigator. https://investmentpolicy.unctad.org/international-investment-agreements (accessed May and August 2022).

Wang, D. T. and W. Y. Chen. 2014. Foreign Direct Investment, Institutional Development, and Environmental Externalities: Evidence from China. *Journal of Environmental Management.* 135. pp. 81–90.

Wei, Y., S. Ding, and Z. Konwar. 2022. The Two Faces of FDI in Environmental Performance: A Meta-analysis of Empirical Evidence in China. *Journal of Chinese Economic and Business Studies.* 20 (1). pp. 65–94.

White, L. V., R. Fazeli, W. Cheng, E. Aisbett, F. J. Beck, K. G.H. Baldwin, P. Howarth, and L. O'Neill. 2021. Towards Emissions Certification Systems for International Trade in Hydrogen: The Policy Challenge of Defining Boundaries for Emissions Accounting. *Energy.* 215, Part A (119139).

World Bank. 1993. *The East Asian Miracle: Economic Growth and Public Policy.* Washington, DC.

———. 2020. *World Development Report 2020: Trading for Development in the Age of Global Value Chains.* Washington, DC.

———. 2022. *State and Trends of Carbon Pricing.* Washington, DC.

———. Deep Trade Agreements : Data, Tools and Analysis. https://datatopics.worldbank.org/dta/dashboard.html (accessed September 2022).

———. Carbon Pricing Dashboard. https://carbonpricingdashboard.worldbank.org/map_data (accessed January 2023).

———. World Development Indicators. https://databank.worldbank.org/source/world-development-indicators (accessed December 2022 and January 2023).

World Meteorological Organization (WMO). 2022. *State of the Climate in Asia 2021.* Geneva.

World Trade Organization (WTO). 2021. Trade and Climate Change. The Carbon Content of International Trade. *Information Brief.* No. 4. Geneva.

———. 2022. *World Trade Report 2022—Climate Change and Trade.* Geneva.

———. Regional Trade Agreements Database. https://rtais.wto.org/UI/PublicMaintainRTAHome.aspx (all accessed May 2022).

———. Statistics on Trade in Commercial Services. https://www.wto.org/english/res_e/statis_e/tradeserv_stat_e.htm (accessed August 2022).

Wu, H., S. Ren, G. Yan, and Y. Hao. 2020. Does China's Outward Direct Investment Improve Green Total Factor Productivity in the "Belt and Road" Countries? Evidence from Dynamic Threshold Panel Model Analysis. *Journal of Environmental Management.* 275 (111295).

Xie, R. H., Y. J. Yuan, and J. J. Huang. 2017. Different Types of Environmental Regulations and Heterogeneous Influence on 'Green' Productivity: Evidence from China. *Ecological Economics.* 132. pp. 104–112.

Xing, Y. and C. D. Kolstad. 2002. Do Lax Environmental Regulations Attract Foreign Investment? *Environmental and Resource Economics.* 21 (1). pp. 1–22.

Xu, X. and Y. Sheng. 2012. Productivity Spillovers from Foreign Direct Investment: Firm-Level Evidence from China. *World Development.* 40 (1). pp. 62–74.

Xu, Y., Y. Wu, and Y. Shi. 2021. Emission Reduction and Foreign Direct Investment Nexus in China. *Journal of Asian Economics.* 74 (101305).

Yang, C., L. Liu, W. Yang, and T. Ahmed. 2021. Environmental Regulation, Outward Foreign Direct Investment, and Low-Carbon Innovation: An Empirical Study Based on Provincial Spatial Panel Data in China. *Mathematical Problems in Engineering.* 3021224.

Yu, P., Z. Cai, and Y. Sun. 2021. Does the Emissions Trading System in Developing Countries Accelerate Carbon Leakage through OFDI? Evidence from China. *Energy Economics.* 101 (105397).

Yu, X. and Y. Li. 2020. Effect of Environmental Regulation Policy Tools on the Quality of Foreign Direct Investment: An Empirical Study of China. *Journal of Cleaner Production.* 270 (122346).

Zhang, C. and X. Zhou. 2016. Does Foreign Direct Investment Lead to Lower CO2 Emissions? Evidence from a Regional Analysis in China. *Renewable and Sustainable Energy Reviews.* 58. pp. 943–951.

Zhang, J., and X. Fu. 2008. FDI and Environmental Regulations in China. *Journal of the Asia Pacific Economy.* 13 (3). pp. 332–353.

Zhang, N., Z. Liu, X. Zheng, and J. Xue. 2017. Carbon Footprint of China's Belt and Road. *Science.* 357 (5356). p. 1107.

Zhang, Y. 2021. Is the EU's Carbon Border Tax a Good Approach? Voices. 24 June. Blavatnik School of Government, University of Oxford. https://www.bsg.ox.ac.uk/blog/eus-carbon-border-tax-good-approach.

Zhao, X. G., Y. F. Zhang, and Y. B. Li. 2019. The Spillovers of Foreign Direct Investment and the Convergence of Energy Intensity. *Journal of Cleaner Production.* 206. pp. 611–621.

Zhou, Y., J. Jiang, B. Ye, and B. Hou. 2019. Green Spillovers of Outward Foreign Direct Investment on Home Countries: Evidence from China's Province-Level Data. *Journal of Cleaner Production.* 215. pp. 829–844.

Annex 7a: Potential Impact of Trade Facilitation on Greenhouse Gas Emissions

Groups	Subgroups	Measures	Impact on Mitigating GHG Emissions (Low-1/Mid-2/High-3)	Possible Channel
General Trade Facilitation	Transparency (5 measures)	Publication of existing import–export regulations on the internet	3	Lesser trips required to comply with requirements; reduction in paper use
		Stakeholders' consultation on new draft regulations (prior to their finalization)	1	Allows for continuous sharing of information in trade facilitation projects
		Advance publication/notification of new trade-related regulations before their implementation (e.g., 30 days prior)	3	Lesser trips required to comply with requirements; reduction in paper use
		Advance ruling on tariff classification and origin of imported goods	2	Speeds up clearances and thus reduces waiting time
		Independent appeal mechanism (for traders to appeal customs rulings and the rulings of other relevant trade control agencies)	1	Unbalanced discretionary power of customs may contribute to delay in the release of goods
	Formalities (8 measures)	Risk management (for deciding whether a shipment will be physically inspected)	1	May speed up movement of shipments
		Pre-arrival processing	3	Reduction in time spent at the border
		Post-clearance audits	1	Improve trader's compliance and facilitate clearance procedures
		Separation of release from final determination of customs duties, taxes, fees, and charges	2	Reduction in time spent at the border
		Establishment and publication of average release times	1	Lengthy release times will advocate for reducing border delays
		Trade facilitation measures for authorized operators	3	Allows qualified operators to benefit from preferential measures like rapid release times, fewer physical inspections, and reduced documentary requirements
		Expedited shipments	3	Reduces waiting time
		Acceptance of copies of original supporting documents required for import, export, or transit formalities	2	Reduces waiting time
	Institutional arrangement and cooperation (5 measures)	Establishment of a national trade facilitation committee or similar body	1	Ensures coordination of various stakeholders for seamless implementation of trade facilitation
		National legislative framework and/or institutional arrangements for border agencies cooperation	2	Provides avenue to expedite crossing of shipments and therefore reduce waiting time
		Government agencies delegating border controls to customs authorities	2	Provides avenue to expedite crossing of shipments and therefore reduces waiting time
		Alignment of working days and hours with neighboring economies at border crossings	2	Provides avenue to expedite crossing of shipments and therefore reduces waiting time
		Alignment of formalities and procedures with neighboring economies at border crossings	2	Provides avenue to expedite crossing of shipments and therefore reduces waiting time
	Transit facilitation (4 measures)	Transit facilitation agreement(s) with neighboring economy(ies)	2	Reduction in time spent at the border
		Customs authorities limit the physical inspections of transit goods and use risk assessment	2	Reduction in time spent at the border
		Support pre-arrival processing for transit facilitation	2	Reduction in time spent at the border
		Cooperation between agencies of economies involved in transit	2	Reduction in time spent at the border

continued on next page

Annex 7a continued

Groups	Subgroups	Measures	Impact on Mitigating GHG Emissions (Low-1/Mid-2/High-3)	Possible Channel
Digital Trade Facilitation	**Paperless trade** (10 measures)	Automated Customs System (e.g., ASYCUDA)	3	Reduction in waiting time; elimination of printed paper; elimination of physical delivery
		Internet connection available to customs and other trade control agencies at border crossings	2	Indirect, but enabler
		Electronic single window system	3	Reduction in waiting time; elimination of printed paper; decrease in the number of procedures involved; lesser trips required to comply with requirements
		Electronic submission of customs declarations	3	Reduction in waiting time; elimination of printed paper; elimination of physical delivery
		Electronic application and issuance of import and export permit	3	Reduction in waiting time; elimination of printed paper; elimination of physical delivery
		Electronic submission of sea cargo manifests	3	Reduction in waiting time; elimination of printed paper; elimination of physical delivery
		Electronic submission of air cargo manifests	3	Reduction in waiting time; elimination of printed paper; elimination of physical delivery
		Electronic application and issuance of Preferential Certificate of Origin	3	Reduction in waiting time; elimination of printed paper; elimination of physical delivery
		E-payment of customs duties and fees	3	Reduction in waiting time; fewer trips required to comply with requirements
		Electronic application for customs refunds	3	Elimination of printed papers; fewer trips required to comply with requirements
	Cross-border paperless trade (6 measures)	Laws and regulations for electronic transactions are in place (e.g., e-commerce law, e-transaction law)	2	Enable the shift from manual to electronic processes
		Recognized certification authority issuing digital certificates to traders to conduct electronic transactions	2	Help facilitate the use and boost confidence on the security of electronic transactions
		Electronic exchange of customs declaration	3	Reduction in waiting time; elimination of printed paper
		Electronic exchange of Certificate of Origin	3	Reduction in waiting time; elimination of printed paper
		Electronic exchange of Sanitary and Phyto-Sanitary (SPS) Certificate	3	Reduction in waiting time; elimination of printed paper; reduction in cargo storage time
		Paperless collection of payment from a documentary letter of credit	3	Reduction in waiting time; elimination of printed paper
Sustainable Trade Facilitation	**Trade facilitation for SMEs** (5 measures)	Trade-related information measures for small and medium-sized enterprises (SMEs)	2	Fewer trips required to comply with requirements; reduction in paper use
		SMEs in Authorized Economic Operators scheme (i.e., government has developed specific measures that allow SMEs to benefit from the scheme more easily)	3	Allow qualified SMEs to benefit from preferential measures like rapid release times, fewer physical inspections, and reduced documentary requirements
		SMEs access single window (i.e., government has taken actions to make single windows more accessible to SMEs, e.g., by providing technical consultation and training services on registering and using the facility)	3	Reduction in waiting time; elimination of printed paper
		SMEs in a national trade facilitation committee (i.e., government has taken actions to ensure that SMEs are well-represented and made key members of national trade facilitation committees)	1	Ensures coordination of various stakeholders for seamless implementation of trade facilitation
		Other special measures for SMEs	1	Other measures may include reduction in inspection and paperwork for a specific minimum shipment value

continued on next page

Annex 7a continued

Groups	Subgroups	Measures	Impact on Mitigating GHG Emissions (Low-1/Mid-2/High-3)	Possible Channel
Other Trade Facilitation	**Agricultural trade facilitation** (4 measures)	Testing and laboratory facilities available to meet SPS of main trading partners	2	Decrease in the number of procedures involved
		National standards and accreditation bodies are established to facilitate compliance with SPS	2	Reduction in cargo storage time; decrease in the number of procedures involved
		Electronic application and issuance of SPS certificates	3	Reduction in waiting time; elimination of printed paper
		Special treatment for perishable goods at border crossings	3	Reduction in waiting time; reduce risk of spoilage
	Women in trade facilitation (3 measures)	Trade facilitation policy/strategy to increase women's participation in trade	1	Information on trade procedures and requirements are accessible to women to reduce burdensome procedures
		Trade facilitation measures to benefit women involved in trade	1	Trade facilitation measures, like the use of digital tools, can ease customs transactions for women entrepreneurs
		Women membership in the national trade facilitation committee or similar bodies	1	Membership of women in committees can help in women's participation in the implementation of trade facilitation measures
	Trade finance facilitation (3 measures)	Single window facilitates traders' access to finance	3	Reduction in waiting time; elimination of printed paper; fewer trips required to comply with requirements
		Authorities engaged in blockchain-based supply chain project covering trade finance	2	Elimination of printed paper; fewer trips required to comply with requirements
		Variety of trade finance services available	1	Available finance options decline
	Trade facilitation in times of crisis (5 measures)	Agency in place to manage trade facilitation in times of crises and emergencies	3	Ensure speedy movement of critical goods and essential supplies
		Online publication of emergency trade facilitation measures	2	Fewer trips required to comply with requirements; reduction in paper use
		Coordination between economies on emergency trade facilitation measures	3	Ensure speedy movement of critical goods and essential supplies.
		Additional trade facilitation measures to facilitate trade in times of emergencies	3	Ensure speedy movement of critical goods and essential supplies.
		Plan in place to facilitate trade during future crises	3	Ensure speedy movement of critical goods and essential supplies

GHG = greenhouse gas, SME = small and medium-sized enterprise, SPS = sanitary and phytosanitary.

Note: A low score (=1) represents a negligible impact on GHG emissions reduction, an intermediate score (=2) represents an indirect impact (or a catalytic impact for green trade facilitation), and a high score (=3) represents a direct impact on abating GHG emissions.

Source: Kim, Basu-Das, and Ardaniel (2022) based on ADB (2021d).

Annex 7b: Analyzing the Environmental Content of International Investment Agreements

To analyze references in international investment agreements that relate to environmental protection and climate change, two main sources were used: United Nations Conference on Trade and Development's (UNCTAD) International Investment Agreement (IIA) Navigator and the Asian Development Bank's (ADB) IIA Agreement database.

UNCTAD's IIA Navigator. The navigator provides a global mapping of the treaty elements of investment treaties and other treaties with investment provisions. The mapping includes information on environmental references in the preamble such as specific references to sustainable development, general public policy exceptions for the environment, and environmental clauses. The following table provides a summary of the categories in the UNCTAD mapping covering references to environmental aspects.

ADB's IIA Database: The IIA Tool Kit provides information on 15 investment provisions for investment treaties concluded by economies in Asia and the Pacific. The database includes a mapping of the relevant article and text for each treaty provision, allowing for textual analysis of the environmental content in the treaty. The following table provides information on the textual information included to identify environmental references.

Information on environmental elements of international investment agreements in the UNCTAD and ADB databases offers a comprehensive view. In general, UNCTAD identifies more agreements including environmental elements than the ADB database. This may be explained by a broader definition of environmental content and the inclusion of the preamble not captured in the database. Also, a number of international investment agreements in ADB database are not mapped by UNCTAD.

Treaty Elements with Environmental Reference in UNCTAD IIA Navigator

Item	Description
Preamble > Reference to environmental aspects	Preamble contains reference to environmental investment aspects or related concepts such as plant life or animal life, biodiversity, climate change, or others.
Preamble > Reference to sustainable development	Preamble contains a reference to the concept of sustainable development.
Exceptions > General public policy exceptions > Public health and environment	Treaty allows the contracting parties to derogate from WTO Agreement on Trade-Related Investment Measures treaty obligations in order to protect the environment (i.e., "human, animal or plan life or health," "conservation of living or nonliving exhaustible natural resources," "prevention of diseases or pests").
Other clauses > Health and environment	Treaty uses the terms "environment" or related terms such as "ecological," "animal," or "plant" in any of its provisions (except the preamble), including general exceptions, reaffirmations of the right to regulate for health and/or environmental purposes, nonbinding clauses, and any others.
Other clauses > Not lowering standards	Treaty contains a provision prohibiting or discouraging the contracting parties from attracting investment through the relaxation of labor, environmental, health, safety, or other domestic standards.
Standards of treatment > Expropriation > Carve-out for general regulatory measures	Treaty carves out from the notion of expropriation regulatory measures of general application undertaken to protect legitimate public welfare objectives (including the environment).

IIA = international investment agreement , UNCTAD =United Nations Conference on Trade and Development, WTO = World Trade Organization.

Source: UNCTAD. Investment Policy Hub: International Investment Agreements Navigator. https://investmentpolicy.unctad.org/international-investment-agreements (accessed August 2022).

Environmental References in the ADB Database

Related Topics/Areas	Main Reference
Energy, environmental, animal, plant, natural, environmentally, UNFCCC	UNCTAD (2004). Key Terms and Concepts in International Investment Agreements: A Glossary
Emissions, emission, GHG, carbon, carbon footprint, Paris Agreement	OECD (2022). Investment Treaties and Climate Change
Air, pollution, waste, disposal, sanitary, phytosanitary, pest, pests, national treasures, archaeological, pollutants, contaminant, contaminants, flora, fauna, habitat, historical monuments, historical monument	Gordon and Pohl (2011). Environmental Concerns in International Investment Agreements: A Survey

GHG = greenhouse gas, OECD = Organisation for Economic Co-operation and Development, UNFCC = United Nations Framework Convention on Climate Change, UNCTAD =United Nations Conference on Trade and Development.
Source: ADB compilation.

Annex 7c: Measures of Asia's Exposure and Vulnerability to the European Union' Carbon Border Adjustment Mechanism[1]

The potential risks to Asian economies from the European Union's (EU) implementation of the Carbon Border Adjustment Mechanism (CBAM) is based on two concepts: exposure (importance of EU trade for domestic economy) and vulnerability (measured by the economy's ability to adapt to CBAM). The methodology to estimate the relative risk index based on these two concepts follows Eicke et al. (2021).

The risk index uses 19 indicators across four dimensions: (i) exposure to CBAM; (ii) reliance on trade with the EU; (iii) emission levels and lack of decarbonization efforts; and (iv) statistical capacity to measure, report, and verify emissions (as shown in the figure below). The framework of Eicke et al. (2021) was modified by adding or replacing

indicators, but the overall concept of combining exposure and vulnerability was followed in estimating the risk indexes. The indicators for each dimension are captured in the box figure. The indicators are normalized using a min-max normalization for all sample years (2015–2019) and for all economies.

An overall risk index was calculated as the simple average of the dimensional indexes. The indexes were aggregated further by region and Asian subregions and presented as a simple average over 2015–2019. The pandemic years 2020–2021 were not included to avoid extreme values during the crisis that might skew the estimated risk indexes.

Framework to Measure Economies' Risk to EU CBAM Implementation

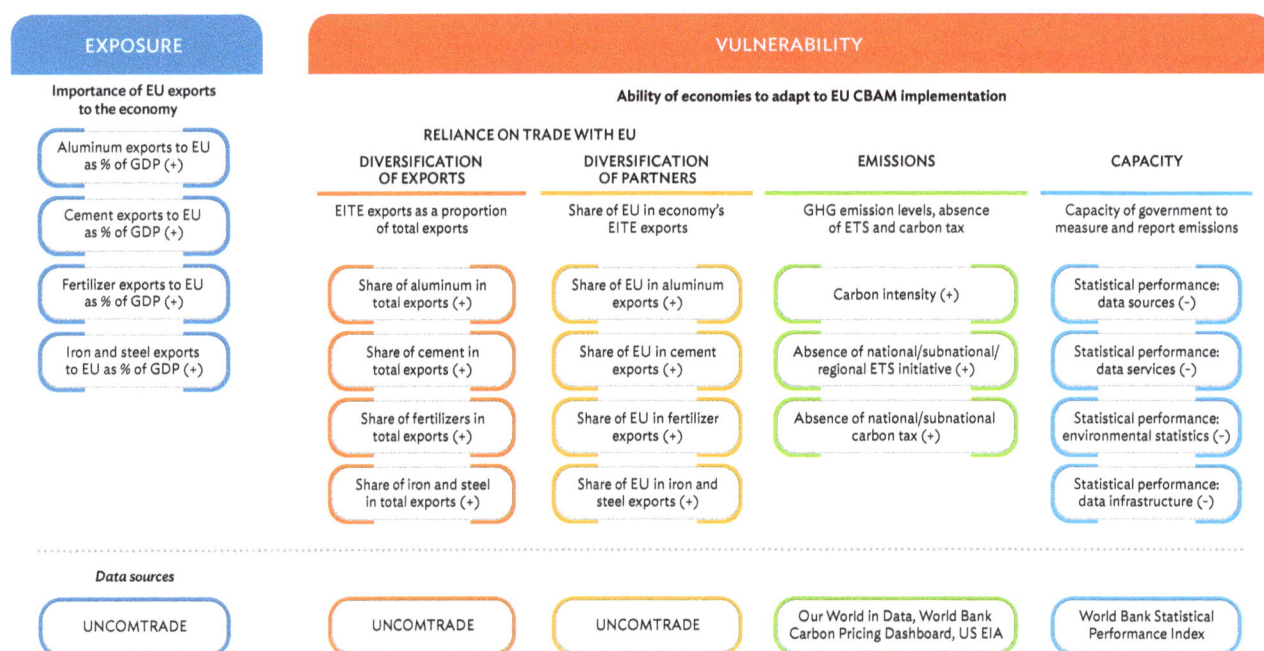

CBAM = Carbon Border Adjustment Mechanism; EITE = emissions-intensive and trade exposed goods (aluminum, cement, iron and steel, and fertilizers); ETS = emission trading scheme; EU = European Union (27 members); GDP = gross domestic product; GHG = greenhouse gas; US EIA = United States Energy Information Administration; UNCOMTRADE = United Nations Commodity Trade Database.
Source: Tan, Tayag, and Quizon (2022) based on Eicke et al. (2022).

---

[1]   Taken from Tan, Tayag, and Quizon (2022).

The Asian region has a low overall risk of exposure and vulnerability to CBAM because its trade with the EU is a small proportion of the region's trade.
Africa, the Middle East, and non-EU Europe are the regions with the highest potential risk for CBAM adoption. These regions have stronger trade linkages with the EU, particularly on emission-intensive and trade-exposed goods, and so are more likely to be affected. However, compared with other regions, Asia has relatively higher carbon dioxide (CO_2) emissions, which could make its products more likely to be subjected to the CBAM. It also has more economies with lower levels of statistical capacity, which could make it more difficult to trade CO_2 emissions.

Overall Risk Index to EU CBAM Implementation, By Region

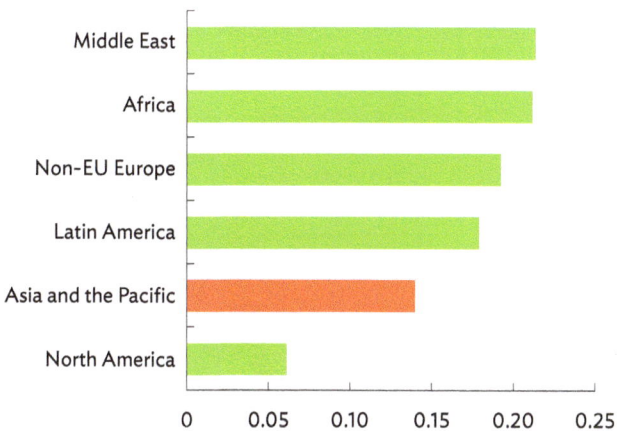

CBAM = carbon border adjustment mechanism, EU = European Union (27 members).
Source: Tan, Tayag, and Quizon (2022).

Within Asia, Central Asia, the Pacific, and South Asia face the highest overall potential risk to CBAM.
Central Asia has the highest level of exposure as EU trade is relatively more important to their economies. In particular, Central Asia's exports of aluminum and fertilizer to the EU as a share of its GDP are the highest among Asian subregions (as shown below). The Pacific subregion posted the highest emission-related risk index given its high carbon intensity of power generation, although carbon emission levels across the Pacific are generally low both in absolute and per capita terms. The Pacific's statistical capacity to measure and report emissions is the lowest among Asian subregions, mainly due to less developed data infrastructure—legislation, standards, skills, and partnerships—and lack of financial resources to deliver useful data products and services. South Asia has the next highest risk in three of the four dimensions. In general, economies in developing Asia have higher risk than developed Asia as their exports are less likely to be diversified, they have higher emissions, have not implemented an ETS or carbon tax, or lack statistical capacity.

Risk Index to EU CBAM Implementation By Dimension—Asia and the Pacific

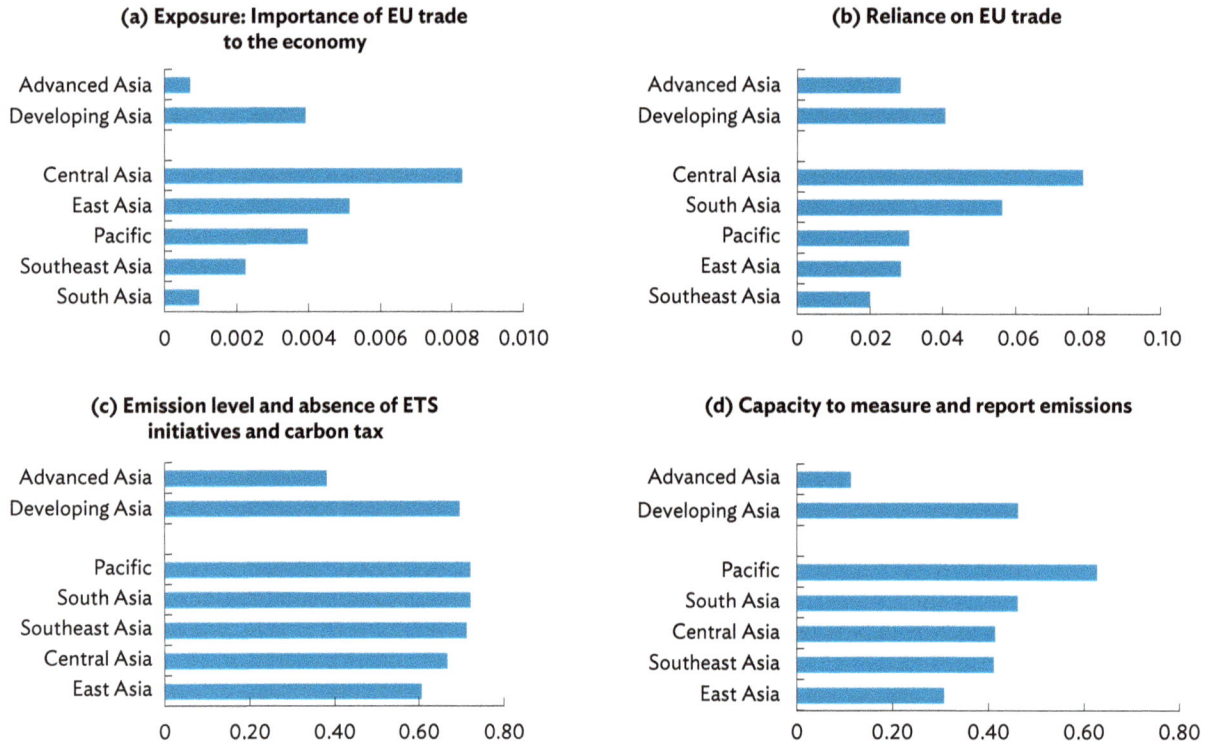

(a) Exposure: Importance of EU trade to the economy

(b) Reliance on EU trade

(c) Emission level and absence of ETS initiatives and carbon tax

(d) Capacity to measure and report emissions

CBAM = Carbon Border Adjustment Mechanism, ETS = emission trading scheme, EU = European Union (27 members).

Note: Risk index is calculated for data between 2015 and 2019.

Source: Tan, Tayag, and Quizon (2022).

8 Statistical Appendix

The statistical appendix comprises 10 tables of selected indicators on economic integration for the Asian Development Bank's (ADB) 49 members from Asia and the Pacific. The succeeding notes describe the economy groupings and the calculation procedures undertaken.

Regional Groupings

- Asia and the Pacific refers to the 49 regional members of ADB.
- Developing Asia refers to Asia excluding Australia, Japan, and New Zealand.
- The European Union consists of Austria, Belgium, Bulgaria, Croatia, Cyprus, Czechia, Denmark, Estonia, Finland, France, Germany, Greece, Hungary, Ireland, Italy, Latvia, Lithuania, Luxembourg, Malta, the Netherlands, Poland, Portugal, Romania, Slovakia, Slovenia, Spain, and Sweden.

Table Descriptions

Table A1: Asia-Pacific Regional Cooperation and Integration Index

The Asia-Pacific Regional Cooperation and Integration Index (ARCII) is a composite index that measures the degree of regional cooperation and integration in Asia and the Pacific. It comprises eight dimensional indexes based on 41 indicators to capture the contributions of eight different aspects of regional integration: (i) trade and investment, (ii) money and finance, (iii) regional value chains, (iv) infrastructure and connectivity, (v) people and social integration, (vi) institutional arrangements, (vii) technology and digital connectivity, and (viii) environmental cooperation. The construction of ARCII follows two steps: first, the 41 indicators have been weight-averaged in each of the eight dimensions to produce eight composite dimensional indexes; second, these eight dimensional indexes are weight-averaged to generate an overall index of regional integration. In each step, the weights are determined based on principal component analysis. For more details on the methodology and to download the data, please see Asia-Pacific Regional Cooperation and Integration Index Database. https://aric.adb.org/database/arcii.

Table A2: Regional Integration Indicators—Asia and the Pacific (% of total)

The table provides a summary of regional integration indicators for three areas: movement in trade and investment, movement in capital, and people movement (migration, remittances, and tourism); for Asian subregions, including the Association of Southeast Asian Nations (ASEAN) plus 3 (including Hong Kong, China). Cross-border flows within and across subregions are shown, as well as total flows with Asia and the rest of the world. Table descriptions of Tables A3 and A7 (movement in trade and investment); Tables A5 and A6 (movement in capital); and Tables A8, A9, and A10 (people movement) provide additional description for each indicator.

Table A3: Trade Share—Asia and the Pacific (% of total trade)

It is calculated as $T_{ij}/T_{iw} \cdot 100$, where T_{ij} is the total trade of economy "i" with economy "j", and T_{iw} is the total trade of economy "i" with the world. A higher share indicates a higher degree of regional trade integration.

Table A4: Free Trade Agreement Status—Asia and the Pacific

It is the number and status of bilateral and plurilateral free trade agreements (FTAs) with at least one of the Asian economies as signatory. FTAs only proposed are excluded. It covers FTAs with the following status: framework agreement signed—the parties initially negotiate the contents of a framework agreement, which serves as a framework for future negotiations; negotiations launched—the parties, through the relevant ministries, declare the official launch of negotiations or set the date for such, or start the first round of negotiations; signed but not yet in effect—parties sign the agreement after negotiations have been completed, however, the agreement has yet to be implemented; and signed and in effect—provisions of the FTA come into force, after legislative or executive ratification.

Table A5: Cross-Border Portfolio Equity Holdings Share—Asia and the Pacific (% of total cross-border portfolio equity holdings)

It is calculated as $E_{ij}/E_{iw} \cdot 100$ where E_{ij} is portfolio equity holdings of economy "i" issued by economy "j", and E_{iw} is the total global cross-border portfolio equity holdings of economy "i". Calculations are based solely on available data in the Coordinated Portfolio Investment Survey (CPIS) database of the International Monetary Fund (IMF). Rest of the world (ROW) includes equity securities issued by international organizations defined in the CPIS database and "not specified (including confidential) category." A higher share indicates a higher degree of regional integration.

Table A6: Cross-Border Portfolio Debt Holdings Share—Asia and the Pacific (% of total cross-border portfolio debt holdings)

It is calculated as $D_{ij}/D_{iw} \cdot 100$ where D_{ij} is portfolio debt holdings of economy "i" issued by economy "j", and D_{iw} is the total global cross-border portfolio debt holdings of economy "i". Calculations are based solely on available data in the CPIS database of the IMF. ROW includes debt securities issued by international organizations defined in the CPIS database and "not specified (including confidential) category." A higher share indicates a higher degree of regional integration.

Table A7: Foreign Direct Investment Inflow Share—Asia and the Pacific (% of total FDI inflows)

It is calculated as $F_{ij}/F_{iw} \cdot 100$ where F_{ij} is the foreign direct investment (FDI) received by economy "i" from economy "j", and F_{iw} is the FDI received by economy "i" from the world. Figures are based on net FDI inflow data. A higher share indicates a higher degree of regional integration. The bilateral FDI database was constructed using data from the United Nations Conference on Trade and Development, ASEAN Secretariat, Eurostat, and domestic sources. For missing data in recent years, bilateral FDI estimates derived from a gravity model are used. All bilateral data available from previous years were utilized to estimate the following gravity equation:

$$lnFDI_{ijt} = \alpha + \beta 1 lnGDP_{it} + \beta 2 lnGDP_{jt} + \gamma X_{ijt} + \delta_i F_i + \delta_j F_j + \delta_t F_t + v_{ijt}$$

where FDI_{ijt} is the FDI from economy "j" (home) to economy "i" (host) in year t, GDP_{it} is the gross domestic product (GDP) of economy "i" in year t, GDP_{jt} is the GDP of economy "j" at year t, X_{ijt} are the usual gravity variables (distance, contiguity, common language, colonial relationship) between economies "i" and "j", and F_i, F_j, F_t are home, host, and year fixed effects, respectively, and v_{ijt} is the error term. Data on distance, contiguity, common language, colonial relationship are from the Centre d'Études Prospectives et d'Informations Internationales (the French Research Center in International Economics) and data on GDP are from the World Development Indicators of the World Bank. For more details on methodology and data sources, please see Asian Economic Integration Report 2018 online Annex 1: http://aric.adb.org/pdf/aeir2018_ onlineannex1.pdf.

Table A8: Remittance Inflows Share—Asia and the Pacific
(% of total remittance inflows)

It is calculated as $R_{ij}/R_{iw} \cdot 100$ where R_{ij} is the remittance received by economy "i" from partner "j", and R_{iw} is the remittance received by economy "i" from the world. Remittances refer to the sum of the following: (i) workers' remittances which are recorded as current transfers under the current account of the IMF's Balance of Payments (BOP); (ii) compensation of employees which includes wages, salaries, and other benefits of border, seasonal, and other nonresident workers and which are recorded under the "income" subcategory of the current account; and (iii) migrants' transfers which are reported under capital transfers in the BOP's capital account. Transfers through informal channels are excluded.

Table A9: Outbound Migration Share—Asia and the Pacific
(% of total outbound migrants)

It is calculated as $M_{ij}/M_{iw} \cdot 100$ where M_{ij} is the number of migrants of economy "i" residing in economy "j" and M_{iw} is the number of all migrants of economy "i" residing overseas. This definition excludes those traveling abroad on a temporary basis. A higher share indicates a higher degree of regional integration.

Table A10a: Inbound Tourism Share—Asia and the Pacific
(% of total inbound tourists)

It is calculated as $V_{ij}/V_{iw} \cdot 100$ where V_{ij} is the number of individuals from economy "i" that have arrived as tourists in destination "j" and V_{iw} is the total number of individuals from economy "i" that have arrived as tourists in all international destinations. A higher share indicates a higher degree of regional integration.

Table A10b: Outbound Tourism Share—Asia and the Pacific
(% of total outbound tourists)

It is calculated as $V_{ij}/V_{iw} \cdot 100$ where V_{ij} is the number of individuals from economy "i" that have traveled as tourists in destination "j" and V_{iw} is the total number of individuals from economy "i" that have traveled as tourists abroad. A higher share indicates a higher degree of regional integration.

Methodological Note and Update—AEIR Cross-Border Investment Firm-Level Data[136]

Background

To assess trends and patterns on foreign direct investment (FDI), this chapter utilizes two types of data: (i) FDI based on standard balance of payments (BOP) data, and (ii) FDI based on firm-level activity. Here, data based on firm-level activity are used to supplement information gathered from the standard BOP data.[137]

The chapter on Cross-Border Investment tracks firm-level data on the creation of new assets—marked as greenfield investment—and the acquisition of existing assets, identified as mergers and acquisitions (M&As). Firm-level data are used to supplement BOP-based data in two ways. First, firm-level data contain information on the mode of entry of an investment and whether FDI arrives primarily through generation of new assets or the purchase of existing assets. Second, sources allow for tracking of global ultimate ownership, allowing the data to offer better insight into investment origins. Besides these essential pieces of information, analysis of firm-level data offers valuable information about the impact of investment from multinational enterprises (MNEs) on recipient economies (UNCTAD 2009).

This combined information is used in the *Asian Economic Integration Report (AEIR)* and the Asia Regional Integration Center (ARIC) data set.

Data Sources

Data on greenfield investment are sourced from the Financial Times' fDi Markets, while data on M&As are gathered from Bureau van Dijk's Zephyr M&A Database. The fDi Markets' database tracks global greenfield investment activity starting from 2003, with a monthly frequency. The database provides details on greenfield projects such as company information (parent and investing), source and destination economies, sector classification, business activity, capital expenditure, and jobs generated. Where data are unavailable, fDi Markets employs its proprietary model to estimate values for capital expenditure or jobs generated.

Meanwhile, the Zephyr M&A Database has information on each M&A deal's company details (target, acquiring, and ultimate owner); source and destination economies; deal values, types, and statuses; and sector classification. Zephyr similarly uses a model to estimate missing or unavailable deal values. Should information on global ultimate ownership be unavailable, these details are obtained as best as possible via the Orbis Company Database.

Sector Harmonization

After cleaning and processing downloaded information, data from fDi Markets and Zephyr M&A Database are matched and merged by economy pair, sector, year, and quarter. The merged data set would then contain bilateral data on greenfield projects (number of projects, capital expenditure, and jobs generated) and M&A deals (number of deals and deal value).

---

[136] ADB staff using ADB. 2018. Online annex. Annex 1: Foreign Direct Investment (Balance of Payments) and Firm-level Investment Activity by Mode of Entry—Data Description and Methodology. *Asian Economic Integration Report 2018: Toward Optimal Provision of Regional Public Goods in Asia and the Pacific.* Manila. https://aric.adb.org/pdf/aeir2018_onlineannex1.pdf; Government of Canada, Statistics Canada. Industry Classifications. https://www.statcan.gc.ca/en/concepts/industry; Government of the United States, Census Bureau. North American Industry Classification System. https://www.census.gov/naics; and United Nations Conference on Trade and Development (UNCTAD). 2009. *UNCTAD Training Manual on Statistics for FDI and the Operations of TNCs: Volume I–FDI Flows and Stocks.* New York and Geneva.

[137] Detailed information on the methodology for BOP-based FDI is available through the *Asian Economic Integration Report 2018: Toward Optimal Provision of Regional Public Goods in Asia and the Pacific* online annex on BOP-based FDI and firm-level activity (ADB 2018).

Sector harmonization is done through a concordance using the North American Industry Classification System (NAICS) 2012 and 2017 codes. While fDi Markets uses its own sectoral classification, an approximate concordance with NAICS 2012 is available.[138] Meanwhile, Zephyr M&A Database has several available economic classifications, and the ARIC data set uses the NAICS 2017.

Data Coverage and Horizon

The ARIC data set covers data from 2003 onward, for all available economies and regions. fDi Markets and Zephyr M&A Database regularly update deal and project information such as statuses and estimates on deal or project values. As such, the latest 3 years from each database are downloaded and updated once a year. These latest years are then appended to the existing data set. Meanwhile, historical data are downloaded as needed. Greenfield projects of all statuses are included, while only completed-confirmed M&A deals are included in the data set.[139]

Revisions on Compilation Method

To better capture and understand how investments from MNEs flow across time and economies, the coverage and compilation process for firm-level data has been updated. From now on, this updated data set will be used in the AEIR and the ARIC database.

Data Coverage

For a better picture of greenfield investments globally, the project types covered in the ARIC data set was expanded. Previously, ARIC covered only new greenfield projects. This was updated to include project expansions, which may also create new assets and additional jobs. An indicator on greenfield project status (announced, opened, or closed) is also now available.

Sector Harmonization and Classification

The ARIC database continues to use NAICS codes as the basis for sector matching and merging. However, instead of converting the sector classification of the M&A data set into the proprietary classification that fDi Markets uses, the greenfield classification is converted to NAICS codes using the approximate concordance previously used. The 2-digit NAICS codes are then obtained for the broader NAICS sectors and the 3-industry economic classification. In addition, the 3-industry classification has been revised into primary, manufacturing, and tertiary (in contrast to the previous data set's classifications of primary, manufacturing, and services).[140]

Project and Deal Type Coverage—Old Compilation versus New Compilation

Project or Deal Type	Old Compilation	New Compilation
Greenfield		
Colocation		
Expansion		■
New greenfield project	■	■
Mergers and Acquisitions		
Acquisition	■	■
Capital increase	■	■
Demerger	■	■
IPO		
Institutional buyout	■	■
Joint venture	■	■
Management buy-in or buyout	■	■
Merger	■	■
Minority stake	■	■
Planned IPO		
Share buyback	■	■

IPO = initial public offering.

Note: Green cells indicate inclusion in the data set.

Sources: ADB calculations using data from Bureau van Dijk. Zephyr M&A Database; and Financial Times. fDi Markets (both accessed March 2022).

---

[138]   A table of the fDi Markets concordance used (Table 1: fDi Markets Concordance) is available through the *Asian Economic Integration Report 2018: Toward Optimal Provision of Regional Public Goods in Asia and the Pacific* online annex on BOP-based FDI and firm-level activity (ADB 2018).

[139]   While data on announced M&A deals are also available, these differ from announced greenfield investment. According to fDi Markets, announced greenfield investment are slated to push through and any canceled greenfield projects are removed from their database. Meanwhile, announced M&A deals may still fall through.

[140]   Government of Canada, Statistics Canada. Industry Classifications. https://www.statcan.gc.ca/en/concepts/industry; and Government of the United States, Census Bureau. North American Industry Classification System. https://www.census.gov/naics.

Process Flow of Firm-Level Data Compilation

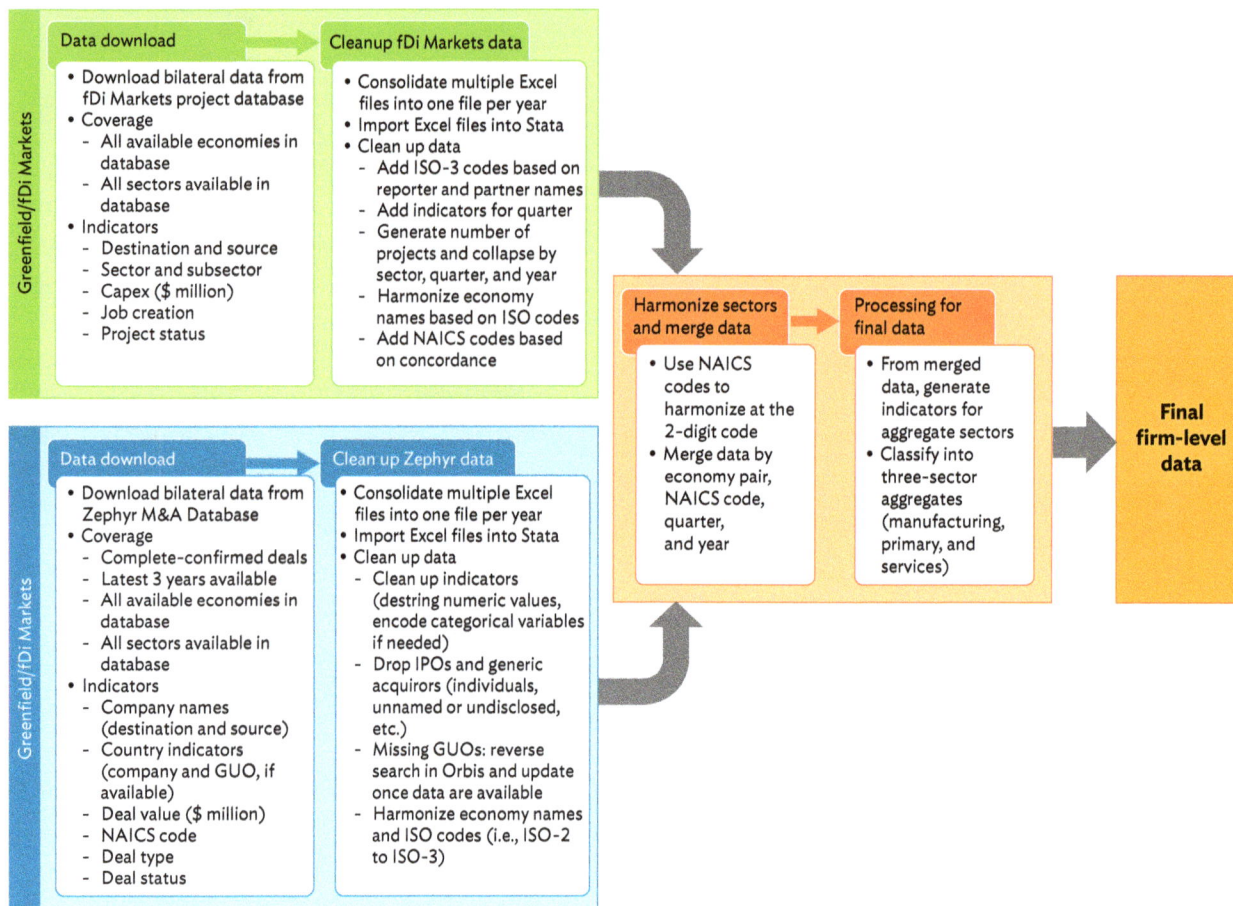

Greenfield/fDi Markets

Data download
- Download bilateral data from fDi Markets project database
- Coverage
  - All available economies in database
  - All sectors available in database
- Indicators
  - Destination and source
  - Sector and subsector
  - Capex ($ million)
  - Job creation
  - Project status

Cleanup fDi Markets data
- Consolidate multiple Excel files into one file per year
- Import Excel files into Stata
- Clean up data
  - Add ISO-3 codes based on reporter and partner names
  - Add indicators for quarter
  - Generate number of projects and collapse by sector, quarter, and year
  - Harmonize economy names based on ISO codes
  - Add NAICS codes based on concordance

Greenfield/fDi Markets

Data download
- Download bilateral data from Zephyr M&A Database
- Coverage
  - Complete-confirmed deals
  - Latest 3 years available
  - All available economies in database
  - All sectors available in database
- Indicators
  - Company names (destination and source)
  - Country indicators (company and GUO, if available)
  - Deal value ($ million)
  - NAICS code
  - Deal type
  - Deal status

Clean up Zephyr data
- Consolidate multiple Excel files into one file per year
- Import Excel files into Stata
- Clean up data
  - Clean up indicators (destring numeric values, encode categorical variables if needed)
  - Drop IPOs and generic acquirors (individuals, unnamed or undisclosed, etc.)
  - Missing GUOs: reverse search in Orbis and update once data are available
  - Harmonize economy names and ISO codes (i.e., ISO-2 to ISO-3)

Harmonize sectors and merge data
- Use NAICS codes to harmonize at the 2-digit code
- Merge data by economy pair, NAICS code, quarter, and year

Processing for final data
- From merged data, generate indicators for aggregate sectors
- Classify into three-sector aggregates (manufacturing, primary, and services)

Final firm-level data

Revised 3-Industry Classification Based on 2-Digit NAICS Code

Primary	Manufacturing	Tertiary
11: Agriculture, Forestry, Fishing, and Hunting 21: Mining, Quarrying, and Oil and Gas Extraction	31–33: Manufacturing	22: Utilities 23: Construction 42: Wholesale Trade 44–45: Retail Trade 48–49: Transportation and Warehousing 51: Information 52: Finance and Insurance 53: Real Estate and Rental and Leasing 54: Professional, Scientific, and Technical Services 55: Management of Companies and Enterprises 56: Administrative and Support and Waste Management and Remediation Services 61: Educational Services 62: Health Care and Social Assistance 71: Arts, Entertainment, and Recreation 72: Accommodation and Food Services 81: Other Services (except Public Administration) 92: Public Administration

GUO = global ultimate owner, ISO = International Organization for Standardization, NAICS = North American Industry Classification System.

Sources: Bureau van Dijk. Zephyr M&A Database; Financial Times. fDi Markets; Government of Canada, Statistics Canada. Industry classifications. https://www.statcan.gc.ca/en/concepts/industry; and Government of the United States, United States Census Bureau. North American Industry Classification System. https://www.census.gov/naics/.

Table A1: Asia-Pacific Regional Cooperation Integration Index

a: Overall Asia-Pacific Regional Cooperation and Integration Index and Dimensional Subindexes—Asia and the Pacific

Year	Overall Index	Dimensional Indexes							
		Trade and Investment Integration	Money and Finance Integration	Regional Value Chain	Infrastructure and Connectivity	People and Social Integration	Institutional Arrangements	Technology and Digital Connectivity	Environmental Cooperation
2006	0.406	0.395	0.401	0.430	0.454	0.567	0.215	0.359	0.244
2007	0.406	0.350	0.389	0.431	0.456	0.577	0.219	0.374	0.256
2008	0.400	0.369	0.360	0.428	0.446	0.560	0.226	0.382	0.258
2009	0.409	0.393	0.374	0.416	0.454	0.563	0.232	0.376	0.267
2010	0.409	0.402	0.393	0.421	0.470	0.584	0.235	0.410	0.269
2011	0.407	0.418	0.355	0.414	0.470	0.578	0.237	0.432	0.269
2012	0.406	0.426	0.362	0.415	0.471	0.581	0.239	0.431	0.267
2013	0.421	0.390	0.405	0.420	0.468	0.578	0.241	0.462	0.269
2014	0.417	0.381	0.391	0.420	0.462	0.578	0.243	0.464	0.269
2015	0.419	0.442	0.413	0.414	0.456	0.568	0.245	0.484	0.274
2016	0.419	0.410	0.377	0.421	0.460	0.562	0.247	0.480	0.277
2017	0.421	0.430	0.383	0.424	0.462	0.568	0.249	0.494	0.277
2018	0.429	0.466	0.393	0.413	0.474	0.574	0.251	0.519	0.280
2019	0.435	0.393	0.382	0.420	0.473	0.583	0.251	0.528	0.279
2020	0.434	0.399	0.384	0.423	0.486	0.566	0.251	0.541	0.280

b: Overall Asia-Pacific Regional Cooperation and Integration Index—Asian Subregions and Subregional Initiatives

	Central Asia	East Asia	Southeast Asia	South Asia	Oceania	ASEAN	CAREC	GMS	SASEC	SAARC	BIMSTEC
2006	0.284	0.460	0.456	0.361	0.459	0.447	0.360	0.445	0.372	0.368	0.389
2007	0.289	0.445	0.454	0.366	0.442	0.450	0.359	0.434	0.362	0.345	0.378
2008	0.291	0.464	0.454	0.354	0.453	0.455	0.371	0.452	0.340	0.330	0.365
2009	0.311	0.462	0.455	0.350	0.471	0.461	0.389	0.453	0.343	0.330	0.366
2010	0.310	0.459	0.462	0.343	0.478	0.467	0.382	0.472	0.366	0.353	0.394
2011	0.314	0.451	0.46	0.374	0.475	0.456	0.389	0.455	0.386	0.374	0.398
2012	0.327	0.460	0.463	0.331	0.480	0.468	0.392	0.465	0.377	0.355	0.393
2013	0.339	0.461	0.467	0.371	0.484	0.483	0.403	0.474	0.368	0.357	0.399
2014	0.321	0.470	0.469	0.380	0.484	0.480	0.406	0.471	0.355	0.347	0.382
2015	0.340	0.467	0.477	0.370	0.478	0.493	0.416	0.494	0.373	0.378	0.410
2016	0.331	0.478	0.472	0.356	0.483	0.488	0.406	0.495	0.371	0.378	0.396
2017	0.346	0.476	0.476	0.368	0.473	0.483	0.426	0.490	0.364	0.367	0.387
2018	0.354	0.478	0.485	0.362	0.470	0.496	0.424	0.498	0.355	0.362	0.403
2019	0.350	0.481	0.481	0.393	0.477	0.492	0.438	0.493	0.358	0.360	0.405
2020	0.346	0.459	0.491	0.373	0.495	0.505	0.429	0.501	0.355	0.360	0.407

c: Regional Integration Index—Asia and the Pacific and Other Regions

	Asia and the Pacific	EU+UK	Latin America	Africa	Middle East	North America
2006	0.406	0.585	0.359	0.309	0.370	0.486
2007	0.406	0.584	0.354	0.292	0.377	0.492
2008	0.400	0.577	0.352	0.305	0.371	0.497
2009	0.409	0.577	0.355	0.306	0.365	0.500
2010	0.409	0.575	0.346	0.326	0.378	0.503
2011	0.407	0.576	0.346	0.323	0.386	0.501
2012	0.406	0.577	0.351	0.332	0.397	0.505
2013	0.421	0.578	0.349	0.333	0.384	0.503
2014	0.417	0.575	0.346	0.343	0.393	0.506
2015	0.419	0.581	0.346	0.352	0.396	0.494
2016	0.419	0.585	0.343	0.345	0.389	0.499
2017	0.421	0.589	0.355	0.342	0.399	0.497
2018	0.429	0.587	0.358	0.352	0.416	0.490
2019	0.435	0.582	0.361	0.363	0.417	0.502
2020	0.434	0.590	0.355	0.371	0.385	0.496

ASEAN = Association of Southeast Asian Nations, BIMSTEC = Bay of Bengal Initiative for Multi-Sectoral Technical and Economic Cooperation, CAREC = Central Asia Regional Economic Cooperation, EU = European Union (27 members), GMS = Greater Mekong Subregion, SAARC = South Asian Association for Regional Cooperation, SASEC = South Asia Subregional Economic Cooperation, UK = United Kingdom.

Notes:
(i)   The Asia-Pacific Regional Cooperation and Integration Index (ARCII) for each subregion (subregional initiative) for each year is calculated by averaging the ARCII scores for all the economies in each subregion (member economies in each subregional initiative).
(ii) The economy coverage for subregions and subregional initiatives includes Central Asia (Armenia, Azerbaijan, Georgia, Kazakhstan, the Kyrgyz Republic, Tajikistan, Turkmenistan, and Uzbekistan); East Asia (the People's Republic of China [PRC]; Hong Kong, China; Japan; the Republic of Korea; Mongolia; and Taipei,China); Southeast Asia (Brunei Darussalam, Cambodia, Indonesia, the Lao People's Democratic Republic [Lao PDR], Malaysia, the Philippines, Singapore, Thailand, Timor-Leste, and Viet Nam); South Asia (Bangladesh , Bhutan, India, Maldives, Nepal, Pakistan, and Sri Lanka); the Pacific (Cook Islands, the Federated States of Micronesia, Fiji, Kiribati, the Marshall Islands, Nauru, Palau, Papua New Guinea, Samoa, Solomon Islands, Tonga, Tuvalu, and Vanuatu); Oceania (Australia and New Zealand); ASEAN (Brunei Darussalam, Cambodia, Indonesia, the Lao PDR, Malaysia, the Philippines, Singapore, Thailand, and Viet Nam); CAREC (Azerbaijan, the PRC, Georgia, Kazakhstan, the Kyrgyz Republic, Mongolia, Pakistan, Tajikistan, Turkmenistan, and Uzbekistan); GMS (Cambodia, the PRC, the Lao PDR, Thailand, and Viet Nam); SASEC (Bangladesh, Bhutan, India, Maldives, Nepal, and Sri Lanka); BIMSTEC (Bangladesh, Bhutan, India, Nepal, Sri Lanka, and Thailand).
(iii) The regional integration index for each region (Table A1c) is calculated in the same method as ARCII but is based on worldwide normalization, i.e., normalizing raw indicator values using global minimum and maximum values.
(iv) Estimates for the subregional initiatives (i.e., ASEAN, CAREC, GMS, SASEC, SAARC, and BIMSTEC) represent intra-subregional integration. Indicators are normalized only across the set of economies covered by the included subregional initiatives.
(v)   Remittance data used in Indicator V-c (Proportion of intraregional remittances to total remittances) was changed to outward remittances.
(vi) Indicator VIII-c (Environmental health score) is revised in the current estimation to ensure compatibility of values across time. It was recomputed using the time series data published by the Environmental Performance Index (EPI) team. Issue categories under the environmental health policy objective which do not have good data coverage from 2006 to 2020 were excluded from the computation (e.g., waste management).
(vii) The following indicators are excluded in this round of estimation due to lack of available 2020 data: Indicator II-d (Capital account openness: Chinn-Ito Index), III-e (Value-added contributions), IV-d (Logistics Performance Index), V-a (Outbound migration), V-c (Remittance), and VIII-d (Ecological footprint of production as a share of biocapacity).

Sources: ADB. Asia Regional Integration Center. Asia-Pacific Regional Cooperation and Integration Index Database. https://aric.adb.org/database/arcii (accessed November 2022); and methodology from C. Y. Park and R. Claveria. 2018. Constructing the Asia-Pacific Regional Integration Index: A Panel Approach. *ADB Economics Working Papers*. No. 544. Manila: ADB; H. Huh and C. Y. Park. 2018. Asia-Pacific Regional Integration Index: Construction, Interpretation, and Comparison. *Journal of Asian Economics*. 54. pp. 22–38; and H. Huh and C.Y. Park. 2017. Asia-Pacific Regional Integration Index: Construction, Interpretation, and Comparison. *ADB Economics Working Papers*. No. 511. Manila: ADB.

Table A2: Regional Integration Indicators—Asia and the Pacific (% of total)

| | Movement in Trade and Investment | | Movement in Capital | | People Movement | | |
| | Trade (%) | FDI (%) | Equity Holdings (%) | Bond Holdings (%) | Migration (%) | Tourism (%) | Remittances (%) |
	2021	2021	2021	2021	2020	2020	2019
Within Subregions							
ASEAN+3 (including HKG)[a]	45.6 ▼	59.8 ▼	18.7 ▼	16.0 ▲	36.8 ▼	59.2 ▼	30.2 ▼
Central Asia	9.0 ▲	1.5 ▼	0.0 ▼	0.2 ▲	8.8 ▼	62.5 ▲	6.2 ▼
East Asia	35.1 ▼	57.7 ▼	16.2 ▲	10.3 ▲	33.6 ▲	22.5 ▼	32.5 ▼
South Asia	6.1 ▲	0.8 ▲	0.3 ▼	0.0 —	19.5 ▼	13.4 ▼	7.1 ▼
Southeast Asia	21.0 ▼	43.4 ▼	6.0 ▼	7.0 ▼	30.1 ▼	73.0 ▲	12.7 ▼
Oceania and the Pacific	4.5 ▼	17.6 ▲	4.1 ▼	4.2 ▼	53.8 ▼	24.7 ▲	36.6 ▲
Across Subregions							
ASEAN+3 (including HKG)[a]	12.4 ▲	3.6 ▼	3.3 ▲	5.1 ▼	13.2 ▲	7.2 ▲	8.7 ▲
Central Asia	26.7 ▼	52.3 ▲	7.4 ▼	20.2 ▲	0.7 ▲	1.0 ▼	0.2 ▼
East Asia	21.2 ▲	10.0 ▲	2.4 ▼	7.3 ▲	16.2 ▲	33.5 ▲	14.7 ▼
South Asia	34.0 ▼	37.0 ▲	8.7 ▼	10.7 ▲	7.5 ▲	17.7 ▼	8.0 ▲
Southeast Asia	47.6 ▼	11.6 ▼	30.4 ▼	32.2 ▼	20.2 ▲	16.6 ▼	17.5 ▲
Oceania and the Pacific	71.6 ▲	25.5 ▼	11.8 ▼	15.7 ▲	4.6 ▼	41.4 ▲	7.2 ▼
TOTAL (within and across subregions)							
Asia and the Pacific	58.2 ▼	60.5 ▼	21.1 ▼	20.9 ▼	35.1 ▼	62.5 ▼	26.9 ▼
ASEAN+3 (including HKG)[a]	58.0 ▼	63.5 ▼	22.0 ▼	21.1 ▼	50.0 ▲	66.5 ▼	38.9 ▼
Central Asia	35.8 ▼	53.8 ▲	7.4 ▼	20.3 ▲	9.5 ▼	63.5 ▲	6.5 ▼
East Asia	56.3 ▼	67.7 ▼	18.6 ▲	17.6 ▲	49.8 ▲	56.0 ▼	47.2 ▼
South Asia	40.2 ▼	37.9 ▲	9.0 ▼	10.7 ▲	27.0 ▲	31.1 ▼	15.1 ▲
Southeast Asia	68.5 ▼	55.0 ▼	36.4 ▼	39.2 ▼	50.2 ▲	89.5 ▼	30.2 ▼
Oceania and the Pacific	76.2 ▲	43.2 ▼	15.9 ▼	19.9 ▲	58.4 ▼	66.1 ▲	43.8 ▲
With the rest of the world							
Asia and the Pacific	41.8 ▲	39.5 ▲	78.9 ▲	79.1 ▲	64.9 ▲	37.5 ▲	73.1 ▲
ASEAN+3 (including HKG)[a]	42.0 ▲	36.5 ▲	78.0 ▲	78.9 ▲	50.0 ▼	33.5 ▲	61.1 ▲
Central Asia	64.2 ▲	46.2 ▼	92.6 ▲	79.7 ▼	90.5 ▲	36.5 ▼	93.5 ▲
East Asia	43.7 ▲	32.3 ▲	81.4 ▼	82.4 ▲	50.2 ▲	44.0 ▲	52.8 ▲
South Asia	59.8 ▲	62.1 ▼	91.0 ▲	89.3 ▼	73.0 ▲	68.9 ▲	84.9 ▼
Southeast Asia	31.5 ▲	45.0 ▲	63.6 ▲	60.8 ▲	49.8 ▼	10.5 ▲	69.8 ▲
Oceania and the Pacific	23.8 ▼	56.9 ▲	84.1 ▲	80.1 ▼	41.6 ▲	33.9 ▼	56.2 ▼

— = unchanged from previous period; ▲ = increase from previous period; ▼ = decrease from previous period.

ASEAN = Association of Southeast Asian Nations; FDI = foreign direct investment; HKG = Hong Kong, China.

[a] Includes ASEAN (Brunei Darussalam, Cambodia, Indonesia, the Lao People's Democratic Republic, Malaysia, the Philippines, Singapore, Thailand, and Viet Nam) plus Hong Kong, China; Japan; the People's Republic of China; and the Republic of Korea.

Trade—no data available on the Cook Islands and Niue.

Equity and Bond Holdings—based on investment from Australia; Bangladesh; Hong Kong, China; India; Indonesia; Japan; Kazakhstan; Malaysia; Mongolia; New Zealand; Pakistan; Palau; the People's Republic of China; the Philippines; the Republic of Korea; Singapore; and Thailand.

Migration—share of migrant stock to total migrants in 2020 (compared with 2015).

Tourism—share of outbound tourists to total tourists in 2020 (compared with 2019).

Remittances—share of inward remittances to total remittances in 2019 (compared with 2018).

Sources: ADB calculations using data from ASEANStats. ASEANStats Data Portal. https://data.aseanstats.org (accessed July 2019); CEIC Data Company; Eurostat. Balance of Payments. https://ec.europa.eu/eurostat/web/balance-of-payments/data/database (accessed July 2022); International Monetary Fund (IMF). Coordinated Portfolio Investment Survey. https://data.imf.org/CPIS (accessed September 2022); IMF. Direction of Trade Statistics. https://data.imf.org/DOT (accessed December 2022); United Nations Department of Economic and Social Affairs, Population Division. International Migrant Stock 2020. http://www.un.org/en/development/desa/population/migration/data/index.shtml (accessed May 2022); United Nations Conference on Trade and Development (UNCTAD; UNCTAD. World Investment Report 2022 Statistical Annex Tables. https://worldinvestmentreport.unctad.org/annex-tables (accessed July 2022); United Nations World Tourism Organization. Tourism Satellite Accounts. http://statistics.unwto.org (accessed November 2022); and World Bank. Global Knowledge Partnership for Migration and Development. Bilateral Remittance staff estimates (May 2020).

Table A3: Trade Shares—Asia and the Pacific, 2021 (% of total trade)

Reporter	Asia and the Pacific	PRC	Japan	EU+UK	US	ROW
Central Asia	**35.8**	**17.4**	**1.1**	**26.1**	**1.9**	**36.3**
Armenia	24.0	15.0	0.7	19.5	2.5	54.1
Azerbaijan	14.7	5.2	0.8	46.8	1.5	37.0
Georgia	31.7	10.3	1.4	21.8	5.9	40.6
Kazakhstan	36.3	17.9	1.6	30.5	2.0	31.3
Kyrgyz Republic	47.3	21.1	0.3	8.1	1.5	43.2
Tajikistan	48.1	12.2	1.5	7.5	0.8	43.6
Turkmenistan	63.9	52.3	0.3	12.3	0.8	23.0
Uzbekistan	43.2	17.6	0.4	9.9	0.8	46.1
East Asia	**56.3**	**15.2**	**5.3**	**12.7**	**11.8**	**19.2**
China, People's Republic of	46.6		6.2	15.6	12.5	25.3
Hong Kong, China	81.1	51.8	3.8	6.5	5.1	7.3
Japan	58.3	22.9		11.3	14.3	16.0
Korea, Republic of	58.4	23.9	6.7	11.2	13.5	16.9
Mongolia	73.4	62.7	2.9	5.1	1.5	20.0
Taipei,China	74.2	32.3	8.6	8.1	11.2	6.6
South Asia	**40.2**	**13.0**	**2.2**	**13.4**	**10.9**	**35.5**
Bangladesh	48.2	16.5	3.1	20.1	8.0	23.7
Bhutan	98.3	4.2	0.3	1.1	0.2	0.5
India	37.3	11.5	2.1	12.6	11.7	38.4
Maldives	57.4	11.8	1.6	9.4	2.5	30.6
Nepal	84.3	13.6	0.4	2.2	2.4	11.0
Pakistan	42.5	23.3	2.3	15.1	9.7	32.6
Sri Lanka	52.5	15.2	2.0	17.1	10.9	19.5
Southeast Asia	**68.5**	**19.6**	**7.0**	**9.0**	**10.8**	**11.7**
Brunei Darussalam	80.4	14.2	13.1	2.3	1.2	16.1
Cambodia	64.7	23.6	3.7	10.5	16.5	8.3
Indonesia	71.0	24.2	7.3	7.8	8.4	12.8
Lao People's Democratic Republic	92.5	28.1	1.7	4.3	1.6	1.6
Malaysia	72.2	18.9	6.7	8.9	9.8	9.2
Philippines	75.1	20.0	11.3	8.7	10.1	6.1
Singapore	66.8	13.4	4.4	9.5	8.8	14.9
Thailand	67.0	19.3	11.3	8.4	10.4	14.2
Timor-Leste	92.1	13.7	2.1	1.0	0.5	6.4
Viet Nam	64.4	25.1	6.4	9.6	16.8	9.1
Oceania and the Pacific	**76.2**	**31.9**	**9.7**	**10.7**	**6.6**	**6.5**
Australia	77.1	33.3	10.3	10.3	6.5	6.1
Cook Islands	—	—	—	—	—	—
Fiji	79.4	12.3	3.3	3.2	13.2	4.3
Kiribati	86.2	13.9	5.2	4.3	1.4	8.1
Marshall Islands	77.8	21.0	8.0	18.4	1.7	2.1
Micronesia, Federated States of	42.5	5.3	5.3	0.5	15.4	41.6
Nauru	76.8	3.8	4.5	0.4	1.1	21.7
Niue	—	—	—	—	—	—
New Zealand	66.9	27.5	6.1	13.1	9.5	10.5
Palau	36.9	19.2	5.1	2.5	27.4	33.2
Papua New Guinea	89.7	17.6	10.2	7.9	0.8	1.7
Samoa	83.1	12.3	3.6	1.0	10.4	5.5
Solomon Islands	86.0	41.6	1.6	9.7	1.9	2.4
Tonga	83.7	8.0	7.7	0.8	11.0	4.4
Tuvalu	71.8	1.1	4.3	0.4	1.0	26.9
Vanuatu	84.2	10.0	1.3	8.7	3.0	4.2
Asia and the Pacific	**58.2**	**16.7**	**5.6**	**12.1**	**11.2**	**18.6**
Developing Asia	**57.3**	**15.3**	**5.9**	**12.2**	**11.1**	**19.4**

— = unavailable, EU = European Union (27 members), PRC = People's Republic of China, ROW = rest of the world, UK = United Kingdom, US = United States.

Source: ADB calculations using data from International Monetary Fund. Direction of Trade Statistics. https://data.imf.org/DOT (accessed December 2022).

Table A4: Free Trade Agreement Status—Asia and the Pacific, as of November 2022

Economy	Under Negotiation		Signed But Not Yet In Effect	Signed and In Effect	Total
	Framework Agreement Signed	Negotiations Launched			
Armenia	0	3	2	13	18
Australia	0	4	1	18	23
Azerbaijan	0	1	0	10	11
Bangladesh	0	3	1	4	8
Bhutan	0	1	0	3	4
Brunei Darussalam	0	1	0	11	12
Cambodia	0	1	1	9	11
China, People's Republic of	0	9	2	21	32
Cook Islands	0	0	0	4	4
Fiji	0	0	0	6	6
Georgia	0	0	0	14	14
Hong Kong, China	0	1	0	8	9
India	0	16	0	16	32
Indonesia	0	6	3	15	24
Japan	0	6	0	20	26
Kazakhstan	0	5	2	13	20
Kiribati	0	0	0	4	4
Korea, Republic of	0	12	3	19	34
Kyrgyz Republic	0	3	2	13	18
Lao People's Democratic Republic	0	1	0	10	11
Malaysia	1	6	1	17	25
Maldives	0	1	2	1	4
Marshall Islands	0	0	0	5	5
Micronesia, Federated States of	0	0	0	5	5
Mongolia	0	0	0	2	2
Nauru	0	0	0	4	4
Nepal	0	1	0	2	3
New Zealand	0	5	1	14	20
Niue	0	0	0	0	0
Pakistan	1	7	1	9	18
Palau	0	0	0	4	4
Papua New Guinea	0	0	0	7	7
Philippines	0	3	0	10	13
Samoa	0	0	0	5	5
Singapore	0	8	1	27	36
Solomon Islands	0	0	0	6	6
Sri Lanka	0	4	0	6	10
Taipei,China	0	2	0	8	10
Tajikistan	0	0	0	8	8
Thailand	1	9	0	15	25
Timor-Leste	0	0	0	0	0
Tonga	0	0	0	4	4
Turkmenistan	0	0	0	5	5
Tuvalu	0	0	0	4	4
Uzbekistan	0	1	0	9	10
Vanuatu	0	0	1	5	6
Viet Nam	0	3	0	15	18

Notes:
(i)   Framework agreement signed: The parties initially negotiate the contents of a framework agreement, which serves as a framework for future negotiations.
(ii) Negotiations launched: The parties, through the relevant ministries, declare the official launch of negotiations or set the date for such, or start the first round of negotiations.
(iii) Signed but not yet in effect: Parties sign the agreement after negotiations have been completed. However, the agreement has yet to be implemented.
(iv) Signed and in effect: Provisions of free trade agreement come into force, after legislative or executive ratification.

Source: ADB. Asia Regional Integration Center. Free Trade Agreements. https://aric.adb.org/database/fta (accessed November 2022).

Table A5: Cross-Border Portfolio Equity Holdings—Asia and the Pacific, 2021 (% of total cross-border portfolio equity holdings)

	Partner					
	Asia and the Pacific	of which				
Reporter		PRC	Japan	EU+UK	US	ROW
Central Asia	**7.4**	**0.1**	**5.0**	**19.2**	**67.3**	**6.1**
Armenia	—	—	—	—	—	—
Azerbaijan	—	—	—	—	—	—
Georgia	—	—	—	—	—	—
Kazakhstan	7.4	0.1	5.0	19.2	67.3	6.1
Kyrgyz Republic	—	—	—	—	—	—
Tajikistan	—	—	—	—	—	—
Turkmenistan	—	—	—	—	—	—
Uzbekistan	—	—	—	—	—	—
East Asia	**18.6**	**6.3**	**1.1**	**13.6**	**29.8**	**38.0**
China, People's Republic of	58.1		1.3	8.1	21.1	12.7
Hong Kong, China	24.4	19.4	1.7	10.9	6.2	58.4
Japan	4.8	0.6		15.2	40.0	40.0
Korea, Republic of	12.7	3.2	3.6	20.4	58.2	8.7
Mongolia	—	—	—	—	—	—
Taipei,China	—	—	—	—	—	—
South Asia	**9.0**	**2.4**	**0.7**	**31.9**	**53.5**	**5.6**
Bangladesh	100.0	0.0	0.0	0.0	0.0	0.0
Bhutan	—	—	—	—	—	—
India	9.1	2.5	0.7	32.6	54.6	3.7
Maldives	—	—	—	—	—	—
Nepal	—	—	—	—	—	—
Pakistan	0.0	0.0	0.0	4.0	14.5	81.5
Sri Lanka	—	—	—	—	—	—
Southeast Asia	**36.4**	**10.8**	**4.5**	**13.2**	**25.4**	**25.0**
Brunei Darussalam	—	—	—	—	—	—
Cambodia	—	—	—	—	—	—
Indonesia	98.8	0.1	0.5	0.0	0.0	1.1
Lao People's Democratic Republic	—	—	—	—	—	—
Malaysia	47.3	6.5	4.2	20.8	24.4	7.5
Philippines	15.2	0.0	0.0	61.0	20.2	3.6
Singapore	35.8	12.2	4.8	10.7	25.8	27.7
Thailand	18.0	0.4	0.8	34.0	26.1	21.9
Timor-Leste	—	—	—	—	—	—
Viet Nam	—	—	—	—	—	—
Oceania and the Pacific	**15.9**	**1.8**	**4.3**	**11.6**	**52.0**	**20.4**
Australia	14.0	1.9	4.4	11.8	52.8	21.4
Cook Islands	—	—	—	—	—	—
Fiji	—	—	—	—	—	—
Kiribati	—	—	—	—	—	—
Marshall Islands	—	—	—	—	—	—
Micronesia, Federated States of	—	—	—	—	—	—
Nauru	—	—	—	—	—	—
New Zealand	29.8	0.7	3.4	10.6	46.1	13.5
Niue	—	—	—	—	—	—
Palau	0.0	0.0	0.0	0.0	0.0	0.0
Papua New Guinea	—	—	—	—	—	—
Samoa	—	—	—	—	—	—
Solomon Islands	—	—	—	—	—	—
Tonga	—	—	—	—	—	—
Tuvalu	—	—	—	—	—	—
Vanuatu	—	—	—	—	—	—
Asia and the Pacific	**21.1**	**6.4**	**2.1**	**13.3**	**32.3**	**33.3**
Developing Asia	**31.8**	**10.9**	**2.8**	**12.6**	**23.5**	**32.7**

— = unavailable, EU = European Union (27 members), PRC = People's Republic of China, ROW = rest of the world, UK = United Kingdom, US = United States.

Source: ADB calculations using data from International Monetary Fund. Coordinated Portfolio Investment Survey. https://data.imf.org/cpis (accessed September 2022).

Table A6: Cross-Border Portfolio Debt Holdings—Asia and the Pacific, 2021 (% of total cross-border portfolio debt holdings)

Reporter	Partner					
	Asia and the Pacific	of which		EU+UK	US	ROW
		PRC	Japan			
Central Asia	**20.3**	**8.8**	**4.2**	**16.3**	**39.0**	**24.4**
Armenia	—	—	—	—	—	—
Azerbaijan	—	—	—	—	—	—
Georgia	—	—	—	—	—	—
Kazakhstan	20.3	8.8	4.2	16.3	39.0	24.4
Kyrgyz Republic	—	—	—	—	—	—
Tajikistan	—	—	—	—	—	—
Turkmenistan	—	—	—	—	—	—
Uzbekistan	—	—	—	—	—	—
East Asia	**17.6**	**5.4**	**1.7**	**25.8**	**40.1**	**16.6**
China, People's Republic of	34.0		2.4	10.8	20.4	34.7
Hong Kong, China	49.0	27.5	7.9	13.8	20.2	17.0
Japan	8.2	0.8		30.7	46.7	14.3
Korea, Republic of	14.4	2.7	3.3	22.3	46.2	17.0
Mongolia	—	—	—	—	—	—
Taipei,China	—	—	—	—	—	—
South Asia	**10.7**	**0.0**	**3.3**	**34.2**	**53.6**	**1.5**
Bangladesh	—	—	—	—	—	—
Bhutan	—	—	—	—	—	—
India	10.7	0.0	3.4	34.9	54.5	0.0
Maldives	—	—	—	—	—	—
Nepal	—	—	—	—	—	—
Pakistan	10.3	0.0	0.0	0.0	12.9	76.8
Sri Lanka	—	—	—	—	—	—
Southeast Asia	**39.2**	**9.6**	**9.1**	**4.7**	**35.5**	**20.6**
Brunei Darussalam	—	—	—	—	—	—
Cambodia	—	—	—	—	—	—
Indonesia	62.0	1.9	0.1	1.7	13.2	23.1
Lao People's Democratic Republic	—	—	—	—	—	—
Malaysia	40.4	6.8	4.0	13.0	18.2	28.3
Philippines	34.2	1.8	0.6	7.3	36.9	21.6
Singapore	38.4	10.3	9.5	4.2	37.4	20.0
Thailand	53.1	4.0	13.9	9.9	9.5	27.4
Timor-Leste	—	—	—	—	—	—
Viet Nam	—	—	—	—	—	—
Oceania and the Pacific	**19.9**	**2.1**	**7.3**	**20.7**	**34.1**	**25.3**
Australia	18.7	2.4	7.5	21.5	33.8	26.0
Cook Islands	—	—	—	—	—	—
Fiji	—	—	—	—	—	—
Kiribati	—	—	—	—	—	—
Marshall Islands	—	—	—	—	—	—
Micronesia, Federated States of	—	—	—	—	—	—
Nauru	—	—	—	—	—	—
New Zealand	28.3	0.0	6.2	15.5	35.8	20.4
Niue	—	—	—	—	—	—
Palau	0.0	0.0	0.0	0.0	100.0	0.0
Papua New Guinea	—	—	—	—	—	—
Samoa	—	—	—	—	—	—
Solomon Islands	—	—	—	—	—	—
Tonga	—	—	—	—	—	—
Tuvalu	—	—	—	—	—	—
Vanuatu	—	—	—	—	—	—
Asia and the Pacific	**20.9**	**5.9**	**3.2**	**22.3**	**39.1**	**17.7**
Developing Asia	**38.2**	**13.2**	**6.8**	**11.1**	**29.5**	**21.2**

— = unavailable, EU = European Union (27 members), PRC = People's Republic of China, ROW = rest of the world, UK = United Kingdom, US = United States.

Source: ADB calculations using data from International Monetary Fund. Coordinated Portfolio Investment Survey. https://data.imf.org/cpis (accessed September 2022).

Table A7: Foreign Direct Investment Inflow Share—Asia and the Pacific, 2021 (% of total FDI inflows)

Reporter	Asia and the Pacific	of which		EU+UK	US	ROW
		PRC	Japan			
Central Asia	**53.8**	**32.0**	**3.8**	**193.9**	**42.8**	**(190.5)**
Armenia	4.2	2.6	0.0	277.2	19.3	(200.7)
Azerbaijan	(2.4)	(0.7)	(0.4)	(9.0)	(1.1)	112.5
Georgia	1.7	(2.4)	0.4	84.2	1.4	12.7
Kazakhstan	99.4	58.3	7.5	342.0	88.3	(429.7)
Kyrgyz Republic	168.2	135.2	0.3	70.6	2.1	(141.0)
Tajikistan	35.7	11.8	9.1	38.2	8.4	17.7
Turkmenistan	0.0	0.0	0.0	0.0	0.0	100.0
Uzbekistan	0.0	0.0	0.0	0.0	0.0	100.0
East Asia	**67.7**	**9.4**	**3.2**	**5.1**	**5.9**	**21.3**
China, People's Republic of	84.2		2.2	3.6	1.4	10.8
Hong Kong, China	44.0	20.4	4.0	8.0	3.8	44.2
Japan	102.3	3.3		(17.8)	34.4	(18.9)
Korea, Republic of	34.0	19.3	7.2	30.8	31.3	3.9
Mongolia	55.1	44.7	3.5	7.5	2.2	35.2
Taipei,China	85.2	22.8	20.0	4.0	2.1	8.6
South Asia	**37.9**	**2.0**	**3.9**	**18.1**	**17.6**	**26.5**
Bangladesh	30.0	7.2	3.8	17.3	3.4	49.2
Bhutan	900.6	0.0	0.0	386.6	702.5	(1,889.2)
India	37.3	0.0	4.1	17.2	19.1	26.5
Maldives	4.7	0.0	4.7	7.0	6.9	81.5
Nepal	38.9	11.6	4.5	14.6	4.7	41.8
Pakistan	67.7	34.6	0.6	39.7	11.7	(19.1)
Sri Lanka	32.3	5.8	4.0	24.9	5.1	37.8
Southeast Asia	**55.0**	**3.7**	**1.4**	**5.8**	**2.0**	**37.1**
Brunei Darussalam	70.7	7.6	7.0	14.6	4.1	10.6
Cambodia	12.5	1.4	1.0	2.5	0.7	84.3
Indonesia	5.2	0.4	0.3	1.3	0.3	93.2
Lao People's Democratic Republic	10.4	2.2	1.0	2.4	0.6	86.6
Malaysia	318.2	8.0	2.7	9.3	2.1	(229.7)
Philippines	3.4	0.4	0.3	0.5	0.8	95.3
Singapore	54.3	4.7	1.7	7.9	3.0	34.9
Thailand	9.0	1.3	0.9	2.2	0.6	88.2
Timor-Leste	0.0	0.0	0.0	0.0	0.0	100.0
Viet Nam	12.0	2.9	1.2	2.6	0.7	84.7
Oceania and the Pacific	**43.2**	**7.0**	**13.1**	**4.0**	**7.3**	**45.4**
Australia	17.7	5.8	10.0	5.4	0.0	76.9
Cook Islands	—	—	—	—	—	—
Fiji	11.5	0.7	1.0	3.7	3.5	81.2
Kiribati	—	—	—	—	—	—
Marshall Islands	—	—	—	—	—	—
Micronesia, Federated States of	—	—	—	—	—	—
Nauru	—	—	—	—	—	—
New Zealand	173.9	1.6	11.0	(13.8)	6.9	(67.0)
Niue	—	—	—	—	—	—
Palau	33.4	6.0	22.6	0.0	22.3	44.3
Papua New Guinea	255.1	14.3	20.4	62.1	36.3	(253.5)
Samoa	—	—	—	—	—	—
Solomon Islands	63.4	5.6	8.5	17.0	18.5	1.1
Tonga	—	—	—	—	—	—
Tuvalu	—	—	—	—	—	—
Vanuatu	195.9	12.3	17.7	73.6	51.8	(221.3)
Asia and the Pacific	**60.5**	**7.4**	**3.2**	**8.3**	**6.2**	**24.9**
Developing Asia	**59.9**	**7.7**	**3.0**	**9.7**	**5.3**	**25.1**

( ) = negative, — = unavailable, EU = European Union (27 members), FDI = foreign direct investment, PRC = People's Republic of China, ROW = rest of the world, UK = United Kingdom, US = United States.

Sources: ADB calculations using data from ASEANStats. ASEANStats Data Portal. https://data.aseanstats.org (accessed July 2019); CEIC Data Company; Eurostat. Balance of Payments. https://ec.europa.eu/eurostat/web/balance-of-payments/data/database (accessed July 2022) and United Nations Conference on Trade and Development (UNCTAD); UNCTAD. World Investment Report 2022 Statistical Annex Tables. https://worldinvestmentreport.unctad.org/annex-tables (accessed July 2022).

Table A8: Remittance Inflows Share—Asia and the Pacific, 2019 (% of total remittance inflows)

Reporter	Asia and the Pacific	Middle East	EU+UK	US	ROW
Central Asia	**6.5**	**0.9**	**9.0**	**2.5**	**81.1**
Armenia	17.6	0.4	9.9	12.2	60.0
Azerbaijan	14.1	4.2	4.3	2.3	75.1
Georgia	12.8	2.1	20.2	3.9	61.0
Kazakhstan	1.5	0.5	26.8	0.8	70.3
Kyrgyz Republic	3.4	0.7	14.2	1.2	80.4
Tajikistan	5.4	0.4	6.4	1.2	86.7
Turkmenistan	0.0	0.0	0.0	0.0	100.0
Uzbekistan	0.0	0.0	0.0	0.0	100.0
East Asia	**47.2**	**0.2**	**9.8**	**30.2**	**12.5**
China, People's Republic of	49.5	0.2	9.7	27.5	13.1
Hong Kong, China	40.4	0.0	13.1	23.9	22.6
Japan	22.9	0.3	17.4	42.9	16.6
Korea, Republic of	41.1	0.0	5.3	50.6	3.1
Mongolia	42.0	0.3	24.6	0.0	33.1
Taipei,China	—	—	—	—	—
South Asia	**15.1**	**59.1**	**9.5**	**12.6**	**3.7**
Bangladesh	38.3	51.0	5.9	3.7	1.1
Bhutan	83.4	0.0	4.6	0.0	12.0
India	8.7	60.7	8.1	17.3	5.3
Maldives	69.4	0.5	18.2	0.0	11.8
Nepal	43.8	44.6	4.8	6.0	0.9
Pakistan	7.6	67.2	15.8	8.2	1.1
Sri Lanka	19.7	52.9	20.5	3.4	3.4
Southeast Asia	**30.2**	**22.6**	**10.7**	**33.3**	**3.2**
Brunei Darussalam	—	—	—	—	—
Cambodia	65.6	0.0	8.3	23.1	3.0
Indonesia	41.1	51.2	4.1	2.6	1.0
Lao People's Democratic Republic	72.7	0.0	4.5	21.3	1.5
Malaysia	87.9	0.0	4.8	4.6	2.6
Philippines	17.8	31.5	9.2	38.8	2.6
Singapore	—	—	—	—	—
Timor-Leste	84.7	0.0	14.9	0.0	0.4
Thailand	32.4	2.1	25.3	29.3	10.9
Viet Nam	28.5	0.0	14.9	53.5	3.2
Oceania and the Pacific	**43.8**	**0.7**	**28.6**	**17.0**	**9.9**
Australia	25.4	1.3	45.9	17.0	10.5
Cook Islands	—	—	—	—	—
Fiji	60.6	0.0	3.3	24.2	11.9
Kiribati	89.4	0.0	7.6	0.0	3.0
Marshall Islands	1.8	0.0	0.2	95.8	2.2
Micronesia, Federated States of	2.8	0.0	0.8	55.2	41.1
Nauru	—	—	—	—	—
New Zealand	82.8	0.1	10.6	5.0	1.5
Niue	—	—	—	—	—
Palau	20.3	0.0	7.0	0.0	72.7
Papua New Guinea	14.5	0.0	0.8	0.0	84.8
Samoa	70.9	0.0	0.8	18.6	9.7
Solomon Islands	83.4	0.0	13.3	0.0	3.3
Tonga	49.8	0.0	0.7	31.4	18.1
Tuvalu	55.9	0.0	1.6	0.0	42.4
Vanuatu	34.5	0.1	21.9	0.0	43.5
Asia and the Pacific	**26.9**	**31.8**	**10.0**	**21.8**	**9.4**
Developing Asia	**26.9**	**32.5**	**9.7**	**21.6**	**9.3**

— = unavailable, EU = European Union (27 members), ROW = rest of the world, UK = United Kingdom, US = United States.

Source: ADB calculations using data from World Bank. Global Knowledge Partnership for Migration and Development. Bilateral Remittance staff estimates (May 2020).

Table A9: Outbound Migration Share—Asia and the Pacific, 2020 (% of total outbound migrants)

Reporter	Asia and the Pacific	of which PRC	of which Japan	EU+UK	US	ROW
Central Asia	**9.5**	**—**	**—**	**16.4**	**0.8**	**73.3**
Armenia	18.9	—	—	10.3	4.3	66.4
Azerbaijan	14.5	—	—	4.5	0.8	80.3
Georgia	11.0	—	—	20.9	0.8	67.3
Kazakhstan	1.4	—	—	28.8	0.1	69.7
Kyrgyz Republic	3.7	—	—	13.4	0.2	82.7
Tajikistan	6.2	—	—	6.2	0.3	87.2
Turkmenistan	2.5	—	—	4.6	0.2	92.7
Uzbekistan	22.5	—	—	3.9	0.7	72.9
East Asia	**49.8**	**2.5**	**8.5**	**10.8**	**31.6**	**7.8**
China, People's Republic of	55.2		7.4	10.9	27.7	6.2
Hong Kong, China	39.2	20.8	—	12.6	26.7	21.5
Japan	24.0	0.7		19.5	43.4	13.0
Korea, Republic of	38.4	6.6	20.7	5.6	49.2	6.8
Mongolia	42.6	—	—	27.6	—	29.8
Taipei,China	—	—	—	—	—	—
South Asia	**27.0**	**0.0**	**0.2**	**9.1**	**1.4**	**62.4**
Bangladesh	42.2	0.0	0.2	6.1	0.3	51.3
Bhutan	86.8	—	—	3.5	—	9.7
India	18.3	0.0	0.2	7.9	2.5	71.3
Maldives	78.8	—	—	13.6	—	7.5
Nepal	58.2	—	—	3.0	0.1	38.7
Pakistan	20.5	0.1	0.3	14.6	1.5	63.4
Sri Lanka	22.4	0.2	1.3	19.1	0.7	57.8
Southeast Asia	**50.2**	**1.7**	**3.1**	**7.5**	**8.3**	**33.9**
Brunei Darussalam	75.0	—	—	13.5	—	11.5
Cambodia	75.8	—	0.4	7.5	10.8	5.9
Indonesia	42.7	0.7	1.2	3.8	1.1	52.4
Lao People's Democratic Republic	80.8	—	—	4.4	13.2	1.6
Malaysia	88.0	0.3	0.6	5.6	1.8	4.6
Philippines	17.0	0.9	4.5	8.8	15.0	59.2
Singapore	64.7	—	0.9	20.1	3.7	11.5
Timor-Leste	86.9	—	—	12.9	—	0.2
Thailand	43.4	1.1	4.9	24.6	9.8	22.2
Viet Nam	38.5	8.9	9.9	13.1	16.0	32.4
Oceania and the Pacific	**58.4**	**0.2**	**0.8**	**19.8**	**5.1**	**16.7**
Australia	28.1	0.7	1.9	45.5	7.1	19.3
Cook Islands	99.9	—	—	0.0	—	0.0
Fiji	63.4	—	—	3.0	6.8	26.8
Kiribati	92.9	—	—	4.8	—	2.3
Marshall Islands	1.3	—	—	0.0	10.0	88.7
Micronesia, Federated States of	2.8	—	—	0.6	11.0	85.6
Nauru	97.0	—	—	0.9	—	2.1
New Zealand	79.0	—	0.4	12.4	1.9	6.7
Niue	99.5	—	—	—	—	0.5
Palau	12.1	—	—	7.6	—	80.3
Papua New Guinea	48.9	—	—	38.7	—	12.4
Samoa	67.3	—	—	0.7	8.4	23.6
Solomon Islands	88.2	—	—	11.0	—	0.7
Tonga	57.8	—	—	0.7	14.3	27.2
Tuvalu	81.1	—	—	1.6	—	17.2
Vanuatu	26.9	—	—	16.1	—	57.0
Asia and the Pacific	**35.1**	**0.8**	**2.2**	**10.0**	**7.9**	**46.9**
Developing Asia	**34.9**	**0.9**	**2.3**	**9.7**	**7.7**	**47.8**

— = unavailable, EU = European Union (27 members), PRC = People's Republic of China, ROW = rest of the world, UK = United Kingdom, US = United States.

Source: ADB calculations using data from United Nations. Department of Economic and Social Affairs, Population Division. International Migrant Stock 2020. http://www.un.org/en/development/desa/population/migration/data/index.shtml (accessed May 2022).

Table A10a: Inbound Tourism Share—Asia and the Pacific, 2020 (% of total inbound visitors)

Destination	Asia and the Pacific	of which PRC	EU+UK	US	ROW
Central Asia	**70.6**	**0.4**	**2.1**	**0.3**	**26.9**
Armenia	15.0	1.1	23.1	7.8	54.1
Azerbaijan	29.7	0.2	3.0	0.3	67.0
Georgia	45.3	0.3	5.5	0.5	48.6
Kazakhstan	66.3	0.7	1.7	0.3	31.7
Kyrgyz Republic	91.6	0.2	0.3	0.1	8.0
Tajikistan	87.3	0.3	0.5	0.3	11.9
Turkmenistan	—	—	—	—	—
Uzbekistan	—	—	—	—	—
East Asia	**83.7**	**29.4**	**5.1**	**6.1**	**5.1**
China, People's Republic of	—		—	—	—
Hong Kong, China	83.0	64.2	6.5	3.5	7.0
Japan	85.9	25.9	5.2	5.3	3.6
Korea, Republic of	78.9	27.5	5.2	8.8	7.1
Mongolia	38.5	22.9	3.2	1.9	56.3
Taipei,China	88.5	8.2	3.5	6.1	1.9
South Asia	**42.6**	**3.0**	**28.0**	**11.1**	**18.4**
Bangladesh	—	—	—	—	—
Bhutan	88.3	2.4	6.0	3.6	2.1
India	44.6	1.4	23.6	14.3	17.4
Maldives	25.4	6.0	45.0	3.5	26.1
Nepal	73.8	10.0	15.4	9.2	1.6
Pakistan	—	—	—	—	—
Sri Lanka	35.9	5.1	38.4	3.3	22.5
Southeast Asia	**77.6**	**15.8**	**11.4**	**3.7**	**7.2**
Brunei Darussalam	88.2	16.1	9.1	1.4	1.4
Cambodia	75.7	25.1	14.4	4.3	5.6
Indonesia	83.1	6.1	9.0	2.3	5.6
Lao People's Democratic Republic	90.2	16.5	6.1	2.2	1.6
Malaysia	90.5	9.1	4.9	1.1	3.5
Philippines	64.5	12.4	11.7	15.4	8.5
Singapore	77.2	13.6	13.9	4.7	4.2
Thailand	65.4	19.6	18.2	3.3	13.0
Timor-Leste	83.3	17.1	12.1	3.1	1.5
Viet Nam	76.9	24.8	9.4	4.9	8.7
Oceania and the Pacific	**59.3**	**9.2**	**20.6**	**11.0**	**9.2**
Australia	57.1	11.3	22.7	10.2	10.0
Cook Islands	75.4	0.3	11.0	7.0	6.5
Fiji	76.7	7.4	6.7	13.6	3.1
Kiribati	44.0	—	7.8	46.2	2.0
Marshall Islands	—	—	—	—	—
Micronesia, Federated States of	—	—	—	—	—
Nauru	—	—	—	—	—
New Zealand	58.2	5.9	20.4	12.6	8.8
Niue	—	—	—	—	—
Palau	83.0	18.3	5.6	9.9	1.5
Papua New Guinea	87.2	6.7	5.5	5.4	1.9
Samoa	84.3	3.8	1.7	7.1	6.9
Solomon Islands	88.4	3.1	4.5	5.8	1.3
Tonga	81.2	2.1	3.1	14.9	0.8
Tuvalu	76.5	2.5	9.0	5.4	9.1
Vanuatu	78.7	3.8	—	—	—
Asia and the Pacific	**73.7**	**14.4**	**10.6**	**4.7**	**11.1**
Developing Asia	**73.6**	**13.6**	**10.4**	**4.2**	**11.9**

— = unavailable, EU = European Union (27 members), PRC = People's Republic of China, ROW = rest of the world, UK = United Kingdom, US = United States.

Source: ADB calculations using data from United Nations World Tourism Organization, Tourism Satellite Accounts. https://statistics.unwto.org (accessed November 2022).

Table A10b: Outbound Tourism Share—Asia and the Pacific, 2020 (% of total outbound visitors)

| Origin | Destination | | | |
	Asia and the Pacific	EU+UK	US	ROW
Central Asia	**63.5**	**1.2**	**0.2**	**35.1**
Armenia	57.6	1.9	1.3	39.3
Azerbaijan	29.4	1.0	0.1	69.5
Georgia	27.6	7.6	0.3	64.4
Kazakhstan	50.5	1.0	0.3	48.1
Kyrgyz Republic	86.9	0.1	0.1	12.9
Tajikistan	74.0	0.0	0.0	25.9
Turkmenistan	58.5	0.5	0.1	40.8
Uzbekistan	86.1	0.4	0.0	13.5
East Asia	**56.0**	**7.1**	**6.4**	**30.5**
China, People's Republic of	51.8	5.2	2.7	40.3
Hong Kong, China	48.3	1.1	1.2	49.4
Japan	54.4	13.6	19.4	12.6
Korea, Republic of	65.0	10.6	10.8	13.6
Mongolia	43.6	0.9	2.9	52.6
Taipei,China	78.8	6.7	4.8	9.7
South Asia	**31.1**	**3.9**	**5.1**	**59.9**
Bangladesh	74.7	0.6	1.0	23.7
Bhutan	86.4	0.4	1.4	11.8
India	28.8	5.9	7.9	57.4
Maldives	89.1	1.1	0.2	9.6
Nepal	58.0	1.9	4.9	35.2
Pakistan	7.4	1.6	2.0	89.0
Sri Lanka	64.4	2.2	1.5	31.9
Southeast Asia	**89.5**	**1.2**	**1.0**	**8.3**
Brunei Darussalam	98.6	0.1	0.1	1.2
Cambodia	98.4	0.1	0.3	1.2
Indonesia	76.4	1.3	0.8	21.5
Lao People's Democratic Republic	99.9	0.0	0.0	0.1
Malaysia	92.3	0.6	0.5	6.6
Philippines	62.2	5.6	3.7	28.5
Singapore	95.8	0.9	1.1	2.2
Thailand	94.9	1.1	0.6	3.4
Timor-Leste	100.0	0.0	0.0	0.0
Viet Nam	94.3	0.7	1.9	3.1
Oceania and the Pacific	**66.1**	**12.4**	**7.7**	**13.8**
Australia	63.7	13.3	8.1	15.0
Cook Islands	95.5	0.3	0.5	3.7
Fiji	90.4	0.4	5.9	3.4
Kiribati	76.5	2.6	2.2	18.7
Marshall Islands	25.5	2.5	12.1	60.0
Micronesia, Federated States of	3.9	0.4	2.6	93.1
Nauru	82.2	3.8	1.0	13.0
Niue	72.9	10.4	7.2	9.5
New Zealand	85.4	0.7	0.7	13.2
Palau	10.5	2.5	2.5	84.5
Papua New Guinea	98.1	0.2	0.5	1.2
Samoa	96.8	0.3	0.0	2.9
Solomon Islands	92.9	1.6	1.3	4.2
Tonga	91.9	0.3	5.5	2.2
Tuvalu	85.6	1.6	2.2	10.7
Vanuatu	85.5	0.6	0.6	13.4
Asia and the Pacific	**62.5**	**4.7**	**4.1**	**28.8**
Developing Asia	**62.8**	**3.6**	**2.8**	**30.8**

— = unavailable, EU = European Union (27 members), ROW = rest of the world, UK = United Kingdom, US = United States.

Source: ADB calculations using data from United Nations World Tourism Organization, Tourism Satellite Accounts. https://statistics.unwto.org (accessed November 2022).